# Politics of
# Latin America

# Politics of Latin America

## The Power Game

SIXTH EDITION

### Harry E. Vanden
*University of South Florida, Tampa*

### Gary Prevost
*College of Saint Benedict/*
*Saint John's University*

New York   Oxford

OXFORD UNIVERSITY PRESS

*This work is dedicated to those who teach Latin American politics, with special thanks to those who showed us the way: Gary Wynia, who taught Gary Prevost, and C. Neale Ronning, John C. Honey, and Mario Hernández Sánchez-Barba, who guided Harry E. Vanden.*

Oxford University Press is a department of the University of Oxford.
It furthers the University's objective of excellence in research, scholarship, and education by publishing worldwide. Oxford is a registered trade mark of Oxford University Press in the UK and certain other countries.

Published in the United States of America by Oxford University Press
198 Madison Avenue, New York, NY 10016, United States of America.

For titles covered by Section 112 of the US Higher Education Opportunity Act, please visit www.oup.com/us/he for the latest information about pricing and alternate formats.

Library of Congress Cataloging-in-Publication Data
Names: Vanden, Harry E., author. | Prevost, Gary, author.
Title: Politics of Latin America : the power game / Harry E. Vanden, University of South Florida, Tampa, Gary Prevost, College of Saint Benedict/Saint John's University.
Description: Sixth Edition. | New York : Oxford University Press, [2017] | Includes bibliographical references and index.
Identifiers: LCCN 2017011159 | ISBN 9780190647407 (paperback : alk. paper) | ISBN 9780190647414 (ebook)
Subjects: LCSH: Latin America—Politics and government.
Classification: LCC JL960 .V36 2018 | DDC 320.98—dc23
LC record available at https://lccn.loc.gov/2017011159

9 8 7 6 5 4 3 2 1
Printed by Sheridan Books in the United States of America

# Brief Contents

# CONTENTS

# MAPS AND FREQUENTLY CITED ACRONYMS

## Maps

## Frequently Cited Acronyms

| | |
|---|---|
| AD | Democratic Action Party, Venezuela |
| AID | Agency for International Development, U.S. Department of State |
| AMNLAE | Association of Nicaraguan Women, Luisa Amanda Espinosa |
| ANDI | National Association of Industrialists, Colombia |
| APRA | American Popular Revolutionary Alliance, Peru |
| ARENA | National Republican Alliance, El Salvador |
| ARENA | National Renovating Alliance, Brazil |
| BPR | People's Revolutionary Bloc, El Salvador |
| CACIF | Coordinating Committee of Agricultural, Commercial, Industrial, and Financial Associations, Guatemala |
| CAFTA-DR | Central America–Dominican Republic Free Trade Agreement |
| CDR | Committees for the Defense of the Revolution, Cuba |
| CDT | Democratic Workers' Confederation, Chile |
| CGT | General Confederation of Labor, Argentina, Colombia, Chile, Brazil |

| | |
|---|---|
| CIA | Central Intelligence Agency, United States |
| CONAIE | Confederation of Ecuadorean Indigenous Nationalities |
| COPEI | Social Christian Party, Venezuela |
| CORFO | Development Corporation, Chile |
| CPC | Confederation of Production and Commerce, Chile |
| CPD | Coalition of Parties for Democracy, Chile |
| CSTC | Trade Union Confederation of Colombian Workers |
| CSUTUB | Confederation of Peasant Unions, Bolivia |
| CTDC | Democratic Confederation of Colombian Workers |
| CTV | Confederation of Venezuelan Workers |
| CTC | Confederation of Cuban Workers, Confederation of Colombian Workers |
| CUT | Unitary Labor Central, Brazil, Chile, Colombia |
| ECLA/ECLAC | Economic Commission for Latin America/and the Caribbean |
| EGP | Guerrilla Army of the Poor, Guatemala |
| ELN | National Liberation Army, Colombia |
| ERP | Revolutionary Army of the People, Argentina |
| ERP | Popular Revolutionary Army, El Salvador |
| EZLN | Zapatista Army of National Liberation, Mexico |
| FAL | Armed Forces of Liberation, El Salvador |
| FALN | Armed Forces of National Liberation, Venezuela |
| FAR | Fuerzas Armadas Rebeldes, Guatemala |
| FARC | Revolutionary Armed Forces of Colombia |
| FEDECAFE | National Federation of Coffee Growers, Colombia |
| FDNG | New Guatemala Democratic Front |
| FDR | Democratic Revolutionary Front, El Salvador |
| FMLN | Farabundo Martí National Liberation Front, El Salvador |
| FrePaSo | Front for a Country in Solidarity, Argentina |
| FSLN | Sandinista National Liberation Front, Nicaragua |
| FTAA | Free Trade Area of the Americas |
| GAM | Group of Mutual Support, Guatemala |
| IMF | International Monetary Fund |
| ISI | Import substitution industrialization |
| M-19 | April 19 Movement, Colombia |
| M-26 July | July 26 Movement, Cuba |
| MAS | Movement Toward Socialism, Venezuela, Bolivia |
| MDB | Brazilian Democratic Movement |
| MERCOSUR/ MERCOSUL | Common Market of the Southern Cone |
| MINUGUA | United Nations Verification Mission, Guatemala |
| MIR | Movement of the Revolutionary Left, Chile, Peru, Venezuela |
| MNC | Multinational corporation |
| MNR | National Revolutionary Movement, Bolivia |
| MST | Landless Movement, Brazil, Bolivia |
| MVR | Fifth Republic Movement, Venezuela |
| NAFTA | North American Free Trade Agreement |

| | |
|---|---|
| NAM | Non-Aligned Movement |
| OAS | Organization of American States |
| PAC | Civil Defense Patrol, Guatemala |
| PAN | National Action Party, Mexico |
| PCC | Cuban Communist Party |
| PDC | Christian Democratic Party |
| PDS | Social Democratic Party, Brazil |
| PDVSA | Venezuelan National Petroleum Company |
| PJ | Justice [Peronist] Party, Argentina |
| PLF | Party of the Liberal Front, Brazil |
| PMDB | Brazilian Democratic Movement Party |
| PP | Patriotic Pole, Venezuela |
| PPD | Party for Democracy, Chile |
| PRD | Democratic Revolutionary Party, Mexico |
| PRI | Institutional Revolutionary Party, Mexico |
| PSDB | Brazilian Social Democratic Party |
| PSN | Nicaraguan Socialist Party |
| PT | Workers' Party, Brazil |
| RN | National Renovation, Chile |
| UCR | Radical Civic Union, Argentina |
| UFCo | United Fruit Company |
| UNO | National Opposition Union, Nicaragua |
| UNT | National Workers Union, Venezuela |
| UP | Popular Unity, Chile |
| UP | Patriotic Union, Colombia |
| URNG | Guatemalan National Revolutionary Unity |

# LIST OF TABLES AND FIGURES

## Tables

## Figures

# PREFACE

The political reality in Latin America has changed once again and another group of regimes quite different from those they have replace is in power. Thus the need for a new edition to put this change in context. It should also be noted that the sixth edition of *Politics of Latin America* is animated by the same passions that guided the first five editions, our love and fascination for Latin America and how politics are practiced there. We were motivated to proceed to a sixth edition by the continuing positive reactions we received from students and the community of scholars who study Latin America and who have adopted our textbook. We are most indebted to our students at the University of South Florida, Saint John's University, College of Saint Benedict, and Hamline University who have provided invaluable commentary. We are also indebted to the country chapter authors who have so graciously updated their work for the new edition.

The new edition continues to focus on power politics and recent developments in the region, but not only the post-2002 election and reelection since of numerous progressive governments chosen by their populations to provide an alternative to the Washington-driven neoliberal policies of the 1990s, but similarly, the backlash that began with the coup in Honduras in 2009 and congressional coup in Paraguay in 2010, and continued with the narrow election of neoliberal Mauricio Macri in 2015 in Argentina and the impeachment of Dilma Rousseff in Brazil in 2016. These events suggest that once again elitist sectors continue to seek ways to resist the assertion of popular power and new internal and external power alignments and that such reactionary actions will find favor, if not support, from many sectors in the United States. Pursuant to this new reality, there have been important changes in the sixth edition of *Politics of Latin America: The Power Game*:

## New to This Edition

- Updated country elections in Argentina, Brazil, Chile, Paraguay, Honduras, and Bolivia.
- Tables and charts have been updated, and a new chart has been added to show the evolution over time of the Gini coefficient in selected countries.
- In several chapters there is an analysis of the resurgence of the political forces of the right marked by electoral successes in Argentina, Brazil, and Venezuela at national or local levels.

- The U.S.–Latin American relations chapter draws a balance sheet on eight years of Obama administration policies in the region and the challenges facing the Trump administration, including the growing role of China.

Many people have helped us in this endeavor. We continue to learn and benefit from the voices and actions of Latin American peoples and from our many colleagues who study the region from around the world. In this regard we are especially grateful to Dorothea Melcher for assistance with the section on colonial Latin America, Kwame Dixon for contributing heavily to the section on Afro-Latins, David Close who helped us update the Nicaragua chapter, Richard Stahler-Sholk who provided an update on the Zapatistas, Marc Becker for his updates on Ecuador, Nathalie Lebron for her input on contemporary feminist movements, and Shawn Schulenberg who contributed the section on gays and lesbians contained in Chapter 5. Gary Prevost is especially indebted to the office staff of Saint John's University and the College of Saint Benedict. Special recognition goes to Sheila Hellermann for invaluable secretarial help and to student assistant Charles Pults, who updated the electoral systems table and appendices on electoral results. We are most indebted to Adam Golob at the University of South Florida for constructing the majority of the tables, and to Mariela Noles Cotito from ISLAC at USF for securing photos for this edition. The index was prepared by Sheila Hellermann at St. John's University and the College of St. Benedict. We also thank the Latin American Public Opinion Project (LAPOP) and its major supporters (the United States Agency for International Development, the United Nations Development Program, the Inter-American Development Bank, and Vanderbilt University) for making data available. Finally, we are grateful to the following reviewers for their suggestions: Megan Sholar, Loyola University, Chicago; Daniel S. Haworth, University of Houston, Clear Lake; Erica Townsend-Bell, Oklahoma State University; Natasha Borges Sugiyama, University of Wisconson, Milwaukee; and Maria Rosa Garcia, California State University, Northridge.

We hope this new edition continues to excite and enlighten students and buttress the teaching of the professors who use it, and we beg the indulgence of the reader for any errors, which, of course, remain our responsibility.

*Harry E. Vanden*
Tampa

*Gary Prevost*
Collegeville

# Notes on Studying Politics in Latin America

Latin America is a dynamic, complex, and rapidly changing reality. It ranges from small pastoral villages to two of the largest urban megalopolises on earth. Both democratic and dictatorial, its governments are sometimes replaced by voting in clean elections and other times by military coups. Although exciting to study, Latin America's complexity often challenges the ideas and intellectual approaches we use to study it—indeed, one approach alone is usually just not sufficient to understand what is going on there. The authors of this work maintain that it takes all the conceptual tools and insights that can be mustered to begin to understand such a complex reality. Because the political history of the nations that comprise Latin America has been quite different from that which developed in the United States, Canada, Britain, or Australia, most of us who study Latin American politics believe it is imperative to know this history because most political practices grew out of it. The authors speak of dictatorial *caudillos* and of authoritarian political culture, yet they acknowledge the great political changes and democratic reforms that have also marked Latin American history. Each nation has a political history marked by periods of dictatorship and democracy. Each nation has struggled with the need to change social and economic structures and traditional economic practices that have vested most of the land in a few families and left the vast majority of citizens with no or little land or means of adequately sustaining themselves. Latin America has experienced more revolutions than any other part of the world, yet the comparative conditions for the lower classes in most countries are only little better than they were at the end of the colonial period in the early 1800s. As reflected in the two introductory chapters on broad historical periods in Latin America (Chapters 2 and 3) and the detailed political history provided for each of the ten country case studies presented here, the authors strongly believe that one cannot begin to understand Latin American politics without knowing the region's history. Equally, they know just how great the political variations have been and thus strongly believe that one must equally study the particular historical evolution of each country to comprehend its own brand of politics and see how it conforms to and diverges from general political trends and practices in the region. The often influential role of the

United States in Latin American politics and inter-American relations is explored in Chapter 11. Similarly, there are certain events, such as the Mexican and Cuban revolutions, and certain figures—such as Victor Raúl Haya de la Torre of Peru, Juan Perón of Argentina, and Cuba's Fidel Castro—whose historical trajectories need to be studied because of their lasting influence in their own countries and in the region as a whole.

It should further be noted that there are many ways of remembering or interpreting what went on before. Indeed, it has been suggested that much of history has been written by the elite. Using the term perfected by the influential Italian thinker Antonio Gramsci, we would say that the "superstructure," or the culture and institutions controlled by the dominant class, have dictated much of the history that has been written. For instance, we now know that much that was written by patriarchal European elites was but one version of what transpired. Class, gender, race, nationality, religion, and ideology all influence how we see an event and how we evaluate it. Slavery, one imagines, will always be seen somewhat differently by slave and slaveholder. And the descendants of each may keep many of their foreparents' views of things. The chapters in this book endeavor to present a view of the present and past that is inclusive of views of native peoples, Africans who were brought as slaves, women, dominated classes, and others who were subordinated as well as the more standard history written from the perspective of the dominant elites in Latin America, the United States, and Europe. By incorporating more diverse views, the authors hope to supply a better and more complete picture of how the region evolved and what it is like today.

But history is not enough. Similarly, before we deploy specific concepts gleaned from the study of comparative politics, most students of Latin American politics believe that a great deal of the political behavior in the region has been heavily influenced by internal and international economic forces and that one cannot fully comprehend politics without understanding the economics of the region. The internal economies of the indigenous societies were totally disrupted by the conquest and the imposition of economic systems designed to export wealth to Europe and thus incorporate the Americas into the international system on terms favorable to Europe. Economic power was seized by the European elite. Thereafter, the structure and functioning of Latin American nations would be heavily influenced by their trade and commercial relations with more economically developed areas; their economies, societies, and political institutions would also be transformed by this external orientation. Latin America was to fit into the international system as a producer of primary (unfinished) goods such as sugar, tin, tobacco, copper, coffee, and bananas. According to classical Western capitalist theories of free trade economics, such trade was to be equally advantageous to peripheral areas such as Latin America as it was to metropolitan areas such as Europe and the United States. Yet, after World War II, a careful study of the terms of trade for Latin America by the Economic Commission for Latin America of the United Nations suggested just the opposite—that benefits from trading patterns were accruing primarily to the developed areas, not to Latin America. As scholars of Latin America and other social scientists studied the full implication of this phenomenon, they arrived at a theory that explained the continuing underdevelopment and dependency of Latin America. Dependency theory, as the paradigm came to be called, soon heavily dominated thinking among social scientists who studied Latin America. For most scholars, it became the principal way of understanding Latin American society, politics, development, and the region's relations with the outside world. This approach predominated from the late 1960s into the 1990s, supplanting many classical economic assumptions and displacing other theories of underdevelopment, such as modernization theory, which was championed by many U.S. scholars. Chapter 7 explores dependency theory in greater detail and makes the general argument that since economic and political power are so closely entwined in Latin America, an approach that combines both—political economy—is necessary. More recent theories of neoliberal economics and globalization are also explored.

But even if, as Karl Marx believed, economic relations form the basis for social structures, it is still necessary to examine those social structures carefully. Nor can economic relations be fully comprehended until elements of social, gender, race, and class relations are introduced. Family and gender relations, race, and subordination have all played key roles in the development of Latin American politics and economics. The subordinate position of indigenous peoples, Afro-Latins, and women has conditioned politics and been conditioned by them. Class is of equal importance, given the hierarchical nature of the societies that developed. The authors believe familiarity with these issues is necessary and thus have included one chapter on indigenous and African peoples (Chapter 4) and a second that explores the status of women and gender roles (Chapter 5).

The rise of fundamentalism in domestic politics in the United States, the Islamic resurgence in a variety of Muslim countries, and the rise of religious parties in India have once more brought religion to the center of the political stage. Yet in Latin America, the role of the Catholic Church and religion has always been an important factor in politics. For five centuries, the Church has remained the bulwark of the status quo in most countries. Yet, there have always been radicals in the Church who were not afraid to challenge entrenched political interests, even though most of the Church hierarchy usually worked hand in glove with the state. Such was the case in the sixteenth century when Chiapas Bishop Bartolomé de las Casas became a crusader against the enslavement of indigenous people. At the beginning of the nineteenth century, two progressive priests—Hidalgo and Morelos—waged the first phase of the mass-based independence movement in Mexico. Adapting Marx to the specific conditions in the region, the most original Marxist thinker in Latin America, José Carlos Mariátegui, argued that religion could be a revolutionary force. Stimulated by his thought and progressive theological trends in Europe, the Peruvian priest Gustavo Gutiérrez developed a radical new "theology of liberation." The advent of liberation theology and growing support for the radical transformation of socioeconomic structures by the Conference of Latin American Bishops after 1968 made religion a major political force for change in many countries in the region. Priests supported guerrilla groups, resisted dictatorships, became guerrillas themselves, and, in the case of four priests in Nicaragua, became part of the leftist Sandinista government. Lay people formed participatory Christian base communities and used their faith as a potent political force. Meanwhile, more conservative Protestant evangelical groups converted millions to their faith. The new flock was often exhorted to support fellow Protestant (and usually conservative) candidates and not to be involved in (radical) politics. It is difficult to comprehend the dynamics of Latin American politics without understanding the religious forces and factions at work there. Thus the authors have also included a chapter on religion (Chapter 6).

Democracy and dictatorship have been two contrasting themes running through Latin American history and the conduct of politics in each nation. Their dynamic and dialectical interaction have defined the political game and created unique political cultures in the region. Thus, democracy and authoritarianism are explored in Chapter 8, as is Latin America's special brand of political culture.

Chapters 1 through 11 provide the national and hemispheric context in which Latin American politics are played out. Different readers and instructors may choose to emphasize different areas; others may opt to also read an accompanying novel, like Isabel Allende's *House of the Spirits* (1985), *El Señor Presidente* by Miguel Angel Asturias (1987), or Gabriel García Márquez's *One Hundred Years of Solitude* (1970). Films and videos also illustrate many of these factors and bring figures like Juan and Eva Perón to life (*Evita*, 1996). The authors believe that astute students of the political game in Latin America must develop some appreciation for such background factors before they begin to focus on politics.

Most political scientists believe that politics concerns power and influence—how resources are allocated in a society. In his classic work, *Politics: Who Gets What, When, How,* Harold Lasswell suggests that the study of politics is the study of influence and the influential. In a context that is particularly relevant to Latin America, he argues that the "influential are those who get the most of what there is to get" and further adds that those who get the most are the elite, and the rest are the masses (Lasswell 1958: 13). He further invokes the early political economist David Ricardo to the effect that the distribution of wealth suggests one of the principal avenues of influence in a given society. Thus Lasswell notes that in the early part of the twentieth century, 2,500 individuals in Chile owned 50 million of the 57 million acres of privately held land in the nation (p. 17). That is, the large landowners were dominant economically and could use this base to influence—if not dominate—the political process. The study of politics and the subfield of comparative politics have evolved considerably since the time Lasswell originally wrote those pages (the 1930s). At that time, he and other social scientists in the United States were more willing to focus on concepts of class and the domination of wealth. That was before the advent of the Cold War and the dichotomization of the world into two opposing camps, with social science often reflecting each camp's dominant values.

Social science in Latin America has been much more willing to use class and Marxist concepts in its study of the Latin American reality. This is reflected in the work of many Latin Americanists outside the region as well. In the United States, comparative politics evolved from traditional-legalistic approaches that looked at history and constitutions, to behavioral approaches that studied interest groups and voting behavior and other quantifiable political actions to explain politics, to postbehavioral approaches that came to include policy analysis, aspects of dependency theory, and world systems analysis, as well as a postmodern literary/cultural deconstructionist analysis. Currently, political scientists in the United States are focusing a great deal of interest on rational choice theory. Yet, those conceptual tools most frequently employed by Latin Americanists who focus on politics do not usually include deconstruction (although there are exceptions among literary-oriented Latin Americanists and Latin American intellectuals) or rational choice theory. Conceptual approaches most often and most successfully employed include elitist analysis, class analysis, a pluralist analysis of interest groups, mass organizations and others who exercise power in the political process, analysis of voting and political preferences where conditions allow for relatively clean elections and free expression of opinion, dependency analysis and political economy, and a careful consideration of powerful groups like the military or armed guerrilla groups that have the capacity to use force to take power or heavily influence policy decisions. All these are employed in this work. The authors also rely on the approach to understanding Latin American power relations developed by Gary Wynia in *The Politics of Latin American Development* (1990).

Latin Americanists have followed their own evolution. As suggested earlier, they have found political history to be of great importance. From this they extracted useful political concepts such as *caudillismo, golpe de estado* (coup d'état), and junta. These and similar concepts like authoritarianism and machismo are, nonetheless, explained well by the concept of political culture as developed in comparative politics in the 1960s, during the time when behaviorism was dominant. In that political values and beliefs in Latin America are generally so different from those found in Anglo-American political cultures, special treatment is given to general outlines of Latin American political culture in Chapter 8. The authors examine the development of political values from family, gender, race, and class relations as well as historical factors. They do so in the confines imposed by class, authoritarian rule, and the use and abuse of power by those who rule. Later, the country-chapter authors make frequent use of these concepts as they analyze the politics of individual nations.

Of equal importance is a fundamental subtext in most writing about Latin American politics: power rules, and absolute power rules absolutely. This is manifest in the title of a highly respected work on Guatemala by Richard Adams, *Crucifixion by Power* (1970). Frequently it is not what the constitution says; it is the power of the dictator or the president to ignore the constitution, have Congress amend it, or simply arrange for the nation's Supreme Court to make a favorable interpretation. Ultimately, it may not be the constitution, elections, public opinion, civilian politicians, or the party system that decides the issues. Rather, it may be a coup, as in Ecuador in 2000 and Honduras in 2009, or a political understanding with the military that allows the president to dismiss Congress and the Supreme Court and rule on his own, as in Peru in 1992. In most Latin American countries, there is always the possibility that naked power can and will be used. This has been the case since the *conquistadores* established their rule through brute force. Naked power—and violence—can be used by the government to suppress the rulers' political enemies, by the military to take over the government or threaten to do so or by opposition groups that contend for power through the use of arms. One is here reminded of Mao Zedong's oft-quoted dictum: "Power flows out of the barrel of a gun." Even when democratic processes are being followed, the threat of the use of force is often present. Thus, the military could often veto policy decisions by a civilian government, as was the case in El Salvador and Guatemala for many years; the oligarchy can threaten to mobilize their friends in the military on their behalf; or, as was the case in Nicaragua and Colombia, the opposition groups that grew out of revolutionary organizations can threaten to take up arms again.

At the local level the amount of power a large landowner can wield may be a more important factor in politics than the election of a reformist in the last election or the composition of the government. The local notable's power allows him to manipulate the policy process, control public officials, pay off the local police, or hire his own armed guards and also heavily influence the electoral process—indeed, most likely the reformer would have never been elected. Yet the notable's power could be challenged by a well-organized popular organization like the Landless in Brazil or neutralized by the presence of an active guerrilla group like the Fuerzas Armadas Revolucionarias de Colombia (FARC) in Colombia. Of considerable significance is the emergence of powerful social movements like those in Bolivia and Ecuador and the massive "take the streets" protest movement in Brazil in June 2013.

In Latin America, politics are dictated by power and the powerful. This book examines those who play the power game in separate chapters on political actors and political institutions (Chapter 9) and revolutions and change (Chapter 10). The way the game is played is conditioned not only by the historical, social, and economic factors mentioned previously, but it also has developed its own rules and practices. They are explored in these chapters, beginning with a discussion of how the constitution is often best described as an ideal to strive for rather than a basis for the rule of law.

Country chapters on Mexico, which is in North America; the South American Southern Cone countries of Argentina, Brazil, and Chile; the South American Andean countries of Colombia, Venezuela and Bolivia; the Caribbean nation of Cuba; and Guatemala and Nicaragua from Central America follow. They provide specific examples of how the power game is played in ten different Latin American nations. This is a representative—but not inclusive—sampling of the Latin American political reality. Each of the Latin American nation-states has developed its own way of conducting politics. Reference is made to some key events in the countries not necessarily included in the case studies, but it was not possible to fully explore the particular political nuances of all aspects of national politics in each country. Those who carefully study general trends and how they develop in the included case studies will, we believe, have a good basis to explore how politics are conducted elsewhere in Latin America.

# Bibliography

Adams, Richard. *Crucifixion by Power*. Austin: University of Texas Press, 1970.

Allende, Isabel. *House of the Spirits*. New York: Knopf, 1985.

Asociación Latinoamericano de Sociología, Centro de Estudios sobre America, Editorial Nueva Sociedad. *Sistemas políticos: Poder y sociedad (estudios de caso en América Latina)* [Political Systems: Power and Society (Latin American Case Studies)]. Caracas: Editorial Nueva Sociedad, 1992.

Asturias, Miguel. *El Señor Presidente*. New York: Antheneum, 1987.

Borón, Atilio A. *Reflexiones sobre el poder, el estado y la revolución* [Reflections on Power, the State, and Revolution]. Córdoba, Argentina: Espartaco Córdoba, 2007.

Eckstein, Susan, ed. *Power and Popular Protest: Latin American Social Movements*. Updated and expanded edition. Berkeley: University of California Press, 2001.

García Márquez, Gabriel. *One Hundred Years of Solitude*. New York: Harper & Row, 1970.

Lasswell, Howard D. *Politics: Who Gets What, When, How*. New York: World, 1958.

Mills, C. Wright. *The Power Elite*. New York: Oxford University Press, 1956.

Wynia, Gary. *The Politics of Latin American Development*. New York: Cambridge University Press, 1990.

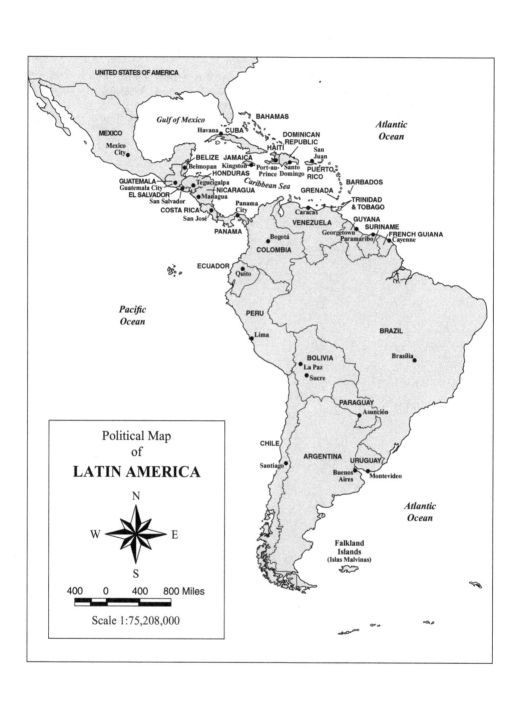

Political Map
of
**LATIN AMERICA**

N

W · E

S

400    0    400    800 Miles

Scale 1:75,208,000

# ONE

# AN INTRODUCTION TO TWENTY-FIRST CENTURY LATIN AMERICA

A million people took to the streets in Brazil in June of 2013 to challenge government unresponsiveness to their needs and demands. They contested the political direction of a government led by Brazil's first woman president, Dilma Rousseff. Protests and political maneuvering continued in 2015 and 2016. Amidst a major corruption scandal that blossomed in 2016, the machinations of opposition politicians culminated in the impeachment and removal from office of Brazil's president only to have thousands go into the streets to protest Dilma Rousseff's successor, Michel Temer in 2017. The people are on the move in Latin America and their anger and frustration are ever more frequently intensified by the revelation of corruption. Before Brazil, protesters mobilized by the thousands to force leaders out of office in Ecuador, Argentina, and Bolivia and force policy change in those and many other countries. Massive demonstrations against the government have characterized Venezuela in 2017. A whole generation of more responsive, progressive leaders took the helm in the region and then conservative political forces found ways to challenge their power and forced progressive leaders out of office in Honduras, Paraguay, Argentina, and Brazil. And a new generation of media-savvy, participating citizens are mobilizing in original and increasingly intense ways throughout the hemisphere. The traditional dominance of the United States and international financial institutions, like the International Monetary Fund (IMF), is being challenged throughout the region, and China is becoming a much more important player in Latin America. Old norms were put aside as Bolivia has been governed by its first indigenous president; women recently served as elected presidents in Brazil, Chile, Costa Rica, and Argentina; and a progressive former guerrilla headed Uruguay.

Such are the changes that are buffeting the region. Latin America—a term coined by a Frenchman to describe this area—is not a homogeneous part of the world that just happens to lie south of the border that runs from Florida to California. It is an immense region that is striving to establish its place in the world in the twenty-first century. A diverse area of twenty nations and peoples that includes Mexico, Central America, the Spanish- and French-speaking Caribbean nations, and the Spanish and Portuguese nations in South America, Latin America is home to some 625 million people (more than 8 percent of the world's population) who well represent the rich racial and cultural diversity of the human family. Although a U.S. commonwealth, some also include Puerto Rico as part of Latin America. Its people include Amero-Indians from pre-Columbian civilizations, such as the Incas, Aztecs, and Maya; Europeans from countries such as Spain and Portugal (but also England, France, Holland, Italy, Poland, and Germany); West Africans from areas such as what is now Nigeria, the Congo, and Angola; Jews from Europe and elsewhere; Arabs and Turks from countries such as Lebanon, Syria, Egypt, and Turkey; Japanese; Chinese; and different peoples from the Indian subcontinent. These and other racial and cultural groupings have combined to create modern nations rich in talent and variety. The dynamic way the races have combined in Latin America even led one observer to predict that the Latin American region would be the birthplace of the fusion of the world's major racial groupings into a new *raza cosmica*—a cosmic race.

Latin America still has some places where the siesta follows the large midday meal. More commonly, the modern Latin American has a heavy meal in an urban setting and returns to the job for a full afternoon of work. The rapid pace of globalization, urbanization, commercialization, industrialization, and political mobilization continues to radically change the face of the region. Nicaragua, Guatemala, and Costa Rica still gear much of their economies around the export of excellent coffee. Meanwhile, Mexico is making more and more automobiles and automobile components as a result of the North American Free Trade Agreement (NAFTA; between Mexico, Canada, and the United States); Brazil is selling its passenger planes, jet trainers, and modern fighter aircraft in the globalized international market while it is developing a common market in the Southern Cone of South America (*Mercosur*); new clothing-assembly plants are moving to Nicaragua and Guatemala; and Costa Rica is manufacturing Intel chips and exporting software for hospital administration.

Latin America constitutes an enormous and extremely rich region. The area ranges from Cuba and Mexico in the north to Argentina and Chile's southern tip in Tierra del Fuego some 7,000 miles to the south. *El continente,* as the region is called by many of its Spanish-speaking inhabitants, is extremely diverse in geography and population. Geography as conceptualized in Latin America sees the mainland region of Latin America from Mexico south as one continent and not two as seen in the United States. It encompasses hot and humid coastal lowlands, steamy interior river basins, tropical rain forest, highland plateaus, coastal deserts, fertile lowlands, and high mountain peaks of almost 7,000 meters (23,000 feet). Subregions include Central America, the Caribbean, and South America.

The term *Latin America* is an ingenious attempt to link together most of this vast area. Strictly speaking, it refers to those countries in the Western Hemisphere south of the United States that speak Latin-based (Romance) languages: Spanish, Portuguese, and French.[1] In a more general sense, Latin America and the Caribbean can be said to include the English- and Dutch-speaking parts of the Caribbean and South America as well as Belize in Central America.[2] The focus of this book will be on the Latin part of the region, although the English- and Dutch-speaking countries will be included in some of the maps and tables and are occasionally referred to for the sake of comparison. Nor would we minimize their importance or the many similarities they share with the Latin part of the Americas.

# Geography

Latin America is huge and diverse; it runs from 32.5° north latitude to 55° south latitude. With a total area of 20 million square kilometers (8 million square miles), it is one of the largest regions of the world. Taken on the whole, it is almost as large as the United States and Canada combined and larger than Europe.

The climatic and topographic diversity of Latin America is remarkable. Its range of environments is greater than in North America and Europe: rain forests, savanna grasslands, thorn scrub, temperate grasslands, coniferous forests, and even deserts. Plateaus extend down from the United States into Mexico and Central America. The Andes extend from the Caribbean island of Trinidad to Tierra del Fuego at the southern tip of South America and form the largest mountain chain on earth. They are most prominent as they parallel the west coast of South America. Many peaks are over 5,486 meters (18,000 feet); Mount Aconcagua in northern Argentina reaches almost 6,982 meters (22,840 feet) and is the highest point in the Western Hemisphere. Snow-capped peaks can be found from Venezuela in northern South America to Argentina and Chile in the south. A fault line that runs from California through the middle of Mexico and Central America and down the west coast of South America and another that runs through the Caribbean make the region prone to earthquakes. Volcanoes are found in Mexico, the Caribbean, and Central and South America. Other major geographic areas include the Guiana Highlands in northern South America, the Brazilian highlands, and the Pampas in the south. River systems include the Orinoco in the north, the Río de la Plata in the south, and the mighty Amazon in the middle of the South American continent.

Even at the same latitude, one can find very different climates. *Altitudinal zonation*, as this phenomenon is called, refers to the range in altitude from sea level to thousands of meters that occurs as one travels as few as 80 kilometers (50 miles) horizontally. It makes for very different climates. Land from sea level to 915 meters (3,000 feet) is termed *tierra caliente*; from 915 to 1,930 meters (3,000 to 6,000 feet), *tierra templada*; from 1,930 to 3,660 meters (6,000 to 12,000 feet), *tierra fría*; and above 3,660 meters (12,000 feet), *tierra helada*, which experiences frost, snow, and ice through all or most of the year. Even close to the equator, the temperature cools 2.05° C (3.7° F) for each 305 meters (1,000 feet) of altitude. Although at the same latitude, Quito, the capital of Ecuador at 2,835 meters (9,300 feet), has an average annual temperature of 12.6° C (54.6° F), while Ecuador's largest city, Guayaquil, located on the coast, has an average temperature of 25.7° C (78.2° F). Each zone is suitable for different crops. Tierra caliente, when it is humid, is usually ideal for tropical fruits, while tierra templada is suited for growing crops like coffee, potatoes (which can be grown up to 3,355 meters [11,000 feet]), corn, and coca plants. Because of the temperature variation, crops requiring very different climates, such as bananas (humid, tropical lowlands) and coffee (cooler, shaded highlands), can be grown in the same Caribbean island (Jamaica) or small Central American nation (Costa Rica, El Salvador, Nicaragua, Honduras, or Guatemala). It is interesting to note that there are some crops that are extremely adaptive and can grow at a variety of altitudes. Corn is grown throughout Mexico, Central America, and the Andean region and formed an essential part of the classical Aztec, Mayan, and Incan economies. Coca cultivation has remained an essential part of agriculture in the area occupied by the Incan Empire (concentrated in Peru, Bolivia, and Ecuador but extending into Colombia, northern Chile, and Argentina). The cultivation and consumption of coca leaves has been an essential

Physical Map of **LATIN AMERICA**

400 0 400 800 Miles

Scale 1:120,000,00

part of indigenous culture in most of the Andean region since pre-Incan times. The coca plant can live up to forty years and produces the best leaves for chewing when grown at altitudes of 915 to 1,220 meters (3,000 to 4,000 feet). Coca thrives in the shaded areas of the eastern Andean slopes, but it also can be grown at much higher altitudes or in the dryer mountainous regions such as the eastern Colombian Andes. It will also grow in hot, humid rain forests at much lower elevations. The leaves are not as good from these latter locations, but this is a less important consideration when they are used for a newer economic activity—the production of cocaine.

The Amazon is the second-longest river in the world, carrying more water than any other. It runs from the jungles of eastern Peru for some 6,275 kilometers (3,900 miles) to its mouth at the Atlantic Ocean. Large riverboats and many ocean-going ships with a draft of 4.3 meters (14 feet) or less can go as far as Iquitos, Peru, where they still transport all the heavy cargo for that jungle city.

## Once There Were Rain Forests

During the first century, tropical rain forests covered 2.02 billion hectares (5 billion acres) on our planet and represented 12 percent of the land surface. In the last 100 years alone, more than half that forest has been actively destroyed. The deforestation is extensive. According to one study, the size of the deforested areas rose from 78,000 square kilometers (30,110 square miles) in 1978 to 230,000 square kilometers (88,780 square miles) in 1988. By the mid-1990s, the annual deforestation rate was 15,000 square kilometers (5,790 square miles) per year and has continued to rise. In 2002, as we began the new millennium, over 20.2 million hectares (50 million acres) of tropical rain forest were lost every year. In Latin America, the Amazon basin alone houses the largest tropical rain forest in the world and contains one-fifth of the earth's freshwater, 20 percent of the world's bird species, and 10 percent of the world's mammals. More than 20 percent of the planet's oxygen is produced by the trees and plants in the area. Yet, 14 percent of the rain forest has disappeared in a recent ten-year period. According to Greenpeace, the last forty years has seen Brazil alone losing more than 18 percent of its rainforest. This represents an area about the size of California, and most of what remains is under threat.

In 1964, a military government staged a coup and displaced the civilian government in Brazil. During their two decades in power, the development-minded military leadership built the Trans-Amazon Highway and embarked on a policy of exploiting the resources in the Amazon basin and encouraging settlement. During the 1960s, Peru's civilian president, Fernando Belaunde Terry, tried a similar developmentalist strategy for Peru's jungle area that lay on the eastern side of the Andes. However, most of the Peruvian settlers found the jungle's "green wall" much more impenetrable than did their Brazilian counterparts.[3] In Brazil, the migration into the Amazon was enormous. In 1960, there were 2.5 million people living in Brazil's six Amazon states. By the early 1990s, the population had grown to 10 million and continues to grow today. There are more than 18 million landless people in Brazil. Thousands of landless peasants, rural workers, urban slum dwellers, entrepreneurs, and well-heeled Brazilian and foreign businesspeople arrived each day to see how they could carve a fortune from the land and resources in the forest.

The land is often crudely torn open to search for gold, iron ore, or other minerals in places like the huge open-pit gold mine at Serra Pelada. Indigenous populations, like the Yanomami, are pushed farther into the jungle and even shot if they resist the encroachment on their ancestral lands. When other local inhabitants, like rubber tapper Chico Mendes or environmental activist Sister Dorothy, try to resist the brutal destruction of the rain forest, they are often bullied by local officials, *fazenderos* (large landowners), or their hired henchmen or, as were Mendes and Sister Dorothy, assassinated.

The rain forest problem in Brazil alone is enormous. In 1998, the Brazilian government released figures indicating that destruction of the Amazon rain forest reached record levels in the mid-1990s. In 1994 and 1995, for example, an area larger than the state of New Jersey (12,610 square kilometers [7,836 square miles]) was destroyed. Indeed, according to a satellite imaging study by Brazil's National Institute of Space Research, 11,280 square kilometers (7,010 square miles) of Amazon rain forest were lost in 2001, and the figure increased to 15,835 square meters (9,840 square miles) in 2002. Not only is the rain forest cut down, but also, in classic slash-and-burn fashion, the vegetation is burned to prepare the land for agriculture or pasture. This means that not only are thousands of oxygen-producing trees lost every year but also enormous amounts of carbon dioxide are released into the atmosphere when the biomass is burned. This process is also accelerating in Central America and the rain forest

The immense Iguazu Falls on the Brazilian-Argentinian border. (*Cro Magnon/Alamy Images*)

in southern Mexico. Since 1960 almost 50 percent of Central American forests have been destroyed. Environmentalists see the resultant drastic reduction in oxygen production and dramatic increase in carbon dioxide as significant causal factors in the greenhouse effect linked to climate change.

As Latin America strives to develop and as its population grows, its ecosystems are put under increasing stress. In Haiti, Brazil, and elsewhere, the ecosystem has suffered severe stress because of the intense population density. In Haiti, most of the trees have been cut down for building materials and firewood, and the number of birds and other dependent species has been reduced drastically. In Haiti and elsewhere, the commercialization of agriculture, demographic pressure, and policies that favor large commercial producers over small peasant farmers are also combining to increase land degradation. This set the stage for a huge loss of life as rain and mud flowed uncontrolled down the hills and into heavily populated areas when a hurricane swept across Haiti in 2004. Deforestation, overgrazing, and over-exploitation of the land are endangering entire ecosystems throughout the region. Desertification is advancing. It has been estimated that desertification and deforestation alone have affected about one-fifth of Latin America. As early as 1995, some 200 million hectares (494 million acres) of land—almost one-third of the total vegetated land—were moderately or severely degraded.

## The People

Latin America is endowed with enormous human resources. Its 625 million people come from all corners of the globe and are rich in their diversity and skills. Fertility rates are high in Latin America, and population growth rates have been some of the highest in the world. Currently, these rates have declined to 2 percent per year or less. Even at this rate, the population will double approximately every 35 years.

The original inhabitants of the region crossed to the Western Hemisphere on the Bering land and ice bridge that once united Asia and North America. This happened some 20,000 to 35,000 years ago during the Ice Age. The Asian migration flowed into North America and then spread into the Caribbean and through Central America to South America. Varied indigenous civilizations grew up throughout the region. By the time the Spaniards and Portuguese arrived in the late 1400s and early 1500s, at least 50 million indigenous people lived in the region (some estimates are more than double this figure). Population concentrations included the Aztec civilization in central Mexico, the Maya civilization in southern Mexico and northern Central America, and the Incan Empire in the west coast central Andean region in South America. Other groupings could be found throughout the region, including the Caribs, Taínos/Arawaks, Guaraní, and Araucanian. These peoples and their civilizations will be discussed more fully in the following chapter.

The Spanish and Portuguese were the first Europeans to arrive in Latin America. As they came in ever-increasing numbers, they began to populate the region as well. Informal and formal unions between Iberian men and indigenous women soon produced offspring, who came to be known as *mestizos*. Later, as the Amero-Indian population was drastically decimated and additional inexpensive labor was needed, Africans were brought to the hemisphere as enslaved peoples. At least 7 million survived the Middle Passage from western and southern Africa to Latin America and the Caribbean. The culture, religion, and cuisine they brought with them would forever change the face of the societies they helped to form. Indians, Europeans, and Africans populated Latin America during the first centuries. The fact that early Spaniards and Portuguese came without their families and claimed access to women in subordinate positions began a process of racial melding that continues to the present day. These pairings and their children were thrown together in dynamic new societies. Mestizos, mulattos, and *zambos* (the children of unions between native peoples and Africans) appeared in growing numbers.

Most Latin Americans trace their ancestry to Amero-Indian, Iberian, and/or African sources. However, by the middle of the nineteenth century, there was a general realization that new laborers, artisans, and those with other skills could add to the growing nations. Most nations had outlawed slavery by the time of the Civil War in the United States. Brazil was the last; slavery was outlawed there in 1888. Thus, other sources of abundant and inexpensive labor were often needed. Chinese laborers were brought to Peru in the latter part of the nineteenth century. Thousands of Italians were lured to Argentina and southern Brazil to supply the labor for the growing agricultural and industrial production. Workers and indentured servants from India and the Chinese mainland were brought to the British Caribbean and British South America. Many Europeans came to their colonies or former colonies or from other nations to make their way in these new societies. French, Germans, Swedes, Irish, Poles, and others from Europe arrived on Latin American shores to make a better life or as refugees from famine, war, and revolution. European Jews came to seek opportunity and escape pogroms and persecution. Japanese came to southern Brazil and to other countries like Peru for better opportunities, often with their passages paid by the Japanese government (which wanted to alleviate population pressures on the home islands). Turks and Arabs came to explore new horizons. As the United States expanded its economic sphere into Latin America and the Caribbean, some U.S. citizens chose to stay in the lands where they went to make their fortunes. One, an early aviator who came to Peru, stayed to found what was that nation's best-known private airline, Faucett. The Spanish Civil War and World War II began a new wave of immigration from Spain and other countries taken over by the Fascists. Many Jews and others targeted by the Nazis owe their lives to the liberal immigration and visa policies of Latin American nations. (Ironically, as World War II was ending, Nazis, Fascists, and accused war criminals were often able to take advantage of these same liberal immigration policies and Argentine neutrality during World War II to make their way to countries like Argentina and Paraguay.) Today, new immigrants from Eastern Europe and elsewhere continue to arrive to make their places in these dynamic new societies.

## The Land

When the first Europeans arrived in the Western Hemisphere, they found abundant land and resources. Most of the native peoples incorporated the concept of the earth mother, as most notably articulated in Andean culture as the earth mother *Pachamama*, the giver of all life. The land was a sacred trust, to be used with respect and care, and was not the property of any one person. Land either existed in a state of nature or was used or owned collectively by and for the whole community. It was never to be harmed or destroyed and always to be used for the benefit of all creatures. Thus, the native people used but did not abuse the land. Early reports suggest that food was in abundance and generally well distributed to the entire population.

The regime the Iberians brought was far different. The crown, not the earth mother, was sovereign. Lands that had been inhabited by native peoples for thousands of years were unhesitatingly claimed for Spain and Portugal. Those who had been living on the land and working it were thought to have only those rights granted by the crown. Europeanization had begun. Hereafter, the land was to be used, owned, and abused for the benefit of the crown or its subjects. The native peoples, their needs, and their descendants were and would continue to be secondary and subordinate. The land and the people who lived in harmony with it would no longer be respected. There were empires to be carved and fortunes to be made.

At the time of the conquest (late 1400s and early 1500s), Spain and Portugal were very much dominated by feudal institutions. The landowning system was no exception. Both countries were dominated by huge feudal estates and powerful landlords. The peasants were poor and subordinate. This would be the basis of the system brought to the newly conquered lands. Initially, the Spanish and Portuguese monarchs gave huge land grants and grants to use the native peoples in a specific area. The *mercedes* (land grants, *sesmarias* in Brazil) and *encomiendas* (right to use the native peoples and the land on which they lived as long as the *encomendero* took responsibility for Christianizing them) were given to the *conquistadores* and others to whom the crown owed favors or debts. Thus, Europeans soon established domain over huge stretches of land and the people who lived on them. These initial grants were later turned into large landed estates, or *latifundios*, which were not too different from the huge feudal landed estates in the Iberian peninsula. Often ranging for hundreds of thousands of acres, they were frequently larger than whole counties. They were ruled over by the *patrón* and his family, who were the undisputed masters. The lowly *peon* was like a feudal serf and had little, if any, power or recourse, even after protective laws had been enacted. From colonial times to the present, the land tenure system reflected the nature and power configuration of the whole society. Well into the twentieth century, the subordinate status of the peasant and agricultural laborer was maintained. Vestiges of this system were still in evidence in the 1970s. In many areas, the humble *campesino* was expected to approach the *patrón* with eyes cast down, bowing and scraping. As late as the 1960s, there were still instances (mostly in the Andes) of what had become a widespread practice in colonial times: *primera noche/prima nocta*, the landlord's right to spend the wedding night with a newly married woman on his estate.

In time, many of the *latifundios* were divided or otherwise changed and became modern-day large landholdings: *haciendas, fazendas* (in Brazil), and *estancias* (in Argentina). Still owned by one family and comprising hundreds, if not thousands, of hectares (1 hectare = 2.47 acres) these farms still control a disproportionate amount of the land and resources in the countryside. Their continued existence attests to the concentrated nature of land ownership in Latin America.

Currently, land is also being concentrated in large commercial farms, including land used for soy, sugar cane, and other ethanol-producing crops.

The original indigenous population and later the mestizos, Africans, mulattos, *zambos*, and Europeans who became *campesinos* (anyone who owns or has control over the small- or medium-sized land parcels they work) were left with the rest. Their holdings were never large and were further reduced by division through inheritance, illegal takings by large landowners, or the need to sell off part of the land to survive. The resulting small landholdings, or *minifundios*, were and are the most common type of agricultural unit. Comprising less than 10 hectares (24.7 acres), these small family farms afford a meager living during good times and near starvation during bad. In Colombia, traditionally they accounted for 73 percent of the farms, yet they covered only 7.2 percent of the agricultural area. In Ecuador in 1954, 0.04 percent of the landholdings accounted for 45.2 percent of the farmland; in contrast, the *minifundios* comprised 73 percent of the landholdings but only 7 percent of the land. In Guatemala, per the 1979 agrarian census, less than one-tenth of 1 percent of the landholdings comprised 22 percent of the land, while the largest 2 percent of the farms had 65 percent of the land. In El Salvador in 1971, 4 percent of the landowners (the *latifundistas*) owned 64 percent of the land, and 63 percent of the landowners (the *minifundistas* and *microfundistas*) had only 8 percent of the land. At the beginning of the 1980s, 40.9 percent of rural families were landless altogether, and land concentration is still continuing in many areas. In Brazil, 70 percent of the rural population did not own any land at all, but 1 percent of the country's farms (*fazendas*) occupied 43 percent of the arable land in the 1950s. This inequity continued and later engendered a growing Landless Workers Movement (Movimento dos Trabalhadores Rurais Sem Terra; MST) in the 1980s. Their occupations of unused land have often met with brutal repression by local authorities and the *fazendero*'s hired gunmen (see Table 2). The conflict was so intense that some 1,600 Brazilians have been killed in land disputes since 1985.

The process of the fractionalization of small holdings has continued. The *microfundio*, a very small farm of less than 2 hectares (5 acres), is unable to sustain a family. The food and income from this small holding must be supplemented by income from outside labor by one or more family members. The capitalization, commercialization, and related mechanization of agriculture have put even greater stress on the *microfundistas* and many of the *minifundistas*. The reduction in demand for rural labor has forced many to abandon their holdings altogether and flee to the cities in hope of better opportunities. In recent times, large-scale agricultural production has undergone a transformation. The heavy reliance on cheap labor and abundant land in the absence of mechanization is rapidly giving way to more capital-intensive production that relies on mechanization and more intensive use of irrigation (where necessary), chemical fertilizers, and the application of insecticides by aerial spraying. As has been the case in U.S. agriculture, land is also in the process of being consolidated into larger units that can most benefit from the efficiencies of large-scale production. This has signaled a move from the traditional agricultural economy to an integrated capitalist mode of production.[4] The large plantations and commercial farms devote more and more of their production to cash crops that are sold on the world market, while the production of basic foodstuffs for local consumption more

**TABLE 1.**  *Minifundios* and *Latifundios* in Select Countries: Traditional Landholding Patterns, 1970

| Country | Minifundios | | Latifundios | |
|---------|------------|-----------|------------|-----------|
| | % of Farms | % of Land | % of Farms | % of Land |
| Argentina | 43.2 | 3.4 | 0.8 | 36.9 |
| Brazil | 22.5 | 0.5 | 4.7 | 59.5 |
| Colombia | 64.0 | 4.9 | 1.3 | 49.5 |
| Chile | 36.9 | 0.2 | 6.9 | 81.3 |
| Ecuador | 89.9 | 16.6 | 0.4 | 45.1 |
| Guatemala | 88.4 | 14.3 | 0.1 | 40.8 |
| Peru | 88.0 | 7.4 | 1.1 | 82.4 |

*Source*: Michael Todaro, *Economic Development in the Third World*. 2nd ed. New York: Longman, 1985, p. 295.

frequently occurs on the small farms. China has emerged as a new market for many of these crops and for mineral and other primary products. Not surprisingly, the production of corn and grains for local consumption is decreasing amidst growing malnutrition. Fewer of the poor have the funds to augment their consumption of staples. Groups such as OxFam, Bread for the World, and Food First have noted the decrease in protein consumption among the poor with increasing alarm. More and more land is being used for the production of export crops like beef or soy, yet in most of Latin America few of the poor are able to afford beef or other meats more than a few times a year.

Although Latin America is industrializing and urbanizing at an amazing rate, agriculture is still very important. In 1990, agriculture still accounted for 40 percent of the exports for the region. The capitalization and commercialization of agriculture that have buttressed the consolidation and reconcentration of the land have radically decreased opportunities for labor and sharecropping in the countryside. Thirty-nine percent of the rural population in Brazil is now landless. There is also a high incidence of landlessness in Colombia, Ecuador, Guatemala, and Peru. Consequently, there are fewer opportunities for peasants and landless laborers to sustain themselves. Currently, more than 60 percent of the rural population lives in poverty. Global economic forces are driving people off the land in record numbers. In Brazil, many flee to the Amazon region to mine gold or engage in a cycle of slash-and-burn agriculture that pushes them ever farther into the virgin rain forest. More generally, new, rural refugees flock to the cities, where they try to establish themselves in the growing shanty towns that ring large urban centers.

## The Mega Cities: Urbanization

Latin America is no longer the land of sleepy peasants and small villages. It has changed dramatically. Some three-fourths of the population now live in urban areas (see Table 2) compared to 41.6 percent in 1950. There are three cities in Latin America that are now larger than New York City. Mexico City alone has some 22 million people and is the largest city in the world. São Paulo, Brazil, has 18 million and is

**TABLE 2.** Basic Statistics for Latin America, Canada, and the United States

| Country | Total Population (2015) (in thousands) | Annual Population Growth Rate (%) | Urban Population (%) (2015) | Cities with 100,000 or More Inhabitants (2015)~ | Gross National Income (International $) (in millions) (2015)# | Per Capita Gross National Income (International $) (2015)# | Life Expectancy at Birth (2015) | Literacy Rate (15+ yrs old) (2015) | Female Economically Active Rate (%) (2012)> | Estimated Infant Mortality Rate (per 1000 live births) (2016)^ |
|---|---|---|---|---|---|---|---|---|---|---|
| Argentina | 43,298.26 | 1.03 | 91.8 | 27 | 586,170.69 ** | 13,640 ** | 76.1 | 98.0 | 47 | 10.1 |
| Bolivia | 10,737.27 | 1.61 | 69.1 | 10 | 73,380.39 | 6,840 | 67.8 | 94.5◊ | 64 | 36.4 |
| Brazil | 207,749.81 | 0.94 | 85.7 | 250 | 3,122,692.58 | 15,020 | 74.2 | 91.5 | 60 | 18 |
| Chile | 18,088.73 | 1.08 | 88.9 | 30 | 390,191.20 | 21,740 | 81.0 | 96.7▪ | 47 | 6.7 |
| Colombia | 48,228.61 | 0.98 | 79.4 | 61 | 651,946.99 | 13,520 | 73.8 | 93.6▪ | 56 | 14.1 |
| Costa Rica | 4,820.78 | 1.13 | 76.6 | 10 | 71,526.51 | 14,880 | 79.2 | 97.4▪ | 46 | 8.3 |
| Cuba | 11,421.59 | 0.15 | 77.0 | 13 | 210,992.15▪ | 18,630◊ | 79.2 | 99.8◊ | 43 | 4.5 |
| Dominican Republic | 10,530.93 | 1.24 | 78.8 | 20 | 142,837.60 | 13,570 | 73.3 | 90.9 | 51 | 18.1 |
| Ecuador | 16,144.35 | 1.56 | 64.4 | 16 | 180,674.67 | 11,190 | 75.6 | 93.3 | 54 | 16.9 |
| El Salvador | 6,298.49 | 0.40 | 69.0 | 10 | 50,383.05 | 8,220 | 72.7 | 86.8 | 47 | 17.3 |
| Guatemala | 16,381.75 | 2.08 | 56.0 | 5 | 122,755.40 | 7,510 | 71.5 | 77.0 | 49 | 22 |
| Haiti | 10,749.64 | 1.39 | 52.0 | 4 | 18,895.68 | 1,760 | 62.6 | 48.7▾ | 60 | 48.2 |
| Honduras | 8,075.03 | 1.47 | 53.6 | 3 | 38,243.26 | 4,740 | 72.9 | 85.5 | 42 | 17.7 |
| Nicaragua | 6,085.53 | 1.17 | 57.6 | 5 | 30,715.10 | 5,050 | 74.6 | 78.0◊ | 47 | 19 |
| Panama | 3,929.11 | 1.64 | 66.6 | 2 | 81,359.88 | 20,710 | 77.4 | 94.1◊ | 50 | 10.1 |
| Paraguay | 6,639.16 | 1.34 | 66.4 | 7 | 57,576.13 | 8,670 | 72.8 | 93.9◊ | 58 | 19.4 |
| Peru | 31,383.48 | 1.32 | 78.7 | 23 | 375,324.84 | 11,960 | 74.2 | 93.8◊ | 68 | 19 |
| Puerto Rico | 3,683.24 | -0.14 | 93.6 | 5 | 86,328.62▸ | 24,030▸ | 79.2 | 92.0◊ | 36 | 7.4 |
| Uruguay | 3,430.28 | 0.34 | 95.3 | 2 | 69,861.73 | 20,360 | 77.0 | 98.4 | 56 | 8.5 |
| Venezuela | 30,553.59 | 0.95 | 89.5 | 45 | 536,731.79▸ | 17,730▸ | 74.1 | 94.8▪ | 52 | 12.5 |
| **NAFTA Countries** | | | | | | | | | | |
| Canada | 35,362.91^ | 0.74^ | 81.8^ | 52 | 1,576,518.82 | 43,970 | 81.9^ | 99.0* | 58 | 4.6 |
| Mexico | 124,612.40 | 1.38 | 77.3 | 85 | 2,178,018.67 | 17,150 | 76.5 | 94.0 | 44 | 11.9 |
| United States | 323,995.53^ | 0.81^ | 81.6^ | 284 | 18,138,314.00 | 56,430 | 79.8^ | 99.0* | 62 | 5.8 |

*Sources:* Economic Commission on Latin America. *ECLAC/CEPAL Statistical Yearbook for Latin America and the Caribbean.* http://interwp.cepal.org/anuario_estadistico/anuario_2015/en/index.asp. All data from ECLAC/CEPAL Statistical Yearbook 2015 unless otherwise noted.

▸Data from 2013  ◊Data from 2012  ▪Data fvrom 2011  ◊Data from 2010  ▾Data from 2006  ◊Data from 2005
^2016 CIA World Factbook https://www.cia.gov/library/publications/the-world-factbook/rankorder/2091rank.html  *Data from 2013 World Factbook estimates.
https://www.cia.gov/library/publications/the-world-factbook/rankorder/2103rank.html  **Data from 2014 Atlas method.  ~United National Statistical Division.
Demographic Yearbook 2015. Population of Capital Cities and Cities of 100,000 or More Inhabitants. http://unstats.un.org/unsd/demographic/products/dyb/dyb2014.
htm  #The World Bank 2015 Data. http://data.worldbank.org/indicator/NY.GNP.MKTP.PP.CD  >Data from Statistics and Indicators on Women and Men. U.N. Statistics
Division. July 2013. http://unstats.un.org/unsd/demographic/products/indwm/Dec.%202012/5a.xls

the third-largest city in the world, and Buenos Aires, the capital of Argentina, has more than 12 million. By 1990 Latin America had 40 cities with 1 million or more inhabitants. This was more than Canada and the United States combined. More than 140 million Latin Americans live in these modern megalopolises compared to fewer than 100 million in the United States. Urban areas in Latin America continue to explode with new people as more children are born and millions flock to the bright city lights each year. Municipal services can in no way keep up with the steady stream of new arrivals. The streets are clogged with all types of vehicular traffic, and the air is polluted by thousands of cars, trucks, and buses. Mexico City has some of the most polluted air in the world. Oxygen is sold at booths on the street. Thousands suffer and many die from pollution-induced respiratory problems. Mexico City is immense and unmanageable. The quality of life for all too many of its residents is marginal. Nor is it easy to escape. It can take more than two hours to traverse it. São Paulo suffers from similar problems and, like Mexico City, has a very high crime rate. Other cities seem headed in this direction. As the growing middle class exercises its consumers' right to own private vehicles, gridlock is the norm in rush hour, and parking is often nearly impossible. The impoverished masses endure long hours on crowded buses and vans. The congestion is sometimes alleviated by subways, but they rarely cover more than a few areas of the city, may be more expensive, and cannot keep up with the growing number of new neighborhoods and urban squatter settlements.

Often, one-third or more of the population in the large cities lives in slums and shanty towns. Of the 18 million people in greater São Paulo, close to 8 million live in the *favelas*, as the urban slums are called in Brazil. Because many of these new agglomerations often grow quickly where unused land is illegally occupied, city services are often minimal or unavailable altogether. Living conditions are frequently horrible, with no running water, sewer, or trash collection (see Table 7 in Chapter 5). Sometimes the only electricity is provided by illegal taps to lines that run close to the neighborhood. Crime, violence, and growing gang activity are often at uncontrollable levels. Little, if any, police protection is available in most of the larger slums, and poor neighborhoods are often infiltrated if not run by drug gangs, juvenile gangs, and other types of organized crime. The rapidly growing Mara Salvatrucha and M-18 gangs control entire neighborhoods throughout El Salvador, Guatemala, and Honduras, and gangs control entire neighborhoods in Brazilian cities like Rio de Janeiro. Gangs often assert de facto control of specific slum neighborhoods, and the police are often reluctant to enter unless as part of a concerted, massive action led by heavily armed special police. (See the Brazilian films *Cidade de Deus* and *Tropa de Elite* for graphic depictions.) Slum areas are referred to as *barriadas, colonias, pueblos jovenes, villas de miseria,* or *tugurvios* in different Spanish-speaking countries and as *favelas* or *mocambos* in Brazil. They continue to grow dramatically. In these places, there is an abundance of misery and drugs, while hope is often in short supply.

Originally, towns in Spanish America were planned around gracious central plazas, often called the *Plaza de Armas* or *Zócalo*. Here, one would find a pleasant plaza with the main church or cathedral, government buildings, and the palaces of prominent officials ringing it. Others of means and social standing would occupy neighborhoods adjacent to the center. The outskirts of the cities were reserved for

Mexico City, 2000. *(Photo by Patrice Olsen)*

the poor and marginalized. However, the once-majestic colonial centers are now generally overwhelmed with traffic problems and pollution. Towns in Portuguese America were not always planned affairs; often, they grew around a fort or business center and then expanded. In all of Latin America, the worst slums are still generally found on the peripheries of the cities, although poor neighborhoods and scattered makeshift dwellings can also be found inside traditional cities, as is the case in Rio de Janeiro. Many of the wealthy and upper middle class have also begun to move to well-protected, gated, and guarded urban high-rises or flee the centers to populate more removed, attractive, exclusive neighborhoods characterized by gates and guards and high-walled, luxurious houses or high-rise condominiums staffed by numerous servants and well-armed private guards and with easy access to the newest in Latin American consumerism—the mall. Suburban-style *urbanizaciones* are also being constructed to cater to the housing needs of the rest of the growing middle class, which is also flocking to shopping centers and malls in growing numbers. The contrast between the lives of the urban poor and their middle- and upper-class fellow urbanites becomes ever more stark each day and increased in much of the region with the turn to neoliberal economics.

Ironically, many are afraid to shop outside of the privately guarded malls and shopping centers. Fed by deteriorating socioeconomic conditions for the poor, urban crime and delinquency have grown dramatically in recent years. One can see the homeless and the hustlers living and sleeping on the streets in most of the major cities. Many middle- and upper-class drivers are afraid to stop at traffic lights—particularly at night—in many areas for fear they will be robbed at knife- or gunpoint or even by street children who threaten with broken shards of glass. Sometimes the merchants and the police take matters into their own hands. Brazil in particular has become infamous for the way street children have been beaten, run off, and even killed in groups to clear the area and discourage their perceived criminal activity. Some 5 percent of Brazil's children live in the streets. Of these, more than 4,000 were murdered between 1988 and 1991. Even Charles Dickens's impoverished souls would find life hard in the modern Latin American city.

Throughout Latin American society, crime and violence are growing to astronomical levels. Economic and social disparities, the suffering caused by International Monetary Fund-dictated economic adjustments and austerity, the ravages of globalization, a brand of free market economic policy called *neoliberalism* (see Chapter 7), narco trafficking, and the fallout from the guerrilla wars that have raged throughout the region all add to the general level of violence, which is now very high. For instance, El Salvador had one of the highest murder rates in the world at more than 100 per 100,000 per annum in the beginning of 2016. A few year ago, the homicide rate in Honduras was the highest in the world at 82 per 100,000. A few years ago, Colombia was at 80 murders per 100,000, while Brazil had 20 per 100,000. The cost in human suffering and lives is horrendous, and the economic cost is staggering. In 1998, the head of the Inter-American Development Bank reported that violence cost the region about $168 billion per year, or 14.2 percent of the regional economic product. Just in Brazil, the cost was $84 billion, or 10.5 percent of the gross domestic product. The figure for Colombia was 24.7 percent. Nor is Central America immune to the growing crime rates. Violent crime increased by 14 percent in the first half of 2004 alone in Guatemala and has now reached epic proportions. Throughout northern Central America violent street gangs, or *maras*, are on the rise. They got their start when thousands of Salvadoran and other street gang members from Los Angeles and elsewhere in the United States lost their residency because of criminal convictions and were deported to their home countries. Gang activity has been so virulent in El Salvador, Honduras, and even Guatemala that their governments have engaged in heavy-handed, often violent, crackdowns on the Mara Salvatrucha, M-18, and other gangs. Yet neither the police nor judicial authorities are able to stop the rapid growth of gangs (*maras*) in the three Central American countries, where they may include as many as 100,000 members. Also on the increase are violent kidnappings and carjackings in Mexico, Central America, Colombia, and elsewhere. The resultant personal insecurity and added economic expense weigh heavily on the region's future and cloud its growing dynamism. Crime and measures to combat it are consuming more of the region's gross national product (GNP) and slowing development. Many are now fleeing the cities to heavily guarded high-rises or gated suburban communities, or they are leaving their countries completely. More and more of the upper and middle classes live in fear of their own countrymen and try to isolate themselves from the masses. As well as economic refugees, there is a growing flood of refugees to the United States because of high levels of crime generally and gang and cartel persecution in Central America and Mexico in particular. These problems, and their causes, will need to be addressed before the region can realize its full potential.

Yet, the growing personal insecurity and environmental degradation that the region is suffering would seem to contradict an essential tenet of Latin American life—*Hay que gozar de la vida* (Life is to be enjoyed). Many Latin Americans note that North Americans (meaning those who are from the United States) live to work and worry much too much about things. In contrast, Latin Americans work to live and *no se preocupan tanto*—do not worry so much. Whenever there is a bare modicum of economic security—and sometimes even when there is not—they live very well indeed. When one is free from the imminent threat of crime, kidnapping, or economic deprivation, life can be an enjoyable experience to be savored. One rarely turns down an invitation to a social gathering and frequently enthusiastically dances until dawn at a *fiesta*. Of those with any means, it is common practice to stop for a coffee or lunch with friends and family, and most business meetings begin with a *cafecito* and talk of family and friends. Indeed, work is generally not the all-consuming activity it has become in the United States, Japan, and parts of Western Europe. However, when the pollution from the street makes it difficult to sit in sidewalk cafes and the frequency of attacks on nocturnal travelers or gang extortions or assassinations make it dangerous to go out at night, the very essence of Latin American existence is challenged. Many are even afraid to leave their houses unattended or in the hands of poorly paid servants because of the frequent break-ins and house takeovers. In countries like Colombia, Guatemala, and El Salvador, and in cities like Mexico City, any person of means or position must also live in fear of kidnapping for ransom or extortion. Thus, rapid urbanization, industrialization, and the persistence of unresolved social and economic problems such as high unemployment, exploitation, and economic injustice have combined with rapid social and cultural change to produce conditions that threaten the very essence of the Latin American lifestyle. Yet, the indomitable Latin American spirit and passion for life propel "the continent" ever onward.

## Notes

1. *Latin* here refers to modern languages that were derived from classical Latin: Spanish, Portuguese, and French in this case. Haiti is included as part of the region (indeed, it was the first country to gain independence—in 1804) and receives its fair share of attention and interest. Those areas still under French colonial rule receive much less attention. French colonies in Latin America include the Caribbean islands of Martinique, Guadeloupe, Saint Martin, and Saint Pierre and Miquelon as well as French Guiana (site of Devil's Island) on the South American continent.

2. Although we will generally not include those areas that do not speak Spanish, Portuguese, or French in our study, it should be noted that the English-speaking part of the region includes not only Belize in Central America and Guyana in South America but also the Caribbean countries of Barbados, Dominica, Grenada, Jamaica, Saint Kitts-Nevis, Saint Lucia, Saint Vincent, and the Grenadines, and Trinidad and Tobago; English-speaking territories include Anguilla, Cayman Islands, Falkland Islands (which Argentina claims as the Islas Malvinas), Montserrat, Turks and Caicos Islands, British Virgin Islands, and U.S. Virgin Islands. Dutch is spoken in the South American nation of Suriname and in the Caribbean Dutch islands of Aruba, Curaçao, Bonaire, Saba, Saint Eustatius, and Saint Maarten.

3. See the award-winning 1970 Peruvian film *La Muralla Verde* (written, produced, and directed by Armando Robles Godoy with Mario Robles Godoy) for a graphic depiction of the struggle with the jungle.

4. Because of the feudal nature of the original *latifundio* system and the way many small producers were primarily subsistence farmers who sold little, if any, of their production for the world market, many spoke of a dual rural economy with aspects of both feudal and capitalist modes of production. The integration into the capitalist world system that authors such as Andre Gunder Frank (1967) emphasized in his *Capitalism and Underdevelopment in Latin America* has now become almost universal as the large farmers and plantations become ever more oriented to the production of cash crops for export and more and more of the smaller farmers are forced to sell their labor in the globalized national economy to survive.

# Bibliography

Black, Jan Knippers, ed. *Latin America, Its Problems and Promise*. 5th ed. Boulder, CO: Westview, 2010.

Blouet, Brian W., and Olwyn M. Blouet. *Latin America and the Caribbean: A Systematic and Regional Survey*. 7th ed. New York: Wiley, 2015.

Burch, Joann J. *Chico Mendes, Defender of the Rain Forest*. Brookfield, CT: Millbrook, 1994.

Dimenstein, Gilberto. *Brazil: War on Children*. London: Latin American Bureau, 1991.

De Jong, Wil, Dianna Donovan, and Ken-ich Abe, *Extreme Conflict and Tropical Forests*. Dordrecht, The Netherlands: Springer, 2007.

Elkin, Judith. *The Jews of Latin America*. 3d ed. Boulder, CO: Lynne Rienner, 2014.

Frank, Andre Gunder. *Capitalism and Underdevelopment in Latin America*. New York: Monthly Review, 1967.

Garrett, James L., ed. *A 2020 Vision for Food, Agriculture, and the Environment in Latin America*. Washington, DC: International Food Policy Research Institute, 1995.

Haralambous, Sappho, ed. *The State of World Rural Poverty: A Profile of Latin America and the Caribbean*. Rome: International Fund for Agricultural Development, 1993.

Hillman, Richard, ed. *Understanding Contemporary Latin America*. 4th ed. Boulder, CO: Lynne Rienner, 2011.

Janvry, Alain de. *The Agrarian Question and Reformism in Latin America*. Baltimore: Johns Hopkins University Press, 1981.

Klich, Ignacio, and Jeffrey Lesser. *Arab and Jewish Immigrants in Latin America: Images and Realities*. London: F. Cass, 1998.

Levine, Robert. *Tropical Diaspora: The Jewish Experience in Cuba*. Gainesville: University Press of Florida, 1993.

Miller, Shawn William, *An Environmental History of Latin America*. New York: Cambridge University Press, 2007.

Page, Joseph A. *The Brazilians*. New York: Addison-Wesley, 1995.

Perfecto, Ivette, and John Vandermeer, *Breakfast of Biodiversity: The Truth about Rainforest Destruction*. 2d ed. Oakland, CA: Food First, 2005.

Place, Susan E., ed. *Tropical Rainforests: Latin American Nature and Society in Transition*. Revised and updated. Wilmington, DE: Scholarly Resources, 2001.

Preston, David, ed. *Latin American Development: Geographical Perspectives*. 2d ed. Harlow, UK: Longman, 1996.

Rifkin, Jeremy. *Biosphere Politics: A New Consciousness for a New Century*. New York: Crown, 1991.

Skole, D. L., and C. J. Tucker. "Tropical Deforestation, Fragmented Habitat, and Adversely Affected Habitat in the Brazilian Amazon: 1978–1988." *Science* 260 (1993): 1905–1910.

Trigo, Eduardo J. *Agriculture, Technological Change, and the Environment in Latin America: A 2020 Perspective*. Washington, DC: International Food Policy Research Institute, 1995.

Vasconcelos, José. *The Cosmic Race: A Bilingual Edition*. Baltimore: Johns Hopkins University Press, 1997.

## FILMS AND VIDEOS

*Bye, Bye Brazil.* Brazil, 1980. A madcap introduction to Brazil.

*Cidade de Deus/City of God.* Brazil, 2003. A modern classic on (very) violent gang activity in the largest slum in Rio de Janeiro.

*Like Water for Chocolate.* Mexico, 1992. Excellent portrait of Mexican family, food, and the daughter who stays at home to care for her mother.

*Mexican Bus Ride.* Mexico, 1951. Classic film by the Spanish director Luis Buñuel on Mexico, life in Latin America, and the institution of the bus in Mexico and Latin America.

*La Muralla Verde/The Green Wall.* Peru, 1970 (video, 1990). An excellent film about a young Lima family that fights bureaucracy and the jungle's green wall to colonize the Peruvian Amazon.

*Pejote.* Brazil, 1981. Gives a glimpse of the life of street children in a large Brazilian city. For a more general view of city life, see *Central Station*, Brazil, 1998.

*Tropa da Elite.* Brazil, 2007. Graphically depicts how an elite police unit in Rio de Janeiro operates in the city's slums.

## WEBSITES

http://lanic.utexas.edu/　　Latin American Center Homepage, University of Texas.

http://www.blueplanetbiomes.org/　　On rain forests in the Amazon.

# TWO

# EARLY HISTORY

For many years, people in the Western Hemisphere have widely celebrated Columbus's 1492 "discovery" of what the Europeans called the "New World." Accordingly, Columbus Day is celebrated as a national holiday in the United States. More broadly, throughout the Americas, the year 1992 was celebrated as the five hundredth anniversary of the "discovery of the Americas;" but not all celebrated. Many Native Americans banded together to solemnly mark the same period as 500 years of mourning because of the many injustices that the European invasion wrought on their people. Indeed, in the first 100 years of colonization, European rule attacked native religion and culture, razed temples and cultural centers to the ground, and forbade the practice of native religions. In so doing, the colonists attacked the very essence of the original Americans, called "Indians" because Columbus and the original explorers mistakenly believed they had reached the East Indies. Colonization was, as the French Antillean author Frantz Fanon suggests, a brutal, violent imposition of European on native. The effect of European rule was so devastating to the native peoples of Latin America that their numbers were reduced by as much as 90 percent during the first 100 years of European occupation.

There are several versions of how the Iberians treated the native people they encountered. The indigenous version is one of conquest, domination, and subordination. Yet Spain maintained that it brought Christianity and Western civilization to the world it found. In contrast, England long propagated the Black Legend about the cruelties of Spanish colonial rule in the Americas and attributed much of the native population's decline to the barbarities they suffered at the hands of the Spaniards. Another explanation of this precipitous decline is found in several recent studies that make an ever-stronger case for the disease theory of population decline—that is, the main cause of the radical decline in population of the original Americans was not the undeniable cruelty practiced by many of the Spaniards but the unstoppable epidemics of smallpox, measles, typhus, and other diseases that swept through the native population. The first Americans had not, it seems, acquired any natural immunity to these and other diseases the Europeans brought with them. Thus, they were ravaged by them. Many also argue this was the principal factor in the Spaniards' astounding conquest of millions of people with a few hundred *conquistadores.* Indeed, the diseases often spread so rapidly that they arrived before the Spaniards. Evaluating these different perspectives, one might conclude that the story does indeed sometimes change over time but that each new version adds to our understanding of the past. Not surprisingly, then, we find that our historical views of what happened in the sixteenth century are heavily colored not only by the cruelty that gave rise to the Black Legend but also by our present understanding of epidemiology.

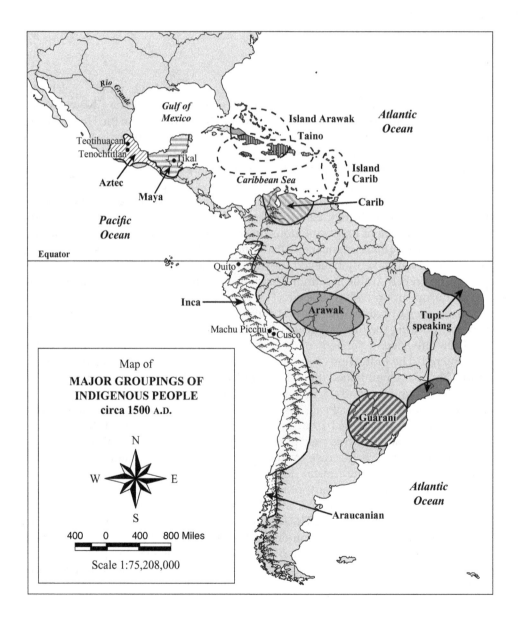

Map of
**MAJOR GROUPINGS OF INDIGENOUS PEOPLE circa 1500 A.D.**

400    0    400    800 Miles

Scale 1:75,208,000

# People in the Americas before the Conquest

To understand the historical context in which political power is exercised in Latin America, we need to briefly trace the human past as it developed in the Americas. Human history did not begin when Europeans began arriving in the Western Hemisphere in large numbers after 1492. Indeed, the common ancestry of all racial groups who found their way to the Americas was neither European nor Asian. Currently, it is believed that the earliest humans emerged on the shores of Lake Victoria in East Africa some 3 million years ago. The famous Leakey family of anthropologists' discovery of tools and bone fragments from our most ancient human predecessors suggests an African birthplace for our species. From there, it is believed, humans spread south in Africa and north to the Middle East, Asia, and eventually Europe. Later, they crossed the land and ice bridge that spanned the Bering Strait from what is now eastern Russia to arrive in Alaska during the Ice Age.

## INDIGENOUS CIVILIZATION

The movement of peoples from Asia to North America occurred in waves and began as early as 40,000 years ago. It continued until about 8000 B.C.E. These immigrants first populated the Western Hemisphere and were the first Americans. They swept down from Alaska and spread across North America and into the Caribbean and Central America; from there they spread down the west coast of South America and then eastward across the continent. As their productive forces increased, they moved from a nomadic existence to one of sedentary agriculture. By 1500 B.C.E., there were villages of full-time farmers. Corn, beans, and squash became staples in Mesoamerica (the southern two-thirds of Mexico, all of Guatemala, and most of El Salvador, Belize, Honduras, and Nicaragua), while potatoes, manioc, and amaranth were dominant in areas of South America. The large numbers of different ethnic groups practiced sedentary or semisedentary agriculture. As they further developed their productivity, they formed larger groups: tribes, chiefdoms, and states. This also led to more concentrated political power.

Native American settlements were scattered throughout the region. The population did, however, become concentrated in three areas: present-day central Mexico, southern Mexico, and northern Central America; along the Pacific Coast; and in the Andean highlands in what is now Peru, Bolivia, and Ecuador. Here, agricultural production was sufficiently advanced to sustain a large, relatively concentrated population. Each of these areas eventually developed a dominant, centralized state civilization that came to be known, respectively, as Aztec, Mayan, and Incan. Smaller political groupings developed elsewhere.

Many aspects of these empires have influenced the culture and even the political organization of subsequent polities in these areas. In that little about these civilizations is usually included in most general courses, the following section presents a rudimentary description of their key aspects.

Large draft or meat animals that could be domesticated were not available to the native civilizations. In the west coast civilization in South America, the guinea pig was domesticated as a source of food, and the llama was used as a pack animal

DISPUTED BY
ENGLAND, RUSSIA
AND SPAIN

NEW
FRANCE

ENGLISH COLONIES

EFFECTIVE FRONTIER
OF SPANISH
SETTLEMENT

FLORIDA
Ceded to England,
1763–1783

ATLANTIC
OCEAN

VICEROYALTY OF
NEW SPAIN

HAITI
(SAINT DOMINGUE)
Ceded to France, 1697

Guadalajara •   • Mexico City

• Santo
Domingo

JAMAICA
Conquered by
England, 1655

Guatemala •

• Caracas

VICEROYALTY OF
NEW GRANADA

Bogotá •

GUIANA

Separated from
Viceroyalty of Peru,
1717, 1739

• Quito

Pernambuco •

VICEROYALTY OF
PERU

VICEROYALTY OF
BRAZIL

PACIFIC
OCEAN

Lima •   • Cusco

Salvador
(Bahia)

Chuquisaca
(La Plata, Sucre) •

Sao Paulo •

• Rio de Janeiro
(Capital, 1763)

VICEROYALTY
OF LA PLATA
Separated from
Viceroyalty of Peru,
1776

Santiago •

Map of

**COLONIAL
LATIN AMERICA**

N

W        E

S

AUDIENCIA OF CHILE
Retained by
Viceroyalty of Peru,
1776

ANDES MTS.

Buenos
Aires •

CLAIMED BUT
NOT SETTLED
BY SPAIN

0      500      1000 Miles

and as a source of wool and meat. The Aztecs bred a small mute dog for food in Mexico. Unlike in Europe, there were no cattle, horses, or oxen.

The use of baskets and of stone, bone, and wood gave way to the development of pottery and more sophisticated stone (obsidian) weapons and tools and eventually to the use of bronze in the Aztec and Incan Empires. In the first more developed societies to emerge, such as the Olmecs and Toltecs in Mexico and the Mochica in coastal Peru, large temple-centered cities emerged. They were beautifully designed and employed sophisticated stone and adobe construction. Only in the thirteenth and fourteenth centuries did these city-centered societies begin to expand and form empires. They were still in the process of expansion when the Europeans arrived.

Our knowledge of these societies is incomplete, in part because there were few chronicles and inscriptions in Incan and pre-Incan civilizations on the west coast of South America and because many of the written texts, inscriptions, and chronicles that did exist for the Aztecs and Mayans were destroyed by the Europeans. The story of these peoples is only now being reconstructed through the laborious work of archaeologists and ethnologists from around the world.

**The Maya.** Mayan civilization flowered between 300 B.C.E. and 1100 C.E. During this time, Europe witnessed the disintegration of the Roman Empire, the rise of the Holy Roman Empire, and the beginning of the Middle Ages. Mayan civilization consisted of a series of city-states that developed in the Petén region of northern Guatemala, the Yucatán, and Chiapas in what is now Mexico. Their cities later spread into Belize and part of Honduras and eventually numbered about fifty. The Mayans developed what was then a very sophisticated native civilization. Their political-social organization was, however, hierarchical, with a king, nobles, and priests on top and the common people and slaves on the bottom; decision-making was authoritarian.

In the original Mayan states, the common people lived in thatched roof huts, not unlike those of the poor Mayan peasants of today, and nourished themselves on a balanced diet consisting of beans, corn, and squash. These crops could be cultivated in the same field. Planting the corn first ensured that it grew upward toward the all-important sun; the beans then used the stalk of the corn to follow the same path, while the broad leaves of the squash spread out on the ground to shade the soil from the desiccating rays of the sun and inhibit the growth of weeds. Further, the beans added nitrogen to the soil as the corn and squash removed it. The Mayan calendar also specified times when the land was to lie fallow. Terraces were used in highland areas to increase land area and stop soil erosion.

It is currently believed that the Mayan peasants paid tribute to the political and religious rulers in the cities. They in turn engaged in warfare with other city-states to gain more riches and obtain additional tribute. They also established extended commercial relations with civilizations to the north and even used the sea as a trade route.

In about 900 C.E., Mayan civilization suffered a rapid decline. The major cities and ceremonial centers were eventually abandoned, to be reclaimed by the jungle. Current research suggests the causes for this disaster were probably lack of adequate food production and soil exhaustion from overfarming, which had been induced by what evidently became an unsustainable population density.

The Maya's accomplishments in astronomy, mathematics, ideographic writing, architecture, and art and their highly sophisticated calendar mark them as one of

Rising some 148 feet out of the jungle in the Petén region of Guatemala, the Temple of the Jaguar in Tikal is one of the greatest Mayan structures. Apparently used for ceremonial purposes, it dates from the classical Mayan period and was constructed about 700 C.E. *(Photo by H. Vanden)*

the most developed civilizations of their time. They had incorporated advances in timekeeping from the Toltec and Olmec and employed the resultant extremely accurate 365-day calendar of eighteen months of twenty days with five additional days or "dead" days (which were considered unlucky). Their mathematical system used units of one, five, and twenty (which could be written as dots for ones and dashes for fives, with twenties denoted by position) and included a place value system employing a sign for zero. During their classical period, their calendar, astronomical observations, and use of zero as a place in written numbers marked their civilization as more advanced than any in Europe in these areas. Their hieroglyph-type writing recounted great events in their history and mythology and was carved or painted on their temples, pyramids, or upright stone *stelae* or recorded in their bark-paper codices. Recent research suggests symbols for syllables were also sometimes used to phonetically sound out words. Although only four of the original glyph codices survived, an early Spanish transcription of the Quiche Mayan creation story, the Popol Vuh, is now part of world literature. Mayan civilization thrived in the classic period from 250 to 900 C.E. in the lowlands in northern Central America and southern Mexico. Great city-state centers like Tikal, Palenque, and Copan flourished.

Although there were occasional female rulers, the societies were patriarchal, and the royal succession was decided through primogeniture. The kings and the nobles made up the ruling class but worked closely with the priests, who were also the astronomers and chroniclers as well as the theologians. Human sacrifice and bloodletting were integral parts of the ceremonial functions, with special importance placed on blood derived from puncturing the royal penis. The losers in a version of Mayan soccer were often beheaded or rolled down the steps of the great pyramids after being tied together as human balls.

Postclassical Mayan civilization lived on in the Yucatán centers like Chichén Itzá and Uxmal after other Mayan lands were conquered by the Spaniards beginning in 1527. As had been the case with the Aztecs, much of the remaining Mayan culture was destroyed by the Spanish authorities, who, despite some initial efforts by priests to preserve Mayan culture, eventually burned many invaluable codices as works of the devil, thus depriving the Mayan people of a good part of their history and heritage. Perhaps because of the strength and sophistication of their culture, Mayan resistance to European domination lived on in more remote areas for centuries and bubbled to the surface occasionally. The Caste Wars in the Yucatán in the nineteenth century (isolated pockets of rebellion lasted into the twentieth century), the indigenous support for some guerrilla groups in the Guatemalan highlands in the 1980s, and the Zapatista uprising in Chiapas in the 1990s were more recent manifestations. Mayan languages are still spoken in these areas, and some religious practices are still honored.

**The Aztecs.** The Aztecs replaced previous native civilizations like that of Teotihuacan and the Toltecs in central Mexico and the Olmecs in eastern Mexico and incorporated many of the values, knowledge, and technology of their predecessors' cultures. By the time Hernán Cortés arrived in central Mexico in 1519, there were perhaps 25 million inhabitants in the region (there is some controversy as to the exact number here and elsewhere in the region). The Aztecs, who migrated from northern Mexico, arrived in the Valley of Mexico in the early 1200s. They were relegated to marshy land not occupied by any other ethnic group. There, they established their capital, Tenochtitlán, on an island in Lake Texcoco about 1325. As their myths explain, they picked the spot because they saw the promised sign of an eagle clutching a snake perched atop a cactus (this symbol graces the Mexican flag).

The Aztec capital became very populous; it had between 150,000 and 200,000 inhabitants by the time of the conquest. As many as 60,000 came to an open-air market each day. Aztec civilization was characterized by military prowess, which extended control beyond the mountains ringing the Valley of Mexico through most of central Mexico and as far south as the Guatemalan border. Once they subjugated other peoples, the Aztecs forced them to pay tribute but did not directly occupy their land save in times of rebellion. Their frequent military campaigns provided many prisoners from the loose-knit empire.

Aztec traders and merchants ranged far and wide. The thriving merchant class lived well. There were large houses for the nobility and the priests, palaces for the emperor, monumental limestone-covered pyramids, temples and other public buildings, and thatched-roof huts for the commoners. Agriculture and trade provided the economic base for the society, which had also developed a well-respected artisan class. The common people consumed corn, beans, and vegetables garnished with chili sauces as their daily meals. The nobility and emperor had diets that included abundant fowl, venison, and the drink reserved solely for them—chocolate. Aztec civilization excelled in engineering, architecture, astronomy, and mathematics. Based on earlier achievements of the Toltecs and Maya, the Aztecs adopted the same 365-day calendar, divided into eighteen months of twenty days, with five additional or "hollow" days added. The calendar also marked the beginning and end of religious rituals. A type of pictorial writing had been developed that was linked to some phonetic elements and was found in their codices, or paper-like books. They did elaborate metal work in gold and silver but not iron. Like other civilizations in the Americas, the Aztecs had not yet learned how to work hard metals and did not use the wheel, nor, as noted before, had nature provided draft animals or beasts of burden.

Power was concentrated and vertical. The Aztec polity was a hierarchical theocracy headed by an emperor who was assisted by four great lords. Next came the politically powerful priests and nobles. The power of the ruler was not unlike that exercised by Mexican leaders in the last two centuries. The ruler exercised power absolutely and often despotically. The new Aztec emperor was chosen by a tribal council, where priests, state officials, and warriors dominated. He was chosen from among the sons, brothers, or nephews of the previous ruler. When Cortés arrived in 1519 and began to subjugate the Aztecs, Moctezuma II was the ruler. He had succeeded his uncle.

By the late fifteenth century, the number of private estates belonging to the nobles had begun to grow, with the subsequent conversion of small farmers into farm workers and tenant farmers. Slavery was a recognized institution and, as in African society, was used as a punishment for a variety of offenses. There was continuing incentives for the frequent wars and uprisings that occurred within the empire. The continuing conflicts provided an almost constant flow of prisoners, who were sometimes sold as slaves to be used as forced labor but were most often sacrificed in large numbers to Aztec deities like Huitzilopochli, the god of war.

Conflicts within the Aztec Empire hastened its demise. With the help of the Tlaxcalans and other Aztec enemies, the Spaniards (whose numbers never exceeded 600) finally defeated the last Aztec emperor, Cuauhtemoc, in 1521. This signaled the formal end of what had been a great, although autocratic, civilization. When the capital had been stripped of its gold and silver, Cortés ordered the temples burned and the city of Tenochtitlán razed. As a way of legitimizing European rule, orders were given to have Mexico City built on the ruins of the old city. It can be argued, however, that the hierarchical power configurations, brutality of those who ruled, and political patriarchy were part of the legacy that did survive and that they left indelible marks on subsequent society and the polities that emerged in the centuries that followed.

**The Incas.** The third great pre-Columbian civilization in the Americas at the time of the conquest was the Incan Empire. The Incas date their early development back to the 1200s but did not begin to expand into an empire until the middle of the fifteenth century. This expansion was led by a series of extremely capable rulers. outstanding among these was Pachacuti Inca Yupanqui (ruler from the late 1400s to 1525), who many consider to be one of the great rulers and conquerors in the annals of history. The empire was centered in the Andes Mountains around the valley of Cuzco in southern Peru and eventually extended from what is now Colombia's southern border for 3,621 kilometers (2,250 miles) through Ecuador, Peru, and Bolivia into northern Chile and northwest Argentina. At its zenith in the early 1500s, it was tied together by an excellent system of often narrow stone roads, which facilitated communication and troop movement. A system of relay runners could carry messages at the rate of some 241 kilometers (150 miles) a day. The llama was used as a pack animal, but the wheel was not part of their technology. There was no written language, and history and events were kept by official memorizers. Also employed was the *kipu*, a memory device composed of a handle with cords of different colors attached to it. Knots were tied in the different color strands at different lengths to signify quantity and events.

The land was intensively tilled, and terraces were built in the highlands to improve and expand the fields. The cultivation of a variety of different types of potato (which originated in the Andes) was highly perfected, as was the cultivation of corn. The common people primarily ate potatoes and corn. The latter crop was also collected by the rulers as a form of tribute. A portion of the grain harvest was given to the state to be kept in state storehouses. It was distributed to the elderly, the infirm, and the widowed or to villages in times of famine or natural disaster. Coca leaves (which are still used today), beans, amaranth, and other crops were also grown.

The state was more developed than other pre-Columbian civilizations and ruled by a semidivine hereditary king called the *Inca*. Power was centralized in his hands, and he was assisted by other members of the royal family, the nobility, and the royal administrators, who were responsible for running the far-flung empire. A lesser nobility also existed. The artisans and agriculturists were on the bottom of the social pyramid and lived in humble, adobe-sided, thatched-roof huts with simple furnishings. Priests and public officials also received grain from the storehouses, as did those pressed into public labor. The state owned or administered most of the society and could require unpaid labor on roads, other public works, or the land of the ruler or estate holders. Writers such as the Peruvian indigenist José  Carlos Mariátegui have characterized this as a form of state socialism. Even today,  there is still a strong communal heritage in the Indian villages in the Andes.

Some have also noted the importance of the collection of tribute in this system and have further suggested that, as was the case in the Aztec Empire, the tradition of tribute made it very easy for the Spaniards to also extract tribute from the indigenous population.

The Incan Empire was administratively divided into four parts, with each part subdivided into provinces. The basic unit was the *ayllu*, which was organized around the extended family. Villages were formed by a collection of *ayllus*, and a grouping of these was ruled over by a *curaca*, or ethnic lord.

Like their Mayan and Aztec counterparts, the Incas had a developed theological system. They had a pantheon of gods beginning with Viracocha, the creator, and Inti, the sun god. Also included was Tumi, the god invoked in human sacrifice. They gave special attention to events like the summer solstice, which occasioned great ceremony and feasting. This is still a major festival in the Peruvian highlands.

The Incas excelled in pottery and weaving and had the proficiency to open the skull in a form of brain surgery. Their architecture was impressive and marked by their ability to move huge stones (on wooden rollers) that weighed tons and then carefully cut and fit them together without mortar. The Cuzco fortress of Sacsahuaman is an excellent example of this. In metallurgy, they were quite proficient in the production of gold, silver, and copper, and they even made some of their tools from bronze. They did not, however, utilize iron.

**Less Centralized Societies.** There were many other less centralized native civilizations as well. These societies were based on hunting, gathering, and agriculture. When they did grow foods, they often practiced slash-and-burn agriculture. Their social organization was much more decentralized than that of the Aztecs, Incas, or Maya. Carib (the origin of the word *Caribbean*), Taíno, and other Arawak peoples populated Antilles islands like Hispaniola, Cuba, and Puerto Rico and were the first to have contact with the Spanish explorers. At the time of Colombus's arrival, there were Arawak settlements extending from Florida to the Amazon basin. Also of importance were the Taíno, who were a native people found in Puerto Rico, Cuba, Hispaniola, and elsewhere in the Caribbean. Their treatment by the Europeans and susceptibility to disease caused them to virtually disappear during the first generation after the conquest.

Other less politically centralized groups fared better. The Mapuche (whom the Spaniards called Araucanians) of Chile and Argentina offered such spirited and sustained resistance to the European invaders that they were not completely conquered until 1883. Similarly, the Apaches of northern Mexico battled on until the last decades of the nineteenth century. The Mapuche of southern Chile continue to struggle for their cultural survival today.

# The Conquest

The first clash of European and Native American civilizations occurred when the Spanish explorers and *conquistadores* consolidated their power in the Caribbean in the 1490s and early 1500s. Santo Domingo and later Havana in particular had become major staging areas for expeditions to other areas. Native people in the Caribbean were rapidly subjugated, and the conquerors looked elsewhere for gold and glory. By the second decade of the sixteenth century, rumors of a rich civilization in central Mexico reached the new colonial rulers in the Caribbean.

Like many of the *conquistadores*, Hernán Cortés was a poor noble, or *hidalgo*, who came to the New World to make his fortune. Commissioned by the colonial authorities to explore the Mexican gulf coast, he led an expedition of 600 men from Cuba to Mexico in 1519. Violating orders established by the governor of Cuba, Cortés landed on the coast and soon made allies with local tribes that had been forced into tributary status by the Aztecs. He was given a resourceful native woman by one of the chiefs. Malinche (Marina), or "la Malinche" as she was called by subsequent generations, became Cortés's translator, advisor, and eventually mistress. Because of this collaboration, she has often been equated with the betrayal of Latin American culture and autonomy and is sometimes seen as a symbol of selling out to outside interests. Others note that a more nuanced reading of her life reveals her to be a woman trying to survive in a complex time in which both indigenous and European societies cemented relationships through the use of native women.

Cortés sent some of his force back to Cuba for more proper authorization and reinforcements and left other men installed in the newly formed municipality of Vera Cruz on the coast. He then ordered his ships burned and directed his main force toward the Aztec capital. They were greatly aided not only by their horses (which were unknown to the natives), diseases, steel swords, steel armor, guns, and cannons but also by an Aztec myth. Cortés was coming in the year that was foretold for the return of the deposed plumed serpent king Quetzalcóatl. The Spanish leader was seen by the Aztec ruler Moctezuma II as Quetzalcóatl returning to claim his throne, and his arrival was not resisted, although Aztec resistance did spring up once the avaricious nature of the Spaniards became evident and the indecisive Moctezuma was replaced by more aggressive rulers.

Christopher Columbus landed in Central America in 1502 on his fourth voyage to the Americas. After Vasco Núñez de Balboa crossed the isthmus and discovered the Pacific Ocean in 1513, settlements were set up on the Caribbean side of Panama. They were later used as transit points between the two oceans. On the Pacific coast, Panama City was not founded until 1519. As expeditions went north from Panama into what is now Costa Rica and Nicaragua, no large, centralized civilizations were encountered and the indigenous groups were soon subjugated. By the second decade of the sixteenth century, Cortés was sending expeditions south from Mexico. By this time, the Maya in Central America were not highly organized in city-states, although there were heavily populated areas in Guatemala. Guatemala City, founded in 1524, eventually became the administrative center for the part of Central America north of Panama. From the time of the earliest European arrivals, there were rivalries among different groups and leaders and a great deal of conflict. Indeed, within two years of the founding of the cities of Granada and León in present-day Nicaragua, the two centers were engaged in a conflict that might be best described as a civil war. This pattern of behavior has persisted in most of the Central American isthmus to the present.

After reports of the riches of the empire to the south had reached the Spanish settlement in Panama, considerable interest in conquest developed. After going back to Spain for special authorization to colonize the great civilization in South America, Francisco Pizarro sailed from Panama with a band of some 200 *conquistadores*. They landed on the Peruvian coast in 1532. The Incan Empire was then at the height of its territorial expansion and encompassed more than 10 million people. However, it was engaged in civil war. The last *Inca*, Huayna Capac, had died without naming his successor, and his two sons, Huáscar and Atahualpa, were both competing for the throne. Atahualpa had just captured Huáscar as the Spaniards arrived, but many followers of the latter were still ready to continue the conflict. Pizarro arranged a meeting with the victor in Cajamarca but used the occasion to capture Atahualpa and slaughter many of his surprised followers. Atahualpa ordered the execution of Huáscar lest he mobilize his supporters and soon offered his Spanish captors a surprising ransom to gain his freedom. Realizing the Spaniards' obsession with gold, he offered to buy his freedom by filling the room where he was kept with gold and silver to the height of his raised arm. As pack trains of llamas were bringing the ransom from the far corners of the empire, Atahualpa's cruel captors nonetheless executed him by garrote. From there, Pizarro and his men went on to capture and loot the Incan capital Cuzco, despite the heroic resistance led by the new *Inca*, Manco Copac. By 1535 the empire was, for all intents and purposes, under Spanish control.

## How Could They Do It?

One question remains unresolved: How could a few hundred Spaniards conquer empires of millions? One reason would surely be the indomitable Spanish spirit forged in the crucible of Iberian culture, where for centuries men had symbolically pitted themselves against huge bulls and reveled in the seemingly impossible victory. It is difficult to explain all the reasons for the ease of the conquest, but authors, such as Benjamin Keen, note some of the following:

1. The Spaniards and Portuguese had honed their fighting and tactical skills in the 700-year reconquest of the Iberian peninsula from the Moors.
2. The Spaniards came outfitted as the soldiers of the great power of the time and enjoyed the latest in military armament and technology: steel swords and armor from foundries like those in Toledo, guns and cannons, horses, cavalries, and huge attack dogs. The Amero-Indian armies had neither steel nor guns and had never seen horses. Further, their notion of war was more limited, and their tactics were generally more ritualistic and emphasized advance warning of attack and capturing the enemy to increase the pool of sacrificial victims. The Europeans focused on swift, sure victory and dispensed with their enemies quickly.
3. As suggested earlier, the diseases that the Europeans brought wiped out whole native populations and greatly debilitated the native armies.
4. The Indian peoples often first saw the Spaniards as gods or demigods and were initially reluctant to destroy them.
5. The three most highly advanced indigenous civilizations had become quite sedentary over the years and would not think of fleeing their agricultural land to regroup elsewhere.
6. The hierarchical and often cruel nature of the political leadership in the native civilizations had accustomed the common people to authoritarian decision-making and arbitrary acts from above and had conditioned the common people not to rebel against the current leaders or those who wielded power. The Spaniards were at least initially perceived as just one more ruling group that had taken over.

# Early Colony

The conquest was a joint endeavor between the crown and private entrepreneurs. The conquistador leader was expected to equip his band with the necessary arms and supplies or find financial backers who would. In turn, he and his mates had a royal license to hunt treasure and native peoples who had not embraced Christianity, for their own profit. The only requirement was that they pay the royal fifth, or *quinto real*, to the crown. Much of the nature of the early colony was dictated by the conditions of the conquest. The Spaniards came for gold, glory, and God and competed fiercely for the former. Many were poor noblemen, or *hidalgos*, but most came from more humble origins. The wealth from looted native cities and civilizations was shared among the members of the conquering military bands. *Encomiendas* and titles were handed out later but usually just to the captains and leaders. Cortés, for instance, proved to be as successful in business as he was in conquest. He amassed a series of large and very profitable holdings in Mexico and proved very apt in his business dealings.

However, only a few of the *conquistadores* achieved the fortunes they desired, and many remained disappointed and bitter. After the initial years of the conquest, more and more Spaniards came in search of fortune at a time when there were few additional native civilizations to loot. In Peru, much of the early sixteenth century was spent in fighting, assassination, and intrigue among the conqueror Francisco Pizarro, his brother, and other Spaniards. Treachery and betrayal were common. The native peoples were often completely brutalized in the plundering of their societies and were at best seen by most as instruments of lucre and occasionally lust: slaves to capture and sell, laborers to exploit, owners of land or property to be seized, women to be used. The colonialists often rose in rebellion when reforms were attempted.

The Spaniards conquered an area forty times the size of Spain. They and the Portuguese had the power and the audacity to enslave the better part of the population on two continents. They did not come as equals but as forceful conquerors. It was their belief that they were morally superior, possessed of the true faith (which was to be imposed more than practiced), and presented with the opportunity of their lives for fame and wealth. The nature of the colony was foretold by Columbus's action on the island of Hispaniola during his second voyage. Anxious to prove the economic viability of the lands he had found, he began to force the natives to bring him a tribute of gold dust. When they refused and rebelled against their would-be masters, Columbus gave the orders to have large numbers of the locals captured and held. As a way of continuing to extract value from the natives, he sent several hundred to Europe as slaves. To placate the gold-starved settlers on the island, he distributed most of the remaining prisoners to them as a form of bounty. As was to be the case throughout the region, the original Americans would be enslaved outright or divided among the European settlers who took their land and then forced them to contribute their labor to the new European enterprise. The original inhabitants of Hispaniola declined rapidly because of disease and the harsh treatment handed out by the Europeans. Of the several hundred thousand inhabitants on Hispaniola at the time of Columbus's arrival, only some 29,000 were alive two decades later. By the mid-1500s, hardly any natives were left.

Ironically, the original *conquistadores* proved to be an endangered group as well. They were soon removed from power and replaced by direct representatives of the king whose loyalty to the crown was unquestioned. In this and other areas, European institutions began to replace the military structures and unbridled civilian power that marked the conquest. Thus, the Iberian colonial bureaucracy began to replace the arbitrary rapaciousness of the conquerors.

## ESTABLISHING A NEW SOCIAL STRUCTURE: THE *CASTAS*

Spanish legislation created a complicated system of social classification consisting of the *castas*, defined by descent and color. On the top were the recently immigrated white Spaniards, the peninsular whites; below them were the descendants of the white colonists, called white *criollos*; after them came the brown people, the *pardos* or mestizos, who consisted of people with mixed ancestry. As time went on, the ranks of the lower and middle classes were bolstered by mestizos, mulattos, and *zambos*. The social pyramid that resulted from the conquest and the colonization consisted of a small group of powerful and usually wealthy Europeans or their descendants on top; a large number of natives and, soon, African slaves on the bottom; and a few Spanish artisans, soldiers, or small merchants as a wisp of a middle class.

The society that the Europeans brought with them from the Iberian peninsula was feudal in nature. Land tenure and many of the social institutions of the colony were more feudal than modern. The early colony still labored under the medieval philosophical doctrine of scholasticism. Thus, considerable time was spent debating the true nature of the Indian population and the comparability of their souls with those of the Europeans. Moral argument and ethical debate were, however, rarely a match for the immense influence of a powerful person in the New World. Like the *grand señor* in Spain or Portugal, he (rarely she) was the unchallenged master of his domain. His will could be imposed in high and low places. Judges would listen, and peons, his to use as he saw fit, had very few practical rights (as contrasted to often extensive but unrealized legal rights).

## WOMEN AND POWER

Few European women came in the earliest years of the colony. Those who did were subject to the strict traditional mores of the Iberian peninsula. However, women unprotected by both class (upper) and race (white) might well be available to the person of power to *coger* (generally meaning "to grab or seize," although in parts of Latin America it came to mean "to have sexual relations"). Thus, lower-class women of color were often at the disposal of men of lighter caste and higher class. In mostly Indian Bolivia, for instance, many *latifundistas*, or large landowners, were able to exercise the *derecho de pernada* (the sexual right to women on their estate) well into the twentieth century. Most upper-class women were strongly subordinated to male members of the family. There are, however, cases of a few women running large estates and even participating in colonial administration. There are more cases of women being the owners of record for huge amounts of land or other forms of wealth. Many of these inherited their wealth and prestige from a husband or father. In more general transgender terms, their power and strength were respected (although not necessarily liked or even accepted whenever an opportunity for noncompliance or rebellion presented itself). In that women were socialized to be meek, they were at a distinct disadvantage. Further, domination in many forms was omnipresent, and it colored the colony and subsequent social and political relations in Latin America in gender relations, politics, and many other areas.

## LABOR

Persons of importance in Spain and Portugal did not engage in manual labor, in large part because they were nobles or aspired to be like them. This attitude was carried over into the American colonies and permeated the societies with a disdain for manual labor that is perhaps most poignantly manifest in the low wages and lack of respect such labor still engenders and the hesitancy to engage in it carried by most members of the upper class and many in the middle class. The initial abundance of free Indian labor heightened this characteristic, as did the subsequent importation of large numbers of African slaves. Over time these labor pools were augmented by the progeny of often-illicit unions of Europeans and Amero-Indians (mestizos) and Europeans and Africans (mulattos).

Symbolic of the exploitative use of Amero-Indian labor and land was the *encomienda* (*sesmaria* in Brazil). The *encomienda* originated in a Spanish practice of granting jurisdiction over lands and peoples captured from the Moors to one of the warriors who led the reconquest. In Spanish and Portuguese America, it came to be the assignment of a group of native people to a conquistador or other colonist. He would oversee them and the land on which they lived and be responsible for their proper Christianization. They in turn were to serve him with their labor and by paying him tribute. This form of forced semislave labor was often supplemented with the labor of Indian slaves. The Dominicans and church officials like Bishop Bartolomé de Las Casas championed Indian rights and endeavored to stop some of the worst practices against the indigenous population. In 1512, the crown responded with the Laws of Burgos to outlaw some of the worst abuses of the Native Americans and make Indian slavery illegal. In 1549, the *encomendero's* right to demand labor from his *tributarios* was also outlawed. Both practices did, however, continue well beyond these dates in some areas.

After the decline of the *encomienda,* land, mine, and *obraje* (textile workshop) owners were forced to rely on the *repartimiento* for their free labor. The *repartimiento* was the practice of requiring the Indian population to provide a set amount of free labor to the landowners, the owners of the mines, the workshop or *obraje* operators, or the state for public works. In Peru, where the *repartimiento* was known by the old Incan term *mita*, as much as six months to a year of service could be required from each male every seven years. The Indians were often horribly exploited (thousands died at mines like Potosí, in what is now Bolivia), even though they did receive a token wage. As the historian Benjamin Keen observes, "the repartimiento like the encomienda was a disguised form of slavery." Indeed, there were harsh penalties for those who avoided service and for community leaders who could not provide the required quotas of laborers.

## SLAVERY AND OTHER FORMS OF ORGANIZATION

As is the case in the United States, Latin America is still feeling the effects of slavery. It is not possible to understand society or working conditions in Brazil, Cuba, Haiti, the Dominican Republic, or the other Latin American societies without understanding the lasting effects of this institution. As suggested by the popularity of the Brazilian *telenovelas* (soap operas), Brazilian society is still reverberating from the adoration a rich Brazilian miner showered on Xica da Silva, the mulatto slave woman he called his "African queen." Yet, one of the worst aspects of the process of colonization was enslavement. The Eurocentrism and racism of the European colonizers initially allowed them to see the native peoples as non-Christian pagans who were inferior and, like the rest of what they found, there to be used by the colonizers. Slavery existed in Europe, North Africa, and the Middle East from long before the conquest. From here, the practice of enslaving native people spread to the Americas. Initially, raiding parties were sent out to find slaves to be used for forced labor and thus thousands of the original inhabitants of the Americas were enslaved in the first century of colonization. As the native population was rapidly depleted and as more laws to protect the indigenous population were passed and sometimes enforced by the crown, landowners needed to look elsewhere for exploitable labor. The outlawing of Indian slavery accelerated this process.

As in other areas, slavery was also an institution in Africa, but it was tied to specific functions. It was, for instance, a way of punishing incorrigible criminals in societies that had mores against drawing blood from their clansmen. Slavery became a recognized institution in Middle Eastern Muslim societies. So it was that there was a growing slave trade in Arab lands and from northern African societies that were conquered by them. Slave traders were soon penetrating farther south into Africa from the area around the Sudan and elsewhere. The proximity of the market for African slaves in the Middle East and North Africa helped establish the slave trade as an international activity.

In the process of seeking a route to the Far East that did not have to pass through the Muslim-controlled Middle East, the Portuguese began to penetrate farther and farther south along Africa's west coast. Spurred on by advances in navigation that were supported by Prince Henry the Navigator after 1450, they eventually circumnavigated the African continent to establish sea routes to the Indies. As they did this, Portuguese settlements were established all along the African coast and trade was begun. Soon, the Portuguese took over islands off the Atlantic coast (Madeira and the Cape Verde Islands). Later, they colonized several of the areas where they had settlements (Angola, Guinea Bissau, and Mozambique).

Stimulated by the strong market for sugar in Europe, Arabs had begun the cultivation of sugar cane in North Africa. Slave labor was used to supply the intense labor needed in the cutting and milling process. When the Portuguese decided to cultivate sugar cane in their Atlantic islands, they copied the Arab use of slave labor. The Portuguese then began to use their outposts in western and southern Africa to capture or buy slaves. When the Portuguese took the cultivation of sugar cane to their colony in Brazil in the 1500s, they also installed a plantation system based on slave labor. As the Dutch, English, and French adopted this crop in their Caribbean possessions, they too relied on a system of slave labor. On arriving in the Americas, the European colonists were faced with tremendous expanses of land available to them. It soon became clear that they needed to find crops and the labor to cultivate them if they were to turn their new possessions into paying propositions. In northern Brazil and the Caribbean, native slavery failed, and the native peoples would not otherwise provide the abundant labor needed. The super-utilization of native peoples and their understandable dislike for the European system combined with factors like their rapid depletion by European-borne diseases (particularly in the Caribbean) and their ability to flee farther into the interior of Brazil served to minimize the number of available workers. This ensured that the Europeans' voracious appetite for cheap and easily exploitable labor could not be satisfied by the local supply in these areas. The use of indentured servants was also to become part of colonial life, but this source of cheap labor also proved insufficient for the demand. Nor did the well-to-do European landowning elite have any intention of farming the land themselves. They were much more prone to use the labor of others to accumulate their wealth and finance trips to London, Madrid, or Lisbon.

Slaves, then, had initially been acquired by Portuguese and Arab raiding parties and traders. Later, the Portuguese used their trade connections, outposts, and a series of slave forts to buy more and more slaves for the growing market in the Americas. During the first century of the colony, they enjoyed a monopoly on the importation of slaves in the Spanish colonies and Brazil. In this way, the transatlantic slave trade was begun. As the trade in humans grew, England and other countries also engaged in the lucrative business. The triangular trade took guns, rum, metal tools, and whiskey to Africa, where these were traded for slaves. Those who survived the horrendous Middle Passage were in turn sold in the slave markets in Havana and elsewhere, and the ships were loaded with tobacco, rum, and indigo for the trip back to Europe. From here the journey began anew. More than 7 million souls were brought to the Portuguese and Spanish colonies in this way.

The African diaspora had a major demographic and cultural impact on all areas of Latin America and the Caribbean, from Mexico to the Bahamas, Martinique, Grenada, Guatemala, Cuba, and Brazil. The arrival of African slaves to the Americas started roughly in 1502. African slaves were imported to substitute for the rapidly diminishing indigenous population. These first groups of slaves came from the slave markets of Spain. The slave markets in Seville, while relatively small, were the most active in Europe during this time. With colonization of the Americas, the demand for slave labor increased dramatically. Europeans were looking to satisfy their labor demands in the New World. After 1519, slaves were taken directly from Africa by European slave ships. The transatlantic slave trade dates from 1519 to 1867; by 1530, the Spanish crown had authorized the spread of slavery to Puerto Rico, Cuba, and Jamaica.

**Law and Slavery.** Spanish law legitimized the practice and ownership of other persons in the Caribbean and Latin America. The foundation of Spanish jurisprudence acknowledged the legality of the institution of slavery even while declaring it contrary to natural law. These laws protected enslaved persons from serious abuse by their masters and gave them the right to marry, inherit property, and be manumitted. Spanish slave law was developed from Roman slave codes. The French had no slave laws on the books, so they eventually enacted the Code Noir, a 1685 compilation designed to regulate slavery in the French Caribbean. Like Spanish law, the Code Noir accorded the slaves basic rights such as marriage, manumission, and judicial recourse in the case of mistreatment. The British had no tradition of slavery in their land and had no elaborated slave codes to define relations between slave and master. This left the English slaveholders in the Caribbean to their own devices. They developed slave codes that essentially gave all the power to the slave masters.

**Comparative Slave Thesis.** In the areas of the New World where there were more carefully elaborated slave codes and laws, as in the Spanish colonies, one theory holds that the nature of slavery was more humane or less dehumanizing. The slave—according to the argument—had a legal personality and was recognized by the law. Thus, slaves could learn to read and even buy their freedom. Along with the process of *miscegenation*—the mixing of the races—some scholars believe that the Spanish slave codes created a far different life for slaves.

In contrast to the Spanish-speaking Caribbean, the English had no elaborated slave codes and made them up as they went along. Thus, in British slave codes, slaves were not recognized as persons but as property. They were accorded no rights: slaves were strictly forbidden to learn how to read or write and to own property. Moreover, miscegenation was less frequent.

Nonetheless, the massive degradation and exploitation of millions of human beings uprooted from their homes in Africa combined with the treatment of the Native American population imbued the Spanish and Portuguese colonies with a deep-seated racism, institutionalized callousness toward laborers (particularly when they were of color), and a proclivity toward (often brutal) exploitation that remains today.

Not all exploited the indigenous or African population with the same degree of harshness. The settlements that the Jesuits set up in Paraguay and elsewhere were notable exceptions, although they too enforced cultural assimilation of native peoples like the Guaraní. The Spanish and Portuguese crowns did not take kindly to the independent power of the Jesuits in these or other matters. Further, many of the powerful in the colonies resisted and sharply criticized the protective role progressive sectors in the Catholic Church played in regard to Indian rights. The *encomendero* turned priest and Indian advocate Bishop Bartolomé de Las Casas was repeatedly rebuked and threatened. Bishop Antonio Valdivieso was threatened and eventually assassinated for his pro-native stances in the area that is now Nicaragua. The Spanish crown did eventually decree minimal protection for indigenous peoples starting with the Law of Burgos (1512) and outlawed practices like Indian slavery. Compliance took much longer. Nor was the more humane treatment by the Jesuits always accepted. They were expelled from the colonies by the Portuguese in 1757 and the Spanish in 1767. African slavery continued into the nineteenth century in the remaining Spanish colonies in the Caribbean and until 1888 in Brazil. The status of enslaved or horribly exploited Africans did not attract the attention of enlightened Church officials. Even Las Casas recommended the use of African slave labor to free the indigenous people from slavery. Further, given the power and prerogative of local notables and their influence on local public officials, many of the worst practices toward the natives and former slaves continued long after being outlawed. One could draw parallels between these practices and the way sectors of the old elite in the American South were able to exploit and deny fundamental rights to former slaves and their descendants in rural areas of Mississippi and Louisiana.

The Indian and African slaves and laborers were, it seemed, to be used and exploited (at times to the point of extinction) to achieve the production necessary to enrich the European owners and to funnel wealth and products back to the metropolitan centers of power and wealth in Europe. As pointed out by many observers, the conditions in the mines, workshops, and farms were often horrendous. They were reflective of the callousness of many of the powerful to the condition and suffering of those more lowly than they.

## Production, Trade, and Extraction of Riches

The native gold and silver were quickly expropriated and sent back to Spain in fleets of galleons. The crown always got its *quinto real* (royal fifth; 20 percent commission). After the existing riches in gold, silver, and gems were depleted by the first conquerors, the Spanish administration began to foster the establishment of durable production of mercantile goods and the introduction of trade in Indian societies that had not yet begun to exchange their products for money. Of primary interest to the mercantilist leadership were precious metals, such as gold and silver, pearls, and precious stones. Where these were not found, the colonial leadership sought to grow commercial goods such as dyes, sugar cane, tobacco, and cocoa. Soon after the conquest, they discovered rich silver mines in Mexico and in Potosí Mountain in the Andes in Upper Peru (Bolivia). The extraction of silver and gold in Mexico and Peru stimulated the colonizers' keen interest in the lands of the former Aztec and Incan Empires. In the regions surroundings these centers, the production of food and other necessary supplies began to determine how the land was used. In Chile, the land was used to produce wheat for Spanish bread; in northern Argentina, the land was used to breed cattle, horses, and mules for work in the mines and for hides to make leather. The beef was dried and salted to make *charqui,* jerked meat.

Tremendous amounts of wealth were removed from the colonies in the form of preexisting gold and silver. Next, the conquerors turned to mining, often expending thousands of Indian lives each year to extract the precious metal (as suggested earlier, mining at Potosí is reputed to have consumed as many as 8 million native lives over three centuries). Between 1531 and 1600, over 14,969 metric tons (33 million pounds) of silver were exported back to Spain. By the last quarter of the sixteenth century, silver bullion accounted for about 90 percent of Latin American exports. Some three-fifths came from mines in what is now Peru and Bolivia. The silver mine at Potosí was legendary. The town attracted so many fortune seekers that it was the largest city in Latin America (population 160,000) at the beginning of the seventeenth century.

The silver was extracted by the miners and shipped to Spain in different ways. First, the crown took the *quinto real* of gross production. The other 80 percent stayed in the hands of the mine owners and was used to pay the workforce and for materials, animals for transportation, food, and luxury products for the rich miners. Here, the merchants who worked in the colony itself dominated, as did those who had the exclusive rights to export goods from Spain to the American possessions. This latter group principally resided in the center of Spanish colonial administration in Spain, Seville. Furthermore, the Spanish crown levied taxes on all imported goods. The capacity of the Spanish state to add more and higher taxes on colonial commerce was astonishing. The consequence was that the goods became very expensive because of the excessive taxation imposed by Spain's colonial monopoly.

As a way of ensuring increased consumption of such imported goods, the *repartimiento de mercancias* (distribution of goods) was introduced as a way to tax Native Americans who were not or who were only marginally incorporated in the market economy. Under this system, the *corregidor* or other local official was able to oblige each household in his charge to buy some Western merchandise at a substantial (and usually highly inflated) price. The colonial official became the monopoly supplier to a captive market.

The high taxes on all imported and exported goods caused considerable discontent among the *criollo* producers and merchants in the colonies, and they were soon ready to evade them by trading with unauthorized merchants from other countries. Their trade was principally with Dutch, British, and French *contrabandistas*. The whole of colonial history is characterized by the efforts of the Spanish authorities to eliminate smuggling by patrolling the coasts, controlling the accounts of the merchants, or forming monopolistic companies such as Guipuzcoana in Venezuela. These efforts never enjoyed much success because smuggled goods were much cheaper than those coming from Spain.

## The Church

The Catholic Church was a major political institution in the colony and had responsibility for (Catholic) Christianization and education. In other words, it was in charge of the spiritual conquest of the Americas. It acted as an agent for the crown, incorporating native peoples into the European world and European economy through participation in and payment for baptism and other rites and the still-popular street processions celebrating Church holy days and the lives of favorite saints and local madonnas. The Church's power was exercised in concert with the state and utilized to extend European control and influence. Its autonomy was mitigated by the fact that in 1508 Pope Julius II granted the Spanish monarch the *patronato real*—the right to nominate all Church officials, collect tithes, and found churches and monasteries in the Spanish Americas. This allowed the state a great deal of control over the Church and helped fuse the two. Nonetheless, the Church did engage in a variety of different activities, amassed considerable wealth, and was often the largest landowner in different regions of the colony.

The cultural and political evolution of Spanish America was also influenced by an instrument employed to purify the Catholic faith. The Spanish Inquisition persecuted alleged heretics (mostly Jewish and Muslim converts to Christianity) and was in large part responsible for the mass exodus of non-Christians from Spain in the late fifteenth and sixteenth centuries. In 1569, the institution of the Inquisition began in Latin America in Lima and Mexico City. It was charged with investigating signs of heresy. Later, it spread to other Spanish (but not Portuguese) possessions and became a license to search out any deviant or different thinking or innovation. Although indigenous people were exempted from the Inquisition after the 1570s and its victims were relatively few in number, it did have the effect of enforcing a certain heterodoxy in thought and suppressing an unfettered spirit of inquiry. Some have even seen it as the forerunner of the infamous secret police employed by Latin American dictatorships and military governments. Others speculate that the lax enforcement of the Inquisition in the Portuguese territories helps account for the less constrained approach to thinking and social and business relations that developed in Brazil. The Museum of the Inquisition in downtown Lima attests to the chilling nature of the interrogation and brutality of the instruments of torture employed to induce confessions in Spanish America.

## Colonial State Organization

Political power was highly concentrated in colonial governmental structures as well. A *virrey*, or viceking (viceroy), headed the colonial administration, ruling as the king's representative in his designated area. The region was first divided into the Spanish viceroyalties of Nueva España (Mexico, Central America, and the Caribbean), Lima (all the Andean countries, present-day Panama, Argentina, Paraguay, and Uruguay), and the Portuguese viceroyalty of Brazil. Later, the viceroyalties of New Granada (present-day Venezuela, Colombia, and Ecuador) and Río de la Plata (present-day Argentina, Uruguay, and Paraguay) were separated. Unlike the English colonies in North America, there were no representative assemblies in Latin America. Laws and decrees came from the Iberian monarchs or the Council of the Indies in Seville, Spain, and were implemented by colonial authorities from Spain and Portugal. Communication was slow, imprecise, and greatly filtered by the interests of the powerful. The colonists often felt that they were living under orders or laws imposed from afar that did not respond to their needs. This led to one of the most famous dictums during the colony—*Obedezco pero no cumplo*: "I obey but I do not comply." In other words, I will yield to your orders and authority, but you will be hard-pressed to make me carry them out. The colonial elite that emerged amassed considerable wealth and power. They were all too willing to employ both to frustrate laws or decrees they found objectionable or impractical. The large landowners in Brazil were perhaps the most independent, a tradition that continues to the present. In Spanish and Portuguese America, laws like those that protected the native peoples were often unenforceable because of the concerted power of local elites. There was also a fault line between the newly arrived colonists from Spain and Portugal, the *peninsulares*, and the sons and daughters of the earlier arrivals from the Iberian peninsula, the *criollos*. The *criollos* resented the fact that the best positions in the colonial administration and the Church went to the *peninsulares* even though they had just stepped off the boat and did not have the *criollos'* history, family, or wealth in the Americas.

## Governmental Organization

The viceroy was indeed the king's representative and could truly rule. Executive, military, and some legislative powers were combined in such a way to establish the cultural model of the all-powerful executive that has permeated Latin American political (and business) culture to the present day. Captains general were appointed to rule over smaller and usually more distant divisions of the viceroyalties and governed in much the same way. Thus, the captain general of Guatemala ruled Central

America (excluding present-day Panama) from his headquarters in Guatemala City but was ostensibly subordinate to the viceroy of New Spain in Mexico City. The captains general in colonial Brazil were given even greater power over their domains and enjoyed greater autonomy from the crown and the viceroy.

The viceroyalties of New Spain and Peru were further subdivided into *audiencias*, or advisory councils, that were presided over by judge-presidents and composed of appointed judges, or *oidores*. They were established in Santo Domingo, Mexico City, Panama, Lima, Guatemala, Guadalajara, Santa Fe, La Plata, Buenos Aires, Quito, Santiago, Cuzco, and Caracas. Beneath the *audiencias* were the governors and, at the local level, the notoriously corrupt *corregidores* and mayors (*alcaldes*). At the higher levels of government, the judicial, legislative, and executive functions were mixed, with the viceroys generally also in charge of the military. Functions and powers often overlapped in a system that was designed to encourage mutual suspicion, spying, and checking a potential rival's power and thus the supremacy of the power of the crown. The *cabildo*, or town council (*câmara* in Brazil), was one of the few political structures with any degree of popular participation or democracy. Many councils were all or partly elected and were truly representative of the population. Many others were dominated by powerful and often corrupt political appointees. Offices were, however, frequently sold, and corruption and intense exploitation of the native population were all too often the norm. The official who did not use his office to accumulate a fortune to take back to the Iberian Peninsula might well be considered the exception.

## The Bourbon Reforms

By the beginning of the eighteenth century the Spanish empire was not well administered. With the end of the Hapsburg dynasty, a French-based Bourbon dynasty began with Philip V and continued to make reforms through most of the eighteenth century. The object was to streamline the colonial structure and centralize power in the Spanish throne as well as stimulate commerce. The state also asserted its power over the Church and even expelled the Jesuits from the Americas in 1767. Conditions did improve somewhat in the later part of the eighteenth century, but many of the worst practices had by then become ingrained, and segments of the population were already chafing under the colonial yoke. The local elite also resented the centralization of power in the crown as well. This helped lead to the uprisings in the central Andes, led by Túpac Amaru II (José Gabriel Condorcanqui, a mestizo descendant of the last Inca, Túpac Amaru, who had also rebelled against Spanish rule) in 1780 and Túpac Katari in 1781, and the revolt of the *comuneros* in New Granada (1781). These uprisings and the sentiments that inspired them helped set the stage for the independence movement.

## Historical Time Line in the Americas

**40,000 B.C.E.–8000 B.C.E.**   Migration of Asian peoples to North America across the Bering Strait

**1500 B.C.E.–1000 C.E.**   Mayan civilization develops in the Yucatán Peninsula, Guatemala, and parts of Honduras and El Salvador

**1150 B.C.E.–500 C.E.**   Olmec culture flourishes in Mesoamerica

**1000**   Incan culture emerges in the Cuzco Valley of South America

**1200**   The Aztecs arrive in the central plateau of Mexico

**1466**   The Aztec emperor Moctezuma Xocoyotzín is born in Mexico

**1492**   Christopher Columbus arrives at what he called San Salvador Island in the Caribbean and encounters Native American culture

**1494**   Treaty of Tordesillas is signed by Spain and Portugal, establishing a line of demarcation from pole to pole 370 leagues west of the Cape Verde Islands; Spain receives the right to colonize all territory to the west of that line; Portugal colonizes lands to the east

**1500**   Pedro Alvares Cabral arrives in Brazil and claims it for Portugal

**1508**   In Hispaniola, the first sugar mill is constructed

**1509**   Pope Julius II authorizes the Spanish Catholic monarchs to propagate the Catholic Church in the Americas; *patronato real* gives power to the crown to appoint Church officials

**1510**   250 slaves are imported to the Americas to work in the gold mines in Hispaniola

**1512**   The Laws of Burgos are promulgated to protect the Native Americans from the worst ravages of Spanish conquest

**1516**   Bartolomé de Las Casas is named the official protector of the Indians

**1519**   Hernán Cortés marches into Tenochtitlán and takes Moctezuma prisoner

**1521**   Spaniards complete conquest of the Aztec Empire

**1521**   Conquistador Gil González de Avila converts 30,000 Indians to Christianity in the area called Nicaragua and sends some 500,000 as slaves to other parts of the Spanish Empire

**1524**   Council of the Indies is established by King Charles V (Holy Roman Emperor Charles V)

**1532**   Francisco Pizarro invades the Incan Empire, captures and executes Emperor Atahualpa, and conquers the Incas

**1538**   The first university in the Americas is established: Saint Thomas Aquinas in the city of Santo Domingo

**1541**   Francisco de Orellana discovers the headwaters of the Amazon River in what is now Ecuador

**1542**   The New Laws of the Indies are issued by Spain, officially eliminating the *encomienda*

**1551**   In Mexico and Lima, new universities are created

**1554**   Araucan Indian chief Caupolican, allied with Chief Lautaro, defeats Spaniards, kills Pedro de Valdivia, and defeats the forces of Francisco de Villagrá of Chile

**1739–1780s**   Bourbon Reforms

**1767**   King Charles III expels the Jesuits from the Spanish Empire

**1780**   Incan descendant Túpac Amaru II leads a rebellion against Spanish authorities on behalf of the Indians

**1781**   Túpac Katari leads a rebellion in what is now Bolivia and besieges La Paz in 1781

**1781**   *Comunero* revolt in New Granada

# Bibliography

Adelman, Jeremy. *Colonial Legacies: The Problem of Persistence in Latin American History.* New York: Routledge, 1999.

Bakewell, Peter. *A History of Latin American Empires and Sequels, 1450–1930.* Oxford: Blackwell, 1997.

Burkholder, Mark A., and Lyman L. Johnson. *Colonial Latin America.* 8th ed. New York: Oxford University Press, 2012.

Conniff, Michael, and Thomas Davis. *Africans in the Americas: A History of the Black Diaspora.* New York: St. Martin's, 1994.

Chasteen, John C. *Born in Blood and Fire: A Concise History of Latin America.* 4th ed. New York: W. W. Norton, 2016.

Davis, Darien, ed. *Slavery and Beyond: The African Impact on Latin America and the Caribbean* (Jaguar Books on Latin America, 5). Wilmington, DE: Scholarly Resources, 1995.

Fagan, Brian. *Kingdoms of Gold, Kingdoms of Jade: The Americas Before Columbus.* London: Thames and Hudson, 1991.

Keen, Benjamin, and Keith Haynes. *A History of Latin America.* Vol. 1. 9th ed. Boston: Wadsworth, 2013.

Kicza, John E., ed. *The Indian in Latin American History: Resistance, Resilience and Acculturation.* Wilmington, DE: Scholarly Resources, 1993.

Leon-Portilla, Miguel, ed. *The Broken Spears: The Aztec Account of the Conquest of Mexico.* Translated by Lysander Kemp. Boston: Beacon, 1992.

Newson, Linda. "The Latin American Colonial Experience." In *Latin American Development: Geographical Perspectives*, edited by David Preston, 2d ed. Harlow, UK: Longman, 1996.

Ohaegbulam, Festus U. *Toward an Understanding of the African Experience from Historical and Contemporary Perspectives.* Lanham, MD: University Press of America, 1990.

Rosenberg, Mark B., A. Douglas Kincaid, and Kathleen Logan, eds. *Americas, An Anthology.* New York: Oxford University Press, 1992.

Schele, Linda, and David Freidel. *A Forest of Kings: The Untold Story of the Ancient Maya.* New York: William Morrow, 1990.

Smith, Carol. *Guatemalan Indians and the State: 1540 to 1988.* Austin: University of Texas Press, 1990.

Soustelle, Jacques. *Daily Life of the Aztecs, on the Eve of the Spanish Conquest.* Stanford, CA: Stanford University Press, 1970.

Stavig, Ward. *The World of Túpac Amaru: Conflict, Community, and Identity in Colonial Peru.* Lincoln: University of Nebraska Press, 1999.

## FILMS AND VIDEOS

*The Buried Mirror. Reflections of Spain in the New World. Part Two: The Conflict of the Gods.* United States, 1991. Video version of Carlos Fuentes's insightful commentary on the indigenous world conquered by Spain and the transposition of the new belief system.

*The Mission.* United States, 1986. An excellent feature-length film starring Robert De Niro; graphically depicts the colonization process among indigenous peoples above the Iguassú Falls in southern Brazil.

*Popol Vuh.* United States, 1991. An animated video that portrays the creation myth of the Maya.

*Prayer of Viracocha.* United States. A beautifully animated indigenous lament to the Incan god Viracocha at the time of the conquest.

*Quetzalcóatl.* United States, 1951. A vision of the Mesoamerican winged serpent god.

*The Spanish Conquest of Mexico.* United States, 1999. Tells the story of how the Aztec empire was conquered.

*Sword and Cross.* United States, 1991. Tells the story of the conquest.

*Xica.* Brazil, 1976. The embellished story of Xica da Silva.

# THREE

# Democracy and Dictators

## *A Historical Overview from Independence to the Present Day*

## Independence

The independence movements that created most of the nation-states that currently make up Latin America developed during the first twenty-five years of the nineteenth century as the result of events occurring in both Europe and Latin America. Haiti became an independent republic in 1804, and most of the other Latin American states achieved their independence by the early 1820s. The local elites succeeded in transferring political power into their own hands outside the control of Madrid or Lisbon. However, the underlying systems of social and economic power inherited from the colonial era remained largely intact. Further, the authoritarian tradition inherited from Spanish and Portuguese colonialism was very much in place and would plague Latin America into the twenty-first century. There was a continual and generally unresolved tension between authoritarian rule learned from years of heavy-handed, top-down colonial (and often precolonial) practice on the one hand and the democratic ideals and inspiration that the independence movements chose to rely on to explain and set up the state structures in the independent nations on the other. Nonetheless, the end of direct colonialism did initiate a nation-building process that would eventually modernize governmental structures and bring Latin America closer to the world economic system. The political change also produced a legitimacy crisis that led to nearly a century of political struggle and the eventual hegemony of liberalism. These more profound changes for the Americas began in the last twenty-five years of the nineteenth century, when the region's long-standing social and economic structures were challenged by the arrival of the Industrial Revolution and market capitalism. These forces eventually weakened the traditional elites and laid the groundwork for the political struggles of the twentieth century.

To better understand the independence movements of the early nineteenth century in Latin America, it is necessary to look not only to the growing unrest in Latin America but also to Europe. By the beginning of the eighteenth century, the Spanish

Empire was already well into a decline that proved to be permanent. However, as was suggested in the last chapter, the Bourbon monarchs of Spain, whose family had assumed the crown in 1713, had embarked on a series of political and economic reforms in their American colonies that they hoped would solidify that rule. In reality, these reforms contributed to the eventual triumph of the independence movements. Inspired by Enlightenment political and economic thought, the Bourbons sought to reform the existing overlapping systems of authority by centralizing political power. They created new administrative units in New Granada (1717) and Buenos Aires (1776). More important, Charles III, who ruled from 1759 to 1788, established a new administrative system that resulted in the appointment of local governors by the crown in Madrid. These rulers, called "intendants," were almost all Spanish-born rather than American *criollos*. This approach marginally solidified the hold of the monarchy over the colonies but brought the crown into more direct conflict with the local *criollo* elites, who had prospered under the previous system of less intrusive rule from Madrid. In one significant example, the monarchy sharply reduced *criollo* control of the administrative and court systems, which it had originally established in the late seventeenth century by purchasing judgeships. Charles III also strengthened his hand by taking greater control of the Church. In his boldest move, he expelled the Jesuits from all Spanish colonies in 1767. Charles saw the Jesuits as an independent power base, so he removed them and profited from the sale of their lands. The Spanish crown also engaged in economic reform that freed the various ports of the empire to trade with other ports in Spanish America and in Spain itself. Illegal trade had long flourished on the forbidden routes, with most of the profits staying within the Americas, but now the Spanish crown was gaining a greater share of the wealth through the collection of customs duties. These economic reforms resulted in a more prosperous colonial economy, where new ports such as Buenos Aires flourished, but their most important long-term effect was the resentment generated among *criollos*, who saw the moves as a plot to undermine their status and power. This resentment, more than any other factor, fueled the independence movements of the early nineteenth century.

Ironically, another reform instituted by the Spanish crown unwittingly aided the cause of American independence. During the eighteenth century, the monarchy had authorized the creation of colonial militias as a protection against feared British and French invasions; by 1800, 80 percent of the soldiers serving in Spanish America were American-born. A military career was one of the few remaining avenues of advancement for socially ambitious *criollos*. These forces provided the core of the local forces that would later fight for independence.

## THE FRENCH REVOLUTION, LOCAL UPRISINGS, AND INDEPENDENCE

Events in Europe determined the timing of the independence movement. The French Revolution of 1789 launched ideas of freedom and equality throughout the French Empire, and cries of *liberté, égalité,* and *fraternité* fell on receptive ears among the slave population in Haiti. In 1791, a slave uprising was led by Toussaint L'Ouverture, an extremely able, self-educated freed slave. After a series of successful battles against opposition forces that included a formidable contingent of Napoleon's army in

1802, the popular forces triumphed. Haiti gained its independence from France in 1804 and thus became the first independent Latin American nation. In other parts of Latin America, a few, like the Afro-Venezuelan José Leonardo Chirinos, even spoke of proclaiming a republic of the "law of the French" in 1795. Meanwhile, the Spanish monarchy had tried to save its Bourbon counterparts during the French Revolution in 1789, but having failed that, Spain allied itself with Napoleon Bonaparte in 1796. However, in 1808, Napoleon turned on his Spanish allies and occupied Madrid, placing his brother Joseph on the Spanish throne (1808–1813) and forcing the abdication of Ferdinand VII. This act by Napoleon was the catalyst for rebellion in Spain and the Americas that would eventually lead to independence for most of Spanish America. Some historians argue, however, that the resistance of indigenous peoples in the latter part of the eighteenth century was the real catalyst. As noted in the last chapter, in 1780, Túpac Amaru II, claiming lineage from the ancient Incan Empire, led a revolt that mobilized more than 80,000 mostly indigenous fighters and lasted for two years in southern Peru and Bolivia before it was defeated by the Spanish army. The struggle was joined by Túpac Katari in Upper Peru (now Bolivia) in 1781. There was also a popular revolt of the *comuneros* in New Granada in 1781. These movements are important in the history of indigenous struggles and popular uprisings but may be better understood outside the context of the independence movements. With radical demands for land reform and indigenous rights, the political thrust of these movements was not supported by the *criollo* independence leaders of the early nineteenth century. In fact, the Peruvian rebellions and the later rebellion in Mexico led by Father Hidalgo in 1810 frightened the *criollos* into making common cause with the Spanish-born elites and delayed independence in both Mexico and Peru. It also meant that, outside of Haiti, rebellions against colonial rule by the masses (who were predominantly people of color) did not triumph.

The *criollos*, born in America, increasingly longed to wrest political power from the *peninsulares*. In the late eighteenth century, the *criollos* began to look outward for guidance, increasingly to France. As a result, the French Revolution had more impact than the American Revolution. As suggested earlier, the most dramatic example of the influence in Latin America was in Haiti. Of course, the majority of creoles were not Jacobin revolutionaries. They wanted to reform the local political systems to give themselves power, but they were in no way interested in revolution or in giving all the power to the common people. Napoleon's invasion of Spain in 1808 provided that opportunity.

In the wake of the Napoleonic invasion, the Spanish king, Ferdinand VII, was forced to abdicate and was imprisoned while Napoleon's brother Joseph was put on the throne. To resist the French, the Braganzas, Portugal's royal family, fled Portugal and escaped to Rio de Janeiro. The Brazilians received their royal family warmly and celebrated their extended stay in Rio de Janeiro. In contrast, the initial instincts of Spanish Americans were to pledge loyalty to Ferdinand; but fairly quickly the creole elites began to realize their own power, and by 1810 the creoles had moved from tentative autonomy to open declarations of independence. However, despite the fortuitous circumstances for independence, the events that followed did not easily lead to independence for most of Latin America during the ensuing twenty-five years. Nor did the newly formed United States republic assist in the struggles for independence.

One of the earliest examples of the capacity of resistance by the local population came in Buenos Aires. In 1806, the British occupied the city, forcing the viceroy to flee to Córdoba. The British, however, were driven out by a locally organized citizens' army, which also successfully defended against a counterattack in 1807. This local action independent of Madrid set a powerful example for future actions. The viceroyalty of Buenos Aires was also able to negotiate a better deal in the arena of free trade after the expulsion of the British forces. Ironically, it involved the desire of the local commercial elite to trade directly with the British, who provided the most promising market for their growing production of hides and salted beef. In 1809, Spain granted Buenos Aires limited freedom of trade with nations allied to Spain or neutral in the Napoleonic Wars. This agreement helped strengthen the self-confidence of the local elites.

# Early Drive for Independence in Hispanic America

The first phase of the Spanish American independence movements occurred between 1810 and 1814. In 1810, Napoleon's forces completed their victory over the Bourbons and established a liberal constitution for Spain, but in 1814 Ferdinand VII returned to the Spanish throne and annulled the liberal constitution of 1812. In 1810, Argentine local elites came together to create a provisional government of the provinces of the Río de la Plata. Prior to their declaration of independence of 1816, these local elites pledged their allegiance to Ferdinand VII, but the pattern of local initiative, first shown in the rebellions against the British, was institutionalized.

Venezuela was the scene of a movement similar to that in Buenos Aires. In Caracas, a local council expelled the Spanish governors and organized a new government under Ferdinand VII. The best known of the leaders was Simón Bolívar. Born into a wealthy Caracas family and tutored by the great Latin American liberal thinker Simón Rodríguez, Bolívar was educated in Spain and came in contact with the ideas of the Enlightenment (especially Rousseau and romanticism). In 1805, he committed himself to the independence of his homeland. In 1811, the local Caracas authorities, under his influence, declared Venezuela's independence. After an initial series of military defeats, the exiled Bolívar returned to Venezuela and defeated the Spanish army in a series of exceptional military victories, earning him the title El Libertador (The Liberator).

In the provinces of New Spain (Mexico), this time period also saw exceptional developments. By 1810, a group of *criollos*, including a priest named Miguel Hidalgo, began plotting to seize authority in the name of Ferdinand. When the plot was discovered by the Spanish authorities, Hidalgo led a popular uprising centered in the village of Dolores, thus the famous *grito de Dolores*. A powerful response came not from the local elites but rather from the impoverished mestizos and indigenous people. Uniting under the banner of the long-adored dark-skinned Virgin of Guadalupe, they comprised a fighting force of 50,000. In a decision whose motivation has been debated ever since, Hidalgo turned away from a probable victory over the Spanish authorities in Mexico City and moved to the north. In 1811, his army was defeated near Guadalajara, leading to his capture and execution.

Following Hidalgo's death, leadership of the independence forces was taken by José María Morelos, another priest even more strongly committed to radical social reform, including the end of slavery. A republican, Morelos believed that the whole population should participate in political affairs. In 1813, the Congress of Chilpancingo declared Mexico's independence from Spain and decreed that slavery should be abolished. The Congress's liberal constitution of 1814 created a system of indirect elections and a powerful legislature. However, it was never enacted because Morelos's guerrilla army did not control enough territory to seriously threaten Spanish authority.

In 1814, Napoleon's defeat restored Ferdinand VII to power in Spain. The colonial authorities used this fortuitous event—along with military reinforcements—to regain control in the face of the developing independence movements. Ferdinand annulled the liberal Spanish constitution of 1812 and reestablished himself as an absolute ruler. The king's return divided *criollo* leaders, with many concluding that there was no reason to continue their rebellions. By 1816, with the exception of Buenos Aires, Spanish rule had been reestablished throughout the empire. In Venezuela, even the victorious Bolívar saw his support significantly reduced; he

Simon Bolivar, El Libertador, 1783-1830. *(The Art Archive)*

was forced into exile on the English island of Jamaica. The independence movement in New Spain also suffered serious setbacks. In 1815, Morelos was captured, tried, and executed as the Spanish military commanders regained the upper hand and blocked implementation of the liberal constitution that had been enacted the previous year. Only the government in Río de la Plata survived the reconquest. It struggled to survive and had not yet become a full-blown independence movement.

The Spanish reconquest was short-lived. In 1816, Bolívar returned to Venezuela from his exile on Jamaica and launched a new campaign for the independence of his country. His new ally was José Antonio Páez, the leader of the *llaneros* (cowboys) who had fought alongside the royalists during the previous struggles. In 1819, Bolívar mounted an army of 4,000 and succeeded in defeating the Spanish and their royalist collaborators. Meanwhile in the south, José de San Martín initiated a significant military campaign. San Martín, the son of a Spanish military officer, entered the service at age eleven. In 1812, he offered his services to the junta in Buenos Aires. Over the next five years, he developed the rebel forces into an army and then led 5,000 soldiers across the Andes in a surprise attack on the loyalist forces in Chile. The Spaniards were defeated in the battle of Chacabuco, and San Martín entered Santiago triumphantly. San Martín's next target was the liberation of Peru; in 1820, he prepared for an attack on Lima, the capital of the viceroyalty. He faced a city where monarchist sentiment was quite strong. Both the *criollos* and the *peninsulares* favored the continuation of Ferdinand's rule. Wary of a defeat, San Martín withheld his attack. At that point, decisive events in Spain again intervened. Ferdinand reversed his political course and abruptly embraced the previously annulled Spanish liberal constitution of 1812. Monarchists throughout Spanish America were shocked by the turnabout, which abolished the Inquisition, thus unacceptably weakening the power of the Church. The changes in Spain suddenly altered the climate for independence in both Lima and Mexico City, where the monarchists held sway. The monarchists now viewed independence as a means of preserving the status quo, which would uphold traditional values and social codes. As a result of this sudden change of perspective, in 1821 the municipal council of Lima invited San Martín to enter the city; on July 28, he formally proclaimed the independence of Peru. Meanwhile in the north, Bolívar, after defeating the Spanish forces in New Granada, attempted to create a new state of Gran Colombia, uniting Venezuela, New Granada (Colombia), and Ecuador under republican principles. This effort received little support, so Bolívar moved south, hoping to confront and defeat more of the royalist forces as he sought to achieve his vision of a united continent independent of colonial control and organized along republican principles.

Antonio José de Sucre was sent by Bolívar to liberate Ecuador. Sucre led the combined Ecuadorian, Colombian, and Venezuelan forces against the Spanish and finally defeated them in the battle of Pichincha in 1822. In Ecuador, Bolívar met with San Martín and declared that they were "the two greatest men in America." Personal and political differences, however, precluded the consummation of an alliance. Bolívar rejected San Martín's proposal for a monarchy in Peru and San Martín's offer for Bolívar to serve under his command. Further, Bolívar's plans for the union of Gran Colombia were rejected by San Martín. Disillusioned and unwilling to split the revolutionary forces, San Martín soon after resigned his post and retired to France, where he died in 1850. However, even San Martín's departure did not slow the independence movement. In late 1823, Bolívar's forces confronted the large Spanish force that had retreated inland from Lima, and a year later the royalists were defeated decisively at the battle of Ayachucho, effectively ending three centuries of Spanish rule in the Americas. In 1825, Bolívar entered Upper Peru to press the idea that the two Perus should form a single nation. The leaders of Upper Peru, however, having already struck an independent course, declared their own republic and named it Bolivia in honor of Bolívar. Over the next five years Bolívar tried unsuccessfully to promote his idea of political union. His ideas were resisted by the local elites, including some of his own lieutenants, who feared the reinstatement of centralized control. In 1826, Bolívar tried to implement his vision of a united Spanish America by convening the Congress of Panama. His efforts were not successful, and in 1830 the Liberator died a bitter man who failed to achieve a united Latin America and saw many of his democratic dreams languish. Toward the end of his life he concluded that he and the other independence leaders "had plowed the sea."

Simultaneous to these events in South America, the conservative independence movement went forward in Mexico. The royal government was disintegrating; Agustín de Iturbide, the creole commander of the army in Mexico, seized the moment to declare Mexican independence with little bloodshed on September 28, 1821. Only the Spanish garrison in Veracruz held out against Iturbide's proclamation. It was a conservative revolt that even many Spaniards supported. The new regime was marked by three conservative principles: constitutional monarchy, official Catholicism, and equality of *peninsulares* and *criollos*. Iturbide had himself proclaimed emperor only when "no suitable European monarch could be found." Central America, with its traditional strong ties to Mexico, followed suit and declared its independence from Spain in 1821. In 1822, the Central American landowners, fearing liberal dominance in Spain, transferred their loyalty to royalist Mexico. However, the Mexican monarchy lasted only two years. In 1823, when Iturbide abdicated, the modern-day Central American states from Guatemala to Costa Rica became the Independent United Provinces of Central America. With the independence of Mexico and Central America, Spanish control in the Western Hemisphere was reduced to Cuba and Puerto Rico.

# Brazilian Independence

Brazilian independence was achieved in a manner very different from that of Spanish America. The differences were rooted in the character of the Brazilian state and economy and in the special role played by Britain in the context of the Napoleonic Wars. When the Napoleonic army invaded Portugal in 1807, the entire royal family was able to flee to Brazil with the assistance of the British navy. The royal family ended Portugal's commercial monopoly by opening Brazil's ports. Soon after 1810, Britain gained privileged access to Brazil through low tariffs, a commitment to the gradual end of the African slave trade, and extraterritorial privileges for British citizens living in Brazil.

When Napoleon was decisively defeated, the Portuguese monarchy was free to return to Lisbon; initially, they did not, and instead Dom João proclaimed Brazil to be a coequal kingdom with the same rank as Portugal. Dom João, however, did eventually return to Lisbon and left his son Dom Pedro behind with the prerogative to declare Brazil independent. The new king declared independence on September 7, 1822, with the full support of the Brazilian elites and with only token resistance from a few Portuguese garrisons. In sharp contrast to much of Spanish America, independence was achieved in Brazil without significant bloodshed and without the development of a strong military caste. The nation also remained united despite some small-scale regional revolts. Furthermore, Brazil did not see a strong republican/ monarchist split because the overwhelming majority of the local elite sided with monarchism. Brazilian sugar barons were dependent on the slave trade and thus on the monarchy, which lasted only a year beyond the abolition of slavery in 1888.

## Early Years of Independence

Thus, the Latin American nations became independent of European rule. It was, however, a much longer struggle to liberate themselves from their inherited political and cultural traditions. Foremost among these was the authoritarian proclivity that was strongly ingrained in political culture. For instance, Bolívar, the great liberator, frustrated with regionalism and the assertion of political autonomy by various leaders in the Republic of Gran Colombia, often forsook formal democracy and reverted to dictatorial rule to hold the republic together. Much of the early history of the republics was filled with such local and national *caudillos*—by men on white horses. An even more telling example is that of Dr. José Gaspar Rodríguez de Francia. Soon after independence in Paraguay, the then-leader of the country, Francia, proclaimed himself dictator in perpetuity. His rule from 1816 to 1840 set a pattern for extended dictatorial rule that would continue to plague Paraguay until 1989. This and similar traditions of extended authoritarian rule continued to haunt many other Latin American countries through the nineteenth and twentieth centuries. Indeed, authoritarian rule would predominate in Paraguay, Bolivia, and Haiti through the nineteenth and twentieth centuries. The military-style leaders would dominate the period up until the 1850s in most countries, including Mexico, Argentina, and Peru. The seeds of democracy had been planted, but the early years of republican history seemed to justify Bolívar's previously noted conclusion that "we have plowed the sea."

## The Aftermath of Independence
## and the Monroe Doctrine

The aftermath of independence was a difficult time for most of Latin America. The newly independent nations faced terrible obstacles as they sought to move forward economically, politically, and socially. The consolidation of national rule was even more difficult than in the United States, which, in light of its defeat by Great Britain in the War of 1812, limited its initial contacts with Latin America and formulated the still-controversial Monroe Doctrine in 1823. First stated by President James Monroe and enunciated by his Secretary of State, John Quincey Adams, it was primarily designed to preclude continued European interference in independent Latin America and stop any reimposition of colonial rule in the hemisphere. Within the Latin American nations, it was a considerable struggle to establish national control and move beyond the regionalism that was so strong in most of the nations. Further, politics were generally dominated by upper-class landowning elites, whose concept of democracy was quite limited. With the primary exception of Brazil, the new leaders took over power in the context of the physical devastation brought by the wars for independence. Devastation was particularly heavy in Mexico and Venezuela, but everywhere the burden of supporting the large armies of liberation was significant. Economic activity was also greatly affected by the continuous wars. Trade had almost ceased during the period. Trade with Spain ceased, of course, but inter-American trade was also adversely affected. Communication almost completely collapsed among the new countries. The economies of the newly independent countries also faced challenges related to their very nature. Based almost exclusively on mining and agriculture, the colonies had been marginally integrated into the world economy before independence, but they now faced new challenges not based on their previous colonial commitments. The failure to achieve political unity meant that each new country faced the challenge of creating its own national economy. There were also regional differences; Mexico had a fairly well-developed national economy, but most of the other countries did not. As countries sought to develop themselves, they often faced internal divisions as well as interference from outside political and economic influences. Most new regimes lacked the financial assets even to equip a national army, let alone embark on significant national economic development. Mechanisms for tax collection and other standard methods of revenue collection were simply not sophisticated enough to meet the new nations' considerable needs. As a result, many countries, including Mexico and Argentina, turned to loans from foreign banks as a way out of their crises. Foreign governments, especially Britain, eagerly provided money in hope of significant returns. These loans, made more than 150 years ago, began a dependence on external finance and external actors that has persisted to the present day.

The era of free trade was also launched during this time period, as Latin America slowly adapted itself to the world economy. Exports to the United States and Europe began to increase—nitrates from Chile, hides and salted beef from Argentina, sugar from Cuba, and sugar from Brazil. The growth in exports was also accompanied by a corresponding rise in manufactured imports, especially textiles. Latin American artisans and small producers were often driven out of business in the exchange. This time also saw the arrival of a small number of foreign merchants who took up key positions in the fields of shipping, insurance, and banking. The pattern of losing out to foreign competitors was primarily the result of the technological superiority of the Europeans, but the local elites exacerbated the problem with misguided political choices. The traditional landowning elites first ensured that their holdings were secure and then retreated to the security of their *haciendas* and *fazendas,* not particularly concerned about maximizing production or contributing to the economic modernization of their countries. Political power was left largely in the hands of military men who had become *caudillos,* among them Juan Manuel de Rosas, the governor of Buenos Aires province; Antonio López de Santa Anna, the president of Mexico; and a lieutenant of Bolívar, José Antonio Páez. These military governments, without significant streams of revenue, were vulnerable to being overthrown and incapable of sustaining local economic growth. Some leaders recognized the dangers inherent in a weak central state, so in many countries conflict developed between locally based power brokers and the centralizers. These struggles were to be the forerunners of later battles for political power between conservatives and liberals.

One group negatively affected by independence was the indigenous peoples. They had not been a consistent force for elite-led independence and therefore were not seen by the new governments as important allies. As a result, they lost whatever protections they may have had under colonial administrations. Their land became increasingly vulnerable to takeover and their condition even more impoverished.

# 1850–1880

The second stage of Latin America's integration into the world economy occurred between 1850 and 1880. National unification became the political theme as local *caudillo* rulers were slowly supplanted by national leaders, who began to construct the apparatus of the modern state. Liberal reform leaders like Benito Juárez in Mexico, Domingo Sarmiento in Argentina, and Justo Rufino Barrios in Guatemala appeared.

As Latin American nations were ever more integrated into the commercialized world economy, liberal political (and economic) reforms and modernization that began in the 1850s continued. The epic Argentine struggle between the rural *gaucho* and remaining Indians on the one hand and the Europeanized *porteño* (port) elite from Buenos Aires on the other was indicative of this trend. The 1853 defeat of the *gaucho* dictator Juan Manuel de Rosas by reformist forces ushered in a new regime that opted for the "civilizing" influence of the port city over the rural landowners, the *estanciaros*. The government and economy were modernized, and massive European immigration (mostly from Italy) began. European capital, science, and technology were injected into the development process. Liberal reforms set the stage for the emergence of other sectors in Argentine society. The meat-packing and grain-exporting industries gradually facilitated the emergence of an industrial proletariat and the beginning of a middle class. Argentina became ever more closely tied to England through the sale of its beef and the influx of British investment.

Meanwhile, peasants were beginning to feel the squeeze as their countries were further incorporated into the world market. Economic pressures and social upheaval fomented political restructuring as well. As a result, the region began to witness the emergence of reformist parties like the Radical Civic Union in Argentina, which held sway for most of the second and third decades of the twentieth century.

Periods of democratic rule began to appear, and political participation and the franchise were slowly widened beyond the elite to include common people in most countries. The transformation was in part driven by the slow rise of Latin America's export trade and the need to have a national infrastructure to support such trade. This era saw the beginning of efforts by national governments to transform long-standing land tenure arrangements that were dominated by largely unproductive *latifundios* and government land. This was the era of liberal ascendency almost everywhere in Latin America. During this period, there were significant efforts to undermine Church authority and establish secular, public education. Liberal ideas also made their way into the prison system and even military organizations.

Benito Juárez, The Great Reformer, 1806–1872. *(Photo by Gianni Dagli Orti/The Art Archive)*

All these liberal reforms and nation building occurred in the context of the penetration of North American and European capital.

To transport the region's coffee, sugar, nitrates, and other primary products to Europe and elsewhere, there was a strong need to replace the region's antiquated transportation system with new roads, canals, railroads, and docks. The traditional landowning elites had no need for infrastructure development to prosper, so they had not built it and were indifferent to its construction. The impetus for such development came primarily from abroad. European industrialization created a great thirst for everything from foodstuffs to fertilizers to metals. The developing European industries also sought out new markets for their manufactured goods. These twin European needs laid the groundwork for the next phase of Latin American development. Latin American countries willing to do business with Europe gained rising political power and wealth that challenged the traditional elites. However, the character of this economic arrangement—Latin American primary goods traded for European finished goods—established the pattern of Latin America's role in the world economy that persists to this day. The countries saw very little growth of domestic industry as European producers of machinery, weapons, and other light manufactured goods often blocked the development of indigenous industries. Competing with European entrepreneurs would have been difficult, given Europe's head start in technology; nor were Latin American governments of the time inclined to set up tariff barriers to spur local development. Generally, they were more than happy to welcome unrestricted foreign trade in return for their share of the profits. The era of 1850–1880 was one of laying the groundwork for even more dramatic changes that would occur in the last twenty years of the nineteenth century.

# 1880–1910

The needs of European industrialization that had been developing slowly throughout the nineteenth century came to a head after 1880. The demands for food by Europe's industrial workers and for raw materials to fuel factories were insatiable. Several key Latin American countries were transformed by these demands. Argentina became a great producer of beef, wool, and wheat. Brazil and El Salvador became the world's primary producers of coffee, satisfying Europe's newfound addiction, with Peru, Mexico, and Cuba supplying the sugar. Mexico provided Europe and North America with a variety of raw materials, including hemp, copper, and zinc. Thus, the pattern established in earlier decades of Latin American countries producing primary goods in exchange for European manufactured goods was deepened.

European countries also invested in Latin America. During this period Britain was by far the dominant investor, with almost two-thirds of the total investment by 1913. Railroads and mining were the two key sectors into which Europeans and North Americans placed their money. American investment also began to increase dramatically after 1900. Only modest amounts of Latin American capital went into these sectors, so the pattern of economic control by foreign powers became well established. Thus, Latin American prosperity became increasingly tied to the health of the European and North American economies. It also meant that most of the key decisions about the economic direction of Latin America were not being made in Rio de Janeiro or Buenos Aires but rather in New York, London, and Paris.

The new economic reality was justified and validated by the growing predominance of liberal ideology in most parts of Latin America. Free trade political liberals who favored less centralized state rule formed liberal parties, while traditional agricultural interests and pro-Church conservatives formed conservative parties. Local political leaders and their foreign counterparts extolled the virtues of free trade and open borders. It was viewed as simply "unnatural" to stand in the way of the economic and social progress that such arrangements were supposed to bring. Even the traditional landed elites in large measure cooperated in the modernization process, providing generous concessions to foreign companies while relying on traditional labor practices. To local governments it seemed only logical to collect some revenue from commercial trade, which during colonial times had flourished illegally outside their control. Of course, it was only a tiny slice (less than 5 percent) of the population that benefited from these free trade agreements. Local elites, who viewed the native populations as significantly inferior, excluded them systematically from national political life. Democracy developed slowly. Where elections were held in Latin America in the nineteenth century, less than 10 percent of the population was eligible to vote through most of these years. Most of the countries were organized as republics, but it was in form only. Political participation was limited to segments of the elite, democracy was weak, and popular participation was weaker.

Elitist domination of politics persisted through the end of the nineteenth century but in a different form. The dominance of the local *caudillo* was over. National governments were now dominant, epitomized in the Porfirio Díaz regime in Mexico (1876–1880 and 1884–1911). In some ways, leaders like Díaz were mirror images of the local *caudillo*. Usually military men, they were no longer doing the bidding of a local *hacienda* owner. Instead, they were representing the interests of commercial farmers and merchants whose economic success was predicated on foreign trade and a national infrastructure. To achieve the national power they needed, local authorities had to be put in line, a process that was consummated in Argentina and Mexico during this period. All such national regimes had a law-and-order focus designed to achieve political stability and therefore attract foreign investment.

The turn of the twentieth century saw the beginning of the consolidation of the modern nation-state in Latin America. As suggested earlier, this process had begun with liberal reforms in Mexico under Benito Juárez in the 1850s, by Bartolomé Mitre and Domingo Faustino Sarmiento (1862–1874) in Argentina, and by Justo Rufino Barrios (1871–1885) in Guatemala. In each country, the consolidation of power by newly emerging commercial elites was tied to increasing trade with the industrialized world. This movement of power away from more traditionally oriented elites would continue in the region through the 1940s.

Late-nineteenth-century Brazil and Mexico saw the strong influence of developmental thought associated with Auguste Comte's philosophical positivism. Indeed, it was positivism that inspired the modernization of the Brazilian state and the foundation of the Brazilian republic in 1889. Thus, the new elites in both of these countries began to rely on science and technology and tried to organize their societies to conform to the scientific law of progress. Following the advice of his positivist scientific advisors, or *científicos*, Díaz consolidated the commercial integration of Mexico into the world economy and was responsible for the massive foreign investment and improved infrastructure that characterized his rule. As with elite-run regimes in virtually all Latin American countries save Argentina, these new regimes did little to enfranchise the peasant and laboring masses economically (or politically). Indeed, the economic conditions of the common people had changed little since independence, and conditions that favored the emergence of a substantial middle class developed at a slow pace.

## Post-1910

By 1910, Latin America was being integrated ever more strongly into the world capitalist economy, assigned the role of peripheral producer of primary goods and consumer of industrialized goods from the developed nations at the center of the system. Further, there was increasing investment in plantations like those that grew sugar in Cuba or bananas in Central America and mines in countries like Mexico (silver), Chile (copper), and Bolivia (tin). Likewise, British and American financial capital sought even more investment opportunities in the expanding Latin American economies. The Great Depression temporarily halted the integration of Latin America into the international capitalist economic system, but the pace of integration continued and quickened in the second half of the century.

As we suggest in the chapter on economics (Chapter 7), increased demand for the export commodities and increasing imports helped commercialize Latin American economies. Import substitution industrialization further changed the face of Latin America, as did the subsequent phase of export-led growth and the growing production and export of manufactured goods. The 1970s saw Latin American countries borrow more and more capital from outside the region, greatly increasing their external debts in the process. Debt and debt repayment remained a poignant problem into the twenty-first century. The last decades of the twentieth century witnessed the transformation of the region from what at the beginning of the century was a rural area where wealthy landowners and poor peasants or rural laborers predominated to a modern, urbanized area where three-fourths of the people lived in cities. By the turn of the twenty-first century, the largest class in most countries was the urban working class, which included a growing informal sector. Likewise, a significant middle class had developed and cut its political teeth. As these new classes were joined by new segments of the upper class tied to industrialization and commercialization and the increased involvement of multinational corporations and foreign investors, new political forces were mobilized and new political coalitions developed.

## THE MEXICAN REVOLUTION

These and other factors led to the development of the first great revolutionary movement of the twentieth century, the Mexican Revolution. The dominance of traditional landowners, the Church, and the Díaz dictatorship kept developing social and political forces in check for many years. However, the struggle for change finally erupted in 1910 and spread throughout society. The mostly rural masses soon mobilized with cries of *"pan y tierra"* (bread and land) and participated full force in the many revolutionary armies that fought for the next seven years under such generals as Pancho Villa and Emiliano Zapata. It was indeed a revolution won by *los de abajo*, those from below, to use Mariano Azuela's term. The radical constitution of 1917 manifested many of the new ideas of the revolutionaries, set the stage for the development of modern Mexico, and infected the rest of Latin America with new ideas and expectations. Hereafter, land reform, legislation protecting workers, secular education, reduction of the power of foreign investors, and the Church's power and influence—as well as the ability to break with overly European models in favor of those that recognized the culture, history, and ethnicity of the masses—began to filter through Latin America. They soon combined with ideas from the second great revolution of the twentieth century (in Russia in 1917) to stimulate the development of new, more progressive social movements and political parties that would endeavor to forge a very different Latin American reality. The rest of the twentieth century witnessed myriad struggles between the conservative political and economic forces and mobilized classes and coalitions advocating significant reformist or revolutionary change.

Forces favoring reform and revolution would hereafter battle conservative forces and those tied to the existent system. After the Russian Revolution and subsequent spread of more radical forms of socialism and Marxism, these struggles would often become more class oriented and often quite bloody as the dominant classes fought tooth and nail to preserve their status and privilege.

## DEMOCRATIC REFORMISM IN URUGUAY

The modern reformist era arrived in Uruguay at the turn of the century. Like Argentina, Uruguay had an urban working class and the beginning of a middle class whose interests were quite different from those of the traditional landholders. The dynamic leader of the liberal Colorado Party, José Batlle y Ordóñez, chose his 1903 election as president to enact a series of extensive economic and political reforms that would turn Uruguay into a modern social democracy and welfare state by the 1920s. Further, in a fascinating experiment with less autocratic forms of rule, Uruguay was even governed by a *colegiado,* or collective presidency (where power was shared among members of a presidential council and the titular head of state rotated), from 1917 to 1933 and from 1951 to 1967. Thus, from 1903 until 1973, Uruguay was regarded as the Switzerland of Latin America and as an example of just how democracy and enlightened social democratic-style rule could triumph in a Latin American state.

Later, conditions changed in Uruguay, and the threat of even greater popular mobilizations and the threat to the domestic upper class and foreign capitalists posed by the often-popular Tupamaro guerrillas mobilized conservative forces against further change. Thus, even in democratic Uruguay, the rising tide of bureaucratic authoritarian military governments in the 1970s undermined their hard-won democratic political culture and the working- and middle-class benefits and liberties that had been achieved. This experiment with reformist democracy and a fully developed welfare state was cut short when the military staged a coup in 1973. The military controlled the country for the next twelve years. Full democratic rule was not restored until 1985, but the *colegiado* was no longer employed, and the working and middle classes were forced to accept government cutbacks and other structural adjustments. More recently, a progressive coalition, the *Frente Amplio,* has become a major power contender. Dr. Tabaré Vázquez led an even broader leftist electoral coalition, the Frente Amplio Encuentro Progresista Nueva Mayoria, to a first-round electoral victory in October 2004. The Tupamaro guerrilla group turned political party (Movimiento de Liberación Nacional-Tupamaros) was a member of the winning coalition, which also carried a legislative majority in both houses. The leftist victory is seen as a clear repudiation of neoliberal policies and an assertion of popular control. This leftist tact in Uruguayan politics was further underlined by the 2009 presidential electoral victory of José Mujica. The former Tupamaro guerrilla headed the Frente Amplio slate, which also maintained a majority in both legislative houses. Tabaré Vásquez was returned to power in 2015 as the Frente Amplio candidate.

## DEMOCRACY AND DICTATORSHIP IN ARGENTINA

It was suggested earlier that in the nineteenth century Argentina evolved from the gaucho dictatorship of Juan Manuel de Rosas to the reformist civilian rule of presidents like Domingo Sarmiento. By the turn of the century, Argentine beef and wheat were flooding into Europe, and British investment was pouring into Argentina. The South American nation was developing rapidly and had a higher per capita income than several European nations. It soon spawned a proletariat and a nascent middle class. These groups became the base for a newly formed, European-inspired Radical Party, which promised to bring enlightened democratic rule to Argentina.

Before Argentina could experience sustained economic or political development, the Great Depression dashed hope for continued economic development, and the weakening of the Radical Party and a subsequent coup d'état in 1930 plunged the nation back into a military dictatorship.

After oligarchy-inspired conservative rule in most of the 1930s and early 1940s, a group of officers again intervened to take over the government in 1943. The junta they formed was eventually dominated by Colonel Juan Domingo Perón, who was later able to consolidate his power with the help of Eva Duarte and successfully ran for president in the 1946 elections. Peronism, as his political movement came to be called, became the dominant political party and political movement in Argentina. Peronism displaced the Socialist Party as the party of the masses and remained the largest political party for the rest of the twentieth century. Juan Perón was a dynamic, charismatic, and often dictatorial leader who was famous for his mass rallies and ties to the Argentine labor movement. Eva Perón became the darling of the masses and greatly bolstered the Peronist project. She died in 1952 and Juan Perón was ousted from power in 1955, yet their influence would linger. When again allowed to run for president in 1973, Juan Perón was re-elected, with his then-wife María Isabel Martínez Perón as his vice president. He died the next year, and Isabel Perón became the first female president in Latin America, only to be overthrown by a military coup in 1976.

From 1955 to 1966, Argentina was characterized by frequent alternation between military regimes and weak democratic governments. The country was industrializing and engaging in successful policies of import substitution, but it continued to be plagued by high inflation and a growing foreign debt. Strikes, labor actions, and guerrilla warfare challenged the oligarchy and the government. The military ruled outright from 1966 to 1973 and instituted a brutal "dirty war" against leftists and other political enemies from 1976 to 1983. After the military government initiated and lost the Falkland Islands War in 1982, elections brought a return to civilian government in 1983. Although initially threatened by barracks revolts and plagued by economic difficulties that allowed rightist Peronist President Carlos Menem to impose unpopular austerity measures, democracy continued throughout the rest of the century. His replacement, Fernando de la Rua, was forced from office because of an economic meltdown in 2001 and early 2002. Mass mobilizations, economic chaos, and massive street demonstrations continued until the third congressionally appointed president (Eduardo Duhalde) was able to stabilize the situation and hold presidential elections in 2003. Néstor Kirchner, a leftist Peronist who voiced strong opposition to the neoliberal policies advocated by the International Monetary Fund (IMF), won the presidency. Economic conditions had finally stabilized by 2005 as Kirchner developed policies that contested much of the advice of international financial institutions and neoliberal economists. With Venezuela's help, the Kirchner administration was able to cancel Argentina's debt with the IMF and strengthen its independent, anti-neoliberal stance. In 2007 Kirchner's wife, Cristina Fernández, successfully ran for president to continue his policies. Her attempts to increase the export taxes on agricultural exports did, however, generate considerable opposition, which caused a drop in her popularity. The government's legislative coalition lost its majority in both houses in the 2009 elections, but Christina Kirchner rebounded and won re-election in 2011, even though her husband Néstor died unexpectedly in 2010.

She experienced criticism for some of her policies suffered a decline in popularity that impacted the Peronist party, which lost the 2015 presidential election to Mauricio Macri, a center-right candidate who implemented neoliberal policies once in power.

## AUTHORITARIANISM, APRISMO, MARXISMO, AND DEMOCRACY IN PERU

Peru's defeat in the War of the Pacific (1879–1883) caused a national reexamination that began the consolidation of the modern nation-state and unleashed new social and political forces. Critical writers like Manuel González Prada spawned the radical reformist movements that eventually led to state centralization and consolidation under subsequent presidents and radical political movements like Victor Raúl Haya de la Torre's Alianza Popular Revolucionaria Americana (American Popular Revolutionary Alliance; APRA) and José Carlos Mariátegui's Peruvian Socialist Party (later, the Peruvian Communist Party).

Haya de la Torre, heavily influenced by the Mexican as well as the Russian Revolution, came to believe in a necessary political, economic, and social restructuring of all of Latin America. He founded APRA while visiting Mexico in 1924 and began a lifelong struggle to found political movements that would enfranchise the masses, promote land reform, improve the treatment of indigenous Americans, and resist the dominance of the United States. This movement led to the formation of APRA in Peru (which was kept from power by conservative and then reformist military forces until Alan García's presidency in 1985) and similar political movements in other countries. These movements represented the aspirations of the toiling masses—particularly indigenous peoples—and many sectors of the emerging middle class. The groups were often characterized as national revolutionary parties even though they were generally more reformist than revolutionary by the time they came to power. They came to be dominant parties in Venezuela (Acción Democrática, founded by Rómulo Betancourt), Costa Rica (Liberación Nacional, founded by José Figueres), Bolivia (Movimiento Nacionalista Revolucionario [National Revolutionary Movement, MNR], founded by Víctor Paz Estenssoro), Puerto Rico (Popular Democratic Party [PDP], founded by Luis Muñoz Marín), and the Dominican Republic (Partido Revolucionario, founded by Juan Bosch).

Coming from a more modest background than the aristocratic Haya de la Torre and more specifically focused on the Indian peasants and rural laborers, miners, and the small urban proletariat, the self-educated Mariátegui was heavily influenced by his reading of Manuel González Prada and about the indigenist movement in Peru, Marxist literature, Lenin and the Russian Revolution, and the Mexican Revolution. He supported indigenous rights and the workers' movement in Peru and went on to found the Peruvian Socialist Party, which soon affiliated with the Communist International. In so doing he stimulated the development of a Marxist-Leninist movement in Peru and gave impetus to revolutionary struggle in Peru and elsewhere. Indeed, he argued for a Latin American socialism that was "neither copy nor imitation" of any other, but his early demise in 1930 and strong criticism from the Soviet-controlled Communist International limited his influence for many years. Marxists in Peru and elsewhere in Latin America rarely followed his independent stance, and communist parties were generally subordinate to European influences and Soviet control.

Not until the last decades of the twentieth century was Mariátegui's open brand of Marxism fully appreciated by a broad spectrum of the Latin American left.

Substantial structural change did not come to Peru through a socialist movement or through APRA; rather, it arrived with a reformist military takeover in 1968 that maintained power until 1980. Thus, it was the military—not reformist or radical civilian politicians—that instituted a comprehensive system of land reform in Peru (although they did not set up sufficient financial mechanisms to empower poor peasants and agricultural workers who were the beneficiaries of this reform) and addressed the conditions of the workers. Previously, Peru's political history had been marked by dictators like Augusto Leguía (1919–1930) and Manuel Prado (1949 and 1956–1962) and by intermittent periods of democracy.

There was a return to democratically elected governments after 1980, but the struggle against severe economic conditions for the masses and the rise of the guerrilla group Sendero Luminoso stretched the democratic institutions beyond their limits. By the mid-1990s, events such as the 1992 *auto-glope* (self-coup) of elected president Alberto Fujimori had greatly diminished the practice of democracy. This trend was continued with the 2000 fraudulent re-election of Fujimori for a constitutionally prohibited third term, though he was forced from office in 2001 and new elections were held. By 2004, his elected successor, Alejandro Toledo, who was accused of favoritism and corruption, insisted on following neoliberal policies that became increasingly unpopular. His support was so small (measured in single digits in opinion polls) that some wondered if he would even be able to finish his term. Indeed, 2005 began with an armed uprising demanding his ouster. In 2006 former Aprista president Alan García was elected president in a run-off election against radical nationalist candidate Ollanta Humala. During his five-year term, García continued more conservative policies informed by neoliberal economics and became more closely allied with the United States. A more moderately positioned Humala was finally elected president in 2011 in a run-off election against Keiko Fujimori, the former president's daughter. Once in office Humala tacked to the right, opting for neoliberal policies. In 2016, rightest candidate Pedro Pablo Kuczynski was elected to the presidency in a tight run-off against Keiko Fujimori. This further underlined the reality that in Peru the radical socioeconomic change envisioned by José Carlos Mariátegui has not yet come to pass.

## DEMOCRACY, SOCIALISM, INTERVENTION, AND DICTATORSHIP IN CHILE

Political reform came to Chile earlier. It began with the formation of a parliamentary republic (1891–1924) and came to include a proletariat and a nascent middle class. The predominance of copper mines owned by foreign corporations sparked the formation of a strong socialist-oriented union movement, and the large number of socialist immigrants helped create a socialist political movement in Chile. Like Mariátegui in Peru, the labor leader Luis Emilio Recabarren championed a Marxist party in Chile. Building on the newly developing political forces unleashed by a nitrate boom, the parliamentary republic, and the development of copper mining, Chile continued to evolve, experiencing a short-lived socialist republic under Marmaduke Grove in the early 1930s.

Along with more traditional parties, a substantial socialist movement developed. As its support grew among the miners and urban working class and sectors of the middle class, it was challenged by a strong, reformist Christian Democratic Party that had also created a union movement. The Christian Democrats headed off the leftist challenge, mobilized workers, and, with support from the United States and their Christian Democratic allies in Europe, won two important elections in the 1960s and went on to establish themselves as a major reformist party. Even greater structural change began when the Socialist Party, in coalition with the Communist and Radical parties, finally achieved power in 1970 with the election of Salvador Allende as president. This was a clear triumph of the popular classes.

Up to this point Chile, like Uruguay and Costa Rica after 1948, was considered a nation where the seeds of democracy had taken root and flowered. Indeed, many thought that the thoroughgoing socialist restructuring proposed by Allende might actually be carried out by peaceful, constitutional means. Some significant progress was made during the first years of Allende's Popular Unity government from 1970 to 1973, but Chilean society became increasingly polarized. The United States and conservative sectors in Chile made every effort to destabilize the newly elected government. U.S. military aid to the Chilean military was, interestingly, continued, even though all other aid was cut. Finally, Chilean democracy was shattered by a brutal U.S.-supported and Central Intelligence Agency (CIA)–sponsored military coup in September 1973. The workers had lost. The coup displaced all progressive forces and instituted a repressive military regime run by Augusto Pinochet that lasted until 1990. Thousands were murdered by the state security forces. A return to free market economics was one of the primary goals of the military dictatorship. As the country came to terms with the brutality of the military dictatorship in the post-Pinochet period, five democratic elections were held. The *Concertación* (Coalition of Parties for Democray; CPD) won the first four elections and a socialist once again became president in 2000. From 1990 on, civilian presidents helped soften aspects of the rather austere neoliberal economic policies. On the whole, the country was considered to have developed a thriving economy based on neoliberal principles. Even so, many suffered from poor wages and living conditions. The George W. Bush administration's plan to privatize Social Security was based on a similar plan implemented in Chile, where it became fraught with problems, and many of the privatized pension funds left their participants with very little indeed. The election of former defense minister and Socialist Party member Michelle Bachelet as president in 2005 helped institutionalize more progressive democratic rule in Chile and provided an independent-minded woman president as a new political and personal role model. As democratic rule became more strongly reinstitutionalized, January 2010 saw Chileans elect Sebastián Piñera, of the National Renewal Party in the center-right Coalition for Change. He was the first rightist to be elected president of Chile after the Pinochet dictatorship. Student and other protests undermined conservative rule in Chile, and Michelle Bachelet was re-elected president in 2013.

## CUBA, COLONIALISM, AND COMMUNISM

Much of the inspiration for the democratic attempt at a constitutional socialist revolution in Chile was derived from the Cuban example as well as from Chile's own socialist and democratic tradition. Indeed, the event after the Mexican Revolution that inspired the most attempts at radical change in Latin America was the revolution that took place in Cuba in 1959. As it evolved toward a socialist path that eventually embraced Marxism-Leninism, Cuba became a model for radical change throughout the region.

Cuba, like Mexico, was an example of change delayed. Even independence had come late to Cuba; Cuban patriots lost the Ten Years' War (1868–1878), and slavery was not abolished until 1886. Spanish colonial rule endured until 1898, and independence was not achieved until 1902 (and then only under U.S. tutelage). The system that ensued was dominated by sugar plantations and sugar refineries (*centrales*) that were increasingly owned or controlled by U.S. businesses as American investment capital flooded to the island in the first decades of the twentieth century. A Cuban upper class centered in sugar production also developed, while the masses were generally relegated to positions as cane workers and *guajiros* (peasants). Poverty and seasonal unemployment characterized rural agricultural labor, as did de facto subordination of people of color. A monocrop economy and dependent nation par excellence, Cuba became closely tied to the United States for sugar sales and the importation of finished goods. Indeed, it was often suggested that the American ambassador to Havana was nothing less than a proconsul.

By the 1920s Cuba had already experienced its first dictatorship (Gerardo Machado, 1924–1933), which was only ended by military coup. A second coup was led by a noncommissioned officer, Sergeant Fulgencio Batista, in 1933. Batista maintained good relations with the United States and, promoted to colonel, was elected to the presidency in 1940 as a reformer. In 1952, he executed another coup and established what became a brutal and unpopular dictatorship, which was eventually overthrown by Fidel Castro's 26th of July Movement. Supported by peasants and agricultural workers, segments of the Cuban upper class, and many from the middle class that had emerged in Havana, the revolutionaries took power in 1959 and went about reforming the country, basing many of their ideas on the reformist constitution of 1940. The guerrilla war that put them in power became immortalized in fellow guerrilla leader Ernesto "Che" Guevara's manual on guerrilla fighting, *Guerrilla Warfare*.

The examples of the Cuban Revolution and of forming guerrilla groups to wrest power from dominant elites were of immediate interest to the Latin American left. The Cuban Revolution became Marxist after the United States organized the Bay of Pigs invasion in 1961 and, thus, became an example of the revolutionary transformation of a Latin American society. The notion of overthrowing the status quo with a band of guerrilla fighters and addressing the economic and social injustices and foreign control that had characterized the region was widely acclaimed by progressive forces. A variety of Fidelista guerrilla groups were organized throughout Latin America and set about emulating the Cuban example and fighting their way down from the hills into the corridors of power in the nations' capitals. Guerrilla movements like the Frente Sandinista de Liberación Nacional (FSLN) in Nicaragua, the Armed Forces of National Liberation (FALN) in Venezuela, the Revolutionary Armed Forces of Colombia (FARC), and the Movement of the Revolutionary Left (MIR) in Peru and Chile began to operate from Mexico and Guatemala in the north to Argentina and Chile in the south. Radical change and socialist revolution through violent struggle were now added to the political mix. The revolutions were not led or fomented by Latin American Soviet-oriented communist parties, which generally had very limited success, frequently criticized the young Fidelista revolutionaries, and often did not support the movements. Cuba became the revolutionaries' mecca and source for moral and sometimes material support. The radical regime continued in power into the twenty-first century and proved to be one of the longest lasting socialist governments. Although many expected a radical restructuring of the government when Fidel Castro was no longer the president, 2008 saw a stable, relatively effortless presidential transition to Fidel's brother, Raúl Castro, who did initiate some economic reforms. Diplomatic relations with the United States were restored in 2015, and Fidel died in 2016 at the age of 90.

## Earlier Attempts at Change: Bolivia and Colombia

Before the Cuban Revolution, other less radical attempts at change had been made in Latin America in the post–World War II period. The MNR in Bolivia was inspired by the philosophy and example of the Peru-based APRA and the Mexican Revolution. Led by Víctor Paz Estenssora, National Revolutionary Movement (MNR) radicals had led the strongly indigenous and heavily unionized radical tin miners, indigenous peasants, and middle-class supporters to seize power in 1952. They soon nationalized the tin mines and engaged in a major agrarian reform that distributed large amounts of land to impoverished peasants. Difficult economic conditions and the hostility of the United States made it difficult to maintain the reformist project. The experiment was cut short in 1964 when the vice president took power through a military coup. A series of military governments followed, but the masses mobilized once again in late 2003 to force the U.S.-linked president to resign. The mostly indigenous masses and their social and political movements again mobilized in 2005 to force the former vice president and now president to resign to pave the way for the new elections in December 2005. Indeed, broad indigenous support facilitated the election of Evo Morales as president. He was the first indigenous Bolivian to hold that post and was re-elected in 2009 with 64 percent of the vote. He joined with other progressive political leaders such as presidents Hugo Chávez of Venezuela, Rafael Correa of Ecuador, Daniel Ortega of Nicaragua, and Raúl Castro of Cuba to chart a new course for his and other Latin America nations.

The movement to enfranchise the masses in Colombia was manifest in the figure of progressive liberal politician Jorge Gaitán. He represented the progressive wing of the Liberal Party and promised better conditions for the labor movement and for peasants. Before he could mobilize support for such badly needed reforms, he was assassinated in Bogotá in April 1948. Those committed to change took to the streets, and days of violent rioting followed. Known as the *Bogotazo*, the violent actions in the capital soon spread throughout the country, where bands of liberals attacked conservatives, whom they believed had denied them the change they so badly needed. Soon, the entire country was caught up in a decade of fighting known as *La Violencia*. It was finally ended by the formation of the National Front, a common front based on a political pact between the elites in the Conservative and Liberal Parties whereby they agreed to share power among the mainstream elements of the two parties. A clear example of politics by pact among the elite, the agreement lasted until the early 1970s.

In the meantime, those desiring more fundamental change gravitated to a variety of guerrilla groups that began to operate in Colombia from the 1960s onward. Many of these gained such power that they were able to negotiate special agreements with the government; one of the original and surviving guerrilla groups, the Fuerzas Armadas Revolucionarias de Colombia (FARC), even managed to negotiate a temporary ceasefire with the Colombian government that gave them control over part of Colombian territory. They and other guerrilla groups had been greatly strengthened in the 1990s by agreements with several Colombian drug cartels that guaranteed protection and economic well-being for the peasants in their areas and gave the cartels certain protection from the armed forces as long as they paid their taxes to the guerrilla organization. By 2000, the eroding power and legitimacy of the government and the growing strength of FARC and the Ejército de Liberación Nacional (ELN) suggested that change in Colombia could still come through a revolutionary takeover. This and the continuing power of the drug cartels prompted the United States to greatly increase military, antidrug, and economic aid to Colombia in 2000. The U.S. war on drugs and the continued existence of FARC prompted the Clinton administration to create Plan Colombia, the multibillion dollar plan to eradicate coca fields and stop the production of illegal drugs in Colombia. Conflict continued, but by 2007 the level of U.S. funding for Plan Colombia was being reduced despite President Alvaro Uribe's hard line with guerrilla groups and close cooperation with the United States. Yet, Colombia remained the United States' closest ally in South America and agreed to allow the United States to use sections of several Colombian military bases for military activities, though the Colombian supreme court later ruled this unconstitutional. Uribe's defense minister, Juan Manuel Santos, was elected in 2010 as a continuation of the hard line, pro-U.S. policies activities. He continued to fight the guerrillas but did begin to negotiate a peace process with the main guerrilla force the RevolutionaryArmed Forces of Colombia (FARC). Yet, economic and social conditions were far from ideal; high unemployment and great income disparity continued. The implementation of the U.S.–Colombia Free Trade Agreement in 2012 and the related decline in economic opportunity for many farmers in Colombia helped spark a month-long national strike by Colombian farmers in 2013. In 2014 Juan Manuel Santos was re-elected in a run-off election and oversaw the conclusion of negotiations with the FARC that finally culminated in a peace agreement between the government and the guerrillas in 2016.

## BRAZIL, U.S. FOREIGN POLICY, AND THE NATIONAL SECURITY STATE

Like Cuba, change and social restructuring came late to Brazil. From independence in 1822 until 1889, Brazil was an empire under the control of emperors from the Portuguese royal family. Brazil did not see the consolidation of the modern nation-state until Getúlio Vargas's takeover of the federal government in the revolution of 1930 and his subsequent establishment of the "new state" in 1936. Vargas and his personal style of populism dominated Brazilian politics until his suicide in 1954. Through the efforts of many progressive political movements, change again occurred in the late 1950s. Juscelino Kubitschek was elected in 1955 by promising to move the country forward. His dynamic approach to government action and the founding of the new capital of Brasília helped heighten expectations for a brighter future.

After 1960, the United States became increasingly concerned with political mobilization of the masses and political movements that might, as had occurred in Cuba, become radicalized as they struggled to break away from the stultifying economic and social structures that had condemned the vast majority of Latin Americans to poverty and suffering. U.S. policy toward Latin America in the 1960s was twofold: foment gradual change and restructuring through the Alliance for Progress and related activities (this would undermine the political base of more revolutionary movements), and support the development of counterinsurgency and the national security states to fight and defeat the radical guerrilla movements that did appear. To the latter end, military training in places like the School of the Americas in the Panama Canal Zone, and aid to Latin American militaries were greatly increased. Soldiers and lower-level officers were trained in counterinsurgency tactics. Command officers were imbued with a version of the national security doctrine that suggested that the Latin American governments, and especially the military, were responsible for protecting the nation and state from the threat posed by guerrillas, leftist political movements, and communism. Since many Latin American military leaders already thought of themselves as guardians of the nation, this training—which was replicated and emphasized in national war colleges—served as a further impetus to intervene when there was danger of uncontrollable popular mobilization or unchecked guerrilla activity. In 1965, U.S. president Lyndon Johnson even enunciated the Johnson Doctrine (a corollary to the Monroe Doctrine) to explain the need of the United States to intervene in its sister republics to stop the spread of communism.

The shadow of the Cuban Revolution, peasant mobilization, worker militancy, and domestic radicals who might opt for violent revolution—all seen through the lens of national security doctrine—convinced the Brazilian military and conservative forces that they were facing a revolutionary situation. The United States had already expressed concern and was communicating with the military and sympathetic politicians. A military coup was staged in 1964, and a long period of authoritarian military rule was initiated.

The military regime that took power did not, however, stabilize the situation and then hold elections, as was often the case when military juntas took over. Rather, it usurped power from civilian politicians, closed Congress, arrested some leftist leaders, banned traditional political parties, and generally argued that the Brazilian military could develop the country much better than the civilian politicians could. The peasant mobilization and worker militancy that helped spark the popular movement were suppressed, as were radical groups. There would be no revolution in Brazil. Instead, a long period of military rule (lasting until 1985) was initiated, and the military took it upon itself to guide Brazil in achieving its *grandeza* (greatness) by developing along more conservative, state-directed capitalist lines. Large *fazendas* were continued, foreign capital was invited in, the government went into joint business ventures with multinational corporations, the Amazon was thrown open for development, and indigenous people were seen as expendable in the rapid developmental process that ensued. Growth and development were expected; socioeconomic restructuring and income redistribution were unacceptable.

This long-term economically and politically involved military rule and the resultant national security state designed to stop political or social revolutions like that which occurred in Cuba came to be called *bureaucratic authoritarianism*. Brazil was the proto type for this extended military rule. After Brazil's return to democracy in 1985, new power contenders like the Workers' Party (PT) appeared. Although still dominated by more conservative forces until 2002, the Workers' Party finally managed to win the presidency in that year and again in 2006. By 2010 the Brazilian economy had grown substantially, and the second administration of the Workers' Party President Luiz Inácio Lula da Silva, popularly known as Lula, had consolidated its power after making peace with Brazil's economic elites. Workers' Party rule continued under Lula's hand-picked successor Dilma Rousseff, Brazil's first female president. However, many felt that the impoverished sectors of the population were not benefiting fully from Brazil's economic growth and were still marginalized economically. Poor health care and public education combined with fare increases in public transportation, the perception of widespread government corruption, and inordinate public spending on stadiums and other facilities for the 2014 World Cup and 2016 Olympics triggered massive protests and street demonstrations all over Brazil in June of 2013. Although narrowly re-elected in 2014, widening corruption scandals, severe economic decline, and political maneuvering by the rightest parties precipitated Rousseff's impeachment in 2016 and her replacement by her rightist vice president Michel Temer. Many referred to the process as a congressional coup and by 2017 Temer was also accused of corruption and suffered declining support because of this and his implementation of unpopular neoliberal policies.

# The Cold War and Change

## THE DOMINICAN CASE

In early 1965, political instability and the possibility of the mobilization of the Dominican masses by Juan Bosch and his APRA-style Dominican Revolutionary Party raised the specter of a reformist party taking power but, as had happened with the 26th of July Movement in Cuba, then becoming radicalized as it endeavored to effect change in an economy heavy with U.S. investment. Red flags went up in the White House and the Pentagon, and in April 1965, 25,000 marines were dispatched to Santo Domingo to restore order and staunch any leftist threat. No more Cubas would be tolerated. Conservative rule was restored and continued into the 1980s. More progressive leaders such as Leonel Fernández (Dominican Liberation Party; PLD, 1996–2000, 2004–2008, and 2008–2012) charted a new course in the 1990s and after. With the signing of the Central American Free Trade Agreement (CAFTA) and the inclusion of the Dominican Republic in that agreement, the island nation was drawn even more strongly into the U.S. sphere of influence.

## CENTRAL AMERICA AND U.S. HEGEMONY

The quest for change in Central America came more slowly. American involvement in the region dated from William Walker's intervention in Nicaragua in the 1850s. American investment grew through the latter part of the nineteenth century and all during the twentieth.

The case of U.S.–Nicaraguan relations is addressed in the following discussion. Other attempts were made to transform the traditional reality of Central America. For instance, from 1944 to 1954, reformist forces in Guatemala attempted to consolidate a modern nation-state and make economic and social reforms that would economically and politically empower the peasants, banana workers, and the majority indigenous population for the first time. However, the new government soon found itself in a heated dispute with the Boston-based United Fruit Company, which had very strong ties to the U.S. government. Before the land reform program could be completed, the revolution of 1944 was overthrown by a CIA-organized military coup in 1954. A virtual civil war erupted in the 1960s as Cuba-inspired guerrillas tried unsuccessfully to overthrow the military and conservative forces. The struggle continued into the 1990s and claimed some 200,000 Guatemalan lives. A peace accord was finally negotiated with the help of the United Nations in 1996.

In El Salvador, a small oligarchy reigned as fourteen families ruled and used brutal repression to maintain their virtual monopoly on wealth and power (as in La Matanza of 1932; see Chapter 10). The families frequently used their military allies to maintain an unjust status quo. Military rule predominated in the 1960s and 1970s, and pressure for change grew by 1979. Rather than allow needed land and other reforms, the rulers once again opted for repression. This led to strong civilian opposition and the eventual formation of the Farabundo Martí Front for National Liberation (FMLN). A civil war developed in the 1980s as a coalition of reformers and revolutionaries battled the military and the U.S.-backed civilian government. More than 70,000 lives were lost in the civil war in El Salvador; the United States supplied more than $5 billion in military and economic aid to stop the revolution. Peace was finally negotiated in the 1990s, and the FMLN was transformed into a major political party, although the U.S-backed Alianza Republicana Nacionalista (National Republican Alliance; ARENA) consistently won the presidency and most, but certainly not all, other offices through 2007. The electoral fortunes of FMLN began to change in 2008, and FMLN candidate Mauricio Funes was elected president in early 2009 and former FMLN guerrilla leader Salvador Sánchez Cerén succeeded him in office in 2014. Breaking with right-wing rule in Guatemala, Alvaro Colom was elected president in 2007 as a reform candidate. After former military leader and then–President Otto Pérez Molina was forced from office because of a corruption scandal linked to him and the vice president, comedian Jimmy Morales was elected president and took office in 2016.

But El Salvador and Guatemala had not been able to escape the consequences of the lack of socioeconomic reform or the culture of violence that the brutal civil wars had engendered. Brutal gangs (*maras*) developed. MS or MS-13 (the Mara Salvatrucha) and M-18 (Barrio 18) were reputed to have as many as 100,000 members in Central America by 2008 and could not be controlled by the governments in El Salvador, Guatemala, or Honduras. El Salvador, Honduras and Guatemala were three of the most violent societies in the world. The homicide rate for El Salvador alone was over 100 per 100,000 (as compared to 5 in the United States) in early 2016. There were ten homicides a day in a total population of 6.8 million. By the beginning of 2008, the *maras'* organizations extended through the three countries and reached to the United States, where gang members from Central America began to appear (see box on *maras*). Thousands of Central Americans chose to flee the *maras* and the increasing crime and violence in the region. By 2014 the Mexican drug cartels had also made major inroads in Central America, and the region was becoming the major transshipment point for drugs headed for the United States from South America. These factors, combined with political unrest and government repression, made Honduras one of the most dangerous countries in the world with a homicide rate of 82 per 100,000 in 2013. The gang-generated violence in particular was a major factor in the massive immigration of Central Americans to the United States.

Events were different in Costa Rica. The victory of José Figueres and his National Liberation forces in the Costa Rican civil war of 1948 and the subsequent establishment of a modern social democratic state in the 1950s marked the only example of progressive change to endure in the region. Figueres's strong ties to the United States and his American wife helped facilitate the success of the Costa Rican experiment, which turned into a two-party dominant democracy that valued honest elections and electoral competition. The country opted for a European-style social democracy that continued to achieve high levels of education, health care, and sanitation. It elected Laura Chinchilla as its first woman as president in 2010.

## The Post–Cold War Period and U.S. Hegemony

The 1991 demise of the Soviet Union, the main socialist rival to the ascending hegemony of the United States, and the resultant difficulties for Cuba and the Cuban revolutionary model meant that neither communism nor Cuba was perceived as an immediate threat in Latin America. This, in turn, relaxed the emphasis on the national security state and counterinsurgency in Latin America. Further, the end of bureaucratic authoritarian (military) regimes by the early 1990s signaled a return to greater formal democracy.

---

### MILITARY DICTATORSHIP AND BUREAUCRATIC AUTHORITARIANISM

As suggested in this brief historic overview, there was a strong rightist reaction against the leftist forces that sought social change. After the CIA sponsored the Guatemalan coup in 1954 there was a period of traditional conservative military rule that lasted into the 1980s and was marked by its human rights abuses and brutality. But apart from such traditional military rule, in some countries the strength of the leftist challenge to power elicited a series of military takeovers throughout the region. Labeled "bureaucratic authoritarianism" by the Argentine political scientist Guillermo O'Donnell, it referred to military governments like the one that ruled Brazil from 1964 to the beginning of 1985 and August Pinochet's infamous dictatorship in Chile that ruled from the September 11, 1963 coup until 1990. The Dirty War in Argentina was conducted by the military regime that ruled from 1976 to 1983. Other countries that experienced such rule included Bolivia, Uruguay, and Peru where a progressive nationalist Nasserite military government ruled from 1968 until 1980. The strong push for democratization that sprang up in Latin America in the 1990s was in large part a reaction to the suppression of democratic freedoms and state violence and terrorism during the military regimes, and in all the cases, save possibly Peru, the brutal human rights record that saw massive human rights violations, included the murdering of thousands, massive torture, secret jails, and countless disappearances. The United States pushed its anticommunist, national security state, counterinsurgency stance in the hemisphere. It is often accused of facilitating many of these regimes and generally worked with and supported them despite criticizing their human rights record. After the demise of the Soviet Union and other communist states, the United States strongly advocated democratization, free elections, and free markets. Yet, many of the countries are still coming to terms with such brutality. They have established truth commissions to shed light on the events, allowed for national reconciliation, and, in some cases, paved the way for the prosecution of those who committed crimes. Reminiscent of Nazi atrocities, the refrain "never again" is sometimes heard.

The triumph of capitalism in Eastern Europe further stimulated the process of free market capitalist globalization. In Latin America, nationalist economic policies that protected and promoted import substitution industrialization and the growth of national businesses were rapidly abandoned in favor of free markets, free trade, and the free flow of investment capital. Latin America now seemed to be a safe place for international capital to do business. By 2000, Colombia was the only country to have any significant radical groups contesting power through the use of force and challenging the new Pax Americana. Throughout the region, increasing pressure came from international financial institutions like the IMF to globalize and set aside policies that would directly transfer benefits, income, or wealth to the still-suffering masses of Latin Americans. The new focus was not on socioeconomic change, restructuring, or income redistribution; rather, it was on capitalist growth that would—Latin Americans were told—benefit all. Those suspicious of the continuing intervention of the United States believed that marine uniforms and guns may well have given way to business suits and IMF portfolios. Others felt that Latin American nations might now finally be able to compete in the international economic arena on more equal ground because the globalization of their economies would force them to modernize and become more competitive. By 2011, this latter view was not widely shared as neoliberal economic policies were discredited and the global economic crisis began to be felt across Latin America. However, by the middle of the second decade of the twenty-first century, the rightest forces were once again mobilizing, and leftist regimes were being displaced by more conservative administrations. Many of the initial Pink Tide governments were no longer in office, and neoliberal policies were once again being put in place.

## Venezuela: Dictatorship, Democracy, and the Post–Cold War Bolivarian Republic

The combination of neoliberal-inspired economic policy, continued impoverishment of the masses, and shoddy statesmanship created conditions that generated a movement led by a progressive army officer in the country where Simón Bolívar had started the struggle for independence in South America. In 1810, Bolívar and the junta in Caracas struggled to establish democracy in Caracas and the rest of what is now Venezuela and Colombia. Yet, the march toward democracy was not always easy in Bolívar's homeland. The Venezuelan nation saw its share of dictators in the remaining years of the nineteenth century and experienced a long period of dictatorial rule in the first part of the twentieth century. Indeed, the dictatorship of Juan Vicente Gómez (1908–1935) is one of the most notorious in Latin American history. Before Gómez, Venezuela almost experienced another wave of European intervention. At the turn of the century, several European states, led by Germany, wanted to take over the customs operations of the nation to get funds to repay debts owed by Venezuela. This plan was frustrated by the U.S. invocation of the Monroe Doctrine, but even so, Germany, England, and Italy did engage in a naval bombardment of Puerto Cabezas in 1903. These economic problems were resolved with the beginning of petroleum production under the Gómez dictatorship.

Modern democracy came to Venezuela with the APRA-inspired Acción Democrática takeover in 1945 and the election of civilian president Rómulo Gallegos in 1947. But he too was overthrown by another coup in 1948. From 1952 to 1958 Venezuela suffered the military dictatorship of Marcos Pérez Jiménez. Led by Rómulo Betancourt, Acción Democrática instituted an open democracy, political competition (mostly with the Christian Democratic COPEI Party) that lasted until 1998. A founding member of the Organization of Petroleum Exporting Countries (OPEC), Venezuela was able to build a governmental and physical infrastructure from its increasing petroleum revenues. Although many lived well, the proceeds from petroleum production were concentrated in the middle and upper classes and a few well-paid unionized petroleum workers. The vast majority continued to live in poverty despite the petroleum bonanza. Strong civilian government and a stable two-party system did, however, develop. This system suffered its first challenge when major riots broke out after IMF-inspired austerity measures were met with massive rioting by the poor in Caracas in 1989. The inability of successive governments to govern and increasing corruption led to two serious coup attempts by reformist military officers in 1992 and the eventual emergence of one of the coup leaders as a challenger to the old political system. After serving two years in prison, Hugo Chávez assembled an opposition movement (Fifth Republic Movement) and successfully ran for the presidency in December 1998. He defeated the candidates fielded by the two main parties and swept many of his supporters into office throughout the nation. The two long-dominant parties lost legitimacy in the face of the traditional system's breakdown and Chávez's promises to confront neoliberalism and the conditions that were keeping the masses in poverty. Further, he charged the old political structures with corruption and of only benefiting the elite. He spoke of the need for structural change and made favorable references to the achievements of the Cuban Revolution and Fidel Castro after his visit to the island. In 2000, Chávez managed to have a much-revised constitutional system passed in a national plebiscite and to again hold elections at all levels to legitimize his mandate. He won 60 percent of the vote. The newly restructured state was dubbed the "Bolivarian Republic of Venezuela." His power was threatened by a coup attempt in 2002 and a popular referendum to remove him from office in 2004. Neither was successful, and Chavismo was solidly in control in 2011. Though Chávez was not able to initially secure a majority for all the constitutional reforms he championed, he did get most passed with a second referendum in 2010, but the opposition made substantial gains in congressional elections later in the year. Chavismo and the Bolivarian revolution suffered a major setback with Chávez's death in 2013, and his successor, Nicolás Maduro, in the face of growing opposition, could not maintain a congressional majority and was unable to resolve a growing economic crisis that included shortages of food and medical supplies. By 2017 Venezuela was experiencing a severe political and economic crisis.

## The Pink Tide and The Rightest Resurgence

Hugo Chávez was, however, symbolic of the anti-neoliberal, leftist Pink Tide in Latin American politics that not only brought him to power but also Evo Morales in Bolivia, Rafael Correa in Ecuador, Néster Kirchner and Cristina Fernández de Kirchner in Argentina, Fernando Lugo in Paraguay, and Tabaré Vásquez and former Tupamaro guerrilla José Mujíca in Uruguay. In addition to Raúl Castro in Cuba, by 2014 there were four other former leftist guerrillas who had been elected as presidents: Daniel Ortega in Nicaragua (2006, 2011, and 2016), José Mujica in Uruguay (2009), Dilma Rousseff in Brazil (2010 and 2014) and Salvador Sánchez Cerén in El Salvador (2014). These leaders supported new political organizations like ALBA (Bolivarian Alliance), worked on multiple projects for Latin American unity, and resisted U.S. hegemony and pressure to join free trade agreements like NAFTA. Running on a more progressive platform than in her first election, Michelle Bachelet of the Socialist Party was also elected to a second term in Chile, putting all the ABC powers (Argentina, Brazil, and Chile) under liberal-minded women presidents. Similarly, Laura Chinchilla was elected as Costa Rica's first female president in 2010.

Yet by 2017 Chávez and his hero Fidel Castro were dead, and Chavista policies were under attack as crisis racked Venezuela. Nester Kirchner had also died, and Cristina Fernandez de Kirchner and the Peronists were no longer in power in Argentina. Lugo had been removed from power in Paraguay, and Dilma Rousseff had been impeached and removed from power in Brazil. But Morales and Corea were both in power as were Michelle Bachelet in Chile and Tabaré Vasquez in Uruguay. Although accused of becoming a strong man, Daniel Ortega and the FSLN were still in power in Nicaragua as was Sánchez Cerén in El Salvador. The struggle between leftist policies and rightest reaction was once again being played out in Latin America.

## Growth, Persistent Poverty, and Immigration to the United States

As was the case in Venezuela, by 2005 most Latin American economies experienced some economic growth but maintained a wide gap between upper-class beneficiaries of globalization and the still-prevalent misery of the masses. In many cases, income distribution even widened. However, a few countries, such as Costa Rica and Chile after 1990, developed sufficient social welfare programs to at least soften the savage capitalism that globalization had unleashed in Latin America. It remains to be seen if this new direction in economic policy will engender sufficient benefits to satisfy the masses, if the people will mobilize behind new political leaders and political movements that challenge the status quo and promise greater economic equality as part of a pink tide of leftist governments, if they will opt for rightest governments that champion neoliberal policies, or if they will just leave if they can. As suggested earlier, by 2005 there was an upsurge in popular movements, and leftist leaders had taken power in Argentina, Brazil, Uruguay, and Venezuela. Radical popular movements had displaced less progressive politics in Bolivia and Ecuador, and leftist presidents were elected in both Andean nations. But traditional interests and some right-wing backers in the United States were still capable of resisting and even reversing change. For a while, a leftist was the leading candidate for the 2006 election in Mexico but was narrowly defeated at the polls and defeated more decisively a second time when he ran in 2012. Attempts to improve the economic disparity had some success in Nicaragua after Ortega's re-election in 2006, but innovative progressive presidents who tried to challenge conservative interests in Honduras (Manuel Zelaya), Paraguay (Fernando Lugo), and Brazil (Dilma Rousseff) were removed from office by a congressionally sanctioned military coup in Honduras (2009) and a congressionally orchestrated and highly politicized impeachment in Paraguay (2012) and Brazil (2016)—both referred to as congressional coups.

As greater economic and social justice was not achieved in most of Central America, Mexico, and elsewhere in much of Latin America and cartel and gang-related crime increased drastically in Mexico and Mesoamerica, many decided to flee to the United States. Millions of Latin Americans have been immigrating to the United States as a survival strategy. As suggested by Table 3, the number of documented and undocumented immigrants crossing U.S. borders continued to surge, despite efforts by the U.S. government to retard undocumented arrivals. By 2013 some 11.7 undocumented immigrants were living in the United States. Further new estimates, based on the most recent census data and other official statistics, show that the number of undocumented immigrants did not decline significantly from 2009 to 2012, despite record numbers of about 400,000 deportations each year and stepped-up border enforcement as well as attempts to discourage such immigration. However, the number of undocumented immigrants to cross the United States's southern border did begin to decline by 2016. Economic and political conditions that the United States helped create and maintain in Latin America were forcing millions to migrate north. By backing repressive governments in places like Guatemala, Honduras, and El Salvador earlier and advocating neoliberal economic policies throughout the region, the U.S. government has, during the last few decades, accelerated the flow of Latin Americans into the United States. In the process of doing so, policymakers had given new meaning to the term blowback.

A clear example of the interconnectedness of Latin America and the United States is the juvenile gang phenomena in the northern tier of Central America (Guatemala, El Salvador, and Honduras). By most estimates there are more than 100,000 gang members in these countries, and some estimates suggest as many as 50,000 in each Central American nation. The two most prominent gangs—Mara Salvatrucha (MS or MS-13) and M-18 (Barrio 18 or, in English, the 18th Street gang)—have the vast majority of members and are known for their brutality and viciousness.

**TABLE 3.** Immigrants in the United States by Region and Country of Birth 1996-2014

| Region and Country of Birth | Legal Immigrants | | | Estimated Illegal Immigrants Residing in the U.S. | | |
|---|---|---|---|---|---|---|
| | 1996 | 2006 | 2014 | 1990 | 2008 | 2013> |
| **North America** | **340,428** | **413,992** | **324,354** | **2,789,000** | **8,800,000** | ... |
| Mexico | 163,556 | 173,749 | 134,052 | 2,040,000 | 7,030,000 | 6,194,000 |
| **Caribbean** | **120,000^** | **146,384** | **133,550** | ... | ... | **260,000** |
| Antigua-Barbuda | 406 | 570 | 369 | ... | ... | ... |
| Bahamas | 767 | 847 | 654 | ... | ... | ... |
| Barbados | 1,041 | 959 | 384 | 4,000 | 5,000* | ... |
| Cuba | 26,438 | 45,614 | 46,679 | 2,000 | 7,000* | ... |
| Dominica | 797 | 471 | 345 | 3,000 | 4,000* | ... |
| Dominican Republic | 39,599 | 38,068 | 44,577 | 91,000 | 91,000* | 123,000 |
| Grenada | 785 | 1,068 | 633 | ... | ... | ... |
| Haiti | 18,383 | 22,226 | 15,274 | 67,000 | 76,000* | ... |
| Jamaica | 19,084 | 24,976 | 19,026 | 37,000 | 41,000* | 77,000 |
| Trinidad and Tobago | 7,331 | 8,854 | 3,988 | 23,000 | 34,000* | ... |
| **Central America** | **44,277** | **74,956** | **44,403** | **530,000** | ... | **1,603,000** |
| Belize | 785 | 1,252 | 789 | 10,000 | 8,000* | ... |
| Costa Rica | 1,502 | 3,109 | 1,966 | 5,000 | 17,000* | ... |
| El Salvador | 17,902 | 31,782 | 19,273 | 298,000 | 570,000 | 436,000 |
| Guatemala | 8,762 | 24,133 | 10,238 | 118,000 | 430,000 | 704,000 |
| Honduras | 5,866 | 8,117 | 8,156 | 42,000 | 300,000 | 317,000 |
| Nicaragua | 6,901 | 4,145 | 2,886 | 50,000 | 21,000* | 68,000 |
| Panama | 2,559 | 2,418 | 1,095 | 7,000 | 11,000* | ... |
| **South America** | **61,744** | **137,971** | **73,715** | **185,000** | **800,000** | **690,000** |
| Argentina | 2,450 | 7,327 | 3,874 | 7,000 | 15,000* | 35,000 |
| Bolivia | 1,913 | 4,025 | 1,719 | 8,000 | 13,000* | ... |
| Brazil | 5,888 | 17,903 | 10,429 | 20,000 | 180,000 | 117,000 |
| Chile | 1,706 | 2,774 | 1,581 | 6,000 | 17,000* | ... |
| Colombia | 14,275 | 43,144 | 18,175 | 51,000 | 141,000* | 137,000 |
| Ecuador | 8,319 | 17,489 | 10,960 | 37,000 | 170,000 | 146,000 |
| Guyana | 9,489 | 9,552 | 6,267 | 13,000 | 22,000* | ... |
| Paraguay | 615 | 719 | 391 | ... | ... | ... |
| Peru | 12,869 | 21,718 | 10,606 | 27,000 | 61,000* | 105,000 |
| Suriname | 211 | 314 | 158 | ... | ... | ... |
| Uruguay | 539 | 1,664 | 1,128 | 2,000 | 2,000* | ... |
| Venezuela | 3,465 | 11,341 | 8,427 | 10,000 | 34,000* | 44,000 |

... Data not available.

*Sources: 2009 Yearbook of Immigration Statistics*, Table 2 and Table 3. Office of Immigration Statistics, Department of Homeland Security, https://www.dhs.gov/sites/default/files/publications/ois_yb_2009.pdf.

*2014 Yearbook of Immigration Statistics*, Table 2 and Table 3. Office of Immigration Statistics, Department of Homeland Security, https://www.dhs.gov/sites/default/files/publications/ois_yb_2014.pdf.

*Estimates of the Unauthorized Immigrant Population Residing in the United States*, August, 2008. Department of Homeland Security, https://www.dhs.gov/sites/default/files/statistics/immigration.shtm.

*Estimates of the Unauthorized Immigrant Population Residing in the United States*, January, 2011. Department of Homeland Security, https://www.dhs.gov/xlibrary/assets/statistics/publications/ois_ill_pe_2011.pdf.

*Estimates of the Unauthorized Immigrant Population Residing in the United States*, January, 2012. Department of Homeland Security, https://www.dhs.gov/sites/default/files/publications/ois_ill_pe_2012_2.pdf.

>Data from Migration Policy Institute. *An Analysis of Unauthorized Immigrants in the United States by Country and Region of Birth.* http://www.migrationpolicy.org/research/analysis-unauthorized-immigrants-united-states-country-and-region-birth

^Estimate based on Table 2 "Persons Obtaining Lawful Permanent Resident Status by Region and Selected Country of Last Residence" from *2014 Yearbook of Immigration Statistics.*

*From the year 2000 instead of 2008; DHS does not provide a comprehensive breakdown of illegal immigration in 2008.

# CENTRAL AMERICAN GANGS—THE *MARAS*

The *maras* (juvenile gangs) were formed in the 1970s and the 1980s when thousands of people escaped from the violent civil wars in Central America, leaving societies with prevalent violations of human rights and a culture of violence. Many of them came to the United States where they lived in poor neighborhoods of Los Angeles and other cities. There the young Salvadorans, Guatemalans, and some Hondurans met American gangs, such as the Crips and the Bloods, that dominated many of those neighborhoods. As a form of defense, some formed their own gangs, such as the Mara Salvatrucha (MS or MS-13) or took over what used to be a Mexican gang, such as the 18th Street gang (M-18). They learned the tactics and practices of American gangs as well as the culture of violence that was predominant in the neighborhoods where those gangs operated.

When their gang-related criminal activities were documented in their criminal records, the immigration authorities became aware of their existence as noncitizens (residents or undocumented arrivals) and deported thousands. These young people were deported to El Salvador, Honduras, and Guatemala, where they re-formed as gangs and adopted the culture of extreme violence of the Central American civil wars. Assignations, brutal rapes, threats, torture, and beheadings—often as warnings to any who crossed them—became the norm for the gangs. Homicide rates skyrocketed, and the general population became fearful. None of the three governments was able to control the spread of the gangs or their violence.

According to the psychological orientation that most of the young *mareros* have, the *mara* has to overcome any resistance by any means necessary; this includes threats and intimidation, violence, rape of women, and murder. If the objects of the gang's attention agree to incorporate themselves into the gang, they have to suffer an initiation ceremony that consists of a severe beating by the entire group, which lasts thirteen seconds for the MS-13 gang and eighteen seconds for the MS-18 gang. In some cases, a young woman can opt for "the train"—having sex with all the boys in the group, one after another.

These *maras* are not like cartels; they are not even like the gangs of the *favelas* in Rio de Janeiro or other cities in Brazil. They are juvenile gangs, and the members are young: some only nine years old when they join. The most common age ranges between twelve and nineteen years, although some are between twenty and twenty-two, and a few are older. The general rule is that one cannot quit the *mara* when they are younger, and an attempt to do so will cause the local group, *la clica* (the click), to put a green light on the person, meaning that any member of the *mara* can and should kill him. The dominant mentality of the *maras* is that of an insecure juvenile machismo. They abuse women and are very violent and irrational, although each click has its own set of rules and discipline. Since their inception in Central America in the 1980s, they have now spread to the United States. The Mara Salvatrucha has been declared a transnational criminal organization by the U.S. Department of the Treasury.

Yet another indicator of how closely events and policy in the United States and Latin America were becoming was the tremendous flow of cash that Latin immigrants were sending back to their home countries. Indeed, remittances sent home by Latin Americans working in the United States became a major source of income in many countries, like Mexico and the Dominican Republic (see Table 4). This also began to change the population dynamics and politics on both sides of the U.S. border. People and thus labor—like capital—became ever more fluid and able to flow past borders. There were many dimensions to the globalization process in the twenty-first century in the Americas, and fences, walls, or increased border patrols could not even begin to stop it. It should also be noted that there was increased migration within the region as well, especially to economic centers such as southern Brazil, Argentina, and Costa Rica. However, the economic crisis that spread to Latin America in 2008 not only discredited many neoliberal tenets and temporarily reduced immigration to the United States and better-off countries in the hemisphere, it also drastically reduced the amount of the remittances sent to the poorer countries and, for a time, stimulated some reverse migration as jobs disappeared in the United States. This temporary trend was reversed as the U.S. and world economies improved.

**TABLE 4.** Remittances to Latin America and the Caribbean Countries (2014)

| Country | Remittances (US$ millions) | Percentage of GDP |
|---|---|---|
| Argentina | 1,069 | 0.2 |
| Belize | 126 | 4.5 |
| Bolivia | 1,164 | 5.4 |
| Brazil | 1,910 | 0.1 |
| Chile | 488 | 0.4 |
| Colombia | 4,073 | 1.1 |
| Costa Rica | 559 | 1.3 |
| Dominican Republic | 4,571 | 7.9 |
| Ecuador | 2,462 | 3.4 |
| El Salvador | 4,217 | 17.4 |
| Guatemala | 5,544 | 11.8 |
| Guyana | 438 | 15.9 |
| Haiti | 1,923 | 18.9 |
| Honduras | 3,353 | 18.6 |
| Jamaica | 2,160 | 14.5 |
| Mexico | 23,645 | 2.1 |
| Nicaragua | 1,136 | 15.0 |
| Panama | 847 | 2.2 |
| Paraguay | 608 | 2.9 |
| Peru | 2,639 | 1.4 |
| Suriname | 151 | 3.7 |
| Trinidad and Tobago | 138 | 0.5 |
| Uruguay | 134 | 0.3 |
| Venezuela | 897 | 0.3 |

*Source:* Multilateral Investment Fund, *Remittances to Latin America and the Caribbean. Data located at* http://www.fomin.org/en-us/HOME/Knowledge/DevelopmentData/Remittances.aspx

# Nineteenth-Century Time Line

**1804**   Following mass slave rebellion led by Toussaint L'Ouverture, Haiti becomes the first independent republic in Latin America

**1807**   Napoleon Bonaparte invades Spain and Portugal; Ferdinand VII imprisoned and forced from Spanish throne, and Napoleon names his brother as successor; in the Americas, creoles begin plotting the independence of their Spanish American countries; the Portuguese court escapes and, with the British navy's help, flees to Brazil

**1810**   Mexico declares independence from Spain under the leadership of Father Miguel Hidalgo

**1811**   Venezuela declares its independence by forming a junta that expels the Spanish governor

**1813**   Father José María Morelos revives the Mexican independence movement; José de San Martín and the Army of the Andes liberate Argentina

**1816**   The United Provinces of the Río de la Plata declare their independence

**1817**   Chile is liberated by Bernardo O'Higgins; Spain outlaws the slave trade in all of its provinces to the north of the equator

**1819**   The United States buys Florida for $5 million

**1821**   On July 28, San Martín proclaims Peru independent; Dom Pedro defies summons of Cortés by remaining in Brazil, creating the only durable monarchy in Latin American history; Stephen F. Austin and other settlers move into Texas; Mexico and Central America gain independence

**1822**   Agustín de Iturbide is crowned emperor of Mexico

**1823**   The Central American Federation is established; the Monroe Doctrine is announced by U.S. president James Monroe; Peru passes its constitution

**1824**   The defeat of the Spanish army in Ayachucho, Peru, marks the end of Spanish rule in the Americas

**1825**   Bolivia gains its independence

**1825–1828**   War between Brazil and United Provinces of the Río de la Plata (present-day Argentina); the peace treaty created the independent state of Uruguay

**1826**   Congress of American Republics held in Panama; independence leaders sign concordats with the Vatican making Catholicism the state religion

**1830**   In Chile, beginning of the Conservative Republic; the Conservative Party holds power for thirty years

**1835**   Texans revolt

**1836**   Texans declare independence from Mexico

**1845**   U.S. Congress annexes Texas

**1846**   War between the United States and Mexico begins

**1848**   The Treaty of Guadalupe Hidalgo brings end to war between United States and Mexico; the United States gains approximately half of Mexico's territory

**1855**   U.S. citizen William Walker and former troops from the Mexican–American War invade Nicaragua; Walker declares himself president and holds power until 1857

**1857**   In Mexico, the Laws of the Reform are promulgated by Benito Juárez

**1864**   Maximilian given Mexican throne by Napoleon III

**1867**  President Juárez expels the French and marches into Mexico City

**1868–1878**  Ten Years' War; nationalist Cubans lose fight for independence from Spain

**1871**  Chilean constitution is changed, disallowing consecutive presidential terms; Brazil passes "law of the free womb"—all children born to Brazilian slaves are considered free; also in Brazil, ex-Liberal Party members found the Republican Party

**1876–1880, 1884–1911**  General Porfirio Díaz rules over Mexico

**1879–1883**  War of the Pacific between Chile, Peru, and Bolivia; Bolivia loses land access to sea

**1886**  Slavery ends in Cuba

**1887**  In Chile, the Democratic Party is founded

**1888**  Brazil passes "golden law," which frees all slaves without compensation

**1889**  On November 16, Brazil is declared a republic as Emperor Dom Pedro II and his family leave in exile

**1890**  Increasing commercial relations between United States and Latin America and formation of the Pan-American Union

## Contemporary Time Line

**1910–1917**  Mexican Revolution

**1911**  Francisco Madero elected president of Mexico

**1912**  Universal male suffrage granted in Argentina; U.S. military intervenes in Nicaragua; U.S. troops stay until 1925

**1913**  Madero killed

**1914**  Panama Canal opens

**1915–1934**  United States occupies Haiti

**1916–1922**  U.S. marines occupy Dominican Republic

**1916**  Hipólito Yrigoyen, leader of the Unión Cívica Radical (UCR, or Radicals), elected president of Argentina; workers' compensation laws passed in Chile

**1917**  Chile passes employer liability laws; Venustiano Carranza assumes presidency in Mexico and a new constitution is written; U.S. military intervenes in Cuba; Puerto Rico is legally annexed to the United States; Puerto Ricans given U.S. citizenship

**1919**  Chile passes retirement system for railway workers in the same year that 100,000 workers march past presidential palace; Emiliano Zapata murdered

**1922**  Communist Party formed in Brazil; oil found in Venezuela

**1924**  Military junta in Chile; Alianza Popular Revolucionaria Americana (APRA) formed by Victor Raúl Haya de la Torre

**1926**  Augusto César Sandino returns to Nicaragua to fight with liberals; begins guerrilla war against newly occupying U.S. forces

**1926–1929**  Mexican Church suspends worship, protesting state harassment; many priests and civilians killed in the Cristero rebellion

**1926**  Democratic Party founded in São Paulo, Brazil

**1929**  Ecuador is the first Latin American country to grant suffrage to women

**1930**  On September 6, the military of Argentina overthrows the Yrigoyen government; October coup in Brazil; Getúlio Vargas takes over government

**1932** Brazil and Uruguay grant suffrage to women; Chaco War between Bolivia and Paraguay; Paraguay gains more territory; uprising in El Salvador is brutally repressed in la Matanza

**1933** U.S. troops leave Nicaragua; Anastasio Somoza begins to take power; U.S. president Franklin Roosevelt announces Good Neighbor Policy

**1934** Lázaro Cárdenas becomes president of Mexico; during his term, he redistributes 17,806,168 hectares (44 million acres) of land to landless Mexicans; Sandino murdered in Nicaragua

**1938** Mexican oil industry nationalized under Cárdenas

**1939** El Salvador grants suffrage to women

**1943** Juan Perón and other military officers take over in Argentina

**1944** Democratic revolution in Guatemala

**1945** Modern democratic era begins in Venezuela with takeover by APRA-inspired Acción Democrática, led by Rómulo Betancourt; Guatemala and Panama grant suffrage to women

**1946** Juan Perón elected president of Argentina; Eva "Evita" Duarte Perón becomes first lady

**1947** Argentina and Venezuela grant women suffrage

**1948** José Figueres and APRA-inspired Liberación Nacional Party lead reformist revolution in Costa Rica and establish modern democratic social welfare state; Costa Rican army banned by its new constitution; *Bogotazo* in Colombia; *La Violencia* begins

**1949** Chile and Costa Rica grant women suffrage

**1952** Evita Perón dies of cancer; Fulgencio Batista takes direct power in Cuba; Puerto Rico becomes a commonwealth of the United States; Marcos Pérez Jiménez stages coup in Venezuela, initiating a dictatorship that lasts until 1958; Bolivia grants women suffrage; Bolivian revolution led by Movimiento Nacionalista Revolucionario (MNR) and Víctor Paz Estenssoro

**1954** Alfredo Stroessner takes over as president of Paraguay and rules until 1989; in Guatemala, CIA-organized coup deposes constitutional president Jacobo Arbenz and begins three decades of often brutal military rule; United Fruit regains land nationalized in land reform program during 1944 revolution

**1955** Juan Perón ousted from power by the military and goes into exile; Honduras, Nicaragua, and Peru grant women suffrage

**1956** Juscelino Kubitschek de Oliveira inaugurated president of Brazil; construction of Brasília begins

**1957** François "Papa Doc" Duvalier elected president of Haiti; Colombia grants women suffrage

**1958** Dictator Pérez Jiménez ousted in Venezuela; Acción Démocratica's Rómulo Betancourt elected president, beginning modern democratic era

**1959** Batista flees Cuba; Fidel Castro and the 26th of July Movement take power

**1960** Construction of Brasília completed

**1961** Paraguay is the last Latin American country to grant suffrage to women; the United States organizes unsuccessful Bay of Pigs invasion by Cuban exiles

**1962–1965** The Second Vatican Council (Vatican II) commits the Church to work for human rights, justice, and freedom

**1962** Peronists again allowed to run for office in Argentina; Cuban Missile Crisis; Jamaica gains independence from Britain

**1963** Rural unionization legalized in Brazil; peasant leagues grow

**1964** Eduardo Frei Montalva elected president of Chile; military coup in Brazil; bureaucratic authoritarian military stays in power until 1985

**1965** U.S. marines invade the Dominican Republic

**1966** Brazil's government unveils Operation Amazonia, a plan to develop the Amazon basin

**1967** Ernesto "Che" Guevara dies in Bolivia

**1968** October 2 student massacre in Tlatelolco, Mexico City; meeting of Latin American bishops in Medellín; Colombia adopts a "preferential option for the poor" under the influence of liberation theology; reformist military leaders take over in Peru under Juan Velasco Alvarado

**1970** Salvador Allende elected president of Chile; he is the first freely elected Marxist president in Latin America; the Communist Party of Peru—Sendero Luminoso (PCP-SL)—emerges after an ideological split in Peru's Communist Party; origins of the group can be traced to a study group formed in the early 1960s by Professor Abimael Guzmán Reynoso at the University of San Cristóbal de Huamanga; Sendero Luminoso, the Shining Path, later takes the form of a revolutionary movement

**1971** Haitian president "Papa Doc" Duvalier dies; his son, Jean-Claude "Baby Doc" Duvalier, takes control; U.S. Peace Corps accused of sterilizing Indian women without their knowledge, expelled from Bolivia

**1973** Juan Perón re-elected president of Argentina; his wife Isabel becomes vice president; Salvador Allende dies in a September 11 military coup in Chile; General Augusto Pinochet initiates a brutal military dictatorship that rules until 1990

**1974** Juan Perón dies; Isabel Perón becomes first female president of a Latin American country

**1975** UN Conference on Women held in Mexico City, kicking off the Decade for Women; Cuba passes law requiring men and women to share responsibilities for housework and childrearing

**1976** Argentine military ousts Isabel Perón; General Jorge Rafael Videla takes power, and the Dirty War begins; the Mothers of the Disappeared begin to hold weekly vigils challenging the military government's human rights abuses

**1978** John Paul II becomes pope; the Catholic Church becomes more conservative; conservative Church leaders begin to attempt to eliminate liberation theology

**1979** Somoza regime collapses; the Frente Sandinista de Liberación Nacional (Sandinista National Liberation Front; FSLN) takes power

**1980** Archbishop Oscar Romero of San Salvador assassinated; four American church women murdered by Salvadoran military; Farabundo Martí National Liberation Front (FMLN) formed in El Salvador

**1981** United States inspires contras to war against Nicaraguan government; 30,000 die before 1990

**1982** Falklands/Malvinas War begins between Argentina and Britain; Brazil elects first freely elected governors since 1965; General Efrain Rios Montt becomes

Latin America's first evangelical dictator in Guatemala and embarks on a brutal counterinsurgency that often targets entire Indian communities

1983   U.S. marines land in Grenada

1985   Brazil elects Tancredo Neves as first freely elected president since military government; the night of his inauguration he has surgery and never recovers; Vice President José Sarney becomes president

1986   "Baby Doc" Duvalier flees Haiti

1988   Amid well-documented charges of election fraud, Institutional Revolutionary Party (PRI) candidate Carlos Salinas defeats Cuauhtémoc Cárdenas and Party of the Democratic Revolution (PRD) to gain presidency of Mexico

1989   Carlos Menem elected president of Argentina; Patricio Aylwin elected president of Chile, the first elected president of Chile since Allende took power; Pinochet maintains his position as commander-in-chief of the Chilean armed forces and as senator for life; in Brazil, Fernando Collor de Mello elected president, defeating Workers' Party (PT) leader Luiz Inácio "Lula" da Silva; U.S. troops invade Panama to oust Manuel Noriega; six Jesuit priests assassinated in El Salvador by U.S.-trained troops after the FMLN overruns much of San Salvador; announcement of austerity package in Venezuela causes riots, in which 276 die

1990   Alberto Fujimori elected president of Peru; stays in office until 2001; President Salinas of Mexico announces his intention to negotiate the North American Free Trade Agreement (NAFTA) with the United States; Jean-Bertrand Aristide elected president of Haiti; a military coup prevents him from taking power; Violeta Barrios de Chamorro elected president of Nicaragua, defeating FSLN candidate Daniel Ortega

1991   Jorge Serrano of Guatemala becomes Latin America's elected evangelical president

1992   In Brazil, Collor is impeached, and Vice President Itamar Franco becomes president; Fujimori closes Congress in an *auto-golpe,* or self-coup; leader of the Sendero Luminoso Abimael Guzmán captured; World Summit on the Environment and Development held in Rio de Janeiro; guerrilla war ends in El Salvador; two military coup attempts occur in Venezuela

1993   Eduardo Frei Ruiz-Tagle (son of the president 1964–1970) elected president of Chile; Carlos Andrés Pérez forced to step down in Venezuela

1994   Fernando Henrique Cardoso elected president of Brazil; NAFTA goes into effect on January 1; Zapatista National Liberation Army revolts in Chiapas; Ernesto Zedillo elected president of Mexico after first PRI candidate is assassinated; United States occupies Haiti; Aristide assumes presidency

1995   Menem re-elected president of Argentina; Fujimori re-elected president of Peru; new quota in Argentina making sure that one in four members of Congress are women; Mercosur, or Southern Cone Common Market, is founded, including Argentina, Brazil, Uruguay, and Paraguay.

1998   Pinochet loses post as commander-in-chief of Chilean armed forces; Cardoso re-elected president of Brazil, once again defeating Lula; former coup leader Hugo Chávez elected president of Venezuela, ending domination by two traditional parties, Acción Democrática and the Social Christian Party (COPEI)

**1999** Mireya Moscoso elected first female president of Panama; Plan Colombia initiated

**2000** Socialist Ricardo Lagos elected president of Chile as the Concertación candidate; Confederation of Indigenous Nationalities of Ecuador (CONAIE) and military officers briefly take over Congress in Ecuador; Fujimori re-elected in Peru after forcing constitutional changes allowing him to run for a third term; opposition candidate Vicente Fox elected president of Mexico, breaking seven decades of presidential domination by the PRI; in Venezuela, president Hugo Chávez re-elected for six-year term under new constitution

**2001** Argentina experiences severe economic and political crisis; President Fernando de la Rua resigns; Alejandro Toledo elected president in Peru after Fujimori forced out of office

**2002** Workers' Party candidate Luiz Inácio "Lula" da Silva elected to presidency of Brazil on fourth run; attempted coup in Venezuela reversed by massive street demonstration supporting President Hugo Chávez; hard-liner Alvaro Uribe elected president of Colombia

**2003** Massive mobilization by *cocaleros,* indigenous peoples, unions, and others force Bolivian President Gonzalo Sánchez de Lozada from office; Argentina elects leftist Peronist Néstor Kirchner as president

**2004** Dr. Tabaré Vázquez of leftist Broad Front wins presidency in Uruguay; Venezuelan president Hugo Chávez registers strong support in referendum on his rule

**2005** Ecuadoran president Lucio Gutiérrez is forced from office by popular mobilizations; Bolivian president Carlos Mesa also forced to resign, and former *cocalero* leader Evo Morales elected first indigenous president of Bolivia later in the year

**2006** Lula and Worker's Party government survive scandal to win second presidential term in Brazil; left-leaning Rafael Correa elected president of Ecuador; Alvaro Uribe continues hard line on negotiating with guerrillas and is re-elected president of Colombia; Sandinista leader and former president Daniel Ortega is again elected president in Nicaragua; in a hard-fought campaign in Mexico, PAN candidate Felipe Calderón wins presidential election by razor-thin margin; leftist PRD candidate Miguel López Obrador contests vote and vows parallel government; Hugo Chávez re-elected president of Venezuela with 62 percent of vote; Michelle Bachelet becomes first female president of Chile

**2007** Evo Morales continues reforms in Bolivia and asserts nation's right to own and control all natural gas; Hugo Chávez asserts socialist nature of Venezuelan regime and continues strong leadership style while confronting George Bush and increasingly hostile U.S. foreign policy; Nobel prize winner Rigoberta Menchú makes poor showing in Guatemalan presidential election, which is won by Alvaro Colom; Néstor Kirchner decides not to run for a second presidential term in Argentina in favor of his wife Cristina Fernández de Kirchner, who wins vote to become first woman elected to the presidency

**2008** Leftist former archbishop, Fernando Lugo elected president of Paraguay; Fidel Castro resigns as president of Cuba, and Raúl Castro is elected president by National Assembly; United Socialist Party advocated by Venezuelan government; relations between Venezuela and the United States become more tense. Evo Morales faces secessionist movement in Bolivia

**2009**　Obama administration takes more conciliatory tone with Venezuela and eases travel restrictions for Cuba, opening a dialogue with Raúl Castro and Cuban leadership; Hugo Chávez continues move toward United Socialist Party for Venezuela and finally wins referendum allowing elected officials to serve more than two terms; 2009 coup d'état against progressive Honduran President Manuel Zelaya met with street demonstrations and universal international condemnation (including that of Obama administration) and calls for the restitution of constitutional democratic government. Honduran leaders ignore international condemnation and hold presidential election, which is accepted by the United States amidst intense criticism from most Latin American states. Evo Morales re-elected president of Bolivia with 64 percent of the vote

**2010**　United States negotiates base agreement with Colombia; former defense minister Juan Manuel Santos elected Colombian president. Center-right candidate Sebastián Piñera elected president in Chile. Former Tupamaro guerrilla José Mujíca elected president on Frente Amplio ticket in Uruguay. Workers' Party candidate Dilma Rousseff elected as first female president of Brazil; Laura Chinchilla elected first female president of Costa Rica

**2011**　Daniel Ortega re-elected president in Nicaragua despite constitutional provision against second term; Ollanta Humala elected president in Peru; Cristina Fernández de Kirchner re-elected president of Argentina

**2012**　PRI candidate Enrique Peña Nieto elected president of Mexico, PRD candidate López Obrador comes in second; Fernando Lugo removed from office in Paraguay in congressional coup

**2013**　Massive protests and street demonstrations in Brazil shake PT government; Hugo Chávez dies; Nicolas Maduro is elected as Chávez successor in tight election; former Chilean president Michelle Bachelet elected president for second time

**2014**　Dilma Rousseff re-elected president in Brazil in close election; former FMLN guerrilla leader Salvador Sánchez Cerén elected president in El Salvador

**2015**　Otto Pérez Molina implicated in corruption scandal in Guatemala and forced from presidency by massive protests and then placed under arrest; Jimmy Morales elected president of Guatemala; Pedro Pablo Kuczynski elected president of Peru in run-off against Keiko Fujimori; "Car Wash" corruption scandal widens in Brazil; Juan Manuel Santos re-elected president of Colombia; United States and Cuba restore diplomatic ties; murder and disappearance of 43 normal students in Guerrero State in Mexico initiates major scandal for Mexican government

**2016**　Daniel Ortega re-elected president of Nicaragua; Dilma Rousseff impeached and removed from office in Brazil, replace by Vice President Michel Temer; increased opposition protests and deteriorating economic conditions in Venezuela; peace agreement with the FARC reached in Colombia, ending half a century of war.

# Bibliography

Azuela, Mariano. *The Underdogs: A Novel of the Mexican Revolution*. New York: Penguin, 1962.

Beezley, William H., and Judith Ewell, eds. *The Human Tradition in Latin America*. Wilmington, DE: Scholarly Resources, 1997.

Bethell, Leslie, ed. *The Cambridge History of Latin America*. Vols. 4 and 5. Cambridge: Cambridge University Press, 1986.

Blum, William. *Killing Hope: U.S. Military and CIA Interventions since World War II*. Monroe, ME: Common Courage, 1995.

Bulmer-Thomas, Victor. *The Economic History of Latin America since Independence*. 3d. ed. New York: Cambridge University Press, 2014.

Butler, Smedley D. *War Is a Racket*. Los Angeles: Feral House, 2003.

Charlip, Julie A., and E. Bradford Burns. *Latin America: An Interpretive History*. 10th ed. Englewood Cliffs, NJ: Prentice Hall, 2016.

Chasteen, John C. *Born in Blood and Fire: A Concise History of Latin America*. 4th ed. New York: W. W. Norton, 2016.

Cortés Conde, Roberto, and Shane J. Hunt, eds. *The Latin American Economies: Growth and the Export Sector, 1880–1930*. New York: Holmes and Meier, 1985.

Galeano, Eduardo. *Open Veins of Latin America: Five Centuries of the Pillage of a Continent*. New York: Monthly Review, 1997.

Galeano, Eduardo. *We Say No: Chronicles 1963–1991*. New York: W. W. Norton, 1992.

Keen, Benjamin. *A History of Latin America: Independence to the Present*. Vol 2., 8th ed. Boston: Houghton Mifflin, 2009.

LaFeber, Walter. *Inevitable Revolutions*. 2d ed. New York: W. W. Norton, 1992.

Langley, Lester. *The Americas in the Age of Revolution 1750–1850*. New Haven, CT: Yale University Press, 1996.

Leo Grande, William. *Our Own Backyard: The United States in Central America, 1977–1992*. Chapel Hill: University of North Carolina Press, 1998.

Lynch, John. *The Spanish–American Revolutions 1806–1826*. New York: W. W. Norton, 1986.

Macauley, Neil. *The Emergence of Latin America in the Nineteenth Century*. New York: Oxford University Press, 1988.

Mariátegui, José Carlos. *José Carlos Mariátegui, An Anthology*, edited and translated by Harry E. Vanden and Marc Becker. New York: Monthly Review, 2011.

McSherry, J. Patrice. *Predatory States: Operation Condor and Covert War in Latin America*. Lanham, MD: Rowman & Littlefield, 2005.

Oliva Campos, Carlos, and Gary Prevost, eds. *The Bush Doctrine and Latin America*. New York: Palgrave, 2007.

Orozco, Manuel. *Migrant Remittances and the Development in the Global Economy*. Boulder, CO: Lynne Reinner, 2013.

Prevost, Gary, Carlos Olive Campos, and Harry E. Vanden, eds. *Social Movements and Leftist Governments in Latin America*. London: Zed, 2012.

Rodríquez, O. Jaime E. *The Independence of Spanish America*. Cambridge: Cambridge University Press, 1998.

Russell-Wood, A. J. R. *From Colony to Nation: Essays on the Independence of Brazil*. Baltimore, MD: Johns Hopkins University Press, 1975.

Schoultz, Lars. *Beneath the United States: A History of U.S. Policy Toward Latin America*. Cambridge, MA: Harvard University Press, 1998.

Skidmore, Thomas E., Peter H. Smith, and James N. Green. *Modern Latin America*. 8th ed. New York: Oxford University Press, 2013.

Smith, Peter H. *Talons of the Eagle: Dynamics of U.S.–Latin American Relations*. 4th ed. New York: Oxford University Press, 2013.

Vanden, Harry E. "Maras, Contragoverned Spaces, and Sovereignty." In *US National Security Concerns in Latin America and the Caribbean*, edited by Gary Prevost, Harry E. Vanden, Carlos Oliva Campos, and Luis Fernando Ayerbe. Basingstoke, UK: Palgrave Macmillan, 2014.

Vanden, Harry E. "Nicaraguan Foreign Relations." In *Revolution and Counterrevolution in Nicaragua: 1979 through 1989*, edited by Thomas Walker. Boulder, CO: Westview, 1991.

Vanden, Harry E. "State Policy and the Cult of Terror in Central America." In *Contemporary Research on Terrorism*, edited by Paul Wilkinson and A. M. Stewart. Aberdeen, UK: Aberdeen University Press, 1987.

Vanden, Harry E. "Terrorism, Law and State Policy in Central America: The Eighties." *New Political Science* 18/19 (Fall/Winter 1990): 55–73.

Vanden, Harry E., and Thomas Walker. "U.S.–Nicaraguan Relations." In *The Central American Crisis*. 2d ed. Edited by Kenneth M. Coleman and George C. Herring. Wilmington, DE: Scholarly Resources, 1991.

## Films and Videos

*The Battle of Chile*, Chile, 1976.
*Evita*. United States, 1997.
*Machuca*. Chile, 2004.
*Missing*. United States, 1982.
*The Official Story*. Argentina, 1985.
*Que Viva Mexico*. Russia/USSR, 1931.
*Reed: Mexico Insurgente*. Mexico, 1971.
*Romero*. United States, 1989.
*Sin Nombre* (Nameless). Mexico and United States, 2009.
*State of Siege*. France, 1973.

## Websites

http://www.presidencia.govgob.bo/   Presidential website in Bolivia
http://www.gobiernoenlinea.ve/home/homeG.dot/   Governmental website in Venezuela

# FOUR

# THE OTHER AMERICANS

Details of the Spanish and Portuguese colonization of Latin America were provided in earlier chapters in this volume. The purpose of this chapter is to explore the contemporary consequences of that conquest on the indigenous peoples of the Americas who lived in the region prior to 1492 and to examine the fate of the more than 10 million Africans who were brought to the Caribbean and Latin America as slaves.

In 1992, the 500th anniversary of the first voyage of Columbus provided renewed focus on the current conditions of those segments of Latin American society who have been often ignored and marginalized by governments and scholars alike. It is estimated that close to 70 million indigenous people are alive today. Indigenous people constitute a clear majority in Bolivia, close to half the population in Peru and Guatemala, and a substantial minority in countries such as Ecuador, Mexico, Panama, and Nicaragua. In the 1980s, conflict and then negotiation between the revolutionary government of Nicaragua and the peoples of the Atlantic Coast focused international attention on the region's indigenous people. In recent years, indigenous people have become more politically active in both Latin America and worldwide. In 1990, a nationwide indigenous uprising paralyzed Ecuador. A decade later the national indigenous group, the Confederation of Indigenous Nationalities of Ecuador (CONAIE), was one of the primary political actors in a government takeover that forced out President Jamil Mahuad. In 1994, an indigenous-based guerrilla movement, the Zapatistas, drew international attention to the southern Mexican state of Chiapas. In the early 2000s, indigenous groups helped bring down unpopular governments in Ecuador and Bolivia. In many countries, indigenous movements have been in the forefront of struggles over the control of natural resources and the environment and have begun to move from a position of marginalization to one of centrality in Latin American society. In 2005, the Bolivian people elected their first indigenous president, Evo Morales. Once in office Morales moved to bring the country's natural resources under government control and sponsored constitutional reforms that codified Bolivia as a multinational state, thus acknowledging the Aymara, Quechua, and other indigenous nationalities that comprise the nation. After Morales took office, the polychromatic indigenous flag flew beside the nation's flag outside the presidential palace.

## People of Color under Colonialism

In 1492, Spain turned westward in search of wealth and empire. That same year the Spanish monarchy had recovered Granada from the Moors, the culmination of a struggle that had lasted seven centuries. It was an era of reconquest for Spain, undertaken in the context of its Christian vision. Queen Isabella became the patroness of the Inquisition, which was designed to root out all alien religions (Judaism, Islam, and others) in Spain. Pope Alexander VI, who was Spanish, ordained Isabella the master of the New World. Three years after the discovery, Columbus directed a military campaign against the native population in Hispaniola. His cavalry decimated the native inhabitants, and more than 500 were shipped to Spain and sold as slaves. Most died within a few years. Throughout the conquest of the Americas, each military action began with the Indians being read a long narrative (in Spanish, without an interpreter) exhorting them to join the Catholic faith and threatening them with death or slavery if they did not comply. The brutality of the proselytization notwithstanding, in many ways the religious arguments were only a cover for the primarily commercial basis of the conquest.

The newly powerful Spanish government had decided to establish its own direct links to the east, hoping to bypass the independent traders who up until that time had monopolized the trade there for spices and tropical plants. The voyages also sought precious metals. All of Europe needed silver. The existing sources in central Europe had largely been exhausted. In the Renaissance era, gold and silver were becoming the basis of a new economic system, mercantilism. Those nations that had supplies of these precious metals could dominate the Western world. Despite that, most of the expeditions that came to the Americas in search of wealth were not sponsored by governments (Columbus and Magellan were the exceptions) but by the *conquistadores* themselves or by businessmen who backed them. The *conquistadores* did indeed find gold and silver in large quantities; but to mine it, they needed local labor. That drive for labor produced what Eduardo Galeano has called the "Antillean holocaust":

> The Caribbean island populations were totally exterminated in the gold mines, in the deadly task of sifting auriferous sands with their bodies half submerged in water or in breaking up the ground beyond the point of exhaustion, doubled up over the heavy cultivating tools brought from Spain. Many natives of Haiti anticipated the fate imposed by their white oppressors: they killed their children and committed mass suicide.

The civilizations confronted by the Spaniards in Mexico and Peru were large and prosperous ones. The Aztec capital Tenochtitlán (present-day Mexico City), with 300,000 people, was then five times larger than Madrid and double the population of Seville, Spain's largest city. Tenochtitlán had an advanced sanitation system and engaged in sophisticated agricultural techniques in the marshland around the city. It was a majestic city dominated by the Templo Major, its most sacred site.

When the conqueror Pizarro arrived in South America, the Incan Empire was at its height, spreading over the area of what is now Peru, Bolivia, and Ecuador and including parts of Colombia and Chile. The third great civilization was that of the Maya, who inhabited the Yucatán peninsula of Mexico and south into Guatemala.

The Mayas were skilled astronomers and mathematicians who had developed the concept of the number zero.

Despite their high level of civic and scientific development, the indigenous people in the Americas were defeated by a variety of factors that favored the European invaders. The European military commanders were also quite skillful at exploiting divisions among the indigenous people. In Mexico, Cortés allied with the Tlaxcalans against Moctezuma and the Aztecs of Tenochtitlán. Pizarro also succeeded in exploiting family disputes among the Incas to foster his advantage in Peru.

The brutality of their conquest was unlimited. They took the gold and melted it into bars for shipment to Spain. Sacred temples and other public places were simply destroyed. Later, in Mexico City, the Spanish would build their metropolitan cathedral and government buildings on the foundations of the primary religious and political buildings of the old Aztec capital, as if to symbolize the total subjugation of the original inhabitants. Pizarro's forces in Peru did the same, sacking the Temple of the Sun in Cuzco, the capital of the Incan Empire.

The Europeans also brought with them diseases not found in the Americas—smallpox, tetanus, leprosy, and yellow fever. Smallpox, the first to appear, had devastating consequences. The indigenous people had no defenses against these plagues and died in overwhelming numbers. As much as half the existing population may have died as a result of the first contact.

As suggested in Chapter 2, the scope of the genocide against the indigenous people of the Americas is staggering. There were probably upward of 70 million people living in the Americas when the Europeans arrived, between 30 and 40 million in Mexico alone. By the middle of the seventeenth century, that number had been reduced to 3.5 million. In some countries, such as Cuba, the native population had been completely exterminated, while in one region of Peru, where there had been more than 2 million people, only about 4,000 families survived. Over the course of three centuries, silver production at Potosí consumed 8 million lives.

In addition to such dramatic loss of life through forced labor, the mining system indirectly destroyed the farming system. Forced to work in the mines or as virtual slaves on crown lands, indigenous people were forced to neglect their own cultivated lands. In the Incan Empire, the Spanish conquest resulted in the abandonment of the large, sophisticated farms that had grown corn, peanuts, yucca, and sweet potato. The irrigation systems that had been built over centuries were neglected, and the land reverted to desert, a condition that persists today.

## European Justification

While millions of indigenous people perished, Europeans engaged in marginalized debates over the legal status of their victims. The Spanish court in the sixteenth century acknowledged in principle their legal rights and entitlement to dignity. Various religious leaders spoke out against the inhumane treatment that the native people received, but these legal statements and religious proclamations ultimately had no meaning because the exploitation of indigenous labor was essential to the functioning of the colonial system. In 1601, Philip III formally banned forced labor in the mines but in a secret decree allowed it to go forward; his successors, Philip IV and Charles II, continued the exploitation.

The ideological justifications for the exploitation of the indigenous people were many and varied. Political and religious leaders often characterized the native people as "naturally wicked" and viewed their back-breaking work in the mines as retribution for prior transgressions. Many religious leaders offered the opinion that as a race indigenous people lacked a soul and therefore could not be "saved" by the Church in the traditional sense. Many Church leaders never accepted Pope Paul III's declaration of 1537 that the indigenous people were "true men." Others viewed them as natural beasts of burden, better suited for much of the region's manual labor than its four-legged creatures. The Spanish and Portuguese colonizers were not alone in consigning the indigenous to a subhuman status. Some European intellectuals of the Enlightenment, such as Voltaire and Montesquieu, refused to recognize them as equals.

The indigenous population of the Americas, though conquered and defeated by the Spanish and Portuguese during the sixteenth century, continued its resistance on an ongoing basis. Probably the most dramatic example of that resistance occurred in Peru near the end of the eighteenth century. At that time, Spanish pressures and demands on the Peruvian Indians increased considerably. In particular, under the *repartimiento de mercancias* the natives had to purchase goods from Spanish traders whether or not the items were useful. Locals were often unable to pay for these purchases and, as a result, were forced from their villages to earn money in mines or on *haciendas*, neglecting their own productive enterprises. During this time, the Spanish rulers also sought to dramatically increase silver production at Potosí and did so with harsh forced labor programs. These conditions fostered a strong desire among the indigenous population to return to the glories of the Incan Empire of three centuries earlier. Their aspirations led to the great revolt of 1780–1781. These dramatic events had many forerunners; 128 rebellions took place in the Andean area between 1730 and 1780. From 1742 to 1755, a native leader, Juan Santos, waged partisan warfare against the Spaniards. The memory of his exploits was still alive when the revolt of José Gabriel Condorcanqui erupted. A well-educated, wealthy mestizo descendant of Incan kings, Condorcanqui took the name of the last head of the neo-Incan state and became Túpac Amaru II. His actions began with an ambush of a hated local Spanish commander; by early 1781, the southern highlands of Peru were in full revolt. The objective of Amaru's revolt was the establishment of an independent Peruvian state that would be essentially European in its political and social organization. His vision was that caste distinctions would disappear and that the *criollos* would live in harmony with Indians, blacks, and mestizos. The Catholic Church was to remain the state church. However, the Indian peasantry who responded to his call for revolt had clearly more radical goals, no less than total inversion of the existing social order and a return to an idealized Incan Empire where the humble peasant would be dominant. The peasants exacted their revenge on all those viewed as European, including the Church hierarchy and its priests. These actions frustrated Amaru's strategy of forming a common pro-independence front of all social and racial groups. Some Indian leaders, fearing the radical direction of the revolt, threw their support to the Spaniards. Despite some initial successes, the rebel movement soon suffered a complete rout. Amaru, members of his family, and his leading captains were captured and brutally executed in Cuzco. While the most spectacular indigenous rebellion of that era, it was not unique. The revolt of the *comuneros* in New Granada in 1781–1782 had its origin in intolerable economic conditions. Unlike the Peruvian upheaval, it was more clearly limited in its aims. Its organization and its effort to form a common front of all colonial groups with grievances against Spanish authority were advances over Amaru's rebellion. A central committee elected by thousands of peasants and artisans directed the insurrection, which carried out an assault on Bogotá. Negotiations followed the rebellion, and an apparent agreement reached in June 1781 satisfied virtually all the rebels' demands. However, the Spanish commissioners secretly voided the deal and, following the demobilization of the rebel army, regained control by crushing the leadership of the *comuneros*.

The exploitation of the indigenous population did not end with Spanish and Portuguese colonial rule. The continuing oppression was never more graphic than in Bolivia, which always had one of the highest percentages of indigenous people. Well into the twentieth century, *pongos*, or domestic servants, were being offered for hire as virtual slaves. As they had in colonial times, the locals acted as beasts of burden for the equivalent of a few pennies. Throughout much of the continent, they continued to be marginalized, driven from the little good land they had been able to maintain during colonial times. In the latter part of the nineteenth century, and the early part of the twentieth century, the dramatic expansion of commercial farming fell heavily on those indigenous communities that had survived the earlier genocide of the mining operations. The *pongo* system in Bolivia came to an end in the 1953 agrarian reform brought on by a popular rebellion with indigenous support.

## The Role of Sugar and Slavery

Gold and silver were the primary targets of the conquest, but on his second voyage Columbus brought sugar cane roots from the Canary Islands and planted them in what is now the Dominican Republic, where they grew quite rapidly. Sugar was already a prized product in Europe because it was grown and refined in only a few places (Sicily, Madeira, and the Cape Verde Islands). Over the next three centuries, it would become the most important agricultural product shipped from the Western Hemisphere to Europe. Cane was planted in northeast Brazil and then in most of the Caribbean colonies—Barbados, Jamaica, Haiti, Santo Domingo, Guadeloupe, Cuba, and Puerto Rico. In the places where it was developed, the sugar industry quickly became dependent on the importation of slaves from western Africa. This industry became central to the development of significant parts of Latin America and left a legacy of environmental destruction and racism that still influences the region.

This is not to say that all slave systems in the Caribbean and elsewhere were based on the sugar plantation. Also, not all black people in the Americas are descendants of slaves, and not all slaves worked on sugar plantations. An important exception is the role slaves played in the extraction of gold in Brazil, which will be discussed later. However, it was the development of the sugar plantations of Brazil and the Caribbean in the seventeenth century that provided the impetus for the massive importation of Africans throughout the Americas. A full-blown transatlantic slave trade began after 1518 when Charles I of Spain authorized the direct commercial transfer of Africans to his possessions in the New World. It took some time for slavery to develop as we would come to know it, but it is estimated that eventually the slave trade moved more than 10 million Africans into various parts of the Americas between 1518 and 1870. Of those 10 to 11 million, more than 4 million wound up in the Caribbean islands. Brazil was the only area of the Americas to receive more slaves than did the Caribbean, with more than 5 million. The North American colonies received fewer than 1 million. Brazil was the first place where a slave society was established in the Americas, and it was the last country in the Western Hemisphere to abolish slavery, doing so only in 1888, two years after it was ended in Cuba and twenty-three years after it came to an end in the United States.

The contemporary condition of northeast Brazil is a testament to the destructive power of the sugar industry. From the beginning of Portuguese colonization early in the sixteenth century, Brazil was the world's largest producer of sugar; initially in the Spanish colonies, it was only a secondary activity. Brazil would remain the largest producer of sugar for over 150 years; from early on, it required the importation of African slaves because of scarce local labor and the large-scale loss of life among the native population. The sugar industry was labor intensive, needing thousands of workers to prepare the ground and plant, harvest, grind, and refine the cane. Ironically, although the Portuguese crown initiated the colonization of northeast Brazil, Dutch entrepreneurs actually dominated the sugar industry, including participation in the slave trade. In 1630, the Dutch West India Company conquered northeast Brazil and took direct control of sugar production. From there the sugar-production facilities were exported to the British in Barbados. Eventually, sharp competition developed between the two regions, with the Caribbean island eventually winning out as the Brazilian land began to deteriorate. The land was left permanently scarred by the 150 years of sugar monoculture. It had been a vast and fertile area when the colonists arrived, but the agricultural methods used were not sustainable. Fire was used to clear the land, and as a result considerable flora and fauna were permanently destroyed. The conditions of life for the African slaves who worked on the plantations were horrendous. No food was grown; all had to be imported, along with luxury goods, by the owners of the plantations. In this way, the plantation workers were totally dependent on the landowners. The result was chronic malnutrition and misery for most of the population. The current legacy of the sugar monoculture is that northeast Brazil is one of the most underdeveloped regions of the Americas, inhabited by more than 30 million people who are primarily the descendants of African slaves brought there more than four centuries ago. Sugar remains an important crop for the region, but today less than 20 percent of the land is used for sugar production; much of the rest is simply unusable because of environmental degradation. Other regions of Brazil have gone on to produce more sugar. As a result, this once fertile region must import food from other parts of Brazil, and more than half the people in the region live below the poverty line.

Northeast Brazil is not the only region to be permanently scarred by the production of sugar and the slavery that accompanied it. The islands of the Caribbean have suffered much the same fate. The Spanish had originally grown sugar cane in Cuba and Santo Domingo but on a relatively small scale. Barbados under Dutch entrepreneurship became the first great sugar experiment in the Caribbean, beginning in 1641. In just twenty-five years, Barbados had 800 plantations and over 80,000 slaves. The island's previously diverse agricultural production was slowly destroyed as virtually all good land was given over to sugar production. However, before long, the island's ecology was destroyed and its sugar production was no longer competitive, leaving behind a destitute people. From Barbados, sugar production shifted northward to Jamaica, where by 1700 there were ten times as many slaves as white inhabitants; by the middle of the eighteenth century, its land had also become depleted. In the second half of the eighteenth century, sugar production shifted to Haiti, where more than 25,000 slaves per year were being imported to increase the size of the industry to meet growing European demand. Haiti soon ceased to be the center of Caribbean sugar production, not as the result of an ecological disaster but rather as the result of revolution.

Revolution erupted in Haiti in 1791, and over the course of the next twelve years the sugar economy of the island was devastated. The rebellious slaves eventually succeeded in driving out the French army in 1803 and establishing Haiti as an independent nation. However, independence had high costs, including an embargo by both the United States and France. Although Haiti eventually won its recognized independence from France in 1825, the island's economy was devastated by continual attacks by French expeditionary forces and because of a large cash indemnity paid upon recognition of independence. As a result, Haiti ceased to be at the center of sugar production; that focus shifted northward to Cuba.

After the Haitian rebellion and subsequent reduction in production, the price of sugar in Europe doubled, and after 1806 Cuba began to sharply increase its production. Sugar production had begun its shift toward Cuba in 1762 when the British briefly took control of Havana. To expand the sugar industry, the British dramatically increased the number of slaves brought into Cuba. During the eleven-month British occupation, Cuba's economy turned toward sugar. Previously vibrant Cuban production of fruit, beef, and light manufactured goods was largely set aside for the growth of the sugar industry. This period also saw the destruction of Cuba's forests and the beginning of the process of degrading the fertility of Cuban soil. Following the Haitian revolution, Cuban sugar production was also given a boost when Haitian sugar producers fled with their slaves to set up production in eastern Cuba. The doubling of the capacity of the Cuban sugar industry after 1806 also required the continued importation of slaves over the ensuing decades even as the slave trade was gaining more and more international condemnation. More than 1 million Africans were brought to Cuba as slaves and in the process transformed the face of Cuban society forever. Today, close to 50 percent of the Cuban population is of African heritage.

# Resistance to Slavery

Similar to the long history of indigenous resistance to colonialism, Africans who survived the voyage and sold into slavery did not willingly accept their fate. *Marronage* (flight from slavery) was a recorded fact almost from the first days that Africans were brought to the island of Hispaniola. Indigenous people and slaves fled into the inaccessible mountains of the interior, sustaining a condition of liberation and keeping alive a sense of independent identity. In 1514, on the island of Puerto Rico, two Taíno/Arawak chiefs and their people allied with Africans against the representatives of the Spanish crown. A second uprising occurred seventeen years later when the enslaved black population rose up against its oppressors. In 1522, an uprising in Santo Domingo began with the revolt of forty sugar-mill workers. Although these uprisings were eventually defeated and no full-scale rebellion would succeed prior to 1803, *marronage* was common throughout the Americas where large numbers of African slaves were concentrated. These maroon communities were common through four centuries of slavery in the Americas. Known by a variety of names (*palenques, quilombos, mocombos, cumbes, ladeiras,* and *mambíses*), these communities ranged from tiny, ephemeral groupings to powerful states encompassing thousands of members and surviving for generations or even centuries. Such maroon communities were generally well organized. They had political and military organization and were not, as is sometimes said, groups of wild, runaway, disorganized blacks. Some of these maroon communities were so powerful that they were able to negotiate treaties with European powers.

In some places throughout the Americas, these communities still exist, often maintaining their cultural heritage and bearing living witness to the earliest days of African presence in the Americas. One of the best examples of such a community is the maroons of the Cockpit Country of northwestern Jamaica, who trace their roots back to the sixteenth century and have survived as a community to the present day. Today, their early leaders are recognized as national heroes by the Jamaican government. The maroons of Jamaica are probably the best-known group in North America, but many other similar communities exist throughout the Americas. San Basilio de Palenque near Cartagena, Colombia, is a surviving example. There, the inhabitants of the ex-maroon community speak Palenquero, a dialect that fuses Spanish and elements of several West African languages. Most black people of the Pacific lowlands of Panama, Colombia, and Ecuador do not see themselves as so directly connected to Africa. They lay full claim to their own homeland—the coastal section of this tropical rain forest.

In Brazil, fugitive slaves organized the black kingdom of Palmares in the northeast and throughout the seventeenth century successfully resisted military expeditions of both the Dutch and the Portuguese. The independent kingdom of Palmares was organized as a state, similar to many that existed in Africa in the seventeenth century. Encompassing an area one-third the size of Portugal, it boasted a diversified agriculture of corn, sweet potatoes, beans, bananas, and other foods. Land was held in common, and no money was circulated. The ruling chief was elected from the ranks of the tribe and organized a defense of the territory that successfully protected it for several decades. When the Portuguese finally conquered Palmares in the 1690s, it required an army of several thousand, the largest colonial army of the time.

# The Slave Trade

The slave trade, which left its lasting legacy on the Americas, was driven in large measure by the profits it generated in Europe. Britain is probably the best example of that profiteering. Queen Elizabeth I was reportedly opposed to the slave trade on moral grounds when the first English slave traders landed in Britain, but she quickly changed her perspective when shown the financial benefits that could flow from the trade. Once its lucrative nature was clear, the British moved quickly to overcome the Dutch dominance of the early trade. A key factor in the success of the British was the concession of the trade monopoly granted to them by the weakened Spanish. The South Sea Company, with significant investment from Britain's most powerful families, including the royal court, was the chief beneficiary of the monopoly. The impact of the slave trade on Britain's economy was significant. Traffic in slaves made Bristol Britain's second most important city and helped make Liverpool the world's most important port. Ships left Britain for Africa with cargoes of weapons, cloth, rum, and glass, which served as payment for the slaves who were obtained in West Africa and then shipped to the Americas. The African chiefs who cooperated in the slave trade used the weapons and the liquor to embark on new slave-hunting expeditions. Conditions on the ships were horrific, and often as many as half of the people on board died during the voyage. Many died of disease, while others committed suicide by refusing to eat or throwing themselves overboard. Those who survived the voyage but were too weak to impress buyers were simply left on the docks to die. The healthy survivors were sold at public auction.

Despite the losses at sea, the trade was highly lucrative as the ships sailed back to Britain with rich cargoes of sugar, cotton, coffee, and cocoa. Liverpool slave merchants were making more than £1 million in profits per year, and there was considerable spin-off to the rest of the economy. Liverpool's dockyards were improved considerably to handle the increased commerce. Banks in Britain's largest cities prospered through the trade. Lloyd's of London became a dominant force in the insurance industry, covering slaves, ships, and plantations. Almost 200,000 textile workers labored in Manchester to provide needed products for the Americas, while workers in Birmingham and Sheffield made muskets and knives. Although initially dominated by the Portuguese, it was the slave trade that positioned Britain to be the dominant world power by the end of the eighteenth century. At the start of the nineteenth century, Britain turned against slavery, not primarily out of any newfound moral revulsion but through a calculation that its growing industrial production needed wage earners throughout the world to buy its products.

The British were by no means alone as a nation that participated in the slave trade. Equally important were the Portuguese, who supplied the millions of Africans necessary for the exploitation of their primary colony, Brazil. In addition to providing slaves for the sugar industry, the Portuguese developed gold extraction in Brazil using slave labor. From 1700 onward, the region of Minas Gerais in central Brazil was the focal point of the extraction. For more than a century, gold flowed out of the region, with Portuguese and British slave traders gaining massive profits. The region itself was left destitute, a condition that persists today for the descendants of those slaves who worked the mines. Subsistence farming replaced the mines and, as in northeast Brazil, became, in Galeano's words, "the Kingdom of *fazendas.*"

## Concept of Race

Race must be understood as a socially constructed, not biologically determined, concept. According to Michael Hanchard, race in Latin America determines status, class, and political power. In this respect, race relations are power relations. Being black in Brazil generally signifies having a lower standard of living and less access to health care and education than whites have, but in the minds of many it also signifies criminality, licentiousness, and other negative attributes considered to be related to African peoples. It follows, then, that the meaning and interpretation of racial categories are always subject to revision, change, and negotiation. Most important, racial constructs are dynamic and fluid insofar as racial groups are not categorized in isolation but in relation to other groups who have their own attendant values of class, status, and power. The concepts of blackness and race have long been controversial in Latin America, and only in recent years have scholars and political activists for black and indigenous rights begun to create a dialogue that can shed light on the issues. The term "black" is an adjective derived from Latin, meaning in a literal sense "sooted, smoked black from flame." In practical terms, in Latin America, it has been defined as being "not white" and as having a connection to Africa. As in North America, blackness can equally be the target of unrelenting racism or the basis of deeply held religious and aesthetic attachment to a heritage of struggle, survival, and achievement. The dominant, lighter-skinned ruling elites of Latin America historically have viewed the population of African descent with a mixture of fear and hatred. The blacks who lived free in isolated areas such as the Cauca Valley of Colombia have been the targets of campaigns of fear, labeling them as subhuman beasts who had brought a "primitive" culture with them from Africa. Such historical labeling meant that these groups in Colombia were marginalized from national political life.

The racism of the dominant classes of the Americas comes through in the historical treatment of the greatest of Latin America's heroes, Simón Bolívar. In the wars of liberation led by Bolívar between 1813 and 1822, black troops from revolutionary Haiti helped overthrow colonial governments in the territory that became the Republic of Gran Colombia. The liberation of these territories helped foster an era of black consciousness among the indigenous black communities. It has often been speculated that Bolívar may have had black ancestors, but this idea has generally been rejected in Colombia and Venezuela by white and mestizo biographers who were clearly uneasy about the implications of such a possibility. That unease was rooted in an unwillingness by the mestizo majority to acknowledge the positive role of Afro-descendants in the development of the continent.

Race is a powerful ideological concept in contemporary times throughout the Americas. There are two competing concepts that vie for recognition. Mestizaje is the ideology of racial mixture and assimilation, which is the adopted perspective of most of the political elites of the region. Negritude, on the other hand, is a concept that celebrates the positive features of blackness. At the national government level, only in Haiti is negritude the explicit national ideology. In most countries where there is a significant population of African heritage, the concept of negritude has been both the basis of societal discrimination and a symbol of racial pride for the oppressed. Of course, such pride is often seen by the dominant political culture to be a threat to the sovereignty and territoriality of the nation.

## Contemporary Manifestations of Racial Inequality

Not unlike in the United States the legacy of slavery has strong ramifications down to the present in those parts of Latin America where there are significant numbers of Afro-descendants, countries like Brazil, Colombia, Venezuela, and Cuba. Modern day Afro-descendants have faced higher levels of poverty, lower levels of political representation, lesser social mobility, and lower levels of education and continue to be victims of overt acts of racism. As was true in the United States, Latin Americans of African heritage have generally been invisible in the historical narrative their country's modern history despite their real contributions to the development of the region. The myth of the racial equality embedded in the previously discussed concept of mestizaje and the rejection of the more affirming concept of negritude allowed the predominately mestizo leaders of the region to deny the significance of the challenge of racism in contemporary Latin America and for decades after independence to not foster meaningful political dialogue. This denial of racism was especially powerful in Brazil where more than 100 million people are descendants of slaves—almost half the population—disproportionally live in poverty, and are underrepresented in the political sphere. Until the restoration of democracy in the 1980s there was little race-based discussion from either the political left or right. Even in a country like Cuba, where a significant part of the population are Afro-descendants and overall great social progress was achieved for all Cubans regardless of race after the 1959 revolution, serious discussion of racial discrimination within the revolutionary process has only surfaced in the last decade. The result was a recognition that some of the benefits of the country's economic reforms were not flowing equally to Cuba's black population.

## Contemporary Afro-Descendant Movements

When reviewing their own history and social movements, black social activists and movement leaders in Latin America inevitably raise the comparison with the U.S. civil rights movement and state with deep regret that black Latin America never had an equivalent movement. However, black-based social movements over the years have gained momentum and are now challenging centuries of domination. For example, black social movements are gaining strength in Brazil, Colombia, Ecuador, Venezuela, Uruguay, Nicaragua, Costa Rica, Honduras, and other Latin American countries. These movements are fighting for social inclusion and development, equality before the law, human rights protections, and democratic reform.

Black organizations in Brazil are some of the best organized and politically developed in the region. The black movements in Brazil are not monolithic and are quite diverse in scope, practice, and philosophy. Like all social movements, there are basic points of convergence and divergence. However, most of the progressive black movements agree that racism is an obstacle to Afro-Brazilian progress. One of the most powerful examples of a movement that has promoted black liberation is Brazil's black consciousness movement, a loosely linked network of nearly 600 organizations that has the goal of preserving ethnic heritage and fighting against the discrimination and poverty of contemporary Brazil. The groups are not united by a single ideology, and they pursue their campaign against racism using a variety of methods. Some organizations focus almost exclusively on culture, believing that the rediscovery of African roots can transform the consciousness of Brazil's black population. Other groups, such as the São Paulo–based Unified Black Movement (MNU), are politically focused, arguing that racism must be combated through changes in political, social, and economic structures. The groups have demonstrated against police violence and have fought in the courts for the enforcement of existing laws against discrimination in the workplace. During the writing of Brazil's constitution in the 1980s, MNU was instrumental in convening the National Convention of Blacks for the Constitution. The grassroots debates of this initiative, together with the efforts of Carlos Alberto de Oliveira and Benedita da Silva, two black members of Congress elected in 1986, resulted in the inclusion of a constitutional amendment that outlawed racial discrimination. The activity of the black consciousness movement has also forced the traditional Brazilian political parties to react with statements against racism and to make commitments to include blacks among their lists of political candidates and appointments to public office. These efforts have borne some fruit with the appointment of a number of blacks to key positions by the centrist Brazilian Democratic Movement Party (PMDB), but there are only a handful of black deputies in the national legislature. Pressure on the political elites has helped break down the long-held elite-generated myth that Brazil is a "racial democracy."

However, the black movement is currently far from the mass political phenomenon that it aspires to be. Part of the limitation of the movement is its narrow social base. Black consciousness groups are composed primarily of professionals, intellectuals, and upwardly mobile students. The movement is relatively small in total numbers, with probably 25,000 sympathizers out of an Afro-Brazilian population of some 104 million. Despite these limitations, the movement does represent an important contribution to the cause of racial justice in the continent's largest country. The recent use of quotas to ensure adequate Afro-Brazilian admissions to universities was one gain achieved by the black movements. Afro-Colombians have also struggled for equality and have modestly succeeded in raising consciousness of their separateness from the majority of the Colombian nation. President Hugo Chávez's self-identification as a descendant of slaves has brought the issue forward in contemporary Venezuela.

## Contemporary Struggle of the Indigenous People

The history of exploitation of the indigenous people at the time of the conquest and the century that followed is generally not disputed. Rather, it is the history that follows that is controversial. Even those who have sympathy and understanding for the oppression of the indigenous people have tended to avoid a systematic

**TABLE 5.** How Many Afro-descendants in 2016?

| Country | Estimated Population of Afro-descendant | % of Total Population |
|---|---|---|
| Antiqua & Barbuda | 86,095 | 92.0% |
| Barbados | 278,378 | 95.5% |
| Belize | 21,585 | 6.1% |
| Brazil | 104,352,598 | 50.7% |
| Bolivia | 109,696 | 1.0% |
| Colombia | 9,606,614 | 21.0% |
| Costa Rica | 380,058 | 7.8% |
| Cuba | 4,006,926 | 35.9% |
| Dominican Republic | 1,166,755 | 11.0% |
| Ecuador | 997,008 | 6.2% |
| Grenada | 108,550 | 97.6% |
| Guyana | 345,141 | 46.9% |
| Haiti | 9,961,510 | 95.0% |
| Honduras | 177,865 | 2.0% |
| Jamaica | 2,916,874 | 98.2% |
| Nicaragua | 537,012 | 9.0% |
| Peru | <922,231 | <3.0% |
| Puerto Rico | 561,755 | 15.7% |
| St. Vincent & The Grenadines | 86,998 | 85.0% |
| Suriname | 240,188 | 41.0% |
| Trinidad & Tobago | 698,114 | 57.2% |
| Uruguay | 134,041 | 4.0% |
| Venezuela | 14,534,000 | 47.0% |
| **Total** | **136,773,760** | |

*Note:* Table accounts for both black and mixed-race populations.

*Sources:* CIA World Factbook. 2016.

https://www.cia.gov/library/publications/the-world-factbook/fields/2075.html; http://www.pewresearch.org/fact-tank/2016/03/01/afro-latino-a-deeply-rooted-identity-among-u-s-hispanics/ft_16-02-22_afrolatino_map_420px/

understanding of its contemporary reality. There was a common perception that Native American cultures were primarily relics of the past, doomed to be abandoned as modernity spread to the deepest regions of rural Latin America. To the degree that indigenous cultures survived, it would be as rural, isolated communities clinging to traditional ways of life. Although such communities exist, they make up only a tiny fraction of the approximately 70 million native peoples who live in the Americas today. Because the stereotype of the isolated rural community is not actually the norm, our understanding of the issues and needs of this population must change.

The indigenous people who survived the conquest recovered their numbers slowly but steadily. Contrary to the predictions of assimilative policies, native peoples have remained demographically stable; bilingualism has increased without the disappearance of native languages. The native peoples have not been defeated or eliminated. Indigenous peoples still live in nearly all the regions where they lived in the eighteenth century. They have expanded into new territories and established a presence in urban, industrialized society that challenges the stereotypical image of indigenous peasants. Indigenous people are prominent throughout the major cities of the continent. In the new century indigenous people increasingly carry their identity with pride and organize on a hemisphere-wide basis. As noted at the beginning of the chapter, the emergence of the Zapatistas in Mexico in 1990s and the election of Evo Morales to the presidency of Bolivia in 2005 were the most prominent manifestation of renewed indigenous politics, but important developments also occurred in Ecuador and Mexico deserving of our attention.

## ECUADOR

One of the strongest contemporary movements of indigenous peoples is CONAIE, a nationwide organization that has sought to represent the native peoples of Ecuador, who make up between 25 and 30 percent of the population—the fifth-largest percentage of indigenous people in the hemisphere.

Provincial and regional indigenous organizations were created in the 1970s. In 1980, the Confederation of Indigenous Nationalities of the Ecuadorian Amazon (CONFENAIE) was founded to represent the indigenous population of the Oriente, an important step toward a national organization. In the highlands, indigenous organizations dated back to the founding of the Ecuadorian Indigenous Federation (FEI) in the 1940s. CONAIE was established in 1986 to form a single, national organization. In the 1970s and 1980s, the organizations tended to have a local focus, but in the 1990s the movement adopted a broader agenda: the right to self-determination, the right to cultural identity and language, and the right to economic development within the framework of indigenous values and traditions. Land became the focal point for the indigenous movement in Ecuador. It has also been the issue on which it has connected most successfully with nonindigenous groups.

Indeed, land was the focal point of CONAIE's first national actions in 1990. After weeks of organizing and stagnated discussions with the national government, CONAIE orchestrated an uprising that paralyzed the country for a week. The protests ended when the government agreed to national-level negotiations with CONAIE. While not succeeding in most of its demands, CONAIE did win the right to name the national director of bilingual education programs and the granting of some significant tracts of land to indigenous organizations. These mobilizations laid the groundwork for the larger and more powerful actions of 1994. CONAIE reached greater prominence in June 1994 when it sponsored a strike that shut down the country for two weeks. The target of the protest was the Agrarian Development Law, approved by the Ecuadorian Congress, which called for the elimination of communal lands in favor of agricultural enterprises. The 1994 protests in Ecuador also demonstrated the ability of the indigenous movement to link up successfully with other nonindigenous social and political movements. Commerce was brought to a halt throughout Ecuador when CONAIE set up roadblocks and boycotted marketplaces. Trade unions joined in the action by calling a general strike and stopped the delivery of goods to the cities. In parts of the Amazon, indigenous communities took over oil wells to protest the privatization of Petroecuador, the state-owned oil company.

CONAIE succeeded in getting a broad range of organizations to unite behind its own progressive agrarian reform proposal, which called for the modernization of communal agriculture but not through the government's plan of commercialization. Rather, CONAIE's proposal called for government support for sustainable, community-based projects that emphasized production for domestic consumption rather than foreign export. CONAIE also proposed the use of environmentally sound farming techniques. At the heart of their counterproposals was the idea that organized groups of civil society in the countryside would play a central role in implementing the new law.

The protests and counterproposal met stiff resistance from the government of Sixto Durán Ballen, which viewed the Agrarian Development Law to be at the center of its broader package of neoliberal reforms. The government declared a state of emergency and put the armed forces in charge of dealing with the protests. The armed forces arrested protest leaders and violently suppressed street demonstrations. The army occupied many indigenous communities, destroying homes and crops. However, the repression was not fully successful at stopping the protest movement. The government was forced to negotiate with CONAIE and ultimately to make modifications in the agrarian reform law that limited its potentially worst features. However, probably the most important result of the 1994 protests was the recognition that the indigenous movement is a significant actor in contemporary Ecuadorian politics. CONAIE and the indigenous people as a whole achieved this position through their mobilizations, successful linking with nonindigenous groups, and dynamic formation of political demands.

In January 2000, CONAIE organized several thousand indigenous people to protest the government's handling of an economic crisis and to call on the president, Jamil Mahuad, to resign. Working with cooperative members of the military, the protesters occupied the national parliament and declared a new government headed by a three-person junta including indigenous leader Antonio Vargas. However, their victory was short-lived. Under pressure from the United States and the Organization of American States (OAS), the military withdrew from the junta and conceded the presidency to Mahuad's vice president Gustavo Noboa. CONAIE was defeated in the short term in its efforts at radical reform, but its considerable power was made dramatically evident to the country's traditional rulers. In 2002, support from CONAIE was crucial to the success of the presidential campaign of populist Lucio Gutiérrez. Gutiérrez swept to victory promising to challenge the neoliberal orthodoxy and appointing indigenous representatives to government positions. However, by 2004, Gutiérrez had betrayed his promises, and CONAIE was back in the streets as a leading opposition force. In April 2005, CONAIE was a small part of a broad coalition of opposition forces that drove Gutiérrez from office following an ill-fated scheme to overhaul the nation's court system to his benefit. CONAIE has continued to press its agenda of indigenous rights in the era of Rafael Correa, the progressive Ecuadorian president first elected in 2006 and re-elected in 2009 and 2013. Given Correa's generally progressive stance, CONAIE had some expectation for progress under Correa but have primarily found themselves at odds with a president who has aimed his policies primarily at the urban poor and middle classes who also voted him into office. Correa has often upstaged CONAIE by backing CONAIE initiatives such as the declaration of Ecuador to be a plurinational country. The issue that has most separated Correa from CONAIE has been his advocacy of large-scale mining. This strong difference of perspective led to a demonstration of thousands of indigenous people in January 2009 opposing the new mining law by shutting down the Pan-American Highway for a brief period. Violent response from the Correa government only served to alienate the two sides to an even greater degree. At its 2009 congress in April, CONAIE denounced Correa for "governing from the right" and for setting up parallel indigenous organizations to compete with CONAIE. CONAIE was also wary of supporting Correa after their experience with Gutiérrez. Correa initially supported a CONAIE-initiated proposal not to drill for oil in the Yasuni National Park in the Amazon forest but in June 2013 reversed that policy, announcing that the government would exploit the resource to support his government's antipoverty programs and increase the nation's economic development. Not surprisingly, the indigenous movements, citing the oil's contribution to climate change and the extraction's damage to native lands, opposed the plan vigorously, leading to more violent confrontations and arrests. The Correa government has remained committed to its use of the oil revenues as a social development strategy, lending to the characterization of the divide as red and green, socialist and environmentalist. As Ecuadoran expert Marc Becker observes, the debate reveals how difficult it is to break from the capitalist logic of an export-driven economy even when many of the political forces involved share the same goal of sustainable development.

The Confederation of Ecuadorean Indigenous Nationalities (CONAIE) in action. *(Photo by Dolores Ochoa/AP Images)*

Despite its strong confrontation with Correa and divisions within the indigenous movement, CONAIE and its allied political party, Pachakutik, remain an important political force, especially in the province of Zamora Chinchipe in the southeastern Amazon where its candidate Salvador Quishpe triumphed in the 2009 regional election. This victory, in an area of the mining sector, gives CONAIE a continuing base from which to challenge the government in Quito.

## BOLIVIA

The election of Evo Morales to the presidency of Bolivia in 2005 was the culmination of decades of indigenous and nonindigenous political organizing. Development of uniquely indigenous movements occurred later in Bolivia than in Ecuador despite Bolivia being the only country in the region with a majority indigenous population. In Bolivia, social-movement organizing from the grassroots had a stronger labor union-organizing focus coming out of the 1952 revolution. That revolution was spearheaded by powerful mining unions who also took up the cause of land rights without explicitly framing the issue as one of indigenous rights. In the 1960s and 1970s an Aymara (Bolivia's largest indigenous group) political movement broadly known as Katarismo developed, drawing its name from the leader Tupac Katar from Tupac Amaru's 1780s uprising discussed earlier in the chapter.

As Marc Becker has observed students who came from rural areas to study in the capital but faced discrimination as second-class citizens often provided leadership for these new ethnic-based movements. They promoted new ethnic ideologies that rejected the homogenizing, purely class-based perspectives of the 1952 revolution that treated all peasants, indigenous and nonindigenous, as the same. They resurrected the *Wiphala*, the rainbow-colored flag of the Inca's Tawantinsuya as their symbol, and spread their message, the Aymara language.

Also in the late 1970s a new peasant organization formed, the Confederation of Peasant Unions (CSUTUB) and was headed for almost twenty years by an Aymara Indian, Genaro Flores, who also headed the previously discussed Tupac Katari Revolutionary Liberation Movement. By the 1980s, new peasant and indigenous groups were formed to protest U.S.-sponsored coca eradication and neoliberalism. As Bolivian scholar Trudi Morales has observed, these movements used direct action tactics—strategic roadblocks, property seizures, hunger strikes, mass marches, and "chew-ins" of the sacred coca leaf—to pressure and even remove governments. By 1988 the national Peasant Coca Growers Union and Evo Morales became the voice of the *cocalero* movement. The indigenous right to grow the coca plant led to increased demands for greater indigenous rights and autonomy. The indigenous focus, combined with an alliance with the parties of the left, elected an unprecedented number of *campesino* and indigenous delegates to the legislature in the 1990s. This development was facilitated by the 1994 Law of Popular Participation and the 1994 Law of Civic Associations and Indigenous Peoples that permitted indigenous and traditional communities to participate in the political process directly, independent of the political parties. These reform laws directly contributed to the historic electoral victory by Morales in 2005 and the subsequent 2009 constitution, which further strengthened Bolivian indigenous rights.

Once the 2009 pro-indigenous constitution was ratified many expected that it would be easily implemented, but divisions emerged with similarity to the red–green divide in Ecuador came to the fore in Bolivia. The Bolivian focal point was the government plan to build a highway through an ecological reserve, TIPNIS, to facilitate delivery to international markets of Bolivia's natural resources. In 2011 indigenous groups that had previously supported the government demonstrated against the highway and became highly critical of the government, accusing it of hypocrisy for supporting the international environmental movement abroad but endangering a vital bioreserve at home. The Bolivian confrontation has only further underscored the challenges that social movements based on indigenous rights will make to the extractivist model for social development being pursued by the progressive governments of the Andean region.

## BRAZIL

In Brazil, the issue that most marks the indigenous struggle is the contest for land. Land is the subsistence base of indigenous groups, whether they are hunters and gatherers in the Amazon or small farmers in the northeast. It is the issue that unites Brazil's 206 indigenous societies.

Brazil's indigenous people are only 0.9 percent of the national population, speaking 170 languages, with legal rights to about 11 percent of the national territory. Much of the indigenous land is rich in natural resources. Nearly 99 percent of indigenous land is in the Amazon region, occupying more than 18 percent of the region, but little more than half the indigenous population lives there. In the other densely populated parts of the country, almost half the indigenous population lives on less than 2 percent of the indigenous land.

The current struggle over land is not a new one. Expropriation of indigenous lands and decimation of the indigenous population have usually paralleled the drive by Europeans for a particular raw material, whether timber, gold, sugar, or rubber. The administration of President José Sarney (1985–1990) was especially aggressive in moving forward with Amazonian development projects. The army's Northern Tributaries Project, begun in 1987, had as its goals the reduction of indigenous land areas and the subsequent opening up of large new areas for both farming and mining. As a result, between 1987 and 1990 the Yanomami's 9.5 million hectare (23.5 million acre) territory was reduced by 70 percent and divided into nineteen different unconnected parcels of land. Protests at the 1992 Earth Summit led to the creation of land reserves by the governments of both Brazil and Venezuela. Despite the newly created reserves, conflict between the gold miners and the Yanomami continued. In 1993, many Yanomami were massacred in an attack by the miners and with no effective intervention by the Brazilian government. The 1988 Brazilian constitution contained progressive provisions for environmental protection and indigenous people's rights, but the reality was that they were generally not implemented. Powerful private economic interests moved forward with their projects, often buying off government officials with large bribes. The government itself moved forward with environmentally questionable projects such as the planned Paraná-Paraguay River seaway.

However, sole focus on these devastated and isolated groups would miss an important part of the story. In the last thirty years, the indigenous people have begun to change their situation through political organization. The demographic decline reached its low point in the mid-1970s, and the population has risen ever since. The first complete indigenous census, in 1990, counted about 235,000 indigenous people. By 2000, the number had grown to 300,000. Between 1990 and 1995, the area of indigenous land with complete legal documentation increased more than fourfold.

At the same time, the Brazilian indigenous movement also made important links in the international community, most especially with the environmental community. During the 1980s, there developed among environmentalists internationally a significant consciousness of the destruction of the Amazon rain forest. In developing international attention about the problem in Brazil, groups like Greenpeace and the World Wildlife Fund made common cause with Brazil's indigenous groups. Both sets of groups began to speak the same language—sustainable development. Both indigenous peoples and environmentalists argued that the rain forest was not a wilderness to simply be preserved but rather an area that was inhabited and contained important resources for the world that the people who currently lived there could provide—medicines, rubber, and foodstuffs. The activists argued that the kind of development being projected and carried out by the Brazilian government—primarily slash-and-burn agriculture—was inappropriate for the fragile character of the land. They pointed to vast tracts of land that had been exploited in the 1960s and 1970s and were now worthless semidesert. Considerable international attention was also brought to the region by the work of Francisco "Chico" Alves Mendes, leader of the National Council of Rubber Tappers, who was assassinated in 1988 after his organization, the Alliance of the Peoples of the Forest, organized to block further dam construction and defend the environment. Internationally, consciousness has clearly developed on this and related environmental issues and has placed significant pressure on the Brazilian government since the mid-1980s. However, this has not stopped the government from moving forward with its development plans. Often, the government has successfully created a nationalist backlash against international pressure by characterizing it as a form of neocolonialism. However, in 2007 an important development occurred when President Luiz Inácio da Silva announced an agreement with several indigenous groups acknowledging their autonomy and claim to resources.

## MEXICO

On January 1, 1994, a rebellion led by the Zapatista National Liberation Army (EZLN) began in the state of Chiapas in southern Mexico. This rebellion, more than any other indigenous political action in the 1990s, captured the attention of scholars and political activists alike. On that day, within a few hours after the takeover of San Cristóbal de las Casas, computer screens around the world sparked with news of the uprising. The Zapatista uprising generated extensive online publicity as the EZLN communicated its cause directly and electronically. The indigenous explosion in Chiapas, in which several hundred people lost their lives in twelve days of fighting, was only the beginning. Over twenty years later, the government continued to renege on accords it had signed recognizing indigenous rights and culture, and federal troops still occupied the indigenous parts of the state, though the rebels forged ahead with autonomous structures of local government.

**TABLE 6.** How Many Native People in 2016?

| Country | Estimated Native Population (2016) | % of Total Population |
|---|---|---|
| Argentina | 1,316,602 | 3.0% |
| Belize | 61,217 | 17.3% |
| Bolivia | 5,753,579 | 55.0% |
| Brazil | 1,809,087 | 0.9% |
| Canada | 1,485,242 | 4.2% |
| Chile | 1,747,361 | 9.9% |
| Colombia | 1,605,509 | 3.4% |
| Costa Rica | 116,941 | 2.4% |
| Ecuador | 3,111,900 | 19.4% |
| El Salvador | 123,133 | 0.2% |
| Guatemala | 6,151,933 | 40.5% |
| Guyana | 66,968 | 9.1% |
| Honduras | 622,528 | 7.0% |
| Mexico | 34,486,690 | 28.0% |
| Nicaragua | 298,340 | 5.0% |
| Panama | 455,745 | 12.3% |
| Paraguay | 343,141 | 5.0% |
| Peru | 13,833,478 | 45.0% |
| Suriname | 11,716 | 2.0% |
| USA | 3,725,949 | 1.2% |
| Venezuela | 865,544 | 2.8% |
| **Total** | **77,992,604** | |

*Sources:* CIA World Factbook 2016. https://www.cia.gov/library/publications/the-world-factbook/fields/2075. html; International Work Group for Indigenous Affairs. http://www.iwgia.org/regions/latin-america/venezuela; Indigenous People in Ecuador. http://ecuador.nativeweb.org

The EZLN had its origins in the indigenous- and peasant-organizing initiatives of the 1970s, which began to link up with leftist political organizers arriving in the Lacandón jungle of Chiapas from other parts of Mexico. A combination of growing repression and the impact of neoliberal policies in the early 1980s radicalized some of these groups, leading them to join an armed movement initially known as the National Liberation Forces (FLN), the precursor of the EZLN, which burst on the scene as the North American Free Trade Agreement (NAFTA) went into effect. The roots of their rebellion ran very deep. The indigenous people of Chiapas, mostly Maya, have labored under conditions of semislavery and servitude for centuries. The state is the principal source of the nation's coffee, and just over 100 people (0.16 percent of all coffee farmers) control 12 percent of all coffee lands. The large coffee farms have the best land, most of the credit, and the best infrastructure. Even more important are the cattle lands. Some 6,000 families hold more than 3 million hectares (7.4 million acres) of pastureland, equivalent to nearly half the territory of all Chiapas rural landholdings. Many of these vast cattle ranches were created through violent seizures of community and national land. The current struggles here date back to the early period of the twentieth century when the local oligarchs resisted any attempt at land reform. The program of the Institutional Revolutionary Party (PRI) president Lázaro Cárdenas, which distributed millions of acres of land elsewhere in Mexico in the 1930s, lagged in its implementation in Chiapas. In 1974, the local elites harshly repressed indigenous efforts at political organizing for land reform. The massive repression of the 1970s was followed by a more selective repression, consisting of the assassination of several peasant leaders. The peasants responded by creating networks of self-defense, but the authoritarian PRI governors responded with harsh tactics. The state repression was carried out by a combination of the federal army, state and local police forces, and so-called white guards—hired security forces at the service of the big landowners. PRI leaders deliberately provoked conflicts among peasants, between peasants and small proprietors, and between PRI village leaders and opponents of the regime. The local PRI leadership operated through a loose organization known as the "Chiapas Family." The family was made up primarily of big ranchers, owners of coffee farms, and lumber barons who controlled local elected offices. The control was enhanced by the co-option of local indigenous leaders, many of whom were bilingual teachers. Operating through PRI-dominated organizations like the National Peasant Confederation (CNC), the local leaders were given economic advantages that were passed on to their closest supporters in the communities. This divide-and-conquer strategy led to many violent confrontations in the period of the Zapatista uprising.

Despite the historic dominance of the region politically and economically by the PRI and its supporters, an independent civil society began to develop after 1975. Organizers from the outside participated, including liberation theology–inspired Catholic clergy and members of Mexican leftist parties. Two grassroots organizations formed in the 1970s exist today: the Regional Association of Collective Interest Union of Ejido Unions (ARIC-UU) and the Emiliano Zapata Peasant Organization (OCEZ). The organizations use a variety of tactics, including direct action, to press their grievances against the Mexican government. A new phase in the impact of civil society began on October 12, 1992, with a demonstration in San Cristóbal de las Casas to commemorate the 500th anniversary of indigenous resistance to the European conquest. Thousands of people from different ethnic groups took over the colonial capital and destroyed the statue of the conquistador Diego de Mazariegos. The event foreshadowed the EZLN uprising a little more than a year later.

A fundamental catalyst for the 1994 uprising was the reform of Article 27 of the Mexican constitution announced by President Carlos Salinas de Gortari in 1992. This reform, for the first time since the programs of Cárdenas, halted land redistribution and permitted the sale of communal lands that up until that time had been protected. For the peasants of Chiapas, this meant the end of agrarian reform, which had been slow and arbitrary but was now effectively dead. The peasants felt that they could no longer turn to the government as a mediator in land disputes. For the landowners, the reform was a green light to end once and for all peasant resistance to their plans for greater commercialization of agriculture in the region. Government troops first confronted a column of Zapatistas in May 1993, but the Salinas government, in the midst of an intense effort to win support for NAFTA, did not wish to tarnish its image by acknowledging the existence of a significant armed challenge within its borders. It was in that context of political change and resistance that the Zapatistas burst onto the scene.

From the beginning of their appearance, it was clear that the EZLN insurgency, made up of several thousand indigenous people and their "support base" communities throughout the highlands and the jungle, was a different kind of political movement from the traditional guerrilla armies that preceded them in Mexico and Central America. From the beginning they were a civil-resistance organization seeking basic change using revolutionary tactics. The EZLN never claimed as a goal the overthrow of the Mexican state. Rather, it called for the immediate resignation of Salinas, subsequent fall elections, and the expansion of peaceful, popular political participation. From the beginning its actions were the catalyst for generalized civil resistance throughout Chiapas.

Within a month of the launching of the Zapatistas' war, the National Mediation Commission (CONAI) headed by Bishop Samuel Ruiz brokered a ceasefire between the warring parties and began negotiations that continued on and off until June 1998, when Bishop Ruiz resigned from CONAI and the commission dissolved, charging the government with pursuing a path of war rather than peace. The Mexican Congress formed the Commission for Concord and Pacification (COCOPA) in January 1995 to continue negotiations with the Zapatistas while a ceasefire was in place. The government broke the truce in February 1995 with an army offensive that unsuccessfully attempted to capture the Zapatista leaders. The 1995 offensive was made possible by a massive deployment of 60,000 Mexican soldiers into the region. The army, with U.S., Argentinean, and Chilean advisors, employed counterinsurgency tactics honed during Latin America's guerrilla wars of the previous three decades. Between 1996 and 2014, the United States provided over $2.4 billion in military and police aid to Mexico, including helicopters that can be used in counterinsurgency operations. The Mexican army cooperated on its southern border with the Guatemalan army, well trained in counterinsurgency warfare. During its February 1995 offensive, the army destroyed the basic resources of a number of villages suspected of collaborating with the Zapatistas. The offensive forced the EZLN to retreat into more remote areas, but the Mexican government was not able to destroy the EZLN, in part because of the presence of many international human rights observers in the area and the mounting of large demonstrations on behalf of the EZLN in Mexico City. Unable to destroy the EZLN militarily, the government returned to negotiations, and in February 1996, the government and the EZLN signed accords on the rights of indigenous communities. The San Andrés Accords included two key demands of the EZLN, official recognition of the rights of indigenous communities to choose their own leadership and to control the natural resources in their territory. However, in reality, the Mexican government did not implement these measures. The primary point of conflict centered on the autonomous municipal councils created by the Zapatistas since 1994. The Zapatistas claimed the right to local self-governance under Article 39 of the Mexican constitution, which gave people "the inalienable right to alter or modify the form of their government," and the International Labor Organization's Convention 169 (ratified by the Mexican government in 1991), which gave indigenous peoples control over their habitats. In scores of communities, local councils were elected only to be denied recognition by the Mexican government, which continued to recognize local government structures dominated by politicians from the major parties. As a result, many villages split into pro-government and pro-EZLN factions. Despite the lack of official recognition, these autonomous municipal councils no longer recognize the official judicial system and have established alternative methods of conflict resolution. They have also set up community development projects, such as community corn and coffee fields and vegetable gardens, as well as autonomous schools and clinics. These alternative institutions have gained some financial backing from international solidarity groups and collectives in sympathy with the Zapatistas.

The end of the 1990s saw a dramatic increase in violence in the Chiapas region, much of it carried out by paramilitary organizations with links to the government. The most horrific incident occurred on December 22, 1997, when forty-five residents of the Tzotzil indigenous town of Acteal (including thirty-six women and children) were killed in an attack on their chapel by a heavily armed paramilitary gang. It has been reported that one group, the Anti-Zapatista Indigenous Revolutionary Movement (MIRA), received $1,250 a month from the PRI-led state government. From April through June 1998, the government launched a series of joint military and police invasions (often coordinated with paramilitaries) that dismantled the Zapatista autonomous municipalities of Ricardo Flores Magón, Tierra y Libertad, and San Juan de la Libertad and raids on Zapatista communities such as Unión Progreso, where eight indigenous residents were taken away by public security forces and their mutilated bodies later returned.

When this militarization provoked the dissolution of CONAI in 1998 and the collapse of negotiations, the Zapatistas launched a national "consultation" in which nearly 3 million Mexicans participated, expressing support for compromise legislation drafted by COCOPA to implement the San Andrés Accords on indigenous rights. Hopes for implementing legislation were briefly raised by the 2000 election of President Vicente Fox from the opposition National Action Party (PAN), who had boasted during the campaign that he would solve the Chiapas problem "in 15 minutes." Later that year, Pablo Salazar was elected state governor on an "Alliance for Chiapas" coalition ticket of anti-PRI parties, and the Zapatistas announced three conditions for resuming peace talks: (i) fulfillment of the San Andrés Accords approving the COCOPA law, (ii) freeing of all Zapatista prisoners, and (iii) closing seven (out of 259) military bases in areas of major Zapatista influence. In response, the government closed four bases and released a few dozen out of about 100 prisoners, and Fox presented an indigenous law to Congress but backpedaled from the COCOPA version. The Zapatistas then took their case directly to the public and to Congress, organizing a caravan from Chiapas to Mexico City in February–March 2001 that included twenty-three indigenous EZLN commanders plus Subcomandante Marcos. The caravan culminated in one of the largest gatherings in Mexico City's *zócalo* (main plaza) in modern history and a historic address to the Congress by ski-masked Comandante Esther. However, after the Zapatistas returned to Chiapas, Congress passed an indigenous law that gutted the key provisions of the San Andrés Accords and the COCOPA law. The sham legislation was rejected by the congresses of all six Mexican states with the largest proportion of indigenous populations and denounced by indigenous and human rights organizations, which filed 329 constitutional challenges in the Supreme Court. Nevertheless, it was entered into law in August and upheld by the Supreme Court in September 2001.

The struggle for recognition of indigenous rights and for participatory democracy continued. On January 1, 2003, 20,000 indigenous people marched in San Cristóbal to demand revision of the indigenous rights law, and the EZLN broke a two-year silence to condemn the three major parties for betraying the spirit of the San Andrés Accords. Meanwhile, in late 2002, government agencies and paramilitaries began a new escalation of violence against Zapatista support communities in the Montes Azules Biosphere Reserve near the Guatemalan border. This region was coveted by transnationals for its potential hydroelectric and biodiversity resources, in the wake of President Fox's multibillion-dollar Plan Puebla Panama (PPP), which would turn all of southern Mexico and Central America into a giant free trade zone. Grassroots organizations in Chiapas joined their counterparts in Central America in cross-border networks to resist the PPP. Meanwhile, the Zapatistas continued their patient construction of autonomous government from the bottom up, announcing in July 2003 that their five *Aguascalientes* resistance centers in Chiapas would be renamed *Caracoles* and would be the seats of a new regional structure of "Good Governance Councils" (Juntas de Buen Gobierno). Each junta became a regional rebel government, incorporating rotating delegates from over thirty Zapatista rebel autonomous municipalities.

In June 2005, the EZLN issued the "Sixth Declaration of the Lacandón Jungle," inaugurating a national initiative called "The Other Campaign" to link progressive struggles across Mexico. Subcomandante Marcos headed the first phase of the campaign in early 2006 as "Delegate Zero." The tour was temporarily halted following massive government repression of some allied organizations in San Salvador Atenco (near Mexico City) in May 2006, in which two protesters died and dozens of women were raped by police. After a disputed presidential election in July 2006 in which conservative PAN candidate Felipe Calderón claimed victory, the government appeared to shift to more militarized responses to social movements. Federal forces were deployed against protesters in Oaxaca in November 2006, and in September 2007 the EZLN announced the suspension of the second phase of the Other Campaign (scheduled for south-central Mexico from October–December) due to escalating paramilitary attacks on Zapatista communities. In October 2007, a caravan carrying Marcos and other Zapatista leaders was detained at one of the growing number of roadblocks across Mexico as they traveled to an encounter of indigenous peoples in Vícam, Sonora, highlighting the escalating government threat against the movement.

After a period of several years in which the Zapatistas concentrated on developing structures of autonomy within their communities and skeptics claimed the movement had faded, in May 2011 tens of thousands of ski-masked Zapatistas marched silently into San Cristóbal in support of the civic Movement for Justice with Peace and Democracy of the poet Javier Sicilia. That movement was a protest cry against the militarized "war on drugs" that had claimed 60,000 lives (including Sicilia's son) during President Calderón's six-year administration, and the Zapatistas' gesture of solidarity highlighted their commitment to a vision of justice that was broader than indigenous rights. Some 50,000 Zapatistas marched into town again in December 2012 as a reminder that the organized struggle continues. The EZLN subsequently announced the promotion of a new indigenous subcommander, Moisés, and also launched "little schools" in Zapatista territories beginning in August 2013, a new outreach initiative to explain their organizing model to civil society supporters and showcase the progress of their autonomy after twenty years. After a Zapatista teacher known as Galeano was killed by paramilitaries in May 2014, Subcomandante Marcos announced that the identity of Marcos was also dead and that "the voice of the Zapatista National Liberation Army will no longer come from my voice." The former Marcos took on the name of Galeano and stepped into the background, leaving Subcomandante Moisés as principal voice of the movement.

Beyond Chiapas, repression continued to fall on indigenous expressions of autonomy and resistance. The indigenous community of Cherán in the state of Michoacán declared a form of autonomy in 2011, fighting off drug cartels and expelling the police. Indigenous groups in Oaxaca and elsewhere used autonomy claims to protect lands and territories against mining and energy megaprojects of transnational corporations, often leading to confrontations between the communities and state authorities. Indigenous groups in Guerrero, tired of collusion between organized crime and the government, formed their own community police whose leader Nestora Salgado was jailed for two years on trumped-up charges and later left for the United States in March 2016. In September 2014, 43 poor and indigenous students at a rural teachers college in Ayotzinapa, Guerrero were forcibly disappeared in an incident pointing to collusion between drug cartels, police, and the military, amidst international denunciations of the government's failure to conduct a credible investigation. The Zapatistas held a number of public meetings jointly with the National Indigenous Congress (Congreso Nacional Indígena; CNI), and in a joint communiqué in October 2016, the CNI and EZLN announced a series of community consultations to nominate an indigenous woman candidate for Mexico's 2018 presidential election, clarifying that "our struggle is not for power, which we do not seek. Rather, we call on all of the ordinary peoples and civil society to organize to put a stop to this destruction and strengthen our resistances and rebellions."

With or without official recognition from the state, the Zapatista movement continues to represent innovative forms of resistance to the dictates of global capital and oppressive government. As a result, the region is likely to remain a focal point of indigenous resistance that will be modeled elsewhere in the Western Hemisphere.

## Conclusion

As Latin America proceeds through the twenty-first century, its image as a continent populated only by Spanish- and Portuguese-speaking mestizos is gone forever. The election of Evo Morales as Bolivia's first indigenous president and the massive indigenous mobilizations in Bolivia in 2003 and 2005 that paved the way for his victory are symbolic of this new reality. The indigenous peoples of the region and the descendants of the African slaves have clearly asserted their claim to a role in the future of the region. No longer forgotten and marginalized, these groups will assert their power ever more strongly and increase their political and social roles in the coming years.

# Bibliography

Andrews, George Reid. *Afro-Latin America 1800–2000*. New York: Oxford University Press, 2004.

Applebaum, Nancy. *Race and Nation in Modern Latin America*. Chapel Hill: University of North Carolina Press, 2003.

Bailey, Stanley. *Legacies of Race: Identities, Attitudes, and Politics in Brazil*. Palo Alto, CA: Stanford University Press, 2009.

Becker, Marc. *Indians and Leftists in the Making of Ecuador's Modern Indigenous Movements*. Durham, NC: Duke University Press, 2008.

Becker, Marc. *Pachakutik: Indigenous Movements and Electoral Politics in Ecuador*. Lanham, MD: Rowman & Littlefield, 2012.

Benjamin, Thomas. *The Atlantic World: Europeans, Africans, Indians, and Their Shared History, 1400–1900*. New York: Cambridge University Press, 2009.

Benson, Devyn Spence. *Antiracism in Cuba: The Unfinished Revolution*. Chapel Hill: University of North Carolina Press, 2016.

Conniff, Michael, and Thomas Davis. *Africans in the Americas: A History of the Black Diaspora*. New York: St. Martin's, 1994.

Cook, Noble David. *Born to Die: Disease and New World Conquest, 1492–1650*. Cambridge: Cambridge University Press, 1998.

Dixon, Kwame. *Afro-Politics and Civil Society in Salvador de Bahia, Brazil*. Gainesville: University Press of Florida, 2016.

Dixon, Kwame, and John Burdick, eds. *Comparative Perspectives on Afro-Latin America*. Gainesville: University Press of Florida, 2012.

French, Jan Hoffman. *Legalizing Identities: Becoming Black or Indian in Brazil's Northeast*. Chapel Hill: University of North Carolina Press, 2009.

Gates, Henry Louis, Jr. *Black in Latin America*. New York: NYU Press, 2011.

Gois Dantas, Beatrice. *Nago Grandma and White Papa: Candomble and the Creation of Afro-Brazilian Identity*. Chapel Hill: University of North Carolina Press, 2009.

Graham, Richard, ed. *The Idea of Race in Latin America, 1870–1940*. Austin: University of Texas Press, 1990.

Hanchard, Michael. *Racial Politics in Contemporary Brazil*. Durham, NC: Duke University Press, 1999.

Klein, Herbert. *Slavery in Latin America and the Caribbean*. New York: Oxford University Press, 1986.

Krogel, Alison. *Food, Power and Resistance in the Andes: Exploring Quechua Verbal and Visual Narratives*. Lanham, MD: Lexington, 2013.

Laguerre, Michel. *American Odyssey*. Ithaca, NY: Cornell University Press, 1984.

Madrid, Raúl L. *The Rise of Ethnic Politics in Latin America*. Cambridge: Cambridge University Press, 2012.

Mattiace, Shannon. *To See with Two Eyes: Peasant Activism and Indian Autonomy in Chiapas, Mexico*. Albuquerque: University of New Mexico Press, 2004.

Menchú, Rigoberta. *I Rigoberta Menchú: An Indian Woman in Guatemala*. Edited by Elizabeth Burgos-Debray. London: Verso, 1984.

Merleaux, April. *Sugar and Civilization. American Empire and the Cultural Politics of Sweetness*. Chapel Hill: University of North Carolina Press, 2015.

Postero, Nancy Grey. *Now We Are Citizens: Indigenous Politics in Postmulticultural Bolivia*. Stanford, CA: Stanford University Press, 2006.

Postero, Nancy Grey, and Leon Zamosc, eds. *The Struggle for Indigenous Rights in Latin America*. Brighton, UK: Sussex Academic Press, 2004.

Reiter, Bernd, and Gladys L. Mitchell, eds. *Brazil's New Racial Politics*. Boulder, CO: Lynne Reinner, 2010.

Telles, Edward. *Pigmentocracies: Ethnicity, Race and Color in Latin America*. Chapel Hill: University of North Carolina Press, 2014.

Urban, Greg, and Joel Sherzer, eds. *Nation-States and Indians in Latin America*. Austin: University of Texas Press, 1991.

Van Cott, Donna Lee. *From Movements to Parties in Latin America: The Evolution of Ethnic Politics*. Cambridge: Cambridge University Press, 2005.

Wade, Peter. *Blackness and Racial Mixture: The Dynamics of Racial Identity in Colombia*. Baltimore: Johns Hopkins University Press, 1993.

Wade, Peter. *Race and Ethnicity in Latin America*. 2d ed. London: Pluto, 2010.

Yashar, Deborah. *Contesting Citizenship in Latin America: The Rise of Indigenous Movements and the Postliberal Challenge*. Cambridge: Cambridge University Press, 2005.

## FILMS AND VIDEOS

Black in Latin America (PBS series). United States, 2011.

*Blood of the Condor*. Bolivia, 1969.

*Café*. Mexico, 2014.

*Cocalero*. United States, 2007.

*Granito: How to Nail a Dictator*. United States, 2012.

*How Tasty Was My Little Frenchman*. Brazil, 1973.

*Quilombo*. Brazil, 1984.

*Silvestre Pantaleon*. Mexico, 2011.

*10th Parallel*. Brazil, 2011.

*They Are We*. United States, 2014.

*We Women Warriors*. United States/Colombia, 2012.

*Zapatista*. United States, 1999.

# FIVE

# SOCIETY, FAMILY, AND GENDER

The social milieu in Latin America is a fascinating, complex, and often magical reality that frequently seems to defy description. Societies in the region were forged over five centuries from a multitude of diverse, dynamic influences. Foremost among these are the European values and social institutions the colonists brought with them. To these are added those of the preexisting native societies as well as those of the African cultures carried to the Americas by enslaved western and southern Africans. They have blended in different ways to form societal characteristics that have evolved over the centuries and are manifest in a fascinating array of different forms in each country. They have been molded and modified by land tenure, subsequent immigration, trade and commercialization, industrialization, intervention, the modern media, and, now, globalization. There are, however, some constants that will help us understand this reality.

To gain some insight into Latin American society, we can look at how competition among groups and individuals is carried out on the playing field. We need to see how the game is played. Sports are often an excellent reflection of culture: by understanding athletic interactions, we can often better understand other forms of societal relation.

Like politics, *futbol* (soccer) is an area of great passion in most Latin American countries. *Futbol* unifies regions, classes, racial groupings, and even gender in ways few other activities can. When the national team is competing for World Cup standing, it provides a focus, a commonality, and a sense of community much more strongly than most other activities, save a real or possible foreign military threat. World Cup victories are also used by governments to bolster their legitimacy.

Regional and team rivalries also exist. Fans show their spirit and team allegiance by wearing team colors, driving with team banners flowing, and engaging in rhythmic chants through the course of the game. Passions run so high that the field and the players are protected by high barbed wire fences and water-filled moats. In 1969, passions exploded after a game at a regional World Cup match between El Salvador and Honduras; the event became the spark that ignited long-standing tensions to create the so-called Soccer War.

Like (American) football and basketball in the United States, hockey in Canada, and soccer in Great Britain and continental Europe, *futbol* has provided a way out of slums and poverty. *Futbol* further offers one of the few ways to transcend classism and the omnipresent barriers to socioeconomic mobility. To carry the analogy further, it could be argued that the soccer field is one of the few places in society where one is not excluded from play or at least handicapped by class, color, or lack of connections to the powerful.

Traditionally, soccer was a male domain, and there were few opportunities for young women to learn or play the game, although women were welcome to watch, cheer, and support the men who played. Only in recent years has the internationalization of women's sports begun to change this; the Brazilian women's soccer team made it to the 1999 World Cup semifinals before being defeated by the U.S. women's team and in 2007 reached the finals before falling to Germany. The Brazilian star, Marta, has been World Player of the Year on numerous occasions.

These analogies are equally valid for baseball in those societies where the ongoing (usually military) presence of baseball-playing North American men has made the U.S. pastime the primary national sport: Cuba, Nicaragua, Panama, and the Dominican Republic. U.S. and Canadian oil technicians introduced baseball in Venezuela, where both baseball and *futbol* are played. The ease of baseball assimilation suggests not only the strong U.S. cultural influence but also the instant enthusiasm displayed by Latin Americans when they too could compete on a level playing field with occupying military forces or technologically sophisticated foreign workers. Their success is brought home by the presence of growing numbers of Latin American players in the U.S. major leagues. The success of the Chicago Cubs in the 2016 World Series depended to a significant degree on their Latin players.

The popularity of ball games dates back to indigenous civilizations in Mexico and Central America, although the current version of soccer was brought from Europe. In these indigenous civilizations, hotly contested matches were played for as long as days, and the winners could enjoy great success as bestowed by the wealthy and powerful. The losers were, however, often killed or sacrificed. Like the losers of ball games in pre-Columbian times, those in Latin American society who cannot win the wealth–status–power game (the poor) suffer from powerlessness and repression and are frequently sacrificed to poverty, exploitation, humiliation, malnutrition, and occasionally torture and death. Their blood, it could be argued, flows to satisfy the new—now globalized—gods of the day. Why do the poor lose so often? Culture defines much of the playing field and most of the rules of the game. Latin American culture is quite distinct from that in the United States, Canada, Great Britain, or Australia. The sections that follow discuss some of the key aspects of Latin American culture.

From classical Mayan times to the present, the rules of the game have been dictated by those with power and wealth. This began with the Incan and Aztec emperors, Mayan kings, and aristocrats and priests—those who ruled. After the conquest, new hierarchies and dominant classes developed. Society in colonial times could be described as a sharply pointed upper-class pyramid seated on a broad base of indigenous and African peoples (see Figure 1). The small European elite enjoyed wealth, status, privilege, and power—they became the new ruling class.

Even European artisans enjoyed a status well above virtually all the indigenous masses. The exceptions to these classifications would be the mestizo sons and daughters

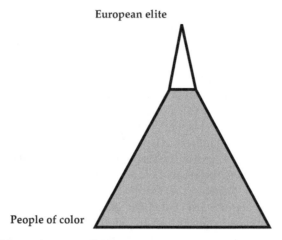

**FIGURE 1.**   Colonial Latin American Society.

of the Spanish and Portuguese elite and native women (who sometimes came from pre-Columbian royal families). Also in this category would be the mulatto children of Portuguese colonists and Africans in Brazil. However, the African and indigenous masses enjoyed neither wealth nor privilege and could exercise little power—they were the lower class. As the subaltern, those who were subjected to elite power, they most commonly led lives characterized by economic deprivation and exploitation.

This basic structure set the tone for Latin American society. A few continued to have it all, while the darker masses suffered the vicissitudes of poverty and powerlessness. With some exceptions, the elite upper class, or oligarchy as it is sometimes called, still makes the rules of the game and dominates the lives of the many. Lighter generally rules darker, and male has traditionally dominated female. Even by the rather optimistic statistics used by the regions' governments, some 40 percent still lived in poverty as of the mid-1990s. Indeed, in 1999, the newly elected populist president of Venezuela, Hugo Chávez, spoke of the 80 percent of Venezuelans who lived in poverty. Today, nearly twenty years into the twenty-first century, progress has been made, but those living in poverty still account for between 40 and 60 percent of the population in most Latin American countries. Conversely, the wealthy and the super-wealthy—the upper class—live very well indeed. For instance, it is estimated that the wealthiest 10 percent of the population receives close to 50 percent of the income, while the bottom half of society receives only about 4 percent of the income. The richest 20 percent of the Brazilian population receives an income that is thirty-two times the income received by the poorest 20 percent. However, as demonstrated in Figure 2, Latin America has made progress in the last decade in reducing poverty.

The inequitable distribution of wealth and power continues to plague Latin American societies. In pre-Columbian times, it was the Aztec, Mayan, and Incan royalty and nobility and, later, the *conquistadores*, viceroys, *encomenderos*, and *latifundistas* who ran the game. Still later, power was monopolized by the rural

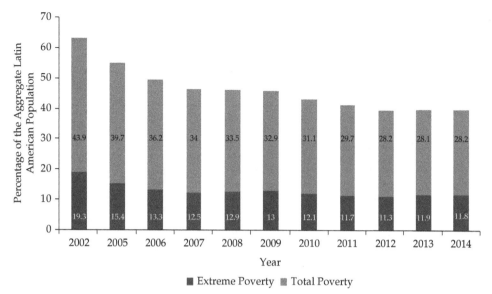

**FIGURE 2.** Latin American Population Living Below the Extreme Poverty and Poverty Lines by Percentage.

landowners (the *hacendados, estanciaros,* and *fazendeiros*), *caudillos,* and Church leaders. By the twentieth century, it was not only the wealthy—the oligarchy—but also the military leaders, dictators, and civilian politicians who frequently shared and held absolute power on a recurring basis, using their political-military power to consolidate their place in the upper class. They were joined by emerging commercial, financial, and industrialist elites and by multinational corporations and their foreign managers.

Power, like wealth, remained concentrated—often absolutely (see Table 7 Gini Coefficients). Indeed, some observers suggest that a requisite for belonging to the ruling class is to know, to have, and to exercise power. This was not only true with the hierarchical native civilizations but has been so since colonial times, when a small European elite allocated resources for larger societies whose majorities were made up of indigenous, African, mestizo, and mulatto majorities. For the sake of simplicity, one could argue that up to 1950 most of Latin America, outside of a few major cities like Buenos Aires, was comprised of an upper class including hacienda-, *fazenda-,* plantation-, or mine-owning *patrones* and a lower class including peasant or rural laborer *peones,* or plantation or mine workers. The basic structure of the system was most often brutal for those on the bottom. Most struggled on in grinding poverty; a few fled to the interior like the runaway slaves (maroons); and occasionally there were local rebellions. In what became a classic part of Latin American society, some decided that they could best survive and maximize their lot by formalizing their position in a classic patron–client relationship. In this way, they made their well-being in large part a function of the paternalism of the patron and his family. In return for their loyalty and support, the power and influence of the patron would, they hoped, be employed to protect and promote them. Leaving the area and enlisting in reform or revolutionary movements were less frequently exercised options.

**TABLE 7.** Gini Coefficients of Selected Latin American Countries

| Country | 1998 | 2006 | 2014 |
|---|---|---|---|
| Argentina | 0.507 | 0.483 | 0.427 |
| Bolivia | . . . | 0.569 | 0.484 |
| Brazil | 0.596 | 0.559 | 0.515 |
| Chile | 0.555 | 0.518 | . . . |
| Colombia | . . . | . . . | 0.535 |
| Costa Rica | 0.457 | 0.493 | 0.485 |
| Dominican Republic | . . . | 0.519 | . . . |
| Ecuador | 0.497 | 0.532 | 0.454 |
| El Salvador | 0.545 | 0.454 | 0.418 |
| Guatemala | . . . | 0.549 | 0.487 |
| Honduras | 0.574 | 0.574 | 0.506 |
| Mexico | 0.490 | 0.480 | 0.482 |
| Nicaragua | 0.452 | . . . | 0.470 |
| Panama | 0.575 | 0.551 | 0.507 |
| Paraguay | . . . | 0.536 | 0.517 |
| Peru | 0.561 | 0.517 | 0.441 |
| Uruguay | 0.438 | 0.472 | 0.416 |
| Venezuela | 0.498 | 0.469 | . . . |

*Source*: The World Bank, World Development Indicators (1998, 2006, 2014). GINI index (World Bank estimate). http://data.worldbank.org/indicator/SI.POV.GINI

*Note*: The Gini coefficient is an internationally recognized measure of the income inequality in a country; the greater the value the greater the inequality.

Yet, there have been changes. The advent of urbanization, industrialization, and the diffusion of advanced technology, as seen in the proliferation of televisions, cellular phones, computers, and cars, has stimulated the growth of new groups. There were hardly any members of the middle class through the nineteenth century in Latin America, yet their numbers have increased drastically in recent decades. They now account for as much as one-third of the population in many countries and have lifestyles that are not totally unlike their North American or European counterparts. Further, the middle class has the added advantage of access to very affordable domestic help. Limited employment horizons for lower-class women and men, low wages, and a tradition of subordination make domestic help plentiful and affordable for most middle- and all upper-class households. Industrialization, *maquiladora*-style assembly plants, and a growing demand for services have burgeoned throughout the region, stimulating demand for middle-class positions in the clerical, supervisory, and technical fields. The social pyramid is now a little flatter and might look more like Figure 3.

By the second decade of the twenty-first century, one also sees contentious social movements and massive demonstrations like those in June 2013. Broad segments of the population challenge the political and economic ruling classes and insist on participating in the power game. They have toppled governments in Ecuador, Bolivia, and Argentina and facilitated the election of many governments of the left in the twenty-first century. These governments have pursued policies aimed at reducing poverty and have demonstrated significant progress, especially in reducing extreme poverty.

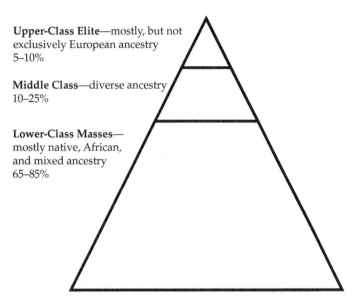

**Upper-Class Elite**—mostly, but not exclusively European ancestry 5–10%

**Middle Class**—diverse ancestry 10–25%

**Lower-Class Masses**—mostly native, African, and mixed ancestry 65–85%

FIGURE 3. Latin American social pyramid.

In the twenty-first century, the vast majority of Latin Americans are urban workers of different types and peasants. As Latin America has industrialized in recent years, the number of industrial workers has skyrocketed and the number of peasants has fallen. Indeed, Karl Marx's vision of a large, brutally exploited, poorly treated proletariat driven from the land and unable to change its lot without total revolution could be coming to pass in Latin America in the twenty-first century. Unlike the nineteenth-century Europe of Marx, in most of Latin America, neither reformers nor the labor movement have been able to change the working conditions of most workers to any appreciable extent. Many still work for less than $5 a day, and few make more than $10. The boss is still very much the authoritarian figure, and the workers are still very much subordinate. The programs of the leftist governments outside of Cuba do not challenge that fundamental framework but rather seek to mitigate its effects.

This domination of the many by the few has not changed as more women enter the formal workforce. In Brazil, 60 percent of women are employed in the formal sector; in Mexico, the figure is 44 percent (see Table 11). If informal sectors (street vendors and in-home producers) are added, the figures would be 72 percent for Brazil and 62 percent for Mexico. Women are thought to be less apt to resist management decisions—or to strike—and more willing to work for lower wages. Further, the proclivity of predominantly male management to hire female workers has also helped reinforce authoritarian control systems and feminize some of the worst worker poverty. It has also exposed a new generation of younger Latin American women to new forms of patriarchy and sexual harassment that are outside the protective familial and community contexts in which they were raised.

As the new millennium develops, the conditions in which most Latin Americans live are very difficult indeed. Although literacy rates have improved, educational

Soccer match between Argentina and Brazil, July 2009. *(AFP/Getty Images)*

levels are still relatively low, and basic indicators like infant mortality reflect a great deal of suffering (see Table 1 in Chapter 1). Out of every 1,000 live births in Bolivia, 39 infants die in their first year of life. In Haiti, 50 of every 1,000 children born die in their first year. Bolivia's number will likely improve as the progressive government's health programs take hold, but little change seems in the offing for Haiti. Cuba, Costa Rica, Chile, and Uruguay are the only Spanish-, Portuguese-, or French-speaking countries in the hemisphere to have an infant mortality rate lower than 10 per 1,000 live births. Elsewhere in Latin America, thousands of children live on the streets and must struggle to survive each day. More than 7 million children live on the streets in Brazil alone. Large numbers die of neglect, disease, or outright murder each year, and many are eliminated as nuisances by merchant-paid death squads or off-duty police.

As seen in Table 8, many who have dwellings do not even have water in their homes, and fewer still have sewer services. Conditions are hard for the masses. Caloric intake and the availability of protein (Table 9) are low among many, and malnutrition is a severe problem for the poorer sectors in most Latin American countries. Cuba is one of the few countries to radically improve such conditions. Even there, as late as 1950, 30 to 40 percent of the general population and 60 percent of the rural population were undernourished. Twenty years after the revolution, malnutrition had been lowered to 5 percent, and today Cuba has a life expectancy and infant mortality rate comparable to the United States.

**TABLE 8.** Population and Social Conditions

| Country | Total Population (2015) (in thousands) | Annual Population Growth Rate (%) | Life Expectancy at Birth (2015) | Access to Improved Drinking Water Sources 2015 (%) | | | Access to Improved Sanitation Systems 2015 (%) | | | Female Economically Active Rate (%) (2012)> |
|---|---|---|---|---|---|---|---|---|---|---|
| | | | | National | Urban | Rural | National | Urban | Rural | |
| Argentina | 43,298.26 | 1.03 | 76.1 | 99 | 100 | 99 | 90 | 96 | 78 | 47 |
| Bolivia | 10,737.27 | 1.61 | 67.8 | 90 | 97 | 76 | 50 | 61 | 28 | 64 |
| Brazil | 207,749.81 | 0.94 | 74.2 | 98 | 100 | 87 | 83 | 88 | 52 | 60 |
| Chile | 18,088.73 | 1.08 | 81.0 | 99 | 98 | 93 | 99 | 100 | 91 | 47 |
| Colombia | 48,228.61 | 0.98 | 73.8 | 91 | 97 | 74 | 81 | 85 | 68 | 56 |
| Costa Rica | 4,820.78 | 1.13 | 79.2 | 98 | 100 | 92 | 95 | 95 | 92 | 46 |
| Cuba | 11,421.59 | 0.15 | 79.2 | 95 | 96 | 90 | 93 | 94 | 89 | 43 |
| Dominican Republic | 10,530.93 | 1.24 | 73.3 | 85 | 85 | 82 | 84 | 86 | 76 | 51 |
| Ecuador | 16,144.35 | 1.56 | 75.6 | 87 | 93 | 76 | 85 | 87 | 81 | 54 |
| El Salvador | 6,298.49 | 0.40 | 72.7 | 94 | 100 | 99 | 75 | 82 | 60 | 47 |
| Guatemala | 16,381.75 | 2.08 | 71.5 | 93 | 98 | 87 | 64 | 78 | 49 | 49 |
| Haiti | 10,749.64 | 1.39 | 62.6 | 58 | 65 | 48 | 28 | 34 | 19 | 60 |
| Honduras | 8,075.03 | 1.47 | 72.9 | 91 | 97 | 84 | 83 | 87 | 78 | 42 |
| Nicaragua | 6,085.53 | 1.17 | 74.6 | 87 | 99 | 69 | 68 | 77 | 56 | 47 |
| Panama | 3,929.11 | 1.64 | 77.4 | 95 | 98 | 87 | 75 | 84 | 58 | 50 |
| Paraguay | 6,639.16 | 1.34 | 72.8 | 98 | 100 | 95 | 89 | 96 | 78 | 58 |
| Peru | 31,383.48 | 1.32 | 74.2 | 87 | 91 | 69 | 76 | 83 | 53 | 68 |
| Puerto Rico | 3,683.24 | −0.14 | 79.2 | 94 | 94 | 94 | 99 | 99 | 99 | 36 |
| Uruguay | 3,430.28 | 0.34 | 77.0 | 100 | 100 | 94 | 96 | 97 | 93 | 56 |
| Venezuela | 30,553.59 | 0.95 | 74.1 | 93 | 95 | 78 | 94 | 98 | 70 | 52 |
| **NAFTA Countries** | | | | | | | | | | |
| Canada | 35,362.91^ | 0.74^ | 81.9^ | 100 | 100 | 99 | 100 | 100 | 99 | 58 |
| Mexico | 124,612.40 | 1.38 | 76.5 | 96 | 97 | 92 | 85 | 88 | 75 | 44 |
| USA | 323,995.53^ | 0.81^ | 79.8^ | 99 | 99 | 98 | 100 | 100 | 100 | 62 |

*Sources:* All data from ECLAC/CEPAL Statistical Yearbook 2015 unless otherwise noted ECLAC/CEPAL Statistical Yearbook for Latin America and the Caribbean http://interwp.cepal.org/anuario_estadistico/anuario_2015/en/index.asp

^2016 CIA World Factbook https://www.cia.gov/library/publications/the-world-factbook/rankorder/2091rank.html

>Data from Statistics and Indicators on Women and Men. U.N. Statistics Division. July 2013 Located at http://unstats.un.org/unsd/demographic/products/indwm/Dec.%202012/5a.xls

**TABLE 9.**   Nutrition and Health Care

| Country | Nutrition and Health Care | | | | | |
|---|---|---|---|---|---|---|
| | Availability of Calories per Day (cal/day per capita)* | Availability of Protein per Person per Day (grams) (2008-2010)** | Physicians Ratio (10,000 hab.)* | % of Births Attended by Trained Personnel* | Number of Deaths due to AIDS* | Public Expenditure on Health as Portion of GDP (%) (2014)* |
| Argentina | 3,155.00^ | 94 | 32.1˟ | 99.7˜ | 1,422ᵋ | 2.7 |
| Bolivia | 2,254.00^ | 61 | 8.9˜ | 73.5˜ | 16ᵠ | 4.6 |
| Brazil | 3,263.00˜ | 90 | 15.1ᐞ | 99.1˜ | 12,048ᵋ | 3.8 |
| Chile | 2,989.00^ | 90 | 18.2ᵋ | 99.8˜ | 456ᵋ | 3.9 |
| Colombia | 2,804.00˜ | 69 | 17.7ᵋ | 98.6ᵋ | 2,354^ | 5.4 |
| Costa Rica | 2,898.00^ | 75ᵉ | 22.8ᵉ | 98.0ᵉ | 147ᵋ | 6.8 |
| Cuba | 3,277.00^ | 84 | 75.0˜ | 99.9ᵉ | 299ᵋ | 10.6 |
| Dominican Republic | 2,614.00˜ | 58 | 21.2ᵉ | 98.6˜ | 457^ | 2.9 |
| Ecuador | 2,477.00^ | 57 | 15.9^ | 94.7˜ | 710ᵋ | 4.5 |
| El Salvador | 2,513.00^ | 72 | 15.5ᵉ | 84.9ᵠ | 287ᵋ | 4.5 |
| Guatemala | 2,419.00˜ | 61 | 7.5ᵉ | 62.8˜ | 474ᵋ | 2.3 |
| Haiti | 2,091.00˜ | 44 | 2.3˜ | 50.0˜ | 77˟ | 1.6 |
| Honduras | 2,651.00^ | 67 | 10.0˜ | 83.0ᵋ | 151˜ | 4.4 |
| Nicaragua | 2,564.00^ | 66 | 8.8ᵉ | 96.1ᵉ | 208ᵋ | 5.1 |
| Panama | 2,733.00˜ | 76 | 16.0ᵉ | 92.8˜ | 475ᵋ | 5.9 |
| Paraguay | 2,589.00˜ | 65 | 15.8˜ | 96.8˜ | 191ᵋ | 4.5 |
| Peru | 2,700.00˜ | 71 | 11.9ᵉ | 91.4ᵉ | 696ᵋ | 3.3 |
| Puerto Rice | … | … | 22.0ᵝ | 99.0˜ | 333ᐞ | … |
| Uruguay | 2,939.00^ | 81 | 47.3ᵉ | 99.9ᵉ | 183ᐞ | 6.1 |
| Venezuela | 2,880.00^ | 83 | 13.0ᵝ | 99.5ᵉ | 1,733ᵠ | 1.5 |
| **NAFTA Countries** | | | | | | |
| Canada | 3,419.00^ | 103 | 25.0ᵋ | 99.9˜ | 303^ | 7.4 |
| Mexico | 3,072.00˜ | 91 | 21.2^ | 96.1˜ | 4,868ᵋ | 3.3 |
| USA | 3,639.00^ | 114 | 26.0^ | 99.3ᵋ | 8,371ᐞ | 8.3 |

ᵠ2003 ˟2004 ᵝ2007 ᵠ2009 ᐞ2010 ^2011 ᵋ2012 ˜2013 ᵉ2014

*Sources*: *Pan American Health Organization, Health Information and Analysis Unit. Regional Core Health Data Initiative, Washington DC, 2015.

http://www1.paho.org/English/SHA/coredata/tabulator/newsqlTabulador.asp

**Food and Agriculture Organization of United Nations. *FAO Statistical Yearbook, 2014*.

http://www.fao.org/docrep/019/i3592e/i3592e.pdf

Health care for most Latin Americans is poor. The public hospitals that serve the great majority are generally of very low quality outside of a few countries such as Cuba and Costa Rica (Table 9). Good health care is usually in short supply and rationed by wealth and power. The combination of lack of health care, poor sanitation, and malnutrition fed a major cholera epidemic that appeared in Peru in the early 1990s and then spread throughout the region. A similar epidemic involving the Zika virus occurred in 2016. As with wealth, health care is also very poorly distributed in the region. The bulk of the best physicians and medical facilities are for the wealthy and the middle class and are concentrated in the capitals and largest cities. Many—particularly in rural areas—do not have access to modern health care at all and simply suffer, die, or seek relief from practitioners of folk or traditional medicine. Yet, the medical care provided for the upper classes in exclusive private clinics is often quite good, although many prefer to go to the United States for specialized treatment. These unequal conditions are being challenged in countries where governments of the left have come to power vowing to improve social services. In the new century, Venezuela, Ecuador, Brazil, and Bolivia have all succeeded in reducing poverty and creating better health outcomes.

Conditions for the upper class rival or exceed upper-class lifestyles in industrialized, northern nations; conditions for the masses in areas like Brazil's northeast and Haiti rival those of the poor in less developed nations in Africa and parts of the Indian subcontinent. It could well be argued that this inequality of wealth and disparity of power and influence are Latin America's greatest curses and are at the root of many of the developmental, social, and criminal problems that continue to plague the region. Yet, if varied social strata have very different economic realities, cultural similarities and interconnecting social relations tie them together into national societies that share many characteristics as well as a few differences. To fully understand the complexity of these relations, one needs to understand the nature and importance of the family and gender roles in Latin American society.

## Family and Gender Roles

Throughout Latin America the family is of fundamental importance. The family and family ties are the bases of identity and orientation to the greater society and political system. Much of one's life revolves around the family, and young people (especially, but not exclusively, women) usually stay with the family at least until they marry, even if this does not occur until their late twenties or afterward. Unmarried daughters often stay in the family house and, according to some traditions—as depicted in the Mexican film *Like Water for Chocolate*—are to stay and care for their parents in their old age, though this tradition is weakening as more women enter the workforce. Government and private pension systems are often unreliable in Latin America. Children, in fact, may be the main or only pension system that aging parents have.

Personal ties and relationships form the bases for much of Latin American society and politics, and these begin with the family. If the world outside the family unit is often perceived as hostile and dangerous, the world within is seen as safe and secure. It is a given that family members help and protect each other, and in Latin America the traditional family has been large. Most early social interaction occurs within the sphere of the extended family, which includes not only father, mother, and children but also grandparents, aunts, uncles, and first and second cousins on both sides. As beautifully depicted in novels like *One Hundred Years of Solitude* by Gabriel Garcia Marquez and *The House of the Spirits* by Isabel Allende, three or even four generations often live in the same household. Nor has the nuclear family been small. Families of eight to ten children were not uncommon in rural areas; now, three or four children are still common and double that number are still seen, although less so in urban areas. Treasured, doted on, and highly valued, children generally receive special attention from all adults. Cultural values and the adamant stand of the Catholic Church against artificial means of contraception and abortion have combined with traditional practices of measuring women's and men's worth by how many children they have to maintain large families. Yet, as Latin America becomes increasingly urbanized (about 75 percent), financial pressures and the increasing need for a second income have begun to reduce family size but not necessarily the importance of the family unit.

## Women and Patriarchy

Patriarchy is strong in Latin America and is manifest in the old Roman term *patria potestas* (powerful patriarch). This term was frequently found in Latin American constitutions and legal codes; it means that the father is all powerful in the family and in family matters. The term preceded *pater familias* in Roman times and originally meant that the father had unrivalled authority in the family and even held life-and-death power over other family members. Property for the family was most commonly held in the elder male's name (although there have been significant exceptions since colonial times), and women often had to go through fathers or brothers to exercise property-owning rights. Today, fathers and husbands enjoy a great deal of power in the Latin American family. Male prerogative often seems unbounded. While traditionally the woman is expected to come to the marriage pure and virgin and to protect the family honor by remaining above reproach, it is expected that the male has considerable sexual experience before marriage. Further, it has frequently been the norm that any extramarital affairs he might have are considered by the general society to be something that men do and typically not sufficient to jeopardize the marriage or to besmirch the family's reputation or honor. Mistresses have been maintained, often openly, and the tradition of the *casa chica* (the little house or second household) continues. Wealthy and not-so-wealthy men often maintain an entire second family in a second household, acknowledge their children, and give them their name. Eva (Evita) Duarte Perón was the product of such a union. Even today one still hears of well-known public figures being seen with their mistresses, but the dual standard suggests a very different code of behavior for married women. For instance, in rural areas of Brazil and elsewhere in the region, a husband who discovers his wife in bed with another man and shoots them dead may argue that his actions were necessary to protect family honor. In the past judges and juries have at times found this sufficient grounds for acquittal. In a related vein, daughters are carefully guarded and protected by their fathers and brothers.

Effective political action in the greater society is often equated with the strong, dominant, uncompromising ruling style that most Latin American patriarchs display. The traditional expectation for the Latin American politician, or *politico*, is that the leader exhibits characteristics most often identified with the strong, dominant male—the macho. Strength and resolve are valued; weakness and an overly conciliatory orientation are not. Indeed, when a country is passing through a time of crisis, one can frequently hear the oft-repeated opinion that what is needed is a *mano dura*, a strong hand, and someone with the maleness to exercise it. It is interesting to note that the first woman elected to the presidency of a South American country,

Michelle Bachelet in Chile in 2006, was the daughter of a military officer who was executed by Pinochet. Soon after, Christina Fernández de Kirchner was elected president of Argentina but only after the election of her husband, Néstor. Former Brazilian president, Dilma Rousseff, is a former guerrilla combatant. Women are winning public office but not necessarily breaking the stereotype of the leader required to have male qualities.

Gender roles are in the process of transition in Latin America, yet machismo, or maleness, is still very much a part of Latin American culture and defines traditional male–female relations. In its less violent form, it frequently robs women of their confidence and independence by socializing them to believe they need a male to protect them, do things for them, provide for them economically, and guide them in their daily lives and development. From an early age, the socialization of male children is generally much different from that of female children. Males are taught to be assertive, and their aggressiveness is tolerated, if not encouraged, while female children are most often taught to not cause a commotion, not challenge authority frontally, and at least appear submissive.

Traditional roles for women also coexist with modern feminist views. Of importance in traditional culture is *marianismo*, the glorification of the traditional female role. The term comes from the cult of the pure Virgin Mary (Maria)-like woman, who is expected to be the bastion of family honor, the submissive woman, and long-suffering family anchor. Violence against women has been a long-standing problem in the region. Some men feel that they have some ownership of the women in their lives and thus feel justified in restricting their action or social contacts and, worse, abusing them physically. Traditionally, such action was generally tolerated by society and even by the police. It was thought to be a family matter or a matter between the man and woman of the household. These patriarchal attitudes are still seen in some places in society and may be especially strong in rural areas. Over the past few years, there is less tolerance for these abusive actions among women and the wider society, and new legislation is being formulated—and sometimes enforced—to better protect women. Special police units, often primarily staffed by women, are on the rise, and there are some safe houses provided by nongovernmental organizations and some municipalities.

In the past Latin American women were limited to the private space of the house and family while the public space outside the home was the sole preserve of the male. Traditionally, the woman's place was at home with the children. She was to support her spouse in his endeavors in the external public space. While this was generally true, it should be noted that Latin American women have sometimes used their traditional roles to penetrate public space. Thus, a very competent, ambitious Mexican noblewoman of the seventeenth century joined a convent and became Sor Juana Inés de la Cruz so that she could pursue her studies and be free to write some of the best (and most passionate) poetry and prose of the colonial era. Latin American universities started as seminaries and excluded women for many years. Only toward the middle of the twentieth century was it possible for women to pursue university education in large numbers, but most were concentrated in traditionally female fields like education, nursing, and social work. This has changed radically today, and one sees a large number of female students in conventionally male bastions, like engineering, in most of Latin America. In the political sphere, those women who did aspire to public position often used their upper-class position or ties to a famous father or husband to gain access (as was the case for Violeta Chamorro in Nicaragua). Talented women like Eva Perón, President Mireya Moscoso of Panama, and President Cristina Fernández de Kirchner of Argentina sometimes traded in part on their husband's position to acquire visibility and power in their own right. Aside from a few such famous personages, competent *políticas* were, however, all too often assigned "female" posts, such as minister of education or minister of social welfare (Table 10). However, the election of women to the presidency of some key countries in the region shows that the region is changing.

Many have observed that some of the most assertive political actions by women in the twentieth century have come from their traditional, private roles as mothers or wives. This was seen in the weekly protests begun by the Mothers of the Disappeared during the dirty war in Argentina in the late 1970s and early 1980s. The Madres de la Plaza de Mayo, as they came to be known, became politically active as

**TABLE 10.** Women Occupying Positions in Parliament

| Country | Women Holding Parliamentary Seats in Single or Lower Chamber (%)* | | | |
|---|---|---|---|---|
| | 2010 | 2012 | 2014 | 2016 |
| Argentina | 39 | 37 | 37 | 36 |
| Bolivia | 25 | 25 | 25 | 53 |
| Brazil | 9 | 9 | 9 | 10 |
| Chile | 14 | 14 | 16 | 16 |
| Colombia | 8 | 12 | 20 | 20 |
| Costa Rica | 39 | 39 | 33 | 33 |
| Cuba | 43 | 45 | 49 | 49 |
| Dominican Repub | 21 | 21 | 21 | 27 |
| Ecuador | 32 | 32 | 42 | 42 |
| El Salvador | 19 | 26 | 27 | 32 |
| Guatemala | 12 | 13 | 13 | 14 |
| Haiti | 4 | 4 | 4 | 0 |
| Honduras | 18 | 20 | 26 | 26 |
| Mexico | 26 | 37 | 37 | 42 |
| Nicaragua | 21 | 40 | 42 | 41 |
| Panama | 9 | 9 | 19 | 18 |
| Paraguay | 13 | 13 | 15 | 15 |
| Peru | 28 | 22 | 22 | 28 |
| Uruguay | 15 | 12 | 13 | 16 |
| Venezuela | 18 | 17 | 17 | 14 |

*Note*: The percentage of parliamentary seats occupied by women is calculated for the lower chamber in countries with bicameral assembly only. The numbers shown reflect changes, if any, after the most recent election prior to those dates, such as results of by-elections or replacements following a parliamentarian's resignation or death.

*Sources*: *Inter-Parliamentary Union, "Women in National Parliaments".

**ECLAC/CEPAL *Statistical Yearbook for Latin America and the Caribbean, 2015.*

they sought to find and, if possible, save their children and other family members. They marched every week in the Plaza de Mayo in the center of Buenos Aires, carrying pictures of their disappeared relatives. In Chile, women publicized the disappearance and murder of their family members by sewing together *arpilleras* (quilts) that told the stories of their loved ones.

## Changing Role of Women

Led by the prominent role of women in the revolutionary movements in Nicaragua and El Salvador, the role of women in the movements against the military dictatorships, and the election of women to executive office validated by the statistics on the percentage of economically active women (Table 10), the traditional role of the woman in Latin America is rapidly being redefined. This process is being moved forward by the following:

- Women who work outside the home.
- Women who exercise more independence by having their own apartments and entering into a relationship with a *compañero*, exploring the full dimension of their sexuality.
- Revolutionary women like guerrilla *comandantes* in El Salvador and Nicaragua and the third of the Sandinista combatants who were women.
- The emerging figure of *la presidenta*. With the election of Mireya Moscoso in Panama in 1999, Dilma Rousseff in Brazil and Laura Chinchilla in Costa Rica in 2010 (Rousseff was re-elected in 2014 but impeached and removed from office in 2016), Michelle Bachelet in Chile in 2006 and 2013, and Cristina Fernández de Kirchner in Argentina in 2007 and in 2011, Latin America witnessed the election of six female presidents (Violeta Chamorro in Nicaragua was the first). Elected as vice president, Isabel Perón also served as president of Argentina for more than a year after husband Juan Perón died in office. Before this, three other Latin American women served as unelected chief executives in Bolivia, Haiti, and Ecuador for shorter periods. More and more women are running for and winning office at other levels as well.
- Radical feminists who challenge many vestiges of machismo maintain a coherent line through their creative work, writing, magazines, journals, organizing, and personal example.
- The new generation of young women who politely but persistently decide not to be bound by the same constraints that restricted the occupational and relational horizons of their mothers and grandmothers.
- Strong national women's movements that are often linked to trade unions and progressive political parties and growth of community-based women's organizations in Latin America's inner cities and suburbs that work on local issues often in cooperation with organized women in trade unions. The prominent role of the unions in the feminist movement has served to refocus the attention of the movement to a class-based agenda in the face of neoliberal ideas.
- The development, especially in Brazil, of feminists organizing in the Afro-descendent community on issues that challenge both racism and sexism.

In the Brazilian case, this organizing is occurring in both urban and rural settings and often in tandem with trade unions.

- The growth and continued development of transnational feminists organizing, which was embodied in the World March of Women, an international nongovernmental organization founded in Quebec, Canada, in 1995 early in the development of the worldwide Global Justice Movement in response to the neoliberal agenda. The international headquarters of the march is located in Brazil. The Brazilian affiliate frequently organizes mass marches in Brasilia, the capital, focused on demands for rural development.
- The increase at universities of research centers devoted to the study of gender issues, which is parallel to a significant rise in the number of women faculty and students, especially in the humanities and social sciences.

A key manifestation of the changing role of women in politics in Latin America is the adoption of the system of quotas to legislate greater women's political representation in the national legislature. Internationally quotas have been used in the last twenty years to mandate women's representation through stating that a legislature must have a certain percentage of women legislators or, more commonly, that political parties must nominate through their party lists a certain minimum percentage of women. During that twenty-five-year time frame, going back to the first mandated quotas in Argentina in 1991, a solid majority of Latin American countries have now adopted some form of quotas for women's representation. The list of countries with legal quotas include Argentina, Bolivia, Brazil, Colombia, Costa Rica, Ecuador, El Salvador, Guyana, Mexico, Paraguay, Peru, Uruguay, and Venezuela. In some countries like Uruguay and Venezuela, the adoption of quotas came with the election of progressive governments, but the majority of quotas were voted in by centrist or conservative governments. As demonstrated by Table 10, the increase in women legislators has been significant. One of the most dramatic changes has occurred in Bolivia where women are now 53% of legislators. Other countries using quotas to make significant progress include Ecuador, Mexico and Nicaragua, all surpassing the 40% mark. There has been a definite increase in women's legislative representation in recent years, but it is not clear that the change has resulted in significant new legislation benefiting women but that may well be inevitable over time.

There is growing participation by women in education, the professions, government, and business (Table 11). Gender roles are rapidly and radically being redefined. Feminism and women's movements have grown substantially in recent decades. There are a variety of women's organizations and feminist publications in Mexico, Argentina, Chile, Brazil, and the other larger countries. Strong women's movements can also be found in Nicaragua, Costa Rica, and Cuba. Women's groups are also active in the smaller countries and in cities and intellectual centers throughout the region. It should, however, be noted that feminism in Latin America is well rooted in Latin American culture and can be quite distinct from North American or European feminism. Thus, most Latin American feminists would define the female role as eventually including a role as spouse or *compañera* and mother. Attitudes on abortion—but not birth control—can also be quite divergent from those held by most feminists in the United States. Progress in the region remains slow on issues of reproductive freedom

**TABLE 11.**   Women in High-Level Positions and Decision-Making Occupations

| Country | Legislators, Senior Officials, and Managers (%/year)* | Share of Women in Adult Labor Force (%) (2012)** |
|---|---|---|
| Argentina | 23(2006) | 47 |
| Bolivia | 35 (2009) | 64 |
| Brazil | 37(2013) | 60 |
| Chile | 33 (2002) | 47 |
| Colombia | 53(2010) | 56 |
| Costa Rica | 35 (2011) | 46 |
| Cuba | . . . | 43 |
| Dominican Republic | 37(2013) | 51 |
| Ecuador | 40 (2012) | 54 |
| El Salvador | 37(2012) | 47 |
| Guatemala | . . . | 49 |
| Haiti | . . . | 60 |
| Honduras | . . . | 42 |
| Mexico | 31(2008) | 44 |
| Nicaragua | 41(2006) | 47 |
| Panama | 46(2011) | 50 |
| Paraguay | 34(2014) | 58 |
| Peru | 30(2013) | 68 |
| Puerto Rico | 43(2008) | 36 |
| Uruguay | 44(2011) | 56 |
| Venezuela | . . . | 52 |

. . .Data not available.

*Sources*: *The World Bank. Indicators.

http://data.worldbank.org/indicator/SG.GEN.LSOM.ZS?locations=AR

**Statistics and Indicators on Women and Men. U.N. Statistics Division. 2013.

in large measure due to the continued political strength of the Roman Catholic Church, but legalization of abortion in Uruguay in 2013 represented a significant step. Prior to that, the only Latin America country with legal abortion was Cuba.

Nathalie Lebon observes in *Women's Activism in Latin America and the Caribbean*, which she and Elizabeth Maier edited, "The past four decades have witnessed the rapid and profound transformation of gender roles and gender ideologies in Latin America and the Caribbean, much of which has revolved around women taking their destinies in their own hands, individually and collectively." Indeed, as we travel through the new century, Latin American women are seeking and gaining empowerment in a variety of ways that they define on their own terms, but gender is not the only impediment to equality or upward mobility. Racism and a rigid class structure pose equally formidable barriers.

## Class, Gender, Race, and Mobility

Even though women are gaining power at an ever increasing rate, their mobility is still limited. Cuba is one of the Latin American countries with the highest degree of equality. Socialist Cuba legislated equality some years ago and even passed the

Cuban Family Code in 1975. It requires men and women to share household tasks and childrearing equally. In a trend that is beginning to spread throughout the region, women can enter most career paths and most professions. Although conditions for women in Cuba are very good in comparison to most Latin American countries, they have not reached full potential. Although thousands belong to the ruling Communist Party in Cuba, their representation is less than equal in the party congresses. As one moves upward to the Central Committee and higher levels of government, the representation of women diminishes even further. Women generally experience greater equality at the lower levels: the higher women go in the political and party structure, the greater the barriers to their upward mobility. This is even more the case in most other Latin American countries. In countries where capitalism is dominant, women have generally found it very difficult to obtain management positions and even more so to rise to positions of power or prominence. Positions in the government bureaucracy or educational institutions have been easier to obtain. Not surprisingly, gender is frequently a barrier to upward mobility even in Cuba and Costa Rica (which has also passed progressive legislation guaranteeing legal equality), not to mention other more traditional areas of Latin America.

The class system in most of Latin America is fairly rigid, and it is very difficult for most to experience much upward mobility. As was suggested in the discussion of Amero-Indian and African peoples in Chapter 4, race has also remained a barrier to acceptance and mobility. This reality has been unpacked through the concept of intersectionality and its applicability to Latin America. The work of Mala Htun on Afro-descendent women is particularly important. There have been examples of successful indigenous Latin Americans, such as Benito Juárez of Mexico, who ascended to the presidency of the republic without ever repudiating his native heritage. More commonly, native peoples have had to assimilate to some extent to occupy positions of responsibility outside their native communities. Even in countries like Guatemala and Bolivia, which are inhabited predominantly by native peoples, Hispanicizing family names, the predominant use of Spanish, and adoption of Western dress were generally necessary for upward mobility. Indeed, many native people feel obliged to pass as mestizos (*ladinos* in Guatemala). The election of Evo Morales as the first indigenous president in Bolivia (55 percent indigenous) is indicative of both the historic inclusion of indigenous people and the sea change that is underway. Yet, as suggested by the testimony of Domitila Barrios de Chungara (*Let Me Speak*) in Bolivia and Rigoberta Menchú (*I Rigoberta*) in Guatemala, indigenous peoples are still second-class citizens, particularly when they come from the working class. When they are also female, they suffer even more discrimination. When they are openly gay, their lives may be a living hell even as some countries legalize same sex unions.

The lot of Afro-Latins has also been fraught with difficulty. Racial discrimination in Latin America was never as institutionalized as it was in the United States, but it nonetheless existed. Slavery continued in many countries until the second half of the nineteenth century. When it ended, black Latin Americans emerged from slavery into societies where official segregation was not legislated but was practiced in more subtle forms. Some observers have noted that most of the governments of Latin America have espoused a philosophy of racial democracy but have simultaneously instituted a social order that in large part excluded their African populations

Two Zapatista guards at entrance to EZLN encampment in Chiapas, 1996. As with other mass and revolutionary organizations in Latin America, more and more women are participating in all aspects of activity. *(Photo by H. Vanden)*

from many key aspects of national life. As suggested by the eloquent testimony of Brazilian congresswoman Benedita da Silva, lower-class origins and being female make the struggle of people of color even more difficult. Afro-Latin women have made a significant contribution to the women's movement in Latin America and have played a key role in social transformation. There is, however, a paucity of literature and research in this area.

Black women—like indigenous women—are at the bottom of the social pyramid in Latin America. Afro-Latin women have had to form their own organizations to address issues of specific concern. Indeed, many black women in Latin America complain that mainstream white organizations do not understand the intersection of race and gender. For many black women's organizations, this nexus provides a much-needed framework of understanding. Field research by Kwame Dixon suggests that in the human rights area, this framework allows researchers to see the racial and gender bases for many rights violations. For instance, as a result of the war in Colombia, displaced persons tend to be disproportionately female and Afro-Colombian or indigenous. This suggests the intersection of multiple forms of discrimination. There are also distinct forms of discrimination that occur against a person when gender and race or ethnicity intersect. That is, women who are black or indigenous are more apt to suffer discrimination than a white woman or a black or indigenous man. Sexual orientation compounds these factors if it is acknowledged.

As noted in Chapter 4, there is, however, growing black consciousness and movements in several countries to pass legislation prohibiting racial discrimination. Currently, black women's organizations are developing frameworks that incorporate race, class, and gender. Within the black community in Brazil, one finds several groups that also focus on gender inequality. Among these are the Geledés Instituto da Mulher Negra and the Centro de Referencia da Mulher Negra in Bahia.

Initial colonial society set up a rigid system in which classism, racism, patriarchy, and elitism in many forms were pervasive. Even today, one is still often judged by her or his birth and family name. Indeed, the Iberian tradition of using the maternal maiden name as well as the paternal name (paternal family name followed by maternal family name) is still in practice; for example, in Hispanic Latin America, José Sánchez López is the son of his father Sánchez and his mother, whose father's name is López (in Brazil both names may also be used, but the mother's family name appears first). Thus, mobility and entrance to social circles or employment opportunities are often defined more by who one is in terms of class, race, and gender and the circles in which one's family travels than by one's actual accomplishments and abilities. Indeed, it may take a generation or two for a family to gain access to social institutions like the Club Nacional in Peru, even if they have achieved economic or artistic success in their time. This process may take even longer in some countries if a person is primarily of indigenous or African ancestry. Some have even suggested that a process of whitening by wealth, great success (e.g., Pelé in Brazil), or substantial power (e.g., Batista in Cuba or Somoza in Nicaragua) must occur first. Indeed, many of the competent professionals who immigrate to the United States do so because they find that they have a much better chance of being hired or accepted for their actual accomplishments and demonstrated abilities rather than being prejudged by class, race, gender, or family in their home countries. In this and other areas, cultural norms and mores strongly preconditioned perceptions.

## Sexual Orientation and Gender Identity

Open discussion of sexual orientation and gender identity is still generally taboo throughout much of Latin America, but this is changing rapidly as lesbian, gay, bisexual, and transgender (LGBT) movements challenge traditional views on these subject. To properly see how these topics are understood in the region, one must cast aside U.S.-centric preconceived notions and labels. By doing this we can see many variations in how sexuality and gender have been understood throughout Latin America, from pre-Columbian times to the present.

Because most precolonial history was lost, destroyed, or interpreted through the eyes of the conquistadors, accurate records of how indigenous societies dealt with these issues preconquest are scarce. Most evidence that did survive focuses on male–male relationships, and here we see great variation in how indigenous societies understood and treated them. For example, Aztec and Mayan civilizations for the most part interpreted them through a gendered lens of an honor–shame paradigm. In this systemization, there was a clear difference between the active and passive roles in intercourse modeled after traditional male–female gender roles: The active partner supposedly embodied the masculine characteristics of strength and virility, whereas the passive role resembled the weakness and frailty of women. These discourses of penetration were frequently evoked in a number of ways to symbolize power and domination. In other parts of these empires, male–male sex acts were understood very differently in what is referred to as the age-stratified model, which is similar to how ancient Greek civilizations conceptualized male–male sexuality. According to this model, sodomy signified a mentoring relationship among men where knowledge and power were transmitted through blood and semen from community elders to coming-of-age young men. In contrast to the former understanding, being the passive participant in the sex act was a masculinizing, not a feminizing, experience.

Pre-Columbian indigenous groups in the Andes conceptualized sexual and gender variations quite differently. As opposed to focusing on the act of penetration as a means for domination or preserving masculinity, Incan civilizations celebrated individuals—both male bodied and female bodied—who deviated from gender and sexual norms, often designating them as having a third gender. Some today prefer to use the label "two-spirited," emanating from the belief that a two-spirited persons does not just have one spirit living within them but two—one male and one female. Consequently, they were revered as enlightened and blessed individuals, often occupying very prestigious social roles within the tribes, such as chiefs and shamans.

These paradigms changed significantly with the conquest. The conquistadors from the Iberian Peninsula brought with them their own ideas about gender and sexual deviance, of which two distinct, and sometimes contradictory, strains of thought were particularly influential: the views of the Catholic Church and Mediterranean ideas of masculinity/femininity. Over time these foreign ideas overtook indigenous views and formed the basis of the social stigma and legal persecution that came to dominate the region for centuries, including today.

The same Mediterranean gender norms that formed the basis of machismo/marianismo also significantly influenced how colonial Latin American societies treated gender and sexual variants. Homosexuality was understood according to a gender-stratified model, whereby one's sexual role (*activo/pasivo*) strongly influenced one's gender identity. Today in the West, we consider homosexuality and transgenderism to be two distinct categories or identities, but under this regime there is more blurring of the two: one either performs his or her proper gender/sex role or he or she does not. In this understanding, it matters less the sex of the person with whom one is having sex, but the more the role they perform in the sexual acts. The *activo* in this case is not necessarily a homosexual because he is still performing the masculine role of "penetrator," while the *pasivo* is a both a sexual and a gender deviant by being penetrated.

Catholicism was central to both the Spanish and Portuguese Empires at the beginning of the 1500s, so Church teachings also played a significant role in how gender and sexual transgressions were treated. The official position of the Church was that sex for any purpose other than procreation was lustful, violating the Sixth Commandment. Sodomy, or *pecado contra natura*, was a sin, whether man–man, woman–woman, or man–woman. Homosexuality was understood to be a behavior as a result of a moral failing, rather than a person with a distinct identity. In other words, there were no homosexual people—just homosexual sex acts.

As Latin American countries achieved independence from Spain and Portugal, they fashioned their constitutions and laws according to the Napoleonic code, removing most explicit prohibitions against sodomy. In Argentina, for example, Article 19 of the 1853 Constitution states: "Private activities that do not affect public order and morality and do not harm other people are reserved to the judgment of God and off-limits to the authority of magistrates." However, this does not mean that homosexuality and gender variance were, by any means, more socially accepted. Similar to the United States at the time, inherent in this system was an implicit agreement that sexual and gender deviance would be tolerated in private as long as they were not openly discussed or visible in public. To reinforce this, most countries had vague laws against vagrancy, public decency, and cross-dressing that were used at the discretion of police to enforce this public–private divide. This social-legal system dominated the region for centuries.

Within the past few decades, globalization has enabled another paradigm shift in thinking about homosexuality in Latin America as the Western industrialized world's gay-egalitarian model is slowly replacing the gender-stratified model. Whereas before identity was based on the gendered notion of one's sexual role (*activo* or *pasivo*), this new understanding instead links one's identity to his or her object of sexual choice (male or female).

As this new model is taking hold, homosexuality in Latin America has two characteristics that fundamentally influence how it has developed socially and politically in the twentieth century. First, because same-sex attraction is not necessarily an outwardly visible characteristic, gays and lesbians exert some power in controlling who "knows." Strategically, this can be important, as LGBT people can hide their sexuality/gender to avoid discrimination in ways that other marginalized groups such as women and people of color cannot generally do so easily. Second, sexual/gender variation is not necessarily a condition shared with members of one's core social group—the family—meaning that the home is not necessarily a safe space for many. Earlier parts of this chapter discussed how the family plays such a fundamental role in social life in Latin America. For LGBT people, this has especially dangerous implications as coming out may risk both one's primary social unit and economic livelihood. It may also increase the risk of brutal anti-gay attacks. Moreover, because young adults often live with their parents until they are married (and sometimes even longer), gay barrios have not formed in most large Latin American cities like they have in the United States, impeding the ability for LGBT communities to form a collective identity and organize politically. Because lesbians and gays lived in isolation from one another, they could do little to challenge the public–private divide.

However, over the past several decades, two things have worn down this public–private barrier. First, the emergence of HIV/AIDS (VIH/SIDA) in the 1980s forced many out of the closet. Individuals who earlier were able to compartmentalize their lives became visibly sick and could no longer hide it from their friends and families. Also, as gays and lesbians witnessed their friends get sick and die en masse, group identity solidified and these new communities sought ways to slow the spread of the epidemic and treat those who were sick. To fight the disease, visibility became one of the primary political tactics. Second, social movement organizations representing sexual and gender minorities began to appear in many Latin American countries starting in the 1970s. In South America, many groups began to form as repression eased with the end of the military dictatorships and the reemergence of democracy. However, these organizations faced hurdles of both internal divisions and rejection from political parties.

In the early years of organizing (and still today in many countries), the LGBT movement was fractured. In many places, groups representing lesbians and transgender persons have splintered off from traditionally male-dominated gay rights organizations because of their patriarchal propensities. Moreover, although gay men, lesbian women, bisexuals, and transgender persons all face stigma, repression, and violence from society at large, the problems they face are often very different.

LGBT people in the Americas have had great difficulty finding allies on any part of the political spectrum. The right has been almost universally unfriendly to LGBT people, both in the past and today. Likewise, the left did not initially welcome LGBT people, following the doctrines of the Communist Parties of the Soviet Union and China that homosexuality was bourgeoisie decadence and not an issue for the working class. Since LGBT people are represented in every social class, incorporating them might threaten group solidarity among the working class. Socialist Cuba, for example, after the revolution was repressive to homosexuals in the 1960s and 1970s as exemplified in the film *Before Night Falls*. Leftist organizations continued to discriminate against LGBT people for many decades, although some parts of the left have changed their views significantly in recent years. For example, lesbians and gays played fairly active roles in the Sandinista revolution in Nicaragua, and the Cuban government has significantly moderated its position with Fidel himself even apologizing for the revolution's past history of discrimination. Moreover, leftist governments in Argentina, Brazil, and Chile, among others, have openly embraced and supported LGBT issues in recent years.

LGBT movements and organizations have won a number of important social, political, and legal victories in the first two decades of the twenty-first century. In what was once a mostly underground phenomenon that was rarely discussed in public and not organized politically, this nascent movement has recently begun openly challenging social mores and entering public policy debates. Political activism and visibility are both growing: São Paulo, Brazil, is now home to the world's largest pride celebration, which in 2007 attracted more than 3.5 million people. Also, attitudes have warmed on the subject, and the movements have secured some impressive legal victories thought impossible only a decade ago. Politically, a few issues have dominated the agendas of most gay rights organizations: decriminalizing sodomy and homosexuality, passing nondiscrimination protections, securing additional funding and protections for persons with HIV, same-sex partnership recognition, and gender-identity laws for transgender rights.

Combating anti-LGBT violence and discrimination are the top priorities for most LGBT groups as both problems are still very commonplace (and increasing, in some cases) throughout Latin America. For example, even though Brazil has the reputation of being a country where "anything goes" because of its widely flamboyant Carnival, it is actually home to some of the most savage violence against transgender women, with LGBT groups estimating that one person is killed per day on average because of their gender identity or sexual orientation. Rates of violence are especially high in several Central American countries, which is much less accepting,

on average, of LGBT people compared to South America. As a result of this violence, a handful of countries (some at the local and some at the national level) have
enacted some types of ordinances making it a crime to discriminate based on sexual
orientation, gender identity, or both, or they have increased the penalties if an act of
violence is rooted in anti-LGBT hate. Enforcement of such laws is, however, generally lax. Beyond hate crime and anti-discrimination laws, many LGBT organizations
have also made HIV activism one of their top priorities. Brazil notably stands out,
as it has provided HIV medication universally and free of charge since 1996 and has
fought to obtain the rights to produce low-cost generic antiviral drugs to treat HIV.
Finally, laws giving transgender persons more rights have also hit the agenda for
LGBT groups. Argentina passed a gender identity law in 2011 that in most respects
is considered the most progressive in the world for transgender people. Many other
countries are considering similar legislation.

Recently, same-sex partner recognition has become an important issue for lesbians and gays. LGBT organizations initially sought relationship recognition in a
piecemeal fashion—first seeking health-care benefits, inheritance rights, access to
partner's pensions, and so forth—sometimes winning significant concessions in
either the legislature or the courts. Within the past decade, LGBT groups shifted
their strategies to push for broader social recognition in the form of state-sanctioned
unions (e.g., civil unions). Buenos Aires, Argentina, became the first city in Latin
America to pass such a law in 2002, with other parts of Argentina, Mexico, and
Brazil soon following suit. Uruguay, Colombia, and Ecuador then took steps to recognize civil unions nationwide. Argentina became the first country to recognize
same-sex marriage through legislation in 2010, followed by Uruguay in 2013. Both
Brazil (2013) and Colombia (2016) today also recognize same-sex marriage, but they
only made these advancements as a result of judicial intervention. Notably, even
socially conservative Chile passed a civil union bill in 2015, and the current government today is considering legislation to also recognize marriage. This is a remarkable turn of events for a country that did not legalize divorce until 2004.

The main opposition today to LGBT people still comes from religious conservatives repeating many of the same arguments used centuries before. However,
in some South American countries, the Catholic Church has lost some of its political effectiveness. In places such as Argentina and Chile, the Church's reputation
was tarnished during the 1960s and 1970s as it was seen as being too complicit in
human rights abuses at the hands of the military dictatorships. Because of this, it
has had to carefully walk the fine line between arguing against homosexuality but
not against human rights. In addition, clergy abuse scandals have also plagued
the Church in some parts of Latin America, in some ways severely crippling their
moral authority. However, the recent rise in Protestantism presents a unique challenge to lesbians and gays, as many of these denominations are more antigay than
Catholicism.

As Latin America becomes more urban and educated and as egalitarian values
are championed by women, indigenous organizations, Afro-Latins, landless workers, neighborhood organizations, gays and lesbians, and many others, the nature
and structure of Latin American society will continue to change, and many of the
old barriers will be challenged.

Christina Fernandez de Kirchner and Dilma Rousseff when they were presidents of Argentina and Brazil.

# Bibliography

Alvarez, Sonia E., Evelina Dagnino, and Arturo Escobar. *Cultures of Politics/Politics of Culture: Revisioning Latin American Social Movements*. Boulder, CO: Westview, 1998.

Balderston, Daniel, and Donna J. Guy. *Sex and Sexuality in Latin America*. New York: New York University Press, 1997.

Benson, Devon Spence. *Antiracism in Cuba: The Unfinished Revolution*. Chapel Hill: University of North Carolina Press, 2016.

Bouvard, Margante Guzman. *Revolutionizing Motherhood: The Mothers of the Plaza de Mayo*. Wilmington, DE: Scholarly Resources, 1994.

Chase, Michelle. *Revolution Within the Revolution: Women and Gender Politics in Cuba, 1952–1962*. Chapel Hill: University of North Carolina Press, 2015.

Cubit, Tessa. *Latin American Society*. 2d ed. Harlow, UK: Longman, 1995.

Dore, Elizabeth, ed. *Gender Politics in Latin America: Debate in Theory and Practice*. New York: Monthly Review, 1998.

Dore, Elizabeth, and Maxine Molyneux, eds. *Hidden Histories of Gender and the State in Latin America*. Durham, NC: Duke University Press, 2000.

Eckstein, Susan, ed. *Power and Protest: Latin American Social Movements*. 2d ed. Berkeley: University of California Press, 2001.

French, William, and Katherine Elaine Bliss, eds. *Gender, Sexuality and Power in Latin America since Independence*. Lanham, MD: Rowman & Littlefield, 2006.

Hanchard, Michael, ed. *Racial Politics in Contemporary Brazil*. Durham, NC: Duke University Press, 1999.

Horswell, Michael J. *Decolonizing the Sodomite: Queer Tropes of Sexuality in Colonial Andean Culture*. Austin: University of Texas Press, 2005.

Htun, Mala. *Inclusion Without Representation in Latin America: Gender Quotas and Ethnic Reservations*. Cambridge Studies in Gender and Politics. Cambridge: Cambridge University Press, 2016.

Imaz, José Luis de. *Los Que Mandan/Those Who Rule*. Translated by Carlos A. Astiz. Albany: State University of New York Press, 1970.

Jesus, Carolina Maria de. *Britita's Diary: The Childhood Memories of Carolina Maria de Jesus*. Armonk, NY: M. E. Sharp, 1998.

Kampwirth, Karen. *Women and Guerrilla Movements*. State College: Penn State University Press, 2002.

, Gaby, ed. *Compañeras: Voices from the Latin American Women's Movement*. London: Latin American Bureau, 1994.

, Elizabeth, and Nathalie Lebon, eds. *Women's Movements in Latin America and the Caribbean: Engendering Social Justice, Democratizing Citizenship*. New Brunswick, NJ: Rutgers University Press, 2010.

Pierceson, Jason, Adrianna Piatti-Crocker, and Shawn Schulenberg, eds. *Same Sex Marriage in Latin America: Promise and Resistance*. Lanham, MD: Lexington Press, 2013.

Randal, Margaret. *Sandino's Daughters*. New Brunswick, NJ: Rutgers University Press, 1995.

Sigai, Peter Herman. *Infamous Desire: Male Homosexuality in Colonial Latin America*. Chicago: University of Chicago Press, 2003.

Stahler-Sholk, Richard, Harry E. Vanden, and Glen Kuecker, eds. *Latin American Social Movements in the Twenty-First Century: Resistance, Power and Democracy*. Lanham, MD: Rowman & Littlefield, 2008.

Telles, Edward, and Project on Ethnicity and Race in Latin America. *Pigmentocracies: Ethnicity, Race and Color in Latin America*. Chapel Hill: University of North Carolina Press, 2014.

Thiesenhusen, William C. *Searching for Agrarian Reform in Latin America*. Boston: Unwin Hyman, 1989.

Trexler, Richard C. *Sex and Conquest: Gendered Violence, Political Order, and the European Conquest of the Americas*. Ithaca, NY: Cornell University Press, 1995.

Windance Twine, Francis. *Racism in a Racial Democracy: The Maintenance of White Supremacy in Brazil*. New Brunswick, NJ: Rutgers University Press, 1998.

## FILMS AND VIDEOS

*108 Cuchillo de Palo*. Paraguay, 2010.
*Black Orpheus*. Brazil, 1958.
*Blossoms of Fire*. Mexico, 2000.
*Buenos Días Compañeras/Women in Culm*. Cuba, 1974.
*Burnt Money*. Argentina, 2000.
*Café*. Mexico, 2014.
*Central Station*. Brazil, 1998.
*Doña Herlinda and Her Son*. Mexico, 1985.
*Eles nao usam Black Fie*. Brazil, 1980.
*Housemaids*. Brazil, 2012.
*In Women's Hands* (Americas Series). United States, 1993.
*Like Water for Chocolate*. Mexico, 1992.
*Mirrors of the Hea*rt (Americas Series). United States, 1993.
*Place without Limits*. Mexico, 1978.
*Portrait of Teresa*. Cuba, 1979.
*Shoot to Kill*. Venezuela, 1990.
*Strawberry and Chocolate*. Cuba, 1994.
*We're All Stars*. Peru, 1993.

## WEBSITE

http://www.presidencia.cl/   President's office in Chile

# SIX

# RELIGION IN LATIN AMERICA

The Catholic character of Latin America came into sharp focus on March 20, 2013, when Argentinian Jorge Mario Bergoglio, the archbishop of Buenos Aires, was elected as the head of the Roman Catholic Church and became Pope Francis. His election focused even greater attention to the role of the Church in Latin American affairs. Treatments of contemporary Latin American politics often pay relatively little attention to the role of religion. Such an omission is a serious one because from the era of the great Meso-American civilizations to the present time spiritual factors have had a great impact on the political scene. This chapter will explore that evolution over time. The Roman Catholic Church will be a major focus but not to the exclusion of other religions, especially the rapid rise of evangelical Protestantism in the last forty years.

The primary religious character of Latin America is Roman Catholic. For five centuries, the Catholic Church had a virtual monopoly on religious life. During that time, religious and political authorities were tightly bound together. The North American concept of separation of church and state was not known in Latin America until almost the twentieth century. Today's reality in Latin America is somewhat different, although close to 70 percent of the population still identify themselves as Roman Catholic. During the last forty years, the most important development in Latin American religiosity has been the exponential growth of evangelical Protestantism. In 1970, only 2 to 3 percent of the population in most Latin American countries was evangelical; today, that number has reached close to 15 percent. The last forty years have also witnessed significant turmoil within the Catholic Church. Following the historic Second Vatican Council in the early 1960s, the region's bishops began meeting regularly; in 1968, at a meeting in Medellin, Colombia, they issued a groundbreaking document that seemed to commit the Church to a much greater role in promoting social justice. If the Medellin document had been fully implemented, it would have marked a dramatic reversal of the historical role played by the Catholic Church as the ally of the wealthy and powerful. However, the promise of Medellin to stand with the poor brought resistance from the more conservative clergy in both Latin America and Rome, leaving a divided Church that has been vulnerable to inroads from Protestantism. It is also inaccurate to view the totality of Latin American religion as falling within the scope of Protestantism and

Catholicism. A variety of spiritual religions and movements also continue to exist in the region, many with their roots in the large number of slaves brought to the Western Hemisphere from Africa in the sixteenth through the nineteenth centuries. In many cases, the indigenous peoples of the Americas have also maintained a spiritual identity independent of Western religions.

Historically, religion and politics have been deeply intertwined in Latin America. This interconnection began with the role the Roman Catholic Church played in the military conquests of the Spanish and Portuguese in the fifteenth and sixteenth centuries. Church authorities came ashore with the *conquistadores* in search of souls to convert and provided ideological justification for the military conquests and for monarchical rule. Ultimately, the Church was rewarded for this role with vast amounts of wealth and power. The Church set up parallel institutions to the royal administration. It was granted significant tracts of land from which it generated wealth and was given free rein to develop the region's educational system.

The relationship between religion and politics is a complex one. Strong religious communities help set the value structure of a society by stating what is important in life. In doing so, religious values help frame what the citizenry expects out of their lives and therefore, on one level, what they may expect from government authorities. For example, traditional Roman Catholic teaching, which emphasized the glories of eternal salvation rather than the material pleasures of one's current life, seemed to dampen the expectations of the citizenry and therefore reduce the pressure on the political authorities to provide a good life in the here and now. Catholic theology rooted in Thomas Aquinas also provided a direct justification for monarchy and elite rule. All humans were deemed to be born in original sin, and it was only through God's grace that some people were better suited to rule than others. The essence of politics was then to elevate such people to power so that they could be responsible to God's will, not to the will of the people. This reasoning was used to justify the Spanish and Portuguese monarchies. It was only in the eighteenth and nineteenth centuries that ideas began to develop in Church teaching that provided justification for democratic thinking. Religious authorities can also play a more direct role in politics by influencing their followers to support a particular political leader or party. In recent times, Argentina and Chile have shown contrasting examples of Church policy. In Argentina, the Catholic hierarchy actively supported the two military regimes that ruled between 1966 and 1983. Such support was important in a country where military rule had earlier been supplanted by constitutional democratic governance. In contrast, the Catholic hierarchy became an outspoken critic of the Chilean military regime during the 1980s. That opposition helped pave the way for the defeat of a military-sponsored referendum in 1988 and the return to civilian rule in 1990. Despite these contrasting examples, historically most interventions by the Church have been to support the status quo.

The question of separation of church and state has long been a contentious one, with the establishment of such a principle being slow to arrive in Latin America in comparison with the United States. As elsewhere, the impetus for such a separation came from those who sought independence in spiritual matters from an overbearing government that gave favors only to persons from a particular religion. In Latin America, the challenge to the tight relationship between church and state came from the Liberal political movements of the nineteenth century. In response, the Church closely allied itself with the Conservatives in an attempt to maintain its historically privileged position. When Liberal regimes came to power, the Church was usually disestablished, meaning that the hierarchy lost its direct control over political matters. The dates of disestablishment range from the initial case of Colombia in 1848 to Mexico in 1857 and Brazil in 1889. Unlike the liberal establishment in the United States, which granted freedom of religion and then largely stayed out of church affairs, the Latin American Liberals granted official freedom of worship but then sought to interfere in the affairs of the Church by attempting to compel priests to marry and reorganize diocesan boundaries. By 1910, virtually all Latin American countries, with the exception of Colombia, which reversed its disestablishment from 1886 until 1930, had granted formal religious liberty. As a result, the Catholic hierarchy ended its sole association with the Conservatives and broadened its relations to include the Liberal elites with whom they had fought so bitterly. The terms of their dealings with the state were now different, lacking the legal and financial privileges of the previous centuries.

In the early twentieth century, the Catholic Church also faced for the first time a significant thrust of Protestant missionary work into the region. However, Catholics retained a strong position based on their large following and the rootedness of their ideas in the popular culture. Also, as the fierce anticlericalism of the nineteenth century began to fade, the Church, without official representation in government, began to regain its political influence with the elites as newer, more powerful challenges from revolutionary movements united Liberal and Conservative elites. The Church concentrated its political efforts on protecting its own position in society by pushing for mandatory religious education and public funding of its organizations and projects. The new tactic of accommodating both Liberal and Conservative elites, and even the populist leaders in Brazil and Argentina, actually succeeded in winning back some privileges previously lost and guaranteeing the Church a prominent societal position through education and public festivals.

Today, Roman Catholicism remains the dominant religion of Latin America, but it is facing increasing challenges from both evangelical Protestantism and the overall secularization of society (see Table 12). In several countries, Protestants may surpass Catholics in numbers of adherents if current trends continue. Phillip Berryman has observed that because of the relatively low percentage of Catholics attending mass regularly, the number of churchgoing Protestants may be roughly equal to that of Catholics. As Protestantism grows, the political implications of this development are unclear. Many of the evangelical movements are closely connected with right-wing political movements based in the United States, but, overall, the evangelical movement is quite pluralistic and may represent a liberalizing trend in comparison to the most conservative forces within the Catholic Church. In this chapter, we analyze all the religious movements in greater depth, with an emphasis on their relationship to politics.

**TABLE 12.** Religious Affiliation in Latin America

| Country | Roman Catholic | Protestant | Hindu | Muslim | Jewish | Other | Non Believers/ No Affiliation | Unspecified |
|---|---|---|---|---|---|---|---|---|
| Argentina | 92.0% | 2.0% | | | 2.0% | 4.0% | | |
| Belize | 40.1% | 33.2% | | | | 10.5% | 15.5% | 0.6% |
| Bolivia | 76.8% | 16.0% | | | | 1.7% | 5.5% | |
| Brazil | 64.6% | 22.2% | | | | 4.7% | 8.0% | 0.4% |
| Chile | 66.7% | 17.4% | | | | 3.4% | 11.5% | 1.1% |
| Colombia | 90.0% | | | | | 10.0% | | |
| Costa Rica | 76.3% | 15.0% | | | | 5.5% | 3.2% | |
| Dominican Republic | 95.0% | | | | | 5.0% | | |
| Ecuador | 74.0% | 11.6% | | | | 6.4% | 8.0% | |
| El Salvador | 57.1% | 23.1% | | | | 3.0% | 16.8% | |
| Guatemala | 55.5% | 35.5% | | | | 9.0% | | |
| Guyana | 8.1% | 31.6% | 28.4% | 7.2% | | 19.6% | 4.3% | 0.9% |
| Haiti** | 54.7% | 28.5% | | | | 6.7% | 10.2% | |
| Honduras | 97.0% | 3.0% | | | | | | |
| Jamaica | 2.2% | 66.7% | | | | 7.6% | 21.3% | 2.3% |
| Mexico | 82.7% | 8.0% | | | | 1.9% | 4.7% | 2.7% |
| Nicaragua | 58.5% | 24.1% | | | | 1.6% | 15.7% | |
| Panama | 85.0% | 15.0% | | | | | | |
| Paraguay | 89.6% | 6.2% | | | | 1.1% | 1.1% | 1.9% |
| Peru | 81.3% | 12.5% | | | | 3.3% | 2.9% | |
| Suriname | 22.8% | 25.2% | 27.4% | 19.6% | | 5.0% | | |
| Trinidad and Tobago | 21.6% | 33.6% | 18.2% | 5.0% | | 8.4% | 2.2% | 11.1% |
| Uruguay | 47.1% | 34.3% | | | 0.3% | 1.1% | 17.2% | |
| Venezuela | 96.0% | 2.0% | | | | 2.0% | | |

* Includes Evangelical, Pentecostal, Seventh Day Adventist, Anglican, Mennonite, Baptist, Methodist, Nazarene, Jehovah's Witness, and other Protestant.

** "Other" includes 2.1% of the population which practices voodoo as their primary religion. Voodoo is an official religion in Haiti, and roughly half the population practices voodoo in addition to another religion.

https://www.cia.gov/library/publications/the-world-factbook/geos/ve.html unless otherwise marked.

< Spain Exchange Country Guide. Study Country. http://www.studycountry.com/guide/GT-religion.htm

# Indigenous Religious Practice

Any discussion of religion in Latin America must begin with a discussion of the spiritual practices of the indigenous peoples who lived in the Americas prior to the conquest. What are the traditional spirits of the indigenous people? Juan Schobinger argues that indigenous religious practice as it evolved to the time of the conquest was significantly different from that of European religious tradition. He argues that indigenous religion was intuitive, open to nature, communitarian, and tended to see everything visible as a symbol of something greater on which the people depended. This religious tradition was seen as contrasting with the more individualistic thrust of European religion. Religious rites became more sophisticated over time, and practices were passed from one generation to the next and from one civilization to the next. Several high points are worth noting. The classic Mayan period from 300 to 900 C.E. in what is today southern Mexico and Guatemala was governed by a priestly elite who were inspired by deities. The civilization was sophisticated in that there was both an official religion of the upper classes and a popular spiritualism. This spiritual divergence may help us understand the painful nature of the encounter between the two civilizations.

Anthropological research on the indigenous civilizations of the Americas demonstrates a broad evolution of religious and spiritual practices. Our knowledge of these activities comes primarily from wall art and carvings that survived to the twentieth century, when the majority of research was done. The pattern that can be observed is one of a growing religiosity of the lower classes. The spiritual life was constructed around both official ceremonies or feast days and series of myths and stories that framed a world view.

Mayan religious life was centered on the magnificent stepped pyramids, which symbolically reached toward the cosmic world. Their world view was embodied in the story of the Popol Vuh, the basic idea of which was that there had been four ages previous to the one in which they were living. Each previous age had been brought to a cataclysmic end by gods dissatisfied with the imperfections of humans. Life was focused on activities and rites designed to convince the gods not to bring their civilization to an abrupt end. The ceremonies were elaborate and preceded by strict fasts. Sacrifices played an important part, but in the classic Mayan period human sacrifice was not involved. That practice emerged only later; it originated in Mexico with the Toltecs and was then adopted by Mayans under their influence.

The arrival of the Spanish and Portuguese conquerors had a devastating impact on the spiritual life of the indigenous civilizations, especially the ones that were at the height of their development in the sixteenth century, the Aztecs and the Incas. The conquerors often destroyed the public religious buildings and, through the missionaries who accompanied them, forcibly converted the local population to Catholicism. Perhaps the most blatant example of this was in the capital of the Aztecs, Tenochtitlán, where the Spanish conquerors constructed the Catholic metropolitan cathedral on top of the foundations of the destroyed Templo Mayor of the Aztecs, destroying the official and public form of indigenous religion. Indigenous leaders were subjugated and, with them, the ability to conduct the festivals that had dominated their religious practice. This approach by the conquerors led to two parallel phenomena: the maintenance of indigenous religious beliefs through popular culture and the quiet practice of indigenous religions in former Mayan lands and Bolivia and the adoption of European religious forms as a way to maintain traditional practices in the face of a superior power.

## Colonial Catholic Church

From its first appearance in the New World, the Catholic Church was an essential element in the conquest and colonization of the native peoples by Spain and Portugal. From the beginning, it held a privileged position with considerable

economic and political power. It provided ideological justification for the subjugation of the native peoples encountered by the conquerors. As a reward for its role,
the Church was granted significant landholdings and a central role in the new
colonial societies as the primary provider of education. The Church viewed the natives as people who could be converted to the faith, thus augmenting the Church's
ranks worldwide. The Church had no respect whatsoever for the existing spiritual
beliefs of the native peoples. This aggressive and intolerant Catholicism reflected
that era when the Spanish monarchy defeated the Moors in southern Spain and
expelled the Jews. The early sixteenth century was also marked by Catholicism's
vigorous reaction to the Protestant Reformation. The Church's stature was further
enhanced when Pope Alexander VI in 1494 adjudicated the division of the continent between Spain and Portugal and conferred on their monarchies the right
and duty of propagating the Catholic faith. The model of social order the Iberian
conquerors brought was that of "Christendom." Ironically, this model arrived in
Latin America just as it was beginning to unravel in Europe. Berryman has called
the Latin American form "colonial Christendom." Under this system of patronage,
the Spanish and Portuguese monarchs exercised full administrative control over the
churches in their territories.

In many ways, the role played by the Catholic Church in Latin America was
simply an extension of the role that it had played in Europe. After its first four
centuries of existence as a movement that struggled to survive in the face of hostile opponents, the Church succeeded in gaining recognition from the political and
economic elites who allowed it to carry out its spiritual mission without significant
interference from government authorities. It protected its position by endorsing
governments and social systems that were willing to further Catholic values and
protect Church interests. The Church always had an ambivalent view toward secular life. It tended to view the difficult human existence of the majority of the people
as a burden to be endured in the hope of a glorious afterlife. Secular authorities
were viewed with a skeptical eye, but as long as they permitted the Church authorities to carry out their pastoral mission, the Church leaders gave their backing to the
political and economic leaders.

The Latin American Catholic Church adopted this model and applied it
throughout the New World, but it is important to note that from the beginning of
the Church's presence in Latin America there were missionaries who protested the
cruelty of the conquest. The most famous is the Dominican priest Bartolomé de Las
Casas, who came to Hispaniola in 1502. Although he initially held Indian slaves
and initially favored the importation of slaves, Las Casas experienced a conversion
and spent the remainder of his life arguing that the indigenous people should be
treated with respect and won over to Catholicism with the power of the gospel
rather than the force of arms. He wrote in *In Defense of the Indians*, "With what
swords and cannons did Christ arm his disciples when he sent them to preach the
gospel. Devastating provinces and exterminating natives or putting them to flight,
is this freely sharing the faith?" Many Dominican bishops followed Las Casas in
the defense of the Indians. The tradition continued in the late twentieth century
with Church leaders like Bishop Samuel Ruiz defending indigenous peasant interests in Chiapas.

# The Church in Modern Latin America

In the first twenty-five years of the nineteenth century, Latin America broke away from Spain and Portugal. The independence movement and its aftermath created a crisis for the Catholic Church. Most of the bishops sided with the Spanish crown, and popes made pronouncements against independence in 1816 and 1823. Some clerics, including the Mexican priests Miguel Hidalgo and José Morelos y Pavón, were leaders of the independence movement, but for the most part the Church found itself on the losing side of the political change. The Vatican only began to recognize the new states in 1831, and in many countries the clergy left, leaving some dioceses vacant. Those clerics who remained in most cases allied themselves with the newly created conservative parties, who pledged to support the historic role of the Church in Latin American society. In societies where the Conservatives held sway, the Church was able to prosper, albeit in a more limited way. However, in those countries where the Liberals came to power, the Church faced new laws that enabled the government to confiscate their lands. In the eyes of the Liberals, the Church represented an obstacle to their vision of progress and development. The nineteenth century also saw the rise of Freemasonry in Latin America as a challenge to the dominance of the Church in secular matters. As a result of attacks from the Liberals and Freemasons, the Catholic Church was thrown into crisis in much of Latin America in the nineteenth century. The Church came to rely on a steady flow of priests from Europe as it could not recruit enough clergy from within the region. Even today Catholic clergy are primarily foreign in many Latin American countries, including Guatemala, Venezuela, and Bolivia.

The Catholic Church entered the twentieth century in considerable disarray, weakened by attacks from Liberal governments and facing an increasingly aggressive Protestant challenge. Protestant missionaries began arriving in the last decades of the nineteenth century and often received favorable treatment from the Liberal governments, which saw them as a useful tool in breaking the hold of the Catholic Church. Inroads in Catholic dominance did occur, but most Latin Americans continued to view themselves as Catholic. In the early twentieth century, the Catholic hierarchy initiated changes in response to the challenges it faced. The Church embraced new values as it sought to maintain its hold on a population that was also undergoing significant change. Religious freedom was embraced, and there was a limited recognition of the principle of separation of church and state. The latter was limited because Catholic schools continued to receive government subsidies and Catholic teaching was promoted in public schools. The Church also embraced the concept of social justice as it sought to relate the gospel to people's actual living circumstances on this earth as opposed to being concerned only with heavenly salvation. Church leaders also began to speak out on a variety of universal issues, such as freedom, equality, and women's rights. This era was marked by serious efforts to combat what the Church saw as alien influences on its traditional followers. The Church created organizations like Catholic Action to resist the influence of liberalism, Masonry, and Marxism. Catholic Action especially targeted university students and middle-class youth, who were seen as the likely future leaders.

The Vatican originally developed Catholic Action to combat socialism among working-class Europeans, but Pope Pius XI saw benefits in the Latin American incarnation. The organization was firmly rooted in such early social encyclicals as Rerum Novarum, but its success in Latin America was limited because the sectors to which it was targeted were so much smaller than in Western Europe. One exception to this pattern was in Chile, where the efforts of Catholic Action contributed to the formation of the Christian Democratic Party as a centrist alternative between Conservatives and the Socialists and Communists.

The Church also organized competing unions or "workers' circles" to directly compete with socialist- and communist-led unions, which were gaining significant influence in the Latin American working class. In this period, the rural poor were largely ignored. In another break with tradition, the Church hierarchy also sanctioned a much greater role for laypeople. These changes occurred very slowly over the early decades of the century, but the pace of change accelerated in the 1950s and 1960s as the Latin American Church increasingly shaped its teaching and practice of Catholicism to the particular conditions of Latin America.

The first plenary meeting of the Latin American Bishops' Conference (CELAM) occurred in 1955 in Rio de Janeiro. This conference would become influential in shaping the direction of the Church over the remainder of the century. The Latin American Church had been moving closer to greater acceptance of a role in social change and social justice, but the Second Vatican Council in Rome (1962–1965) accelerated the process. The documents produced by the council committed the Church to oppose governments that restricted religious or political freedoms and to acknowledge the significance of working for social justice in a variety of settings. During the early 1960s, the Catholic Church became involved in various movements that sought agrarian reform, expanded voting rights, and greater government spending on health and education. The Church also became the direct vehicle for improving people's lives through health training, literacy programs, and production cooperatives. Such programs contributed to a wider movement for nonviolent, reformist-oriented change.

In addition to promoting social justice, Vatican II articulated a more collegial model for the bishops. Rather than simply being subordinates of the pope, bishops came to be seen as peers who needed to work together to address concerns in their particular geographical area. Although the Vatican Council was an important turning point, socially conscious activity by the Church predated it in some places. In Brazil in the late 1950s, the Catholic hierarchy united with the government of reformer Juscelino Kubitschek to oppose the country's landowning oligarchy. The Church was instrumental in the formation of a development agency for northeast Brazil. Kubitschek used the Christian language of social justice to justify his reforms. It was in this era that Paulo Ereire, a Catholic educator in the northeast, developed a new method for teaching literacy. Catholic Action movements of students and workers organized in many places to promote a progressive agenda. The activities of Catholic Action led to discussion of the need for political action to change the basic structural inequalities that were limiting the effects of reform and social work. Before these discussions were fully consummated, the 1964 Brazilian military coup occurred, placing the Church and its activists in a more defensive mode and setting the stage for its next important contribution to Latin American political life. During the 1950s, bishops in Chile became involved in programs of land reform, literacy, and rural cooperatives. These efforts went beyond the Church's traditional social work and, as a result, brought the Church into conflict with the traditional elites.

# A New Political Role

From the 1960s through the 1980s, the Catholic Church became a focal point in many areas of resistance to military rule. In Brazil after the military coup of 1964, the Catholic hierarchy broke from its traditional role of absolute defender of the status quo. This stance in Brazil contrasted with the role that the Catholic Church had played during the Cuban Revolution. The Church had stood with the Batista dictatorship to the end, and few Catholic activists had been involved in the revolutionary movement. After the 26th of July Movement took power, the Church became the focal point of resistance to the new government and suffered significant repression, including the expulsion of foreign priests, which further debilitated an already weak Cuban Church. As a result of the Cuban Revolution, the Latin American hierarchy saw the potential danger to the future of the Church in an uncompromising stand toward revolution and radical reform. In societies under dictatorial rule, like Brazil, the Church was just about the only institution that could provide a haven against the overwhelming power of the state. Aided by the Church's organizational and financial resources, local parishes were able to provide material and legal assistance for those who were repressed. Agencies established by the Church monitored human rights violations and provided lawyers for those accused of political crimes. The Church also set up programs that distributed food and clothing to the families of those who were imprisoned, and upon release from jail political prisoners received aid from the Church in the form of counseling and employment assistance.

In many countries, Catholic clerics and laypeople became part of nonviolent resistance movements that argued for the restoration of civilian rule. Catholic leaders not only criticized specific military governments but also rejected authoritarianism as a method of rule, a significant break from the past. In the context of that ferment, CELAM met in Medellin, Colombia, in 1968. The conference came on the heels of the historic Second Vatican Council, which had turned the Church to a social justice vision and encouraged the regional conferences of bishops to look more closely at the specific challenges of their areas. The Latin American bishops picked up this challenge and in the process produced a document that has influenced the Church's work ever since. In 1967, Pope Paul VI's encyclical On the Development of Peoples focused on third-world development issues, containing a mild rebuke of the existing international economic order. Soon after the pope's encyclical, groups of bishops and priests began to lay out a program for Latin America in advance of the conference. A group of eighteen bishops, half from Brazil, went beyond the pope's statement while also drawing heavily upon it. They wrote approvingly of both revolution and socialism. In Argentina, Peru, Colombia, and Mexico, new groups of priests formed to press a progressive agenda as the gap between the rhetoric of the

Vatican Council and the reality of everyday life in Latin America became more obvious. They raised fundamental questions about the wealth of the Church, its historic support for the status quo, and the need for political action to achieve change. These groups did not speak for anywhere near a majority of the clergy, but their ideas shook up the complacency of the Church and dominated the discussion leading into the conference.

The task of those at CELAM who convened in Medellin, Colombia in 1968 was to apply the work of the Second Vatican Council to Latin America, but they met at a particularly significant moment in the history of the struggle for social change. The year had been one of dramatic developments—students had occupied universities in the United States, factory workers and students had united in France, Mexican police had repressed student demonstrations, and the Soviet invasion of Czechoslovakia had ended the drive for reform in that country. Combined with the force of Pope Paul's encyclical, these events pushed the bishops to produce a philosophy and plan of action that would be more progressive than its conservative past and probably more radical than most were actually prepared to carry out in practice. The documents emerging from the conference were striking in that such topics as justice, peace, and education received greater attention than did the traditionally dominant topics of pastoral work and Church structures.

At the most basic level, the bishops called for Catholics to be involved in the transformation of society. "Institutionalized violence" in the form of poverty, repression, and underdevelopment was decried and categorized as "sin." Such a categorization represented a significant expansion of the concept beyond its traditional meaning of individual transgression. They called for "sweeping, bold, urgent, and profoundly renovating changes." Revolutionaries were presented in a very positive light and not tainted with an identification with violence. The Church made a number of commitments that included the defense of human rights and the sharing of the conditions of the poor. The conference also raised the idea of neighborhood-based, lay-led ecclesial communities that would soon begin springing up all over Latin America. The term "liberation" was used often and placed primarily in human rather than spiritual terms. However, the bishops stopped short of endorsing the right of the oppressed to fight for their rights. Some feared being labeled as condoning violence, while others remained committed in a principled way to nonviolence. The conference came to grips with the realization that a new Catholic theology needed to emerge from the Latin American condition. Theology was no longer viewed as universal and could not simply be imported from Europe or North America. A key figure in the development of liberation theology, as it came to be called, was the Peruvian theologian Gustavo Gutiérrez. Gutiérrez had first used the term "liberation theology" shortly before Medellin, and soon afterward Gutiérrez and the Brazilian theologian Hugo Assmann published full-length books on the subject. From the early 1960s, Catholic theologians had begun to discuss the necessity of developing a specific Latin American theology, but they were slow to break with the long-standing tradition of a universal theology. Ultimately, the pressure of events resulted in the breakthrough works of Gutiérrez and Assmann. For decades Catholicism had struggled to be relevant to the modern world, but with liberation theology it sought to find in Christianity guidance in the struggle for change. As Berryman states, "it is a critique of how social structures treat the poor and how Christians and the church itself operate."

As Gill points out, a key element of liberation theology is the reliance on Marxist methodology. The theologians based their understanding of Latin American poverty on dependency theory, a perspective that views poverty and oppression in the third world as a direct consequence of the world capitalist economy dominated by Western Europe and the United States. Some theologians, such as Ernesto Cardenal of Nicaragua, also embraced the Marxist idea of class struggle and from that justified participation in revolutionary movements. In the wake of the 1968 CELAM conference, Catholic clergy and laypeople throughout Latin America increasingly took up the Church's call for greater attention to matters of social justice and political involvement. Thousands of Catholic nuns and priests moved out of traditional convents and religious houses and into poor neighborhoods, where they shared the difficult living conditions of the poor. Part of the motivation was to make the Church more relevant to its majority poor constituency. Traditionally, the Church had devoted a great proportion of its time and resources to the middle and upper classes and had sustained itself in significant measure through the tuition payments it received to educate the sons and daughters of the wealthy. The move to the poor neighborhoods was seen by those who did it as a means to better carry out their religious vocation. Although the moves did involve some personal hardship, the nuns and priests who engaged in this new form of pastoral work were freer than their counterparts who remained in traditional roles as parish priests and educators.

Most of the clergy who went into the poor neighborhoods adopted the educational approach of the Brazilian educator Paulo Freire, called *conáentizaáón* (consciousness-raising), detailed in his classic work *Pedagogy of the Oppressed*. Rather than imparting their wisdom to the people in the neighborhoods, the clergy saw their role as drawing out conclusions through group reflection. These discussions were often carried out in what became known as ecclesial-based communities, meetings in homes to read and discuss the scriptures with the purpose of drawing conclusions about their relevance to everyday life. Those leading the discussions, religious or lay, urged people to search for the underlying causes of their poor situation. In rural areas, these discussions would often move from immediate problems to matters such as land ownership and class structures. Similar developments occurred in urban settings, where people would seek to understand the root cause of poor sanitation or poor public transportation in their neighborhoods. More often than not, the consciousness-raising led to the formation of groups that had a variety of purposes—soup kitchens, peasant associations, cooperatives, and so forth. Some were primarily self-helping in their focus, while others were oriented more toward political action. Self-help activities included programs to teach job skills or to serve as Alcoholics Anonymous centers. In Brazil, the groups formed an important core of the resistance to military rule at a time in the 1970s when few other outlets for political opposition existed. Political activities ranged from voter registration to serving as centers for revolutionary organizing in Nicaragua and El Salvador.

# Impact of Liberation Theology

The impact of liberation theology and the work of nuns, priests, and laypeople in advancing an agenda for social change was considerable, but it never succeeded in fully transforming the historic role of the Church as a bastion of the status quo in Latin America. Within five years of the historic conference at Medellin, conservative Latin American bishops, especially in Brazil and Mexico, began a systematic counterattack against liberation theology. As the first step in their strategy, they took control of CELAM, the very organization that had initiated the progressive changes. Their counterattack was not initially a frontal assault. For example, no attempt was made to repeal the documents that were passed in Colombia. As the Argentine generals took power in 1976 and carried out the dirty war, they largely retained the support of the Catholic hierarchy. The Conservatives were given a large lift with the ascension of Pope John Paul II in 1978. John Paul had been archbishop of Kraków, Poland, and a staunch anticommunist. It was natural that he would side strongly with those in the Latin American Church who saw themselves as working against the influences of Marxism within the Church. The papacy's assault on liberation theology proceeded on many fronts during the 1980s. In 1984, the Vatican issued a document that strongly criticized liberation theology; in the same time period, Rome was successful in marginalizing the influential Brazilian theologian Leonardo Boff. The revolutionary government in Nicaragua, which contained several priests sympathetic to liberation theology, was singled out for harsh criticism during a papal visit in 1983. Those priests in the Nicaraguan government were prevented from carrying out their religious duties. However, the papacy's strongest move against liberation theology may have been its appointment of new bishops who would hold steadfastly to Rome's conservative stance. Archbishop Helder Camera of Recife, Brazil, one of the region's harshest critics of military rule and a strong proponent of the strategy of working with the poor, was replaced by a conservative, who moved almost immediately to reverse the fruits of Camera's work. In Cuernavaca, Mexico, there was a high concentration of Christian base communities as a result of the work of Bishop Sergio Méndez Arceo, but when he retired in the late 1980s the Vatican appointed a conservative to replace him and the grassroots work suffered. Overall, the counterattack of the conservative forces in the Church was directly related to the growing strength of the left and the high stakes that were involved. In Brazil, the Workers' Party (PT) was on the verge of winning the national presidency in the late 1980s, and only a united front of all the conservative forces succeeded in defeating their candidate, Luiz Inácio da Silva, in the 1989 election. In Central America throughout the 1980s, revolutionary forces were on the upswing in Nicaragua, El Salvador, and Guatemala. The revolutionary shock waves were felt as far north as Mexico. In that context, the papacy weighed in on the side of the anticommunist forces, a decision that dovetailed with the foreign policy initiatives of the United States. Progressive Church forces came to be seen as part of a revolutionary upsurge that had to be suppressed.

The diminishing impact of liberation theology in the 1990s cannot be blamed exclusively on the counterattack by the Vatican. Part of the failure of liberation theology to fully transform the Church lies within the movement itself. Liberation theology never really succeeded in becoming a mass movement within the Church. Fewer than 10 percent of the nuns and priests actually moved into communities to work directly with the poor. Christian base communities (CEBs) did arise in significant numbers in some select places, such as in Brazil during the military government in the 1970s, but they never came close to their goal of transforming the manner in which the Church functioned. In Brazil, close to 100,000 CEBs developed by the mid-1980s, but that accounted for only about 2.5 percent of the Catholic population. Significant lay leadership was involved in the CEBs, but most remained dependent on the leadership of clergy, which limited the CEBs' ability to grow into a mass movement. However, one very positive result of the work of the CEBs was a significant increase in the proportion of women in leadership roles in comparison to the past. The CEBs also gave the Catholic Church a significant presence in working-class neighborhoods that had been previously ignored. The decline of liberation theology, acknowledged by Gutiérez in 1994, was also the result of a changing political climate. Born in the era of 1960s revolutionary idealism, liberation theology has declined with the assault on the progressive agenda marked by the collapse of Eastern European socialism and the defeat of the Sandinista revolutionary project in Nicaragua. These setbacks led many within the progressive Church community to scale back their short-term expectations for dramatic social change and to work for more reformist goals within the existing system. The restoration of democratic systems throughout the region in the 1980s facilitated this change in strategy.

The horizons of the reformers may have been limited by world events and their own shortcomings, but their political legacy has not been unimportant. In several key situations in the 1980s, progressive Roman Catholic bishops played an important political role as mediators. In El Salvador, Archbishop Arturo Rivera y Damas, who assumed the leadership of the Church after the military assassinated outspoken Archbishop Oscar Romero, made numerous attempts to bring an end to that country's devastating civil war. The military initially rejected such appeals as treason, but the archbishop's efforts eventually contributed to the 1992 peace agreement. The Guatemalan bishops played a similar role against the wishes of the military to help broker the eventual agreement in that country that ended a forty-year civil war in 1997. Chilean bishops were also instrumental in bringing about a negotiated end to the Pinochet regime. In the conflict in Chiapas in the 1990s, Bishop Samuel Ruiz played an important role as a mediator between the Mexican government and the Zapatistas. During the 1970s and 1980s, scores of human rights monitoring organizations were formed in the region, often with the protection and funding of the Church. Under different political circumstances, most of these organizations are now independent of the Church, but their work continues; they represent an important legacy of the movement for liberation theology. A focus on liberation theology alone tends to miss an important impact that the Catholic Church continues to have on the question of reproductive rights and the rights of sexual minorities. Until the recent legalization of abortion in Uruguay Cuba had been the only country in the region where the procedure was not illegal. Most governments of the left including Venezuela and Nicaragua chose not to challenge the position of the Roman Catholic Church despite outcry from advocates of women's rights. Political pressure has been building in many countries to allow abortion at least in limited circumstances, but continued Church opposition makes widespread legalization unlikely in the near future. As discussed in the previous chapter, gay, lesbian, and transgender rights are making progress in Latin America in recent years, but the Catholic Church hierarchy is remaining firm in opposition to gay marriage while speaking out against homophobia. The opposition of the Catholic Church together with that of the evangelicals may well keep gay marriage limited in the region for the foreseeable future.

It is too early to assess the impact that Pope Francis will have on the direction of the Catholic Church in Latin American social and political affairs, but there are some definitive hints that come from his tenure as the leader of the church in Argentina. What is clear from his work in Argentina has been his humility, his concern for the poor, and his commitment to dialogue across social, political, and religious divisions. That stance is giving support to those priests, nuns, and laypersons within Latin America that have advocated and worked for the poor and the marginalized in the spirit of the 1968 document of liberation theology. Pope Francis has made clear that the Church's teachings on sexuality will not change but that its broader message of social justice should take center stage. Because more conservative elements within the Latin American church and worldwide will push back against that emphasis, it is not yet clear whether the renewed emphasis on social justice will take hold in the wake of the two profoundly conservative popes that preceded Francis.

## Protestantism and Pentecostalism

The most important development in the Latin American religious sector in the last forty years is the remarkable growth of Protestantism, especially Pentecostalism. Fewer than twenty years ago, these groups made up no more than 2 to 3 percent of the population, but today they have reached the significant level of 15 percent continent-wide, with a much greater presence in some countries, such as Guatemala, Brazil, and Colombia. It also should be pointed out that a focus on absolute numbers is misleading because, in comparison to those who identify themselves as Catholic, the evangelicals tend to be more active in church life. Pentecostal churches were founded mostly in the early part of the twentieth century. They are often connected to Charles Parham's spiritual revival in Topeka, Kansas, in 1901 and a subsequent revival in Los Angeles in 1906. From those revivals came churches such as the Assemblies of God, the Church of God, and the Church of God in Christ.

It is important to not place any single label on the Pentecostal churches, which are quite diverse in both their religious and political practices. Some, such as the Universal Church and the Deus e Amor Church, are not built around fixed church structures but instead draw followers to tents and warehouses where the emphasis is on singing and spiritual healing. Their services are dramatic, with considerable moaning, screaming, and crawling on hands and knees. The object of the services is to drive out the demons that have "infected" the members. These churches also have a considerable presence on the radio, with hundreds of hours of programming in countries such as Brazil. The Universal Church tends to draw a middle-class constituency, while the Deus e Amor Church followers are overwhelmingly poor. The largest single Pentecostal group in Latin America is the Assemblies of God, who have 8 to 12 million followers and 35,000 churches in Brazil alone. In contrast to lack of institutionalism in the previously discussed evangelicals, the Assemblies of God, with their origins in North America, are highly organized and have considerable financial resources. Although the majority of their members are very poor, their relative wealth belies their North American ties.

Berryman has attributed the appeal of the Pentecostals to a simple message of love and prayer that provides community and a sense of self-respect. Another basis of the success of the movement among the region's poorest citizens is that most evangelical ministers come from the same social class as their congregants. In contrast, most Catholic priests, even those who espouse liberation theology, come from middle- and upper-class backgrounds. It is also very difficult to characterize the political impact of the evangelical movement. Unquestionably, some churches, such as the Word of God movement in Guatemala, have directly promoted right-wing politics through the born-again leader General José Efraín Rios Montt, who carried out massive repression as president in the early 1980s. Later Jorge Serrano based his Guatemalan presidential campaign on evangelical votes, and conservative Alberto Fujimori reached out to evangelicals in his 1990 run for the presidency in Peru. Evangelical representatives are an important voting bloc in the Brazilian congress and have in 2016 been credited with backing conservative candidates, winning many major municipal elections. However, beyond these examples, the evangelicals have not really developed anything close to a clear, coherent political message. Not all evangelicals are politically conservative. The Brazilian PT has many evangelicals within its ranks, including one of its congressional leaders, Benedita da Silva, an active member of the Assemblies of God. Many Pentecostals consciously reject any significant involvement in politics, but the overall political thrust of the movement seems to serve as a barrier to progressive political movements.

## African-Inspired Religions

After indigenous religion, Catholicism, and Protestantism, the fourth religious tradition in Latin America is that of African-inspired religion. This religious trend is present to some degree throughout the continent but is especially prevalent in countries such as Cuba, Haiti, Brazil, and Puerto Rico where millions of slaves were imported from West Africa. The Africans brought their spiritual beliefs with them and have maintained them for more than three centuries in the face of efforts by both political and religious authorities to marginalize them. In some instances, the well-developed Yoruba religion was transferred to the New World without significant modification (Santería in Cuba and Puerto Rico and Candomblé in Brazil). In other instances, the African beliefs have commingled with Catholic and Protestant spirituality to form a hybrid. Generally speaking, those practicing these religious traditions believe that the dead continue to live and communicate with the world through a variety of means. They believe that these spirits influence the manner in which the living exist, sometimes for good and other times for evil. A series of deities, or Orishas, are also prominent in the Yoruba-based religions.

One of the strongest movements is the voodoo of Haiti, which developed among the slave population and was influential in the abolitionist and independence movements at the end of the eighteenth century. It also would later become a tool of the Duvalier dictatorships from the 1950s to the 1980s. Voodoo spirits are called loas, and the objective of the religion is to connect the living with the loas. The spirits' help is sought to cure ailments and to provide advice for solving daily problems. Priests, called hougans, facilitate the connection between the spiritual world and the followers of voodoo. The priests have an authority that can be based on either their charisma or the patrimony of a local political or military leader.

Following an instrumental role in achieving Haitian independence in 1804, the voodoo movement was largely driven underground for the next 150 years at the behest of the country's mulatto and Catholic elite. However, a strong underground

Shrine to the Black Virgin in Regia, outskirts of Havana. Type and placement of candles also suggest the shrine is worshipped by practitioners of Santería, who frequent the church along with the Catholic parishioners. *(Photo by Patrice Olsen)*

network of priests and their followers was constructed in Haiti's poorest communities, and the religious beliefs were passed on from generation to generation. Then, in the late 1950s, these local voodoo organizations became the power base for the political movement of François Duvalier, who won the 1957 elections and later established a harsh dictatorial rule that was eventually passed on to his son. The feared Tonton Macoute militias organized by Duvalier for use against his political foes came from his voodoo power base. The younger Duvalier was driven from power in the mid-1980s, but voodoo retains a strong spiritual following in contemporary Haiti without the politicization that it had during the Duvalier period.

A lesser-known but equally important African-based movement called Santería has a very important presence in contemporary Cuba and Puerto Rico. Like voodoo, Santería has its origins in the African slaves brought to Cuba to harvest sugar cane. Santería came from the Yoruba people of what is today Nigeria. Like voodoo, Santería provided a link to their African past and some respite from the brutality of slavery. As in Haiti, the bonds of the Santería communities helped pave the way for independence and abolitionist movements that developed in the latter part of the nineteenth century in Cuba. However, in contrast to voodoo, Santería, out of an instinct for survival in strongly Catholic Cuba, often linked its rituals and spirits to those of the Roman Catholic Church. The key figures of the Catholic Church, such as Jesus and various saints, were masked as Yoruba deities. The Santeristas also timed their main festivals according to those of the Catholic Church, such as Easter and Christmas. Such accommodation simply reflected the relationship of forces that existed in Cuba and Puerto Rico during the long years of Spanish and Catholic rule. However, it was a very successful accommodation because it allowed the spiritual beliefs of the Afro-Cuban population to survive into the twentieth century. The movement went into decline with the advent of the revolutionary government in Cuba in 1959 but underwent a revival in the 1990s with the more tolerant attitude toward religion by the government and is today probably the dominant religious practice in Cuba.

Brazil is another country where African-based religious movements have a significant following. There are two major variants in the country. Umbanda shares the practice with Santería of pairing its deities with those of the Catholic Church. Similar to voodoo and Santería, Umbanda's followers seek advice from the spirits on problems of everyday life. There are many Umbanda centers, especially in Rio de Janeiro, which hold full schedules of cultural activities alongside exercise programs and social services. The intermediaries between the people and the spirits, called mediums, often obtain a large personal following. Even more akin to Santería is Candomblé, also brought by slaves from the Yoruba region of West Africa. Like Santería, it sometimes links its deities with those of the Catholic religion. Candomblé generally appeals more to the poor. The spirits are also less connected to practical advice and more to pageants of dancing and eating. The movements in Brazil can be credited with helping the poor maintain their cultural identity in the face of the dominant white and Catholic culture and in the process contributed to the success of Afro-descendant political movements.

## Judaism

Any discussion of religion in Latin America should make mention of the region's Jews. They are not large in number, probably under 500,000 in the region as a whole, with the largest communities in Argentina (240,000), Brazil (100,000), and Mexico (35,000). Most Jews who live in Latin America came as part of nineteenth- and twentieth-century immigration, but they have faced persistent anti-Semitism and marginalization that dates to the time of the conquest.

By the fifteenth century, Jews had lived in Spain for a thousand years. Always a minority, the Jews were often caught in the battle between Catholicism and Islam and manipulated by both. Over the 1,000 years, periods of great Jewish contribution to Spanish life alternated with periods of persecution and forced conversion. Their situation worsened after 1391 when pogroms broke out, first in Seville and then throughout Spain. In 1492, the Spanish crown expelled the Jews from Spain and soon established a series of laws that excluded all Jews, even those who had converted to Catholicism, from Spanish public life. Anyone who had any Jewish or Moorish "blood" was excluded from positions in the professions, the Church, the military, and the government. This indelible labeling of those with Jewish ancestry, converted or not, led to the widespread labeling of Jews as a "race," a perspective that was imported to Latin America and continues to the present time.

The exclusion of Jews from Spain was extended to Spanish lands in the Americas. In her first instruction to the governor of Hispaniola, Queen Isabella forbade Jews and "new Christians" (as the converts were called) from settling in the Indies. This legal prohibition continued throughout Spanish rule into the nineteenth century. Many new Christians and some Jews did succeed in settling in the Western Hemisphere by subverting the law. However, the local missionaries laid the groundwork for long-term anti-Semitism among the native population. Jews were singled out as the tormentors and killers of Christ. Primary among the charges leveled against Jews was subversion. Popular opinion blamed converted Jews for the Dutch defeat of the Portuguese in Brazil in 1630. It was alleged that the new Christians assisted the invaders because they hoped to reestablish Judaism under more tolerant Dutch rule. The stereotype of Jews as subversives persists in Argentina, the country with the largest Jewish population. The generals who carried out Argentina's Dirty War in the 1970s attacked Jews as subversives and Marxists. Their most famous target was the Jewish journalist Jacobo Timmerman, but the campaign revived anti-Semitism in contemporary Latin America.

## Conclusion

In contemporary Latin America, the impact of religion on society is more complex than ever before. The absolute hold of Catholicism on the region is now part of history, and, despite the Church's attempts to remake itself in the last fifty years, there will likely be no return to its former dominance. Protestantism has made great strides in recent years, especially with the rapid growth of evangelical sects.

However, it should be remembered that these groups claim the allegiance of less than one in five Latin Americans. The political impact of the rapid growth of Protestantism is difficult to measure but seems to be trending in a conservative direction or simply discouraging of any involvement in politics. Although generally critical of liberation theology, the evangelicals have largely failed to develop their own strategy for confronting the region's ongoing social ills. That failure may yet derail the long-term growth of the evangelical movement as a coherent and influential political force.

It would seem that the work of liberation theology begun in the 1960s has run its course, but that does not mean that its future impact will be marginal. The Catholic Church's commitment to social justice seems to have been firmly established. Pope John Paul's visit to Mexico in early 1999 underscored this fact. Twenty years earlier, on his first visit to Mexico, he spoke harshly of liberation theology and emphasized his opposition to communism of any kind. That message inevitably bolstered the status quo and, by implication, was pro-capitalist. On the 1999 visit, the pope's message was strikingly different. In reference to the contemporary emphasis on neoliberalism and free markets, he said, "The human race is facing forms of slavery which are new and more subtle than those of the past." The pope called on both governments and international organizations to carry out plans aimed at third-world debt relief and wealth redistribution. Some called this perspective "post-liberation theology." Pope John Paul passed from the scene, and his successor, Benedict, while conservative theologically, continued the Church's strong impetus for social justice. The wave of center-left governments in the region over the last twenty years resonate well with the Church's message of social justice and often work closely with Church leaders. Emblematic of this connection is the Ecuadoran president Rafael Correa, whose progressive politics are firmly rooted in Catholic social teaching. The election of Pope Francis, the first Jesuit pope, the first pope from the Americas, and the first pope from the Southern Hemisphere has deepened the Catholic connection to the continent's identification with progressive social change and the commitment to political democracy.

# Bibliography

Berryman, Phillip. *Religion in the Megacity: Catholic and Protestant Portraits from Latin America.* Maryknoll, NY: Orbis, 1996.

Berryman, Phillip. *Stubborn Hope: Religion, Politics, and Revolution in Central America.* Maryknoll, NY: Orbis, 1994.

Betances, Emelio. *The Catholic Church and Power Politics in Latin America.* Lanham, MD: Rowman & Littlefield, 2007.

Cleary, Edward, and Hannah Stewart-Gambino. *Power, Politics, and Pentecostals in Latin America.* Boulder, CO: Westview, 1997.

Cleary, Edward, and Timothy Steigenga, eds. *Resurgent Voices in Latin America: Indigenous Peoples, Political Mobilization, and Religious Change.* Piscataway, NJ: Rutgers University Press, 2004.

Davis, Darien. *Beyond Slavery: The Multilayered Legacy of Africans in Latin America and the Caribbean.* Lanham, MD: Rowman & Littlefield, 2006.

de Castro, Christina Maria. *The Construction of Muslim Identities in Contemporary Brazil.* Lanham, MD: Rowman & Littlefield, 2013.

Elkin, Judith Larkin. *The Jews of Latin America.* 3d ed. Boulder, CO: Lynne Reinner, 2014.

Gill, Anthony. *Rendering unto Caesar: The Catholic Church and State in Latin America*. Chicago: Chicago University Press, 1998.

Hess, David. *Samba in the Night: Spiritism in Brazil*. New York: Columbia University Press, 1994.

Languerre, Michael S. *Voodoo and Politics in Haiti*. New York: St. Martin's, 1989.

Levine, Daniel. *Politics, Religion, and Society in Latin America*. Boulder, CO: Lynne Reinner, 2012.

Matibag, Eugenio. *Afro-Cuban Religious Experience: Cultural Reflections in Narrative*. Gainesville: University Press of Florida, 2004.

Preire, Paulo. *Pedagogy of the Oppressed*. New York: Herder and Herder, 1970.

Ramirez, Daniel. *Migrating Faith: Pentecostalism in the United States and Mexico*. Chapel Hill: University of North Carolina Press, 2015.

Rieger, Joerg, ed. *Across Borders: Latin Perspectives in the Americas Reshaping Religion, Theology, and Life*. Lanham, MD: Lexington, 2013.

Selka, Stephen. *Religion and the Politics of Ethnic Identity in Bahia, Brazil*. Tallahassee: University Press of Florida Press, 2009.

## FILMS AND VIDEOS

*Americas 6, Miracles Are Not Enough*. United States, 1993.

*Prom Faith to Action in Brazil*. United States, 1984.

*Onward Christian Soldiers*. United States, 1985.

*Remembering Romero*. United States, 1992.

# SEVEN

# The Political Economy of Latin America

## On Economics and Political Economy

In Latin America, one cannot fully understand the political game without understanding its economic underpinnings. The initial encounter between the Old World and the Americas resulted from Iberian desire for the economic advantage gained from new trade routes to the East Indies. From the onset, the Americas were an economic enterprise for European colonizers; subsequently, local elites have used the region for their gain. Since the conquest, the economic good of the masses has frequently been sacrificed for the enrichment of foreign and domestic interests. Political power and economic power have generally reinforced each other in Latin America. Those with the wealth have written the political rules. Thus, an understanding of the economics of the region enriches our understanding of its politics, and vice versa.

We note that the discipline of economics studies how goods and services are produced, distributed, and consumed. It has its immediate origins in the eighteenth century in works such as Adam Smith's *An Inquiry into the Nature and Causes of the Wealth of Nations* (1776). In more recent times, economists—like political scientists— often have tried to separate the study of politics and economics. Yet, this was not the original intent of Smith, his fellow political economist David Ricardo, or a subsequent student of political economy, Karl Marx. Indeed, if we go back to the original writings of Adam Smith and David Ricardo, we find that they preferred the concept of "political economy" because such an approach took into account the complexity and unity of political and economic phenomena.

Modern students of political economy thus believe that an approach that encompasses both politics and economics is much more effective in studying how scarce resources are allocated and how political values and political power affect that allocation. Given the considerable concentration and interconnection of economic and political power in Latin America, a more comprehensive approach would seem in order.

When Adam Smith was writing in the late 1700s, the dominant economic system for Great Britain, Spain, Portugal, and the American colonies was mercantilism, in which the state implemented a policy of increasing exports and acquiring bullion and raw materials through carefully restricted commerce. This was a politically directed policy that used state control of trade and colonization. The government exercised considerable control by regulating production, directing foreign trade and tariffs, and exploiting commerce, particularly with a European nation's colonies. Thus, Smith and Ricardo realized the fundamental role of the state and the political power that defined the policymaking process. Indeed, they hoped to induce the state to exert less control over economic interactions. As the discipline of economics evolved over the years, the difficulty in understanding economic phenomena led some commentators to refer to economics as the "dismal science." Yet, by looking at economics and politics jointly and taking into consideration historical context and sociological factors, a more comprehensive approach to understanding resource and power allocation in different nations can be achieved. This is very much the case in Latin America. Such an approach will be employed in this text.

## The Latin American Economy

As in the rest of the world, economies in the Americas began as small, local spheres that were isolated from events outside their valley, village, or small region. As time and productive forces progressed, this initial isolation slowly began to break down in many regions. Civilizations such as the Olmec in eastern Mexico (1500-400 B.C.E.), the early Maya (1500 B.C.E.–900 C.E.), and the Mochica (400–1000 C.E.) in northern Peru appeared and began to bring the hitherto isolated population clusters together. As the Aztec and Incan Empires grew, trade and commerce over much wider regions developed. Such economic intercourse was, however, limited to regions and did not extend far beyond the actual political entities. Latin America's integration into the world economy only began when the Europeans arrived. However, even after centuries, one could still find isolated villages and valleys that were only marginally integrated into the world economy. During colonial times and well into the twentieth century, haciendas were often near self-contained economic units with minimal contact with the outside, save the sale of one or two cash crops for national consumption or export to Europe or North America. Indeed, a few native Amazonian groups, such as the Yanomami, were being integrated into the world economy only as the twentieth century ended.

A substantial sector of agriculture made up of Native American and other subsistence farmers who used the bulk of their production to feed themselves and their families was only slowly integrated into the international system. These farmers' growing need for goods that they could not produce themselves led to their gradual integration into the national and international economy as they sold small amounts of a cash crop, handicraft, or their labor to landowners, plantations, or tourist enterprises. Yet, as the sad history of the Yanomami in recent times suggests, integration into the international economic system did not necessarily benefit those who were losing their isolation. Indeed, as their consumption and nutritional patterns changed, they were more likely to suffer from malnutrition.

Latin America was integrated into the world economy after 1500. Due to improvements in navigation and seafaring, Portugal and Spain established world trade routes that circumnavigated Africa and eventually came to include the

Americas. From Columbus's second voyage on, the Americas were used to extract wealth for European powers—beginning with gold and silver bullion and slaves. As suggested previously, a pattern was soon established whereby land, people, and resources were used to benefit nations outside the region and for the advantage of the local European or mostly European elite, rather than the native masses. As gold and silver stocks were eventually depleted, new crops and minerals were found to export to Europe and other industrializing areas such as the United States. Indigo, cacao, brazilwood, and sugar were exported in colonial times, as were rubber, nitrates, copper, and tin in the nineteenth century and coffee, grains, beef, bananas, and petroleum in the twentieth century.

As time passed, Western and Western-trained economists came to believe in the economic doctrine of comparative advantage, whereby a country that is especially well endowed by climate, resources, soil, or labor can produce a product comparatively better and more efficiently than any other. Coffee exports from Colombia are an example. By specializing in the production of that product and trading it in the international market for products that other countries could produce better and more cheaply because of their comparative advantage, the producing country can maximize revenues in world trade. That is, Colombia currently produces coffee cheaply and uses the money from the sales of the coffee to buy, for example, computers from Japan, where these products are produced best and most cheaply. This view holds that it would be expensive, inefficient, and all but impossible for Japan to produce coffee and difficult and costly for Colombia to produce computers. Both countries, it is argued, gain when they specialize in the production of one or a few products that they are best able to produce. After World War II, the Latin American experience with international trade and the pioneering work of the Economic Commission for Latin America (ECLA) challenged this view. However, before this view is explored, a more thorough explanation of the production and export of commodities will be offered.

After 1500, Latin America became tied to the Western economic system that had become the basis for the international economic system in two distinct ways: First, products were exported according to the demands of the market and development in Europe, and, second, the region became an outlet for European products. Much like the old South in the United States, most of the local economy revolved around the production of one crop and most of the infrastructure was geared to gathering that commodity to ports where it could be loaded on boats and shipped (see Table 13). As cotton was king in the antebellum South, so sugar was king in northern Brazil, Cuba, the Dominican Republic, Haiti, and much of the rest of the Caribbean. Coffee and bananas became the prime export crop in Central America and Colombia. Economies also revolved around the extraction and export of minerals: copper in Chile, tin in Bolivia, and oil in Venezuela. Luxury goods for the landowning elite or for mine owners came from the advanced industrialized areas, as did the tools and most of the finished products that could not be made by the local blacksmith or carpenter.

During colonial times, manufacturing was often outlawed (in 1785 all manufacturing was prohibited in Brazil) and was usually discouraged. Thus, most of the finished products came from outside. Indeed, such practice was consistent with the

**TABLE 13.** Major Exports of Latin American Countries (2003–2014)

| Country | Commodity | 2003 | 2004 | 2005 | 2006 | 2007 | 2008 | 2009 | 2010 | 2011 | 2012 | 2013 | 2014 |
|---|---|---|---|---|---|---|---|---|---|---|---|---|---|
| Argentina | oil seed cake and meal and other vegetable oil residues | 11.2 | 10.7 | 9.7 | 9.7 | 10.6 | 10.5 | 14.9 | 12.5 | 12.3 | 13.6 | 14.4 | 18.0 |
| | Lorries and trucks, including ambulances, etc. | ... | ... | 2.7 | 3.0 | 3.1 | 2.7 | 2.7 | 3.7 | 4.3 | 4.9 | 5.5 | 5.8 |
| | soya beans | 6.2 | 5.1 | 5.7 | 3.9 | 6.2 | 6.6 | 3.1 | 7.5 | 6.7 | 4.1 | 5.5 | 5.7 |
| | soya bean oil | 7.0 | 6.8 | 5.6 | 6.1 | 8.0 | 7.1 | 6.0 | 6.3 | 6.4 | 5.5 | 5.5 | 5.2 |
| Bolivia | natural gas | 24.3 | 28.1 | 36.2 | 40.7 | 42.4 | 46.7 | 38.0 | 40.7 | 43.8 | 51.0 | 52.4 | 52.3 |
| | oil seed cake and meal and other vegetable oil residues | 13.4 | 12.0 | 7.7 | 5.4 | 5.2 | 4.3 | 6.8 | 5.0 | 4.4 | 5.0 | 5.5 | 6.0 |
| | ores and concentrates of zinc | 7.8 | 6.8 | 7.3 | 13.4 | 14.8 | 10.9 | 13.3 | 13.0 | 10.7 | 6.9 | 6.5 | 8.5 |
| | ores and concentrates of silver | 4.5 | 4.0 | 3.2 | 4.0 | 4.6 | 7.5 | 11.5 | 10.0 | 12.3 | 9.4 | 7.4 | 6.3 |
| | crude petroleum | 6.1 | 7.7 | 11.4 | 8.4 | 5.7 | 4.6 | 1.5 | 2.7 | 2.6 | 3.7 | 4.4 | 5.1 |
| Brazil | iron ore and concentrates | 4.7 | 4.9 | 6.2 | 6.5 | 6.6 | 8.4 | 8.7 | 14.8 | 16.5 | 12.9 | 13.6 | 11.6 |
| | soya beans | 5.9 | 5.6 | 4.5 | 4.1 | 4.2 | 5.6 | 7.5 | 5.6 | 6.4 | 7.2 | 9.5 | 10.4 |
| | crude petroleum | 2.9 | 2.6 | 3.5 | 5.0 | 5.6 | 6.9 | 6.2 | 8.3 | 8.5 | 8.5 | 5.4 | 7.3 |
| Chile | refined copper including remelted ores and concentrates of copper | 21.9 | 26.6 | 25.6 | 30.5 | 30.3 | 30.2 | 31.6 | 34.1 | 32.7 | 28.8 | 25.0 | 24.0 |
| | ores and concentrates of copper | 12.9 | 16.8 | 18.4 | 21.2 | 21.6 | 15.4 | 18.1 | 19.6 | 18.2 | 20.9 | 22.4 | 22.3 |
| Colombia | crude petroleum | 19.8 | 18.5 | 19.6 | 19.2 | 19.0 | 25.4 | 25.7 | 35.5 | 42.5 | 46.7 | 48.9 | 48.4 |
| | coal | 11.1 | 10.9 | 11.9 | 11.9 | 11.4 | 12.6 | 16.8 | 14.6 | 14.5 | 12.8 | 11.1 | 12.1 |
| Costa Rica | thermionic valves and tubes, transistors, etc. | ... | 3.4 | 11.4 | 17.0 | 15.1 | 11.0 | 7.6 | 10.5 | 18.7 | 18.8 | 21.0 | ... |
| | medical instruments | 8.0 | 8.0 | 7.0 | 8.2 | 7.3 | 6.3 | 5.9 | 8.0 | 7.9 | 8.8 | 9.8 | ... |
| | other fresh fruit | 3.5 | 4.4 | 4.7 | 6.1 | 5.5 | 6.0 | 5.1 | 7.6 | 7.1 | 7.1 | 7.3 | ... |
| | fresh banana including plantains | 9.7 | 9.4 | 6.9 | 9.0 | 7.7 | 7.3 | 5.1 | 7.8 | 7.1 | 6.3 | 6.8 | ... |
| Cuba | cigars and cheroots | 11.7 | 8.7 | 9.8 | 7.2 | ... | ... | ... | ... | ... | ... | ... | ... |
| | raw sugar, beets & cane | 16.7 | 11.5 | 7.1 | ... | ... | ... | ... | ... | ... | ... | ... | ... |
| | medicaments | 1.7 | 6.0 | 9.4 | 7.4 | ... | ... | ... | ... | ... | ... | ... | ... |
| Dominican Republic | | | | | | | | | | | | | |
| Ecuador | crude petroleum | 39.4 | 51.3 | 54.8 | 54.6 | 54.1 | 56.4 | 45.5 | 51.4 | 53.1 | 54.2 | 54.8 | 52.3 |
| | fresh banana including plantains | 18.2 | 13.5 | 11.0 | 9.6 | 9.5 | 8.8 | 14.5 | 11.7 | 10.1 | 8.9 | 9.5 | 10.5 |
| | crustacea and mollusks, fresh chilled, salted, dried | 4.6 | 4.3 | 4.6 | 4.7 | 4.4 | 3.8 | 4.8 | 4.9 | 5.3 | 5.5 | 7.3 | 10.4 |
| | coffee, green or roasted | 3.4 | 3.7 | 4.8 | 5.1 | 4.7 | 5.6 | 6.1 | 4.8 | 8.9 | 5.7 | 4.3 | 2.1 |
| El Salvador | under garments (knitted or crocheted) | 1.5 | ... | 28.2 | 25.3 | 24.0 | 25.2 | 21.2 | 21.5 | 18.9 | 19.3 | 19.5 | 19.2 |
| | over garments (knitted or crocheted) | ... | ... | 12.6 | 11.2 | 10.2 | 7.3 | 9.1 | 9.3 | 8.6 | 8.6 | 9.9 | 10.9 |
| | articles of artificial plastic materials | 1.2 | 1.5 | 2.2 | 2.4 | 2.9 | 3.3 | 3.8 | 4.1 | 4.0 | 4.3 | 4.4 | 4.9 |

(continued)

**TABLE 13.** Major Exports of Latin American Countries (2003–2014) (*continued*)

| Country | Commodity | 2003 | 2004 | 2005 | 2006 | 2007 | 2008 | 2009 | 2010 | 2011 | 2012 | 2013 | 2014 |
|---|---|---|---|---|---|---|---|---|---|---|---|---|---|
| Guatemala | coffee, green or roasted | 11.4 | 11.2 | 8.6 | 14.5 | 8.4 | 8.4 | 8.1 | 8.4 | 10.5 | 9.5 | 7.1 | 6.1 |
| | fresh banana including plantains | 9.0 | 8.5 | 4.9 | 7.3 | 4.7 | 4.4 | 6.1 | 4.6 | 4.7 | 6.1 | 6.5 | 6.6 |
| | raw sugar, beets & cane | 8.1 | 6.4 | 4.4 | 9.3 | 5.2 | 4.9 | 7.0 | 8.6 | 6.4 | 7.8 | 9.4 | 8.7 |
| Haiti | | ... | ... | ... | ... | ... | ... | ... | ... | ... | ... | ... | ... |
| Honduras | coffee, green or roasted | 19.1 | 22.2 | 26.1 | 21.4 | 21.4 | 21.1 | 23.2 | 38.1 | 29.8 | ... | ... | ... |
| | insulated wire and cable | ... | ... | ... | 14.0 | 9.8 | ... | 5.4 | 5.0 | 5.1 | 11.1 | ... | ... |
| Mexico | crude petroleum | 10.2 | 11.3 | 13.2 | 13.9 | 14.0 | 15.0 | 11.4 | 12.3 | 14.4 | 12.9 | 11.4 | 9.2 |
| | passenger motor cars, other than buses | 7.6 | 6.3 | 6.3 | 7.0 | 6.9 | 7.5 | 6.6 | 7.8 | 7.8 | 8.0 | 8.6 | 8.2 |
| Nicaragua | insulated wire and cable | ... | ... | ... | ... | ... | 5.5 | ... | ... | ... | ... | ... | ... |
| | coffee, green or roasted | 15.0 | 17.8 | 15.4 | 28.8 | 16.8 | 11.0 | 18.4 | 21.1 | 22.5 | 12.8 | 8.5 | 8.7 |
| | meat of bovine animals, fresh chilled, salted, dried | 14.7 | 15.5 | 14.5 | 11.2 | 15.9 | 7.8 | 17.7 | 18.9 | 22.3 | 11.0 | 9.2 | 9.8 |
| | under garments (knitted or crocheted) | ... | ... | ... | ... | ... | ... | ... | ... | ... | 3.1 | 3.4 | 9.6 |
| | crustacea and mollusks, fresh chilled, salted, dried | 12.9 | 12.0 | 11.0 | 10.3 | 6.7 | 4.3 | 6.7 | 7.0 | 6.3 | 4.4 | 5.7 | 6.0 |
| Panama | fish, fresh, chilled or frozen | 36.1 | 35.7 | 32.4 | ... | ... | ... | ... | ... | ... | 8.5 | 8.6 | 10.3 |
| | other fresh fruit | ... | ... | 2.2 | 3.5 | 3.1 | 3.4 | 2.9 | ... | 5.3 | 5.3 | 5.7 | 3.9 |
| | fresh banana including plantains | 13.3 | 12.3 | 10.1 | ... | ... | ... | ... | ... | ... | 12.8 | 12.4 | 12.0 |
| | crustacea and mollusks, fresh chilled, salted, dried | 9.0 | 8.5 | 9.5 | ... | ... | ... | ... | ... | ... | 6.3 | 9.8 | 10.1 |
| Paraguay | soya beans | 42.9 | 36.9 | 34.0 | 22.8 | 30.5 | 33.3 | 24.9 | 24.3 | 29.5 | 21.8 | 26.7 | 23.9 |
| | electric energy | ... | ... | ... | ... | ... | ... | ... | 30.5 | 29.2 | 30.8 | 23.8 | 22.6 |
| | meat of bovine animals, fresh chilled, salted, dried | 3.7 | 9.4 | 14.6 | 21.9 | 12.4 | 13.4 | 17.5 | 13.5 | 9.3 | 10.4 | 10.7 | 13.3 |
| | oil seed cake and meal and other vegetable oil residues | 11.1 | 11.0 | 8.3 | 7.3 | 10.3 | 12.0 | 11.7 | 5.0 | 5.0 | 2.7 | 9.8 | 11.5 |
| Peru | refined copper including remelted ores and concentrates of copper | 11.4 | 12.5 | 12.4 | 15.5 | 10.0 | 10.4 | 9.3 | 9.2 | 7.7 | 5.4 | 6.2 | 5.7 |
| | ores and concentrates of copper | 6.1 | 10.7 | 10.0 | 14.5 | 19.3 | 19.0 | 19.6 | 22.4 | 21.8 | 23.2 | 22.5 | 21.1 |
| Puerto Rico | ... | ... | ... | ... | ... | ... | ... | ... | ... | ... | ... | ... | ... |
| Uruguay | meat of bovine animals, fresh chilled, salted, dried | 16.5 | 20.7 | 21.9 | 23.8 | 17.9 | 20.3 | 17.8 | 16.5 | 16.5 | 16.3 | 14.5 | 15.8 |
| | soya beans | ... | 3.1 | 3.0 | 3.5 | 4.7 | 5.6 | 8.5 | 10.6 | 10.3 | 16.0 | 20.9 | 17.8 |
| Venezuela | crude petroleum | ... | ... | ... | 91.6 | ... | 73.2 | 63.3 | 66.0 | 66.9 | 72.5 | 85.1 | ... |
| | petroleum products | ... | ... | ... | ... | ... | ... | ... | ... | ... | 25.9 | ... | ... |

*Source: All data from ECLA C/CEPAL Statistical Yearbook 2015. ECLAC/CEPAL Statistical Yearbook for Latin America and the Caribbean* http://interwp.cepal.org/anuario_estadistico/anuario_2015/en/index.asp

free trade concepts of specialization and comparative advantage. There was very little industry in Latin America until well into the twentieth century—after World War II in most countries—and very little interregional trade existed within countries or among them, given the external orientation of the infrastructure. A new group of merchants sprung up as part of these trade patterns. The comprador class made their living from selling finished goods that were imported from the outside. From importer to wholesaler to distributor to merchant, each made a considerable markup on each product sold. The state also charged high import taxes on imported goods, particularly if they were classified as luxuries. Monopoly was not uncommon, and personal and political ties helped secure import licenses, exclusive rights, and favorable terms. The little manufacturing that existed was usually protected by power and privilege and was not forced to compete directly with foreign products. The quality of products was often well below that of similar products on the world market.

## Agrarian Production

Until the second half of the twentieth century, most of Latin America was agrarian. Traditional landed estates (*latifundios*, haciendas, *fazendas*) produced crops such as cotton, cattle, sugar, or coffee. Their feudal-like origins in the Iberian peninsula often meant very traditional forms of production as well as social relations. Workers were subordinated to the patron (landlord) and his family, paid poorly, generally treated miserably, and often held in debt peonage through the monopolistic sale of necessary goods at high prices at the estate store. Armed guards and control over the roads into and out of the estate were—and sometimes still are—used to further control the labor force. The original landed estates were not overly efficient, relying principally on abundant land and inexpensive labor. The earnings from the sale of cash crops were generally used more to support the upper-class lifestyle of the family than for capital improvements on the estate. The owners often spent a considerable amount of their time in their city home in the regional or national capital or in Europe and thus were absentee landowners. The more abundant small farmers, or *minifundistas,* had very little land and thus had to use very labor-intensive forms of cultivation. Nor did they have capital or credit to invest in their land. The abundance of land (often left fallow or otherwise unused) in the hands of the landed elite and the paucity of land for the *campesinos* (farmers or tenant farmers) and rural landless laborers have perpetuated the disparity of income derived from the original distribution of land and power. Of equal importance, these inequities fueled demands for land reform, economic restructuring, and occasionally revolution. In more recent times, small farmers had to increasingly turn to paid labor outside their own land (usually for large landowners or commercial farms or plantations) to survive. Pressured by debt and intense poverty, they often sell what little land they have and become rural laborers or move to urban areas.

As the national economies developed, regions and often whole nations became what is referred to as monoculture or monocrop economies—dedicated to the production of one crop or commodity (see Table 13). As late as 1985, more than 50 percent of Colombia's official export earnings were derived from the sale of coffee on the international market. In the twenty-first century Colombia's dependence on coffee has been replaced by petroleum exports. In El Salvador, the focus on coffee was even greater—67 percent. Mexico also derived some 67 percent of its export earnings from the sale of one commodity—petroleum. In Venezuela, that figure was more than 84 percent for the same product. Chile derived 46 percent of its export earnings from the sale of copper. Reliance on one export commodity was even higher in previous decades. For instance, in 1958, the Bolivian economy centered on the production of tin; 58 percent of its export earnings derived from the sale of that commodity. Since the latter part of the nineteenth century, coffee and bananas have been big in Central America. By the middle of the twentieth century in Honduras, more than 50 percent of export earnings were derived from bananas (31 percent) and coffee (23 percent).

## Dependency and Underdevelopment

The problems with monocrop or near monocrop are twofold. By making the entire economy dependent on one primary product, the nation's economic health becomes heavily wed to the fortunes of that product in the international market. Boom periods are often followed by devastating busts. Coffee trees planted during a time of high coffee prices often mature a few years later when the coffee price is depressed. When their beans are sold on the international market, the excess supply only depresses coffee prices further. A dip of a few cents in the international price for coffee—or sugar or copper—can mean a recession or worse in the national economy. For instance, copper prices fell to five cents a pound during the Great Depression and rose steadily in the 1940s, only to fall to four cents a pound in 1950. When this occurs, the resultant worsening economic conditions often stimulate unrest and have contributed to the downfall of many presidents and other political leaders in Latin America.

## Foreign Investment and Enclave Production

Mining and sugar and banana plantations have often been dominated by foreign investment as they are much more capital intensive and strongly employ U.S. and Canadian concepts of business efficiency. Initially, these foreign corporations created types of enclaves, where the company, upper-level management, and even middle-level management were all foreign and often lived in a special compound fenced off from local inhabitants. Tools, explosives, fertilizers, and other elements in the productive process were shipped into the country and taken directly to the mine or plantation. Products were shipped directly out of the country—often on foreign-owned railroads—and profits were sent back to corporate headquarters in New York, Boston, or London. More local people and products were eventually incorporated into local production, but ownership, upper-level management, and the end source for profit remission (the countries where the profits ended up) remained foreign. An example would be a company known to much of North America, Chiquita Banana. United Brands (formerly United Fruit Company) started as a Boston-based company founded by a New England sea captain in the 1880s. It grew to become a huge producer and exporter of bananas and one of the largest multinational corporations (MNCs) operating in Central America. It conducted operations in Guatemala, Honduras, Nicaragua, Costa Rica, and Panama and came to exercise considerable power over local governments, particularly in Honduras and Guatemala. The CIA organized a coup against the constitutional government in Guatemala in 1954 that was directly related to United Fruit's pressure on the U.S. government to stop the expropriation of its unused land by the reformist Jacobo Arbenz government.

---

### THE CROP THAT COULD

Since Latin America was brought into the international system as a producer of primary products, the region has sought a product that could demand a good price on the world market and that its farmers could produce using traditional methods without making huge investments. In this way, small and large farmers could easily grow the crop and earn a good living from its sale. They needed a crop that would hold its value in the markets in the north and could be turned into a finished product in the south with minimal investments in equipment and technology. To date, the only major crop to fill that bill has been coca. Unlike any other commodity, cocaine's manufacture, transport, and distribution in the north is controlled by Latin America-based business organizations (cartels) that bring most of the profits back to their home countries. Further, the coca leaves from which cocaine is made have been part of traditional indigenous culture for more than 1,000 years and are thought to have special spiritual and medicinal qualities by large parts of the populations of Peru, Bolivia, and Ecuador. In these Andean nations, chewing the coca leaf is legal and common among indigenous peoples in the highlands. The leaves are also used to make tea or moistened and applied directly to heal sore or swollen eyes. Thus, it is difficult for the local population to conceive of many of the pernicious effects of the highly refined extract of the coca leaves—cocaine.

It is estimated by the U.S. Drug Enforcement Agency (DEA) that drug trafficking in the United States is more than a $200 billion business each year. A great deal of this figure results from the sale of powdered or crack cocaine. South America exports some 600 metric tons of cocaine each year. As with other products from the region, the primary markets are the United States, Canada, and Western Europe. For instance, it is estimated that Colombia alone exports 245 metric tons of cocaine each year. Using the street value price, this would mean that cocaine exports for Colombia account for some $2.7 billion per year. The official figure for all goods and services exported from Colombia was $56.5 billion in 2014 (drug sales are not reported and thus not part of official figures). About half of this resulted from the sale of petroleum, with coal coming second at $7.6 billion. Using these figures, cocaine would rank as the country's third most important export and on par with a traditional Colombian export, coffee. Eager to protect the right to grow coca as a traditional medicinal product, Bolivian President Evo Morales has significantly reduced Bolivia's contribution to the cocaine trade under the slogan, "*Coca si, cocaine no.*"

Unlike the production of most other Latin American products, all who work in production are relatively well paid, from the peasant who grows the leaves to the pilot who flies it into the United States. It is only as the finished product begins to be consumed in the producing countries that the full extent of the hazard becomes known. Nor do many in the producing countries see the negative effect on tourism and investment or the damage done to legitimate businesses that are crowded out of the market by enterprises that sell on a very low or negative profit margin to launder huge amounts of money.

Efforts by the U.S. government to eradicate Latin America's most lucrative export commodity have been less than successful for the previously discussed reasons and because many local and national police officers usually make less than $200 per month and are hard put to make ends meet. One way to increase income has been to accept payments for not reporting traffic or other violations or for simply looking the other way. Commanders and military officers make relatively modest salaries, as do most judges. Governmental officials and politicians seem particularly susceptible to bribes and campaign donations. Even former Colombian president Ernesto Samper was accused of taking a large campaign donation from a drug cartel. The corruption has also spread to transshipment points in Central America, the Caribbean, and especially Mexico. In that country, drug-induced corruption has spread widely. Many police officers, upper-level officials, military officers, and government officials have been indicted for accepting bribes. In recent years the drug trade passing through the country is responsible for thousands of deaths. Throughout these countries, the amounts of money available to bribe or otherwise induce local and national officials to ignore certain activities or give intelligence on impending government actions is many times more than most officials make in a year, if not a lifetime. The temptation is too great for many, and for those who will not be bought, there are always other ways. Indeed, many police and other public officials are given a choice: *plata o plomo* (money or lead). Others are assassinated outright.

Attempts to organize producers into international cartels or producers' associations have generally had only the most minimal effect on the stabilization or maintenance of commodity prices. Attempts have been made to organize international associations of coffee producers to maintain the price of coffee. In the early 1960s, the International Coffee Agreement was signed and later the International Coffee Organization was established. Production quotas were assigned to all producing members in an effort to control the supply of coffee and thus the price. However, in part because of the resistance of African nations, who preferred to set their own production quotas, these efforts failed, and coffee continues to be subject to market fluctuations. The Organization of Petroleum Exporting Countries (OPEC), of which Venezuela was a founding member, was for many years the only producers' association that was able to influence the price of its product. Yet, by the late 1990s, petroleum prices had fallen significantly. These falling prices helped put considerable strain on the long-dominant Social Christian Party (COPEI) in Venezuela. As Venezuelan petroleum prices fell to a low of less than $10 per barrel at the end of 1998 (from a high of $35 a barrel in the early 1980s), the presidential election campaigns of candidates from these parties wilted in the face of the newly organized Patriotic Pole coalition formed to back Hugo Chávez. Former coup leader Chávez won with 57 percent of the vote. Throughout his years in office, Chávez, and his successor Maduro, depended on world oil prices that have stabilized for several years around $100 per barrel. Without these oil prices, Venezuela and its Bolivarian Alliance for the People of Our America (ALBA) allies, Bolivia and Ecuador, could not have afforded their extensive social welfare programs. However, the fall of oil prices to under $50 a barrel in 2014 threw the Venezuelan economy into turmoil and Maduro's party was decisively defeated in December 2015 legislative elections and the Venezuelan economy subsequently suffered severe decline in 2017 with a resulting radical decline in support for the government.

Many national leaders and thinkers have wondered why Latin America has remained less developed than its neighbor to the north, the United States. Most Latin American nations have abundant resources and sufficient land. Gradually, national leaders and scholars have learned the same bitter lessons that U.S., Canadian, and many European farmers have found to be all too true: if unprotected by government price controls, prices for primary products fluctuate greatly and rise very slowly. Like U.S. farmers, Latin Americans have produced more and more at ever greater efficiency, but they have received comparatively less and less for it—while paying increasing prices for cars, machinery, and other finished goods from industrial, more developed national and international centers.

## Raúl Prebisch and ECLA

Such an economic understanding by Latin Americans was stimulated greatly by the pioneering work of ECLA (the Economic Commission for Latin America and the Caribbean) and its director Raúl Prebisch. Prebisch, an Argentine-born and educated economist, had previously held high-level economic positions in the Argentine government. In the late 1940s, he gathered a team of Latin American economists at the Santiago, Chile, headquarters of ECLA. He and his fellow economists made extensive studies of the prices for primary products exported by Latin America and compared them to those of the finished goods that were imported. Their studies indicated that the relationship between these product prices, or the terms of trade, were unfavorable to Latin America. Posited as the now-famous Prebisch thesis, the theory argued that there is a structural tendency for Latin American terms of trade to deteriorate over time because of the concentration of exports in primary commodities. As suggested by Figure 4, over time the price for finished goods rises much faster than the price for primary goods.

These findings, which were initially considered controversial by Western economists from industrialized nations, called into question the argument for specialization in the production of any one primary product in the international market. Interestingly, later studies by the Economic Commission for Africa of the United Nations Economic and Social Council found that the terms of trade for African primary exports vis-à-vis finished imports from Europe and the United States were also unfavorable to Africa.

## Dependency Theory

ECLA's work and the Prebisch thesis were fascinating examples of how Latin American economists working from a perspective grounded in their own reality could see how their relationship with the industrialized center (Europe and United States) was less than satisfactory. This gave great impetus not only to new economic policy direction in the Latin American nations but also to the development of a

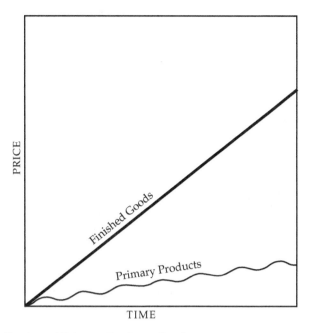

**Figure 4.**  Finished Goods and Primary Products Graph.

whole new way to view Latin American development—dependency theory. The ECLA studies were symbolic of the post–World War II decolonization process and the subsequent willingness to assign negative consequences to the relations imposed by actual or formal colonial masters on the development of native peoples. This also represented a significant break with metropolitan theorists and economists who saw underdevelopment as inherent to Latin America and other third-world nations and caused primarily by economic, social, or cultural patterns that had developed within those societies.

The late 1940s also provided alternative explanations for the lack of development in Latin America, Africa, and Asia. Basing their understanding in large part on V. I. Lenin's classic work *Imperialism, the Highest Stage of Capitalism* (1916), scholars familiar with this Marxist analysis argued that the colonies were used as places to invest surplus capital and sell goods from the colonizing countries and as sources of cheap raw materials and cheap labor. Indeed, according to this view, the high return on investment and low prices paid for raw materials and labor meant that value was extracted from the colonized countries and exported to the developed countries, where it further fueled their development. It was further argued that such surplus value was the difference between what was paid and what it would have cost if fair value had been paid at the industrial center. As with the initial taking of gold bullion in the colonial era, this extracted wealth helped continue the impoverishment of the colonized country and made the colonial country rich.

This thesis was updated by the African leader and intellectual Kwame Nkrumah. The first president of Ghana and intellectual author of Pan-Africanism argued that imperialism had taken on a new but equally pernicious form—neocolonialism. In his work *Neocolonialism, the Last Stage of Imperialism* (1965), Nkrumah argued that former colonizers now controlled their former colonies and other former colonies by less direct means. They established economic spheres of influence—pound or franc areas where the former colonial currency and its financial sector dominated. They dominated the area by investment and a foreign economic presence and bought the same raw materials at the same prices and sold the same finished goods. Further, the former colonizers were aided in this endeavor by native politicians and pro-Western elements of the native bourgeoisie, who often did the bidding of the former colonial masters and generally helped maintain their neocolonial dominance in the face of any radical reformers or revolutionaries who attempted to change the subordinate nature of this relationship. The Latin American intellectual Eduardo Galeano labeled this group "the commission bourgeoisie." Foreign aid and missionaries were but more subtle means of continuing neocolonial control. Political and economic control was exercised in a more indirect way than under direct colonialism, but the effect was very similar for the native people.

Other advocates of dependency theory argued that Latin America was maintained in a neocolonial state under the tutelage of the United States and European powers. Given that the Latin American nations had been independent much longer than the African states, the mechanisms of control were different and often more subtle. Thus, one finds more discussion of cultural imperialism in Latin America. It is often asserted that economic relations, foreign aid and diplomacy, and the media and other forms of control were employed to keep Latin America subordinate. Neocolonialism was thus manifest throughout Latin American society, as could be seen in U.S. movies, television series, religious evangelization, the spread of Western consumption patterns, the canonization of Mickey Mouse and Donald Duck, and the mass pilgrimage to Miami and Florida's Disney World by Latin America's elites and many from the middle class.

Andre Gunder Frank's *Capitalism and Underdevelopment in Latin America* (1967) brought dependency theory to the fore. As suggested earlier, Frank and other dependency theorists argued that the relationship between the developing area (satellite or periphery) and the developed area (center or *metropol*) was one of dependence. Thus, the *dependentistas* argued that underdevelopment in Latin America resulted from the region being brought into the capitalist system to satisfy the economic needs of the metropolitan powers. Decisions as to when and where to develop mines, plantations, or infrastructure were made according to the requirements of the metropolitan powers, not the Latin American nations. From colonial times on, economic decisions responded more to the needs of the industrializing center than to the needs of the agrarian periphery. Over time, the national economic systems in Latin America thus became dependent on the production and export of primary products to Europe and the United States (the industrialized center or metropol).

It is argued, then, that the economic development and even the political autonomy of Latin American nations became dependent on the outside forces of the metropolitan powers. They did not possess full independence and, hence, were dependent on and subordinate to outside forces. Latin American underdevelopment was thus a result of the exploitation and control of forces outside the region. As Latin America had been incorporated into the international capitalist system, it had lost its wealth and autonomy. The plundering of the gold and silver of the region was symbolic of how the capitalist system had served the interests of the Latin American nations. Indeed, capitalism and economic penetration by the metropolitan capitalist powers were responsible for a great deal of Latin American underdevelopment. Frank and others argued that even the feudalistic *latifundios* had been incorporated into the international system and were part of the worldwide spread of capitalism. Latin America's problems thus resulted from the nature of capitalism itself and the way it subordinated classes in nations and even developing nations themselves.

The dependency perspective also contradicted what had become a common view about Latin American economies. The dual-economy view held that the economies were divided into two sectors. One was comprised of near-feudal social and economic relations on the *latifundio* and in landowner–sharecropper relations and subsistence agriculture; the other was centered in the modern export sector that tended to employ modern capitalist practices. Each national economy was divided in two, one traditional and feudal-like and the other modern and capitalist. The *dependisteis* saw only one economy well integrated into the world capitalist system. Frank and the early dependency writers thus focused on external linkages and the international capitalist system in particular to explain Latin underdevelopment.

There were, however, later dependency writers who enriched this perspective by also looking more closely at the specific historical, social, and economic configurations of nations such as Brazil and Argentina. They examined internal factors such as class and intraclass competition to further explain the complex phenomenon of development in the region. Foremost among these was the Brazilian social scientist Femando Henrique Cardoso, who, together with Chilean sociologist Enzo Faletto, wrote *Dependency and Development in Latin America* (1971). The more subtle analysis of internal class formations and historical development patterns and the role of multinational corporations made this one of the most useful analyses of the Latin American reality.

## Import Substitution Industrialization

As these new perspectives stimulated a rethinking of how development should be pursued, policies began to change more rapidly. ECLA recommended import substitution industrialization (ISI) as a way to reduce the importation of finished goods. From the 1930s on, several of the larger nations had begun to focus on what became known as inward-looking development, reasoning that the path to development was through developing internal economic capacity, including industrial capacity, while continuing to export primary products. ECLA recommended strongly that internal industrialization be pursued. This would mean that less of the foreign exchange earned through the sale of primary products would be expended on finished goods and more capital would stay in the country. In this way, the negative effects of the terms of trade would be minimized. Latin American domestic manufacturing was officially and continually encouraged. A growing number of new industries began to produce for the domestic market. Sporadic industrialization had occurred in some of the large countries, such as Mexico, Argentina, and Brazil—particularly during World War I and II and even the Great Depression, when Latin America was cut off from its external supplies of finished goods. This time, however, ISI became official policy and was pursued vigorously through increasing domestic manufacturing. Domestic entrepreneurs were encouraged to set up new industries and expand old ones, and MNCs were invited to set up plants to supply the domestic market. Even car companies set up assembly plants, as was the case with Volkswagen in Mexico and Brazil and Fiat in Argentina. Chrysler also began assembling cars in Latin America and was joined by Toyota in the 1970s. Panasonic, Motorola, and other electronics companies began to manufacture in Latin America, as did most of the major pharmaceutical companies and even food processors like Nabisco and Nestlé.

Attempts were made to control the national content of the components used in the finished product, the percentage of nationals in middle- and upper-level management, and the amount of profit that could be remitted to the home office of the MNC each year. These attempts to assert national sovereignty met with varying success and were often skillfully circumvented by sophisticated MNCs.

A modern textile factory in Latin America. *(Glow Images/Alamy Images RF)*

From the late 1940s on, Mexico required that 51 percent of all companies doing business in Mexico be owned by Mexican nationals or Mexican corporations (the dropping of this provision after NAFTA caused some controversy in Mexico). There was some nationalization of foreign corporations by Latin American governments (Bolivian tin mines after 1954, foreign assets in Cuba after 1960, copper mines in Chile in the 1960s and 1970s, and the International Petroleum Company in Peru in 1968), but the general trend was for more and more foreign investment to flock to the region further enhancing foreign ownership. This wave of investment was particularly strong after military coups in Brazil in 1964 and Chile in 1973. Manufacturing and MNCs became part of the economic panorama in Latin America. Smaller and relatively less developed nations such as Guatemala, El Salvador, Costa Rica, and even Honduras experienced increases in manufacturing and the arrival of MNCs that produced finished products. The trend had been encouraged by U.S. government policies beginning with the Alliance for Progress programs after 1961.

## Export Orientation

Industrial production was initially destined for internal national markets or those of neighboring nations who had entered into an agreement such as the Central American Common Market (1960), the Latin American Free Trade Association (1960), or the Andean Pact (1967). This was a great stimulus for the industrialization of Latin America; for example, Mexico and Brazil further developed their own steel and automobile industries. The nature of production also changed. Domestic manufactured products became more similar to those manufactured for Western consumer taste. Gradually, as the domestic demand for manufactures faltered, Latin American nations began to take on an externally oriented perspective. Hereafter, manufacturing and crop diversification would be done with an eye toward external sales as well as the domestic market.

The influx of international capital, more sophisticated technology, and the opening up of internal markets made for more and better manufactured goods. The entrance of the MNCs drove some local producers out of business, and others were forced to upgrade the quality of their products. Of those local producers who survived, many soon realized that they too could enter the global market with their more sophisticated products. Nor were the products limited to those produced by sophisticated MNCs and high-technology national producers. Other domestic industries also grew: weaving and handcraft in Guatemala, wine in Chile, shoes in Brazil. Indeed, the Brazilian shoe industry eventually became one of the largest producers of footwear on the world market. As another way of gaining more foreign exchange, many countries encouraged the production of nontraditional exports, not only producing more finished goods that could be exported but also diversifying production of primary products. Such was the case in Colombia, where a vigorous export industry in flowers developed. As this process occurred over the 1960s, 1970s, and 1980s, Latin America became more integrated into the international economic system, primarily through ties to industrialized capitalist nations— the United States, Western Europe, and later Japan.

The transformation of Latin American economies can be seen in the following:

- More extensive use of capital-intensive technology.
- Increased training in manufacturing-related engineering for those who employed and replicated technology in capital-intensive techniques used in advanced industrial nations. Many engineering students were sent to the United States or Europe and brought back advanced capital-intensive technology with them.
- Lack of development of appropriate technology that could take advantage of Latin America's abundant and inexpensive labor supply.
- The spread of Western-style consumerism to the upper, middle, and lower classes.
- State intervention to encourage and protect export-oriented domestic industries and sometimes to nationalize them or, as in the case of Brazil, to set up key industries such as aircraft production.
- The growth of middle sectors who worked in management and technologically sophisticated aspects of production (e.g., engineers, skilled technicians, accountants).
- The growth of an industrial proletariat.

## Increasing Foreign Debt and the Debt Crisis

Newer plants created in Latin America were often copies or near copies of standard plants from a particular MNC, although often using the less advanced technology and relatively outdated standards that operated in the developed world, where capital was plentiful and labor was expensive. The employment created for such plants was modest, but the investment in new machinery and patented processes was not. This type of production used up local sources of capital quickly. Thus, even as there were more goods to export, it became necessary to borrow money from abroad to satisfy these capital needs. The growing demand for Western consumer goods also meant that more and more products were being imported to keep consumers satisfied. This also used up scarce foreign exchange. These two processes and the acquisition of expensive military hardware by countries like Peru, Chile, Brazil, and Argentina meant that more external borrowing was necessary to compensate for the net outflows of funds. This caused what came to be called "debt-led growth." The result of this outward-directed orientation and debt-led growth was that the external indebtedness of Latin American nations began to grow. Brazil is a prime example of this.

Prior to 1970, most of the Latin American external debt was owed to individual states or to multilateral lending institutions such as the Inter-American Development Bank. Interest rates were minimal. The petroleum crisis of 1973–1974 changed this. First, it meant that those Latin American nations that were net importers of petroleum were forced to use more of their foreign exchange to pay for the hydrocarbons they imported. Second, it meant that petroleum-producing countries began to amass significant foreign exchange surpluses and needed to find places to invest these funds. Most of these petrodollars ended up in Western banks, which soon had more than ample funds for lending but, because of the stagnation in developed countries, could not find borrowers in those countries. Large banks like Chase Manhattan and Bank of America began to make large loans readily available to private and public borrowers in Latin America. These factors combined to radically increase the external debt in Latin America, which jumped from less than $30 billion in 1970 to more than $230 billion in 1980. By the beginning of the 1980s, debt service payments alone were some $18 billion per year. Drops in commodity prices and world recessions in the 1980s did not improve this picture. Economic growth slowed in most countries and shrank in a few. Indeed, the 1980s were referred to as the "lost decade" because growth rates were so abysmal in most of Latin America—for many countries, only 1 or 2 percent per year. A few countries even experienced negative growth rates.

Mexico and Brazil experienced high levels of economic growth in the 1960s and 1970s; each had periods of economic growth during this time that were referred to as economic "miracles." Both, however, continued to borrow from abroad. This situation was aggravated by increases in petroleum prices in the 1970s and early 1980s. The Latin American nations' indebtedness grew, and both Mexico and Brazil acquired external debts in excess of $110 billion (Table 14). By 1982, Mexico declared that it could not meet all the loan payments that were due. This caused considerable concern in the international investment community. Large banks in the United States were particularly concerned and sought relief from the Reagan administration. After some discussion, the U.S. government tendered an emergency loan package to Mexico to stop it from defaulting. Other countries came close to defaulting as well; Peru, under the Alan Garcia presidency, even declared a moratorium on repaying its external debt. The prospect of widespread default created near panic among many large banks in the United States and Europe since many of them had made very high percentages of their loans (mostly unsecured) to Latin American public and private institutions. Since a large portion of their capital had been loaned out and could not be called back, they were, in bankers' language, "overexposed." There was also talk of the Latin American nations joining together and negotiating terms of debt repayment or even refusing to pay altogether. This movement never materialized, but Western nations and international financial institutions such as the International Monetary Fund (IMF) and the World Bank, fearful of a default, were instrumental in renegotiating more favorable repayment packages and reducing interest rates.

As the Latin American nations became even more dependent on external sources to solve their financial problems, the role of international financial institutions such as the IMF, the World Bank, and the Inter-American Development Bank became ever stronger. This was also true for the role of the Agency for International Development (AID) of the U.S. Department of State. In addition to the growing importance of AID, the United States and its Western capitalist allies were able to exercise a tremendous amount of control over decision-making in these international bodies. Further, pursuant to the victory of the conservative economic policy embodied in Thatcherism in the United Kingdom and the Reagan revolution in the United States, the policies advocated by AID and the international financial institutions became ever more conservative. Indeed, the free market/free trade ideas of Milton Friedman and the Chicago School soon began to appear as policy recommendations.

**TABLE 14.**   Total External Dept, Year-End Totals (In Millions of Dollars)

| Country | 2008 | 2009 | 2010 | 2011 | 2012 | 2013 | 2014 |
|---|---|---|---|---|---|---|---|
| Argentina | 124,711.49 | 116,697.62 | 130,818.92 | 143,170.71 | 141,107.86 | 141,075.52 | 147,853.17 |
| Bolivia | 5,929.83 | 5,801.23 | 5,874.50 | 6,297.70 | 6,711.30 | 7,755.80 | 7,849.30 |
| Brazil | 198,491.51 | 198,136.31 | 256,803.72 | 298,204.05 | 312,898.39 | 308,625.06 | 338,630.51 |
| Chile | 64,318.00 | 74,041.00 | 86,737.75 | 98,894.61 | 117,568.90 | 130,723.56 | 137,416.50 |
| Colombia | 46,368.80 | 53,718.81 | 64,723.40 | 75,903.28 | 78,763.37 | 91,922.91 | 93,868.04 |
| Costa Rica | 9,105.25 | 8,237.99 | 9,135.26 | 10,919.43 | 14,509.45 | 17,654.31 | 18,678.77 |
| Cuba | 11,591.20 | 12,310.20 | ... | ... | ... | ... | ... |
| Dominican Repub | 7,218.83 | 8,214.62 | 9,946.91 | 11,625.43 | 12,871.50 | 14,919.42 | 15,641.70 |
| Ecuador | 16,899.51 | 13,513.67 | 13,914.23 | 15,210.33 | 15,913.13 | 18,672.38 | 22,970.64 |
| El Salvador | 9,994.20 | 9,881.80 | 9,698.40 | 10,669.50 | 12,530.30 | 13,290.70 | 13,663.10 |
| Guatemala | 11,163.38 | 11,247.92 | 12,025.50 | 14,020.60 | 15,339.44 | 17,492.90 | 18,259.70 |
| Haiti | 1,917.40 | 1,278.44 | 353.27 | 726.80 | 1,173.00 | 1,474.14 | ... |
| Honduras | 3,464.00 | 3,344.88 | 3,772.58 | 4,188.28 | 4,844.00 | 6,641.70 | 6,729.30 |
| Mexico | 129,423.60 | 165,932.00 | 197,727.00 | 209,742.50 | 228,764.40 | 261,038.80 | 279,000.00 |
| Nicaragua | 3,511.50 | 3,660.90 | 4,068.19 | 4,263.15 | 4,480.80 | 4,723.67 | 4,724.03 |
| Panama | 8,477.29 | 10,150.15 | 10,438.53 | 10,857.78 | 10,782.40 | 12,231.10 | 12,689.44 |
| Paraguay | 3,124.28 | 3,044.24 | 3,621.06 | 3,863.75 | 4,580.39 | 5,130.64 | 5,324.00 |
| Peru | 34,997.14 | 35,157.34 | 43,673.50 | 47,976.99 | 59,375.68 | 60,823.16 | 63,464.55 |
| Uruguay | 15,424.82 | 17,969.37 | 18,425.20 | 18,344.95 | 21,122.00 | 22,862.00 | 24,244.00 |
| Venezuela | 53,223.00 | 70,246.00 | 84,058.00 | 97,888.00 | 115,495.00 | 110,485.00 | ... |
| **Totals** | **759,355.04** | **822,584.48** | **965,815.92** | **1,082,767.84** | **1,178,831.31** | **1,247,542.77** | **1,211,006.73** |

. . . Data not available.

*Source: Statistical Yeearbook of Latin America, 2015.*

http://interwp.cepal.org/anuario_estadistico/anuario_2015/en/index.asp

# Structural Adjustment and the Move to Neoliberalism

As conditions for continued borrowing, international financial institutions began to first suggest and then insist on economic structural adjustments to the national economies. Indeed, more and more of the loans were conditional on such adjustments. It was argued that the Latin American nations must take the bitter pill of austerity through these structural adjustments. Government costs and inflation had to be reduced through measures such as fiscal reform, monetary restraint, cutting back jobs and services in the public sector, and stopping government subsidies for basic goods or petroleum. Likewise, wages were to be held down as a way of checking inflation and keeping wage costs at bay in the evermore important export industries. Orthodox economic thought became more widely accepted, and the ISI advocated by ECLA fell from favor.

As Eastern European socialism weakened and then began to disappear in the late 1980s and as the Soviet Union's breakup moved the world from the Cold War and a strong bipolar system to one dominated by Western capitalism and the United States, economic policy recommendations became ever more dominated by the orthodox capitalist economic thinking advocated by the conservative govern-ments in power in the United States and United Kingdom. Keynesian economics and its advocacy of state intervention in the market economy and deficit spending to stimulate business activity was no longer in favor. Rather, the free market and free trade ideas championed by economists like Milton Friedman became popular. Indeed, the conservative economic thought of opponents of state intervention and planning, such as Friederich A. von Hayek, became influential. By the early 1990s, such thought was dominant in the IMF, the World Bank, the Inter-American De-velopment Bank, and AID. Since the headquarters of all these organizations are located in Washington, D.C., this thinking became referred to as the "Washington Consensus."

## NEOLIBERALISM

In Latin America, this type of economic policy was characterized as neoliberal-ism because it seemed to be a new version of the classical eighteenth-century economic liberalism of Adam Smith and other earlier economic liberals. Classi-cal economic liberals believe that the magic hand of the market, not government control or trade barriers, should regulate the economy. Indeed, political liberal-ism in nineteenth-century Latin America included a belief in increasing commerce through free trade.

---

### KEY COMPONENTS OF NEOLIBERALISM AND THE WASHINGTON CONSENSUS

1. Radically reducing government size and spending by cutting back on govern-ment jobs and programs—especially social programs.
2. Fiscal and monetary reform.
3. Minimizing government regulation in economic matters (deregulation).
4. Liberalizing commerce through the reduction and eventual elimination of all tariff barriers and trade restrictions.
5. Opening up the national economy to foreign investment and allowing the free flow of capital.
6. Privatization of government-owned corporations, industries, agencies, and utilities.
7. Eliminating government subsidies for essential consumer goods, such as bread or tortillas and petroleum products.

---

## GLOBALIZATION

Other factors were at work as well. The success that a variety of MNCs, such as Nike, had with moving all or part of their production to plants they established in Asia became widely known. More and more assembly plants, or *maquiladoras*, were established first just across the U.S. border in northern Mexico and then spread throughout the Caribbean basin and into some South American countries, such as Ecuador. Electronic components, the unsown pieces of cloth that make up clothing, and other unassembled parts in other industries were manufactured in the United States, Japan, Western Europe, and even Taiwan and then assembled in Latin America in an ever-growing number of *maquiladoras*. Regular manufacturing for export production was also encouraged, and MNCs came to Latin America in increasing numbers to take advantage of low wages, lax labor and environmental protection, minimal regulations and taxation, and generally sympathetic governments. Free trade zones (*zonas francas*) were also set up, where companies could be completely free of any governmental regulation. The process of neoliberal globalization, it was argued, would be beneficial for all; thus, all were expected to expedite its implementation.

As the world became increasingly subject to economic globalization, capital and production plants became ever more fluid, moving freely from one country to another according to who offered the most favorable terms. The new wisdom was for each nation to produce everything it could as efficiently as possible and to export as much of it as possible to maximize export earnings. This allowed the nation to keep up with external debt payments, pay for an expanding number and amount of imports, and hopefully have some foreign exchange earnings left over to add to foreign exchange reserves. The national borders were to be open to imports so that national consumers could get the lowest prices on the goods they consumed. If some national industries could not compete with the increased number and variety of imported goods then so be it. They should be closed, and capital and labor should be shifted to those industries that could compete and export their goods.

## Privatization and Neoliberalism

The new mantra was "globalize, globalize, globalize," and in Latin America it was combined with the specifically neoliberal mantra of "privatize, privatize, privatize." As suggested earlier, mines had been nationalized in Bolivia and Chile, and considerable state-owned industry existed in Brazil and elsewhere. Most of the states owned all or part of the national telephone and telecommunication companies, and many had autonomous state-owned agencies, such as the Peruvian national fishing company PescaPeru. In Mexico, all aspects of petroleum production had been nationalized since 1936; the resulting state-owned enterprise, PEMEX, is one of the largest national companies. It was also thought that it might be possible to privatize some governmental infrastructure, such as new highways. Thus, much new superhighway construction in countries like Brazil and Mexico was financed by private capital and/or run by private companies through their direct administration of the roadways and collection of tolls.

The movement toward privatization was especially strong in Latin America because state-owned entities had generally been little more efficient than the government bureaucracies themselves. Often, they had been subject to cronyism, bloated employment practices to accommodate payback for political or personal support, and corruption. Thus, one could easily wait up to two years for the installation of a phone line (unless phone company employees were "motivated" through monetary inducements) or suffer frequent loss of electricity or water service.

As Latin American nations returned to international lending agencies (the IMF in particular) for additional short- and long-term loans, they found that the imposed neoliberal conditions (conditionality) included the privatization of major public enterprises, such as the telephone companies. They were to be sold or auctioned off, and a substantial part of the proceeds were to be used to pay off part of the external debt. This led to increasing pressure on the political leaders to sell off these enterprises (usually to foreign corporations or consortia) to meet the conditions of the loans. However, utility rates were generally very low for consumers, and thousands of jobs were at stake. Not surprisingly, there were substantial popular and political mobilizations, union strikes, and job actions to resist the sales. The mobilization to protest the privatization of the water company in Cochabamba, Bolivia, was one of the most notable. Nonetheless, many of these entities were partially or wholly sold off, frequently at bargain prices. The lucrative entities that made good profits attracted considerable investment interest and sold rapidly, whereas those that lost money and were government liabilities went begging for buyers. This in turn led to the perception on the part of some that decisions were once again being made because of foreign influence and for the benefit of foreign corporations, not the national populace. As will be discussed later, these and other factors led to growing political discontent and new political mobilizations.

Latin America soon became a place where MNCs could go to reduce their production costs. By the early twenty-first century, more and more manufacturing jobs from the United States were moving to Latin America.

## Regional Integration, NAFTA, and the Globalization Process

In 1826, Simón Bolívar convened the Congress of Panama to foster the uniting of Spanish America into one political and economic entity. He dreamed of a united Latin America to rival the growing power of the United States in North America, but his proposal failed. Others had visions of unity in Central America. From 1824 to 1840, the Central American states that were part of the Captaincy General of Guatemala in colonial times (Guatemala, El Salvador, Honduras, Nicaragua, and Costa Rica) were united in the Central American Federation. However, the Central American states could not remain united. Their shattered dreams of unity lay dormant until after the Europeans began a process of regional economic integration out of the ashes of World War II. The beginnings of a united Europe and the creation of the European Common Market in 1957 proved to be a catalyst for Latin American efforts at economic integration.

Encouraged by the ECLA and the United States, the Central American Common Market was formed in 1960. Its common tariff walls were to encourage import substitution and internally oriented economic growth within the region. Promoted more by Latin American initiative, the Latin American Free Trade Association was also founded in 1960, and the Andean Pact was forged in 1967 with the same expectations. However, internal political pressure and vested national economic interests made it difficult to reduce tariffs among the respective member nations. None of these pacts had any appreciable success. The next stage in regional integration was not forged until the era of globalization.

In 1989, President George H. W. Bush launched the Enterprise for the Americas Initiative. This plan envisioned a common area of economic cooperation for the Americas extending from the frozen north in Canada to Tierra del Fuego in southern South America. All the Americas would move toward one gigantic economic zone that could easily rival a united Europe. Unlike the European Union, however, no attempt would be made to gradually integrate while ensuring that all member states had similar costs of production and approximately the same labor and political rights. Under this plan, Canada and the United States would combine with their less powerful sister republics in the south on the assumption that free trade and increased commerce could cure all ills and benefit all member nations. The first concrete action in this process developed among the United States, Mexico, and Canada. NAFTA was signed in 1992 and went into effect on January 1, 1994, following ratification by the legislatures of the three governments. Building on a bilateral U.S.–Canadian agreement initiated in 1989, NAFTA created one of the two largest trading blocs in the world, with a population of 370 million and a combined economic production of $6 trillion, a worthy rival to the European Union. NAFTA also removed most restrictions on cross-border investment and allowed the free flow of goods and services.

The agreement was vigorously pursued by the Salinas administration in Mexico in the hope that increased investment in Mexico and a greater North American market for its products would stimulate the Mexican economy and create jobs for the millions of unemployed and underemployed Mexicans. In contrast, the U.S. labor movement feared that thousands of jobs would head south, where wage rates were approximately one-tenth of what they were in the United States and labor rights and safety regulations were minimal. The movement convinced presidential candidate Bill Clinton to oppose the agreement in the 1992 election campaign. However, once in office, President Clinton bowed to pressure from large U.S. corporations that wanted to set up more factories and retail stores in Mexico and investment firms and business interests that saw lucrative investment opportunities. Clinton led a difficult but successful battle for ratification of the agreement that had been negotiated by President Bush. After the agreement went into effect, many more U.S. firms moved their plants to Mexico to set up regular factories and *maquiladoras*. They took thousands of jobs with them, although some new jobs were created in the United States to supply the now-open Mexican market. There was, however, a net loss of U.S. jobs. Ford, General Motors, and Chrysler set up factories in Mexico to manufacture cars for Mexico, the United States, and Canada that were not only put together locally but also made mostly from parts manufactured in Mexico, including the engines and transmissions.

In Mexico, many small- and medium-size industries and businesses were not able to compete with their larger U.S. or Canadian counterparts and went bankrupt.

Mexican agriculture in general and corn farmers more specifically were especially hard hit as they were unable to compete with heavily subsidized U.S. agriculture. These and related events caused considerable political turmoil in all three countries. In Mexico, they led to charges that the Mexican elite was selling out the country to U.S. corporate interests, especially since most of the jobs created were at or around the minimum wage of less than US$4 per day. Many, in both Canada and the United States, feared that their political leaders entered into an agreement that would be more a net exporter of jobs than a bonanza for the common people. As with the general process of globalization and the implementation of neoliberal reforms elsewhere, the benefits of growth have been distributed very unevenly but not that differently from the United States. (see Table 7 in Chapter 5 and Table 15 in this chapter). As labor, political groups, and mass organizations have mobilized against the negative effects of many of these changes in a variety of countries, including Venezuela, Ecuador, Costa Rica, Nicaragua, Argentina, and Brazil, political leaders have felt internal pressure against neoliberal changes while still being pressured by international financial institutions and the United States to make them. There is considerable consensus among Latin American intellectuals and quite a few politicians in South America that neoliberal policies have not worked well in Latin America and have caused unnecessary pain and suffering. The appeal of the argument that U.S. workers have not benefited from free trade deals helped propel Donald Trump to the U.S. presidency calling for a renegotiation of NAFTA.

Buoyed by the successful implementation of NAFTA at the beginning of 1994, the Clinton administration promoted and hosted the Summit of the Americas in Miami in December 1994. Attended by thirty-four heads of state, with the conspicuous absence of Fidel Castro, it was the first such hemispheric gathering since 1967. The 1994 meeting represented an assurance from the United States to Latin America that it would not be neglected in the twenty-first century. The primary achievement of the meeting was to create a framework of negotiations for the creation of a hemisphere-wide customs union, the Free Trade Area of the Americas (FTAA) by 2005.

Clinton's statement that the gathering was "a watershed in the history of the continent" was overblown. As a first step, Chile was to be integrated quickly into NAFTA, then Clinton—with renewed "fast-track" negotiating authority from the U.S. Congress—would lay the groundwork for the FTAA. In the years since the Miami summit, the prospects for hemispheric economic integration have dimmed considerably. Difficulties for the FTAA project and the expansion of NAFTA began at the end of 1994. At that time, the Mexican peso had to be sharply devalued and was rescued from disaster only by a multibillion-dollar bailout from the IMF spearheaded by the United States. The bailout stabilized NAFTA, but it undercut political support within the U.S. Congress for making new trade agreements and potential commitments for further financial bailouts. As a result, an anti-FTAA coalition developed in the U.S. Congress with support in both major parties.

In 2001, President George W. Bush recommitted to the FTAA project and began the process of lobbying Congress for the renewed fast-track authority necessary for a deal. Bush, aided by the events of September 11, 2001, regained fast-track authority in 2002. The year 2003 was to be the breakthrough year for completing the treaty along the line of the U.S. vision. However, renewed Latin American skepticism, fueled by the election of Luiz Inácio Lula da Silva (Lula) in Brazil in 2002 and Néstor Kirchner in Argentina in 2003, derailed U.S. plans. Meeting in the Argentine capital in October 2003, the two leaders formulated the Buenos Aires Consensus as an alternative to the Washington Consensus. This Argentine–Brazilian skepticism about FTAA as projected by the United States doomed the project to failure. The November 2003 FTAA meeting in Miami went ahead as scheduled, and countries meeting there did not officially end the idea, but rather talked of a scaled-back treaty, a so-called FTAA lite. In reality, no further FTAA meetings have been held, and efforts at regional integration have moved along several parallel lines, reflecting the political differences in the hemisphere.

Following the defeat of the FTAA, the United States moved to implement an alternative strategy based on the Central American Free Trade Agreement (CAFTA) and selected bilateral agreements with willing Latin American countries. That U.S. strategy has seen some success. Negotiations for CAFTA were completed in late 2003, and the pact was eventually approved by most Central American governments and the U.S. Congress in 2006. The final piece of the CAFTA puzzle came into place in October 2007 with its approval by a narrow margin in a Costa Rican referendum. Thus Costa Rica joined Nicaragua, Guatemala, and El Salvador in the pact.

The agreement was intended to boost trade and investment among the countries involved, including more access to U.S. markets for the Central American countries and CAFTA's other member, the Dominican Republic. Ten years into its implementation, the agreement has largely not lived up to its promise to increase prosperity in the region. As the result of the lowering of tariff barriers by the CAFTA-DR countries, U.S. trade to the region has almost doubled but with some of the same consequences of NAFTA as the region's farmers have been negatively impacted by subsidized agricultural goods from the United States. On this question the full impact will only be known after 2020 when the CAFTA-DR countries must fully eliminate agricultural tariffs. The supporters of the agreement also argued that more manufacturing jobs would be created in the region, but manufacturing exports to the United States have actually fallen more than 20 percent since 2005 as U.S. textile manufacturers have moved some production to even lower wage countries in Asia. The agreement did little to give greater access to the U.S. market for CAFTA-DR countries as those tariffs had largely been eliminated in the 1980s. The agreement also promised to improve labor and environmental conditions in the region, but, as with NAFTA, these promises have proven to be false as labor and environmental activists continue to be targeted with no assistance from treaty provisions, which mainly favor the transnational corporations. The ongoing drug wars and gang violence in the Northern Triangle countries of the region and the subsequent flow of refugees northward is an ongoing indictment of the failure of the agreement to deliver on its promises.

The United States also aggressively pursued bilateral agreements with sympathetic neoliberal governments in Peru, Ecuador, Colombia, and Panama. With all but Ecuador, the United States succeeded in crafting agreements along the lines of the 2004 U.S.–Chile agreement. Negotiations with Ecuador broke down when the neoliberal Lucio Gutiérrez was forced from office by mass demonstrations in 2005 and eventually replaced by Rafael Correa, a clear anti-neoliberal. The agreements with Columbia, Peru, and Panama were strongly resisted in the U.S. Congress but with support from U.S. president Barack Obama, all three were enacted by 2012, a blow to those in Latin America opposing such agreements.

The success of the bilateral agreements with select Latin American governments has also fit well with a U.S.-driven multilateral initiative, the Trans-Pacific Partnership (TPP). The TPP is a high-priority, free trade pact, modeled on the neoliberal principles of the defeated FTAA, that seeks to link several Latin American countries (Mexico, Costa Rica, Panama, Columbia, Peru, and Chile) with Asian Pacific Rim countries, including Australia, New Zealand, Japan, Singapore, and South Korea. Negotiations proceeded over a seven-year time period ending with a signed deal in 2015 that included three Latin American countries, all close U.S. allies: Mexico, Peru, and Chile. Progressive Latin American leaders like Evo Morales, together with Latin American social movements, denounced the pact once details were revealed for its neoliberal character and as a ploy to divide Latin America and counter its autonomous regional integration projects. However, implementation of the agreement requires approval from the U.S. Congress and opposition forces in that body, supported by the new U.S. president, Donald Trump, are now confident that there is no path to its approval. The apparent demise of the TPP demonstrates the ongoing doubts about the economic benefits of globalization when the process is controlled by the nations of the global north.

## Latin America's Regional Integration Projects

Even as the United States pursued its own projects, the nature of Latin American efforts at regional integration independent of the United States began to take different forms. MERCOSUR, the Common Market of the South, was formed in 1994 and is a customs union that links Argentina, Brazil, Paraguay, Uruguay, and Venezuela. Several others, including Bolivia, Chile, and Ecuador, are associate members. Over its twenty-year history, built on the region's two largest economies, the project has seen significant success in promoting regional trade, a tenfold increase among the participating countries. The body has also succeeded in creating a MERCOSUR parliament that oversees the trade and investment procedures among the member states. MERCOSUR was formed as a trade pact on broadly neoliberal principles, but it has never endorsed the investor-friendly concepts promoted by the United States in the FTAA. To the contrary, MERCOSUR, together with the Andean Pact, came to be seen by Brazil and Argentina as a counterweight to neoliberal initiatives. The long-term prospects for MERCOSUR are uncertain, marked by ongoing trade disputes between Brazil and Argentina and concerns by the smaller states in the pact that their interests are not fully served. It is also unclear whether MERCOSUR can contribute to the creation of a continent-wide customs union as envisioned in the Union of South American Nations (UNASUR) discussed later in Chapter 11.

Under Hugo Chávez, the Venezuelan government, bolstered by strong oil and gas revenues, embarked on a bold path of challenging U.S. dominance in the region through government-to-government direct financial aid and through its support for two multilateral projects, the Bank of the South and ALBA. In 2007 alone, Venezuela pledged close to $10 billion in aid to Latin American governments—three times the amount given by the United States. These were unprecedented amounts for a Latin American country. The most dramatic example of Venezuelan assistance was to Argentina. Saddled with billions of debt to the IMF and wishing to free itself from the neoliberal constraints of the fund's conditionality programs, Argentina and president Néstor Kirchner turned to Chávez for help, and Venezuela responded by purchasing more than $5 billion of Argentina's IMF debt, allowing them to repay the IMF and walk away from the IMF-imposed neoliberal policies. The independence from the IMF proved to be a boon to the Argentinean economy and to the recovery of its social indicators. Other significant government-to-government aid went to Bolivia, Ecuador, and Nicaragua following the election of progressive presidents in those countries in 2005 and 2006.

Venezuela took the lead in promoting the idea of the Bank of the South, a project designed to sideline the role in Latin America of the U.S.-dominated Inter-American Development Bank, World Bank, and IMF. With seven initial members (Argentina, Brazil, Bolivia, Ecuador, Paraguay, Uruguay, and Venezuela), the bank had a projected initial capital base of $20 billion and was designed to give member states access to loans for emergency situations and to develop programs for social services. The bank represented another potential challenge to U.S. hegemony in the region, but its implementation was not a high priority for Brazil, and when oil revenues in Venezuela plummeted, the project was put on hold.

A very different project under Venezuelan and Cuban leadership is ALBA. Launched in 2005 as the Bolivarian Alternative, initially as a project of bilateral cooperation between Cuba and Venezuela, it was broadened to include Bolivia, Ecuador, Honduras (which later withdrew after 2009 coup), Nicaragua, and three Caribbean island nations following the change of the political landscape in those countries. Presenting itself as an alternative to the neoliberal model of free trade deals, ALBA involves the exchange of services, primarily in the fields of education and health care. Cuba contributes its human resources, cultivated over the long years of the Cuban Revolution in the form of teachers and medical personnel who did extended service in the other member countries of ALBA. In return, energy-poor Cuba receives oil and gas from the energy-rich members of the group, Venezuela and Bolivia. The current economic value of the exchange is smaller than the size of Venezuela's other aid programs, but it has the potential to change the social dynamics in the impoverished countries that are participating. The exchange is especially important for Venezuela as it seeks to deliver its promises to improve the

**TABLE 15.** Share of Aggregate Income Received by U.S. Households (Percentage) by Quantile and Top 5 Percent, 1967 to 2015

| Year | Number (thousands) | Lowest Fifth | Second Fifth | Third Fifth | Fourth Fifth | Highest Fifth | Top 5 Percent |
|------|------|------|------|------|------|------|------|
| 2015 | 125,819 | 3.1 | 8.2 | 14.3 | 23.2 | 51.1 | 22.1 |
| 2014 | 124,587 | 3.1 | 8.2 | 14.3 | 23.2 | 51.2 | 21.9 |
| 2013 | 123,931 | 3.1 | 8.2 | 14.3 | 23.0 | 51.4 | 22.2 |
| 2012 | 122,459 | 3.2 | 8.3 | 14.4 | 23.0 | 51.0 | 22.3 |
| 2011 | 121,084 | 3.2 | 8.4 | 14.3 | 23.0 | 51.1 | 22.3 |
| 2010 | 119,927 | 3.3 | 8.5 | 14.6 | 23.4 | 50.3 | 21.3 |
| 2009 | 117,538 | 3.4 | 8.6 | 14.6 | 23.2 | 50.3 | 21.7 |
| 2008 | 117,181 | 3.4 | 8.6 | 14.7 | 23.3 | 50.0 | 21.5 |
| 2007 | 116,783 | 3.4 | 8.7 | 14.8 | 23.4 | 49.7 | 21.2 |
| 2006 | 116,011 | 3.4 | 8.6 | 14.5 | 22.9 | 50.5 | 22.3 |
| 2005 | 114,384 | 3.4 | 8.6 | 14.6 | 23.0 | 50.4 | 22.2 |
| 2004 | 113,343 | 3.4 | 8.7 | 14.7 | 23.2 | 50.1 | 21.8 |
| 2003 | 112,000 | 3.4 | 8.7 | 14.8 | 23.4 | 49.8 | 21.4 |
| 2002 | 111,278 | 3.5 | 8.8 | 14.8 | 23.3 | 49.7 | 21.7 |
| 2001 | 109,297 | 3.5 | 8.7 | 14.6 | 23.0 | 50.1 | 22.4 |
| 2000 | 108,209 | 3.6 | 8.9 | 14.8 | 23.0 | 49.8 | 22.1 |
| 1999 | 106,434 | 3.6 | 8.9 | 14.9 | 23.2 | 49.4 | 21.5 |
| 1998 | 103,874 | 3.6 | 9.0 | 15.0 | 23.2 | 49.2 | 21.4 |
| 1997 | 102,528 | 3.6 | 8.9 | 15.0 | 23.2 | 49.4 | 21.7 |
| 1996 | 101,018 | 3.6 | 9.0 | 15.1 | 23.3 | 49.0 | 21.4 |
| 1995 | 99,627 | 3.7 | 9.1 | 15.2 | 23.3 | 48.7 | 21.0 |
| 1994 | 98,990 | 3.6 | 8.9 | 15.0 | 23.4 | 49.1 | 21.2 |
| 1993 | 97,107 | 3.6 | 9.0 | 15.1 | 23.5 | 48.9 | 21.0 |
| 1992 | 96,426 | 3.8 | 9.4 | 15.8 | 24.2 | 46.9 | 18.6 |
| 1991 | 95,669 | 3.8 | 9.6 | 15.9 | 24.2 | 46.5 | 18.1 |
| 1990 | 94,312 | 3.8 | 9.6 | 15.9 | 24.0 | 46.6 | 18.5 |
| 1989 | 93,347 | 3.8 | 9.5 | 15.8 | 24.0 | 46.8 | 18.9 |
| 1988 | 92,830 | 3.8 | 9.6 | 16.0 | 24.2 | 46.3 | 18.3 |
| 1987 | 91,124 | 3.8 | 9.6 | 16.1 | 24.3 | 46.2 | 18.2 |
| 1986 | 89,479 | 3.8 | 9.7 | 16.2 | 24.3 | 46.1 | 18.0 |
| 1985 | 88,458 | 3.9 | 9.8 | 16.2 | 24.4 | 45.6 | 17.6 |
| 1984 | 86,789 | 4.0 | 9.9 | 16.3 | 24.6 | 45.2 | 17.1 |
| 1983 | 85,407 | 4.0 | 9.9 | 16.4 | 24.6 | 45.1 | 17.0 |
| 1982 | 83,918 | 4.0 | 10.0 | 16.5 | 24.5 | 45.0 | 17.0 |
| 1981 | 83,527 | 4.1 | 10.1 | 16.7 | 24.8 | 44.3 | 16.5 |
| 1980 | 82,368 | 4.2 | 10.2 | 16.8 | 24.7 | 44.1 | 16.5 |
| 1979 | 80,776 | 4.1 | 10.2 | 16.8 | 24.6 | 44.2 | 16.9 |
| 1978 | 77,330 | 4.2 | 10.2 | 16.8 | 24.7 | 44.1 | 16.8 |
| 1977 | 76,030 | 4.2 | 10.2 | 16.9 | 24.7 | 44.0 | 16.8 |
| 1976 | 74,142 | 4.3 | 10.3 | 17.0 | 24.7 | 43.7 | 16.6 |
| 1975 | 72,867 |  | 10.4 | 17.0 | 24.7 | 43.6 | 16.5 |
| 1974 | 71,163 | 4.3 | 10.6 | 17.0 | 24.6 | 43.5 | 16.5 |
| 1973 | 69,859 | 4.2 | 10.4 | 17.0 | 24.5 | 43.9 | 16.9 |
| 1972 | 68,251 | 4.1 | 10.4 | 17.0 | 24.5 | 43.9 | 17.0 |
| 1971 | 66,676 | 4.1 | 10.6 | 17.3 | 24.5 | 43.5 | 16.7 |
| 1970 | 64,778 | 4.1 | 10.8 | 17.4 | 24.5 | 43.3 | 16.6 |
| 1969 | 63,401 | 4.1 | 10.9 | 17.5 | 24.5 | 43.0 | 16.6 |
| 1968 | 62,214 | 4.2 | 11.1 | 17.6 | 24.5 | 42.6 | 16.3 |
| 1967 | 60,813 | 4.0 | 10.8 | 17.3 | 24.2 | 43.6 | 17.2 |

Source: U.S. Census Bureau, Historical Income Tables: Households, http://www.census.gov/data/tables/time-series/demo/income-poverty/historical-

Note: Households as of March of the following year.

daily life of poor Venezuelans. The ALBA project continues, but the major economic challenges facing Venezuela and the shaky political future of ruling PSUV make ALBA's long-term viability questionable.

## Economic Legacy

Neoliberalism, the structural adjustments of the 1990s, and the globalization process generally did have a considerable effect on the Latin American economies. They generally recovered from the "lost decade" of the 1980s and began to experience growth in the early and mid-1990s, although growth did begin to slow in many economies by decade's end. Another clear area of success was the reduction of inflation to single-digit figures in most of Latin America. This was particularly noteworthy in Brazil and Argentina, which had both experienced inflation in excess of 1,000 percent per year in past decades (see Table 16). Real-wage rates for the vast majority of workers did not, however, improve. Unemployment remained a severe problem in most countries, and growing numbers of workers were forced to go into the informal sector to survive. Indeed, the number of those selling all manner of fruits, vegetables, clothing, household products, and auto products on the streets and at traffic lights in larger cities all over Latin America increased significantly. A type of dual economy developed where the working class was forced to buy its necessities in the markets and on the streets, where quality and prices are lower, while the upper and upper middle classes went to supermarkets, specialty shops, and the growing number of malls to make their purchases. The lower segments of the middle class may frequent all these places, depending on their precise need, income that month, and interest in being seen in the right place. More consumer goods of better quality are available at better prices, but many cannot begin to afford them.

Poverty and misery continue and have increased in some countries. Income and wealth have become even more concentrated in the hands of the wealthy few, although the spread continues to the middle class. Many argued that the social costs of this form of development are too high. This consensus spread as far as the international financial institutions themselves, as suggested by the title of a book by the Inter-American Development Bank, *Facing Up to Inequality in Latin America: Economic and Social Progress in Latin America, 1998–99 Report.* Even the neoliberal World Bank began to insist that loan packages contain programs specifically designed to improve living conditions for the masses and mitigate some of the worst aspects of the reforms. However, such concerns are not sufficient to prompt a reevaluation of the neoliberal model by the international financial institutions that advocate it.

The economic scene is changing radically in Latin America. One sees major stock exchanges in São Paulo, Mexico City, Lima, Santiago, and Buenos Aires; more and more manufactured goods or key components are being made in the region; and modern aspects of Western consumption such as computers, cable TV, mass retail stores, and the omnipresent auto are inundating national societies. Brazil is already the sixth-largest economy in the world, and more and more

TABLE 16. Latin American Inflation: Variations in the Consumer Price Index (Average Annual Rate; General Level), 1990–2014

| Country | 1990 | 1991 | 1992 | 1993 | 1994 | 1995 | 1996 | 1997 | 1998 | 1999 | 2000 | 2001 | 2002 | 2003 | 2004 | 2005 | 2006 | 2007 | 2008 | 2009 | 2010 | 2011 | 2012 | 2013 | 2014 |
|---|---|---|---|---|---|---|---|---|---|---|---|---|---|---|---|---|---|---|---|---|---|---|---|---|---|
| Argentina | 2313.9 | 171.7 | 24.9 | 10.6 | 4.2 | 3.4 | 0.2 | 0.5 | 0.9 | -1.2 | -0.9 | -1.1 | 25.9 | 13.4 | 4.4 | 9.6 | 10.9 | 8.8 | 8.6 | 6.3 | 10.5 | 9.8 | 10.0 | 10.6 | 21.4 |
| Bolivia | 17.1 | 21.4 | 12.1 | 8.5 | 7.9 | 10.2 | 12.4 | 4.9 | 7.7 | 2.2 | 4.4 | 1.6 | 0.9 | 3.3 | 4.4 | 5.4 | 4.3 | 8.7 | 14.0 | 3.3 | 2.5 | 9.9 | 4.5 | 5.7 | 5.8 |
| Brazil | 2947.7 | 432.9 | 951.8 | 1942.2 | 2105.3 | 66.0 | 15.8 | 6.9 | 3.2 | 4.9 | 7.0 | 6.8 | 8.5 | 14.7 | 6.6 | 6.9 | 4.2 | 3.6 | 5.7 | 4.9 | 5.0 | 6.6 | 5.4 | 6.2 | 6.3 |
| Chile | 26.0 | 21.8 | 15.4 | 12.7 | 11.4 | 8.2 | 7.4 | 6.1 | 5.1 | 3.3 | 3.8 | 3.6 | 2.5 | 2.8 | 1.1 | 3.1 | 3.4 | 4.4 | 8.7 | 1.5 | 1.4 | 3.3 | 3.0 | 1.2 | 4.6 |
| Colombia | 29.1 | 30.4 | 27.0 | 22.4 | 22.8 | 20.9 | 20.8 | 18.5 | 18.7 | 10.9 | 9.2 | 8.0 | 6.3 | 7.1 | 5.9 | 5.0 | 4.3 | 5.5 | 7.0 | 4.2 | 2.3 | 3.4 | 3.2 | 2.0 | 2.9 |
| Costa Rica | 19.0 | 28.7 | 21.8 | 9.8 | 13.5 | 23.2 | 17.5 | 13.3 | 11.7 | 10.0 | 11.0 | 11.3 | 9.2 | 9.4 | 12.3 | 13.8 | 11.5 | 9.4 | 13.4 | 7.8 | 5.7 | 4.9 | 4.5 | 5.2 | 4.5 |
| Cuba | ... | ... | ... | ... | ... | ... | ... | ... | ... | 0.3 | 12.0 | 0.3 | -5.2 | 2.0 | -2.2 | 2.8 | 5.1 | 7.1 | 1.6 | -1.2 | 1.3 | 1.3 | 1.9 | 0.6 | 0.7 |
| Dominican Republic | 50.5 | 47.1 | 4.3 | 5.2 | 8.3 | 12.5 | 5.4 | 8.3 | 4.8 | 6.5 | 7.8 | 8.8 | 5.2 | 27.5 | 51.5 | 4.2 | 7.6 | 6.1 | 10.6 | 1.4 | 6.3 | 8.5 | 3.7 | 4.8 | 3.0 |
| Ecuador | 48.5 | 48.7 | 54.6 | 45.0 | 27.3 | 22.9 | 24.4 | 30.7 | 36.1 | 52.2 | 96.1 | 37.7 | 12.5 | 7.9 | 2.7 | 2.2 | 3.3 | 2.3 | 8.4 | 5.2 | 3.6 | 4.5 | 5.1 | 2.7 | 3.6 |
| El Salvador | 24.0 | 14.4 | 11.2 | 18.5 | 7.2 | 9.7 | 9.8 | 4.5 | 2.5 | 0.5 | 2.3 | 3.8 | 1.9 | 2.1 | 4.4 | 4.7 | 4.0 | 4.6 | 7.3 | 0.5 | 0.9 | 5.1 | 1.7 | 0.8 | 1.1 |
| Guatemala | 41.0 | 35.1 | 10.2 | 13.4 | 12.5 | 8.4 | 11.1 | 9.2 | 6.6 | 5.2 | 6.0 | 7.3 | 8.1 | 5.6 | 7.6 | 9.1 | 6.6 | 6.8 | 11.4 | 1.9 | 3.9 | 6.2 | 3.8 | 4.3 | 3.4 |
| Haiti | 20.8 | 15.2 | 19.3 | 36.5 | 37.3 | 25.1 | 18.3 | 16.4 | 10.6 | 8.7 | 13.7 | 14.2 | 9.9 | 33.0 | 24.5 | 15.8 | 13.1 | 8.5 | 15.5 | 0.0 | 5.7 | 8.4 | 6.3 | 5.9 | 4.6 |
| Honduras | 23.4 | 34.0 | 8.8 | 10.7 | 21.7 | 29.5 | 23.8 | 20.2 | 13.7 | 11.6 | 11.1 | 9.7 | 7.7 | 7.7 | 8.1 | 8.8 | 5.6 | 6.9 | 11.4 | 5.5 | 4.7 | 6.8 | 5.2 | 5.2 | 6.1 |
| Mexico | 26.7 | 22.7 | 15.5 | 9.8 | 7.0 | 35.0 | 34.4 | 20.6 | 15.9 | 16.6 | 9.5 | 6.4 | 5.0 | 4.5 | 4.7 | 4.0 | 3.6 | 4.0 | 5.1 | 5.3 | 4.2 | 3.4 | 4.1 | 3.8 | 4.0 |
| Nicaragua | 7485.2 | 2945.1 | 23.7 | 20.4 | 7.8 | 10.9 | 11.6 | 9.2 | 13.0 | 11.2 | 11.5 | 7.4 | 4.0 | 5.2 | 8.4 | 9.4 | 10.0 | 10.7 | 19.6 | 3.0 | 5.9 | 8.5 | 7.5 | 7.1 | 6.0 |
| Panama | 0.8 | 1.2 | 1.8 | 0.4 | 1.3 | 1.0 | 1.3 | 1.2 | 0.6 | 1.3 | 1.4 | 0.3 | 1.1 | 1.4 | -0.3 | 2.9 | 2.5 | 4.2 | 8.8 | 2.4 | 3.5 | 5.9 | 5.7 | 4.0 | 2.6 |
| Paraguay | 38.2 | 24.2 | 15.2 | 18.2 | 20.6 | 13.4 | 9.8 | 7.0 | 11.6 | 6.7 | 9.0 | 7.3 | 10.5 | 14.2 | 4.3 | 6.8 | 9.6 | 8.1 | 10.2 | 2.6 | 4.7 | 8.3 | 3.7 | 2.7 | 5.0 |
| Peru | 7479.0 | -49.0 | 73.5 | 48.6 | 23.7 | 11.1 | 11.5 | 8.5 | 7.3 | 3.5 | 3.8 | 2.0 | 0.2 | 2.3 | 3.7 | 1.6 | 2.0 | 1.8 | 5.8 | 2.9 | 1.5 | 3.4 | 3.7 | 2.8 | 3.2 |
| Uruguay | 112.5 | 102.0 | 68.5 | 54.1 | 44.7 | 42.2 | 28.3 | 19.8 | 10.8 | 5.7 | 4.8 | 4.4 | 14.0 | 19.4 | 9.2 | 4.7 | 6.4 | 8.1 | 7.9 | 7.1 | 6.7 | 8.1 | 8.1 | 8.6 | 8.9 |
| Venezuela | 40.7 | 34.2 | 31.4 | 38.1 | 60.8 | 59.9 | 99.9 | 50.1 | 35.7 | 23.6 | 16.2 | 12.5 | 22.4 | 31.1 | 21.7 | 16.0 | 13.7 | 18.7 | 31.4 | 28.6 | 29.1 | 27.1 | 21.1 | 38.5 | 43.0 |
| Latina America | 567.6 | 55.3 | 16.0 | 12.4 | 735.2 | 37.7 | 21.6 | 13.0 | 10.0 | 9.3 | 9.5 | 7.2 | 8.6 | 11.1 | 7.3 | 6.4 | 5.3 | 5.5 | 8.1 | 5.6 | 5.7 | 6.7 | 5.7 | 6.6 | 7.8 |

... Data not available.

Source: Statistical Yearbook of Latin America, 2015. http://interwp.cepal.org/anuario_estadistico/anuario 2015/en/index.asp

products on the world market come from Brazil and other countries in the region. Although conditions for the masses in Mexico are still not that positive, Mexico is generating more and more millionaires and now counts some of the wealthiest people in the world among its population. On an international scale, Brazilian managers are among the very best paid. The rise of progressive governments in the region in the last ten years have resulted in successful poverty-alleviation programs in key countries like Brazil, Bolivia, Chile, Ecuador, and Venezuela, but the serious problems of highly inequitable distribution of wealth and income remain a challenge in the region.

## Environmental Issues

Since the founding of Earth Day in the United States in 1970 and the convening of the first United Nations conference on the environment in Stockholm in 1972, there has been a worldwide dramatic increase in awareness and activism on environmental issues. Latin America has been no exception to that environmental focus, especially since the 1992 Rio de Janeiro Environment Summit on twentieth anniversary of the Stockholm meeting. That meeting brought international focus to a range of issues from biodiversity to deforestation to climate change. The twenty-five years since the Rio meeting have seen a dramatic increase in environmental issues, and in each case there is a very important Latin American component. An exposition of contemporary Latin American environmental issues reveals some very important trends with significant ramifications for the Latin American political economy.

Scholars Armijo and Rhodes have articulated a framework that helps us understand the dynamics of Latin American environmental issues in a manner that acknowledges the political diversity of the region. The governments in the region vary quite widely in their perspectives on environmental protection. For example, senior policymakers in Brasilia (and in Washington, D.C.) focus on preventing climate change through "green growth," while governments like Venezuela, Bolivia, and Ecuador link the environment to the rights of indigenous people and avoiding exploitation by market-based capitalism. The result of these sharply variant views is that while there is considerable pressure from nonstate actors for joint environmental actions at this juncture, there is very limited transnational action.

The green-growth model has long been palatable to Brazilian leaders, even predating the Workers' Party governments of Lula and Rousseff. In the 1980s Brazilian governments came under harsh scrutiny for promoting policies of agricultural development that were leading to a rapid process of deforestation in the Amazon jungles. In the last twenty years, Brazilian governments have pushed back against the international criticism in a variety of ways. First, they no longer encourage the type of slash-and-burn agriculture that led to rapid deforestation. More significant, the Brazilian government has continued old practices and initiated new ones that it categorizes as green growth. Going back decades, Brazil has generated the bulk of its electricity needs from hydroelectric power (which is largely climate change neutral) and has funded new, large-scale projects to keep its hydroelectric dependence at more than 80 percent. In addition, Brazil has made large-scale successful investment in the production of biofuels from sugar cane. These state-driven but market-oriented initiatives leave Brazil's green-growth model at odds with its more politically radical neighbors.

The Brazilian position accepts some responsibility for the lesser-developed countries to contribute to the climate-change challenge, but the anticapitalist position embodied by both Bolivia and Venezuela places the onus for confronting climate change on the northern, developed, capitalist countries, who they argue are primarily responsible for greenhouse gas emissions and therefore must curtail them. This view links the concepts of indigenous rights and protection of natural resources. In the anticapitalist view, the solution to environmental problems lies in socialism. This view was embodied in the statement by Bolivian president Evo Morales at the World People's Conference on Climate Change and the Rights of Mother Earth in 2009 with the pronouncement that "either capitalism dies or it will be Mother Earth." Environmental rights are now stipulated in the Bolivian Constitution. Consistent with the need to protect and revere *pacha mama* (the Earth Mother), Bolivia has developed the concept of *vivir bien*, or living well, without wasteful and unnecessary consumption. This concept, which is also being developed in Ecuador under the rubric of *el bien vivir*, is based on the indigenous concept of *sumak kawsay* (in Quechua), challenges ideas of continual economic growth, and suggests that having a satisfying life that does not pillage nature is more important. Many find this to be a viable conceptualization of a sustainable economy that challenges capitalist—and traditional socialist—concepts of economic development through growth and the consumption that it implies.

Anticapitalist stances are represented mostly forthrightly in the myriad of environmental nongovernmental organizations that have arisen across the region, which are often linked with indigenous rights movements. These groups often have rhetorical support from the region's progressive governments like Venezuela, Bolivia, and Ecuador, but the reality of the political economy of these countries has brought serious conflict with environmental activists and their indigenous allies. These countries are heavily dependent on the extraction of oil and natural gas both to maintain their comparative advantage in the world economy and to pay for social programs in health, education, housing, and food security, which are at the heart of their domestic socialist agendas. As a result, all three countries are pursuing an extractive strategy with no end in sight. Conflict with the indigenous and environmental activists has been inevitable, no more so than in Ecuador where in 2013 President Rafael Correa approved drilling in the Yasuni National Park, rejecting the Yasuni-ITT initiative over the strong objection of CONAIE, the main indigenous organization. CONAIE accuses Correa of hypocrisy in claiming to embrace a pro-environment agenda but acting otherwise. On his part, Correa condemns the environmental activists for standing in the way of his antipoverty agenda. This confrontation has been dubbed the red–green divide.

Confrontations between environmentalists and Latin American governments are not limited to the ALBA states or to the long-term climate effects of oil and natural gas extraction. Traditional battles between mining interests and local communities have come to the fore in countries as varied as Peru, Honduras, El Salvador, and Mexico. In virtually all these cases, indigenous peoples resist strip-mining operations being carried out by transnational mining companies that have the support of a market-oriented central government. Such confrontations are not new to Latin America but are today receiving much greater international attention in the context of worldwide environmental consciousness.

## Twenty-First-Century Prospects

Starting in the second decade of the twenty-first century, the expanding market in China and other areas of the global economy greatly increased the demand for mined resources and other primary products. For the first time in many years, focusing on the production of primary goods became an excellent way of earning foreign exchange. This even led to what Henry Veltmeyer and James Petras has called the "new extractivism" in their book by that title. This stimulated growth in Latin American economies like Brazil even during the financial crisis after 2008. Further, it helped to bolster a neoliberal model that would use financial resources gained from selling mining products, soy, natural gas, petroleum and ethanol to distribute to the poorer classes to compensate for their lack of wealth and income. That is, proceeds from the sale of natural resources such as iron ore and petroleum and crops like soy would ameliorate some of the worst aspects of the now-globalized neoliberal model and help to maintain the basic structure of the system. This also had another effect.

China was not only able to drastically increase trade with countries like Brazil and Ecuador but also to help to finance infrastructure projects and provide loans and investment funds from the China Export-Import Bank and Chinese Development Bank. As Kevin Gallagher notes in his 2016 book, *The China Triangle: Latin America's China Boom and the Fate of the Washington Consensus*, between 2008 and 2012 more than 85 percent of Latin American exports to China were raw materials, and between 2003 and 2012 China invested $50 billion in Latin America. Given the increased importation of Chinese manufactured goods, this was also a negative stimulus to continued Latin American industrialization.

Fueled in part by higher commodity prices for the region's primary exports (beef, oil, corn, soybeans, coffee, etc.), the major economies generally expanded in the early years of the new century with annual growth rates between 5 and 10 percent. This new-found macroeconomic economic prosperity, coming in the wake of almost two decades of economic stagnation, found democratic governments in power throughout the hemisphere and their historically influential militaries largely consigned to the barracks. With the exception of a few countries, such as Colombia, Peru, and Guatemala, left of center governments were in power, having been placed there by electorates who grew weary of the unfulfilled promises of Latin America's neoliberal governments in the 1990s (headed by Carlos Menem in Argentina and Fernando Henrique Cardoso in Brazil). The first wave of this new political leadership, headed by Néstor Kirchner in Argentina and Lula in Brazil, stopped the U.S.-inspired FTAA dead in its tracks by 2003. That reversal was stunning because it had been unanimously endorsed by the Latin American presidents present at the 1994 Miami summit.

Leaders of Venezuela, Bolivia, and Ecuador offered varied visions of achieving "twenty-first-century socialism" built primarily on the premise of spending the available fossil fuel revenue on health, education, and food security programs for the majority poor in these countries. The Workers' Party in Brazil offered a less radical vision than Venezuela, Bolivia, and Ecuador with its signature poverty-alleviation program. The Family Allowance (*bolsa família*) is a wealth-transfer plan connected to education aimed at mitigating extreme poverty. These programs have made a real difference in the lives of some of Latin American's poorest citizens but their sustainability is not guaranteed. The drop in world commodity prices following the 2008 Great Recession and the slowing demand in China had a very significant impact on countries dependent on commodity exports that had left governments in power, particularly Argentina, Brazil, and Venezuela. In each case the progressive government was punished at the polls because they had to cut back on popular social programs in the face of declining government revenues. In addition, as discussed in the previous section on the environment, even among progressive forces, there is not agreement on the wisdom of the resource extractive strategy even for laudable purposes. The recent dramatic drops in commodity prices have underscored that Latin American economies are still heavily weighted toward the production of primary products, not finished goods, reflecting the region's long-standing limited role in the world economy. Asia's thirst for Latin American oil, mineral resources, and foodstuffs at decent price levels remained strong for some time, but dependence on resource exportation to Asia and other markets is not a long-term plan for productive or sustainable Latin American growth. The drop in commodity prices beginning in the early 2010s has also had political implications for the success of the region's progressive governments. First, the long rule of the Peronists was ended by the victory of conservative, Mauricio Macri in November 2015, followed by a decisive defeat of the PSUV in Venezuela's mid-term legislative elections and the impeachment and removal from power of Dilma Roussoff in 2016. The conservative governments taking power have yet to reveal a new strategy going forward.

The reality is that the economies of Latin America now face major challenges from their industrial competitors in Asia, who are generally better positioned in manufacturing in the new century. Brazil and Argentina have signed long-term trade deals to provide agricultural commodities to China. These agreements can be lucrative in the short term but, over the long haul, they may serve to perpetuate Latin America's centuries-long standing as a relatively impoverished region providing the more-developed world, which now includes China, with raw materials and foodstuffs. In the process, Latin America will remain vulnerable to the inevitable swings in commodity prices—and as dependent as ever—and without long-term solutions to its deep-seated history of poverty and inequality. To avoid that fate, Latin American governments must craft policies that use the current position in the world economy to diversify their economies beyond commodity production while systematically working to reduce absolute poverty and make significant investments in health care and education. Yet, the economic slowdown in China and the resultant decreased demand for petroleum and other primary products has caused an economic contraction in much of Latin America and a severe economic crisis in Brazil. This will challenge the commodities-led growth that Latin American experienced in the last decade.

# Bibliography

Baran, Paul A. *The Political Economy of Growth*. New York: Monthly Review, 1957.

Berry, Albert, ed. *Poverty, Economic Reform, and Income Distribution in Latin America*. London: Lynne Reinner, 1998.

Blumer-Thomas, Victor. *The Economic History of Latin America since Independence*. 3d ed. Cambridge: Cambridge University Press, 2014.

Cardoso, Fernando Henrique, and Enzo Faletto. *Dependency and Development in Latin America*. Berkeley: University of California Press, 1979. First published as *Dependencia y Desarrollo en America Latina*, 1971.

Chilcote, Ronald. *Development in Theory and Practice: Latin American Perspectives*. Lanham, MD: Rowman & Littlefield, 2003.

ECLA. *Study of Inter-American Trade*. New York: United Nations, 1956.

ECLA. *Towards a Dynamic Development Policy for Latin America*. New York: United Nations, 1963.

Frank, Andre Gunder. *Capitalism and Underdevelopment in Latin America*. New York: Monthly Review, 1967.

Franko, Patrice. *The Puzzle of Latin American Economic Development*. 3d ed. Lanham, MD: Rowman & Littlefield, 2007.

Gasllagher, Kevin P. *The China Triangle: Latin America's China Boom and the Fate of the Washington Consensus*. Oxford: Oxford University Press, 2016.

Hearn, Adrian and Margaret Myers, eds. *The Changing Currents of Transpacific Integration: China, The TPP, and Beyond*. Boulder, CO: Lynne Reinner, 2016.

Inter-American Development Bank. *Beyond Facts: Understanding Quality of Life, Development in the Americas 2009*. Cambridge: David Rockefeller Center, 2009.

Jameson, Kenneth P., and Charles Wilber, eds. *The Political Economy of Development and Underdevelopment*. 6th ed. New York: McGraw-Hill, 1996.

Kingstone, Peter. *The Political Economy of Latin America: Reflections on Neoliberalism and Development*. New York: Routledge, 2011.

Lenin, V. I. *Imperialism, The Highest Stage of Capitalism*. New York: International, 1979.

Merleaux, April. *Sugar and Civilization: American Empire and the Culture of Sweetness*. Chapel Hill: University of North Carolina Press, 2015.

Miller, Shawn William. *An Environmental History of Latin America*. New York: Cambridge University Press, 2009.

Nkrumah, Kwame. *Neo-Colonialism, The Last Stage of Imperialism*. London: Nelson, 1965.

Rodney, Walter. *How Europe Underdeveloped Africa*. Washington, DC: Howard University Press, 1981.

Sanchez-Ancochea, Diego, and Iwan Morgan, eds. *The Political Economy of the Public Budget in the Americas*. London: Institute for the Study of the Americas, 2009.

Tucker, Richard. *Insatiable Appetite: The United States and the Ecological Destruction of the Tropical World*. Lanham, MD: Rowman & Littlefield, 2007.

Veltmeyer, Henry and James Petras. *The New Extractivism. A Post Neo-Liberal Development Model of Imperialism in the Twenty-First Century*. London: Zed, 2014.

Veltmeyer, Henry, and Darcy Tetreavlt, eds. *Poverty and Development in Latin America: Public Policies and Development Pathways*. Boulder, CO: Lynne Reinner, 2013.

FILMS AND VIDEOS

*Amazonia: The Road to the End of the Forest*. Canada, 1990.
*The Battle of the Titans*. Denmark, 1993.

*Coffee: A Sack Full of Power*. United States, 1991.
*Deadly Embrace, Nicaragua, the World Bank and the International Monetary Fund*. United States, 1996 (available through Ashley Eames, Wentworth, NH, 03282).
*The Debt Crisis*. United States, 1989.
*Lines of Blood—The Drug War in Colombia*. United States, 1992.
*Mama Coca*. United States, 1991.
*Traffic*. United States, 2000.

## WEBSITES

http://www.cepal.org/en/ Economic Commission for Latin America and the Caribbean. The political economy of Latin America

# EIGHT

# DEMOCRACY AND AUTHORITARIANISM

## *Latin American Political Culture*

In June 2009 Manuel Zelaya was rousted from his bed by a group of soldiers with their rifles trained on him. He was told he was being deposed as president of Honduras and then taken to a plane while still in his pajamas and flown out of the country. Honduras and Latin America had experienced their most recent coup d'état. Even more remarkably, many members of the Congress, judges on the Supreme Court, and many members of the public thought this was the right thing to do. They were following a long tradition of forcing a president from office when he had engaged in political action that powerful interests—including the military—did not like. He had recently doubled the minimum wage and was organizing a referendum to see if the voting public wanted to change the constitution to allow for a second consecutive term. The economic threat to the business class was too great, and others feared he would use any constitutional revision to extend his stay in office beyond the current one-term limit. So powerful interests in Honduras connived to use the military to oust the constitutional president from office and replace him with their appointee. He had, after all, threatened the interests of the powerful. Such actions would be met with universal condemnation if they occurred in Great Britain, Canada, Australia, or the United States, and it is very doubtful indeed that many members of the military could be convinced to engage in such an action. Yet, this coup, or *golpe de estado*, scenario had been played out hundreds of times before in Latin America, often with the support of a significant section of the population and usually with the support of a substantial part of the upper class and most, if not virtually all, of the military officers. One might rightly conclude that political values and attitudes about changing the president and government are quite different in Latin America. This tradition was extended in Paraguay in 2012 when the constitutionally elected president Fernando Lugo was removed from office by what has been described as a congressional coup. The members of Congress were angered about how he had handled a land dispute and feared that the peasants and small farmers would threaten landed interests. Using revelations about his personal life (he had fathered a child while a priest), the Congress indicted and impeached him as a way of removing him from office and protecting traditional class interests. Following their colleagues in Honduras, the Paraguayan right had found a way to oust a progressive leader and roll back the clock and protect traditional conservative interests. In 2016 conservative political interests and opposition members of Congress used Brazilian congressional maneuvering to impeach elected President Dilma Rousseff and remove her from office in what many in Brazil also considered a coup. This ended Workers Party rule and placed the pro-neoliberal vice president Michel Temer in office.

The right had executed a military coup against Hugo Chávez in Venezuela in 2002, but it was overturned by a mobilized populace. Such was not the case when protests were brutally repressed in Honduras, controlled in Paraguay, and minimized in Brazil. As demonstrated in Figure 5, such values are still found in Latin American society and can be manipulated by those who would challenge the rule of law for political benefit. This would seem to be a tactic that the right is refining as a way to challenge the pink tide and progressive policies in Latin America.

To better understand the very unique context in which politics are conducted in Latin America, it is necessary to understand not only general aspects of Latin American society, economics, and culture but also those specific beliefs and views that affect how Latin Americans see, judge, and participate in politics. In the study

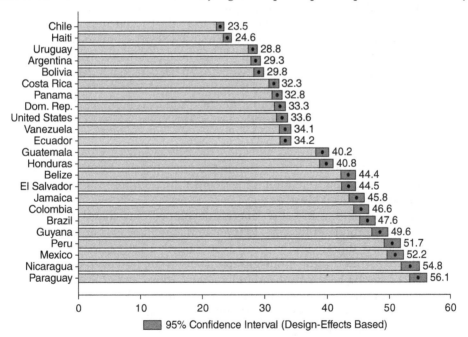

**FIGURE 5.** Support for a Military Coup if Corruption Exists, 2014

*Source:* Guilherme Russo, and Latin American Public Opinion Project. "Amid Brazil's Protests, a Troubling Surge in Support for Military Intervention." *AmericasBarometer: Topical Brief,* March 23, 2015. http://www.vanderbilt.edu/lapop/insights/ITB019en.pdf

of comparative politics, the term "political culture" was developed to describe the associated values, attitudes, and orientations toward politics that individuals have in a specific area or group. This term has proven very useful in studying the way politics are conceived and practiced in different countries and regions. This conglomerate of attitudes and beliefs about politics, or political culture, develops in a society over a period of time. The concept helps us focus on the political beliefs and values that are embedded in a particular national society or in a specific group. As developed through the study of politics in different nations, political culture is defined as those attitudes and beliefs that affect the way we think about, engage in, and evaluate politics and political events. There have been several major studies of political culture dating back to the 1960s. Perhaps the most famous were Gabriel Almond and Sidney Verba's *The Civic Culture* (1965) and Almond and Verba's *Civic Culture Revisited* (1980). These studies used (not always perfect) survey research to examine the ways in which the civic—or, as they conceived it, Western democratic—culture was manifest in five different democracies: the United States, Great Britain, Germany, Italy, and Mexico. Not surprisingly, the values, beliefs, and practices regarding democracy were quite different in the five democratic nations in regard to fundamental dimensions like political participation and respect for and expectations of government and its actions.

Political values can differ sharply between countries, within countries, and from one group to another in a particular nation or region. Thus, coups d'état, strongman rule, and authoritarian decision-making that are common in Latin America might be totally unacceptable in Great Britain, Canada, or the United States, where moderation, compromise, and consensus are more highly valued. Conversely, the political vacillation for which U.S. President Bill Clinton became famous would be little tolerated in a Latin American president, even though his personal indiscretions might. Further, it can be argued that if indeed there is a political culture of authoritarianism in Latin America, as manifest in dictatorial rulers and their support, there is another that values democracy and constitutional rule. This culture is seen in practitioners of open democracy in Costa Rica and in those who, though not always victorious, insist on honest, transparent elections and the rule of law in what were recently reformed and reinvigorated democracies in Uruguay, Bolivia, El Salvador, Ecuador, and countries struggling to maintain the democratic tradition in Paraguay, Brazil, Venezuela, and post-2000 Mexico.

The nature of politics in Latin America developed over many centuries, with the most remote origins in the pre-Columbian hierarchical and authoritarian rule that characterized the governing process among the Aztecs, Mayas, Incas, and other highly structured indigenous groups. There were, however, more participatory practices among less centralized indigenous groups and at lower levels in the far-flung Incan Empire. The communally based *ayllu* would be an example of the latter and one that has recently helped engender community-based participatory politics in indigenous Andean areas where this kinship unit existed from Incan if not pre-Incan times. To this was added the authoritarian, hierarchical, and often dictatorial forms of governing that were brought from the Iberian peninsula and developed in the colonial and early republican eras. Of particular note is the absolutist tradition (from the absolute monarchies in the Iberian peninsula) that became manifest in the Americas in the unchecked power of the viceroy and other governmental leaders in the colonies and the fusion of political and military power in the hands of the viceroy or captain general. Similarly, the seignorial large landowner, or *latifundista*, enjoyed almost virtually unchecked power on his estate and often in the area in which it was located. All these factors combined to make for a tradition and thus a political culture that was generally far from democratic in all too many instances.

# Authoritarian Legacy and Weak Democratic Tradition

## THE *CAUDILLO* TRADITION

Many believe that this authoritarian, dictatorial cluster of values that is commonly found throughout Latin America and which is an integral part of Latin America political culture is most clearly manifest in the person of the *caudillo*, or strong, usually dictatorial, leader. The term originally meant a local or regional strongman but was widened to describe a national leader who ruled in the same authoritarian, dictatorial manner as a local strongman. Thus the local Argentine gaucho leader Juan Manuel de Rosas came to be a national *caudillo* as he and his gaucho bands took over the province of Buenos Aires in 1829 and later established a Latin American dictatorship in Argentina that lasted until 1852. Swinging toward democracy, Argentina established a viable democratic tradition after Rosas's military defeat and expulsion. It lasted until the Great Depression of 1929. Dictatorship returned in 1930 and the 1940s saw the emergence of one of the most renowned of the Latin American *caudillos*—Juan Domingo Perón. Nor was he alone in this part of Latin America. The neighboring state of Brazil had seen the emergence of an extraordinary politician, Getulio Vargas. He began his rule as a caudillo from the state of Rio Grande do Sul who took over the national government and used his strongman rule to begin the consolidation of the modern Brazilian state. He dominated Brazilian politics from 1930 until his suicide in the presidential palace in 1954. Argentina's other northern neighbor, Paraguay, fell under the strongman rule of Alfredo Stroessner through a coup in 1954. He ruled over Paraguay with a strong hand until he was finally removed from office by another coup in 1989. In more recent times, many have described Peru's president Alberto Fujimori (1990–2001) as a *caudillo*, particularly after he suspended the constitution and dismissed Congress and the Supreme Court with the help of the military in 1992. Others suggest now-president Daniel Ortega of Nicaragua is a *caudillo* because of the way he ruled the country from 1979 to 1990, his rule from 2006 to present, and his heavy-handed methods in his own Sandinista party.

For the vast majority of Latin American countries that gained their independence in the early nineteenth century, this authoritarian tradition weighed heavily and was further strengthened by the dictatorial practices of the leaders of the independence movement as they took the reins of power in the newly independent nations and by the less statesmanlike dictators who all too often followed. One is here reminded of authoritarian *libertadores* like Simón Bolívar and dictators like the previously mentioned Juan Manuel de Rosas in Argentina and Antonio López de Santa Anna in Mexico.

In *Authoritarian Regimes in Latin America: Dictators, Despots, and Tyrants*, Paul H. Lewis describes what he calls "the undemocratic or authoritarian culture" that predominated in Latin America. Although he does not examine the precolonial origins of this political culture, he argues that it has several roots: first, the hierarchical, autocratic, and crusading character of Spanish and Portuguese society found in the Iberian peninsula; second, the nature of colonial society based on the conquest and later the exploitation of slaves; and third, the independence movement itself, which left behind anarchy and banditry that required a strong hand on the part of those who governed in order to assert control and maintain order in the nascent republics. In a section on *"caudillo* power," he further chronicles the many *caudillos* who emerged as national leaders in the first decades of Latin American independence.

## DEMOCRATIC DEFICIT

As Latin America developed, there was little experience with democracy during the colonial period. There were no legislatures or popular representative bodies where the people could make their views known or participate in governing, above the municipal level. This level was the exception. For instance, in many areas, the town council, or *cabildo*, did allow some degree of participation and democracy in many—but not all—municipalities. Many indigenous villages also exercised some degree of democracy in decision-making practices. But the general lack of experience with democracy led one astute student of Latin America, Mario Hernández Sánchez-Barba, to observe that the democratic constitutions patterned on the United States and France that were enacted in Latin America during the early nineteenth-century independence struggles were attempts to impose a democratic framework on a very authoritarian reality. Although the new Latin American nations (and Brazil after 1889) were launched as democratic republics with constitutional structures similar to those of the United States and the French Republic, democratic experience and a democratic political culture lagged far behind. It was perhaps a little like introducing cricket and cricket rules to players who have never seen the game and have been playing soccer all their lives. Although some countries took to the new game faster than did others, all underwent a long period of assimilation that included periods of play much more like the old game. Some even suggest that in times of crisis the players still revert to the old (authoritarian) patterns of play (see Figure 5). As was suggested in Chapter 3, nineteenth- and twentieth-century Latin American history saw ongoing pendulum swings between periods of democracy and authoritarian rule. Indeed, it might be argued that Latin American political culture in most countries was characterized by a nominal commitment to the practice of democracy and a deep-seated reverence for authoritarian rulers with the strength to govern effectively. As previously noted, some have also suggested that two political cultures existed in these countries, one authoritarian and one nominally democratic, with different groups favoring each at different times in their national history (and often according to their calculation of maximum benefit).

## DEMOCRACY GROWS

The defeat of fascism during World War II and the wartime alliance all the Latin American states save Argentina had with the United States during the war set the stage for a deeper strengthening of democracy. The United States said it was fighting the Axis powers to save democracy. This had a certain resonance in Latin America, particularly after the Allied victory. Thus there were several attempts to break with the authoritarian tradition and initiate a new democratic wave. There was an unsuccessful attempt to rid Nicaragua of the Somoza dictatorship in 1944. The democratic revolutions of 1944 and 1945 strengthened internal democratic trends elsewhere in Central America and other parts of Latin America. After the 1944 revolution in Guatemala, a progressive democratic regime emerged. Costa Rica underwent a revolution in 1948 that established a democratic regime characterized by open and honest elections, respect for political rights, and an aversion to authoritarian tendencies and military involvement in politics (the Costa Ricans even abolished their military). Thereafter Costa Rica has not experienced any subsequent coups or other unconstitutional changes of power and has been characterized by its democratic elections and competitive two-party dominant political system. The democratic revolution in Venezuela launched a new democratic movement centered on the Acción Democrática party and put the Venezuelan novelist Romulo Gallegos in power as the president (1945–1948). Although there was a temporary reversion to authoritarian military rule under the dictatorship of Pérez Jiménez (1948–1958), constitutional democracy continued to develop in Venezuela thereafter. Jorge Gaitán and progressive forces in the Liberal Party started a movement to strengthen popular democracy in Colombia in 1946. The truncation of this process that occurred when Gaitán was assassinated in 1948 sparked the *Bogotazo* and the subsequent *Violencia*, but even here elements of democratic political culture lived on. Uruguay also developed a strong democratic tradition that was sustained until it too succumbed to the wave of military coups that swept through Latin America in the 1960s and 1970s. Chile also developed strong democratic practices and even had a parliamentary form of government in the 1890s. It had a well-seated democratic tradition and a vibrant multiparty system by the 1960s. It was in this democratic tradition that Salvador Allende hoped to organize a democratic socialist revolution when he was elected president in 1970. He, his coalition of socialists, and members of the Radical and Communist Parties were able to do so for three years until the military intervened with strong assistance and support from the U.S. government. The coup d'état and subsequent military dictatorship of Augusto Pinochet did, however, halt the practice of democracy from the date of the coup on September 11, 1973, until the return to democratic rule in 1990.

The 1950s and 1960s then had seen the intermittent growth of democracy in these countries and elsewhere in Latin America as well, although dictatorship and authoritarian rule were also common. As they had done in the nineteenth century, these periods of democratic rule from the 1940s on helped strengthen democratic values and began to strengthen democratic political culture in Latin America.

### MILITARY RULE AND BUREAUCRATIC AUTHORITARIANISM

While Costa Rica and Uruguay, and to a lesser degree, Venezuela, Chile, and Colombia saw the commitment to democracy and democratic means become much more pervasive from the 1950s on, the authoritarian dimension of Latin American political culture was to rear its head in a different way as authoritarian tendencies reemerged. Causes for a return to such authoritarian rule included the Cold War and the strong anticommunism that the United States (and many Latin American economic and political elites) had pushed throughout the hemisphere and the inculcation of the national security doctrine and counterinsurgency that U.S. diplomats, military trainers, and the U.S. Army School of the Americas had taught Latin American politicians and military personnel. These ideas and U.S.-sponsored training and diplomacy mixed with class interests, the threat from left-wing guerrillas, and the authoritarian and autocratic tendencies that characterized the military and many sectors of the ruling economic and political groups set the stage. There was a perceived threat that the left would take over and threaten elite and U.S. interests as occurred in Chile and had occurred in Cuba with the radicalization of the revolution. The result was the reversion to long periods of dictatorial military rule dubbed "bureaucratic authoritarianism" by the Argentine political scientist Guillermo O'Donnell. The term was coined to describe the institutional military dictatorships that arose in the 1960s and the 1970s and remained in power for as long as twenty years, as was the case in Brazil (1964–1985). The initial analysis stems from O'Donnell's work *Modernization and Authoritarianism* (1972, in Spanish) and was expanded later in *Bureaucratic Authoritarianism: Argentina, 1966–1973, in Comparative Perspective* (1988). This long period of institutionalized military rule was to include not only Brazil and Argentina but also Bolivia, Uruguay, Chile, Peru, Panama, Guatemala, El Salvador, and Honduras. All these regimes challenged civilian rule, existent politics and political parties, and many fundamental tenets of democracy itself. The United States accepted and even supported these military regimes (save those of Peru and Panama, which had elements of leftist populism) in varying degrees and saw them as a bulwark against communism and Marxism. Democracy was eroded significantly, and many horrendous abuses of human rights became common. Indeed, the United States soon became seen not as an advocate of democracy but as a supporter of brutal right-wing dictatorships (as in Chile, Argentina, and Brazil) and an enemy of rooted democracy. Many of the worst human rights abuses were denounced by some sectors of the U.S. government under the administration of Jimmy Carter, but the Reagan administration reversed the human rights policy of the Carter administration and embarked on a strong anticommunist policy that often embraced some of the worst regimes in Latin America and formed and supported the murderous *contras* as a means of destabilizing and trying to overthrow the leftist Sandinista government in Nicaragua in the 1980s. But U.S. policy was to change with the demise of Eastern European socialism after 1989. The United States and its Western European allies no longer believed they needed to guard against leftist insurgencies and radical political movements that would challenge U.S. interests and ally themselves with Cuba and the Soviet bloc.

# Democratization

Democratization has grown slowly in most of Latin America. Although the process accelerated dramatically since the end of military rule in the 1980s and 1990s, it started in the early nineteenth century with elitist or aristocratic democracies where power was held in few hands. Gradually, it evolved and incorporated more participants as literacy levels rose, property requirements were abolished, slavery ended, women were afforded the franchise, and lower-class groups mobilized. And democratic ideals continue to inspire and suggest how the republics should function. The persistence of such ideals has helped shape political culture. In *Democracy in Developing Countries: Latin America*, Larry Diamond notes that elitist democracies helped get important players involved and invested in democracy, which in turn allowed for participation, to which others could aspire. The elitist model of democracy was gradually popularized as new groups began to participate effectively in the political systems. Diamond further argues that the constitutional, liberal, and democratic idea delegitimized the authoritarian use of power but ultimately did not radically change the elitist proclivity of the system. Discussing elite politics and the roots of democracy in *Building Democracy in Latin America*, John Peeler observes that the royal absolutism that so heavily influenced the authoritarian tradition became dominant only in the fifteenth century and that it was resisted at the elite level by the medieval tradition of the *fueros*, or special privileges, extended to religious personnel and the nobility. Thus, the idea of special rights and privileges for favored groups and their ability to resist even

Luiz Inácio Lula da Silva, Brazil. *(Photo by Paulo Fridman/WPN/Photoshot)*

the strong control of the state became entrenched in Latin America as well. The local elite often displayed and used its own autonomy to resist state authority, as suggested by the oft-quoted phrase *"Obedezco pero no cumplo"* (I obey but do not comply). This has continued to the present day and helps explain why civilian and military elites are often loath to submit to governmental rule or allow leftist leaders to begin economic and social restructuring. Indeed, they often see themselves as immune from jurisdiction—not controlled by the law. Impunity in such situations is common.

In his seminal work, *Democracy in Latin America*, George Philip is clear on the persistence of the authoritarian as well as democratic beliefs. He acknowledges the variation in the region but sees predemocratic patterns of political behavior surviving democratization. Nor does he see the broad institutional changes that have usually preceded democratization and democratic consolidation taking place in most of Latin America. There is positive institutional change in some countries, but, as suggested by the Honduran and Paraguayan cases, throughout the region authoritarian legacies have survived even the most recent transition to democracy in the 1980s and 1990s. Even more critically, Philip observes that the bureaucracy remains patrimonial, law enforcement is weak, and public opinion is often ready to support open law-breaking by political leaders. Thus, the conflicting values that leaders and the public have about democracy versus authoritarian rule have not allowed for the consolidation of democracy in most of Latin America. Earlier in the work he cites a respected poll taken in Chile in 2001: only 45 percent of those sampled thought democracy was preferable to any other kind of government, while 11 percent agreed that in "certain circumstances an authoritarian government can be preferable to a democratic one." Other polls have shown similar results elsewhere in Latin America (see Table 17 and Figure 6).

Politicians and the public have often shown themselves quite willing to support extra-constitutional uses and assumptions of power at critical times (see Figure 7). Venezuela developed one of the strongest democratic traditions in Latin America. But, even in democratic Venezuela, there was considerable support for the 1992 coup attempt by Hugo Chávez to overthrow the widely discredited Carlos Andrés Pérez government. The polarization of attitudes that transpired after Chávez was elected president and began to transform the state was also very strong. Indeed, the partisanship became so intense that there was also significant support for the short-lived coup that temporarily displaced President Chávez from power in 2002. Nor were most Chávez supporters overly concerned with the leader's tendency to concentrate more power in the presidency or his attempts to extend the presidential term in office. Authoritarian tendencies under Chávez intensified under his successor Nicolás Maduro.

Beginning with the administrations of Ronald Reagan in the United States and Margaret Thatcher in Great Britain, the free market, liberal, capitalist economic model championed by Milton Friedman and the free market/free trade Chicago School became a tenet of U.S. policy. As liberal, free market economics were strongly advocated by U.S. policymakers and offered as the only means to develop for Latin America and other nations, liberal, Western-style representative democracy was advocated

**TABLE 17.** Democracy versus Authoritarianism (Percentages)

Which of the Following Statements Do You Agree with Most?

| Country | "Democracy is preferable to any other type of government." | | | | | | "In certain circumstances an authoritarian government can be preferable to a democratic one." | | | | | |
|---|---|---|---|---|---|---|---|---|---|---|---|---|
| | 1996 | 2001 | 2009 | 2015 | 2016 | Change Since 2015 | 1996 | 2001 | 2009 | 2015 | 2016 | Change Since 2015 |
| Paraguay | 59 | 35 | 45 | 44 | 55 | +11 | 26 | 43 | 29 | 37 | 25 | −12 |
| Costa Rica | 80 | 71 | 74 | 57 | 60 | +3 | 7 | 8 | 9 | 15 | 9 | −6 |
| Panama | 78 | 34 | 64 | 44 | 45 | +1 | 10 | 23 | 13 | 14 | 13 | −1 |
| Argentina | 71 | 57 | 64 | 70 | 71 | +1 | 15 | 21 | 19 | 15 | 13 | −2 |
| Honduras | 42 | 57 | 53 | 40 | 41 | +1 | 14 | 8 | 12 | 13 | 9 | −4 |
| Mexico | 53 | 46 | 42 | 48 | 48 | 0 | 15 | 35 | 14 | 15 | 17 | +2 |
| Bolivia | 64 | 54 | 71 | 65 | 64 | −1 | 17 | 17 | 10 | 12 | 16 | +4 |
| Colombia | 60 | 36 | 49 | 55 | 54 | −1 | 20 | 16 | 14 | 11 | ... | −3^ |
| Guatemala | 50 | 33 | 14 | 33 | 31 | −2 | 21 | 21 | 30 | 15 | 17 | +2 |
| Peru | 63 | 62 | 52 | 56 | 53 | −3 | 13 | 12 | 16 | 16 | 18 | +2 |
| Dominican Republic | ... | ... | 67 | 63 | 60 | −3 | ... | ... | 24 | 15 | 20 | +5 |
| Ecuador | 52 | 40 | 43 | 71 | 67 | −4 | 18 | 23 | 25 | 16 | 12 | −4 |
| Brazil | 5 | 30 | 55 | 54 | 32 | −22 | 24 | 18 | 18 | 16 | 13 | −3 |
| Chile | 54 | 45 | 59 | 65 | 54 | −11 | 19 | 19 | 10 | 12 | 18 | +6 |
| Uruguay | 80 | 79 | 81 | 76 | 68 | −8 | 9 | 10 | 8 | 11 | 12 | +1 |
| Venezuela | 62 | 57 | 85 | 84 | 77 | −7 | 19 | 20 | 7 | 10 | 13 | +3 |
| Nicaragua | 59 | 43 | 55 | 48 | 41 | −7 | 14 | 22 | 10 | 18 | 21 | +3 |
| El Salvador | 56 | 25 | 68 | 41 | 36 | −5 | 12 | 10 | 13 | 17 | 14 | −3 |
| **Total Average** | **58** | **47** | **58** | **56** | **53** | **−3** | **16** | **19** | **16** | **15** | **15** | **−1** |

...Data unavailable or not applicable.
^No statistics available for 2016 for Colombia. The change is calculated from 2015–2009 data.
*Source:* Latinobarómetro 2016. http://www.latinobarometro.org/latOnline.jsp

as a means of achieving an environment in which free markets could flourish. Dominant political and economic elites and U.S. and Western sycophants in Latin America soon picked up the new mantras and advocated for Western, free market capitalism and Western-style representative democracy. Thus the new political mantras became the "transition to democracy" and then "democratization." For those who had always controlled politics in most of the Latin America nations, different skills became necessary. Military interventions, coups, and different forms of brutal repression would be set aside for a while. Gross electoral fraud and election manipulation would be called into question and increasingly open to scrutiny and denunciation from national electoral commissions, international electoral observation teams, or even the U.S. government. The ability to manipulate and control politics through public relations, the media, and orchestrated campaigns soon was championed as the most effective means of controlling the masses and preventing takeovers by the left. Constitutionally questionable parliamentary maneuvering and outright seizures

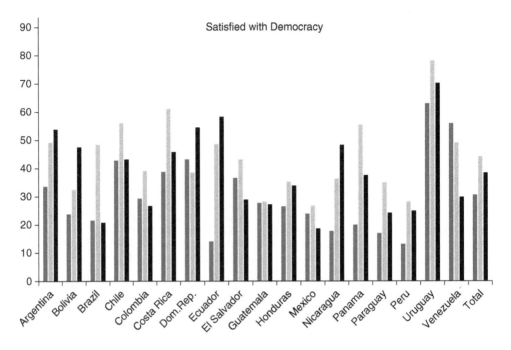

How satisfied are you with the way democracy works in your country?
% responding "very satisfied" or "somewhat satisfied"

■ 2005    ■ 2010    ■ 2015

FIGURE 6.   Satisfaction with Democracy

of power as in Venequela in 2002 and Honduras in 2009 have now been added to the means of stopping or removing leftist regimes. The extent of U.S. initiative in these actions is difficult to determine, but U.S. acceptance of the results is clear. U.S. policy initiatives to unseat Nicolás Maduro in Venezuela are also revealing. These policies explain the ability of the Mexican political and economic elites (with the support of rightist groups in the United States) to keep the popular leftist candidate (López Obrador) from winning in closely contested elections in 2006 and 2012. It also explains how the leftist presidential opposition candidate in the 2013 Honduras election could be kept from power even though she initially led in the polls. As had been the case with military aid and the national security and counterinsurgency doctrines, the United States would be the primary supplier of doctrine, training, and guidance, though homegrown national suppliers would also emerge.

Political consultants and pollsters were enrolled in the new democratization project in Latin America as new mechanisms of control and guidance were developed. For instance, negative campaigning, fearmongering, and scare tactics were propagated through well-orchestrated media campaigns. They would replace security concerns and counterinsurgencies as the preferred means to control the masses and ensure that they did not enroll in any leftist political movements or parties, like the guerrilla-based FMLN party in El Salvador or even the Sandinistas

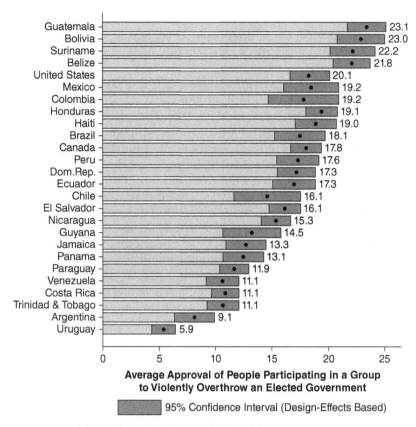

FIGURE 7. Approval for Violent Overthrow of Elected Government

*Source:* Mitchell Seligson, and Latin American Public Opinion Project. AmericasBarometer (2012): 50.3; https://www.oas.org/en/spa/democracia/docs/Mitchell_Seligson.pdf

in Nicaragua. Leftist movements tried to adapt to the new game plan with varying degrees of success but lacked the requisite resources and ties to the U.S. government or even to many private concerns in the United States. One of the early successes of this program was the electoral defeat of the Sandinistas in Nicaragua in 1990. Having been unable to defeat the Sandinista military with the U.S.-trained and directed *contras* (counterrevolutionaries), the United States helped to organize an electoral coalition of fourteen opposition parties, pushed very strongly to pick Violeta Chamorro as their presidential candidate, and funneled millions of dollars and other forms of support to the opposition. Indeed, the U.S. Congress had formed the National Endowment for Democracy to facilitate precisely this type of initiative. The Endowment invested $9 million in the opposition in the 1990 election. Although the Sandinistas also organized a slick campaign and a rock star-type image for Sandinista president Daniel Ortega, Nicaragua became "democratized" as the Sandinistas lost and Violeta Chamorro and her National Opposition Union (UNO) coalition triumphed. Try though they might, the Sandinistas could not regain power for sixteen years and then only after they had connived with a very corrupt political boss and former president (Arnaldo Alemán) to change the electoral rules to allow a presidential candidate to triumph with a plurality of the vote (an absolute majority was no longer required).

Recent events in Mexico provide another case study. By the 1980s the one-party domination of the Mexican political system by the Institutional Revolutionary Party (PRI) was losing support and legitimacy. The leftist Revolutionary Democratic Party (PRD) and the rightist Party of National Action (PAN) began to receive increasing support and to win local elections. The situation came to a head in the 1988 national election. The PRD in all likelihood won the presidential election in that year but was frustrated by what most independent observers saw as massive electoral fraud. Nor was the party successful in its attempts to take the presidency in 1994 or 2000 when a rightist party (PAN) did manage to unseat the long dominant PRI. The 2006 election was symbolic of the new forces in play. The PRD candidate for the presidency, Andrés Manuel López Obrador, had been a popular mayor of Mexico City and started the campaign with a substantial lead over PAN candidate Felipe Calderón. Intense negative media campaigning, support from conservative forces in the United States, and accusations of aid and support from Cuba and Venezuela had erased his lead by the time of the election. Amid some accusations of electoral fraud, the government, business, and Bush administration candidate Calderón managed a razor-thin electoral victory by less than 1 percent. López Obrador contested the election and held massive rallies for his parallel government for months after the election but was shut out of power. The conservative leadership had been sustained in the United States' NAFTA partner. Yet, the upsurge in popular protest suggested that the masses would no longer be so easily manipulated. Nonetheless, López Obrador was again shut out of power through similar tactics in the 2012 election.

The case of Honduras if not Paraguay and Brazil suggests that rightist interests backed by rightist groups in the United States may be willing to return to more heavy-handed and repressive policies to stop leftist rule and staunch the pink tide of leftist regimes coming to power. Manuel Zelaya was thrown out of power by a congressionally sanctioned military coup in 2009 when he embarked on a leftward tack and engineered Honduras's membership in ALBA. His supporters protested his unconstitutional removal from power; they were systematically and often brutally repressed, newspapers were destroyed, and journalists were killed. In these conditions an election was held later in the year to pick a rightest successor, Porfirio Lobo. The repression, the intimidation, and the killings of journalists and peasant and political activists continued through Lobo's term and even intensified during the electoral campaign in 2013. By this time there was an extensive opposition that had morphed into Libre, a new opposition party that ran Xiomara Castro, Zelaya's wife, as their presidential candidate. Although initially ahead in the polls, the extensive use of negative campaigning, political intimidation, and the assassinations of journalists and Libre activists propelled the rightist candidate, Juan Orlando Hernández, to a win amid charges of electoral fraud.

Although the congressional coup in Paraguay suggested the development of a possible trend, generally speaking, as democratization developed, brutal repression declined radically and the citizenry was encouraged to participate in the political process. An interesting thing happened along the way. Popular forces that had been frustrated in their attempts at thoroughgoing change soon found that there was a lot of repression-free political space in which they could mobilize. New movements began to appear. One sees early manifestations of this in Venezuela, where a democratic political culture that included fair elections had been developing since the 1940s. The free market policies advocated by the United States and international financial institutions like the IMF made for a major uprising in 1989 (the Caracazo) and helped spawn two unsuccessful military uprisings in 1992. This in turn engendered a new political movement that rejected the free market, neoliberal economic policies, and the two mainstream parties that had implemented it. Hugo Chávez was able to mobilize his newly formed Fifth Republic Movement to take advantage of the democratic political and hemispheric movement toward democratization to win the 1998 presidential election in Venezuela. As he transformed the constitution and held additional elections, the Venezuelan masses found a framework in which the traditional political elites and their U.S. supporters no longer set the rules of the game or dominated politics. It is, however, less clear whether Chávez was carrying forth other aspects of authoritarianism with his strong presidential rule. But citizenship was being expanded, and the masses were participating in a political process where they began to see palpable benefits reach them.

Elsewhere, new political and social movements sprung up and had even more of a grassroots, popular base. The Zapatistas burst on the scene in January 1994 to graphically demonstrate that insurgencies would soon turn to popular movements that would be nourished by grassroots mobilization and participation and that original Americans and other nontraditional citizens and political actors would no longer be marginalized. The indigenous masses in Ecuador increased their participation in politics, formed the National Confederation of Indigenous Nationalities of Ecuador (CONAIE) and began local and national mobilizations that would depose traditional politicians and even take the national Congress for one day in 2000. They went on to secure the election of Lucio Gutiérrez and then Rafael Correa as presidents. In Bolivia, another indigenous movement composed of peasants, *cocaleros*, miners, and neighborhood residents from Cochabamba and El Alto forced the pro-U.S. neoliberal president Gonzalo Sánchez de Lozado out of office and later elected the Aymara *cocalero* leader Evo Morales as president. The nontraditional leftist Workers' Party (PT) in Brazil would finally capture the presidency in 2002 amid calls for reform, land redistribution, and economic and social restructuring. Liberal Uruguay saw former guerrillas, communists, and other progressives forming the Frente Amplio coalition that would eventually elect two progressive presidents and take control of the national Congress. And in Paraguay, the most traditional and authoritarian of Latin American countries, a former bishop and advocate of liberation theology would mobilize enough of those wanting fundamental change to win the presidency in 2008. Democratization, then, was unleashing new political forces and beginning to enfranchise the formally disenfranchised. Democracy, representative and participatory, was practiced on an expanded scale.

However, after these initial successes by progressive forces, rightest groups in Latin America began to take advantage of anti-incumbent sentiment and economic problems to find means to challenge the popular mandates that enabled the pink tide. Latin American political culture was undergoing root change. The massive mobilizations that had enabled the pink tide were now being replicated to challenge leftist governments in Brazil in 2015 and 2016 and Venezuela from 2003 on and to sanction corruption and even force a president and vice president out of office as in Guatemala in 2015 and 2016. The vestiges of authoritarian and elitist rule would rear their heads in Honduras and Paraguay if not Brazil as constitutional elected leaders were removed from power, yet new social movements sometimes linked to progressive parties continued to challenge traditional authoritarian structures from Mexico to Chile and Argentina (see Chapter 10).

But Latin American political culture is more than an admixture of democratic and authoritarian values. It carries many other attributes from the past. These include the following characteristics and value clusters.

## INDIVIDUALISM

Individualism is strong in Latin American political culture. The individual does not like to be subordinated by government or other powerful political forces and often will only accept such control when there is sufficient power to sustain it. When power weakens or countervailing power can be invoked, rebellion often follows, and the will of another group or individual may become dominant. Political leaders have also sometimes individualized their rule. Power is used by the individual ruler and oftentimes for the individual benefit of the ruler or by or for the group to which the ruler belongs. Equally, power is wielded by small groups, such as the fourteen families in El Salvador or socioeconomic or political elites, and monopolized for their benefit. A commonly held view among many is that, like the colonial rulers, those who hold power will use it in ways that will directly benefit them or their political or socioeconomic group at the expense of the general population. This may result in special projects for home regions or political or business friends or, at times, outright corruption and individual enrichment. Such actions do not buttress the belief that government benefits all the people equally or that special interests or elites do not rule.

## CONFLICTUAL ATTITUDES

Societies and the proponents of political systems in nations like Great Britain often pride themselves on the high degree of consensus on fundamental values and the rules of the game. Others, like politicians in Lebanon and the former Yugoslavia, are divided into factions that have very different views of what the society—or even the nation—is or should be and have held widely divergent ideas of how to achieve their political objectives in those national political systems. There is also a willingness to resolve these issues through the concerted use of organized violence and forms of warfare and to engage in human rights violations of those who challenge their power.

As Latin America developed, different historical epochs added new terms of conflict. Thus, to the struggles of the nineteenth-century Liberals and Conservatives was added the conflict between those advocating radical restructuring on the lines of the Mexican Revolution, such as Alianza Popular Revolucionaria Americana

(APRA) in Peru, or total, comprehensive revolution based on the Cuban process that began in 1959. After 1960 and the radicalization of the Cuban Revolution, leftists and leftist insurgencies challenged mainstream parties in charge of governments and right-wing military groups. Thus, ideological values were often polarized between those advocating a political agenda inspired by socialism or leftist nationalism and those advocating a political agenda based on different conservative ideologies or U.S.-style anticommunism and the national security state. The wide gap between these positions and the lack of consensus on common objectives (and sometimes the rules of the game) made for a political culture that in most instances was not consensual (Costa Rica since 1948 is one notable exception).

As suggested by the title of Kalman Silvert's well-respected work *The Conflict Society*, Latin American society and political culture have strong conflictual elements. Indeed, conflict is often taken to the extreme. Like a high-stakes poker game, there is a willingness on the part of many to take their political struggle to the wall. Politics is seen as a winner-take-all game, and losing often means losing power and thus being forced to fold and cash in one's chips. Players gamble with the power chips they have to win the game. The pot is not to be split. There are winners and losers. Power is to be used to the maximum. In the last hands of the game, push may come to shove—and that means one plays all one's power chips. This may mean buying votes, closing polling places where the opposition is strong, mobilizing friendly army garrisons, or executing a full-blown coup d'état. In such situations, there is frequently a resort to violence or the threat of violence. The willingness at times to take the political struggle to such intense and passionate levels means that violence is regularly employed through intimidation, repression, assassination, rebellion, guerrilla warfare, coups, or even civil war. The authoritarian military regimes in Chile and Argentina were even willing to engage in massive torture, murder, and other human rights violations to make sure that leftist groups would be kept from power. Alternatively, the Shining Path guerrillas in Peru executed a brutal campaign to overthrow the Peruvian government in the late 1980s and early 1990s that included frequent assassinations and massive car and truck bombs. Much of the political conflict in Colombia has been played out in violent confrontations between Liberal and Conservative bands in the late 1940s and 1950s (*La Violencia*) and between guerrilla groups such as the Fuerzas Armadas Revolucionarias de Colombia (FARC) and the Ejército de Liberación Nacional (ELN) and the government from the early 1960s to 2016. The last few years before the end of the conflict saw the interjection of extremely violent paramilitaries begun by wealthy landowners or businessmen and sometimes tied to elements of the Colombian military. They operate extralegally and were notable for their brutality and human rights violations.

## ELITISM AND PACTED DEMOCRACY

Elites have dominated Latin America since the Mayan monarchs and nobles ran the Mayan states in preclassical times. As suggested earlier, there have been a variety of economic, political, and social elites. Early democratization after independence was also controlled by these same elites. Similarly, there are intellectual elites, cultural elites, and even elites that dominate leftist parties and guerrilla movements.

The conscious or unconscious belief that an elite should lead, decide, dictate, or otherwise rule has greatly buttressed authoritarian practices in politics and many other areas of society. From time to time the political and economic elites of a nation get together to form a formal pact as a way of consolidating their rule, minimizing conflict, and sharing power. This was done between the Conservatives and Liberals in the Pact of Benidorm in Colombia in 1958 and by the political leaders of Acción Democrática and COPEI in Venezuela in their Punto Fijo agreement also in 1958. In more recent times, mass mobilization and broad-based social movements in countries like Bolivia and Ecuador have challenged such elitist political perspectives and the parties and power structures that perpetuate them. These developments will be discussed in some detail in Chapter 10.

## PERSONALISM

As suggested in Chapter 5, personal relations are fundamental in Latin America. In societies where trust comes hard, one only wants to deal with those with whom one has *confianza* (trust). Further, since the time of the early *hidalgos* (less-well-off noblemen) and upper-class representatives of the crown, a charming personal veneer has been deemed necessary for successful civil relations. A charismatic manner and personal warmth are thus highly valued commodities that are prerequisites for higher-level positions. Men physically embrace each other if they are friends or close business associates (the *abrazo/abraço*), and opposite-sex and female–female greetings in the same circles include a kiss on one cheek (Hispanic America) or both cheeks (most of Brazil and French Latin America). For new introductions and less-well-known acquaintances, one *always* shakes hands when one is introduced or enters a room and when one departs. The more grace and charm a person displays, the higher his or her presumed social status.

Such is equally the case in politics. *Personalismo* is a valued commodity among politicians. Much of their popularity and following may well be based on their personal charm and warmth. A leader is expected to be able to inspire a personal commitment from his or her following, and this is done in large part through his or her *personalismo*. In this context, the term takes on a meaning closer to *charisma* and has defined some of the region's most successful political leaders: Víctor Raúl Haya de la Torre of Peru's APRA, Juan Domingo Perón of Argentina, and Fidel Castro of Cuba. Each of these leaders was capable of exuding an immense personal charm in virtually all social contacts, be it a private meeting with an individual or small group or a speech to an assembled throng of thousands. Fidel Castro became known for his ability to hold an audience's attention in speeches that lasted hours.

## STRONGMAN RULE: *CAUDILLO, CACIQUE,* AND *CORONEL*

We have established that political leadership in Latin America has often tended to be authoritarian, with the political leader exercising a great deal of power and control. Military dictators who can employ the force and power to maintain their position are tolerated or at least endured until time passes or they can be overthrown. But brutal rulers such as Augusto Pinochet (the military dictator in Chile, 1973–1990) have not always had the *personalismo* of most civilian politicians. Pinochet simply

Juan Perón, Argentina. *(Time & Life Pictures/Getty Images)*

relied on overwhelming force and brutal repression. Since before the conquest, the tradition of the strong local leader became well established. The *cacique* came to mean a local indigenous leader who could be best described as a political boss. In his local community and among his own people, his power base was strong, but it diminished rapidly as he moved away from it. After colonial rule was put in place, other strong men developed. As previously suggested, the *caudillo* initially was a regional political leader or boss who might exercise absolute or near-absolute power in his region. Often a local landowner or other local notable, he usually had an independent base for economic-political power. As time went on, the *caudillo* and *caudillismo* also came to refer to strong, if rather authoritarian, national political leaders such as Juan Perón of Argentina. In the rural areas of traditional Brazil, the large landowners, or *fazendeiros*, were often given the rank of colonel in the state militia. This also came to be an honorific title given to a powerful local notable. Like the colonels in the postbellum American South, *coronéis* were, and sometimes still are, powerful political players in much of rural Brazil. It would be difficult to understand politics in rural Brazil without referring to *coronelismo* or realizing the power and impunity of the *coronel*.

It is interesting to note that the sentiment in favor of strongman rule has sometimes manifest in the phenomenon of *continualismo*. This refers to continuing or remaining in office one term after another as Franklin Delano Roosevelt did in the 1930s and 1940s. This is often the avenue by which a strong leader cum *caudillo* morphs into a dictator, as was the case with Porfirio Díaz who served as president of Mexico repeatedly from 1876 to 1910 and at the beginning of the Mexican Revolution. This tendency led many Latin American countries to limit the president to one term in office, as in Mexico where the president serves one six-year term and is not eligible for re-election. In the 1990s, Alberto Fujimori's attempt to alter the constitution in Peru to allow for more than one term was one of the factors that led to his political demise. In 2008 and 2009, attempts by the presidents of Venezuela and Colombia to lengthen their terms in office caused concern in both countries as did an interest by Bolivian president Evo Morales in extending his term in office in 2016.

## CUARTEL, CUARTELAZO, GOLPE DE ESTADO, AND THE JUNTA

Political culture in Latin America is also influenced by the tendency of the military to leave their barracks, or *cuartel*, to intervene in the political process, the *cuartelazo*. Indeed, when the government is indecisive, ineffective, overly corrupt, or leans too far to the left, many civilians call on the military to intervene (see Figure 5). Military intervention has been an ongoing phenomenon in most Latin American countries. With few exceptions, such as Costa Rica since the 1948 revolution and the subsequent abolition of the armed forces, and Mexico since the 1920s, the militaries have engaged in *golpismo*. They believe themselves to be defenders of the constitution, upholders of national honor, and defenders against subversion, corruption, or tyranny. The Latin American militaries have staged some 250 coups d'état, or *golpes de estado*, since most of the nations became independent in the early part of the nineteenth century. After the successful *golpe*, the dominant military coup makers, or *golpistas*, typically set up a military junta to rule until civilian government is restored. Most commonly, the junta is comprised of upper-level officers from the army, navy, and air force. The period of rule can range from the time it takes to elect or appoint a new civilian president (usually a few months) to more than a decade, as was the case in Brazil (1964–1985) and Chile (1973–1990). This latter type of extended military governance came to be what Guillermo O'Donnell called "bureaucratic authoritarianism." As previously suggested, it was used to refer to the extended period of military rule where the military actively ran the bureaucratic governmental apparatus. Such bureaucratic authoritarianism characterized many of the governments in South America during the 1960s (beginning with the coup in Brazil in 1964), 1970s, and 1980s. Nations under such rule included not only Brazil, Chile, and Argentina but also Bolivia and Uruguay. A progressive Nasserite (a nationalist military government patterned after that led by Gamal Abdel Nasser in Egypt from 1952 to 1970) ruled Peru from 1968 to 1980. A conservative form of extended military rule characterized Guatemala from 1954 until 1985, and the military dominated politics well into the 1990s.

Since democratization has intensified and has buttressed continuing civilian rule in the 1990s, the tendency toward military intervention and *golpes de estado* has diminished. It should be noted, however, that a *golpe* was executed against Hugo Chávez in 2002, and the new government was readily accepted by the Bush administration, which may have had some role in facilitating it. This time, however, the coup was not accepted by the pro-Chávez masses and younger military officers who mobilized to force the end of the coup and Chávez's return to power. However, Honduras experienced a military coup in 2009 that was not reversed, and a new government was eventually recognized by the United States despite strong condemnation by the Organization of American States.

With the return to democracy and greater focus on civil society, democratic (and authoritarian) attitudes are being explored and charted by a number of opinion polls and survey research organizations. Of particular interest are the region-wide surveys done by Latinóbarometro (http://www.Latinobarómetro.org) and Americas Barometer conducted by the Latin American Public Opinion Project (LAPOP: http://www.LapopSurveys.org). Newer works, such as *Democracy in Latin America: Surveying Conflict and Crisis* by George Philip and *Democracy in Latin America: Political Change in Comparative Perspective* by Peter H. Smith and Cameron Sells, also explore democratic attitudes in some depth.

## Políticos and Políticas

Professional politicians are *politicos* or *políticas*. In fact, all those who engage in politics could be described as *políticos*—or *políticas* if they are women. One does not, however, need to be authoritarian to qualify. Different countries have different political cultures. In Brazil, the tradition of the *chefe político* emerged. It came to have special meaning and refers to a *político* with special powers and attributes who could best be described in English as a political boss. The figure of the political boss also exists in Spanish-speaking America and could be referred to as a *jefe político*, although the connotation of power might not be quite so strong. The *caudillo* would be more powerful, if even less likely to abide by the rule of law.

## Corporate Values and Corporatism

Another aspect of Latin American society that strongly influences the political system is corporatism. The concept dates back to the medieval Iberian peninsula when society was conceived organically. The whole society was divided into different bodies (*corpus*) or corporations according to specific function or profession. The identification of individuals is oftentimes stronger to their particular body than to the nation. Church officials highly identify with the Catholic Church and display intense loyalty to it. Military officers in particular frequently display more loyalty to their military institutions than to civilian government or national civilian leaders. Thus, military officers often remain more loyal to their service branch, if not the military more generally, than to the government or civil society. Such feelings facilitate coups and narrow interpretations of the public interest.

## Patron–Client, Clientelism, and Other Special Relations

As was suggested earlier, there is often great disparity in power and prerogative in Latin America. Those who do not have power seek protection from those who do. Thus, alliances between the powerful and the not-so-powerful are often made. Indeed, this practice began on the large landed estates between the *patrón* and the peon, his humble employee. As with patrons and their supporters and followers elsewhere, this type of relationship spread throughout the society. The patron–client relationship refers to the special ties of personal loyalty and commitment that connect a powerful person with those below him. The *patrón* will look after his followers and personally intervene to make sure they are well treated or assist them in a time of trouble, even paying for medical treatment for a family member from personal funds. As the *patrón* rises or falls, his retainers rise or fall with him. The followers give unswerving support to their leader and can always be counted on because of their personal loyalty. The practice is common in politics and the governmental bureaucracy as well as society more generally. It has also characterized many political movements. Indeed, it has been suggested that many Latin American political parties are personal parties grouped around the party leader. Many observers have also noted the existence of personal factions or groups within parties and government—public administration in particular is often rife with these personal groupings. Taken one step further, this can lead to *clientelismo*, which is the practice of filling governmental positions with one's friends and associates to the exclusion of other, often better-qualified job candidates.

Another important social relationship that spills over into business and politics is that of the *compadre* and the *comadre*, the godparents of one's children. Given the traditional importance of the Church, it is not surprising that those who stand with the parents at the christening of their child should play an important role in the life not only of the child but also of the parents. The *compadre* or *comadre* is someone with whom one's relationship has been cemented. Like a blood relative, they generally are people who can be trusted. *Compadres* protect each other, as do *comadres*. They can gain access or special favors and can always count on one's help. If amenable, a person of a higher social status, like the *patrón*, may be chosen as a *compadre* or *comadre*, thus creating a special tie to the *patrón* for the whole family. The terms can also mean a close friend who can be counted on.

Personal or professional networks are always, then, quite significant. The importance of the small group, or *grupito*, cannot be underestimated. The *camarilla*, or clique, is pervasive in Mexican society and politics. In the political context, it specifically refers to a self-promoting political group that maximizes the power and position of its members through concerted collective action. In Brazil, friends, political allies, or associates often form a *panelinha* so that they can do business with each other or be assured of contacts through people they know they can trust.

### IMPROVISATION AND *JEITO*

Finally, improvisation and finesse are greatly valued. Even if extensive preparation was not made, the competent leader is respected for his or her ability to improvise brilliantly. Similarly, one hopes to move things along with the same deftness that world-famous soccer player Pelé moved the ball down the field. Indeed, the Brazilians have a special word for such adroitness, *jeito*. To give a *jeito* is to finesse something, to manage it, to make things happen. In a world where all is not always perfectly organized, the ability to move forward through improvisation is of great importance and is greatly valued.

## Conclusion

Democracy still competes with authoritarian values and elitist proclivities in Latin America. The military, save in Costa Rica, may still be capable of intervening in the political process and deposing an elected president. The constitution is not always followed, and many among the public do not think that such strict adherence to law is necessary during a time of crisis. Democracy is, then, not yet fully consolidated. Philip notes that problems with democratic consolidation in Latin America have a historic and institutional dimension and are at least in part the result of previous authoritarianism. In Latin America, the conduct of politics is a complex process that occurs in a reality far different from that found in the United States, Canada, Australia, Great Britain, or elsewhere. In political and social interactions, all the factors we have discussed—and many others—come into play. Ultimately, power rules, but it is exercised through the culturally based concepts, rules, and techniques that define the power game in Latin America. Further, the nuanced nature of the role these factors play is often the deciding factor in many key political and other events. Their importance in business or economics cannot be underestimated; in the game of politics, their comprehension is essential.

# Bibliography

Almond, Gabriel, and Sidney Verba. *The Civic Culture*. Princeton, NJ: Princeton University Press, 1963.

Almond, Gabriel, and Sidney Verba, eds. *The Civic Culture Revisited*. Boston: Little Brown, 1980.

Almond, Gabriel, G. Bingham Powell, Kaarne Strøm, and Russell J. Dalton. *Comparative Politics Today*. 8th ed. New York: Pearson/Longman, 2004.

Avritzer, Leonardo. *Democracy and the Public Space in Latin America*. Princeton, NJ: Princeton University Press, 2002.

Ciccaariello-Maher, George. *Building the Communes: Radical Democracy in Latin America*. London: Verso, 2016.

Camp, Roderic Ai, ed. *Democracy in Latin America, Patterns and Cycles*. Jaguar Books on Latin America 10. Wilmington, DE: Scholarly Resources, 1996.

Diamond, Larry, Jonathan Hartlyn, Juan J. Linz, and Seymour Martin Lipset, eds. *Democracy in Developing Countries: Latin America*. 2d ed. Boulder, CO: Lynne Rienner, 1999.

Lewis, Paul L. *Authoritarian Regimes in Latin America: Dictators, Despots, and Tyrants*. Lanham, MD: Rowman & Littlefield, 2006.

Manwering, Scott and Aníbal Pérez-Liña. *Democracies and Dictatorships in Latin America: Emergence, Survival and Fall*. New York: Cambridge University Press, 2014.

O'Donnell, Guillermo. *Bureaucratic Authoritarianism: Argentina, 1966–1973, in Comparative Perspective*. Berkeley: University of California Press, 1988.

O'Donnell, Guillermo. *Modernization and Bureaucratic Authoritarianism*. 2d ed. Berkeley: University of California, Institute of International Studies, 1979.

Peeler, John. *Building Democracy in Latin America*. 3d ed. Boulder, CO: Lynne Rienner, 2009.

Philip, George. *Democracy in Latin America: Surveying Conflict and Crisis*. Oxford: Blackwell, 2003.

Silvert, Kalman. *The Conflict Society: Reaction and Revolution in Latin America*. New York: American Universities Field Staff, 1966.

Smith, Peter H., and Cameron Sells. *Democracy in Latin America: Political Change in Comparative Perspective*. 3d ed. New York: Oxford University Press, 2016.

Touraine, Alain. *What Is Democracy?* Translated by David Macey. Boulder, CO: Westview, 1997.

Tulchin, Joseph S., with Bernice Romero, eds. *The Consolidation of Democracy in Latin America*. Boulder, CO: Lynne Rienner, 1995.

Vanden, Harry E., and Gary Prevost. *Democracy and Socialism in Sandinista Nicaragua*. Boulder, CO: Lynne Rienner, 1993.

Walker, Ignacio. *Democracy in Latin America: Between Hope and Despair*. Notre Dame, IL: University of Notre Dame Press, 2013.

## Films and Videos

*Details of a Duel: A Question of Honor.* Chile/Cuba, 1988.
*Evita.* United States, 1997.
*Missing.* United States, 1983.
*The Revolution Will Not Be Televised.* Ireland, 2004.
*State of Siege.* United States, 1982.

## Websites

http://www.latinobarometro.org/   An excellent source for recent survey research on Latin American political attitudes.
http://www.lapopsurveys.org/ and http://www.AmericasBaraometroamericasbaraometro.org/
Good sources for polling data on Latin American conducted by LAPOP, the Latin American Public Opinion Project at Vanderbilt University.

# NINE

# POLITICS, POWER, INSTITUTIONS, AND ACTORS

Power moves politics in Latin America, and naked power often rules. As we suggested in Chapters 5, 7, and 8, politics in Latin America has to do with powerful political and economic actors. Powerful *políticos* (and now *políticas*) have dominated most Latin American societies since classical Mayan and Aztec times. Dictators such as Antonio López de Santa Anna in Mexico, Juan Perón in Argentina, and Anastasio Somoza in Nicaragua have ruled absolutely. Oligarchies such as the dominant fourteen families in El Salvador have dominated politics and brutally suppressed those who challenged them. Military juntas have monopolized power, canceled elections, imprisoned and sometimes eliminated the opposition, and ruled for decades. The military and other groups have ignored constitutions and seized power forcefully, as when the Chilean military bombed the presidential palace to overthrow Salvador Allende in 1973. Also, power can come from the mobilized masses, social movements, protests, demonstrations, or general strikes that challenge government policy and force a government out of office or a dictator to resign. There have been more than 220 extra-constitutional assumptions of power in Latin America since the republics became independent. Indeed, it has been the constellation of power and not constitutional constraints that has conditioned the conduct of politics during most of Latin American history. It is the powerful individual, group, institution, or party that most often rules. Only those who know how to use power can be serious players.

Yet, as Latin American societies have become more complex, those who rule do so through the apparatus of the state and its interaction with political parties, political and social movements, individuals, and interest groups. Those who aspire to power must take over the apparatus of the state and use it to rule. This can be done by a coup d'état, a fraudulent election, a political agreement among political and/ or economic elites to share power, a massive social movement protest, or a relatively honest election with some real political competition. However, once the state apparatus is taken over, any discussion of the nature of political systems in Latin America must begin with a realization of the greater role that has been traditionally assigned to the state, particularly compared to classical models of liberalism. John Locke and other classical liberal thinkers believed that the best government was that which governed least. They were reacting to that absolutist configuration of the state that monarchies like Spain used to rule domestically and over their colonies in the sixteenth, seventeenth, and eighteenth centuries. Yet, it was precisely this absolutist state that served as the model for Latin American rule. Its use and misuse in Latin America have been quite different from the way the liberal state developed in Great Britain and the United States.

When the Latin American nations gained their independence in the early nineteenth century, there was a serious struggle over the political forms that would be adopted by the newly independent nations. During the colonial period, the region experienced different forms of authoritarian rule and state absolutism. The traditional elites who retained power, now independent from Madrid and Lisbon, had little, if any, democratic experience. Indeed, since the conception of the state that was projected from Madrid or Lisbon was absolutist during the colony, the elites had to find informal, noninstitutional (and not institutionalized), more personalistic ways to assert their authority and adapt to local conditions. There was almost no experience with institutionalized representative or popular democracy. The regional assemblies that were found in North America were absent in Latin America. Democracy was little practiced. The post-independence rulers were short on practical democratic models. Indeed, after independence, several countries experimented with monarchical and/or dictatorial rule.

The constitutional structures of the newly independent states were nominally democratic and modeled on the liberal constitutions of France, the United States, and the Spanish liberal constitution of 1812. Yet, political practice and political culture tended to be authoritarian and absolutist, even for committed democrats like Simón Bolívar. Gradually, new groups emerged and democratic practice engendered more democratic and less absolutist attitudes, although the latter have persisted to the present day. A strange hybrid resulted. Most countries adopted a republican, democratic form of government, but in reality traditional authoritarian patterns were most often employed by the elites, and suffrage was very limited initially. In the century and a half after independence, suffrage was gradually expanded, but there was frequent reversion to authoritarian politics and elitist, if not dictatorial, rule. As suggested in Chapter 8, much of the course of Latin American history has been an alternation between the authoritarian tendencies that were acquired during colonial and even precolonial times and the democratic ideas and ideals that were interjected at the time of independence. Democracy has been gaining ground in recent years, but reversions to authoritarian rule are frequent and decision-making practices continue to reflect the authoritarian aspects of the political culture. In his seminal work on Latin American democracy, George Philip observes that predemocratic patterns of political behavior (institutional, organizational, and cultural) have frequently survived democratization. Thus in the region "authoritarian legacies have survived the democratic transition. The bureaucracy remains patrimonial, law enforcement is weak and public opinion will often support open law breaking by political leaders." He goes on to observe that there is more to successful democracy than holding elections. Both he and Peter Smith frequently refer to unconsolidated democracy in Latin America, meaning that following the rule of law, democratic custom, and the constitution is not always done, and personal and authoritarian deviations still occur with some frequency.

# Constitutions

Jurisprudence is a highly developed art in Latin America. Legal documents are beautifully written and comprehensive. Latin American constitutions are no exceptions. They tend to be long, detailed, flowery documents with a large number of articles (the Mexican constitution of 1917 has well over 100 articles, and many other have more than 200 articles and several have more than 300 articles) covering a great many specific situations. As such, they frequently need to be modified, changed, or replaced. The Latin American republics have produced more than 250 constitutions. The Dominican Republic alone has had 32 constitutions. Several others have had 20 or more constitutions. Based on code law, they are not open to case-based interpretation, unlike Anglo-Saxon case law. Nor is legal precedent part of the judicial system. Constitutions have historically been more a norm to strive toward than a strict basis for the rule of law. Presidential power and prerogative are often more important than specific constitutional provisions or prohibitions.

Like the idealism of Don Quixote that permeates the culture, Latin American constitutions represent an ideal to which those who govern and are governed aspire. There have been times and places in Latin American history where the constitutions have been carefully followed (Costa Rica from 1950 to the present; Uruguay and Chile in the 1960s), but they are frequently subordinated to the power of the strong executive, dictator, or military junta. Those who rule have and use power and are less likely to be constrained by the constitution or other legal codes, although they may pay lip service to them. Like U.S. president Franklin Delano Roosevelt in the 1930s, they are more likely to find ways to massage the courts and the constitution to achieve desired policy results. The political tradition in most of Latin America is of strongman rule and the subordination of law and the courts to the executive and other powerful political and economic actors. The concept of the rule of law and protection of the individual against the arbitrary power of the state (through government) that classical liberals from Hobbes on have espoused is not well developed in most of Latin America, although the process of democratization has begun to tentatively incorporate some liberal concepts of human rights and procedural protections. On the whole, though, power and the powerful have generally ruled. Historically, protection for specific groups often came from *fueros* or *amparos*, which protected specific rights—or privileges—for designated groups (rather than as a constitutional right that protected all).

Only in recent decades have Supreme Courts become apt at delimiting presidents' interpretations of what is permissible under the constitution. It should be noted, however, that the process of democratization based on Western concepts of classical liberal democracy that has recently spread through the region has strengthened democratic aspects of political culture in all countries where it is practiced and has begun to place a greater emphasis on the subordination of power and the powerful to the law. Nonetheless, practice is often contradictory. In 2000, the Chilean Supreme Court stripped President Augusto Pinochet of his congressional immunity so that he could be tried for human rights violations committed during his brutal dictatorship—as had been the case earlier for a former general who ruled Argentina during the Dirty War—but Peruvian president Alberto Fujimori was inaugurated for his third term after fraudulent elections were held when he forced the Peruvian Supreme Court to exempt him from a constitutional prohibition against third terms. He was later forced from office by political pressure that developed from an evolving corruption scandal and tried and convicted on his return to Peru in 2007. Others have, however, often skirted constitutional prohibitions against a second term.

Like the constitution in the United States, Latin American constitutions almost universally created three branches of government: executive, legislative, and judicial. However, very rarely are they coequal, even in the constitutions. Two realities common to Latin American systems are a granting of greater power to the executive branch over the legislative branch and a general lack of significant judicial review. Further, while most Latin American constitutions contain a significant listing of human, civil, and political rights, they also include provisions whereby those rights can be suspended by the executive (usually with the consent of Congress) in an emergency or during a time of crisis.

## STATE OF SIEGE

A state of siege (*estado de sitio*) or state of emergency (*estado de emergencia*) may be invoked by most Latin American presidents (usually with the consent of the legislature) for a given period of time, normally ranging from thirty to ninety days. It allows the president to suspend most constitutional guarantees, such as freedom of speech and assembly as well as habeas corpus, and to legislate by decree. After the initial period runs out, it may be renewed. This has often been an avenue by which presidents acquired dictatorial powers. Latin American constitutions are also often contradictory on the question of the military, asserting in one place the primacy of civilian rule but in another granting the military a special responsibility for protecting national sovereignty and maintaining domestic order.

## CODE LAW

The legal systems in Latin America are based on code law. Most analysts of Latin American constitutions and laws stress that the systems are based not on the flexible notions of British common law but rather on strict interpretation of extensive legal codes. Rather than building on a series of case law decisions, Latin American law is deductive. This code-based law has its origin in Roman law, Catholic traditions, and especially the Napoleonic Code. Much of the code law in place was inspired by the Napoleonic Code, which was promulgated in France in 1804, became the basis for the French Civil Code, and was copied across Continental Europe and in the state of Louisiana in the United States. The influence of Roman traditions can be traced to the long Roman domination of the Iberian peninsula, which left more than just its language. This tradition emphasized the importance of a comprehensive, written law that is applicable everywhere, in contrast to the medieval traditions of law on which the English system is based, with its emphasis on limits. What was clearly missing from the Iberian ideas of law transported to the New World were the notions of social contract developed in the English ideas of Hobbes and Locke, which laid the groundwork for the idea of a rule of law based on the consent of the governed.

## CORPORATISM

John Peeler argues that another feature of Latin American constitutionalism drawn from earlier traditions is corporatism. In contrast to the more individualist ideas of the social contract, the Iberian tradition is more corporatist, with a great emphasis on the sociability of humans and their collectivity, and the importance of the groups to which they belong. Latin American constitutions are more likely to acknowledge the legitimacy of the interests of collective groups than of individuals. It is therefore interesting that in contemporary Latin American politics the struggle is often over which groups should have their interests acknowledged. For example, some of the constitutions (Argentina, Brazil, Colombia, and Mexico) specifically acknowledge the rights of indigenous groups, children, senior citizens, workers, and women (see Tables 18 and 19 on women's political rights).

# Institutions

## THE PRESIDENT

Latin American republics are based on the strong presidential form of government. Chile did experiment with parliamentary government around the turn of the twentieth century but has since employed presidential rule. Like France, Haiti and Peru have both a president and a prime minister, but most power resides with the president, who appoints the prime minister. The single most distinctive political feature of Latin American rule is the power of the executive. Contemporary Latin American presidential power is deeply rooted in the autocratic traditions of the colonial period. Presidential power in the twenty-first century has many different underpinnings that are postcolonial, including populist and revolutionary mobilizations, but the continuity with the past is strong. Also, the contemporary Latin American president wears many hats: chief executive, commander-in-chief, head of state, and head of party, to name a few. Multiple powers are not unique to Latin American presidents, just as U.S. and French presidents share similar multiple roles. In Latin America, these multiple roles only further strengthen an already strong presidency, especially because of the president's ability to invoke broad emergency powers. Even during the last few decades, when democratic rule predominated in the region, ruling presidents have occasionally assumed dictatorial power, the most dramatic case being Peruvian president Alberto Fujimori's *auto-golpe* of 1992, where he dissolved the other two branches of government and assumed legislative and judicial powers himself. Latin American presidents often tend to continue in office—*continualismo*. This is often how elected presidents have evolved into dictators. Responding to the period of military dictatorship and traditional *continualismo*, several countries strengthened their democracies constitutionally by prohibiting second presidential terms or at least second consecutive terms. Thus many Latin American constitutions, including those of Peru and Argentina, limit the time in office to two terms. The Mexican constitution of 1917 goes one step further, limiting the president to one six-year term. Several other states also limit the president to one term. Others, like Costa Rica, specify that if a president serves more than one term in office, the terms cannot be consecutive. Popularity and success have pushed several

TABLE 18. Constitutional Guarantees for Women and Equality

| Country | Legal Text | State of Equality |
|---|---|---|
| Argentina | Political constitution of 1994 | All inhabitants are equal before the law. No privileges of blood or birth are recognized, nor personal exceptions nor titles of nobility. |
| Bolivia | Political constitution of 1994 | The State prohibits and punishes all forms of discrimination based on sex, color, age, sexual orientation, gender identity, origin, culture, nationality, citizenship, language, religious belief, ideology, political affiliation or philosophy, civil status, economic or social condition, type of occupation, level of education, disability, pregnancy, and any other discrimination that attempts to or results in the annulment of or harm to the equal recognition, enjoyment or exercise of the rights of all people. |
| Brazil | Federal constitution of 1988 (rev. 2015) State constitutions of 1989 | Everyone is equal before the law, with no distinction whatsoever, guaranteeing the inviolability of the rights to life, liberty, equality, security and property, on the following terms: men and women have equal rights and duties under the terms of this Constitution. |
| Chile | Political constitution of 1980 (rev. 2015) | All are born free and equal in dignity and rights. In Chile there are no privilege persons or groups. In Chile there are no slaves, and any that sets foot on its territory will become free. Men and women are equal before the law. |
| Colombia | Political constitution of 1991 (rev. 2013) | All individuals are born free and equal before the law, shall receive equal protection and treatment from the authorities, and shall enjoy the same rights, freedoms, and opportunities without any discrimination on account of gender, race, national or family origin, language, religion, political opinion, or philosophy. Women and men have equal rights and opportunities. |
| Costa Rica | Political constitution of 1949 | All are equal before the law and cannot commit any discrimination contrary to human dignity. The mother, the child, the elder and the helplessly sick will equally have right to that protection. |
| Cuba | Political constitution of 1976 (rev. 2002) | Discrimination based on race, color of the skin, sex, national origin, religious creeds, or any other type offending human dignity, is prohibited and punished by the law. Women enjoy the same rights as men. |
| Dominican Republic | Political constitution of 2015 | All people are born free and equal before the law, receive the same protection and treatment from institutions, authorities, and other people and enjoy the same rights, liberties and opportunities, without any discrimination for reasons of gender, color, age, disability, nationality, family ties, language, religions, political or philosophical opinion, social or personal condition. Women and men are equal before the law. |
| Ecuador | Political constitution of 2008 (rev. 2015) | The State shall guarantee the enforcement of these collective rights without any discrimination, in conditions of equality and equity between men and women. |

220

| Country | Constitution | |
|---|---|---|
| El Salvador | Political constitution of 1983 (rev. 2014) | All persons are equal before the law. For the enjoyment of civil rights, no restrictions shall be established that are based on differences of nationality, race, sex or religion. |
| Guatemala | Political constitution of 1985 (rev. 1993) | The man and the woman, whatever their civil status may be, have equal opportunities and responsibilities. No person can be subject to servitude or to another condition that diminishes his or her dignity. |
| Honduras | Political constitution 1982 (rev. 2013) | All Hondurans are equal. All forms of discrimination on account of sex, race, class, or any other reason prejudicial to human dignity shall be punishable. |
| Mexico | Political constitution of 1917 (rev. 2015) | Man and woman are equal under the law. Any form of discrimination, based on ethnic or national origin, gender, age, disabilities, social status, medical conditions, religion, opinions, sexual orientation, marital status, or any other form, which violates the human dignity or seeks to annul or diminish the rights and freedoms of the people, is prohibited. |
| Nicaragua | Political constitution of 1987 (rev. 2014) | Unconditional equality of all Nicaraguans in the enjoyment of their political rights, in the exercise of these rights, and in the fulfillment of their duties and responsibilities, is established; there exists absolute equality between men and women. All individuals are equal before the law and have the right to equal protection. There shall be no discrimination based on birth, nationality, political belief, race, gender, language, religion, opinion, origin, economic position or social condition. |
| Panama | Political constitution of 1972 (rev. 2004) | There shall be no public or private privileges, or discrimination, by reason of race, birth, social class, handicap, sex, religion or political ideology. |
| Paraguay | Political constitution of 1992 (rev. 2014) | Men and women have equal civil, political, social, economic and cultural rights. The State will promote the conditions and will create the adequate mechanisms for, making equality real and effective, by leveling the obstacles that prevent or hinder its exercise and facilitating the participation of women in all areas of the national life. No kind of discrimination will be admitted between the workers for motives of ethnic, gender, age, religion, social status and political or syndical preferences. |
| Peru | Political constitution of 1993 (rev. 2009) | Every person has the right to equality before the law. No person shall be discriminated against on the basis of origin, race, sex, language, religion, opinion, economic situation, or any other distinguishing feature. |
| Uruguay | Political constitution of 1966 | All people are equal before the law. |
| Venezuela | Political constitution of 1961 (rev. 2009) | No discrimination based on race, sex, creed or social standing shall be permitted. The State guarantees the equality and equitable treatment of men and women in the exercise of the right to work. The state recognizes work at home as an economic activity that creates added value and produces social welfare and wealth. |

*Sources: Statistical Abstract of Latin America,* Vol. 35. Los Angeles: UCLA Latin American Center Publications, 1999. Constitute: The World's Constitutions to Read, Search, and Compare. https://www.constituteproject.org/

TABLE 19. Women's Political Rights

| Country | Year Right to Vote Granted | Right to Be Chosen Through Popular Election[a] | Year CEDAW[b] Ratified |
|---|---|---|---|
| Argentina | 1947 | Since 2005, candidate lists for both chambers must include women in a minimum of 30% of elected positions. | 1991 |
| Bolivia | 1952 | Since 2010, candidate lists for both chambers must include women in a minimum of 50% of elected positions. | 1960 |
| Brazil | 1932 | Since 2009, candidate lists for the lower chamber must include women in a minimum of 30% of elected positions. | 1984 |
| Chile | 1949 | Same for men and women. | 1989 |
| Colombia | 1954 | As of 2015, candidate lists for both chambers must include women in a minimum of 30% of elected positions. | 1981 |
| Costa Rica | 1949 | As of 2014, candidate lists for the legislature must include women in a minimum of 50% of elected positions. | 1984 |
| Cuba | 1934 | Same for men and women. | 1991 |
| Dominican Republic | 1942 | Since 2000, candidate lists for the lower chamber must include women in a minimum of 33% of elected positions. | 1982 |
| Ecuador | 1929 | As of 2016, candidate lists for the legislature must include women in a minimum of 50% of elected positions. | 1981 |
| El Salvador | 1950 | As of 2014, candidate lists for the legislature must include women in a minimum of 30% of elected positions. | 1981 |
| Guatemala | 1945 | Same for men and women. | 1982 |
| Honduras | 1955 | As of 2016, candidate lists for the legislature must include women in a minimum of 50% of elected positions. | 1983 |
| Mexico | 1953 | Since 2008, candidate lists for both chambers must include women in a minimum of 40% of elected positions. | 1991 |
| Nicaragua | 1955 | Same for men and women. | 1991 |
| Panama | 1946 | Since 2012, candidate lists for the legislature must include women in a minimum of 50% of elected positions. | 1981 |
| Paraguay | 1961 | Since 1996, candidate lists for both chambers must include women in a minimum of 20% of elected positions. | 1986 |
| Peru | 1955 | Since 2000, candidate lists for both chambers must include women in a minimum of 30% of elected positions. | 1981 |
| Uruguay | 1932 | As of 2014, candidate lists for both chambers must include women in a minimum of 33% of elected positions. | 1981 |
| Venezuela | 1947 | Since 1998, candidate lists for both chambers must include women in a minimum of 30% of elected positions. | 1982 |

*Sources: Mujeres Latinoamericanas en Cifras, 1995, pp. 138-139, as cited in Statistical Abstract of Latin America, Vol. 35. Los Angeles: UCLA, 1999.*

[a]Convention on the Elimination of All Forms of Discrimination Against Women, adopted by the United Nations in 1979.

[b]Hinojosa, Magda and Jennifer M. Piscopo. Promoting Women's Right to Be Elected: Twenty-Five Years of Quotas in Latin America. 2013. Prepared for the Electoral Tribunal of the Federal Judicial Branch of Mexico. https://jenniferpiscopo.files.wordpress.com/2013/09/hinojosa-piscopo-final-english.pdf

Latin American presidents to engage in constitutional maneuvers to continue their stay in office; such was the case in Colombia in 2010, which was unsuccessful, and in Nicaragua in 2011, which was successful. The first attempt to extend presidential terms was unsuccessful in Venezuela in 2007, but the second was successful in 2009. Evo Morlaes's attempt to change the Bolivian constitution through a referendum to enable a third term was defeated.

The president is also the personification of the state, as manifest in the presidential sash worn on formal occasions. His or her figure commands a great deal of respect and authority. Some observers place considerable emphasis on the role of the Latin American president as the national *patrón*, replacing the local landowners and *caudillos* of the past, arguing that the president is the symbol of the national society, seen as being responsible for the well-being of the country. Consistent with the classic definition of personalistic politics, the president is seen as being responsible for the allocation of resources through presidential favors and patronage. Another side of this practice is that such a personification of power may lead to corruption; it is not unusual for Latin American presidents to leave the office considerably richer than when they arrived.

## LEGISLATURE

As opposed to the parliamentary system of government, where the legislature is the dominant branch of the political system, or the government of the United States, where the legislature is coequal, in Latin America the legislative branch is seen as clearly subservient, often acting as an advisory body to the executive or occasionally as a rubber stamp. Most of the legislatures in Latin America are bicameral, with a chamber of deputies or representatives and a senate. However, almost all Central American states (not including Belize) follow the model of the Central American Federation and have unicameral legislatures, usually called legislative or national assemblies. Venezuela and Cuba are also now unicameral. The legislatures' budgets are relatively small and their staff support, minimal. In many states, the legislators may have to share a secretary and basic office equipment. The committee system is neither strong nor well developed, nor have Latin American legislatures usually retained the ability to veto acts of the executive or to initiate programs. They have served more modest goals of providing a locus for the political opposition and special interests or for refining laws for implementation. It is too early to definitively declare a new trend for Latin American legislatures, but with the region's wide reestablishment of democratic rule in the 1990s, legislatures in some countries have begun to assert their power and independence. Most significant, in 1992 and 1993, legislatures in Brazil and Venezuela removed sitting presidents from office on the basis of official corruption while reasserting their prerogatives in countries such as Mexico, Argentina, Chile, and Uruguay. Such actions were virtually unprecedented. However, when rightist groups controlled the legislature and not the presidency in Honduras, Paraguay, and Brazil in 2016, congresses were key to deposing a constitutionally elected president. The use of ostensibly constitutional means to challenge or remove an elected president and disenfranchise his or her supporters may be a new tactic the right is developing to remove progressive leaders and block movements that placed them in power. In contrast to such politically motivated surges in congressional power, the Costa Rica Legislative Assembly has remained strong for decades.

Legislators are most commonly elected to four-year terms for the lower house or unicameral legislatures and four- or six-year terms for the upper house. Legislators are usually elected from single-member constituencies, although there has been some experimentation with forms of proportional representation in countries such as Chile. The legislative sessions have historically been short and have been known to last as little as a month. Legislative debate is often acrimonious, with walkouts, protests, and sharp denunciations. Compromise and consensus are often in short supply. As a form of protection against abuse or coercion by the powerful, Latin American legislators enjoy a special right—immunity from arrest or prosecution while the legislature is in session.

## COURTS

The organization of the legal system in Latin America is not unlike that of the United States, with a Supreme Court, appeals courts, and local courts. Judges are generally appointed, although the national legislatures may be involved through nomination or approval of presidential nomination or, in the case of Costa Rica, in the election of Supreme Court justices. Supreme Court justices are not, however, appointed for life, as in the United States. Rather, they serve for a fixed term and must have their term renewed by appointment or election. A tradition of a strong, independent judiciary is not well developed in Latin America. From the Supreme Court down, the judiciary has tended to be susceptible to political pressure from the executive or other powerful groups. Further, certain crimes, such as terrorism or actions by military

The Brazilian legislature in session. *(Photo by Eraldo Peres. AP Images)*

officers, may not be within the purview of civilian courts. Rather, such cases are referred to special military courts. Symptomatic of this trend is the increasing use of *amparo*. The writ of *amparo* allows the individual to protect his or her rights by making a special appeal to the judicial system. It is one way the individual can protect him- or herself from the power of the state. In recent times, Latin American courts, although still weak, have begun to seek more effective ways of attacking official corruption and protecting individual rights.

## GOVERNMENT STRUCTURE AND LOCAL GOVERNMENT

Most Latin American states are unitary, meaning that there are no state-level governmental organizations with autonomous power or independence. The only federal states are Mexico, Brazil, Argentina, and Venezuela. The other nations are divided into provinces or departments. Traditionally, the national government usually appoints prefects or other administrative heads to rule over them. The process of decentralization has allowed for the elections of prefects or governors in many of the unitary states in more recent years. Municipalities exist at the lowest levels and may elect their mayors and councils (although the national government may appoint some council members as well). The organization of the four federal systems is similar to that in the United States, with elected state governors and legislatures and municipalities at the lowest level. Further, any discussion of the relative weights of central and local authorities in Latin American political systems must recognize a certain evolution over time. During the colonial period, the monarchies were largely ineffective at controlling the interiors of their vast empires. Local authorities were generally appointed by the crown, but after appointment they largely functioned in an autonomous way. In rural Latin America prior to the middle of the nineteenth century, local landowners and *caudillos* were the de facto rulers. Later, the process of nation building in the last half of the nineteenth century focused primarily around the communication system—roads, rail, and so on. These systems allowed central governments to extend their authority over the hinterlands, thus replacing the rule of the *caudillos*. As a way of centralizing power, most Latin American countries adopted unitary governmental structures with national/local relations similar to that of France, with almost all authority flowing from the top down—from the central government to local authorities. The local *caudillos* were eventually supplanted as national armies and bureaucracies were created late in the nineteenth century. Rudimentary systems of national taxation were established, although no or little formal authority to raise taxes was given to local authorities (this general lack of revenue-generating authority poses a major problem for local governments today, which most commonly must rely on funding from the national government).

## CENTRALIZATION, DECENTRALIZATION, AND FEDERALISM

This pattern of centralization was the clear intent of most national rulers in the nineteenth century. The majority of Latin American states are unitary, but three countertrends of the twentieth century must be mentioned lest one be left with the impression that Latin American politics has been marked only by centralized rule. First, four countries have adopted federal systems that have devolved some powers to the states—Brazil, Argentina, Venezuela, and Mexico. (Much of the autonomy of the states in Brazil and Argentina was, however, undermined by the long periods of bureaucratic authoritarianism in the 1960s, 1970s, and early 1980s.) Second, the sheer remoteness of some regions in countries like Brazil, Mexico, Argentina, and Colombia has significantly slowed down the integration process, although much of this regional remoteness has disappeared in the last twenty-five years. Finally, local leaders ranging from revolutionary chiefs and guerrilla leaders to drug traffickers and entrenched large landowners have often used the remoteness of their zones of activity to maintain relative independence from the central government. That combination is probably most evident today in Colombia and some areas of Mexico and Honduras where cartels operate. Recent years have seen significant initiatives across the region to decentralize government. They have met with some success and have opened the way for local governments to tax and raise some of their own revenues. This has made for significant reform and renovation in some municipalities.

## ELECTORAL TRIBUNALS

In that their electoral systems have at times been highly susceptible to influence and manipulation, many Latin American nations have established a separate branch of government to oversee elections. Called "supreme electoral councils" or "supreme electoral tribunals," these independent bodies are charged with overseeing the electoral process and guaranteeing honest elections. They have separate budgets and are not under the control of any other branch of government. In countries like Costa Rica, they have become quite strong and independent and have helped ensure electoral integrity. In other instances, they too proved to be vulnerable to powerful influences. As democracy continues to develop in the post-1990s period, their existence is a very positive factor in maintaining honest elections and open political competition.

## THE BUREAUCRACY

Political scientists have long acknowledged the importance of another part of government—the administrative sector, or bureaucracy. Bureaucracies in Latin America have tended to be large, poorly paid and administered, and unmotivated. Staffing is often done as a form of political favor to supporters of winning candidates or ministerial or agency appointees (one form of quid pro quo in a patron–client relationship). Professionalism and motivation are low, and the susceptibility to corruption or being suborned is often great. Indeed, the bribe, or *mordida* (little bite in the hand), is frequent in Mexico and most other countries. Corruption and favoritism often permeate the bureaucracies and feed negative perceptions of government in the general population. Bureaucratic appointments are not always made on the basis of clear standards. Costa Rica is the only Latin American country to have a professional civil service system. Elsewhere, each ministry or agency may have its own recruitment criteria and job classification system, with no general standardization or means of doing cross-agency comparisons. Nor are programs or university training in public administration widespread. Government offices are often open only in the mornings or until 1 or 2 P.M., and many workers have other jobs in the afternoons. In most cases, resources are very scarce. Similarly, phones go unanswered, lines are frequently long, service is poor, and the ability to have a request processed or a problem resolved is minimal. One frequently hears stories of requests simply not being processed until an extra inducement is added to the application. A sense of professionalism based on high levels of training, adequate compensation, and good morale is hard to find among public employees.

Knowledge of the bureaucratic sector is absolutely crucial to an understanding of Latin American politics. The implementation of government policy and programs is totally dependent on different segments of the bureaucracy. Bureaucratic functioning needs to be understood because many casual observers of the region are unfamiliar with the extensive role of government entities in the economy. In reality, most of the large Southern Cone countries, in pursuit of national development in the twentieth century, established significant state sectors to control everything from steel mills to coffee plantations. As in a socialist system, state employees set wages, prices, and production quotas. In the case of Argentina under Juan Perón, a government corporation, Institute Argentino de Promoción del Intercambio (IAPI), was established to purchase all agricultural products from the farmers and then to sell them on the international market with all proceeds going to the government. In some instances, more than 50 percent of the gross national product (GNP) was generated in the public sector. Such large-scale government intervention in the economy allowed many governments to establish significant social welfare programs in education, health, and social services, each with its own administrative bureaucracy. These large bureaucracies provided central governments with vast amounts of patronage that could be used to reward friends and co-opt opposition groups. The bureaucracies generally have lacked significant legislative oversight and, in many cases, have been both highly inefficient and corrupt, allowing both bureaucrats and those who appoint them to become wealthy. The nature and efficiency of these organizations have helped legitimize neoliberal characterizations of a bloated, inefficient government apparatus that needed to be downsized. In the last two decades, however, processes of privatization and downsizing of the state have resulted in a significant decline in the size and role of the bureaucracy in most of Latin America and in the loss of thousands of jobs.

## NEW DIRECTIONS: DEMOCRACY AND DEMOCRATIZATION

In Latin America in the twenty-first century, important questions are being asked about the direction of the region's political systems. The history of the region, as discussed in Chapters 2 and 3, saw the emergence of a wide range of governments: monarchies, rule by a *caudillo* or strong man, civilian and military dictatorships, oligarchic democracies, parliamentary democracies, populist-corporatist regimes, and, in the case of Cuba, a communist-led state. It is difficult to generalize about the location of the different types of regime except to say that the parliamentary or Westminster-style governments developed only in countries, such as Belize and Jamaica, which were formerly under British rule and thus, strictly speaking, are not part of Latin America. Monarchical rule had some presence in the immediate post-independence period in the Latin countries, but by the latter part of the nineteenth century, republican forms of rule, albeit with limited suffrage and strong elite rule, were well established. However, for most of the twentieth century, the trend toward democracy in the major countries of the region was blunted by a series of counter-trends. The most pervasive was the short-circuiting of democratic rule by powerful leaders, both civilian and military. Mexico is a good example of this pattern. After initial flirtation with monarchical rule in the 1820s, republicanism flourished in the middle of the nineteenth century under Benito Juárez as a system was established with limited suffrage and regular elections. However, in the late 1870s, this trend was blocked by the emergence of a classic *caudillo*, Porfirio Díaz, who gained power by legitimate electoral means only to terminate the process and be continuously re-elected through fraud and repression. He ruled for over thirty years, only being defeated and driven from office in 1910 by the powerful forces of the Mexican Revolution. After years of turmoil in the wake of the revolution, Mexico returned to a form of democratic rule with a federal republic in the 1930s. However, Mexican democracy was limited over the ensuing decades by a form of populist and corporatist rule that maintained the same political party, the Institutional Revolutionary Party (PRI), in power through a combination of popular mobilization, clientelism, repression, and voting fraud.

However, the Mexican PRI is not the only twentieth-century example of limitations on democracy that have occurred from regimes operating on a populist and corporatist model. Such regimes have mobilized popular support behind the government from the masses, especially urban dwellers and the working class, by attacking the traditional elites and promising significant increases in the standard of living for the majority classes. The classic examples of such regimes are those of Getúlio Vargas in Brazil and Juan Perón in Argentina. It would be unfair to classify these regimes as simply a continuation of the Latin American trend of strongman rule, although there clearly was an element of that in them. However, they often did operate within an electoral framework and did bring about significant democratic reforms in the areas of social welfare and education. At the same time, limitations on civil liberties and political opposition prevent the placing of such governments completely under the banner of democracy. Venezuelan president Hugo Chávez managed to mobilize popular support under a strong presidency but did so by remaining in the general confines of a democratic system. That fact was underscored when he accepted the defeat of a 2007 referendum that would have significantly expanded his power.

Yet, populist or corporatist rule has not been the primary impediment to democratic rule in Latin America in the last 100 years; that has come from the military. In virtually every country of the region, with the exception of the British colonies that became independent in the last forty years, the military has assumed dictatorial powers, short-circuiting democratic rule for shorter or longer periods of time. The most recent strong intervention of the military into the region's political systems came in the 1960s and 1970s in prominent countries in South America and the almost continual dominance over the last half-century of military regimes in most of Central America (except Costa Rica).

In the late 1950s, many analysts of Latin America were arguing that the era of tyrannical rule was coming to an end. They pointed to long-standing democratic regimes in countries such as Chile and Uruguay and to emerging democracies in Venezuela, Brazil, and Argentina. However, these predictions proved to be short-lived. A military coup in Brazil in 1964 that would begin twenty-one years of dictatorship started a process that would be repeated in Argentina (1966 and 1976), Peru (1968), and Uruguay and Chile (both 1973). In addition, efforts at achieving political democracy in El Salvador, where the military had ruled for decades, came to an abrupt end in 1972 when the military blocked the election of the Christian Democrat José Napoleon Duarte. As the 1970s came to an end, the great majority of Latin American countries were under military dictatorships. The 1980s were dubbed the "lost decade" in Latin America because of dramatic economic declines and rampant social problems. Military rule came to an end throughout the region, in large measure because the military governments had proven themselves incapable of dealing with economic and social woes. In the first years of the twenty-first century, no country in Latin America was under military rule, the last regime falling in Haiti in 1995 under the threat of a U.S. invasion.

It is generally acknowledged that five countries in Latin America stand out for the length and stability of their democratic experiences—Chile, Uruguay, Costa Rica, Colombia, and Venezuela. However, only Costa Rica has not suffered a serious setback or rupture of democratic rule in the period since 1948. What these countries generally have in common is that at some point in their history the economic and political elites found a way to act cooperatively for the purpose of staving off more radical demands for political and economic restructuring. In fact, when democratic rule broke down, as it did in Chile and Uruguay in 1973, it was because the elites came to the conclusion that revolutionary forces could not be contained by constitutional means. It would seem that similar conclusions were reached by the elites in Honduras in 2009 and Paraguay in 2012.

Liberal democratic regimes were established in Uruguay and Chile between 1918 and 1932; Costa Rica established its regime in 1948. Colombia and Venezuela came close to establishing democratic rule in the late 1940s but only fully succeeded a decade later. Peeler argues that the key to the establishment of democracy was an agreement among the competing elites on the process of expanding political participation. He argues by counterexample that the failure to achieve such an agreement in Argentina after Perón's fall in 1955, marked by the continued exclusion of the Peronists, doomed the democratic process in that country.

All five countries conducted elections in the nineteenth century, but these elections were not the principal means of changing governments. Once in power through elections, individuals or parties regularly manipulated the system to maintain themselves in office, often forcing their opponents to turn to force to remove them. If elections were not a sufficient condition for democracy in the nineteenth century, how did that change in these five countries in the twentieth century? Chile may provide the best example. In the nineteenth century, Chile did enjoy a high level of political stability, interrupted only by a civil war in 1891. The basis of the stability was the political domination of an agro-export oligarchy that ruled through a series of limited-suffrage elections. By the 1930s, Chile had developed a clear tripartite system of Liberals, Conservatives, and Radicals. Although some parties would change, this tripartite division has persisted to the present. Key to the system is a center party that often holds the presidency—the Liberal Party until 1912, the Radical Party from 1938 to 1952, and the Christian Democrats from 1958 to 1973 and again from 1990 to 2000.

Chile has had the most openly class-divided politics of any country in the region in the twentieth century. It is argued that the traditional Liberal/Conservative alliance ruled until 1920 and then regained power during Pinochet's military rule. Otherwise, in the twentieth century, the oligarchy protected its interests not by direct rule of its political party but rather by maneuvering within Chile's tripartite system and using the checks and balances established in the 1925 constitution, which was not fully implemented until 1932. Such checks continued through the conservative Chilean Senate, which acted as a check on radical action by the center-left Concertacíon. Various center and center-left governments ruled during the unbroken forty-one years of democratic rule between 1932 and 1973. These governments promoted a series of reforms supporting labor union organization and the creation of an extensive social welfare system. However, they never attacked the serious interests of the traditional oligarchy. There were never any actions to enfranchise rural workers or to redistribute rural property. In fact, the traditional landowners actually gained the cooperation of several reform governments in their efforts to directly obstruct the organization of the rural workers. A variety of constitutional means, including six-year presidential terms with no re-election, a congress chosen on proportional representation, and judges insulated from direct political control, served to deny any sector the possibility of centralizing power and implementing their full agenda. In essence, it was a guarantee for the traditional oligarchy that their fundamental economic power would not be challenged. In return, the oligarchy supported the democratic system and did not turn to the military to defend their interests. The limitation of this system as a guarantor of democracy was demonstrated in 1973 when the oligarchy supported a military coup out of the fear that Popular Unity President Salvador Allende had set in motion political forces that could ultimately lead to the expropriation of their wealth. Democracy was reestablished only in 1990 when the oligarchy was convinced that the radical left was in full retreat and that power could again be placed in a trusted center party, the Christian Democrats, which had successfully mediated class interests prior to Allende's rule. The Chilean example demonstrated that democratic rule in Latin America in the twentieth century was based on cooperation among elites. Only when the traditional oligarchy has been willing to support democracy have there been long periods of rule without military intervention to protect their wealth and property. This also suggests the importance of the idea of "pacted democracy," whereby the political elites make varied agreements to share power or alternate rule for a given period and thus discourage and exclude new political leaders or political movements from challenging their power.

Whether this pattern will persist in the twenty-first century remains to be seen. One could argue that the postmilitary dictatorship period starting in the 1980s and 1990s and extending to the present could best be characterized as nominal democracy. There is a clear tendency to compete for power through ostensibly democratic and constitution means and not to rely on blunt military intervention. Even though the military was used in the 2009 coup in Honduras, Congress and not a military junta controlled and orchestrated the power transition. Although one should not assume that more brutal power machinations involving the military or the brutal use of force will never be used, it would seem that more subtle means will be the order of the day. Rather than intervention to cancel elections, sophisticated campaigning tactics will be employed. Rather that overthrowing an elected president, his or her behavior will be attacked and legal and constitutional means will be manipulated to secure his or her ouster. Further, the growth and power of nonarmed social movements and their ability to depose nonresponsive governments and facilitate the growth of leftist or rightest parties and the election or assumption of power of new presidents (the pink tide) suggests a sea change may be beginning.

# Political Actors

Powerful actors dominate the political game in Latin America. We would agree with the definition of these players offered by Gary Wynia: "any individual or group that tries to gain public office or influence those who do." In Latin America, as elsewhere in the world, the list of such actors is a long one—landowners, businesspeople, peasants, industrial workers, civil servants, and military officers, to name just a few. However, these labels are not sufficient to fully understand the different groups or their interaction. It is important to analyze each and to ascertain the role of each within the Latin American context. Wynia also makes some important observations about Latin American politics in comparison to other parts of the world. For instance, he notes that Latin America's political systems are not replicas of those in North America and Western Europe. They have more varied rules, and there is often not as much consensus among the political actors. Further, many interest groups are not as strong or as well financed as in the United States or Europe.

We have previously discussed individual actors like dictators and the strong president; next, we turn to groups. Looking at each group, we need to ask: Who are the people involved, and from what social class, region, or ethnic group do they come? It is also necessary to ask what, if anything, they want from the political process and when and how they hope to get it. We must also realize that there may be groups that largely wish to be left alone by the political process. However, by and large, we will focus on groups that seek to utilize the political process to their advantage. Another important variable to be studied is the resources that are available to each group—those that can be utilized to influence the political process. Resources can range from sheer numbers and the ability to mobilize them, organizational cohesion, and dedication to wealth and strategic presence in the economy to the capacity to engage in violent activity.

## TRADITIONAL LARGE LANDOWNERS: *LATIFUNDISTAS*

In all the countries of Latin America, with the exception of Costa Rica and Paraguay, the Spanish and Portuguese monarchies granted lands to a group of landowners during colonialization. Initially, the monarchies had primarily been interested in the extraction of gold and silver from the Americas, but as time passed the grant of royal lands for the cultivation of foodstuffs became more the norm for their penetration into the New World. These plantations took on some of the forms of the feudalism of medieval Europe. The local populations were forced to work on the land as virtual slaves. The workers were not paid in wages but rather lived on the *latifundio*, hacienda, or *fazenda* and were given a small piece of land to grow their own food in return for their free labor on the *patrón*'s land. The *hacendados* and *fazendeiros* came to be the dominant class of the colonial period, both politically and economically. They were generally not interested in any significant involvement in the central national government or the distant monarchy in Lisbon or Madrid. All that they needed was the loyalty of local politicians and a local police force that could be called in case of worker unrest.

At the time of independence early in the nineteenth century, this group, made up of *criollo* descendants of the early European settlers, eventually took the lead in breaking ties with Spain and Portugal, taking advantage of the relative weakness of those governments at the time. In the years since independence, this once-dominant class has seen its political and economic power eroded throughout the region. In countries such as Mexico, Bolivia, and Cuba, dramatic twentieth-century revolutions almost eliminated this class altogether. In most countries, over the last century, the large landowners slowly lost political power to the emerging commercial farmers and industrial elites. Beginning in the latter part of the nineteenth century, land ownership and cultivation practices began to change, bringing forward a new class of commercial entrepreneurs who ran their landowning operations as businesses. In some instances, the traditional large landowners transformed themselves into commercial farmers; but in the majority of cases, their lands were eroded by land reform and the cultivation of new land by the commercial farmers, who reduced large landowners' political and economic influence. Changes in the rules of politics over time also cut into their power; but as long as dictatorship and military rule prevailed, the playing field favored the elites, especially the traditional landowners. Later, as republican forms of government emerged in the nineteenth century with greater and greater extension of suffrage, the influence of this group began to erode. However, this erosion of influence has been a slow one because of the enormity of the power once held. In countries where the large landholders continued to dominate the economic landscape, such as El Salvador, they have wielded significant political power to the present time. *Fazendeiros* still have tremendous power in much of rural Brazil, as do their commercial counterparts.

## Business and Industrial Elites

While it is correct that rural elites held a dominant position politically and economically in most of Latin America well into the twentieth century, wealth has never been monopolized by them. Beginning in colonial times, businesspeople who engaged in a wide range of commercial enterprises, from trading to banking, have been a part of the political scene. The turning point for the industrial elites came with the Great Depression of 1929. The depression devastated the region economically, but it also opened the door to entrepreneurs producing goods that were no longer being supplied by depressed European economies. Many of the emerging entrepreneurs in countries like Brazil, Argentina, and Venezuela were new immigrants who generated considerable wealth within one generation. In these large countries, the manufacturing sector began to grow and eventually contributed a greater share of national wealth than agriculture did. The process of becoming more economically independent from Europe was further enhanced by the isolation generated by World War II. As their contribution to national wealth grew, industrial entrepreneurs sought and gained important concessions from the national governments. Unlike the rural elites, who largely favored the import of foreign finished goods without any significant tariff protection, the burgeoning industrialists sought to have their growing industries protected from foreign competition. In addition to government subsidies, the industrial entrepreneurs sought government support for the subordination of organized labor. For obvious reasons, the entrepreneurs generally did not want the interference with their management prerogatives or profits that labor unions generally attempt. Industrialists have had only mixed success in this arena. While military dictatorships like those in Chile, Brazil, and Argentina in the 1970s and 1980s repressed the labor movement, other governments have been less willing to blunt the power of the unions because of their ability to deliver votes, engage in demonstrations, and disrupt the economy.

All members of the business elite do not have the same economic interests or policy agendas. Some elements of the commercial elite have been more engaged in buying and selling traditional primary goods and importing and distributing finished goods. Their interest in import substitution industrialization (ISI) was thus muted. Further, smaller national industries and banks were often at odds with those interests that allied themselves with multinational corporations engaging in manufacturing and finance. The specific financial interests of each group defined their political position. Such elites, since they are few in number, generally did not seek to influence the government through the traditional political process; rather, they served on government boards and commissions or appealed directly to government officials. In many instances, these entrepreneurs sought to bribe government officials for favors for their individual firms. Such bribes were often an accepted part of the political process; however, when such payments came to light, as in Brazil in the 1990s, officials were indicted or forced to resign, as was the case with President Fernando Collor de Mello. Industrialists also sought and gained such overt favoritism as easy credit, export subsidies, and government purchase of only domestically produced manufactured goods. Although some businesspeople espoused the ideology of free trade, very few were actually prepared to go without government subsidies. Until the 1980s, this protectionist mantra generated by the ISI model was largely accepted without question by the governments of the large countries of the region—Mexico, Brazil, and Argentina. This perspective was bolstered by the ideas of the economist Raúl Prebisch and the Economic Commission for Latin America (ECLA). However, the revival of the free trade ideology under the banner of neoliberalism resulted in some profound changes. Begun under the Chilean dictatorship of Augusto Pinochet in the 1970s and 1980s, neoliberal ideas took hold in Argentina, Brazil, and elsewhere in the 1990s. As a result, tariff walls were lowered and government subsidies of industry reduced. New competition from North American, Asian, and European entrepreneurs has weakened the economic and political position of many of the local industrial elites or has forced them to become associated with foreign investors. Commercial business elites may be able to adapt to the new sources of supply, but they may also be challenged by foreign chains like Walmart.

## The Middle or Intermediate Sectors

This is an important and pivotal group in the Latin American political scene. We use the term "intermediate sector" to distinguish it from the concept of middle class, which is prominent in analyses of North America and Europe. Unlike the middle classes in these countries, which gained prominence and stature through economic activity following the Industrial Revolution and industrialization, Latin American intermediate sectors were primarily professional functionaries such as government bureaucrats, doctors, lawyers, shopkeepers, managers, accountants, middle-level military officers, and some teachers. This group has expanded with urbanization and industrialization and is marked by a relatively high level of education and centrality to the functioning of modern society. Their numbers, small until Latin America began to industrialize and urbanize, have grown significantly in recent years. In comparison to the middle classes of Europe and North America, they generally developed less class consciousness and have remained a diverse and fragmented community. Their diversity and specific interests have at times made them forces for change, as was the case with their support for the reformist Radical Party in Argentina during the twentieth century. At other times, they have not been a force for societal change, being largely dependent on the landed and industrial elites that dominated. Most sought to emulate the lifestyle and consumption patterns of the upper classes rather than supplant them, and they have definitely been much less entrepreneurial than their counterparts in the North.

The relationship of the intermediate sectors to the political process has been an interesting one. Not surprisingly, what they have demanded from the political system are resources that further the position of their group—government funds for education, industry, and communication infrastructure. They can move in or out of a particular political camp depending on how well they think their goals can be achieved. They have not been universally consistent in their support of any particular form of government. However, in the twentieth century, more often than not the intermediate sectors have been strong supporters of political reform and multiparty democratic systems. In those situations where these movements have come to the fore, they have clearly favored the expansion of the franchise and the development of defined civil liberties. The intermediate sectors can be connected directly to the development and prosperity of political parties such as the Radical Party in Argentina and the Colorado Party in Uruguay. However, their support for democracy has not been unflagging. The Mexican middle sectors always gave strong support to the one-party domination of the PRI, and in the 1960s and 1970s the middle sectors generally supported the military regimes of Chile, Brazil, and Argentina. Generally, they fear radical or revolutionary movements because the success of such movements might herald the end of their hard-won standard of living. They are horrified by the prospect of slipping into the poverty of the masses. Their ambivalence is partially the result of the resources they bring to the table. In most Latin American countries, this sector has not been large enough to act as a definitive voting bloc, although this is changing in some countries. Instead, they bring to the political process their organizing skills and their central position as cogs in the government, industry, and the business and financial bureaucracies. Such positions lead them to be more comfortable in bargaining with the elites than in mobilizing the masses to achieve their political ends.

## ORGANIZED LABOR

Labor organizing began in Latin America in the 1890s but had relatively little success in its early years. Much as in the United States, it was hampered by divisions among immigrant workers, who often spoke different languages, and by opposition from government authorities, allied with entrepreneurial elites in their implacable opposition to workers' organizations of any kind. The workers' movement may have seemed even more threatening in Latin America than in the United States as it was led almost entirely by political radicals espousing either socialist or anarchist ideas for the complete reorganization of society and the expropriation of the property of the ruling circles. In Argentina, the labor movement organized hundreds of thousands of workers in response to the abysmal working conditions of the time. However, the strong influence of labor was broken by severe repression early in 1919. Hundreds of workers were killed by the police and the army, and the militant leadership was broken. A similar situation occurred in Brazil during the same time period as socialist and anarchist labor leaders were jailed and deported.

Region-wide there was little successful union organizing in the 1920s. Only in the 1930s did labor begin to become a large enough force in the most industrialized countries to become a significant political factor. During the 1930s, significant labor struggles emerged again in Brazil, Argentina, Colombia, El Salvador, Bolivia, and Venezuela. However, even as labor succeeded in organizing many workplaces, the owners of industry and their representatives in government refused to recognize the legitimacy of their organizations or to grant them a significant political role. One exception was Mexico, where the regime of Lázaro Cárdenas (1934–1940) included the labor movement as part of a wider populist strategy aimed at further transformation of Mexican society in the wake of the 1910 revolution. The labor movement has had significant influence to the present time within the PRI. Argentina is also an interesting case of labor influence. By 1943, Argentine labor had recovered from the earlier repression to organize 500,000 workers into its ranks. After initial attempts by the military to repress the movement, Colonel Juan Perón emerged to harness the power of the labor movement behind his nationalist and populist political program. With the support of the labor movement, Perón easily won the 1946 presidential election despite active opposition by the United States. Perón responded by delivering tangible benefits to Argentina's working class over the following decade in the form of higher wages and significant government spending on health care and education. Perón was removed in a 1955 military coup, but the party he created has retained significant labor union support to the present time. In other countries, unions have been allied with other parties.

In contemporary Latin America, the labor movement has many resources at its disposal. While the labor movement does not represent all of the working class, but rather its aristocracy, in a democratic context it has the ability to mobilize considerable votes for its candidates. Yet, women and racial minorities are often underrepresented in leadership positions (see Tables 11 and 22). Between elections, organized labor exercises important economic influence through strategic control of industrial enterprises. Strikes in industries such as transportation, banking, and mining can have great leverage in a society. In extraordinary situations, the labor movement can also be a catalyst for a more far-reaching general strike or even an

armed insurrection. Most labor unions are organized into national labor federations, like the General Federation of Labor or General Confederation of Labor, and
are affiliated with the Communist, Socialist, or Christian Democratic Parties or with
strong nationalist parties, like the PRI in Mexico or the Peronists in Argentina. A few
unions have been formed with the help of the U.S. American Federation of Labor/
Congress of Industrial Organizations (AFL-CIO) and are heavily influenced by the
less political U.S. labor model.

## RURAL POOR

The rural poor have often received considerable attention from scholars, but historically this group has been the most marginalized from political power. First, it
is necessary to state that this group is not homogeneous and that its role in Latin
American society has evolved over time as the result of both land reform programs
and economic transformation. The term *campesino* has been used to label those low-
income agricultural producers who have some attachment to the land in rural Latin
America. Rural laborers comprise another group made up of landless agricultural
workers. In many ways, the basic conditions of their lives have changed very little
over the course of several centuries. The great majority of both groups have lived
in dire poverty, barely earning enough for their survival and reproduction, with
little chance for advancement. Most people born as *campesinos* or rural laborers
died in the same social situation and passed that legacy on to their children and
grandchildren. While having common characteristics, it is also important to see the
significant differences between various groups of the poor based on their different
circumstances of employment.

The first group is known as *colonos*. They work on the large plantations described earlier as the haciendas and *fazendas*. Whether they are tenant farmers or
sharecroppers, they are all too often bound to the plantation by generations of
debt. This group is generally not paid in wages but allowed a small plot of land to
grow food for their sustenance and provided the other basic necessities of life by
the owner of the plantation in return for labor. In the best of situations, this group
can be said to be protected from the greatest uncertainties of harsh rural life by the
*patrón*. As one might expect, their political position is especially precarious. Since
they are wholly dependent on the *patrón*, they have often been either marginalized
from politics or manipulated by the *patrón*'s dictates. In the context of democratic
elections, *colonos, campesinos*, and rural laborers can be coerced into voting for the
chosen political candidates of the estate owner. Because of its numbers, this group
could be a significant political force. However, because they were traditionally isolated from one another on different estates and in different villages, their organizing
power was often muted. Organizing efforts were often resisted with force by local
owners and their allies among the police and judiciary. Currently, better opportunities for exchange of information and interaction are offered by the expanding
modern communication infrastructure, but the forced commercialization of farming
is rapidly forcing this group either off the land and into the cities or to become landless rural laborers.

The second important group is the rural wage laborers, who became increasingly dominant through the economic transformation of Latin America in the

twentieth century. These are the workers on Latin America's commercial farms and plantations who are hired first to plant and then later to harvest the region's primary cash export crops: cotton, coffee, sugarcane, and bananas. Many wage laborers may own small plots of land but are forced to sell their labor to supplement their income to survive. In many places, they are migrants because they often have to travel great distances to find enough work to survive throughout the year. North Americans are somewhat familiar with this class of Latin Americans because many work each year, both legally and illegally, in the agricultural fields of the United States. Like the *colonos*, this group is largely marginalized from the Latin American political process. The combination of their constant travel and precarious economic situation makes it difficult for them to become involved in politics, either as voters or as protestors; but there are important exceptions. Banana workers in Honduras, Costa Rica, Panama, and Guatemala have been very political at times, with involvement in both elections and protest actions. In recent times, many rural laborers have joined the Landless Movement (Movimento dos Trabalhadores Rurais Sem Terra; MST) in Brazil and have begun to exert greater political pressure. Likewise, much of the organizational base of the Zapatistas in Mexico, Confederation of Indigenous Nationalities of Ecuador (CONAIE), and various indigenous groups in Bolivia is rural.

The third group is the subsistence farmers, the *minifundistas* and *microfundistas*. As was pointed out earlier, there may be overlap between the last two categories because many subsistence farmers supplement their income with wage labor. The land that they occupy, sometimes with legal title and sometimes as squatters, is usually less than 10 acres. The crops are grown largely without mechanization or fertilizers because the use of either is out of the financial reach of the cultivator. In good times, the farmer grows enough for the family to survive and sells a small surplus at a local market. If there is crop failure due to storms or drought, there may not be a surplus and the family is driven toward the wage labor–migrant situation. In difficult economic times, the small farmer is also vulnerable to foreclosure if money is owed. This category of existence is generally preferred to that of wage labor, but it faces pressures from many directions. Proponents of land reform programs have often viewed this group's level of economic production as marginal and inefficient, so they have been targeted for elimination, with the hope that their labor can become available for the more efficient larger farms. Others have argued that giving them more land, irrigation, agricultural credit, and technical assistance would resolve much of rural poverty and increase the efficiency of production.

The rural poor have definite grievances to pursue with the political authorities. The *colonos* generally want the opportunity to improve their own lives and those of their children, usually by gaining the opportunity to work their own land. The wage workers want higher wages but are generally frustrated with the government's unwillingness to help them. Those who own small farms seek credit and technical support from the government and protection from their creditors.

For most of Latin American history, the rural poor were not in a strong position to pursue their grievances, divided as they were by both geography and differing interests. However, the twentieth century saw a significant change in their political importance. In Mexico and Venezuela, mass political parties succeeded in organizing the rural poor into the political process as voters behind a clear political agenda. They were even more important in revolutionary movements, playing a key role in such movements in Cuba, Bolivia, El Salvador, Guatemala, Peru, Colombia, and Nicaragua. In addition, the growth of grassroots movements such as the peasant leagues and Landless Movement in Brazil and the peasant unions and other organizations in Bolivia underscore their growing political importance.

## THE MILITARY

The armed forces must definitely be treated as a singularly important group in the political history of Latin America, although that prominence needs to be tempered by the fact that as Latin America enters the twenty-first century, for the first time in its modern history, no country is under military rule. Such a situation represents a stark contrast to the 1970s and 1980s, when more than half the region's governments were military-led. However, a strong process of democratization beginning in the mid-1980s brought civilian governments to power across the region, led by Peru in 1980, Argentina in 1983, Brazil in 1985, and Chile in 1989. Today, the discussion of the role of the military in much of Latin America revolves around its role as a significant bureaucratic interest group. Acceptance of the legitimacy of civilian rule and the subordination of the military to civilian political rule has seemingly become the norm in much of Latin America. Yet, the military still holds veto power in countries, such as Guatemala, and is still able to operate with impunity in some aspects of civil society. The military remains an active force in contemporary politics, and its current position flows from its long-standing power. Indeed, it was the military that removed President Zelaya from office in the 2009 coup in Honduras.

Since World War II and with the strong backing of the U.S. government, Latin American militaries have been competent, professional organizations with considerable modern weaponry. Not surprisingly, the region's largest country, Brazil, has the largest armed forces, with close to 300,000 soldiers in uniform. Brazil spends over $3 billion a year maintaining its forces, which include an aircraft carrier and more than 200 combat aircraft. Other countries that have maintained significant military forces in recent years include Mexico, Argentina, Chile, and Cuba. (Cuba significantly reduced its forces in the 1990s after maintaining close to 50,000 soldiers in Africa, with Soviet help, during the 1970s and 1980s.) Yet, the primary role of most militaries in Latin America has been the maintenance of internal order. However, the size and sophistication of military forces are not in reality the prime determinants of political influence in Latin America or elsewhere. Throughout the twentieth century, the U.S. and British militaries were powerful forces but have never challenged control by civilian authority. In contrast, relatively weak and small military establishments in Latin America have usurped civilian authority and sought to dominate the political process.

The involvement of the Latin American military in politics has its roots in the military nature of the conquest and early settlement, the class character of the military families throughout the course of Latin American history, and other factors. Over the course of Spanish and Portuguese colonial rule, the military officer corps were deeply intertwined with political rulers and the landowning elites. They were often one and the same as leading military people also controlled large tracts of land. If the military leaders did not own significant land, they acted as an important ally against any forces that sought to challenge the landed oligarchy. As a result, the military entered the age of democratic reforms in the twentieth century in a position deeply suspicious of forces that would have curtailed the political and economic power of the old political and economic elites through democratic political means. With few exceptions, the political stance of the military as an enemy of democracy and reform was well established entering the twentieth century. Understanding the military in the twentieth century and especially in the last fifty years becomes a more complex problem. During that time the class character of military officers changed considerably as fewer children of the military continued the family tradition and as the modern, more professional militaries often became an important avenue of social mobility for those who aspired to become members of the middle class or to improve their relative standing in it.

The education system for military officers has long been an important determinant of their orientation toward politics. Military leaders have maintained their system of officer corps education independent of and isolated from the civilian education system. Traditionally, most military education focuses on technical warfare training with little time devoted to the humanities or the social sciences. The Centro de Altos Estudios Militares (CAEM) in Peru, which trained the Nasserite military officers who formed the reformist government of Juan Velasco Alvarado (1968–1975), is an exception; likewise, the training at the National War College (Escola Superior de Guerra) of Brazil viewed strategy as involving some degree of social involvement. Yet, in all military schools, to the degree that matters of history and society are treated, the ideological content very often views the military as the only institution of society that is unambiguously dedicated to the nation's welfare. All civilian politicians are treated with some suspicion, especially those of a center or left persuasion. However, certain interest groups, especially labor unions, are viewed as detrimental to the national interest. At least until recently, there has been little or no shift in this approach to education, which has definitely contributed to the military's willingness to carry out coups against civilian governments.

If military education has provided an ideological justification for certain forms of military intervention, then their disciplined and hierarchical forms of organization provided both the ability to carry out the overthrow of civilian governments and the ability to place themselves at the head of government bureaucracies previously headed by civilians. Military leaders in the 1960s and 1970s in countries such as Brazil argued that their hierarchical forms of organization could bring new levels of efficiency to government bureaucracies previously plagued by bad organization and chaos. This type of military government came to be termed "bureaucratic authoritarianism." In general, claims that the military could be more effective rulers than civilians proved untrue and contributed to the downfall of military governments in the latter part of the 1980s. It is unclear just how readily the military can exercise its power in the current democratized period in Latin America. Yet, they may still have the power to replace a government if they choose to mobilize and have elitist support, as was the case in Honduras in 2009.

## GOVERNMENT BUREAUCRATS

Some have suggested that government bureaucrats should not be treated as distinct and separate actors within the Latin American political process because they simply carry out the wishes of whatever political leaders are in power. However, this view is insufficient for Latin America or most any other region of the world. The key factor in understanding the significant power of government bureaucrats is that while elected politicians serve distinct terms and military leaders can be driven from power, the great majority of bureaucrats stay in their positions for lengthy time periods. In Latin America, government bureaucrats have wielded considerable power because of the post–World War II trend of large-scale government involvement in the ownership of important economic enterprises—banks, airlines, oil refineries, railroads, steel plantations, and many more—leading to the emergence of the nation of "technocrats" who played important political roles, particularly during the authoritarian periods in the 1960s and 1970s, in countries like Brazil, Argentina, Chile, and Uruguay. Privatizations within the last decade have reduced the government's role in countries like Argentina and Brazil, but public ownership remains formidable. A recent acknowledgment of the power of one segment of the bureaucracy came in Venezuela where in 1999 the elected populist president Hugo Chávez spoke of the need to trim the size of the giant bureaucracy of the state-run oil company PDVSA (Petróleos de Venezuela). Chávez acknowledged the power of its bureaucracy, calling it a "government within a government." Other presidents have talked of reducing the size of the bureaucracy at all levels.

This sector has engaged in a significant amount of self-promotion to boost its importance. In contrast to military officers, who stake their right to political office on their duty to country and their organizational skill, government bureaucrats advertise their skill as technocrats who can rise above the squabbling or corruption that may plague elected leaders. Increasingly, many Latin American technocrats are trained at foreign universities in Britain, France, and the United States. Oftentimes they return to their homelands with strong beliefs that their newfound technical skills have given them the right to a say in the political and economic direction of their nation, not just as administrators. In Mexico, the previous four presidents came from the ranks of these *técnicos*.

Government bureaucrats, like those in other sectors, may well be motivated by selfless and patriotic concerns, but those who manage government institutions share many interests. First, they desire to continue their influence over public policy. Second, they seek to administer their agencies with as little interference as possible. Third, they enjoy the power and, in some instances, the wealth that comes from providing goods and services that those in the private sector need.

The means to achieve these ends are fairly well known. The reality is that elected officials are dependent on administrators to carry out their economic and political development plans. If an administrator disagrees with a particular policy initiative, he or she definitely has the ability to sabotage its implementation. While such sabotage may need to be subtle to succeed, the elected officials usually lack the legal authority to remove recalcitrant officials from their posts. It is not yet clear whether the trend toward smaller government bureaucracies promoted by neoliberal reformers in the 1990s will significantly reduce the power of this sector. Ultimately, the sector may well turn out to be an insurmountable barrier to the full implementation of privatization plans or other government reforms. Likewise, oversized bureaucracies have become a fiscal problem that fuels inflation.

## POLITICAL PARTIES

The role of political parties is evolving in Latin America. Wynia argues that political parties have traditionally played at least three separate and distinct roles in Latin American society. Like political parties in the United States and Western Europe, they participate in elections with the aim of gaining state power. In a few countries, like Costa Rica and Venezuela, political parties have played this role for decades, almost exclusively concentrating their energies on winning periodic contests for power. In countries where elections have been the norm, Ronald McDonald and J. Mark Rubl argue that parties tend to serve four functions: political recruitment, political communication, social control, and government organization and policy-making. However, until the 1990s, this role was sporadic in many countries, either because there were no elections, only military rule, or because their role was limited by the lack of constitutional norms. Beyond elections, there are two other roles for political parties, that of conspirators and the creation of political monopoly.

The category of conspirator describes those parties that do not accept the results of elections or operate in the absence of regular elections. These parties generally operate in the extraparliamentary arena, often turning to the use of force to gain power. Such parties can come from a variety of political positions, but most often they are movements that have been denied power through legitimate channels and turn to armed struggle to achieve their goals. Classic examples of this form of political activity occurred in Cuba, when activists in the Orthodox Party, denied the opportunity of gaining power through the 1952 elections because of Fulgencio Batista's cancellation of those elections, formed an armed organization (the 26th of July Movement) that challenged Batista and eventually defeated him.

Parties creating a political monopoly are those that seek to remain in power on a permanent basis. Latin America had two excellent contemporary examples of this type of political movement, the Cuban Communist Party (CCP) and the Mexican PRI up to 2000. Both were very successful in their efforts but used different methods. The Cuban communists have succeeded in part through the establishment of formal rules of the game whereby the constitution enshrines the CCP as the country's only legal party, through its legitimacy as the party of the 1959 revolution, and through its social achievements. The PRI dominated the Mexican political scene for over seventy years, keeping the presidency up to the year 2000, when it finally suffered its first defeat in a presidential election. The party constructed a system where opposition parties competed for power but were limited in their real opportunities for victory by a series of PRI policies, including patronage, co-optation, voter fraud, and occasionally repression. Both movements were born in revolutionary conflict and maintained power in part by presenting themselves as the party of the revolution and as the only political force capable of moving forward the ideals of their revolutions. Conditions have clearly changed in Mexico, and even though the PRI candidate won in the 2012 presidential election, the PRI will now have to alternate power with other parties. The success of such movements is not easy and is usually dependent on some measure of popular support together with the support of the military, although in both Mexico and Cuba the military remained subordinated to civilian politics and heavily influenced by the dominant party.

Latin American political parties emerged in the nineteenth century when most of the region's nations adopted republican forms of government with limited suffrage. Two primary political currents emerged during this time period: the Liberals and the Conservatives. The latter were drawn primarily from the traditional rural elites of the *latifundio* system, who primarily sought from the government a preservation of the economic and political patterns that were established during the colonial period. The Liberals represented the emerging modern upper classes of the nineteenth century, the owners of commercial agriculture, and other newly founded activities. The Liberals wanted the government to undertake a more active role in breaking up traditional landowning patterns, separating church from state, and promoting foreign commerce. Latin American Liberals were not as committed to the political side of liberalism with its emphasis on constitutional rule and freedom of thought. Elections in Latin America were largely an elite matter throughout the nineteenth century, involving only about 5 percent of the adult male population. These parties engaged in electoral contests but also were often the basis for armed conflict as both sides often refused to recognize the results and turned to violence to achieve their political ends.

Representative of elite dominance and patriarchy, women and minorities still struggle for adequate representation in party leadership positions. Internal decision-making is frequently authoritarian and often based on *personalismo*.

**Traditional Parties.** As pressure for increased suffrage succeeded in widening the electoral base and new immigrant groups swelled the Latin American population in the early part of the twentieth century, two distinct patterns of political party loyalty developed: the **Liberals** and the **Conservatives**. They have persisted to the present day. In some countries, Colombia and Honduras being the best examples, the Liberal and Conservative parties, despite being elite driven, succeeded in gaining significant electoral support from the newly enfranchised rural and urban masses. Historically, the Liberals stood for political and economic liberalism (thus greater political rights and the curtailment of Church power on the one hand and free trade and free markets on the other). The Conservatives stood for official religion, centralized government, and state-regulated trade and commerce. This political division basically continued throughout the twentieth century, leaving these countries with essentially two-party systems unchanged over time. The Liberals and Conservatives who succeeded in transforming themselves did so by a variety of means. Hacienda-owning Conservatives, using the strong bonds of the patron–client relationship, have often been able to secure the support of their *colonos* through a combination of reward and punishment. Wage-paying commercial farmers associated with the Liberals may not have had as direct control of their employees, but many did succeed in convincing rural workers that their self-interest lay with support for the Liberal cause. Both parties succeeded in gaining strong familial loyalty to their movements, a connection that has now been passed on through multiple generations.

However, the cases where Liberals and Conservatives succeeded in transforming themselves into broad-based electoral machines were the exception. In some cases, such as in Chile, Liberals and Conservatives were forced to unite (Chile's National Party) to be able to confront new challenges to elite domination.

In the majority of countries, the traditional parties rebuffed the demands of the newly emergent groups with the result that new, **European-inspired political parties** emerged on the scene after 1900. The most interesting were the Chilean Radical Party, the Argentine Radical Civic Union, and the Uruguayan Colorado Party. Modeled after the French Radical Party, these movements stood for suffrage, expanding public education and other government services, and the protection of workers' rights from the power of oligarchies, both urban and rural. Radical politicians succeeded in getting themselves elected in all three countries, drawing primarily on an immigrant and urban constituency, including the emerging proletariat and intermediate (middle) sectors. The Radicals generally did greater damage to the Liberals, who in some ways had attempted to appeal to the same constituency. As the Radicals eclipsed the Liberals, in some countries it turned the primary electoral battlefield into one of Radicals against Conservatives. In some instances, the elite former supporters of the Liberals turned to the Conservatives to form an oligarchic alliance. The heyday of the Radicals was relatively short-lived, although the Argentine party has undergone a rebirth in the last thirty years. The Radical parties faced increased pressure in the 1930s and, unable to deal with the economic challenges of the Great Depression, were either overthrown by the military representing the traditional oligarchy or faced increasing pressure from both populist and socialist movements. They are still important political actors in Argentina and Chile, and the Colorado Party won the presidential election in 2000 in Uruguay. The Liberals have remained relatively strong in Colombia.

**Nationalist Populist Parties.** The 1930s and 1940s saw the emergence of populist parties in both Brazil and Argentina. Each was organized around a single charismatic leader, Getúlio Vargas in Brazil and Juan Perón in Argentina. The populist movement founded by Vargas did not outlive him, but the Peronist Party still plays an influential role in Argentine politics to this day. It is important to understand that the roots of Latin American populism were clearly different from those in the United States, where the movement was primarily a rural-based protest against the railroad monopolies. The success of Latin American populists in the 1930s and 1940s was with the growing urban, industrial working class, whose needs were largely ignored by the dominant parties of the time—Conservatives, Liberals, and Radicals.

The populists saw themselves as the archenemies of the socialist and communist parties that were seeking to appeal to the same constituency—urban industrial workers. However, unlike the Conservatives and Liberals, the populists believed that it was possible to defeat the prospect of revolution by creating government-sponsored worker organizations, which could yield worker discipline in return for better wages and working conditions.

The populism of Juan Perón in Argentina had many similarities to that of Vargas, but there were also some differences. Perón also incorporated elements of Italian fascism, but, unlike Vargas, who first gained power and then later created a movement to sustain his power, Perón gained power through the transformation of the Argentine General Labor Confederation into his personal instrument and the incorporation of conservative, radical, and socialist groups into his political movement. When the military and the traditional oligarchy sought to block his ascendancy to the presidency by arresting him, Perón and his future wife, Eva, mobilized his forces to gain his release and pave the way for his victory in the 1946 presidential election. In power, Perón's strategy was similar to that of Vargas. He implemented programs that delivered social services and a higher standard of living to the urban workers while guaranteeing entrepreneurs labor peace through tight control of the unions. Like Vargas, his rule took on strongly nationalist tones, and policies of economic protectionism were implemented. The government took a strong hold on the economy, the most dramatic example being the creation of a government monopoly over agricultural commodity trading, a strategy that captured the considerable profits of this section entirely for the government. He also nationalized the railroads, airlines, public utilities, and financial system, among other strategic sectors. In typical populist fashion, Perón did not move in any way to redistribute rural land as a revolutionary would have done but, rather, simply brought the rural elites under government control. Perón used the profits from this scheme to finance industrialization, social welfare programs, and the takeover of the country's utilities from foreign owners. Once the Peronist economic strategy began to fail in the early 1950s, Perón fell victim to the power of the old elites, who engineered a military coup in 1955 and sent him into exile. Returning to its populist roots, the Peronists successfully ran Néstor Kirchner for the presidency in 2003.

**Reform Parties.** Another type of political party that emerged during the same era as the populists was the democratic reform parties. Basically, there are two types of reform party: secular and religious. The traits that they shared were

Former President Chávez speaks. *(Ministry of Information, Venezuela)*

based on a rejection of both the populists and the revolutionaries. The democratic reformers did not accept the tendency toward demagoguery and the use of strongarm tactics against political opponents but did embrace the populist strategy of maintaining capitalist, free enterprise systems. The democratic reformers, while sharing some of the short-term desires for social justice with the socialist and communist parties, obviously broke with them over the vision of a classless socialist society.

**APRA Parties.** The secular reform movement began with the American Popular Revolutionary Alliance (APRA), founded by Peruvian Victor Raúl Haya de la Torre while he was in Mexico in 1924. The party was inspired by a range of political ideas, including socialism, indigenism, and anti-imperialism and was more radical in its early years. The charismatic Haya de la Torre led the party through the 1970s. Long persecuted and marginalized in Peruvian politics, APRA only achieved government power under Alan García for a brief period in the 1980s and again in 2006. However, similar political movements inspired by Haya de la Torre in Venezuela and Costa Rica have enjoyed long-term success. The Democratic Action Party (AD) of Venezuela first governed in the late 1940s and has held the presidency of the country for the great majority of the time from 1958 to 1998. In a similar fashion, the National Liberation Party of Costa Rica has held the presidency of that country frequently since its founding at the time of the Costa Rican civil war in 1948. Similar parties developed in Bolivia (MNR), the Dominican Republic (Partido Revolucionario), and Puerto Rico (Popular Democratic Party).

**Christian Democratic Parties.** Religious reformers are grouped in the Christian Democratic movement, which originated in Western Europe after World War II. Drawing heavily on Catholic thought, the Christian Democratic parties emerged as alternatives to the powerful Communist, Socialist, and Labor parties. The rise of Christian Democrats was especially important in Germany and Italy, where earlier pro-capitalist parties had been irredeemably tainted by their association with fascism. Latin American Christian Democrats came to embody very similar political programs to the secular reformists, embracing political democracy in opposition to military rule and a package of reform proposals, especially in the agrarian sector. In contrast to the secular parties, they drew their inspiration from progressive papal encyclicals and reform movements within the Church. Christian Democrats sought to organize throughout the region but ultimately have achieved full success only in Chile and Costa Rica and limited success in Venezuela and El Salvador.

**Left Reform Parties.** A contemporary reform party that clearly bridges the religious and secular boundaries is the Brazilian Workers' Party (PT). The PT emerged in the late 1970s during the growth of opposition to the military dictatorship. From the beginning, the PT had both Marxist and Catholic leadership, the latter being drawn from the powerful ecclesial base communities. The most popular leader was the leader of the resurgent metalworkers union, Luiz Inácio da Silva, known simply as Lula. The PT grew in strength rapidly despite many obstacles thrown in its way, including the jailing of Lula in 1981. With the return of electoral democracy in 1985, the PT established itself as a primary opposition party, supplanting older, more established left parties. In November 1988, the PT's

Luiza Erundina de Souza was elected mayor of São Paulo, Brazil's largest city. The party also demonstrated its mobilization powers through massive industrial strikes in 1988 and 1989. In the 1989 presidential elections, Lula nearly won the presidency in a run-off election against Fernando Collor de Mello, whose well-financed campaign defeated the PT leader by a scant 6 percent. The PT, seeking a more centrist image, voted at its 1991 convention to affirm its commitment to a mixed economy and democracy while retaining socialist ideals. Delegates representing the party's 600,000 members also voted to grant women a minimum of 30 percent of leadership positions. Lula finished a distant second to the well-funded campaign of the centrist Fernando Henrique Cardoso in the 1994 election. He was defeated again when Cardoso was re-elected in 1999. After moving toward the center and reassuring business interests, Lula finally won the presidency in 2002 and was easily re-elected in 2006. His hand-picked successor, Dilma Rousseff, was elected in 2010 and again in 2014. The PT succeeded in becoming the government party but did not hold a congressional majority. Similarly, the Revolutionary Democratic Party (PRD) in Mexico is also representative of this new brand of leftist party, as is the Frente Amplio in Uruguay, which won the presidency and a congressional majority in the 2004, 2009, and 2014 elections. In Bolivia, the widely supported opposition movement coalesced into support for Evo Morales in the Movement to Socialism Party (MAS), which is sufficiently radical to be included in this category. In Venezuela, one saw the formation of the United Socialist Party of Venezuela (PSUV) by the *Chavista* movement in 2007 as a mechanism to achieve twenty-first century socialism. Before Chávez's death, there was speculation that this could be a dominant party that might be able to stay in power for the foreseeable future. This is much less clear today.

**Revolutionary Parties.** The final group of parties to be discussed are the revolutionary parties. Revolutionary movements are discussed in more detail in Chapter 10, but it is necessary to briefly discuss the revolutionary parties in the wider context of other political parties. Two different types of revolutionary party are usually acknowledged in the Latin American context: those whose origins are in Marxist thought and those whose roots are elsewhere. However, it is also necessary to note that not all parties that begin their existence as revolutionary ones remain so. We must also discuss in this context those original revolutionary parties that have become thoroughly reformist in their behavior.

**Communist** and **socialist** parties had their roots in the ideas and political activities of Karl Marx and Friedrich Engels in the last few decades of the nineteenth century in Europe. Initially, the Marxist movement was united, but the 1917 October Revolution in Russia was a turning point. Most European socialist parties had abandoned the possibility of revolution in favor of the achievement of socialism by parliamentary means, but the success of the first socialist revolution in Russia under the leadership of the Bolshevik Party inspired the creation of an alternative set of revolutionary parties, called "communist," that accepted the international leadership of the Soviet Union. Because Latin America industrialized considerably after Europe, the development of socialist or revolutionary parties along Marxist lines was slow to occur. However, during the 1920s and 1930s, these parties did begin to emerge, largely among intellectuals, students, and industrial workers. Overall, these parties did not fare particularly well in the region as they faced wholesale repression from the established governments and fierce competition to organize workers from both the Radicals and the populists. The primary exception was in Chile, where the Marxist parties succeeded in gaining a large following in the working class and entry into coalition governments during the 1930s.

By the 1950s the socialist and communist parties had largely ceased to be revolutionary in orientation. Where possible, in countries such as Guatemala, they sought to work through the political process, working with non-Marxist reform parties to obtain programs for workers' rights and land reform. However, the conservatism of these communist parties only served to open political space to their left, which was soon filled by a new generation of revolutionary parties inspired by the success of the 26th of July Movement in Cuba. Basing themselves on Marxist ideology and co-opting the old, reformist CCP, movement leaders were soon at the head of a new generation of revolutionary parties that came to include the Sandinista National Liberation Front (FSLN) in Nicaragua, the Farabundo Martí National Liberation Front (FMLN) in El Salvador, and the Revolutionary Armed Forces of Colombia (FARC).

The best example of a non-Marxist revolutionary party is the PRI of Mexico. Founded in 1929, twelve years after the triumph of the revolutionary forces over the traditional oligarchy, this party has been one of the most successful in the twentieth-century history of political parties. From its founding in the late 1920s, the PRI won every presidential election in the twentieth century and held an absolute majority in the national legislature until 1997. Some dispute whether the PRI was ever a revolutionary party, but during the rule of Lázaro Cárdenas (1934–1940), the party used tactics of mass mobilization of workers and peasants to secure the gains of the 1910 revolution in the face of continued oligarchic resistance. After the period of Cárdenas's rule, the party became more traditional, maintaining its power through a variety of means ranging from repression to voter fraud to co-optation to maintain its absolute domination of the Mexican political system. By the 1980s, most considered that it had lost any revolutionary orientation.

**Common Characteristics.** Despite their obvious ideological differences, McDonald and Rubl argue that Latin American political parties share some important characteristics—primarily elitism, factionalism, personalism, organizational weakness, and heterogeneous mass support. The elitism revolves around the centralization of decision-making within a small core of (male and mostly European) party leaders who are usually drawn from the upper and middle classes. Some parties engage in a facade of democracy through the conduct of public primaries, but in reality decisions are retained by the core leadership. The latest party to follow this more transparent approach was the Mexican PRI with its first-ever presidential primary in 1999. Newer parties, like the PT and PRD, also display a greater degree of leadership diversity and internal democracy.

Factionalism has also been an enduring problem in Latin American parties. Such factionalism is often most associated with the left, but bitter splits among party leaders on both personal and ideological lines have been common across the political spectrum. Only in the case of the existence of a strong figure, such as Fidel Castro in the Cuban Communist Party (CPP), Juan Perón in the Peronist Party, and Haya de la Torre in the APRA movement, was serious factionalism avoided. When the latter died, his party split into several warring factions.

McDonald and Rubl also argue that Latin American parties have tended to more often be organized around personalities than ideologies. The roots of personalism are deep in Latin American history from the era of the *caudillos*, but they were sustained throughout the twentieth century despite the development of party ideologies and structures. Beyond the obvious examples of Vargas, Perón, and Castro, others abound, including former army officer Hugo Chávez in Venezuela. As party leaders, these personalities in some cases are willing to quickly change their party's position to ensure continuation in office. Identification with a single leader has often proven easier than connection to party symbols and doctrines, especially in the case of the less-educated populations. One has also seen the rise of ad hoc parties organized around a person such as comedian Jimmy Morales in Guatemala or Ollanta Humala in Peru.

Latin America does have some significant examples of well-organized parties—the Mexican PRI, APRA up to the 1980s, the CCP, Argentina's Radical Party, Uruguay's Colorado and Blanco parties, and Venezuela's Democratic Action, but these are the exception rather than the rule. Most Latin American parties are more similar to the U.S. Democratic and Republican parties, coming to life primarily at the time of election, lacking strong ties to grassroots movements, and without a large number of formal members. Some are sustained by a relatively high level of party identification among the voting public, but in general party identification is weak in Latin America compared to Western Europe and the United States.

Class characteristics do tend to carry some weight in Latin American party identification but less so than in Western Europe because of the relatively late development of labor unions. An obvious exception to this rule is the Brazilian PT, which has a very clear worker and peasant allegiance. However, more common in Latin American politics are parties like the Mexican PRI, the Uruguayan Colorados, the Chilean Christian Democrats, and the Argentine Peronists, whose long-running electoral success is based on the creation of a multiclass constituency. Another basis of party identification in Latin America is region. Regional party identification has its roots in the nineteenth century, when warring Liberal and Conservative parties developed regional strongholds. Such patterns continue today in countries like Colombia, Uruguay, Honduras, Peru, and Mexico. In the latter, the opposition National Action Party (PAN) has developed a power base in the states nearest the U.S. border, likely influenced by the tradition of the two-party system in its neighbor to the north.

It should also be noted that the party systems in Latin America are quite often multiparty, with a multiplicity of parties competing for power. The factionalizing of parties is also frequent. In recent years the party systems have also become more fluid with the demise or weakening of traditional parties in Venezuela, Peru, and elsewhere and radical restructuring of the party systems in El Salvador,

Bolivia, and Ecuador. Kenneth W. Roberts (in Levitsky, Loxton, Van Dyck, and Dominguez, *Challenges to Party Building in Latin America*) even argues that established parties have often been displaced by populist figures or new political movements and that while there has been democratic regime institutionalized electoral contestation, on average, party systems have "de-institutionalized." Along these lines, we suggest in Chapter 10 that social movements have also become important political actors as well and may be displacing some parties or revolutionary movements.

# Conclusion

One of the most important issues facing Latin America today is whether democratic rule will continue. Can the large steps taken in the last twenty-five years be sustained? To do so would clearly represent a significant break with Latin America's past. The most daunting issue may be whether democratic governments can be maintained in the face of deep socioeconomic problems that will not be solved overnight.

A series of leftist victories in elections in the last few years suggested the rejection of traditional parties and a new political orientation in Latin America. These elections are part of a trend where new social movements and social actors, especially from the indigenous peoples of the region, have thrust themselves into power. These movements are taking advantage of the democratic openings of the

Bolivian President Evo Morales. *(Photo by Pablo Aneli/AP Images)*

last twenty-five years and, in the process, are raising the expectations of the impoverished masses. However, many of the governments elected have yet to show that they are capable of meeting the high expectations of their people. Rightist parties and conservative interest have begun to use legal, constitutional, and movement mobilization to challenge these regimes in places like Brazil and Argentina. In the past, such a situation often invited the intervention of the military to restore order. However, there is little appetite, even among the business and financial elites, for a return to circumstances of widespread repression and denial of civil liberties that characterized military governments. It is significant that in the cases of Argentina, Ecuador, and Bolivia where large social movements and mass street demonstrations brought down governments in recent years, there was no intervention by the military and eventually, following caretaker rule, new leftist governments were elected and took power constitutionally. The delegitimization of neoliberalism and many of the traditional parties that backed it in most of Latin America has strengthened the search for political alternatives, and by 2017 one began to see greater competition between reformist parties and newly formed or reinvigorated parties on the right.

# Bibliography

Asturias, Miguel Angel. *El Señor Presidente*. New York: Atheneum, 1972.

Black, Jan Knippers, ed. *Latin America: Its Problems and Its Promise*. 5th ed. Boulder, CO: Westview, 2010.

Chávez, David, and Benjamin Goldfrank, eds. *The Left in the City: Participatory Local Governments in Latin America*. London: Latin American Bureau, 2004.

Cleary, Edward. *The Struggle for Human Rights in Latin America*. Westport, CT: Praeger, 1997.

Close, David, ed. *Legislatures and the New Democracies in Latin America*. Boulder, CO: Lynne Rienner, 1995.

Dominguez, Jorge. *Democratic Politics in Latin America and the Caribbean*. Baltimore: Johns Hopkins University Press, 1998.

Foweraker, Joe, Todd Landman, and Neil Harvey. *Governing Latin America*. Cambridge, MA: Polity Press, 2004.

Helmke, Gretchen, and Steven Levinsky, eds. *Informal Institutions and Democracy, Lessons from Latin America*. Baltimore: Johns Hopkins University Press, 2006.

Levitsky, Steven, James Loxton, Brandon Van Dyck, and Jorge I .Dominguez. *Challenges to Party Building in Latin America*. New York: Cambridge University Press, 2016.

Liss, Sheldon. *Marxist Thought in Latin America*. Berkeley: University of California Press, 1984.

Loveman, Brian, and Thomas Davies, eds. *The Politics of Antipolitics: The Military in Latin America*. Wilmington, DE: Scholarly Resources, 1997.

Mainwaring, Scott. *Building Democratic Institutions: Party Systems in Latin America*. Stanford, CA: Stanford University Press, 1995.

Mainwaring, Scott. *Christian Democracy in Latin America*. Palo Alto, CA: Stanford University Press, 2003.

Malloy, James, and Mitchell Seligson, eds. *Authoritarians and Democrats: Regime Transition in Latin America*. Pittsburgh, PA: University of Pittsburgh Press, 1987.

McDonald, Ronald, and J. Mark Rubl. *Party Politics and Election in Latin America*. Boulder, CO: Westview, 1989.

Peeler, John. *Building Democracy in Latin America*. 3rd ed. Boulder, CO: Lynne Rienner, 2009.

Philip, George. *Democracy in Latin America: Surviving Conflict and Crisis?* Oxford: Blackwell, 2003.

Smith, Peter H. *Democracy in Latin America: Political Change in Comparative Perspective.* 2d ed. New York: Oxford University Press, 2011.

Wiarda, Howard. *Dilemmas of Democracy in Latin America.* Lanham, MD: Rowman & Littlefield, 2006.

Wiarda, Howard, and Harvey Kline, eds. *Latin American Politics and Development.* 7th ed. Boulder, CO: Westview, 2010.

Wynia, Gary. *The Politics of Latin American Development.* 3d ed. Cambridge: Cambridge University Press, 1990.

## FILMS AND VIDEOS

*Confessing to Laura.* Colombia, 1990.
*Death and the Maiden.* United States, 1994.
*Death of a Bureaucrat.* Cuba, 1966.
*Doña Barbara.* Mexico, 1943.
*Evita.* United States, 1997.
*La Paz.* Bolivia, 1994.
*Missing.* United States, 1983.
*The Seven Madmen (Los Siete Locos).* Argentina, 1973.
*State of Siege.* United States, 1982.

**TABLE 20.** Overview of Latin American Electoral Systems

| Country | Presidential System | Legislative System | Governors and Municipalities | General Electoral Information |
|---|---|---|---|---|
| **Argentina** | The president is elected for a four-year term with the possibility of one successive term. Presidential elections for Argentina dispense with the 2nd round of elections under two possible situations: (1) where candidate A wins more than 45% of the votes in the 1st round, candidate A is thereby elected; (2) If candidate A wins at least 40% of the votes and is ahead of the runner-up candidate by more than 10 points, candidate A is declared elected. | Bicameral Congress. Proportional Representation. The 257 deputies are elected for four-year terms and may be re-elected. Half of the Chamber of Deputies is renewed every two years. The 72 senators are elected according to procedure established in local provincial constitutions. One third of the Senate is renewed every two years. | Governors and local authorities are elected according to the 25 provincial constitutions. | In December of 1983, Argentina returned to a democracy and since then has had free and fair democratic elections. In April 1994, elections were held to form a Constituent Assembly. The Assembly modified the 1953 Constitution with several reforms, including reduction of the president's term—from six to four years, with the possibility of a second term—and the adoption of a second round of voting if no candidate receives a majority in the first round. In addition, the reforms abolished the electoral college system. Mauricio Macri, of the Republican Proposal party, was elected president in 2015. He is the first non-Radical or non-Peronist president in almost one hundred years. He also won the first presidential runoff in Argentina's history. |
| **Bolivia** | President and vice president elected on the same ticket by popular vote for a five-year term. Per the new constitution, presidents can serve for a total of two consecutive terms. If no candidate receives a majority, the Congress chooses the president from among the top three candidates in a secret ballot. | Bicameral Plurinational Legislative Assembly. Chamber of Senators with 36 seats where members are elected by proportional representation from party lists to serve five-year terms and Chamber Deputies with 130 seats total; 70 uninominal deputies directly elected from a single district, 7 "special" indigenous deputies directly elected from noncontiguous indigenous districts, and 53 plurinominal deputies elected by proportional representation from party lists; all deputies serve five-year terms. | Bolivia is divided into departments and there is one prefecto (governor) per department. The prefectos are elected for five-year terms and have general executive powers. Municipal councils, which in turn elect mayors, are elected every two years. Mayors are elected for five-year terms. | On January 25, 2009, 61.4% of the Bolivian people approved a new constitution, Bolivia's 117th in 184 years that had been at the center of President Evo Morales' pledge for a transformation of Bolivian society. The constitution puts the ownership of Bolivia's natural resources in the hands of the Bolivian government and also, for the first time, declares Bolivia to be a multiethnic state. The referendum passed over the strong objection of the traditional powerbroker in the low lands of the country. |

| | | | | |
|---|---|---|---|---|
| Brazil | The president is elected for a four-year term with the possibility of re-election to one additional term. If none of the candidates receives a majority in the first round of voting, a second round is held between the top two candidates, 20 days after the first round. | Bicameral Congress. The 513 members of the Chamber of Deputies are elected from party lists for four-year terms and may be re-elected. When elections are held, all of the 513 seats are up for election at the same time. The 81 senators are elected to serve eight-year terms and may be re-elected. Members of both houses are elected by proportional representation. | All state legislators and governors are elected for four-year terms. Mayors and city council authorities are directly elected for four-year terms. | In 1993, a popular referendum was held to choose among moving to a parliamentary system, returning to a monarchy, or keeping the presidential system. A great majority of those people who voted supported the existing presidential system. In 1994, an amendment to the Constitution reduced the term of the president from five to four years. 1994 marked the second presidential election held in Brazil since the end of military rule. The Worker's Party held the presidency for several terms, first under Lula da Silva and then under Dilma Rousseff. However, in 2016, she was voted out by the senate and replaced as president by Michel Temer of the Brazilian Democratic Movement Party. |
| Chile | The president is elected for a four-year term without the possibility of immediate re-election. If no candidate receives a majority of the votes, a second round of voting is held. | Bicameral Congress. There are 120 members of the Chamber of Deputies. They are elected from party lists for four-year terms and may be re-elected. There are 38 members of the Senate. The senators are elected for eight-year terms and may be re-elected. Every four years half of the senate seats are renewed. | Chile is divided into regions with one *intendente* (governor) per region. Intendentes are appointed by the president for a six-year term and may be replaced at any time during their tenure. Municipal authorities are directly elected for four-year terms and appoint the mayors. | In October 1988, a plebiscite defeat ended Pinochet's military dictatorship. In July 1989, a referendum approved sixty-four reforms to the Constitution. The measures increased the number of directly elected senators from 26 to 38, reduced the president's term from eight to six years, and prohibited re-election of the president. In 2005, several other constitutional changes went into force, including the elimination of appointed senatorial positions and senators for life, granting the president the authority to remove commanders-in-chief of the armed forces, and reducing the president's from six to four years. In 2014, Michelle Bachelet of the Socialist Party of Chile was re-elect president after four years of Sebastián Piñera's presidency and his National Renewal party. |

*(Continued)*

**TABLE 20.** Overview of Latin American Electoral Systems   *(Continued)*

| Country | Presidential System | Legislative System | Governors and Municipalities | General Electoral Information |
|---|---|---|---|---|
| **Colombia** | The president is elected for a four-year term with the possibility of re-election. If none of the candidates receives a majority of votes in the first round of voting, a second round of voting is held. | Bicameral Congress. The 166 members of the House of Representatives and the 102 members of the Senate are elected for four-year terms and may not be re-elected to consecutive terms. | Governors are elected for four year-terms. Since 1988, mayors have been elected for two-year terms. | In July 1991, the new Constitution was approved which granted rights to minorities and introduced many political reforms aimed at decentralizing authority. In May 1994, vice presidential elections were held for the first time. Indigenous peoples have been allotted two seats in the Senate. In 2005, the constitution was changed to allow for presidential re-election. Juan Manuel Santos, of the National Unity party, was re-elected in 2014. |
| **Costa Rica** | The president is elected for a four-year term with the possibility of re-election. If one candidate receives more than 40% of the vote, no second round voting is held. | Unicameral Congress. The 57 members of the National Assembly are elected for four-years and may not be elected for consecutive terms. | Governors are named by the president for four-year terms. Municipal authorities are elected for four-year terms. | Elections have been free and democratic in Costa Rica since 1949. In 2010, the elected its first woman president, Laura Chinchilla. Luis Guillermo Solís was elected in 2014. He is part of the Citizens' Action party. |
| **Dominican Republic** | The president is elected for a four-year term with the possibility of one consecutive re-election. If none of the candidates receives a majority of the votes, a second round of voting is held. | Bicameral Congress. There are 178 members of the Chamber of Deputies and 32 members of the Senate. All members of Congress are elected for four-year terms and may be re-elected. | The governors of the 31 provinces are appointed by the president. The *síndico* (mayor) of each province is elected. Both serve four-year terms. | The Dominican Republic has existed under four different constitutions since 1990. The most recent form was ratified in 2010. Changes include the re-election of the president, which was outlawed in 1994, the no-exceptions ban on abortion, and a ban on all types of same-sex unions. Danilo Medina, of the Dominican Liberation Party, replaced Leonel Fernández as president in 2012. |

| | | | |
|---|---|---|---|
| **Ecuador** | The president and vice president are elected on the same ticket by popular vote for a four-year term with the possibility of consecutive re-election. If no candidate receives a majority, a second round of voting is held. | Unicameral National Assembly; 124 seats; members are elected through a party-list proportional representation to serve four-year terms. | Governors are appointed by the president for two-year terms. Municipal authorities are elected for four-year terms. | Following his election as president of Ecuador, in 2006, Rafael Correa called for a referendum to form a constitutional assembly to write a new constitution for the country. The referendum, held on April 15, 2007, passed with over 80 percent approval. |
| **El Salvador** | The president is elected for a five-year term without the possibility of consecutive re-election. If none of the candidates receives a majority of the votes, a second round of voting is held. | Unicameral Congress. The 84 members of the National Assembly are elected for three-year terms and may be re-elected. | At the municipal level, local authorities are elected for three-year terms. Governors of departments are appointed by the president. | As a result of the 1992 Peace Accords that ended the country's civil war, elections were held in 1994 that, for the first time, included the former FMLN guerillas. Since then, periodic free and fair elections were conducted and, in 2009, the FMLN won the presidency and a plurality in the national assembly. Salvador Sánchez Cerén was elected in 2014 as the second FMLN president. |
| **Guatemala** | The president is elected for a four-year term without the possibility of re-election. If none of the candidates receives a majority of the votes, a second round of voting is held. | Unicameral Congress. The 158 members of Congress are elected by proportional representation. The candidates are elected by a national and a departmental list procedure. Of the 158 candidates in the last election, 31 were elected from the national lists and 127 were elected from the departmental lists. | Governors are appointed by the president. The duration of their terms is also decided by the president. Mayors are directly elected for terms of four years. | In 1994, the president held congressional elections and presented a referendum of constitutional changes to the Guatemalan people. The level of voter participation in the referendum was extremely low, but the constitutional reforms were approved. These reforms reduced the president's term from five to four years and established the current list system in Congress by population. Jimmy Morales, a comedian by trade, of the National Convergence Front was elected in 2015 in a landslide victory. |

(Continued)

**TABLE 20.** Overview of Latin American Electoral Systems   *(Continued)*

| Country | Presidential System | Legislative System | Governors and Municipalities | General Electoral Information |
|---|---|---|---|---|
| **Honduras** | The president is elected for a four-year term during one round of voting and may not be re-elected. | Unicameral Congress. The 128 members are elected for four-year terms and may be re-elected. Members of Congress are elected on a proportional basis, according to votes cast for the presidential candidate of their party. | Governors are appointed for four-year terms. Municipal authorities are elected for four-year terms. | In June, 2009, President Manuel Zelaya was removed from power in a military coup and sent into exile. Despite widespread regional pressure, Zelaya was not returned to power. At the end of 2009, national elections were held as scheduled and conservative candidate Pepe Lobo was elected and assumed office in January, 2010. In 2013, Juan Orlando Hernández was elected as president. |
| **Mexico** | The president is elected for a six-year term and may not be re-elected. There is only one round of voting. | Bicameral Congress. The 500 members of the Chamber of Deputies are directly elected for three years; 300 are elected from single-member constituencies and 200 chosen under a system of proportional representation. The majority party will hold no more than 300 seats. | Governors are elected for six-year terms, according to the organization and calendar of each state. The Constitution allows for the replacement of governors by re-election during the first two years of their terms and by presidential appointment after that time. Municipal authorities are elected for three-year terms. | Until 2000, the official party, the PRI, won every presidential election since 1929. Measures have been taken in Mexico to open up the electoral process to other political parties. In recent years, through the reforms to the Mexican Congress in late 1993, as well as the creation of the autonomous Federal Electoral Institute (IFE) to oversee federal elections, opposition parties have steadily expanded their representation in the political system. Enrique Peña Nieto was elected in 2012, returning the presidency to the Institutional Revolutionary Party (PRI). |
| **Nicaragua** | The president is elected for a five-year term, and may run for re-election. If none of the candidates receives 45% or more of the vote, a second round of voting will be held. | Unicameral Congress. The 92 members of the National Assembly are elected for five-year terms by proportional representation and may be re-elected. | The Office of Governor does not exist in Nicaragua except in the autonomous Atlantic and South Atlantic regions. Municipal authorities will be elected for five-year terms. | In March 1994, Congress reduced the future terms of the president, members of Congress, and mayors from six years to five years. Daniel Ortega, of the Sandinistas, returned as president in 2006. |

| | | | |
|---|---|---|---|
| **Panama** | The president is elected for a five-year term and may not be re-elected. There is only one round of voting; the candidate who receives a plurality of the votes becomes president. | Unicameral Congress. The 78 members of the National Assembly are elected for five-year terms. | The Office of Governor does not exist in Nicaragua except in the autonomous Atlantic and South Atlantic regions. Municipal authorities will be elected for five-year terms. Governors of the nine provinces are named by the president and may be removed at any time. Municipal authorities are also appointed by the president and serve five-year terms. | In 2009, Ricardo Martinelli's coalition of parties triumphed easily with 59.9 percent of the vote, defeating Balbina Herrera, the candidate of the Revolutionary Democratic Party (PRD), which had held the presidency in the previous term under the leadership of Martín Torrijos. In 2014, Juan Carlos Varela of the Panameñista Party was elected president. |
| **Paraguay** | The president is elected for a five-year term and may not be re-elected. There is only one round of voting. | Bicameral Congress. The 80 deputies and 45 senators are elected for five-year terms and may be re-elected. | Governors are elected for five-year terms. Municipal authorities are elected for five-year terms. | In February 1989, the overthrow of General Alfredo Stroessner initiated a transition to democracy in Paraguay. The year 2009 saw the election of center-left candidate Fernando Lugo, ending the long-term rule of the Colorado Party. However, Lugo was forced from office by the Congress in 2012 before the end of his term. The 2013 election saw the return of the Colorados to power, with President Horacio Cartes. |
| **Peru** | The president is elected for a five-year term and may be re-elected for a consecutive five-year term. If no candidate receives a majority in the first round of voting, a second round is held. | Unicameral Congress. The 120 members of Congress are elected for five-year terms and may be re-elected. | Peru is organized into 25 autonomous regions, and their presidents are elected for a five-year term. Municipal authorities are elected for a three-year term. | In April 1992, President Fujimori dissolved Congress and called for new congressional elections. The new 80-member Congress served for two years and drafted a new Constitution which was approved by a nationwide referendum in October 1993 by 52% of the people who voted. The new Constitution dissolved regional government and created a larger 120-member unicameral Congress. The new Constitution also permits the president to run for re-election. Pedro Pablo Kuczynski, candidate of Peruvians for Change party, won the election in 2016. |

*(Continued)*

257

**TABLE 20.** Overview of Latin American Electoral Systems   *(Continued)*

| Country | Presidential System | Legislative System | Governors and Municipalities | General Electoral Information |
|---|---|---|---|---|
| **Uruguay** | The president is elected by a party list procedure for a five-year term without the possibility of consecutive re-election. The president may run for office again after one term has passed. If no candidate receives a majority in the first round of voting, a second round is held. | Bicameral Congress. The 99 deputies and 30 senators are elected by a system of proportional representation for five-year terms and may be re-elected. | Governors and municipalities are elected for five-year terms. | Since the end of military rule in 1985, seven presidents have been elected. The election of socialist Tabare Vásquez in 2004 marked the end of the long domination of the country's politics by the National Party (Whites) and the Colorado Party (Reds). Broad Front dominance of Uruguay politics continued in 2009 with the election of Jose Mujica. Tabare Vásquez was re-elected in 2015. |
| **Venezuela** | The president is elected for a six-year term by the people. The executive vice president is appointed by the president. There is no second round of election for President. Re-election is permitted. | Unicameral Chamber of Deputies. The 167 seats are elected from the federal territories and various indigenous communities to five-year terms. They may be re-elected to two additional terms. | Governors and municipal authorities are elected for a three-year term. | Venezuela has a long-standing history of democratic rule which bean in 1958; however in 1992 there were two coup attempts and in 1993 President Carlos Andrés Pérez was impeached. After Hugo Chávez was elected president in December of 1998, a Constitution Assembly was convened to draft a new constitution which established a new political framework for the country. Hugo Chávez died of cancer in 2013 and his chosen successor, Nicholás Maduro, won a narrow special election victory. |

*Sources:* Georgetown University and Organization of American States Political Database of the Americas, http://pdba.georgetown.edu/Elecdata/systems.html; Wilfred Derksen, "Elections Around the World," http://www.agora.stm.it/elections/election.htm; International Institute for Democracy and Electoral Assistance, http://www.idea.int/db/countryview.cfm?id=12; Pulsamérica: The Impartial Latin American News Magazine, http://www.pulsamerica.co.uk/2015/11/tonight-argentine-presidential-election-debate-2nd-round/; BBC News, bbc.com/news/world-latin-america

# TEN

# STRUGGLING FOR CHANGE

## Revolution, Social, and Political Movements in Latin America

Latin America has struggled with the need for fundamental change and socioeconomic restructuring from the time that Túpac Amaru and Túpac Katari led uprisings in 1780 and 1781. Most acknowledge the severe inequality that exists throughout the region and very much believe it needs to be changed. The means of doing so are, however, hotly contested. The term *revolution* is employed to evoke the fundamental restructuring that is so much needed in Latin America. Revolutions are, then, much touted and the term is often used to describe any power realignment in Latin America. Nonetheless, it could be argued that thoroughgoing revolutions are much talked about but little done in the region. Even the struggle for independence was more of a change in political elites than a comprehensive restructuring of the social–economic–political structures that the term "revolution" implies. Yet, the vision of a total transformation of oppressive societal structures that revolution involves has continued to inspire political leaders in Latin America. Indeed, many have argued that only through such a revolution can long-standing problems such as massive poverty, inequality, and malnutrition be remedied. Thus, each new revolutionary attempt at thoroughgoing change has been met with utopian enthusiasm by supportive sociopolitical groupings: in Mexico from 1910 to 1917, in Guatemala from 1944 to 1954, in Bolivia from 1952 to 1964, in Cuba from 1959 on, in Nicaragua from 1979 to 1990, in El Salvador during the revolutionary struggle from 1980 to the peace accords in 1992 (and to a lesser extent after the FMLN gained the presidency in 2008), and in Venezuela from 1999 on. But contradictions emerged in these processes as well. The resort to authoritarian methods and the many internal and external difficulties in achieving such revolutionary visions often dampened much of the initial enthusiasm and occasioned many defections from the revolutionary process.

To many analysts, the defeat of the Sandinistas in the 1990 Nicaraguan elections, coming in the context of the collapse of the Communist Party–led governments in Eastern Europe, marked the end of an era of radical revolution in Latin America that had begun with the triumph of the Cuban Revolution in 1959. Many of the same observers noted the flagging fortunes of the revolutionary movements in Guatemala and El Salvador in the early 1990s and predicted the early demise of Fidel Castro's government in Cuba. Others were far less certain that the era of revolution in Latin America had ended. In the 1990s armed insurgencies intensified in Peru, reappeared in Mexico, and continued in Colombia. Further, in El Salvador and Nicaragua, the revolutionary movements were not destroyed. The Sandinista National Liberation Front (FSLN) of Nicaragua and the Farabundo Martí National Liberation Front (FMLN) of El Salvador remained important political movements that could contest power in presidential elections and command an important bloc of votes in their national legislatures and local governments. Yet, such a position is far short of the revolutionary goals that each of them sought. By 2005, the dominant national economic and political elites, aided by a variety of direct and indirect actions by the United States, had been able to blunt the drive for revolutionary takeover outside of Colombia, even though the revolution was still in power in Cuba. Indeed, the struggle for revolutionary change has always been difficult in Latin America, given the forces that have been arrayed against it. However, by the beginning of 2008, new political and social movements and the leaders they supported were once again invoking the need for fundamental change and challenging the neoliberal agenda. This was particularly true with Hugo Chávez in Venezuela and Evo Morales in Bolivia, where socialist revolutions were once again being discussed. Further, the Sandinistas were able to recapture the presidency in Nicaragua in 2006, 20011, and 2016 and the FMLN took that office in El Salvador in 2009 and 2014.

In recent years, many seeking change and social–economic restructuring have begun to harness their vision and creatively mobilize in less violent but highly effective ways. For instance, many had despaired of popular rule in Bolivia after the demise of the Bolivian Revolution led by the Movimiento Nacionalista Revolucionario (MNR) in 1952 and ended by a military coup in 1964. Recent years had even seen the country led by a U.S.-educated member of the elite who seemed only too happy to bow to U.S. policy in such areas as the eradication of coca leaves. Thus, it was all the more remarkable that Bolivian President Gonzalo Sánchez de Lozada was forced out of office by massive displays of popular power by social movements, community organizations, unions, and students in October 2003. A staunch advocate of globalization and neoliberal policies prescribed by international financial institutions like the International Monetary Fund (IMF) and World Bank, he was also symbolic of the upper-class, Western-oriented political elite that have governed Latin America in an authoritarian manner since the Spanish conquest in the early 1500s. His tormentors were equally symbolic of those the political class had long ruled and repressed. They were small farmers, indigenous peoples, workers, miners, students, and intellectuals who dared to challenge the status quo. In 2005, successor president Carlos Mesa was also forced from office by the same forces. Later that year Evo Morales was elected to the presidency with their support. This was not, however, the first time people had risen in the Andean highlands. There had, for instance, been an uprising in 1780 under the leadership of Incan descendant Túpac Amaru. The 1960s had seen the formation of Marxist guerrilla groups in both Bolivia and Peru. Like most other attempts at radical change from Túpac Amaru on, such attempts had been repressed, first by the European forces and then by the national military or the dominant political elite. This occurred in the central part of Mexico in the early 1800s when the mostly Indian, mostly peasant masses answered the famous *grito de Dolores*—the cry for freedom and independence that rang out in 1810. There, a popular movement under the leadership of Miguel de Hidalgo began the struggle for popular control and Mexican independence. The movement was brutally repressed by the Spanish authorities, and Hidalgo and his successor, José María Morelos, faced the same fate as Túpac Amaru: they were executed by the Spanish colonial authorities. The mass uprising was not successful. Rather, Mexican independence, like that in Bolivia and all of Latin America save Haiti, was won by *criollo* political elites who ruled in the name of the majorities but rarely for them.

Dissatisfaction with elite rule, exclusionary political projects, or policies that cause or perpetuate the economic or ethnic marginalization of the masses has continued in Latin America. There have been many other uprisings, like that led by Farabundo Martí in El Salvador in 1932. Indeed, it was the generalized dissatisfaction with Porfirio Díaz's political ruling class in *fin de siglo* Mexico that induced *los de abajo* (those on the bottom) to enroll in the various armies—and thus the revolutionary project—of the Mexican Revolution. Such dissatisfaction and its focus on the failure of the political elite have led to other less successful political rebellions as well. The *Bogotazo* and the ensuing violence in Colombia from 1948 to 1956, the Bolivian revolution in the early 1950s, the popular struggle in Guatemala from the 1960s to the 1990s, the revolutionary struggle of in Cuba in the 1950s, the Nicaraguan Revolution in the 1970s and the decade-long civil war in the 1980s in El Salvador are cases in point. Before the most current forms of radical political mobilization are examined, a more careful discussion of revolutions and revolutionary mobilizations must be undertaken.

It is necessary to review the development of previous movements, tracing the demise of the belief in violent revolution in Latin America to the ascendance of political democracy throughout the region to the temporary political dominance of the ideology of free enterprise embodied in the programs of structural adjustment and neoliberalism and to the resurgence of more radical movements after 2000. As the new century began, prescriptions for revolutionary change needed to undergo some reexamination. The heady days that revolutionaries experienced in the late 1970s were clearly not in evidence, but radical movements and new leadership were considering some of the same policies that these earlier movements had advocated.

## Cuba

The modern wave of revolutions in Latin America began in the Caribbean island of Cuba. That revolution, under the leadership of Fidel Castro and the 26th of July Movement, was a watershed event in Latin American revolutionary history. Following the cancellation of the scheduled 1952 national elections by Fulgencio Batista, Castro and several dozen followers organized an attack on an army barracks in Santiago, hoping to incite a nationwide uprising against the dictatorship. That attack failed, but three years later it led to the formation of the movement, named for the date of the 1953 failed attack. Drawing in part on the earlier experiences of Augusto César Sandino in Nicaragua in the late 1920s, the Cuban revolutionary movement based itself in the isolated Sierra Maestra Mountains of eastern Cuba and sought to build a revolutionary army from the ranks of the local peasants. Given the history of rebellion of that region, the tactics proved successful as the rebel army flourished and eventually engaged in several successful battles against the conscript army of the dictator Batista. Aided by other revolutionary actions in Cuba's cities and the flagging support for Batista both domestically and internationally, the 26th of July Movement succeeded in taking power on January 1, 1959. In the ensuing months, the revolutionary government, with the support of mass mobilizations of workers and peasants, transformed Cuban society. The economy was placed largely in the hands of the state, and by 1961 Fidel Castro had committed Cuba to the socialist path of development, the first country in the Western Hemisphere to do so. Given the popularity of Fidel Castro and the other Cuban rebels, it is not surprising that there was soon a proliferation of self-declared Marxist guerrilla groups through much of Latin America. This proliferation of the Fidelista theory of revolution through armed struggle (*foquismo*) marked what Regis Debray termed the "revolution in the revolution" (a revolution in the Marxist theory of revolution in Latin America).

Although the subsequent wave of guerrilla activity in the region and the virtual canonization of Ché Guevara, the Argentine physician turned dedicated and

Ernesto "Ché" Guevara, 1928–1967. (*Salas Archive Photos/Alamy Images*)

uncompromising socialist revolutionary (see his *Socialism and Man*) helped free Latin American revolutionary thought from the dogmatic, static orientation that had come to characterize it during Joseph Stalin's rule in the Soviet Union, the unyielding emphasis on armed struggle effectively foreclosed a broader examination of the doctrine and the search for more effective ways to mobilize the masses. This new vision of revolution effectively challenged the now-bureaucratized orthodox communist parties, but it did not produce any successful guerrilla movements in the 1960s or well into the 1970s. It did, however, spawn a series of urban and rural guerrilla movements across Latin America and generated a great deal of literature by and about these new Marxist revolutionaries. The introduction of Maoism and Chinese-oriented communist parties in countries such as Colombia and Brazil further stimulated the development of new forms of radical Marxism. However, the subsequent growth in Marxist parties and movements also provided an excellent rationale for the creation and implementation of the U.S.-inspired national security doctrine, counterinsurgency training, and its concomitant strong anticommunism. The U.S.-inspired counterinsurgency defeated most of the original guerrilla movements by the early 1970s. Most significantly, Che Guevara was killed in 1967 in Bolivia by U.S.-trained soldiers and CIA operatives while fighting with a Bolivian revolutionary group and endeavoring to spark a continental-wide revolution. Guerrilla groups did, however, manage to struggle on in Guatemala, Colombia, and Nicaragua, where the FSLN guerrillas did triumph in July of 1979. But by the new century only the FARC in Colombia struggled on.

## OTHER REVOLUTIONARY ENDEAVORS

By 1970, several innovative approaches to Marxist thought were emerging. In Peru, Hugo Blanco was breathing new life into the Trotskyist movement through his work with the highland peasants. In Chile, socialists and communists were contemplating the realization of a peaceful revolution under the leadership of constitutionally elected socialist president Salvador Allende. The far-left Movement of the Revolutionary Left (MIR) did, however, argue that rightist forces would never allow such a transition. In Argentina, leftist theorists began to apply and adapt the theory to their own specific reality. A radical brand of Marxist-inspired Peronism (or Peronist-inspired Marxism) ensued and eventually led to a Marxist faction within Peronism (Juventud Peronista) and the formation of the radical Peronist Montonero guerrilla group. The Montoneros and the Revolutionary Army of the People (ERP) eventually confronted Argentina's military government in an intense struggle in the 1970s. In Uruguay, the Robin Hood–like Tupamaros hoped to foment a popular revolution. Although gains were made toward less dogmatic interpretations and in political education, the lingering emphasis on armed struggle over political education or organization eventually led to intense conflict and violent repression, which the left was ultimately unable to resist.

Revolutionary and socialist movements were profoundly affected by the results of Allende's Popular Unity socialist experiment in Chile. Allende sought to make radical changes in Chilean society (land reform, wealth redistribution, and increased political participation) within the parliamentary process. Some progress was made during the three years he was in power (1970–1973), but the reformist socialist experiment was largely thwarted by Allende's lack of majority control of the legislature. The entrenched power and opposition by the country's elites together with international isolation engineered by a hostile U.S. government disrupted the country's economy and set the stage for a military coup. Allende's rule came to a bloody end on September 11, 1973 when the Chilean military stormed the presidential palace and forced Allende into suicide and then killed thousands of his supporters. A military government under General Augusto Pinochet was established and held power for seventeen years.

The primary impact of the Chilean events was to convince most of the Latin American left that reform-oriented efforts at achieving socialism were fruitless. These views were also bolstered by the 1973 military coup in Uruguay and the subsequent coup in Argentina in 1976. The rightist forces and the military had seized power in a 1964 coup in Brazil. By 1976 military rule had become the norm throughout the region, and the combination of dictatorial rule and unsolved social and economic problems spawned a series of revolutionary upsurges, which were strongest in Nicaragua, El Salvador, Colombia, and Peru. Each had its own characteristics and should be viewed individually, although there were many similarities.

## Nicaragua

Nicaragua's leading revolutionary movement, the FSLN, was formed in 1961 and was directly inspired by the success of the Cuban Revolution. Its early leaders, Carlos Fonseca and Tomás Borge, abandoned the reformist-oriented Nicaraguan Socialist Party (PSN) to form the FSLN. With direct Cuban assistance, the FSLN sought to replicate the Cuban experience and that of their namesake, Augusto Sandino, by establishing a guerrilla army in the mountains of northern Nicaragua that could eventually challenge the power of the dictator Anastasio Somoza. Another element crucial to the revolutionary philosophy of the FSLN was its emphasis on will and the belief that to some degree revolution could be improvised. They turned to the writings of Sandino, José Carlos Mariátegui, and the Italian Antonio Gramsci to craft a philosophy based on revolutionary action, the importance of the subjective factor in making revolution, and the role of ideology in motivating the masses.

In its early stages, the FSLN consisted of just twelve people, including Colonel Santos López, a veteran of Sandino's earlier struggle. Fonseca fought successfully for the inclusion of Sandino's name in the organizational label, but the lack of unanimity on this shows that a variety of revolutionary influences were at work in the early 1960s. Led by Fonseca, the small group studied Sandino's writings and tactics as they prepared for their first guerrilla campaigns in 1963. Those campaigns, like many other similar ones in Latin America at the time, were a failure. The new Sandinistas had failed to do what their namesake had done so well—mobilize the local populace on the side of the guerrillas through well-planned political and organizational activities coordinated with and part of the armed struggle. Over the ensuing years, the FSLN managed to survive by realizing its mistakes and broadening its political work to include neighborhood organizing in the poorest barrios of the capital, Managua. However, the National Guard of the Somoza dictatorship was a powerful force, and it exacted many defeats on the Sandinistas during the

1960s. The Sandinistas survived and slowly built their organization, especially by reaching out to progressive members of the Catholic Church who had been inspired by liberation theology. The FSLN was the first revolutionary organization in Latin America to welcome Christians within its ranks, a position that would bear considerable fruit in the late 1970s.

Between 1967 and 1974 the FSLN carried on what it termed "accumulation of forces" in silence, largely recruiting members in ones and twos and engaging in few armed actions. The silence was broken in a spectacular way with the December 1974 seizure of the home of a wealthy Somoza supporter. An FSLN commando unit held more than a dozen foreign diplomats and top Nicaraguan government officials for several days, finally forcing Somoza to release key Sandinista political prisoners, pay a large sum of money, and broadcast and publish FSLN communiqués. This dramatic act reinserted the FSLN into the political scene at an important time. Popular sentiment against the dictatorship had been growing since it had greedily profited from the devastating 1972 earthquake that had further impoverished more Nicaraguans. However, even as the FSLN reemerged, its own divisions had become clear. By 1975 the organization had split into three tendencies on the basis of tactical differences. The Prolonged People's War group was basically Maoist in orientation. Their strategy and concrete work emphasized rural guerrilla warfare. Relatively isolated in the countryside, they were probably the slowest to realize that a revolutionary situation was developing in the country. The Proletarian Tendency based itself in large measure on dependency theory and the traditional Marxist emphasis on the industrial working class. This tendency saw the Nicaraguan Revolution as unfolding along more traditional lines as a confrontation between the bourgeoisie and the proletariat. Nicaragua's urban working class, small as it was, was seen as the main force of the coming revolution. Political work in the cities was emphasized, and this group also built a base among students. The Insurrectionist, or Tercerista, tendency was the last to emerge. In reality, it did not represent an entirely new approach; rather, it served primarily as a mediator between the two existing tendencies. The Terceristas (or "third force") did not draw a sharp distinction between a rural and an urban emphasis, seeing the need for action in both arenas. Its main and most controversial contribution was its alliance strategy. While not the first group in the FSLN to propose such an orientation, they were the first in the era of Somoza's decline to place it at the center of political work. There was also ample historical precedent for it in the strategies of both Sandino and the 26th of July Movement in Cuba. Both earlier movements incorporated heterogeneous elements while maintaining a revolutionary position. The Insurrectionists believed strongly that it was necessary to mobilize a broad-based coalition to overthrow the dictatorship while maintaining the organizational integrity of the FSLN.

The separation into tendencies did not mean the disintegration of the FSLN. Each current pursued its political work in its own sector, and as the crisis of the dictatorship deepened, all achieved successes. Efforts by the leaders to reestablish unity did not cease, although they were hampered by the imprisonment of key figures such as Borge and the death of Fonseca in combat in November 1976. The three tendencies finally began to converge in the upsurge of mass antidictatorship activity in late 1977 and early 1978 in the wake of the death of popular opposition newspaper

editor Pedro Joaquín Chamorro. In 1978, the three tendencies collaborated to establish the National Patriotic Front (FPN), which created an anti-Somoza front encompassing trade unions, the Moscow-oriented Nicaraguan Socialist Party, student
groups, and some small middle-class parties like the Popular Social Christians—all
under FSLN hegemony.

In September 1978, the FSLN, led by the Terceristas, carried out an insurrection which, while not successful, laid the groundwork for the dictatorship's defeat.
Drawing on the lessons learned from the September 1978 action and with the organization formally reunited in March 1979, the FSLN launched its final offensive in
the late spring of 1979. Somoza's National Guard fought hard to defend the dictator,
who desperately ordered the bombing of Sandinista strongholds in the cities; but in
July 1979, Somoza fled the country, and the FSLN assumed power at the head of a
provisional revolutionary government. The success of the Sandinistas in defeating
the dictatorship and embarking on the fundamental restructuring of Nicaraguan society was a watershed event for Latin America, a second potential socialist revolution. The Nicaraguan Revolution did not fulfill its promises, but that did not change
the significance of the events that unfolded at the end of the 1970s in one of the
region's poorest countries. The FSLN was voted out of office in 1990, but the FSLN
leader Daniel Ortega was re-elected as president in 2006, 2011, and 2016. The Sandinistas once again challenged U.S. influence and opened the possibility for change,
but much of the initial revolutionary zeal had been lost by the second decade of the
twenty-first century.

# El Salvador

Nicaragua was not the only Central American nation convulsed by revolution in
the 1970s and 1980s. Neighboring El Salvador witnessed a bloody confrontation
between the military and revolutionaries that cost 75,000 lives between 1975 and
1992 and sent more than 500,000 Salvadorans into exile in the United States. The
revolutionary period ended with a United Nations–brokered peace agreement that
rewarded the revolutionary coalition, the FMLN, with a prominent role in Salvadoran politics as the country's primary political opposition group. The Salvadoran
military, while still a major political force, stepped down from the controlling position that it had held for more than half a century.

It is not surprising that revolutionary forces came to the fore in El Salvador, for
no Latin American country better fit the profile for revolutionary change. The events
of the 1970s and 1980s followed directly from dramatic confrontations of the early
1930s and the fifty years of direct military rule that followed. By 1932 El Salvador
was the most class-polarized society in the region. In the latter part of the nineteenth
century, El Salvador had become one of the world's largest coffee producers, meeting the ever-growing European demand with the development of ever-larger coffee
plantations dominated by a few wealthy families. The coffee boom enriched a series
of oligarchic families, who came to dominate Salvadoran society, while it further
reduced the peasant population to seasonal labor and marginal lands. From 1907
to 1931, political power rested in the hands of a single family, the Meléndez clan.
The peasantry who were driven off their communal lands during the latter half of

the nineteenth century did not accept their fate passively and engaged in several uprisings, both armed and unarmed, from 1870 onward. The conflict between the ruling oligarchy, made up of coffee farmers, foreign investors, military officers, and Church leaders, and the landless peasants came to a head in 1930–1932. The Great Depression had further impoverished both the remaining small farmers and the plantation laborers as the price of coffee fell precipitously. The possibility of revolution developed very quickly. In 1930, a May Day demonstration in San Salvador against deteriorating economic conditions drew 80,000. Liberal reformer Arturo Araujo won the presidential election in 1931 with the support of students, workers, and peasants. The new government attempted to broaden the political spectrum by announcing that it would permit the newly formed Communist Party, under the leadership of Farabundo Martí, to participate in the 1931 municipal elections. However, the military, under the leadership of Maximiliano Hernández Martínez, seized power in December 1931; the following month, Martí led a premature, mostly peasant rebellion that succeeded in murdering a few landlords and seizing control of some small towns, primarily in the northwestern part of the country.

The response of General Hernández to the uprising was swift and brutal. Known ever since as *La Matanza* (The Massacre), the joint actions of the military and oligarchy killed between 30,000 and 60,000 people, a huge toll in a nation of only 1.4 million. The repression was both selective and widespread. Using voter rolls, the military hunted down and killed virtually everyone affiliated with the Communist Party, including Martí. At the time, the military's actions took on the character of a race war as indigenous people were also singled out for attack.

La Matanza did not end resistance to the rule of the oligarchy, but it reduced it significantly for the next forty years. A series of military leaders ruled the country into the 1960s without even the facade of democracy. In that decade, a reformist challenge to the military developed under the leadership of the Christian Democratic Party and José Napoleon Duarte. Duarte, educated in the United States and the spirit of Kennedy's Alliance for Progress, developed a strong following among intellectuals, students, and a growing middle sector. Duarte's reformist challenge ended with a probable victory in the 1972 presidential elections, but the military voided the results and continued in power. Duarte and other Christian Democratic leaders went into exile, but other, more radical leaders saw the military's actions as proof that the reformist path was not viable in El Salvador. This view was reinforced by the fact that the U.S. government did not intervene, even to promote its seeming prototype for a centrist reformer like Duarte against the Salvadoran generals. As guerrilla groups began to form in the rural areas of the country, other factors also promoted revolutionary prospects. By 1975, about 40 percent of the peasants had no land at all, compared to only 12 percent in 1960. The other surprising force for revolutionary change that developed in the latter half of the 1970s was the Roman Catholic Church. The combination of the reform-oriented ideas of the 1968 Medellín Conference of Latin American Bishops and the repression of the Salvadoran military against the Church itself propelled the clergy and its followers into a central role in the political opposition to the military. The leader of the Salvadoran Church, Archbishop Oscar Romero, was a conservative at the time of his leadership appointment, but the death of a close friend at the hands of the military combined with the growing polarization in the country led him to the unusual position of supporting the right of armed rebellion. In response, the military assassinated Archbishop Romero in 1980 in the midst of growing civil and revolutionary resistance to the military regime.

In 1980, most of the revolutionary guerrilla groups that had begun armed activities in the 1970s came together to form the FMLN. The two primary organizations in the FMLN were the ERP and the Armed Forces of Liberation (FAL). The ERP was founded in 1971 by Marxist and Christian forces that were motivated by the *foco* theory of revolution inspired by Ché Guevara. The FAL was the armed wing of the outlawed Communist Party that developed into a significant force only in the late 1970s. The primary significance of the FAL was that it was one of the few cases where a reformist-oriented Communist Party opted to participate in an armed struggle. Also important in the revolutionary equation was the Democratic Revolutionary Front (FDR), an umbrella alliance also founded in 1980 that encompassed all major popular organizations, labor groups, and community groups. From the beginning, it served as the political arm of the FMLN and after 1982 was recognized internationally as a legitimate political force. The heart of the FDR was the People's Revolutionary Bloc (BPR), the largest of the popular organizations. It was formed in 1975 by diverse organizations of shantytown dwellers, workers, students, teachers, and practitioners of liberation theology. By the late 1970s, despite the severe repression of the military, the organizations of the BPR had succeeded in many places in the country in establishing alternative governing bodies.

Following the decisive triumph of the Sandinista revolutionaries in the summer of 1979, the possibility of revolution in El Salvador seemed very real. Popular mobilizations spread throughout the country. Factories were occupied in San Salvador, and 1980 was declared to be the "year of the liberation." Fearing a repetition of the Nicaraguan Revolution, a section of the Salvadoran elites and the government of the United States carried off a military coup designed to forestall the revolutionary process by appearing to instigate significant reform. On October 15, 1979, a new military junta took power, promising reform. The new government even encompassed figures from the left, including Social Democrat Guillermo Ungo and a minister of labor from the small Communist Party. The new junta promised to reform the security forces, institute land reform, and recognize trade unions. However, the political practice of the new government was far different from its rhetoric. Within a week of taking power, the government security forces broke up strikes, occupied rebellious towns, and killed more than 100 people. In January 1980, Ungo and the entire civilian cabinet quit their posts, acknowledging that the military was already making all key political and security decisions. Three weeks later, the military opened fire on a massive demonstration of 150,000. In March, Romero was assassinated, and the military attacked his funeral procession of 80,000. Thirty people were killed. By March 1980 it was clear to most political activists in El Salvador that open, legal political activity in opposition to the military was impossible. Many political moderates, including a sizeable part of the Christian Democrats, joined with the revolutionary left. This movement soon coalesced into the FDR and FMLN. Christian Democrat Duarte assumed leadership of the junta, claiming to be in the political center between left- and right-wing forces. In reality, Duarte was a figurehead who ruled on behalf of the traditional elites.

In January 1981, on the eve of President Ronald Reagan's inauguration, the FMLN launched an insurrection that was intended to take power. However, the Salvadoran military, with significant resupply by the United States, defeated the offensive and set the stage for a protracted armed conflict. The FMLN had hoped to gain victory before the Reagan administration took office. It gambled that the Carter administration would not resume aid to the Salvadoran government, which had been suspended one month earlier in the wake of the killing of four North American churchwomen by Salvadoran security forces. However, the FMLN's judgment proved wrong. Citing proof of Nicaraguan Sandinista support for FMLN rebels on January 17, 1981, President Carter authorized the shipment of $5 million of military equipment and twenty additional U.S. military personnel. Three months later, the U.S. ambassador in El Salvador at the time of the shipments, Robert White, revealed that there was no real evidence of Nicaraguan involvement, but the announcement of the shipment had served its purpose. The Salvadoran military had been reassured that despite obvious human rights violations even against U.S. citizens, the government of the United States was fully committed to preventing a victory by the Salvadoran revolutionaries. There was not going to be another Nicaragua in Central America.

The civil war continued for ten more years. The FMLN showed considerable resilience in the face of a concerted effort by the Salvadoran army and its U.S. backers to eliminate the guerrilla challenge. At the high point of assistance in the late 1980s, El Salvador was receiving close to $1 billion per year in U.S. aid, ranking behind only Israel and Egypt. Total U.S. aid during this period exceeded $5 billion. The FMLN was a substantial force, with several thousand soldiers in arms. It controlled more than one-third of Salvadoran territory and carried out regular attacks in all but two of the country's fourteen provinces. However, throughout the 1980s, the Salvadoran revolutionaries faced the dilemma that even if they could mount an insurrection that challenged the hold of the Salvadoran military, they faced the prospect of a massive U.S. intervention that would deny them the victory that they sought. As a result, from about 1982 onward, the FMLN argued that the only solution to the civil war would be a negotiated settlement. Sporadic negotiations did occur throughout the 1980s, but the political situation both inside and outside of El Salvador prevented a successful conclusion. To ensure continued support from a reluctant U.S. Congress, the Reagan administration pressed the Salvadorans to hold elections, even though it was clear that these could not be fully democratic in the context of the civil war. There was little freedom of the press, and no candidates of the left could participate without risking assassination by right-wing death squads. With significant U.S. backing, Christian Democrat Duarte won the 1982 presidential election but was largely a figurehead. Throughout the 1980s, real political power lay with the Supreme Army Council and Roberto D'Aubuisson's ultra-right National Republican Alliance (ARENA), which controlled the Salvadoran legislature. Duarte was allowed by the military to remain in power as long as he permitted them free reign against the FMLN. Obviously, such an arrangement did not allow for any real dialogue or hope for a settlement between Duarte and the FMLN. In 1989, with Duarte dying of cancer and the Christian Democratic Party deeply divided, ARENA candidate Alfredo Christiani won the presidency, further entrenching the hold of the far right on Salvadoran politics. The new ARENA government vowed a rapid campaign to defeat the FMLN, but the latter responded in the fall of 1989 with a significant military offensive that reached all the way into the capital. These events served to underscore the fact that after a decade of fighting, the civil war was a stalemate with no end in sight.

However, regional and international events intervened to bring about a negotiated settlement within two years. The electoral defeat of the FSLN in Nicaragua in 1990 and the rapid changes in the Soviet Union and Eastern Europe between 1989 and 1991 weakened the position of the FMLN but also put pressure on the U.S. government and its Salvadoran allies to come to the bargaining table. Under United Nations auspices, brokered settlements moved forward in Cambodia, Angola, Mozambique, and Namibia, placing additional pressure on Central America. In 1990–1991, the FMLN made several concessions toward peace that went largely unreciprocated. In the March 1991 national legislative elections, the FMLN and its sympathizers fielded candidates. Despite significant pressure against the left and intimidation of voters, the left managed to win eight seats and ARENA was denied majority control. In November 1991, the FMLN declared a unilateral ceasefire that was to last until a peace agreement was signed. In January 1992, under mounting international pressure, the ARENA government signed an agreement with the FMLN. The agreement called for the removal of more than 100 military officers implicated in human rights violations during the civil war. The army was to be reduced by 50 percent, the National Intelligence Directorate dismantled, a new police force created to include members of the FMLN, 1980 agrarian reform completed, democratic elections held, and the FMLN disarmed in exchange for land and resettlement compensation for its troops and the right to become a political party.

This agreement was clearly far short of the thoroughgoing social revolution to which the FMLN had committed itself a decade earlier, but it did represent a partial victory for the revolutionaries and a setback for El Salvador's traditional oligarchy. Since the signing of the agreement, El Salvador has remained a contradictory nation. The traditional oligarchy has worked hard to undermine the agreement. The Christiani government was reluctant to purge high-ranking military officers and to disarm the notorious army and police units. In March 1993, a U.N.-appointed truth commission named sixty-two Salvadoran officers responsible for the worst massacres, tortures, and murders of the twelve-year war and called for the immediate dismissal of forty of them. The U.S. Army School of the Americas had trained forty-seven of them. The officers were eventually dismissed but only after pressure from a united opposition within El Salvador and a temporary suspension of aid by the Clinton administration in 1993.

Elections held under the aegis of the accords, especially the first one in 1994, were marked by significant fraud emanating from the government and periodic armed attacks against candidates and supporters of the left. The Christiani government used its control of the Supreme Electoral Tribunal to prevent opposition voters from registering. Especially in the 1994 elections, this fraud definitely denied the FMLN several seats in the National Assembly and control of the local government in several cities. Despite these obstacles, the FMLN succeeded in creating political space for the left that was unprecedented in Salvadoran history. In the March 1997 national and municipal elections, the FMLN fared quite well. It won the mayoralty of San Salvador—the most important political office after the presidency—as well as other key departmental municipalities. Of the country's 262 municipalities, the FMLN governed fifty-three, covering 45 percent of the population. On the congressional front, the FMLN won twenty-seven out of eighty-four seats, just one fewer than ARENA, which was forced into a government coalition with other conservative parties. The FMLN achieved its success in local elections based on its work in the fourteen municipalities it controlled from the 1994 elections and the role it played in the national legislature as an opponent of the government's unpopular economic policies. As a result of the 2003 elections, the FMLN emerged as the largest single party in the National Assembly, with thirty-one seats, three more than the ruling ARENA Party. In 2004, its presidential candidate, the former guerrilla leader Schafik Handal, lost his bid for the presidency to the ARENA candidate Tony Saca, but the party maintained a strong presence in the country and won the presidency in 2009. In 2008 moderate FMLN candidate Mauricio Funes won the presidential election, but did not engage in radical economic and social restructuring. The FMLN presidential candidate Salvador Sánchez Cerén, was elected by a thin margin in in 2014, even though ARENA was still a potent political force in the country and could block radical initiatives.

## Guatemala

A discussion of revolution in Guatemala must encompass a long period of time and does not involve transcendent events like the Cuban Revolution of 1959 or the Sandinista revolution of 1979. The high point of revolutionary forces in Guatemala may well have been in 1944, when an armed uprising succeeded in driving the long-time dictator General Jorge Ubico y Castañeda (1931–1944) from power. The movement against Ubico began with a student strike and escalated into a general strike that forced Ubico's resignation in June 1944. However, the resignation was a front for the continuation of Ubico's system, and it soon led to an armed rebellion of students, workers, and dissident army officers. The rebel movement won an easy victory and set up a junta government known as the October Revolution. The rebellion paved the way for elections that brought Juan José Arévalo to power in 1945. Once in power, the Arévalo government pursued a reformist strategy rather than a revolutionary one. There was unprecedented government spending on schools, hospitals, and housing, and workers were allowed to unionize and engage in collective bargaining. However, rural Guatemala, which held 90 percent of the country's population, was largely untouched by the reforms.

Arévalo was followed in office by Jacobo Arbenz, who deepened his predecessor's reform program but maintained Guatemala fully within the framework of capitalism. In fact, in 1950, Arbenz declared that his primary intent was to make Guatemala "a modern capitalist country." His primary extension of Arévalo's reforms was to carry them to the rural sector by inaugurating a modest land reform that challenged the most blatant policies of the U.S.-owned United Fruit Company. Arbenz also legalized the Communist Party, a reform-oriented organization with significant influence among unionized workers. These reforms, although modest in character, were too much for the country's oligarchy and the government of the United States. In 1954, Arbenz was removed from power in a military coup strongly backed by the United States through the actions of the CIA. The newly installed government of Castillo Armas cracked down on anyone suspected of revolutionary activity. This witch hunt succeeded in setting back the possibility of a Guatemalan revolution by many years. The military coup ushered in a 30,000-strong armed force that brutally repressed any opposition political movements over the ensuing forty years. Peaceful forms of protest were routinely outlawed, and rural villages were often attacked by army patrols seeking to capture "subversives."

The revival of an armed resistance to the Guatemalan military began with the November 1960 revolt of army officers against President Miguel Ydígoras. The revolt was crushed when the United States sent Cuban exiles being trained for the ill-fated Bay of Pigs invasion. However, several rebel leaders escaped and established low-grade guerrilla warfare against the regime. One of the guerrillas' first leaders was Marco Antonio Yon Sosa, originally trained by the United States. Yon Sosa was killed in combat, but guerrillas who survived helped form the Guerrilla Army of the Poor (EGP) in 1972. Inspired by liberation theology, they built a base among the highland Indians, the first revolutionary movement to do so. By 1980 the EGP and other smaller groups had more than 5,000 members. The growing strength of the rebel movement alarmed the Guatemalan oligarchy, and fierce repression was unleashed against the rural areas in the early 1980s. The military's strategy was to destroy the guerrillas' base of operations by terrorizing the civilian population.

During General Romeo Lucas García's rule (1978–1982), there were numerous massacres. With financial support from the U.S. government, the military evacuated Indians from the northern highland guerrilla strongholds in Quiche and Huehuetenango departments and organized them in "model villages," a strategy developed by the United States in Vietnam. The military offered the local population a stark choice: work with us and be housed and fed or die. In 1982, Lucas García was replaced in a coup by General Efraín Ríos Montt, a born-again Christian. Montt declared a state of siege and dramatically increased the level of repression. On July 6, 1982, more than 300 Indian residents of Finca San Francisco in Huehuetenango were massacred outside of their local church. Between 1981 and 1983, it is estimated that 100,000 Indians in 440 villages lost their lives at the hands of government forces. More than 1 million people were displaced from their homes. The repression resulted in the growth of the revolutionary movement. In 1982, the four main guerrilla groups, headed by EGP, united to form the Guatemalan National Revolutionary Unity (URNG). With stepped-up covert U.S. assistance, the Guatemalan military escalated its war against the guerrillas. Newer, more sophisticated weaponry, including helicopter gunships, forced the URNG into retreat by 1983, a move that the Guatemalan government falsely labeled as a defeat of the revolutionary forces. The revolutionary movement survived throughout the 1980s and was bolstered by the growth of strong social protest movements in Guatemala's cities led by labor unions and human rights organizations. In 1987, the labor organizations formed a coalition with the Group of Mutual Support (GAM, an organization of relatives of the victims of repression) and the Peasant Unity Committee (CUC) to demand improved wages, an accounting for the victims of the repression, and land distribution.

These forces of civil society, viewed by the military as allies of the guerrilla movement, also faced harsh repression. Despite the repression, the civil society organizations survived and participated in the 1992 U.N.-brokered negotiations started between the URNG and the government and military. The negotiations occurred because the guerrillas, with their numbers reduced to less than 3,000, realized that military victory was unlikely and the Guatemalan government was under pressure from the administration of George H. W. Bush to reduce emphasis on military aid programs and increase emphasis on consolidating a regional trading bloc. However, given the depths of Guatemala's repression and the reluctance of the oligarchy to accept cooperation with the revolutionaries, the peace settlement did not come easily. In 1993, President Jorge Antonio Serrano attempted to reimpose military rule and return to tactics of harsh repression. However, his coup attempt was reversed by a combination of street demonstrations and opposition from the Clinton administration. Serrano was replaced by Ramiro de León Carpio, the parliament's human rights advisor. His appointment put the stalled negotiations back on track, and a peace settlement was finally achieved on December 27, 1996, bringing an end to Central America's longest civil war. The peace agreement formally ended the civil war but did not end violent conflict in the country, nor did the settlement significantly address the long-standing social inequalities that have fueled the conflict. Most important, there was little change in the pattern of land tenure, with 65 percent of the country's arable land remaining in the hands of just 2.6 percent of the population. The peace agreements called for peaceful settlements of land claims and the return of thousands of displaced families, but the administration of President Alvaro Enrique Arzú Yrigoyen, with the support of the country's traditional oligarchy, did little to further those aspects of the accords. The former revolutionaries, the URNG, operating as part of the civil opposition, used the courts and public protest to press their reform agenda, but despite the term in office of a more progressive president (Alvaro Colom, 2008–2013) fundamental change has not been achieved. There was even a return to more conservative government by ex-military leaders, but in 2015 the elected right-wing president and his vice president were indicted in a major corruption scandal and removed from office after massive popular demonstrations, sometimes referred to as the Guatemalan Spring (see Chapter 20).

# Colombia

Another of Latin America's most important contemporary revolutionary movements is the Revolutionary Armed Forces of Colombia (FARC). In 2010, the FARC had a presence in more than 60 percent of Colombia's municipalities. Although under sharp attack from well-armed paramilitaries and the Colombian government, the FARC sustained itself for more than three decades and contributed significantly to that country's continuing political unrest. The origins of the FARC lie in the peasant struggles of more than a half-century ago. Facing harsh living and working conditions, the workers on coffee plantations began to organize around labor demands and broader political concerns. The movement was most active in central Colombia but faced brutal repression by the army. The peasants responded with armed self-defense groups as early as the 1940s. In 1948, a ten-year period known as *La Violencia* was sparked by the assassination of populist leader Jorge Gaitán. The Colombian Communist Party was very active in this time period and assisted in the organization of self-defense and guerrilla groups. With the triumph of the Cuban Revolution in 1959, the concept of self-defense began to be transformed into the idea of the pursuance of guerrilla warfare with the goal of achieving state power for the purpose of social revolution. It was in this political context that the FARC was founded in 1964.

The organization began among communities of displaced peasants who had settled uncultivated lands in the hope of fleeing the repression of the state. Those who were fleeing state violence traveled in large groups protected by armed self-defense units, a process known as "armed colonization." These settlements were strongly under the influence of the Communist Party. It was these communities that later became the base of the FARC. The nature of national politics in Colombia also contributed to the development of a revolutionary movement. Two political parties, the Liberals and Conservatives, totally monopolized political power and prevented the development of any role within the system for legal means of dissent. To move competition from more violent forms and share power through alternation, they signed a power-sharing agreement in 1956. This alliance, known as the National Front from 1958 to 1974, has dominated the Colombian political scene to the present. Until the implementation of a new constitution in 1991, these two parties ruled under a permanent state of siege designed to curtail virtually all social protest. By blocking almost all possibility of a democratic left, the state created conditions for the emergence of an opposition that was outside of the parliamentary framework.

The FARC was not the only revolutionary group to be founded in this context. The Army of National Liberation (ELN) was formed in 1964, the Popular Liberation Army (EPL) in 1965, and the April 19th Movement (M-19) in 1973. Smaller urban groups were also formed in this time period. In its early years, the growth of the FARC was slow. By the late 1970s, it had established a marginal presence in the central and southern parts of the country, but in the early 1980s, the FARC grew rapidly as the result of a government crackdown on legal opposition. Up until that time it had operated primarily in the political arena but now began to more clearly articulate its role as a military vanguard. It acquired the organizational structure of an army and developed autonomy from the Communist Party. By 1983, it had expanded its military activity to eighteen fronts.

The FARC was committed to fundamental societal transformation through the armed achievement of state power, but it also pursued a flexible tactical position. In 1983, the government of Belisario Betancur made a significant peace overture. Departing sharply from the political stance of his predecessors, Betancur acknowledged many of the socioeconomic demands of the FARC. A ceasefire was arranged, and the possibility of a political resolution of the conflict became real. In the context of the ceasefire, the FARC formed the Patriotic Union (UP), a political front in which the Communist Party played a significant role. The FARC was preparing for a possible electoral role but did not dismantle its military apparatus.

The possibility of a political settlement was scuttled by Betancur's opposition in the Congress, which rejected the reforms proposed in the accords. The political opposition represented the traditional oligarchy and its allies in the military. When a new government under Virgilio Barco came to power in 1986, the government's overture to the armed opposition officially ended. It refused to recognize the demands of the opposition as legitimate and immediately launched harsh repression against the rebels and their supporters in civil society. During 1988 alone, close to 200 UP leaders were assassinated, and in a decade of repression, nearly 3,000 UP members, including mayors, municipal council members, and senators, were killed, virtually eliminating the organization. Despite this repression, the FARC did not officially return to a stance of war until 1991, after the military occupied the town of Casa Verde, the home of the FARC leadership. Although brief peace talks were conducted in mid-1991, the war intensified from that time onward. A constitutional assembly convened in 1991, and the FARC blamed the government for missing an opportunity to incorporate the political opposition through that process.

As the decade of the 1990s wore on, the FARC and other armed rebel groups found themselves at the center of political unrest in the country. The central government in Bogotá was increasingly unable to govern the country effectively as it battled the increasing influence of both drug cartels and rebel political movements. Unable to control the country by normal means, the government turned to paramilitary organizations to deal with problems by sheer force. In essence, it privatized the war against the FARC and the ELN and in the process served to delegitimize the state. As a result, the 1990s saw great ongoing costs in terms of human lives and property. The weakness of the central government opened the door for the FARC to implement a strategy of undermining local ruling structures by its tactic of "armed oversight." By gathering detailed information on local government financing and spending, the guerrillas were able to both target and expose corrupt local officials while also steering some government revenues toward FARC-sponsored projects.

The ongoing crisis of agriculture also contributed to the growing strength of the FARC. As traditional agricultural production declined, the rebels built support among those sectors hardest hit by the decline. The FARC successfully attracted unemployed youth from the countryside into its ranks. As the peasants increasingly looked to coca production to make up for the decline in other production, the FARC stepped forward with protection for those communities. Such actions helped finance the FARC's activities while also raising its political legitimacy among the poorest sectors. The support of the coca growers has contributed to the growing polarization of the society as the government has ignored the real socioeconomic issues and sought with the support of the U.S. government to place the rebels' activities within the militarized scope of the War on Drugs.

The relationship between the FARC and the political process has been more problematic. In 1996, in the midst of sharp conflict between the coca growers and the central government, the FARC organized a highly successful boycott of the municipal elections in the areas where its influence was strongest. In some cities, mayors were elected by as few as seven votes but prevented from taking office by popularly convened local councils. However, the ability of the guerrillas to protect those communities that defied the central government was limited. The government authorized campaigns of terror against these communities, carried out by private paramilitaries. Such growing polarization and the growing importance of the ELN made the prospect of a political settlement to Colombia's long-running insurgent rebellion unlikely in the near future. Heightened U.S. involvement through Plan Colombia further escalated the conflict. The election of hardline President Alvaro Uribe in 2002 dashed any immediate hopes of a negotiated settlement of the long-running civil war. Uribe ruled out negotiations with the FARC and, with the support of the United States through Plan Colombia, vowed to militarily destroy the guerrilla movement. In 2003, the government won some significant victories over the FARC, including targeted attacks on its leadership, but the FARC escalated its own tactics with increasingly bold terror attacks on wealthy Bogotá neighborhoods, including the bombing of the El Nogal club that killed thirty-six persons in February 2003. With the war continuing in stalemate, negotiations between the FARC and Colombia resumed in 2004 over ending the conflict and the prisoners held by both sides. Aided by the Venezuelan and other Latin American governments, a dramatic prisoner release was negotiated in 2007, but the process was stymied after the Colombian armed forces raided a FARC camp just inside Ecuadoran territory and killed the leader who was coordinating prisoner exchanges in 2008. Although suffering some loss of power, the FARC fought on and in 2012 entered into peace negotiations with the government. While the negotiations continued, Colombia saw a massive national protest strike by agrarian producers in 2013, thus suggesting that social movements might be able to engage in nonviolent political contestation. The struggle for change was channeled into less violent forms of political contestation when a peace agreement between the FARC and Colombian government was finally concluded in 2016 (see Chapter 16).

## Peru

One of Latin America's most interesting revolutionary movements was Peru's Sendero Luminoso (Shining Path) of José Carlos Mariátegui. In the late 1980s and early 1990s, they were the most active rebels in Latin America and were seen as seriously challenging state power against an increasingly weak central government in Lima. A decade later, with most of its key leaders either in jail or dead, Shining Path was reduced to a marginal position in Peruvian politics. Its relative demise provide some interesting insight on revolution and revolutionary movements.

Shining Path was founded in 1980 by Abimael Guzmán, a philosophy professor at the university in Ayacucho. He had been doing preparatory work in the area for some years before. For the next thirteen years, the Communist Party of Peru, known as Shining Path, was a central actor in Peruvian politics. Founded on the Maoist principle of a peasant-based revolution that would gain control of the countryside and eventually encircle and overwhelm the central government, Shining Path was quite successful in reaching out from its original student base to gain widespread influence among the indigenous people of the Ayacucho region, long ignored by the central government in Lima. The rebels burst onto the scene by assassinating local officials who refused to cooperate with their efforts and by seeking to create armed, liberated communities out of the reach of the central government. Their political strategy was fiercely sectarian, rejecting all other political movements as part of the status quo. Shining Path was willing to use violence against any reformist forces that refused to cooperate with its strategy—trade unionists, neighborhood organizers, other leftists, or priests and nuns engaged in community organizing. This harsh sectarianism eventually contributed to the movement's decline. Initially, the government's response was almost entirely counterproductive. In the 1980s, the government carried out a military occupation of the highlands region where Shining Path was based. The army's draconian actions did not succeed in defeating the revolutionaries in their strongholds, and popular reaction to the government repression actually helped spread the revolution to other provinces. Between 1989 and 1992, Shining Path stepped up its armed activity in Lima and engaged in a highly effective car- and truck-bombing campaign, badly shaking the government's confidence. However, upon a thorough review of its earlier counterproductive repression, the government began to reformulate its counterinsurgency strategy. Playing on the divisions in the rural communities that were created by Shining Path's sectarian tactics, the government began to succeed in getting rural inhabitants to join government-backed armed self-defense groups. It was a testament to Shining Path's brutality that the government began to succeed despite its own previous brutality. Shining Path's war became one of *campesinos* against *campesinos*. Shining Path's base of support generally did not grow beyond the most marginalized people—students, teachers, and unemployed youth from the shantytowns. It became more a sect than a broad-based popular movement.

In 1992, through stepped-up intelligence activities, the police were able to arrest a number of key intermediate-level officials, weakening the organization's internal structures. This increased repression occurred in the framework of President Alberto Fujimori's auto-coup, or assumption of dictatorial powers, under the guise of fighting Shining Path. Fujimori's efforts culminated later in 1992 with the arrest of Guzmán. Soon after his capture, Guzmán called off the armed struggle and sought political dialogue with the government. However, in 1994, several key Shining Path leaders denounced Guzmán's call for negotiations and vowed to continue the armed struggle. Most of them were later arrested. Shining Path has not been completely destroyed, but as the decade ended it sought to remain politically relevant in the wake of its disunity and numerous defeats at the hands of the government. By 2005, it had been reduced to a few small bands operating in remote areas where the production of coca leaves and the related drug trade could help finance its existence. They began to increase operations in 2013 but were still limited to a remote jungle area and a small number of militants. By 2017 the revolutionary road in Peru was indeed the road less traveled.

## New Social Movements

In recent years, protest and resistance have taken on different forms. New types of mobilization developed all over Latin America. Unlike radical revolutionary movements of previous decades, these new movements did not employ or advocate the radical, revolutionary restructuring of the state through violent revolution. Rather, their primary focus was to contest power by working through civil society to modify the existing political system and pushing it to the limits to achieve needed and necessary change and restructuring. Although there have been some exceptions, like the initial Zapatista uprising of early January 1994 and the very brief participation of the Confederation of Indigenous Nationalities of Ecuador (CONAIE) in a would-be junta that held the Ecuadorian congressional building overnight in January 2000, they were short-lived, and both movements quickly moved from trying to insert themselves as the regional or national rulers to negotiating power with existing national political elites.

These new political movements all contested power but did so in a political environment that was substantially different from what it has been historically. National-level political participation was quite limited at the time of independence. As previously suggested, mass political movements like that led by Hidalgo failed, while those led by the less popularly oriented members of the *criollo* elite, like Iturbide, succeeded and set the stage for the elitist politics of the nineteenth and much of the twentieth centuries. The franchise—and concomitant political participation—were widened in the nineteenth and twentieth centuries. This in turn challenged the political elite to seek mechanisms to incorporate (if not manipulate) ever wider segments of the population. This eventually led to the emergence of mass-based parties, reformist and parties promising revolution, and populism as a means of incorporating the masses into a national project led by a political elite. Some reformist parties, like Liberación Nacional in Costa Rica and Acción Democrática in Venezuela, were able to bring about some economic and political structural change and incorporate wider sectors of the masses into national society and competitive two-party dominant political systems. A few populist projects, like Peronism in Argentina, were also able to achieve significant economic redistribution, break the oligarchy's economic domination, and incorporate the laboring masses and segments of the middle class into the (one party-dominant) party system, albeit under the somewhat demagogic leadership of Juan and Evita Perón. On the other hand, the Cuban Revolution challenged traditional elitist rule in a different way but left little space for the development of autonomous social movements, though it did respond to the needs of the masses and developed the mechanism of *poder popular* that fomented active participation at the neighborhood and local levels. The widespread rebellion against Anastasio Somoza in Nicaragua helped make it possible for the Sandinista revolution to take power and for the FSLN-led government to begin an economic, social, and political restructuring of the Nicaraguan nation. Indeed, as we noted in *Democracy and Socialism in Sandinista Nicaragua*, the strength and relative autonomy of many of the mass organizations in Nicaragua in the early 1980s were significant and helped to show that new organizational structures and political movements that supported them could radically contest and sometimes change the way power was exercised in Latin America. Likewise, the strength and dynamism of neighborhood- and community-based movements that began to flower all over Latin America in the 1980s (even under repressive military regimes) redefined the parameters of political activism and suggested new repertoires of action for emerging social and political movements.

The systems of mass communication and related communication technology as well as easy, low-cost access to the Internet and the ever-widening use of all forms of the social media such as Twitter have greatly enhanced the ability to generate and coordinate mass mobilizations—the stuff of social movements. This was demonstrated vividly by the wide use of cell phones to organize against the 2002 coup in Venezuela and was particularly strong in the massive popular movements and mobilizations that have gripped Brazil since the middle of 2013. These new forms of social media and popular empowerment have combined with higher levels of literacy, widened access to higher education, and much greater political freedom under the democratization process. The result has been a new wave of political and social movements that are often different in their organization and strategy and endeavor to articulate popular needs in new ways. The massive protests and street occupations in June 2013 in Brazil underlined how more evolved forms of social media (cell phones combined with Facebook, Twitter, and Tumblr) could greatly facilitate popular political participation and the contestation of power. These movements have occurred when ideas of grassroots democracy, popular participation, and even elements of liberation theology and Christian-based community organizing have been widely disseminated. Likewise, there is a growing belief that racial, gender, and economic equality should exist and that systems that perpetuate inequality need to be changed.

Ever since the *Caracazo* in Venezuela in 1989, there have been different forms of popular protest against austerity measures and elements of the conservative economic policies that came to be called neoliberalism in Latin America. These have been manifest in diverse forms: the Zapatista rebellion in Mexico in 1994; the neopopulist Movimiento V República led by Hugo Chávez in Venezuela from the late 1990s to 2013; the national indigenous movement led by CONAIE in Ecuador, the growth of its related party Pachakutik, and the election of Rafael Correa; the Movement of Landless Rural Workers (MST) in Brazil; the *Asambleas Barriales* and other protest organizations in Argentina; and the indigenous peasant unions and Cocaleros Federation and their linked political movement, the Movimiento al Socialismo (MAS) in Bolivia. The fact that at least a million media-savvy Brazilians could take to the streets in June 2013 to protest fare increases, corruption, poor-quality public education and health care, and the squandering of scarce resources on megastadiums and infrastructure for the World Cup and Olympics was very significant. However, to not allow such tactics to gain momentum toward radical change, in 2015 and 2016 the right used some of these same means to organize massive popular demonstrations protesting widespread corruption that were able to facilitate the removal of President Dilma Rousseff from office.

## Argentine Manifestation

In Argentina, popular mobilizations, street demonstrations, strikes, and neighborhood *asembleas populares* (or *Asambleas Barriales*) shook the political system and the political class to the core at the end of 2001 and occasioned the resignation of the elected president Fernando de la Rua and the rapid replacement of three other appointed presidents (the vice president had already resigned). In early 2002, a declared anti-neoliberal Peronist president, Eduardo Duhalde, was voted into office by the Argentine Congress. The unresolved economic crisis, default on the foreign debt, and Duhalde's perceived need to make some concession to the IMF other international financial institutions, and U.S. policy kept the population angry and mobilized. Demonstrations and protests continued through early 2003 as the Argentine nation grouped to find a political force capable of ending the crisis. There was so little confidence in traditional parties or politicians that one could frequently hear a popular refrain among many Argentinians—*Que se vayan todos!* (Throw them all out!). However, the limitations of this movement were shown when the Argentine people elected Néstor Kirchner, a more traditional politician from the Peronist Party, to be president in 2003. He promised to move away from neoliberalism and dictates from the IMF and other international financial institutions and return to the traditional nationalist positions of the Peronists. Although radical change was not achieved, many of the worst aspects of neoliberalism were held at bay during Kirchner's terms in office and at least for a time during his wife's (Christina Fernández de Kirchner) term in office.

The nature of the protests in Buenos Aires and other Argentine cities suggested the political sea change that is sweeping across Latin America. Governance is breaking down, and traditional political institutions were losing legitimacy as new movements surge to challenge traditional political leadership. In recent years, a great many of the masses—and some of the middle class—seem to be hit by a feeling that the much-touted return to democracy, celebration of civil society, and incorporation in the globalization process have left them marginalized economically if not politically. The reactions in Argentina, Mexico, Ecuador, Bolivia, Brazil, and Venezuela were strong and significant and, in varying ways, represented a new means of pressuring for much needed restructuring, not from above but by the common people. The 2013 street protests in Brazil underline this phenomenon. It is also quite possible that the democratization and celebration of civil society allow—some would say encourage—the political mobilization that is manifest in the widespread emergence of new social and political movements, if not—as we have argued in *The New Global Politics: Global Social Movements in the Twenty-First Century*—a new way of doing politics.

# Chiapas: Regional Victory

In southern Mexico, local and community organizations began to resist the dire economic consequences engendered by globalization and globalized integration through free trade and NAFTA. It is argued that similar forms of resistance have occurred throughout the hemisphere since the region was interjected into the international capitalist economic system. Yet, these previous struggles were more akin to traditional peasant or indigenous rebellions in that they did not spawn strong national or international links and as such were easily marginalized or defeated. Indeed, localized resistance had bubbled to the surface sporadically since the time of the conquest, if not before. This certainly had been the case in southern Mexico and the Yucatan. Perhaps stimulated by this tradition of rebellion, in the 1980s the indigenous rural population in Chiapas began to resist and organize against the traditional land inequity and the hardships that the commercialization of agriculture and Mexico's further integration into the global market structure caused them. Racial identity and unequal land distribution helped to solidify the movement and led to the formation of a social movement that eventually spawned the Zapatista Army of National Liberation (EZLN). Unlike some other groups, the Zapatistas were successful in linking their struggle to a growing continental indigenous identity and the disastrous effects of globalized free markets on local small farmers. Their ingenious use of the Internet, the mountain

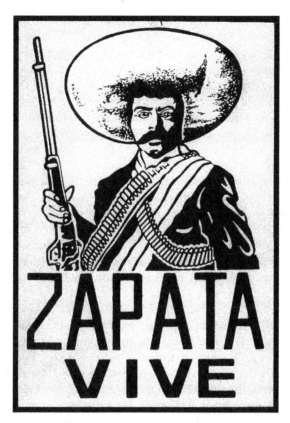

*Zapata lives!* Mexican revolutionary Emiliano Zapata inspires great admiration and emu-
lation. After Zapata became the inspiration and namesake for the Zapatistas, pictures and
Zapata decals like this one were freely circulated in Chiapas and other parts of Mexico.

or ski mask, public relations, marches, and mobilizations kept their cause before the
Mexican nation and the international community. They were able to create a highly
politicized movement with considerable regional power and national visibility—one
that became an international inspiration. They were not, however, able to link their
struggle to other large politicized social movements to form a national coalition. Nor
were they able to mobilize their support behind a nationwide new political party or
political movement (as was done in Ecuador and Brazil) that would be sympathetic
to their demands once it achieved national power or that would at least ensure them
adequate space in civil society to continue to mobilize support and pursue their demands (as was done in Bolivia in 2003 and 2005).

## Ecuador

Southern Mexico was not the only place where the effects of neoliberal policies and
the globalization process generated innovative responses. Since Incan times, local
indigenous communities have been marginalized from important decision-making

processes in Ecuador. This practice was extended to virtually all indigenous people after the conquest and continued during the republic. Yet, by the 1990s, the traditional struggle for land, power, and some modicum of justice for the indigenous, mostly peasant masses was gradually transformed from a local, community-based one to a national one coordinated by CONAIE. CONAIE had become a national organization that was able to mobilize thousands of its people in land takeovers and marches. It connected different ethnic and regional groups and used modern means of communication to forge a national social movement. In the process, it became a major power contender that could challenge governmental action by the late 1990s. After the disastrous dollarization of the economy and imposition of other neoliberal economic policies by President Jamil Mahuad, CONAIE was able to mobilize tens of thousands of its constituents for a march on Quito that culminated in the taking of the congressional building and—backed by a few progressive army officers and civilian politicians—the formation of a short-lived junta in January 2000. This was the first time indigenous people had governed substantial parts of Ecuador since the conquest. Their victory was, however, brief. Although some horizontal contacts with other organizations had been made, the CONAIE militants were not part of a broad-based national coalition that could retain power. With the support of the United States, the traditional political class was able to retake power and negotiate the exit of Mahuad by placing Vice President Gustavo Noboa in power. Once mobilized, CONAIE, learning from the experience, initiated a national political strategy and even started an affiliated political party, Pachakutik, in 1995. In the 2002 elections, they continued to cultivate their now-highly politicized national social movement but were also able to field successful local and congressional political candidates. Eventually, they threw their support behind Lucio Gutiérrez, the army colonel who had been part of the short-lived junta in January 2000. Thus, they helped to elect Gutiérrez to the presidency, though their support was not unconditional. They maintained their autonomy but ensured that their demands would at least receive a hearing at the highest level and might even be received with some sympathy. This stance became important because, once in power, Gutiérrez moved away from his anti-neoliberal positions to the point of seeking a free trade agreement with the United States. CONAIE led the opposition against the turn in the president's politics, and in early 2005, he was forced from office amid large street protests. The support of CONAIE and other indigenous movements was fundamental for the 2006 election of left-leaning candidate Rafael Correa to the presidency and his pursuit of a more progressive political agenda. Later, they would criticize the Correa government for its willingness to extend mining concessions that endangered indigenous communities.

# New Social Movements and New Politics

## The MST

The radically different nature of these new social movements and the new politics can perhaps best be seen in the largest of the new social movements in Latin America, the MST in Brazil. Their ranks exceed 1 million, and on one occasion they were able to mobilize 100,000 people for a march on Brasília. In a pamphlet titled *Brazil Needs a Popular Project,* the organization calls for popular mobilizations, noting that "all the changes in the history of humanity only happened when the people were mobilized" and that, in Brazil, "all the social and political changes that happened were won when the people mobilized and struggled." Their political culture and decision-making processes break from the authoritarian tradition. The movement has been heavily influenced by liberation theology and the participatory democratic culture that is generated by the use and study of Paulo Freire's approach to self-taught, critical education.

The MST was formed as a response to long-standing economic, social, and political conditions in Brazil. Land, wealth, and power have been allocated in very unequal ways in Brazil since the conquest in the early 1500s. Land has remained highly concentrated, and, as late as 1996, 1 percent of the landowners who owned farms of over 1,000 hectares owned 45 percent of the land. Conversely, as of 2001, there were some 4.5 million landless rural workers in Brazil. Wealth has remained equally concentrated. In 2001, the Brazilian Institute of Government Statistics reported that the upper 10 percent of the population averaged an income that was nineteen times greater than that of the lowest 40 percent. The plantation agriculture that dominated the colonial period and the early republic became the standard for Brazilian society. The wealthy few owned the land, reaped the profits, and decided the political destiny of the many. Slavery was the institution that provided most of the labor on the early plantation system and, thus, set the nature of the relationship between the wealthy landowning elite and the disenfranchised masses who labored in the fields. Land has stayed in relatively few hands in Brazil, and agricultural laborers continue to be poorly paid and poorly treated. Further, after the commercialization and mechanization of agriculture that began in the 1970s, much of the existing rural labor force became superfluous. As this process continued, not only were rural laborers let go, but also sharecroppers were expelled from the land they had farmed and small farmers lost their land to larger family or commercial estates. This resulted in increases in rural unemployment and the number of rural landless families. Many were forced to migrate to the cities to swell the numbers of the urban poor, while others opted for the government-sponsored Amazon colonization program whereby they were transported to the Amazon region to cut down the rain forest and cultivate the land. Few found decent jobs in the city, and the poor soil of the former rain forest allowed for little sustained agriculture. As conditions deteriorated, the landless realized that they were fighting for their own existence as a group and, as such, were the authors of their own destiny. The origins of the organization go back to the bitter struggle to survive under the agricultural policies implemented by the military government. The landless in the southern Brazilian state of Rio Grande do Sul began to organize to demand land. Other landless people soon picked up their cry in the neighboring states of Paraná and Santa Catarina. They built on a long tradition of rural resistance and rebellion that extends back to the establishment of *palenques,* or large inland settlements of runaway slaves, and to the famous rebellion by the poor rural peasants of Canudos in the 1890s. In more recent times, it included the famous Peasant Leagues of Brazil's impoverished northeast in the 1950s and early 1960s and the "grass wars" in Rio Grande do Sul and the southern states in the 1970s. When the MST was founded in southern Brazil in 1984 as a response to rural poverty and lack of access to land, wealth, and power, similar conditions existed in many states. Indeed, there were landless workers and peasants throughout the nation. Thus, the MST soon spread from Rio Grande do Sul and Paraná in the south to states like Pernambuco in the northeast and Pará in the Amazon region. It rapidly became a national organization with coordinated policies and strong local participation and decision-making, with frequent state and national meetings based on direct representation. By 2001, there were active MST organizations in twenty-three of the twenty-six states.

This type of national organization had not been the case with the Zapatista movement because conditions and identity were much more locally rooted. Yet, in both cases, traditional politics and traditional political parties had proven unable and unwilling to address the deteriorating economic conditions of the marginalized groups who were suffering the negative effects of economic globalization. Their response was grassroots organization and the development of a new repertoire of actions that broke with old forms of political activity. Developing organization and group actions began to tie individual members together in a strongly forged group identity. The MST decided from the outset that it was to be an organization for the landless workers that would be run by the landless workers for their benefit as they defined it. They engaged in direct actions such as land takeovers from large estates and public lands, construction of black, plastic-covered encampments along the side of the road to call attention to their demands for land, and marches and confrontations when necessary. They even occupied the family farm of President Fernando Henrique Cardoso to draw attention to his landowning interests and the consequent bias they attributed to him. They were at times brutally repressed, assassinated, and imprisoned, but they persevered, forcing land distribution to their members and others without land. Their ability to mobilize as many as 12,000 people for a single land takeover or 100,000 for a national march in 1997 suggested just how strong their organizational abilities were and how well they could communicate and coordinate at the national level. They also created a great deal of national support and helped create a consensus that there was a national problem with land distribution and that some substantial reform was necessary. Struggles that were once local and isolated were now international and linked. The news media and growing international communications links, like cell phones and especially e-mail, greatly facilitated the globalization of struggle and of awareness of local struggles as well as support and solidarity for them. This and the dramatic actions like massive land takeovers by the MST also generated considerable support at the national level and helped define what might have been considered a local problem as a national one that required national attention and national resources to remedy it.

The interaction between the MST and the Workers' Party (PT) is also instructive. Although relations between the two organizations are generally excellent at the local level, with overlapping affiliations, the national leaderships have remained separate and not always as cordial. The MST has maintained a militant line in regard to the need to takeover unused land and assert its agenda, whereas much of the PT leadership has wanted to be more conciliatory. Thus, the landless backed and supported Luiz Inácio "Lula" da Silva and the PT in most local campaigns and the

MST militants on the move. *(Photo by Paulo Santos-Interphoto/AP Images)*

national campaign for the presidency. In this way, they helped achieve significant regime change in Brazil, where Lula was elected with 61.27 percent of the vote in the second round of voting in 2002. Indeed, realizing the PT's historic challenge to neoliberal policies and elitist rule, the landless turned out heavily in the election to join some 80 percent of the registered voters who participated in the voting in both rounds. The landless again supported Lula in the 2006 election but were even more critical after major land reform initiatives failed to materialize in his second term. Once the elections were over, the MST did not press to be part of the government. Rather, they continued to press the government for a comprehensive land reform program and redistribution of the land and the wealth. There would be no return to politics as usual. The PT would press its "0 Hunger" and its successor *Bolsa Familia* programs and other social and economic initiatives, and the MST would press the PT government for structural reforms (e.g., comprehensive agrarian reform) that it considered necessary. By 2013 the MST felt that the PT government had ignored most of their demands, and they too joined the massive June protests (see Chapter 14). As the focus of protest moved to urban areas, the mainstream media gave the MST negative coverage, and with the national obsession with corruption in general and Workers' Party–linked corruption in particular, the MST was a less potent player in national politics.

## Bolivia

In Bolivia, the common people had been marginalized from key decision-making processes in national government since the republic was founded if not from the time of colonial occupation. As Vice President Alvaro García Linera suggested, the subalterns had been excluded. By the twenty-first century things had begun to change radically.

The intensity of the politicalization of social movements in Bolivia was demonstrated by the massive protests and the popular mobilizations that rocked the nation in 2003. As had occurred in Ecuador in 2000, there was a very effective popular mobilization of indigenous peoples and rural peasants through a newly formed national, peasant, indigenous federation that called for the blockading of roads and popular mobilizations. They had quickly been joined by the *cocaleros* of the now-famous Coca Growers Federation led by Evo Morales. The groups that converged on the Bolivian capital of La Paz and other large cities were predominantly lower-class miners and agricultural workers and peasants; people who were mostly indigenous and the poor generally. Theirs was a struggle that had been going at least since the indigenous and peasant uprisings led by Túpac Amaru and Túpac Katari in the 1780s, but this time it was coordinated, effective, and successful. Long before this mobilization occurred, local communities had been forming their own organizations to fight some aspect of colonial rule, exploitation or, more recently, globalization. This reaction can, for instance, be seen in the strong grassroots movement against the privatization of the public water supply in the mostly indigenous community of Cochabamba in 2000. There, the Coordinadora de Defensa del Agua y de la Vida (Coordinating Committee to Defend Water and Life) remained locally rooted, but unlike previous local actions, this struggle was always framed in an international and national context. The protesters publicized their cause through the Internet and sent delegations to international meetings, like the World Social Forums. Further, they were very aware not only of the international dimensions of their struggle and of its globalized causes but also of the possibilities of international links with similar struggles and the international antiglobalization movement generally. This awareness and the electronic and personal links they established with other movements in Bolivia and outside later facilitated their integration into the broad national coalition that set forth a national agenda through support for Evo Morales and his MAS party in the 2005, 2009, and 2014 presidential elections. Extensive networking with other new social movements allowed this and other local or regional movements to become part of a near unstoppable national mobilization that toppled the Sánchez de Lozada government and carried Morales and MAS to power. By linking the local effects of the neoliberal privatization of the water supply in Cochabamba to global policies and national politics, they linked their struggle to a growing regional and international consensus and to a national movement with concrete, achievable objectives.

The intensity of the politicization of this and other social movements in Bolivia was demonstrated by the massive protests and the popular mobilizations that rocked the nation in 2003 and again in 2005. As had occurred in Ecuador in 2000 with CONAIE and its allies, the popular mobilization of indigenous peoples and rural peasants were through the aforementioned local community and regional organizations and a newly formed mostly peasant indigenous federation. The Union of Bolivian Rural Workers under the leadership Felipe Quispe was quickly joined by those who grew the coca leaves that the Sánchez de Lozada government was eradicating under the direction of the U.S. government—the *cocaleros* (coca growers) of the Coca Growers Federation and its indigenous leader Evo Morales. Other groups, like the famous Cochabamba Coordinating Committee to Defend Water and Life, also joined. An ongoing economic crisis and a crisis in traditional politics combined with strong U.S. pressure to open Bolivian markets and virtually elimi- nate the centuries-old cultivation of coca leaves stimulated the masses to meet and mobilize at the local, community level and respond to the movements' calls for action. Communal organization was also strong and had increased since the 1952 Revolution distributed land to the indigenous peasants. By the 1990s, there were peasant unions and local community organizations throughout the Andean region of the country. A strong Landless Movement (MST) had also developed in the non– Andean Santa Cruz region and became an instrument of peasant mobilization there. As indigenous groups met in congresses and assemblies—often termed "Assem- blies to Take Sovereignty"—in the late 1980s and early 1990s, they realized that they needed mechanisms to achieve political power. As their consciousness developed, they began to speak explicitly of the "Sovereignty of the People" and the need to create "Political Instruments for the Sovereignty of the People." As their thinking evolved, they formed peasant unions, neighborhood organizations in places like El Alto, social movements, and political movements like Pachakutik and MAS.

Yet, even in what might be termed one of Latin America's most organized soci- eties, a precipitating event was needed for action, and this was a U.S.-backed pro- posal to sell Bolivian natural gas through a port that landlocked Bolivia had lost to Chile in the ill-fated War of the Pacific (1879–1881). The disastrous failure of the neo- liberal model that Victor Paz Estensoro had inaugurated when the MNR returned to power, and that Sánchez Lozada had advocated, added to the widely shared percep- tion that this new trade deal was but one more ruse to extract wealth from the nation and leave the indigenous masses even more poverty ridden and totally subject to the influence of outside forces. Historically, most peasant and indigenous uprisings and even many strikes by the tin miners had been characterized by their local nature and lack of linkages to national movements and international conditions.

The Union of Rural Workers and the *cocaleros* were soon joined by other social movements, urban unions, and students as they mobilized in massive demonstra- tions in La Paz and other cities. The government futilely tried to repress the demon- strators, causing the loss of eighty lives. This enraged the opposition even more and increased the president's isolation. Meeting in their villages and union headquarters, many more people decided to join the uprising. Bolivian miners and others across the country also joined the protests and decided to march on the capital. As his polit- ical backers dropped away in the face of the mass mobilization, Sánchez de Lozada was forced to resign and leave the country. Morales and MAS were able to ride this wave of protest and mobilization; Morales was elected the first indigenous president of Bolivia, and MAS secured substantial representation in the national legislature (12 of 27 in the Senate and 73 of 130 in the Chamber of Deputies) in the elections of December 2005. Indeed, Morales seems to have well captured the dynamic essence of the combined movements that brought him to power. His support continued and allowed him to gain re-election in December 2009 with 64 percent of the vote and also allowed his MAS party to win a large majority in both houses of the national legislature and in many local and regional governments. To ensure good relations with the social movements, the Morales government set up a Vice-Ministry of Coor- dination with Social Movements and located it in the Office of the Presidency.

This mobilization by the social movements represented a substantial change in politics. The new social movements had been able to take politics out of the presidential palace and the halls of Congress, where elitist politics and the traditional political class dominated, and into their space—the villages, neighborhoods, popular councils, and the streets and rural highways—that they could control. They were beginning to exercise their participatory decision-making in ways that were consistent with their *"usos y costumbres"*—their traditional forms of democracy. They had taken the initiative and had been able to forge a broad, national coalition that cemented the two presidents' downfalls and established the viability of their social movements as key political actors whose demands had to be heeded. They had also mobilized the indigenous and working-class masses like never before. In contrast to the situation in Ecuador in 2000 and the Bolivian Revolution of 1952, they had done so without seizing power themselves but had demonstrated how effectively they could use and mobilize massive political power on a national scale. They had done so from below, through a broad coalition of social movements with strong identities and deep, democratic ties to their constituencies. Vice President García Linares said,

> They had initiated a form of participatory governance that would radically alter the nation's decision making practices in their Andean nation and that suggested that government must indeed serve the people if it was to endure. Further, the push from the social organizations would be necessary to sustain the government and enable it to carry out the necessary transformations.

President Evo Morales said in his inaugural address on January 22, 2006:

> We can continue to speak of our history, we can continue to remember how those who came before us struggled: Túpac Katari to restore the Thuantinsuyo, Simón Bolívar who fought for this larger nation [*patria grande*], Che Guevara who fought for a new more equal world. This democratic cultural struggle, this cultural democratic revolution, is part of the struggle of our ancestors, it is the continuity from Túpac Katari; this struggle and these results are Che Guevara's continuity. We are here, Bolivian and Latin American sisters and brothers; we are going to continue until we achieve equality in this country.

By mid-2010 there were, however, sectors in the Bolivian social movements that expressed concern about policies of the Morales government, even though the government had set up a vice-ministry to coordinate (control) social movements. These tensions came to the surface at the end of the year when mobilized social movements forced the government to rescind an end to petroleum and other consumer-oriented subsidies. Tensions between the Morales government and some social movements have increased in recent years.

# Conclusion

Political scientist Eric Selbin has suggested that, given Latin America's 500-year-old tradition of rebellion and revolution, we should be wary of dismissing the possibility of future revolutions there. An understanding of why revolution and serious study of it must remain integral to our study of Latin America is rooted in the fact that the recent growth of democratic political forms and economic restructuring has done relatively little to eliminate the social inequalities and political disenfranchisement that plague Latin America in the twenty-first century. The greater harbinger for the continued probability of revolutionary upsurges and movements for radical change in Latin America comes from the fact that as the region moves through the new millennium more people live in poverty than was the case twenty years ago and the fact that the gap between the richest and poorest grows wider. Nearly half the region's 625 million people are poor, an increase of more than 70 million in one decade. Most of the regimes that took power during Latin America's recent turn to democratic rule did not seem to make any significant progress in the arena of social justice, with the result that the neoliberal economic models triumphant at the start of the 1990s were increasingly being called into question. By 2011, politics were once again changing. There were myriad new social and political movements that were pressing hard for structural change and were democratizing the decision-making process if not the political culture itself. New leftist presidents had been elected throughout the region, and many were beginning to implement projects for radical change. As U.S. president John F. Kennedy observed in the formulation of the Alliance for Progress, the stifling of reforms makes the violent struggle for change inevitable. Contemporary democratic regimes, as Selbin notes, rely far too often on pacts among elites (pacted democracy) and the marginalization of the indigenous population and masses generally. It would seem that social change will remain on the agenda in the twenty-first century in Latin America. It would also seem that new means of organizing for such change are being developed in communities and new social and political movements throughout the region and that rightest forces are finding new ways, including organizing their own social movements, to resist the radical change motivating these leftist social movements.

Latin America's ruling elites have rarely demonstrated great tolerance for such political opposition. The social movements themselves, often with a single-issue focus, are not necessarily capable of articulating the broader vision for societal change that the region's social and political inequalities demand. It remains to be seen if these new, highly politicized movements or new political parties, like Brazil's PT or Bolivia's MAS, will be able to remedy the region's problems through massive mobilizations and concerted political action. The extent to which they can achieve genuine change and socioeconomic restructuring remains to be seen. If they cannot, then the next question to be asked is whether the traditional forms of revolution and rebellion will remain relevant or whether other forms of struggle will replace them. In the meantime, it is clear that new social movements can challenge governments that no longer listen to the peoples' needs. If those who rule do not pay heed to such needs, they may be driven from power by the mobilized masses as they were in Tunisia, Egypt, Ecuador, Argentina, and Bolivia.

# Bibliography

Alvarez, Sonia, Evelina Dagnino, and Arturo Escobar, eds. *Cultures of Politics/Politics of Cultures: Revisioning Latin American Social Movements*. Boulder, CO: Westview, 1998.

Arnson, Cynthia. *Comparative Peace Processes in Latin America*. Palo Alto, CA: Stanford University Press, 1999.

Bradford, Sue, and Jan Rocha. *Cutting the Wire, the Story of the Landless Movement in Brazil*. London: Latin American Bureau, 2002.

Broad, Robin, ed. *Global Backlash, Citizen Initiatives for a Just World Economy*. Lanham, MD: Rowman & Littlefield, 2002.

Colburn, Forrest. *The Vogue of Revolution in Poor Countries*. Princeton, NJ: Princeton University Press, 1994.

Debray, Regis. *Revolution in the Revolution?* New York: Grove, 1967.

della Porta, Donatella, and Sidney Tarrow, eds. *Transnational Protest and Global Activism*. Lanham, MD: Rowman & Littlefield, 2005.

Eckstein, Susan, ed. *Power and Protest: Latin American Social Movements*. Berkeley: University of California Press, 2001.

Ellner, Steve, and Daniel Hellinger. *Venezuelan Politics in the Chávez Era: Class, Polarization and Conflict*. Boulder, CO: Lynne Rienner, 2003.

Escobar, Arturo, and Sonia E. Alvarez. *The Making of Social Movements in Latin America: Identity, Strategy and Democracy*. Boulder, CO: Westview, 1992.

Hodges, Donald C. *The Latin American Revolution: Politics and Strategy from Apro-Marxism to Guevarism*. New York: William Morrow, 1974.

Guevara, Ernesto Che, and Fidel Castro. *Socialism and Man in Cuba*. 3d. ed. New York: Pathfinder, 2009.

Kampwirth, Karen. *Women and Guerrilla Movements: Nicaragua, El Salvador, Chiapas, Cuba*. University Park: Pennsylvania State University Press, 2002.

Lefeber, Walter W. *Inevitable Revolutions: The United States in Central America*. 2d ed. New York: W. W. Norton, 1994.

Liss, Sheldon. *Marxist Thought in Latin America*. Berkeley: University of California Press, 1984.

McClintock, Cynthia. *Revolutionary Movements in Latin America*. Washington, DC: United States Institute of Peace, 1998.

McLaren, Peter. *Che Guevara, Paulo Freire, and the Pedagogy of the Oppressed*. Blue Ridge Summitt, PA: Rowman & Littlefield, 2000.

Montgomery, Tommie Sue. *Revolution in El Salvador: From Civil Strife to Peace*. 2d ed. Boulder, CO: Westview, 1995.

Palmer, David Scott. *Shining Path of Peru*. 2d ed. New York: St. Martin's, 1992.

Prevost, Gary, Carlos Oliva Campos, and Harry E. Vanden, eds. *Social Movements and Leftist Governments in Latin America*. London: Zed, 2013.

Selbin, Eric. *Modern Latin American Revolutions*. Boulder, CO: Westview, 1993.

Skocpol, Theda. *States and Social Revolution*. Cambridge: Cambridge University Press, 1979.

Stahler-Sholk, Richard, and Harry E. Vanden, eds. *Special Issue: A Second Look at Latin American Social Movements. Latin American Perspectives* 38, no. 1 (January 2011).

Stahler-Sholk, Richard, Harry E. Vanden, and Marc Becker, eds. *Radical Action from Below: Rethinking Latin American Social Movements* Lanham, MD: Roman & Littlefield, 2014.

Stahler-Sholk, Richard, Harry E. Vanden, and Glen Kuecker, eds. *Special Issue: Globalizing Resistance: The New Politics of Social Movements in Latin America. Latin American Perspectives* 34, no. 2 (March 2007).

Stahler-Sholk, Richard, Harry E. Vanden, and Glen Kuecker, eds. *Latin American Social Movements in the Twenty-First Century: Resistance, Power and Democracy*. Lanham, MD: Rowman & Littlefield, 2008.

Stedile, João Pedro, and Bernardo Mançano Fernandes. *Brava Gente: A Trajetórai do MST e a Luta Pela Terra no Brasil*. São Paulo: Fundacão Perseo Abramo, 1999.

Vanden, Harry E. "Globalization in a Time of Neoliberalism: Politicized Social Movements and the Latin American Response." *Journal of Developing Societies* 19, no. 2–3 (2003): 308–333.

Vanden, Harry E. *Latin American Marxism: A Bibliography*. New York: Garland, 1991.

Vanden, Harry E. "New Political Movements, Governance and the Breakdown of Traditional Politics in Latin America." *International Journal of Public Administration* 27, no. 13–14 (2004): 1129–1149.

Vanden, Harry E., Peter N. Funke, Gary Prevost, eds. *The New Global Politics: Global Social Movements in the Twenty-First Century*. London: Routledge, 2017.

Vanden, Harry E., and Gary Prevost. *Democracy and Socialism in Sandinista Nicaragua*. Boulder, CO: Lynne Rienner, 1993.

Webber, Jeffrey R., and Barry Carr, eds. *The New Latin American Left: Cracks in the Empire*. Lanham, MD: Roman & Littlefield, 2013.

Wickham-Crowley, Timothy. *Guerrillas and Revolution in Latin America*. Princeton, NJ: Princeton University Press, 1992.

Wright, Angus, and Wendy Wolford. *To Inherit the Earth: The Landless Movement and the Struggle for a New Brazil*. Oakland, CA: Food First, 2003.

Zebiche, Raul, and Ramon Ryan, *Dispersing Power: Social Movements as Anti-State Forces*. Translated by Ramon Ryan. Oakland: AK, 2010.

Zebiche, Raul and Ramon Ryan. *Territories in Resistance: A Cartography of Latin American Social Movements*. Translated by Ramon Ryan. Oakland: AK, 2012.

## FILMS AND VIDEOS

*1932: Scars of Memory*. United States, 2002 (the 1932 Matanza in El Salvador).

*Americas in Transition*. United States, 1982.

*El Salvador: Another Vietnam*. United States, 1981.

*Even the Rain*. Spain, 2010.

*Grass War! Peasant Struggle in Brazil*. United States, 2001.

*A Place Called Chiapas*. Canada, 1998.

*Raiz Forte/Strong Roots*. Brazil, 2000.

*Romero*. United States, 1989.

*Seven Dreams of Peace*. United States, 1996.

*Tupamaros*. United States, 1996.

*Ya Basta! The Battle Cry of the Forceless*. United States, 1997.

## WEBSITES

http://www.mstbrazil.org/   Landless Workers Movement in Brazil (MST)

http://conaie.nativeweb.org/   The Confederation of Indigenous Nationalities of Ecuador (CONAIE)

# ELEVEN

# U.S.–LATIN AMERICAN RELATIONS

There are many ways of seeing the relationship between the United States and Latin America. That most commonly voiced in North America is that the United States, Canada, and the Latin American nations are sister republics who share a common identity in the Western Hemisphere. This vision is most often expressed as Pan-Americanism and is based on the premise that all the American republics have common interests and objectives no matter their place, power, or national identity within the Western Hemisphere. Accordingly, the Latin American republics are expected to willingly enroll in foreign policy initiatives championed by the United States, be it the fight against fascism during World War II, anticommunism, the war on drugs, free market initiatives, or the war on terrorism. Latin Americans, somewhat like Canadians, do not always see such a commonality of interests and are often resentful of pressure and cajoling by a powerful neighbor. Indeed, they often bemoan their proximity to the colossus of the north as suggested by an adage often heard in Mexico and smaller nations in Central America and the Caribbean—"so far from God and so close to the United States."

One of the earliest statements of the potential conflict with the United States was made by the hero of the struggle for independence from Spain and liberator of South America, Simón Bolívar. His keen awareness of the developing strength of the United States and prescient vision of the need for Latin American strength and unity prompted him to organize an important hemispheric conference that was convened in Panama in 1826, two years after the now-famous declaration of President James Monroe (the Monroe Doctrine) on the need to keep the former colonial powers out of Latin America. This concern could be construed in itself as a tacit recognition of the relative weakness of the Latin American states before the colonial powers of the day and also as a reaction to the United States' troubles in its fight with Britain in the War of 1812.

The 1826 Congress of Panama, as it came to be known, was to bring all the independent Spanish-speaking republics of the hemisphere together to discuss common interests and chart a common course. Brazil and the United States were invited (over Bolivar's objections) only at the last minute, and the U.S. representatives never arrived while the congress was in session. The congress was poorly attended and never achieved its aims, though it did set forth a Latin American position—one that assumed Latin American interests were different from and perhaps conflict-ing with—those of the United States. Fully aware of this developing disparity in power, Bolivar later wrote, in a letter to the British chargé d'affaires in Bogotá dated August 5, 1829, that the United States "seem destined by Providence to plague Latin America with torments in the name of freedom."

As Peter Smith argues in *Talons of the Eagle*, the earliest years of the North American republic reflected the development of the "age of imperialism" and color U.S. attitudes toward Latin America with a sense of superiority and domination that has persisted through more than 200 years down to the present. In *Beneath the United States*, Lars Schoultz notes that in the first half of the nineteenth century, officials in Washington, D.C., began to create a mindset that would continue to influence U.S. policy toward Latin America to the present. From this perspective, the neighbors to the south were inferior to their English-speaking northern neighbors, plagued with problems, and in need of assistance from the United States. Their territory was seen in the context of U.S. security interests and thus might need to be taken, bought, invaded, or otherwise controlled according to U.S. needs.

Imperialism, defined as the quest for land, labor, and resources through empire, fostered a great rivalry among the European powers that lasted for over 200 years and culminated in the cataclysmic world wars of the twentieth century. Thus, by 1898 most of the Western European powers, including tiny Belgium and the Netherlands, had established empires in different parts of what we now refer to as the third world or global south. They used their control to extract wealth for the metropolitan, colonizing countries by obtaining cheap raw materials and markets for their manufactured goods or by investing large amounts of capital. The United States seemingly broke free from this system at its beginning through the successful eighteenth-century war of independence. In reality, the newly independent colonies almost immediately joined that system by looking southward for land and resources. As a result, U.S. behavior in Latin America from the nineteenth century onward would often closely resemble the penetration of the region that marked three cen-turies of Spanish and Portuguese colonial domination (described in Chapter 2). The reality of the U.S. assumption of an imperial role is often overlooked because of the popular myth that U.S. foreign policy was established as a reflection of President George Washington's famous farewell address wherein he warned the new republic to avoid "foreign entanglements." The spin placed on this advice to avoid perma-nent military alliances suggested that the United States adopted an anticolonial, isolationist stance that would dominate U.S. foreign policy well into the twentieth century. The reality was far different, especially regarding U.S. relations with Latin America. First, Washington's views were countered by Alexander Hamilton and others, who argued that the United States should not ignore the conflicts in Europe but rather utilize them to its advantage as the colonies had done during the Revo-lutionary War, when they gained French assistance for the military defeat of the British at Yorktown and enjoyed covert and then overt assistance from Spain in the Louisiana and the Florida Gulf Coast. The differences between Hamilton and Washington were real and have often been manifested in U.S. foreign policy over the decades, but they were not significant in regard to Latin America. The development of a U.S. empire, sometimes defined as a U.S. sphere of influence, was done in stages that reflected the ever-growing power and confidence of the United States. Not surprisingly, the first priority of the new republic was territorial expansion. Thus after purchasing Louisiana (formerly West Florida) after it had been transferred by Spain to France, the U.S. Senate ratified the No-Transfer Doctrine in 1810 whereby it stated that the transfer of any part of (East) Florida into the hands of a foreign power would be troubling and, under certain circumstances, would compel the United States to temporarily occupy that territory. There was considerable uneasiness that Spain would transfer part of Florida to Great Britain, which would in turn use it for bases in the growing conflict with the United States that would become the War of 1812. The political leaders of the new nation were in agreement that European influence in Latin America should be reduced and that there were long-term political and commercial opportunities in the region. From the beginning, the United States did not see Spain and Portugal as long-term threats but rather believed that their declining colonial control would yield great opportunities for the expansion of the British and French Empires. As a result, the United States came reluctantly to support the independence of the former Spanish and Portuguese colonies as a way to reduce European influence in the region.

In the early years of the nineteenth century, beginning with Thomas Jefferson, a policy for Latin America was crafted that culminated in the statement of the Monroe Doctrine in 1823 as official U.S. policy. Still mostly adhered to almost two centuries later, the essence of the doctrine is that the regions of North, Central, and South America and the Caribbean represent a hemisphere "unto itself" naturally dominated by the United States and largely free of significant influence from any other region of the world, especially Europe. Stated by a small young nation at the time, it was an attempt to neutralize European influence in the region that might threaten U.S. interests and a bold declaration representing much more hope than reality. It was the claim of an empire without any real substance, and it would take decades to realize.

As time went on, U.S. leaders looked southward to Florida, Mexico, and Cuba for new territories. Florida was the first prize to be taken from Spain through a combination of military force and negotiation. After opening negotiations with the Spanish in 1817, General Andrew Jackson seized Spanish forts at Saint Mark's and Pensacola on the pretense that the Spaniards had failed to control Indian tribes in the territories. Failing to win British backing for its position, Spain agreed to cede Florida to the United States in return for freedom from claims by U.S. citizens against Spain and U.S. recognition of Spanish control over Texas. The British did not support Spain, fearing that its colonies could eventually fall into French hands, their chief imperial rival. U.S. control was a lesser evil. Of course, the latter concession on Texas would not be honored over time.

## Territorial Expansion: Confrontation with Mexico

By the mid-nineteenth century the United States, often motivated by the concept of Manifest Destiny, began to expand its economic and political power into Latin America. U.S. nationals flocked to the Mexican territory of Texas and soon pushed for independence from Mexico joining *téjanos* (Texas Mexicans) who were already pressing for autonomy. Of great significance was the desire of the United States to obtain territory from Mexico, as it held the vast territories comprising what are now the current states of Texas, Arizona, New Mexico, California, Nevada, Colorado, and Utah. To achieve the dream of Manifest Destiny and realize its potential as a nation from the Atlantic to the Pacific, the acquisition of this vast territory from the Mexicans and the defeat of Indian tribes who lived in the region was seen as essential to the success of the United States if it was to take its rightful place in the imperial world order. The first step in the process was the annexation of Texas in 1845 by President James Polk. Colonists, many of whom were slaveholders from the U.S. South, had declared an independent Lone Star Republic in 1836. However, they were defeated by the Mexican army under the command of Antonio López de Santa Anna at the Alamo, and their declaration was never recognized by the Mexican government. At the time of the annexation, Mexico considered Texas a renegade province and severed diplomatic ties with the United States upon Polk's declaration.

In 1846 Polk sent General Zachary Taylor south to claim the Rio Grande River as the southern border of the United States rather than the traditional Nueces River. After initial border skirmishes, tensions quickly rose between the two parties as the United States stationed a naval fleet off the Mexican coast at Vera Cruz. Diplomatic efforts to settle the dispute included U.S. demands that the acquisition of New Mexico and California, not just Texas, be on the table. Rather than continue to negotiate, Santa Anna instructed his delegation to refuse these terms and war began. From the beginning, the war went badly for Mexico, and, as a result of the Treaty of Hidalgo signed in 1848, Mexico ceded more than 1 million square miles, nearly half its national territory, for the sum of $15 million. Several years later in 1853 under strong U.S. pressure, additional Mexican territory in what is today Arizona and New Mexico was transferred to the United States in the Gadsen Purchase. Ironically, it is to this vast territory that millions of Mexican workers have migrated in the last fifty years, thus reshaping its culture and language and, in the eyes of some, reclaiming lost lands.

As westward expansion increased, the United States showed more interest in Central America as a transit point to the United States' newly acquired West Coast. As the California gold rush started to increase the demand for an easy route to California, Cornelius Vanderbilt established a trans-isthmus transportation route through Nicaragua. This began a period of increasing interest in the Central American isthmus and a U.S. canal through it and would include numerous armed interventions in Nicaragua and the orchestration of the creation of the Panamanian state and the construction of the Panama Canal.

# Dreams of Cuba

The United States also coveted Cuba throughout the nineteenth century, and there was frequent talk of annexation. From Jefferson onward, U.S. presidents viewed Cuba as a natural extension of U.S. territory. U.S. strategy came to be known as the "Ripe Fruit Theory" from a quote by John Quincy Adams:

> There are laws of political as well as physical gravitation; and if an apple severed by the tempest from its native tree cannot choose but to fall to the ground, Cuba, forcibly

disjoined from its own unnatural connection with Spain, and incapable of self-support, can gravitate only towards the North American Union, which by the same law of nature cannot cast her off from the bosom.

The press to annex Cuba reached its zenith in the 1840s and 1850s, following the success of the war with Mexico as James Polk authorized negotiations with Spain to purchase the island. Ultimately these plans failed due to Spain's unwillingness to cede its last remaining major colony in the Americas, northern fears of the admission of a new slave state, and the opposition of the British and French, who were wary of expanding U.S. power. U.S. designs on Cuba would be placed on hold until 1898, but, in the interim, U.S. commercial interests reached out to Cuba, and, by the end of the century, the United States had surpassed Spain as the island's leading trading partner.

## Economic Transformation

With the economic growth and industrialization of the United States and its transformation into a capitalist power on the rise, trade, commerce, investment opportunities, and markets in Latin America became ever more important. As Lars Schoultz notes, from 1865 to 1896, the value of imports from Latin America more than doubled. The consumption of coffee and sugar alone rose sixfold. In the 1880s, Secretary of State James Blaine began a series of initiatives to revive the idea of hemispheric cooperation linked to Bolívar and his exclusively Hispanic America focus in the Congress of Panama in 1826. This new formulation of hemispheric unity would include—despite Bolívar's warnings—the now even more powerful United States. By the end of the decade, commerce and trade became the focus of U.S. interests. Thus, in 1889 U.S. Secretary of State James Blaine created the International Bureau of American Republics, which in turn was transformed into the Pan-American Union in 1890, as a mechanism to facilitate commercial and other interactions between the United States and the Latin American states. Located in Washington, D.C., and sometimes pejoratively referred to as the "U.S. Colonial Office for Latin America," the Pan-American Union would become the symbol of Pan-Americanism and U.S.-dominated hemispheric relations. Half a century later, it would in turn engender the Rio Treaty (the Inter-American Treaty of Reciprocal Assistance; 1947) and the Organization of American States (1948).

The end of the nineteenth century saw an important shift in U.S. policy toward Latin America and the simultaneous emergence of the United States as a significant international player. The defeat of the slave-owning South and the subsequent victory of the northern captains of industry, combined with the conquest of the American West set the stage for the emergence of the United States as a major industrial power in need of raw materials, markets, and places to invest capital. This transformation of the United States in the final third of the nineteenth century meant that the newly industrialized nation turned from the acquisition of new territory to the creation of a U.S. sphere of influence based on economic and political ties, backed by military force. As Peter Smith observes, this shift at the end of the nineteenth century was based in part on the growing racism of that era, which acknowledged that bringing territories such as Puerto Rico and Cuba directly into the United States would clash with the predominantly Anglo-Saxon character of the nation. Second, there was a revaluation by the Europeans of the utility of holding colonies and greater emphasis on commercial advantage. The United States, late to the imperial game, would seek to gain from its newfound position without the costs of maintaining an empire shouldered by the Europeans. In many ways this approach had been successfully utilized in South America in the nineteenth century where the British and French gained significant commercial advantage in Brazil and Argentina without establishing a colonial relationship.

The primary test for the new U.S. strategy came with Cuba in 1898. By that year Cuban independence forces, having relaunched their fight in 1895, were gaining significant ground against the Spanish. Not wanting the independence forces to triumph on their own and sensing Spain's likely defeat, U.S. forces entered the war on the side of the independence forces and secured a quick victory. The imperial nature of the U.S. intervention was made evident when U.S. forces did not allow Cuban independence leaders to be present at the surrender of Spanish forces in Santiago, Cuba, in 1898. Through this act the United States made clear that it would determine the future status of Cuba. Some elements in the United States favored annexation, as it had been desired for a century, but the new imperial strategy won the day. Following a brief U.S. military occupation, Cuba was granted its nominal independence in 1902. The island became a virtual protectorate of the United States over the next fifty-plus years down to the triumph of the Cuban Revolution in 1959. Symbolic of this domination was the Platt Amendment. Written by U.S. Senator Orville Platt and inserted into the Cuban constitution, it granted the right of the United States to intervene on the island "for the preservation of Cuban independence and the maintenance of a government adequate for the protection of life, property, and individual liberty." It remained in effect until 1934 and subordinated Cuban sovereignty to U.S. control. The amendment also provided for a North American naval base at Guantanamo, a site still occupied by the United States against the objections of the Cuban government. Cuban products now went almost exclusively to the United States. U.S. companies invested in all aspects of the Cuban economy—sugar farms and processing plants, mining, communication, and railways. The U.S. Federal Reserve Bank established its only foreign branch in Havana. By 1926, U.S. direct investment on the island totaled nearly $1.4 billion. The Cuban events underscored the importance of the Caribbean basin, including the Central American mainland in U.S. foreign policy.

## Gunboat Diplomacy, the Big Stick, and Dollar Diplomacy

In the period from 1898 to 1933, this region proved to be an important testing ground for the development of twentieth-century U.S. military, economic, and political power. The U.S. leaders sought to reduce European influence in the region, protect important commercial shipping lanes for expanded U.S. trade, and build a transoceanic canal that would facilitate commerce between the West and East Coasts of the United States. This period came to be known as the era of "gunboat diplomacy" and "dollar diplomacy" and would see more than thirty armed interventions.

The most important armed intervention after the Spanish–Cuban–American War came in Panama in 1903. In that year, U.S. forces intervened to quell unrest and to ultimately broker an agreement, the Hay and Herran Treaty, which was signed with Colombia, allowing the construction of a canal through its Panamanian territory. However, the Colombian legislature, fearing violation of its territorial sovereignty, refused to ratify the agreement. The United States responded by inciting a rebellion for independence in Panama and then supporting the independence movement by recognizing the new state of Panama. When Colombia tried to intervene, Teddy Roosevelt ordered the stationing of U.S. warships off the coast to prevent Colombian troops from entering the rebellious province. The United States then arranged an agreement with Panama for a 10-mile-wide canal zone to be subject to U.S. control through a long-term lease so that the Panama Canal could be built. The zone would remain in U.S. hands until the 1977 Panama Canal treaties were negotiated under U.S. President Jimmy Carter and Panamanian president Omar Torrijos, and full control of the Canal Zone was subsequently returned to Panama. The canal was opened in 1914 and immediately became a major international waterway. Protection of the shipping lanes in the Caribbean leading to the canal became a major focus of U.S. policy in the region, and Panama became a long-term compliant ally, opening the Canal Zone to several U.S. bases and the U.S. military's School of the Americas, which engaged in the controversial training of Latin American military officers for decades.

## THE ROOSEVELT COROLLARY

The actions in Cuba and Panama became part of a broader U.S. strategy in the region. Following European intervention in Venezuela in 1902, Theodore Roosevelt declared what became known as the Roosevelt Corollary to the Monroe Doctrine, that the United States, to avoid pretext for European intervention, would maintain order in the hemisphere. The doctrine had little real meaning beyond the U.S. sphere of influence in the Caribbean basin, but it would be the basis of many armed interventions over the next thirty years in Nicaragua, El Salvador, Haiti, the Dominican Republic, and Cuba to name a few.

Although no longer interested in Nicaragua as the preferred location for a transoceanic canal, U.S. involvement continued there with a Marine incursion in 1909. The Mexican Revolution prompted renewed involvement in Mexico, including the naval bombardment of Vera Cruz in 1914 and military incursions in northern Mexico in pursuit of Pancho Villa, the Mexican revolutionary. Theodore Roosevelt's "big stick" became legendary in the Caribbean basin and was a symbolic manifestation of gunboat diplomacy. The U.S. proclivity to send in naval gunboats and marines to sanction, control, and direct the affairs of sovereign nations in Central America and the Caribbean became commonplace. The marines were not only in Nicaragua again (1912–1925 and 1926–1933) but also in Haiti (1915–1934) and the Dominican Republic (1916–1922). As witness to—and participant in—such actions, U.S. Marine Corps Major General Smedley Butler noted:

> I spent thirty-three years being a high-class muscleman for Big Business, for Wall Street and the bankers. In short, I was a racketeer for capitalism. . . . I helped purify Nicaragua for the international banking house of Brown Brothers in 1909–1912.

I helped make Mexico and especially Tampico safe for American oil interests in 1916. I helped make Haiti and Cuba a decent place for National City [Bank] boys to collect revenues in. I helped in the rape of half a dozen Central American republics for the benefit of Wall Street.

## DOLLAR DIPLOMACY

As financial interests intensified, these more primitive instruments of U.S. policy were replaced by "dollar diplomacy," where financial inducements and pressure became the most common means of influencing Latin American nations and favorable financial connections to the United States were emphasized. The United States was concerned that European powers under the guise of collecting debts would intervene militarily in the region, as they had done in Venezuela. In response, the United States developed the new policy, which emphasized the support of private financial interests through U.S. government intervention. U.S. banks were encouraged to assume the debt of countries in the Caribbean basin with the promise that the U.S. government would use whatever means necessary to collect the debts. It was presented by President Howard Taft as representing a shift from "bullets to dollars," but in reality the guarantee to collect debt often resulted in direct military intervention to guarantee payments to the U.S. banks. The Dominican Republic was a good example of this scenario. In 1907 that nation's government signed a fifty-year agreement with the United States to assume control of its debts owed to European powers. Within a decade, in 1916, the United States Marines occupied the island to deal with an armed rebellion against the government and, in the process, asserted its control over the country's treasury, army, and police in addition to the customs houses. U.S. occupation of the island only ended in 1924 when the local government agreed to keep its army under the command of U.S. officers.

## LATIN AMERICAN REACTION

Such heavy-handed interventionist policies on the part of the United States began to elicit considerable Latin American reaction. More removed from the Caribbean basin and the United States' direct sphere of influence, Argentina chaffed under the United States' heavy-handed relations with its fellow Latin American republics. A prominent Argentine jurist, Carlos Calvo, articulated what came to be known as the Calvo Doctrine. In his seminal *Derecho Internacional Teórico y Práctico de Europa y America* (European and American Theoretical and Practical International Law; Paris, 1868), he argued that jurisdiction over a dispute involving a foreign company must be resolved in the courts of the nation where the investments were made. It further prohibited military intervention or even any diplomatic intervention before all recourse to the local courts was exhausted. This doctrine became widely applied throughout Latin America and is at times manifest in a Calvo Clause along these lines inserted in a national constitution. The Drago Doctrine is a narrower application of Calvo's principle. Announced in 1902 by Argentine foreign minister Luis Maria Drago, it stipulated that no foreign power could use force against a Latin American nation to collect debts owed.

By the end of the 1920s, it became clear that better relations were needed if the United States was going to continue to have extensive foreign relations with its Latin

American neighbors. The forces of fascism were also on the horizon, and this helped to further convince the United States that it needed to improve Latin American–U.S. relations. In 1933, the Seventh International Conference of American States was convened in Montevideo, Uruguay. This meeting, which was attended by all the Latin American states and the United States, elaborated what would become one of the most comprehensive statements of modern international law regarding states and their rights. Signed at Montevideo on December 26, 1933, the Montevideo Convention on the Rights and Duties of States stipulates some of the fundamental rights that the Latin American nations considered essential to protect their sovereignty and that were necessary to reign in the actions of their northern neighbor.

Article 1 defines what is necessary to be a state (population, defined territory, a government with capacity to rule and conduct international relations). Reacting to U.S. practice of withholding recognition, Article 3 states, "The political existence of the state is independent of recognition by the other states." Article 4 speaks to equality: "States are jurisdictionally equal, enjoy the same rights, and have equal capacity in their exercise. The rights of each one do not depend upon the power which it possesses to assure its exercise, but upon the simple fact of its existence as a person under international law." Key to the convention and a decided reaction to U.S. interventions, Article 8 states clearly, "No state has the right to intervene in the internal or external affairs of another."

Consistent with the aforementioned Calvo and Drago Doctrines, Article 9 notes, "The jurisdiction of states within the limits of national territory applies to all the inhabitants. Nationals and foreigners are under the same protection of the law and the national authorities and the foreigners may not claim rights other or more extensive than those of the nationals." Taking advantage of the changing winds in U.S. policy and using their majority and developing concepts in public international law, the Latin American states were thus able to fashion a clear normative guide to state practice—one that would, they hoped, moderate U.S. actions.

## GOOD NEIGHBOR POLICY

The era of gunboat and dollar diplomacy came to an end in 1933 with the new administration of Franklin Delano Roosevelt and his declaration of a Good Neighbor Policy for Latin America (the term was first used by President Hoover). In the ensuing years, U.S. policy in the region would undergo a significant shift. As suggested in the Montevideo meeting, the repeated armed interventions and occupations were ending and would be replaced with nominal recognition of the sovereignty of Latin American countries and the view that the security of the region was a collective responsibility.

The Good Neighbor Policy also contained a commitment to shared democratic values and cooperative negotiations of disputes. The policy shift is credited with giving Washington near unanimous support from the region during World War II. However, the shift was a tactical one, not strategic. In reality, the costs of maintaining constant armed interventions had become too costly, and U.S. leaders sought new methods to maintain U.S. hegemony in the region. The high cost of intervention was epitomized by the case of Nicaragua. From 1909 onward, U.S. marines were in almost constant occupation of the nation to deal with Liberal challenges to

U.S. dominance of the country. The occupation turned highly problematic in the late 1920s when a Nicaraguan rebel leader, Augusto César Sandino, fought the marines to a standstill in a bloody seven-year war. The war generated antiwar sentiment in the United States, anti-Yankee sentiment throughout Latin America, and contributed significantly to a reconsideration of U.S. policy in the region by the Hoover administration.

Nicaragua under the Roosevelt administration also became a model for the Good Neighbor Policy, revealing its dark underbelly. Not wishing U.S. troops to be bogged down in the country, the United States worked with the country's elites to create a new force, the Nicaraguan National Guard that would be funded and trained by the United States and replace the duties of the marines. The guard's leader, Anastasio Somoza, chosen by the United States in 1933, also became the country's leader. One of the guard's first acts was the assassination of Sandino after a meeting with the new president in 1933 and the defeat of his remaining rebel army. Somoza and first one son (Luis) and then the other (Anastasio Jr.) would establish a forty-five-year family rule that would last until the Sandinista revolution of 1979. That rule was validated by elections every four years that were hailed by the United States as evidence of Latin American democracy despite the fact that radical parties were outlawed and the opposition conservatives accepted their permanent subordinate position. The Somoza family responded as dutiful U.S. allies, setting an example for neighboring countries.

## Democracy and World War II

Despite U.S. lip service to democracy, by the time of the World War II, many countries in the Caribbean basin had fallen under dictatorial rule. Democracy was, however, advocated during the war. It should also be pointed out that not all of the Latin American countries followed the United States into World War II. Chile was hesitant and remained neutral for a time after the United States declared war on the Axis Powers, and Argentina observed neutrality throughout the conflict. Conversely, both Mexico and Brazil collaborated in the war effort and sent contingents of troops to fight. Brazil also opened its territory to U.S. bases to facilitate the ferrying of U.S. planes to North Africa and Europe. In the process, many women (Women Airforce Service Pilots) became active in the ferrying of military aircraft to North Africa and then Europe through Brazil, and the Brazilian military established a working relationship with their counterparts in the U.S. military.

The Good Neighbor Policy also had an important economic dimension. In what became the mantra of bipartisan trade policy of the United States for the ensuing decades, Roosevelt argued that the United States could best enhance its world position through skillful economic diplomacy. Commercial ties with Latin American countries needed to be a higher priority than military interventions. The depression years, 1929–1932, were a disaster for U.S. trade within the region, with both exports and imports falling more than 50 percent. Cordell Hull, the new Secretary of State appointed by Roosevelt, put liberalization of trade at the top of his agenda and over the next several years established trade agreements with several Latin American countries, including Colombia, Cuba, Honduras, Costa Rica, and Guatemala.

Though the United States was not successful in negotiating other agreements due to Latin American resistance, by 1938 the United States, through its emphasis on commercial lines, had succeeded in becoming the largest trading partner for every Latin American country with the exception of Argentina. This was accomplished despite a vigorous move into the region by Germany in the 1930s. Of course, that German campaign would end with the beginning of World War II, leaving the region more dependent on the United States.

World War II completely restructured the character of international affairs. The formerly dominant powers of Britain and France lost their positions forever and would be forced to relinquish almost all their colonial possessions after the war. The defeated powers of Germany and Japan would recover quickly as economic powers, but in 1945 only the United States and the Soviet Union stood as superpowers. Their inevitable rivalry soon crystallized into the Cold War with its competing nuclear arsenals. For Latin America, the emergence of the United States as a superpower presented a challenge that remained in place for over seventy years, notwithstanding the end of the Cold War in 1992.

## The Rio Treaty and the Organization of American States

Probably the most important result of the expanded U.S. power after World War II was that the United States to a greater degree sought dominant influence beyond the Caribbean basin to all of Latin America. To this end, continental-wide structures were set up, beginning with a comprehensive collective security agreement, the Inter-American Treaty of Reciprocal Assistance, or Rio Treaty (1947). Article 3 lays out the main thrust of the treaty obligations: the parties agreed that "an armed attack by any State against an American State shall be considered an attack against all the American States and, consequently, each one of the said contracting parties undertakes to assist in meeting the attack in the exercise of the inherent rights of individual or collective self-defense recognized by Article 51 of the Charter of the United Nations." Article 6 also gives the body the right to convene for possible action if a party is "affected by an aggression that is not an armed attack." Thus the United States individually, or with the help of other sympathetic American states, could become involved with the affairs of its fellow republics if any perceived threat were registered. The following year, the old Pan-American Union was updated and transformed into a new hemispheric organization. The new organization was named the Organization of American States (OAS in English; OEA in Spanish, Portuguese, and French) and was conveniently headquartered in the old Pan-American Union building in Washington, D.C. It incorporated some functions of the old Pan-American Union, added others, and was premised on collective action. As a regional organization under the United Nations Charter, it too could employ collective security in case of attack on a member state and could engage in "common action" in the event of aggression (Article 4). Thus a U.S.-dominated coalition of American states could be legally empowered to act against an aggressor state or sanction a member state for its actions that were short of direct aggression. This would, from time to time, be used to sanction U.S.-led intervention in Latin American countries, such as the invasion of the Dominican Republic in 1965 and the invasion of Grenada in 1983. Although not always vigorously implemented, much of the thinking of the 1933 Montevideo Convention was also reflected in the charter of the OAS. Thus there was a strong prohibition against intervention: "No State or Group of States has the right to intervene, directly or indirectly, in the internal or external affairs of any other state"(original Article 15). Further, Article 17 states, "The territory of a State is inviolable; it may not be the object, even temporarily, of military occupation or other measures of force taken by another State, directly or indirectly, on any grounds whatsoever." But "measures adopted for the maintenance of peace and security in accordance with existing treaties do not constitute a violation of the principles set forth in Articles 15 and 17." Thus, a strong coalition of Latin American and Caribbean states could, at least, condemn U.S. intervention when it occurred in Panama in 1989 (even though they were hard put to find means to enforce their decision) but could also sanction sending in a U.S.-led OAS mission as was done in Haiti in the early 1990s after President Aristide was overthrown by a military coup. The OAS consists of an assembly of all the states that meets annually, a Permanent Council of Ambassadors appointed by member states, and a secretary general. Meetings of consultation are also called as needed, and several specialized agencies exist, such as the Inter-American Commission on Human Rights and the Pan American Health Organization, which is affiliated with the World Health Organization.

## Guatemalan Case

After World War II, the renewed power of the United States severely constrained the options open to the Latin American countries. Protection from a European power was no longer an option, and the creation of regional alliances to combat the power of the United States was problematic, especially in light of the previously mentioned hemispheric organizations. However, even more difficult was the pursuit of an alternative path of economic and political development that in the lenses of the Cold War could be seen as socialist or Marxist in its orientation. These constraints did not prevent Latin Americans from trying to pursue alternative forms of development, but most of these efforts, with the dramatic exception of the Cuban Revolution, met with determined and successful resistance by the United States during the era of the Cold War and sometimes often employed the structure of the OAS to do so.

Early in this era, the most dramatic example of the price that Latin Americans paid for pursuing a path unsupported by the United States was in Guatemala (see the discussion of Guatemala in Chapter 3). After the 1944 revolution put in place Juan José Arévalo (1945–1950), the democratically elected government of Jacobo Arbenz (1951–1954) pursued a project of radical reform based primarily on indigenous and worker rights and land reform aimed at lands unused by wealthy landowners and the U.S.-based United Fruit Company. Beyond the challenge to U.S. economic interests, U.S. government officials were alarmed by the presence of a few Guatemalan communists at high levels of influence in the Arbenz government. After an extensive lobbying campaign by the United Fruit Company and the heightened Cold War hysteria, the Eisenhower administration began to view the Guatemalan situation as a dire threat to U.S. security and soon mounted a major CIA operation to overthrow Arbenz. The orchestration of the overthrow was not dissimilar to a successful operation in Iran in 1953 (that overthrew the popular constitutional government of Mossadeq, reinstalled the shah, and set the stage for the rise of the Islamic revolution later). The U.S. operation led to the overthrow of the Guatemalan government in 1954 by General Castillo Armas and the imposition of military dictatorship. The cost of this intervention would be long standing for Guatemala. For most of the forty years following the 1954 coup, heavy repression and brutal violent conflict characterized the nation. The struggle was so intense that some 200,000 people (mostly civilians killed by government forces) lost their lives. Only in the last twenty years has the country moved away from this era and haltingly readopted reformist and democratic principles. Guatemala paid a high price for its reformist path, and the lessons weighed heavily on Latin Americans for decades.

However, one case stood out as different. In the 1950s, the 26th of July Movement under the leadership of Fidel Castro, Camilo Cienfuegos, and Che Guevara carried out a successful armed rebellion against the Cuban dictator, Fulgencio Batista. The revolutionaries succeeded in gaining power because U.S. political leaders abandoned Batista in the final months of the rebellion, believing that the rebels, not avowed communists, could be controlled and moderated much like the Bolivian revolutionaries after 1952. This proved to be a major miscalculation by Washington as the revolutionaries moved quickly to institute a series of radical reforms. As the revolutionary government began to implement reforms, the United States responded with harsh sanctions, including the embargo on goods to Cuba. Finally, the new Cuban leaders reached out to the Soviet Union for support and quickly received it, sharply reducing the options available to Washington. Over the ensuing years, the United States would engage in numerous efforts to reverse the Cuban Revolution, including the 1961 Bay of Pigs invasion, but none would prove successful, and over fifty years later Cuba stands independent of the inter-American system dominated by the United States, notwithstanding the establishment in 2015 of full diplomatic relations between the two countries.

## Alliance for Progress

The U.S. setback in Cuba resulted in a fixation by U.S. policymakers to avoid another Cuba. The immediate response of the Kennedy administration to Cuba was the formulation of the Alliance for Progress. Acknowledging that the Cuban Revolution was born of conditions of dictatorship and poverty on the island, Kennedy argued that the United States needed to promote peaceful reform in the region to forestall violent revolution. Thus U.S. policy and aid in the region needed to emphasize democracy, land reform, and industrialization. In many ways it was a restatement of the most idealistic principles of the earlier Good Neighbor Policy. In a few Latin American countries, the spirit of the Alliance would be carried out, but the realities of the Cold War and U.S. instincts for hegemony in the hemisphere trumped the high-minded principles of the Alliance. Thus a growing emphasis on counterinsurgency, military missions, training members of the Latin American armed forces in the U.S. School of the Americas, and the national security state emerged. Betrayal of the Alliance was especially sharp when viewed against the background of armed U.S. intervention in the Dominican Republic in April 1965. This was done as a democratic movement under Juan Bosch was beginning to consolidate power in the island nation.

## National Security Doctrine

In reality, U.S. policy in Latin America after the Cuban Revolution was dominated by a military and security focus that placed the promotion of reform and democracy in a secondary position. The centerpiece of this approach was the concept of a national security doctrine developed jointly by the U.S. policymakers and their counterparts in the Latin American elites to counter the possible influence of the Soviet Union in the region through the repression of all potentially revolutionary forces. The most prominent national security doctrine developed in Brazil through the Superior War School (ESG) founded in 1949 with French and U.S. advisors. As the Cold War escalated, the doctrine viewed Brazil in a state of permanent war where revolutionary forces that could ally with the Soviet Union must be defeated at all costs, including the suspension of civil liberties and democracy. The doctrine was Brazilian nationalist in its orientation but accepted that close ties with the United States and Western Europe were necessary.

In Brazil, the primary manifestation of the national security doctrine was the military coup of 1964 against President João Goulart and the twenty years of military rule that followed. Fearing that Goulart's policies of reform, especially in the rural areas, were fomenting unrest and encouraging revolutionary forces, the generals seized power to "eliminate the danger of subversion and communism." In a short time, more than 50,000 people were arrested and the country's democratic institutions suspended. The Brazilian coup was a key test of the Alliance for Progress. In many ways, Goulart's programs of reform were modeled after the Alliance, yet the United States, now under the leadership of Lyndon Johnson, raised no objections to the coup and quickly developed strong ties with the ruling generals. Acceptance of the Brazilian coup established an important precedent that would see subsequent U.S. presidents either accept or support military rule throughout the region. In 1972 in El Salvador, the Nixon administration stood on the sidelines when the military voided an election won by José Napoleon Duarte, a reform-minded Christian Democrat, who symbolized a decade of the Alliance for Progress programs in that small, Central American country.

## September 11 Coup in Chile

U.S. support for military rule was even better demonstrated on September 11, 1973, when Chilean military forces removed President Salvador Allende from power in a coup that took his life. The United States was complicit in the coup through a range of measures instituted following Allende's election in 1970. It embargoed the country, stating explicitly that the Chilean people would suffer for electing a "Marxist" as their leader. The U.S. economic measures severely damaged the Chilean economy, and behind the scenes the U.S. government maintained military aid and close ties to the Chilean military and urged them to overthrow Allende. For fifteen years after the 1973 coup, the Chilean military governed by brutal, dictatorial means and carried out policies in the framework of a national security doctrine similar to that of the Brazilian generals. Despite international outcry against its violations of human rights including the death and disappearance of at least 10,000 people, the generals maintained the support of the United States until they were defeated in a referendum in 1988, and democracy was returned in 1990.

# Counterinsurgency

The long era of the Cold War deepened the willingness of the United States to place the defense of the status quo in Latin America ahead of all other objectives. The different guerrilla insurgencies that broke out all over Latin America after the Cuban Revolution and challenged traditional oligarchic rule and U.S. domination were seen as a direct threat that, if unchecked, could lead to the implantation of communism all over the region. These insurgencies needed to be stopped, and the United States developed the doctrine of counterinsurgency to do so, often copying counterinsurgency techniques developed in the U.S. war against the Viet Minh and Viet Cong in Vietnam. U.S. military and financial missions carried this doctrine throughout Latin America and invited members of the Latin American militaries to learn it. Through support for such extensive training in counterinsurgency, military coups, the training of Latin American officers at the School of the Americas in Panama and later at Fort Bragg in North Carolina, and close relationships with Latin American financial elites, the leaders of the United States placed themselves in contradiction to not only radical change but to decades of efforts by Latin Americans of many different political orientations to alter that status quo and build more equitable societies. This, and the generous military aid that accompanied it, not only strengthened the Latin American militaries in their fight against different guerrilla groups but also encouraged the militaries to resist many legitimate reform efforts and overthrow civilian governments that were not of their liking. This was a major factor in the long periods of often-brutal military rule (bureaucratic authoritarianism) that developed in Latin America in the 1960s, 1970s, and 1980s.

# Cold War in Central America

The final chapter of the U.S. Cold War policies in Latin America came in response to the Central American revolutionary movements of the 1970s and 1980s. By the mid-1970s strong revolutionary movements had developed in Guatemala, El Salvador, and Nicaragua. In each case the revolutionary movements faced off against military dictatorships that had long received significant U.S. backing under the Cold War national security doctrine. The assistance was significant, including military and economic aid and military training. The Central American events presented a special challenge to the administration of Jimmy Carter, which came to office pledging a foreign policy based on human rights. With regard to Latin America, Carter had completed the negotiation of the Panama Canal treaties, reopened diplomatic relations with Cuba, and condemned U.S. support for the coup in Chile. In Central America, Carter distanced himself from the military governments, including

Somoza in Nicaragua. The Carter administration worked behind the scenes to prevent the triumph of the Sandinista revolutionaries, but once the FSLN was in power in 1979, it recognized the new government and sought to moderate its course through limited U.S. aid.

In El Salvador, the United States supported a progressive coup in the fall of 1979 that briefly brought to power a figurehead civilian government. However, traditional right-wing military forces quickly reestablished control and carried out the assassination of the progressive Archbishop Oscar Romero in March 1980. Romero's assassination spurred the further development of the revolutionary forces united under the banner of the Farabundo Marti National Liberation Front (FMLN), and, by early 1981, they were seemingly on the verge of power. One of Carter's last acts was sending military aid to the Salvadoran generals to successfully fend off an FMLN offensive.

The Reagan administration came to office in January 1981 critical of the Carter approaches in Latin America, which was judged to have been soft on communism. Though he did not reverse the Panama Canal treaties, Reagan had been critical of Carter for that initiative. He ended the overtures to Cuba and reimposed the ban on most U.S. citizen travel to the island. However, the greatest change in policy came in Central America where Reagan committed himself to the defense of the Salvadoran government with a massive package of economic and military aid (approved by a Democrat-led Congress) and a covert plan to overthrow the Sandinista government in Nicaragua through the funding of a rebel army that came to be known as the contras. The latter program was part of a worldwide initiative that came to known as the Reagan Doctrine also involving support for anticommunist rebels in Afghanistan, Cambodia, Angola, and Mozambique. The doctrine was part of a broader reigniting of the Cold War against the Soviet Union following years of detente under Nixon, Ford, and Carter. The Reagan policies in Central America ultimately fostered significant civil society opposition in the United States as tens of thousands of civilians died in wars in Nicaragua, El Salvador, and Guatemala. In the latter case, the Reagan administration did not openly support the Guatemalan military but did nothing to stop the Rios Montt dictatorship from killing thousands of peasants in an early 1980s' counterinsurgency campaign. In the face of citizen pressure, the U.S. Congress cut off aid to the Nicaraguan contras in the mid-1980s, but Reagan continued the operation in secrecy, resulting in his near-impeachment in the Iran–Contra affair. Ultimately, the United States' Central America policies of the 1980s achieved their primary objectives, notwithstanding the devastation that occurred in the three countries (more than 100,000 people killed). The Salvadoran government fended off the revolutionary efforts of the rebels forcing the FMLN to sign a 1992 peace agreement that converted it into a reformist political movement that went on to be a significant force in Salvadoran politics including the holding of the presidency today. In Nicaragua the Sandinistas militarily defeated the contras in 1989 but were driven from office by a war-weary population in a 1990 election. The conservative governments that followed reversed the revolutionary course of the FSLN and brought the country back under U.S. influence. However, the FSLN returned to power in 2007, won re-election in 2011 and 2017, and today dominates the country's politics as a social democratic party. Both governments today enjoy cordial relations with Washington. In Guatemala the rebels were also forced to sue for peace, and eventually in 1994 a peace deal brought an end to the country's forty-year civil war.

## Latin America and the Post–Cold War World

Almost twenty years into the new century, relations in the Western Hemisphere are at a crucial juncture. For the first time in decades there is the possibility of a fundamental shift in the balance of power between the United States and its southern neighbors. What are the key elements in hemispheric affairs at this juncture in the twenty-first century? To answer this question, it is necessary to step back nearly thirty years to the end of the decade of the 1980s, the time of the end of the Cold War. At that moment a variety of factors worldwide and in the Western Hemisphere came together to favor the interests of the United States. The demise of Eastern European socialism, epitomized by the fall of the wall in Berlin in November 1989 and later the unexpected collapse of the Soviet Union, delivered to the United States an unprecedented opportunity to wield its power in international affairs. The renewed ability of the United States to project its military power in world affairs was evidenced in the Persian Gulf War in early 1991, the first major use of force by the United States since its political and military defeat in Vietnam nearly twenty years earlier. U.S. leaders spoke openly in the wake of their easy military victory against Iraq that the "Vietnam Syndrome" had been broken and that the American people had once again sanctioned the use of military power to defend U.S. interests abroad. U.S. leaders were also clear that the changed stance of the Soviet Union had been crucial to the success of its operation in the Persian Gulf. Less than a year after the war, the Soviet Union departed the scene, no longer threatening the United States with its nuclear weapons and leaving the United States as the world's sole military superpower.

Beyond military superiority, the United States also took the ideological offensive. In 1991 President George H. W. Bush declared that the world was entering a new era that would be dominated by democracy and free enterprise. In this perspective, the demise of the Soviet Union proved once and for all the bankruptcy of socialism and dictatorship. President Bush made such declarations despite the fact that the Persian Gulf War had been fought in the interests of Saudi Arabia and Kuwait, two long-standing monarchical dictatorships. While the events in Eastern Europe and the Middle East transformed world affairs, there were important companion developments in Latin America that also favored the interests of the United States. As events unfolded in Eastern Europe, two watershed elections occurred in Latin America that served U.S. interests. In Argentina, Carlos Menem won the presidency and pledged a new direction for Argentina friendly to the United States and its economic ideology, a reversal of forty years of Peronist ideology and less than a decade after the United States sided with Britain in its war with Argentina over the Falklands-Malvinas. In Brazil, the right-wing candidate Fernando Collor de Mello defeated Workers' Party candidate Luis Inácio (Lula) da Silva in an election that had been predicted to go Lula's way until the collapse of Eastern European socialism in the middle of the campaign. In December 1989, the United States, in its first major military action in the hemisphere since Grenada in 1983, invaded Panama and re-moved its former ally Manuel Noriega from power on the pretext of being involved in the drug trade. The invasion of Panama was followed in February 1990 by the electoral defeat of the Sandinistas in Nicaragua, an election they had been expected to win prior to the events in Eastern Europe and Panama. The Sandinista defeat was crucial because it marked the end of an era of revolution in Central America that had begun fifteen years earlier and placed the United States on the defensive in Nicaragua, El Salvador, and Guatemala. The Sandinista defeat was especially bitter for progressive forces because the revolutionaries had been successful in defeating the U.S.-backed contras in a ten-year war.

These political developments allowed the United States to go on the political and economic offensive in the hemisphere, arguing that the triumph of capitalism was complete and that Latin America had to end its decades of economic national-ism and protectionism and open its markets to U.S. goods and investment. This economic penetration had always been true in Central America and the Caribbean but now was to be extended to South America, especially Brazil and Argentina. The centerpiece of the U.S. strategy was the Free Trade Area of the Americas (FTAA) launched with great fanfare by U.S. President Bill Clinton at the Summit of the Americas in Miami in December 1994 and scheduled to be implemented by 2005. It was to be a hemisphere-wide free trade area and was supported with enthusiasm by all the Latin American presidents invited to Miami. At that time in the middle 1990s, momentum for the FTAA and the wider U.S. agenda for Latin America seemed unstoppable. However, more than a decade later, the FTAA project was basically dead, and the United States was on the defensive in many parts of the region. What transpired in the intervening years, and what are the prospects for the future?

In some ways, it is not complicated to understand what happened in Latin America to change the political landscape. The political and economic promises made by Latin American political leaders with the support of Washington (the Washington Consensus) espousing neoliberal principles were not met. Through-out the region, economic programs that cut government services, encouraged the privatization of utilities and other government-owned entities, and opened Latin American economies to more foreign investments and foreign goods proved a disaster for the region's majority poor. Macroeconomic growth rates increased, and the wealthier segments of Latin American societies benefited, but overall the Washington-imposed policies proved a failure for the region. The varied manners in which Latin Americans have responded to the policy failures of that era have framed the present state of hemispheric affairs.

In many ways Venezuela has been at the center of the Latin American resis-tance to U.S. policies, late Venezuelan President Hugo Chávez, following in the footsteps of Simón Bolívar, was a leader of renewed Latin American efforts to reshape their relationship to the United States. Latin American resistance to the U.S. neoliberal agenda began in 1992 in Venezuela with a militant revolt against Carlos Andres Pérez and his policies. A leader of that revolt, army officer Hugo Chávez was jailed, but the seeds of resistance were sown. After his imprison-ment, Chávez formed the Fifth Republic Movement, which had a strong populist, anti-neoliberal platform. He continued his political struggle as a candidate for president in 1998, winning with some 58 percent of the vote. In the fifteen years that followed, Chávez won re-election three times, survived a recall vote, an attempted coup, and withstood an owners' lockout to remain firmly in power and served as the leading Latin American voice for a change in historic hemispheric relations. Chavez died of cancer in 2013, but his movement lives on through Nicolas Maduro, his designated successor. However, Maduro's political standing has been weakened in Venezuela by a severe economic crisis, undermining his hemispheric leadership.

Chávez's 1998 electoral victory foreshadowed a series of election victories by candidates of the left who have since triumphed in Argentina, Brazil, Uruguay, Ecuador, Chile, Nicaragua, Paraguay, and El Salvador. The victories by Lula in Brazil in 2002 (and his subsequent re-election in 2006) and the Kirchners in Argentina in 2003, 2007, and 2011 were especially significant because of the weight of their countries in hemispheric politics and the commitment of their immediate predecessors to definitive neoliberal strategies. Ultimately, it was the opposition of Lula and Kirchner to the completion of the FTAA treaty that doomed the project. When U.S. President George W. Bush took office in 2001, he made completion of the FTAA a priority of his first administration and had the backing of the U.S. Congress to complete the deal. The treaty was to have been finalized at a meeting of the hemisphere's finance ministers in Miami in November 2003, but events played out in a very different manner. One month earlier, Lula and Kirchner met in Buenos Aires and solidified their opposition to the FTAA, and at a special ministerial meeting convened in Washington prior to the Miami conference, the project was placed on indefinite hold over the strong objection of the United States. U.S. efforts to revive the treaty at the Summit of the Americas in Mar de Plata, Argentina, in November 2005 failed as Hugo Chávez led a rally of 50,000 against the FTAA outside the presidential meeting. Faced with the failure of the FTAA project, the United States was forced to retreat to the more modest project of the Central American Free Trade Agreement (CAFTA) and select bilateral agreements with countries such as Chile, Peru, Colombia, and Panama. In 2015, the Obama administration succeeded in including selected Latin American countries in a new free trade pact, the Trans Pacific Partnership (TPP), but that project's implementation was seriously threatened by the election of Donald Trump to the U.S. presidency in 2016. These agreements, if fully implemented, are not unimportant to U.S. interests in the region, but they fall far short of the U.S. domination that could have resulted from the FTAA.

## Latin American Initiatives

The major Latin American countries—Argentina, Brazil, and Venezuela—wary of U.S. dominance of the region, have pursued a series of initiatives over the past twenty years to create greater cohesion, especially among the countries of the Southern Cone. The initial major effort, the Common Market of the South (Mercosur), was a trade pact between Brazil, Argentina, Paraguay, and Uruguay formed in 1994. Mercosur has its origins in the neoliberal era of the 1990s, but in the new century it took on a new role as an alternative to the U.S.-led FTAA. It remains an important project that has facilitated greater trade among its members.

Bolstered by its strong oil and gas revenues in recent years, the Venezuelan government embarked on a path of challenging U.S. hegemony in the region through a series of well-funded initiatives headlined by the Bank of the South and the Bolivarian Alliance for the People of Our America (ALBA). The Bank of the South initiative, formally launched at the end of 2007, aimed at ending or reducing Latin America's dependence on loans from the World Bank, the International Monetary Fund, and the Inter-American Development Bank along with their stringent neoliberal conditionality. The bank had seven initial members (Venezuela, Argentina, Brazil, Ecuador, Bolivia, Paraguay, and Uruguay). All twelve South American countries would be eligible to receive loans from the bank. The founding of the bank came after successful bilateral assistance that Venezuela provided to Argentina in the last five years that allowed the latter to pay off its IMF debts and reverse the neoliberal economic policies that had been imposed on it. Independence from the IMF has proven to be positive for the Argentinean economy and to the recovery of its social indicators. In March 2009, Venezuela, Argentina, and Brazil agreed to contribute $2 billion each to the bank's start-up capital and the other four members a total of $1 billion. However, the bank has been slowed by internal differences over its purpose, and has never been formally implemented.

Another project challenging U.S. hegemony in the region under Venezuelan and Cuban leadership is the Bolivarian Alliance for the People of Our America (ALBA). Launched in 2005 as a bilateral project, then called the Bolivarian Alternative, it has been broadened to include Bolivia, Nicaragua, Ecuador, and the Caribbean island nations following the election of progressive presidents in those countries. Presenting itself as an alternative to the neoliberal model of the FTAA, ALBA involves the exchange of energy-producing products for services, primarily in the field of health care and education. Cuba contributes its human resources, cultivated over the long years of the Cuban Revolution, in return for oil and gas from Bolivia and Venezuela. The exchange is also especially important for Venezuela as Chávez and his successor, Maduro, seek to deliver on promises to improve the daily lives of

Meeting of the Bolivar Alliance (ALBA) Countries: Presidents from second on left to right include , Daniel Ortega (Nicaragua), Raúl Castro (Cuba), Nicolas Maduro (Venezuela), and Evo Morales (Bolivia) (*Photo by Jairo Cajina/ Xinhua/Photoshot*)

poor Venezuelans. As of this writing, the long-term impact of ALBA is uncertain, especially in light of Venezuela's economic and political challenges.

Venezuela is not alone in projecting Latin American independence from the United States in the new century. Presidents Lula and Rousseff of Brazil pursued that country's natural leadership of the region warranted by its sheer size and economic potential. That potential has never been more evident as Brazil dramatically expands its agricultural output and announces important new offshore oil discoveries. Brazil seems poised to become a major international player in the twenty-first century as it increasingly plays a leadership role in the nations of the global south, pressing at the United Nations for the restructuring of the Security Council and taking a leadership role in the World Trade Organization (WTO) negotiations. Brazil's stance lacks the radical rhetoric of Venezuela but may prove in the long run to be the greatest barrier to long-term U.S. dominance of the region. It is not yet clear whether the fall from power by the Worker's Party and their replacement by more pro-U.S. leaders will moderate Brazil's stance.

Brazil together with Argentina and other Latin American countries have also strengthened their ties in recent years with the People's Republic of China. The Chinese, eager to purchase raw materials and foodstuffs, have raised their level of trade in the region by more than tenfold in the last decade. China was not only able to drastically increase trade with countries like Brazil and Ecuador but also help to finance infrastructure projects and provide loans and investment funds from the China Export–Import Bank and Chinese Development Bank. Trade and increased economic interaction with China give the Latin American nations an additional option in international trade, thus reducing their traditional reliance on the United States and Europe.

Another Latin American initiative is the Union of South American Nations (UNASUR), an intergovernmental organization that integrates two existing projects, Mercosur and the Andean Community of Nations (ACN). It was formally launched in May 2008 and has the long-term goal of emulating the European Union. Brazil is the driving force behind the vision, and UNASUR is seen by some observers as a counterweight to the Latin American leadership aspirations of Venezuela and its primary project, ALBA. In December 2010 Uruguay became the ninth nation to ratify the UNASUR treaty, thus giving the union full legality in March 2011. Today there are twelve members. Its secretariat is in Quito, Ecuador, and the parliament is in Cochabamba, Bolivia. A key goal of UNASUR is the creation of a single market beginning with the elimination of some tariffs by 2014 and all tariffs by 2019. A South American Defense Council has also been formed under the umbrella of UNASUR, and there are also cooperative projects in the areas of immigration and energy. However, the momentum behind UNASUR has been slowed since 2011 due to ideological differences among its members and could be slowed further by the recent change of political leadership in both Argentina and Brazil.

## Prospects for the Future

What are the prospects for U.S.–Latin American relations in the coming years? There are a series of potential conflicts over resources, such as oil and water that can bring the United States and key Latin American countries into confrontation.

These conflicts could prove to be significant because now more than ever before Latin Americans are mobilized at the grassroots level to prevent the taking of their resources by powerful European and North American interests that have triumphed so often in the past. This resistance has been best symbolized in Bolivia and Ecuador where grassroots movements, mainly indigenous, have removed presidents from power through street demonstrations when they perceived that their natural resources were being auctioned off by their leaders to foreign interests. In both countries there are now presidents in office placed there by the votes of these movements, vowing to protect their natural resources. Other areas of strong contention include the U.S. desire for additional permanent U.S. bases in the region and its continuing desire to use the issue of drug interdiction as a wedge for U.S. intervention. U.S. efforts to expand its military bases in Latin America suffered a setback when the Ecuadoran government of Rafael Correa in 2009 refused to renew the lease for a U.S. base at Manta that had been agreed to by the previous pro-U.S. government.

For more than twenty-five years, drug interdiction has been the rationale behind U.S. military presence in the Andean region, especially in Peru and Colombia. Pro-U.S. governments in those countries will likely continue to accept a U.S. presence, and the ability of the United States to extend its military power on the pretext of drug interdiction has expanded to include Mexico, Central America, and the Caribbean. At the heart of the renewed security focus in Latin America in the twenty-first century has been a shift in U.S.–Mexico relations. Using the heightened role of Mexico as a transshipment point of drugs into the United States in recent years and the election of the pro–United States National Action Party (PAN) in 2000 and 2006, the two countries entered into the Merida Initiative that resulted in greater cooperation than ever before between the U.S. military and police establishment and their Mexican counterparts. The heightened cooperation has continued even with the election of the traditionally more nationalist Institutional Revolutionary Party (PRI) to the Mexican presidency. The model of the 2006 Merida Initiative was followed by regional agreements of a similar character. The Central American Regional Security Initiative (CASRI) and the Caribbean Basin Security Initiative (CBSI) further integrate these long-standing U.S. allies into arrangements that involve close military and police cooperation. The initiatives are justified by drug trafficking but are also aimed at bolstering U.S. political influence in the hemisphere at a time of renewed Latin American nationalism. However, the limitation of those policies to create prosperity and social stability has been especially clear in the Northern Triangle countries of El Salvador, Honduras, and Guatemala where gang violence and poverty have triggered significant new migration northward in the last five years, severely challenging the immigration authorities in both the United States and Mexico.

As Obama left office in 2017, the United States had succeeded in reversing the decline of U.S. influence in the region, the result of both U.S. policy initiatives and developments in Latin American politics. Beyond the previously discussed success in establishing closer security ties with Mexico, the Obama administration seemingly scored a major victory in 2015 with the successful negotiation of the Trans-Pacific Partnership (TPP), a neoliberal trade pact, that if successfully implemented divides Latin America along ideological grounds by including Mexico, Peru, and Chile, while excluding the ALBA nations, Brazil and Argentina. In the process it would undermine

Former President Obama at the Summit of the Americas meeting in Trinidad in 2009. *(Photo by Andrea Leighton/AP Images)*

the autonomous regional projects of ALBA, UNASUR, and MERCOSUR. However, the election of Donald Trump to the U.S. presidency, an opponent of TPP, makes final approval and implementation of the pact unlikely. Another policy victory for President Obama was the reestablishment of full diplomatic relations with Cuba in July 2015 effectively removing a policy issue that had caused major problems for the U.S. president at the Summits of the Americas in 2009 and 2012. However, as Obama passed the presidency to Republican Trump, the future of the U.S.–Cuban détente was in question. Equally important to restoring U.S. influence in the region has been the changing political fortunes of the progressive political forces in the region. In November 2015, a conservative candidate Mauricio Macri ended the progressive rule of the Argentine Peronists with an upset victory and immediately moved in a pro-U.S. direction that was rewarded with a presidential visit by Barack Obama in March 2016. Subsequently Maduro's PSUV party was decisively defeated in 2015 midterm legislative elections that have raised the question of whether Maduro will be able to survive a recall election and serve out his term. Even if Maduro or the PSUV survive, their ability to fund projects like ALBA that challenge U.S. hegemony has diminished. U.S. influence in the region received an additional boost in September 2016 when Brazilian socialist Dilma Rousseff was impeached and removed from office, replaced by Michel Temer, a conservative who has pledged to resurrect neoliberal economic policies and seek better relations with the United States. Such changes clearly present the incoming Trump administration with an opportunity to make more permanent a new relationship with Latin America, but those efforts may still be limited by U.S. foreign policy priorities located elsewhere in the world and by increased Chinese influence in Latin America spurred on by a Chinese desire for raw materials and increased trade and investment opportunities.

# Bibliography

Butler, Smedly D. *War Is a Racket*. Los Angeles: Feral House, 2003.

Cameron, Maxwell A., and Brian W. Tomlin. *The Making of NAFTA: How the Deal Was Done*. Ithaca, NY: Cornell University Press, 2002.

Ellis, Evan. *China in Latin America: The Whats and Wherefores*. Boulder, CO: Lynne Reinner, 2009.

Gallagher, Kevin P. *The China Triangle: Latin America's China Boom and the Fate of the Washington Consensus*. Oxford: Oxford University Press, 2016.

Gleijeses, Piero. *Shattered Hope: The Guatemalan Revolution and the United States, 1944–1954*. Princeton, NJ: Princeton University Press, 1991.

Grandin, Greg. *Empire's Workshop: Latin America and the Roots of U.S. Imperialism*. New York: Henry Holt, 2006.

Hearn, Adrian, and Margaret Myers, eds. *The Changing Currents of Transpacific Integration: China, TPP, and Beyond*. Boulder, CO: Lynne Reinner, 2016.

LaFeber, Walter. *Inevitable Revolutions: The United States in Central America*. 2d ed. New York: W. W. Norton, 1993.

LeoGrande, William M. *Our Own Backyard: The United States and Central America, 1977–1992*. Chapel Hill: University of North Carolina Press, 1998.

Mora, Frank O., and Michael La Rosa. *Neighborly Adversaries*. Lanham, MD: Rowman & Littlefield, 2015.

Nef, Jorge, and Harry E. Vanden, eds. *Inter-American Relations in an Era of Globalization: Beyond Unilateralism?* Whitby, ON: de Sitter, 2007.

Schmitz, David F. *Thank God They're on Our Side: The United States and Right-Wing Dictatorships, 1921–1965*. Chapel Hill: University of North Carolina Press, 1999.

Schoultz, Lars. *Beneath the United States: A History of U.S. Policy Toward Latin America*. Cambridge, MA: Harvard University Press, 1998.

Schoultz, Lars. *Human Rights and the United States Policy toward Latin America*. Princeton, NJ: Princeton University Press, 1981.

Sikkink, Kathryn. *Mixed Signals: U.S. Human Rights Policy and Latin America*. Ithaca, NY: Cornell University Press, 2004.

Smith, Gaddis. *The Last Years of the Monroe Doctrine, 1945–1993*. New York: Hill and Wang, 1994.

Smith, Peter H. *Talons of the Eagle: Latin America, the United States, and the World*. 3d ed. New York: Oxford University Press, 2008.

Teixeira, Carlos Gustavo Poggio. *Brazil, the United States and the South American Subsystem*. Lanham, MD: Lexington Books, 2012.

Tulchin, Joseph. *Latin America in International Politics: Challenging U.S. Hegemony*. Boulder, CO: Lynne Reinner, 2016.

## FILMS AND VIDEOS

*The Battle of Chile*. Chile, 1976.
*Bloqueo, Looking at the U.S. Embargo against Cuba*. United States, 2005.
*Missing*. United States, 1982.
*Origins of the OAS Charter*. United States (OAS), 2007.
*Panama Deception*. United States, 1992.

## WEBSITES

http://www.alba-tcp.org/   ALBA (in Spanish)
http://www.http://cidh.oas.org/   Inter-American Commission on Human Rights
http://www.mercosur.int/   Mercosur (in Spanish)
http://www.oas.org/   Organization of American States
http://www.paho.org/   Pan-American Health Organization

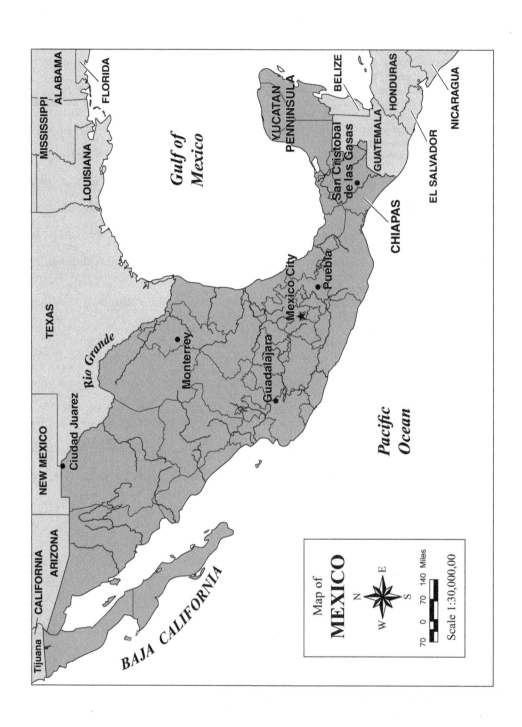

Map of
**MEXICO**

Scale 1:30,000,00

70  0  70  140 Miles

# TWELVE

# Mexico

### Nora Hamilton

## Introduction

Mexico is the second-largest country in Latin America in both population and size, with 121 million people and covering 1,958,000 square kilometers. Geographically part of North America, Mexico is dissected by mountains from north to south, while its varied terrain ranges from northern desert to temperate valleys in central Mexico, with tropical and semitropical zones in the east and southeast.

Mexico's population grew rapidly during most of the twentieth century, although levels of growth were reduced from 2.8 percent per year in the 1970s to just over 1.4 percent as of 2013. Its urban population is now over 79 percent of the total, up from 40 percent in 1950, with 30 percent of the total population in cities of over 1 million and over 20 million in greater Mexico City. Other major cities include Monterrey, a northern industrial city, and Guadalajara, a more traditional, colonial city with a combination of small- and medium-sized industries producing consumer goods and information technology industries, many of them foreign-owned. Some decentralization occurred beginning in the late twentieth century with the growth of cities in the interior and particularly along the U.S. border.

Several factors have been important in shaping both Mexico's history and its contemporary political, social, and economic life. First, it has a rich and varied cultural heritage, largely due to the substantial number of indigenous populations that inhabited the area for centuries prior to the arrival of the Spanish. Evidence of the artistic achievement and complexity of these pre-Columbian civilizations can be found at archaeological sites in various parts of Mexico and in Mexico's museums, especially the National Museum of Anthropology in Mexico City. As a result of the mixture of indigenous populations with the Europeans, Mexico is today a predominantly mestizo country. However, some Mexicans claim pure European heritage, and there is a substantial minority of indigenous populations, estimated at 15 to 25 percent of the total. Mexico also has a small Afro-Mexican population, whose ancestors were brought in to work on plantations during the colonial period.

Second, Mexico has had a special, unequal, and often difficult relationship with the United States, in part due to geographic contiguity. Prior to the Mexican-American War in the mid-nineteenth century, Mexico extended into what is now the southwestern United States. Following the U.S. victory and its annexation of half of Mexico's territory, Mexicans continued to live in the area, and their number has been substantially increased through Mexico–U.S. migration, facilitated by the 2,000-mile border shared by the two countries. Although the threat of U.S. military intervention continued to be a real one until the 1930s, Mexico's subsequent relationship with the United States has been largely demographic and economic. Mexico is dependent on the United States for 78 percent of its merchandise exports and 50 percent of its imports, a relationship formalized in the North American Free Trade Agreement (NAFTA), incorporating Canada, Mexico, and the United States. Also important is Mexican–American migration and the treatment of Mexicans in the United States, where Mexican immigration and settlement have had an important demographic, economic, social, and political impact. In the past three decades, the drug trade and security concerns have become paramount issues.

A third factor is the Mexican Revolution of 1910–1917, a cataclysmic event that shaped much of Mexico's subsequent economic, political, and social life. Although the goals of the various groups that fought in the revolution—democracy, land reform, social justice, and national sovereignty—have been only partially met, they constituted the prevailing ideology in twentieth-century Mexico, and the dominant political party during most of that period, the Institutional Revolutionary Party (PRI), based its legitimacy on claims to represent these goals.

The political structure emerging from the revolution was important to Mexico's long-term political stability, a fourth factor distinguishing Mexico from most other countries of Latin America. Termed the "perfect dictatorship" by Peruvian writer Mario Vargas Llosa, Mexico's dominant party system combined authoritarian controls with flexibility in responding to its constituencies and helped to neutralize protests and dissident groups.

Mexico's political stability benefited from its economic growth between the 1940s and the 1970s. Mexico is one of the most industrialized countries of Latin America; industrial expansion was a factor in Mexico's urbanization and in the emergence of middle-income groups. But the benefits of growth have been unevenly distributed, and Mexico continues to be one of the most unequal countries in the world.

Beginning in the 1980s, Mexico has been undergoing rapid economic and political change, with social and cultural repercussions. Economic globalization and the economic crisis of the 1980s resulted in rejecting old economic models and accepting neoliberalism by Mexican policymakers. This new model is based on opening the economy to foreign trade and investment and the reduction of state intervention in the economy, a process institutionalized when Mexico joined NAFTA in 1994.

Economic crisis and the embrace of economic liberalism in turn led to painful economic and social dislocations due to loss of jobs, reduced wages, and the elimination of previous economic safeguards, in turn leading to increased reliance on the informal sector and/or migration to the United States. Mexicans have also adopted new forms of organization and mobilization, including movements by earthquake victims, middle-class debtors, dissident labor groups, and indigenous organizations. The worsening economic situation undermined one of the major pillars of PRI stability, leading to pressures for political reform and increased support for opposition parties.

International opening, internal economic changes, and social mobilization have in turn led to a process of democratization, involving increased opposition representation in municipal governments, in the national Congress, and among individual state governors. A major milestone in this process was the election of opposition candidate Vicente Fox of the National Action Party (PAN) as president in 2000, ending the seventy-one-year hegemony of the PRI. The subsequent victory of another PAN candidate, Felipe Calderón, in the 2006 presidential election was strongly contested, however, and revealed certain limitations in the democratic process. The election of Enrique Peña Nieto in 2012 brought the PRI back to power, raising fears of a return to the party hegemony and corruption of the past.

## Historical Trajectory

### EARLY HISTORY

Long before the coming of the Spaniards, the area that is now Mexico was the home of numerous distinct populations, ranging from nomadic hunting societies in the northern plains to complex civilizations with high levels of artistic, scientific, and technological sophistication, notably in architecture, sculpture, mathematics, and astronomy. These civilizations were prominent in central and southern Mexico, particularly during the classic period (roughly 150–900 C.E.), when the major cities of Teotihuacán, Monte Albán, Palenque, and others were built and flourished.

The classic civilizations were succeeded by warrior groups. One such group, the Aztecs, established a foothold in central Mexico, where they built their capital, Tenochtitlán. From there they conquered neighboring populations and established an empire that extended from the Gulf of Mexico to the Pacific and from central Mexico into Guatemala, collecting tribute and commissioning labor from the subject populations.

The Spaniards, led by Hernán Cortés, arrived in Mexican territory in 1519 and by 1521 had completed the conquest of the Aztec Empire with the assistance of some of the subject populations. The subsequent 300 years of Spanish colonialism had a profound effect in shaping Mexico's future. First, the hierarchical system of the Aztecs was reinforced by the Spaniards with the addition of strong racial components. Over time, various racial mixtures of Europeans, indigenous populations, and Africans (who had been brought over as slaves) emerged, with mestizos (European and indigenous) eventually becoming the predominant population group.

Second, landowning systems developed during the colonial period resulted in the concentration of much of the land by a small group of large landowners, chiefly Spaniards and their creole descendants, incorporating many of the indigenous communities and exploiting their inhabitants through forms of coerced labor, although some communities maintained their independence and resisted the Spaniards (and later Mexico) until well into the nineteenth century.

Third, as in other parts of Latin America, the Catholic Church became a major force in Mexican history. Efforts by monastic orders to convert the indigenous populations resulted in a synthesis of Catholicism with certain indigenous rituals and practices, evident in the devotion to the Indian Virgin of Guadalupe and the celebration of the Day of the Dead. At the same time, many religious orders became wealthy owners of land, and the official Church became associated with the conservative elements of society, reinforcing the strict hierarchical social order. There have been exceptions throughout Mexican history, however, of dedicated priests and some bishops who worked in the poor communities and sympathized with their needs and interests.

## INDEPENDENCE AND THE MEXICAN REPUBLIC (1810–1910)

The initial independence movements in the early nineteenth century were in fact led by priests—notably Miguel Hidalgo, who led a rebellion not only for political independence but also for the abolition of slavery and of tributes paid by the Indians. The threat of social revolution frightened many of the creole population as well as the Spaniards, who crushed the initial revolts. When independence from Spain was achieved in 1821, it left the existing social system intact. It is Hidalgo, however, who is remembered as the father of Mexican independence and the date of his call to arms, September 16, 1810, that is commemorated as Mexico's Independence Day.

The legacy of the independence movement was a weak state and an oversized military, resulting in several decades of anarchy characterized by internal and external wars, military coups, and economic devastation. Mexico was poorly prepared to defend its borders or to prevent the westward expansion of the United States. In 1834, Texas seceded; and in the 1846–1848 Mexican-American War, Mexico lost most of what is now the U.S. southwest.

Politically, power was contested by Conservatives, representing elite groups who wanted a centralized state and the retention of the colonial socioeconomic hierarchy, and Liberals, representing a mostly urban middle class who opposed land concentration, Church power, and monopoly control of trade. In 1855, the Liberals came to power under the leadership of Benito Juárez, a Zapotec Indian. They passed a series of laws and subsequently the constitution of 1857 calling for a liberal democracy and an end to the privileges of the Church and the military. This period, the Reforma, was interrupted by a Conservative revolt assisted by the French, who took advantage of U.S. involvement in the Civil War to occupy Mexico from 1863 to 1867, when they were finally defeated by the Liberals.

In 1876 a Liberal general, Porfirio Díaz, staged a coup and through a series of increasingly fraudulent elections held on to power until 1910. This period, the Porfiriato, was characterized by the physical, economic, and political integration of the country, the consolidation of the Mexican state, and economic growth through increased integration with the world economy. Díaz sought to modernize Mexico on the basis of foreign investment and European immigration, providing generous concessions to U.S. and European investors in infrastructure, mining, agriculture, and petroleum. Mexican mineral and agricultural exports expanded dramatically, and manufacturing, based on light industries, also grew.

However, the benefits of economic growth were concentrated in the hands of foreign investors and a small number of domestic groups. Díaz's favoritism to foreigners irked domestic investors, and many were genuinely concerned at the growth of foreign, and particularly U.S., control of major sectors of the economy. The small industrial proletariat that worked in the railroads, mines, and manufacturing industries often received low wages for work in harsh conditions and was subject to prohibitions against forming independent labor organizations. The expansion of commercial agriculture for the domestic market and export led to the acceleration of landowner takeovers of land held by peasants and indigenous communities, leaving 96 percent of the population landless. Labor conditions on the plantations and commercial farms were often brutal.

## THE MEXICAN REVOLUTION (1910–1940)

By the first decade of the twentieth century, dissatisfaction with the Díaz regime galvanized large sectors of the population, including liberals and radicals promoting democracy, landowners and mine owners opposed to foreign control, a small but militant proletariat in key industries struggling for decent wages and working conditions, peasants in southern Mexico who had lost land through landowner takeovers, and various regional interests throughout Mexico. A call to arms by Francisco Madero, a leader of the pro-democracy forces, united the disparate groups opposed to Diaz which succeeded in overthrowing the Porfirian government and forcing Diaz into exile.

Madero was subsequently elected president, but after a brief democratic interlude a Porfirian general, Victoriano Huerta, had Madero assassinated and seized power. This action triggered a new revolt in which the Constitutionalist army, led by Venustiano Carranza, a northern landowner, and the Army of the South, led by Emiliano Zapata, defeated Huerta in 1914.

With victory, the fragile unity of the revolutionary forces collapsed. While the leaders of the Constitutionalist Army wanted a return to democracy and national sovereignty, Zapata and Pancho Villa (who had originally fought under Carranza) wanted more fundamental social reforms, particularly a redistribution of land, and distrusted the Constitutionalists. Unable to reach agreement, the revolutionary armies fought each other until the assassination of Zapata in 1919 and the defeat of Villa in 1920. By 1916, however, the Constitutionalists gained control of the capital city and most of the country; Carranza became provisional president and called for a constitutional congress that would formalize the new regime.

The resulting constitution of 1917 reflected to a remarkable degree the heterogeneous goals of different revolutionary factions, in part due to divisions within the Constitutionalists themselves between conservative and more radical groups. It called for a federal system with a separation of powers and no re-election but also for an interventionist state that would, in effect, implement the goals of various revolutionary groups; it reinforced state control of education, eliminating Church-controlled education; called for national control over land and natural resources; enabled the state to expropriate and redistribute land in the public interest; and outlined extensive rights for labor, including an eight-hour day, a forty-hour week, and the right to organize and strike.

The years of violent revolution had resulted in the decimation of an estimated 10 percent of the population, and the immediate postrevolutionary period was one of continued instability as various groups among the revolutionary leadership jockeyed for power. There were also confrontations between the Mexican government and foreign interests over issues involving subsoil rights and mining concessions; peasants and their supporters within the state opposed landowners and their advocates over the expropriation of land; and workers struggled against business groups (and both against the state) over labor rights and organization. The most serious conflict was the Cristero rebellion, a violent struggle resulting from government efforts to implement draconian anticlerical measures.

By 1930, the government had succeeded in consolidating the Mexican state, concentrating political power in the central government, and containing the Cristero rebellion. The formation of a government party, the National Revolutionary Party (PNR), brought together different factions of the revolutionary leadership and provided for periodic changes in government leadership through regular elections without re-election, although the electoral process was far from democratic and social reforms were limited.

This changed under Lázaro Cárdenas, a former governor of the western state of Michoacán, who won the 1934 presidential elections and launched a period of extensive social reforms, supporting workers in their conflicts with business groups and encouraging labor organizing, including the establishment of an independent labor confederation, the Confederation of Mexican Workers (CTM). He also carried out an extensive agrarian reform, distributing land to individual peasants and to communities, and, following a labor conflict between Mexican petroleum workers and the U.S.- and British-owned petroleum companies, expropriated and nationalized the companies, creating a state-owned petroleum company, PEMEX, that has continued to be identified with national sovereignty. The Cárdenas government also pursued an independent foreign policy relative to the United States that continued to distinguish Mexico from other Latin American countries in the following decades.

Through his reforms, Cárdenas established a solid social base among organized workers and peasants, which he sought to consolidate by restructuring the government party. Renamed the Party of the Mexican Revolution (PRM), it had four sectors: labor, incorporating the CTM as well as other confederations and independent unions; peasant, which included peasant organizations, dominated by the National Peasant Confederation (CNC); popular, which drew in various other groups and organizations, including federations of teachers and state employees as well as organizations of women, students, professionals, and small farmers; and military, with elected representatives from each military zone. Party membership was based on membership in an organization in the relevant sector. (The military sector was subsequently dropped.)

# Mexico's Political Economy

## THE "PERFECT DICTATORSHIP": 1940–1982

The reforms and institutions that evolved following the revolution established the basis for political stability and economic development over the next forty years. The corporate structure of the government party facilitated party and government control and co-option of subordinate groups. The establishment of an electoral system involving periodic elections, which opposition parties could contest but only the government party could win, laid the basis for a form of institutionalized authoritarianism with elements of flexibility that distinguished it from more draconian forms of authoritarianism that emerged in Central and South America. The social reforms of the Cárdenas administration, particularly agrarian reform, reinforced the system's legitimacy. The nationalization of Mexico's oil reserves established a precedent for the nationalization of other key economic sectors, generally through negotiated sale rather than expropriation. Mexico also continued to exercise independence in its foreign policy, albeit at a more symbolic level. Finally, the actions of the Cárdenas government affirmed the activist role of the state in social reform and economic development.

For the next sixty years, Mexico was characterized by a hegemonic political system in which the government party (renamed the Institutionalized Revolutionary Party [PRI] in 1947) retained power through periodic but often fraudulent elections. Through its corporate structure, with membership based on belonging to organizations within its three sectors, the PRI penetrated virtually all of Mexican society. The party was closely linked to the state, and clientelistic relations linked state, party, and member organizations, with party and government officials providing favors in return for political support. Member groups were co-opted through limited reforms and concessions; leaders opposed by party or government officials were replaced; and dissidents were neutralized or repressed. However, the fact that repression, particularly in rural areas, was for the most part "hidden" enabled Mexico to retain the reputation of a relatively benign authoritarian regime throughout most of this period.

State control was centralized in the federal government and particularly the presidency. Despite constitutional checks and balances, the president (prior to 1997) controlled legislative as well as executive functions. Although governors and municipal officials were formally elected, the president often had a hand in their selection as well as their removal and replacement, and the federal government exercised monetary control over states and municipalities. At the same time, state governors and local officials could exercise considerable, and even arbitrary, power at the state and local levels, particularly in the southern rural states.

Periodic elections and the principle of non–re-election ensured constant turnover in office and provided a veneer of democracy and flexibility in an essentially authoritarian system. One unfortunate consequence was that government positions were often seen as a one-time opportunity to ensure one's economic future through legal or nonlegal means, such as generous government contracts to family-owned companies or close business associates. Opposition parties gave an appearance of pluralism, but PRI control of the electoral process guaranteed that other candidates rarely achieved political office even at lower levels of government.

## THE "MEXICAN MIRACLE"

The "perfect dictatorship" benefited from economic growth during much of this period. Under the conservative presidents who followed Cárdenas, the focus of government programs shifted from social reform to economic development and particularly the promotion of industry. Mexico's industrial development was based on the import substitution industrialization (ISI) model followed by several Latin American countries and involved the promotion of industry oriented to the domestic market through tax relief and tariff protection as well as substantial state participation in the economy, including investment in infrastructure and state ownership and control of strategic industries such as petroleum, telecommunications, railroads, airlines, and electric power. Many services provided by public sector industries were subsidized to keep domestic industry costs low. Foreign investment was encouraged subject to restrictions such as 51 percent Mexican-ownership of all companies (although this regulation was often weakly enforced) and performance requirements such as the acquisition of an increasing percentage of its inputs from domestic suppliers, and a favorable balance of exports to imports.

The Mexican economy grew rapidly between 1940 and 1970 and more unevenly during the 1970s. Economic growth enabled the Mexican government to increase public sector investment in such areas as education and health, resulting in a dramatic decline in infant mortality and increased levels of education, as well as to provide favors to government and party supporters. By the 1970s, Mexico, along with Brazil, was one of the most dynamic countries of Latin America and was recognized as a semideveloped industrial economy.

However, economic growth was accompanied by growing inequality. Disparities were also evident within and between sectors. Government and private investment favored industry to the relative neglect of agriculture; investment in the rural sector generally focused on commercial farms in northern Mexico oriented to export and neglected small peasant holdings and communal farms in southern Mexico. Similarly, in industry and other sectors, a limited number of large firms controlled the majority of assets.

The combination of industrial growth, centered in the major cities, particularly the federal district and the northern city of Monterrey, and stagnation in the rural area were factors in growing rural–urban migration and the massive growth in the population in and around Mexico City, putting a major strain on its resources. This was also a period of substantial migration to the United States, encouraged by the Bracero Program, initiated during World War II, through which Mexican workers were contracted for specified periods of time to work in U.S. agriculture. The program was extended until the 1960s, leading to a process of cyclical migration whereby Mexican rural workers came to the United States as farm workers for part of the year, returning to their homes during the remaining months. By the 1950s, Mexican migrants were also working in industry and staying longer; some brought their families and settled in the United States.

## ECONOMIC LIBERALIZATION

During the 1970s, in the context of low savings and private-sector investment cutbacks, the government attempted to stimulate the economy by expanding the public sector with investments in steel, chemicals, fertilizer, and heavy industry. With the increase in international oil prices in this period, Mexico also began to develop its petroleum resources for export, drawing on foreign loans and investment, which resulted in a dramatic increase in oil production and exports and the creation of 4 million new jobs in oil, public works, and industry. But the net result was to render the economy more vulnerable to commodity price fluctuations on the international market: oil exports jumped from 15 to 75 percent of total exports between 1976 and 1981, making export earnings heavily dependent on a single product; export earnings were surpassed by imports of industrial inputs and consumer goods; and Mexico's foreign debt increased from $28 billion in 1976 to $75 billion in 1981. An increase in inflation and fear of devaluation led to massive capital flight.

Mexico's vulnerability became evident with the worldwide recession of the early 1980s, which led to a reduction of commodity prices, particularly oil, on the world market by 1981. At the same time, U.S. interest rates had increased from 6.5 percent to 16.7 percent between 1977 and 1981, a further factor in capital flight as well as the increased costs of servicing the debt. In August 1982, Mexico announced that it was unable to meet its debt obligations, portending the economic crisis that would engulf most countries of Latin America in the 1980s.

Similar to other Latin American countries, the Mexican government began to promote a thoroughgoing economic restructuring oriented to a shift from a mixed economy with heavy state involvement to a market economy and from production for the domestic market to production for export. Prompted by changes in the global market, the promotion of economic liberalism, or neoliberalism, by the U.S. government and major international lending agencies such as the World Bank and the International Monetary Fund (IMF), and the technocratic orientation of Mexican economists and policymakers educated in the United States, the government sharply reduced tariffs, cut back public sector employment and government subsidies, reduced regulation, decreased or eliminated previous restrictions on foreign investment, and privatized state-owned industries, reducing the number of state enterprises from 1,155 to 252 by the early 1990s. These changes were institutionalized through NAFTA, between Mexico, Canada, and the United States, which went into effect in 1994 and would eliminate tariffs and other barriers to trade and investment between the three countries by 2008. By the early 1990s, inflation had been reduced to single-digit numbers and growth had resumed. Exports increased from $16.8 billion to $70.3 billion by 1993, and their composition had shifted from primarily oil (75 percent) to primarily manufactured goods (80 percent). Foreign investment, which reached a low point of $183 million in 1987, was up to $33.3 billion by 1993.

Economic restructuring also resulted in significant social transformation. In effect, both agriculture and industry experienced increasing complexity, with the emergence of new middle groups oriented to export, as well as increased polarization—the result of concentration or reconcentration of wealth, deteriorating conditions for many middle- and working-class groups, and increased poverty and destitution of poorer sectors. Competition from cheap imports of consumer goods forced many manufacturing firms to cut back or close down, resulting in wage reductions and loss of jobs. Small and medium farms producing for the domestic market also faced declining incomes due to competition from imports:

peasants and small farmers were forced to supplement their income through casual labor in agriculture or the informal urban sector.

Not surprisingly, migration to the United States increased during this period. The new migrants were more heterogeneous in social composition and geographic origin than earlier cohorts, with an increasing number from urban and middle-class sectors and a substantial contingent from Mexico City, previously a center of attraction for rural migrants. There was also a growing number of migrants from the impoverished indigenous regions of southern Mexico and other rural areas.

Economically, there were several danger signs. Most foreign investment—$28.9 billion—was in portfolio investment, attracted to the Mexican stock market and to the high interest rates of government treasury bonds, which made loans prohibitively expensive for domestic businesses lacking access to foreign credit and saddled those who had borrowed with heavy debts. The growth of imports relative to exports resulted in an $18.5 billion trade deficit by 1994.

The fragility of Mexico's economic situation became evident in 1994. On January 1, the day NAFTA was to go into effect, the Zapatista National Liberation Army (EZLN), an army of indigenous peasants in the southern state of Chiapas, launched a revolt. When the government sent troops to crush the uprising, domestic and foreign media coverage of government repression led to widespread national and international protests, with the result that the government backed down and began negotiations with the Zapatistas.

The uprising in Chiapas was followed in less than three months by the assassination of PRI presidential candidate Luis Donaldo Colosio on March 23. In the meantime, several kidnappings of prominent businessmen heightened the sense of insecurity and crisis. Both foreign and domestic groups began to withdraw investment and export capital, aggravating the hemorrhaging of funds from Mexico. By the end of the year, foreign exchange reserves became dangerously low, immersing Mexico in another economic disaster just as it appeared to be recovering from the previous one.

Foreign loans and the introduction of another major austerity program enabled the economy to recover, but lower and middle sectors of the Mexican population once again bore the combined costs of the crisis and the austerity program, and income distribution again worsened. Government programs to help domestic industries and an antipoverty program aimed at improving health, nutrition, and education levels among poor rural families led to resumed economic growth and a decline in poverty, but many of the gains were lost with the U.S. recession of 2008–2009.

Mexico again recovered, with economic growth fueled particularly by increased manufacturing in such areas as food processing, automotive vehicles and parts, aeronautics, and electronics, much of it oriented to exports. Mexico also expanded its economic relations with other countries in an effort to reduce its dependence on the United States, but the United States continues to account for some 80 percent of its exports. The sharp drop in oil prices in 2014, however, led to another economic crisis and fall in the value of the peso, resulting in anemic growth rates and growing levels of poverty, which increased from less than 30 percent in 2006 to over 40 percent in 2015.

## Uneven Progress Toward Democracy

The political transition from an authoritarian hegemonic party system to a more democratic and pluralist system has been protracted and uneven. Some trace its origins to the student movement of 1968, in which university and high school students carried out a series of marches and demonstrations around several issues, including government expenditures for the upcoming Olympic Games in Mexico rather than the alleviation of poverty. The demonstrations met with escalating violence, culminating on October 2 when government forces fired on a peaceful demonstration killing an estimated 200 to 400 students and onlookers. Although the student movement was temporarily silenced, it raised awareness of the poverty and inequality accompanying Mexico's economic miracle and revealed the coercion and repression underlying the party's "perfect dictatorship."

During the 1970s and 1980s, several groups and movements continued to challenge the status quo, among them rank-and-file workers who mobilized to establish internal democracy within their unions or to form independent unions, nongovernmental organizations (NGOs) concerned with human rights and the inclusion of excluded groups, and opposition parties and coalitions that challenged PRI hegemony in state and local elections. Students of the generation of 1968 took an active role in grassroots organizing in rural areas and urban neighborhoods, resulting in social mobilization around community demands. Women often played an important role in these movements and began to mobilize around women's issues. Other domestic factors, such as the increased independence of the media beginning in the 1970s, and international conditions, such as the process of democratization in South America and other parts of the world in the 1970s and 1980s, were also influential. Finally, the economic crisis beginning in the 1980s and the neoliberal reforms of the 1980s and 1990 resulted in the emergence of new social movements and protest groups, which in turn reinforced support for opposition parties.

The 1988 presidential elections represented a critical turning point. In 1987, a group within the PRI, dissatisfied with the neoliberal direction of the government and the abandonment of the social justice principles of the revolution, formed the "democratic current" within the party and campaigned for the democratization of the internal nomination process for the 1988 presidential candidate. When this effort failed, several left the party and organized around an opposition candidate, Cuauhtémoc Cárdenas, son of Lázaro Cárdenas, who was supported by a number of leftist and other small parties and by popular movements and grassroots organizations that emerged in the 1970s and 1980s.

However, in a clearly fraudulent election (including a computer breakdown during the vote-counting process), the PRI candidate, Carlos Salinas, was declared the victor with 50.7 percent of the vote. Nevertheless, the emergence of a popular opposition candidate who was defeated only through obvious fraud raised hopes regarding the possibility of an electoral defeat of the PRI at the national level. Groups and parties supporting Cárdenas formed the Democratic Revolutionary Party (PRD), protested the election fraud and called for democratic reforms and a return to the principles of nationalism and social justice. Several NGOs that had formed in the 1960s and 1970s began to work with local civic action groups to promote electoral transparency and to monitor local elections. In the meantime, the conservative PAN was expanding, in part through the incorporation of young entrepreneurs, many from northern and central states, who ran for electoral offices in several states.

Although the new Salinas government gave priority to the continuation of economic reforms, the declining PRI legitimacy and its shrinking labor and peasant base as well as the growing strength of the opposition demanded attention to political reform and party restructuring. During the Salinas administration, several laws were passed to reform the electoral process (e.g., the appointment of neutral electoral officials to oversee the elections) and to permit greater participation by minority party representation. The Salinas government also began to acknowledge opposition electoral victories, particularly those of PAN, in gubernatorial races but refused to recognize most victories claimed by the PRD, which it attempted to neutralize.

The 1994 presidential elections were monitored by both domestic and international observers, who generally recognized the electoral process as relatively free of fraud, although the victory of PRI candidate Ernesto Zedillo benefited from government access to financial resources and media coverage and substantial support from business sectors. But as previously noted, Zedillo's inauguration was followed almost immediately by the peso crisis, and the first years of his administration were marked by increased demonstrations, marches, and other forms of protest.

Charges and revelations of corruption affected all levels of government and the party as well as business groups. Mexico's role as the major cocaine route to the United States augmented the corruption and violence. Lawyers and officials involved in prosecuting leaders of drug cartels and journalists exposing high-level corruption were assassinated. In Juarez and other border cities, hundreds of young women, many of them workers in the export platform (*maquila*) industry, "disappeared" and were murdered. Human rights violations included government violence: in 1995 police forces massacred seventeen *campesinos* in the southern state of Guerrero, and in December 1997, forty-five men, women, and children were massacred by paramilitary troops in Acteal, Chiapas.

Repeated economic setbacks and profound disillusion with the PRI led to increased support for the political opposition evident in several opposition victories in gubernatorial, municipal, and legislative elections. In the 1997 midterm elections, the PRI lost control of the legislative assembly to the opposition, and PRD candidate Cuauhtémoc Cárdenas became the first elected mayor of Mexico City (a post previously appointed by the president and that the PRD has retained in subsequent elections).

Finally, in 2000, an opposition candidate, Vicente Fox of PAN, won the presidential elections. Widely seen as a major milestone in Mexico's progress toward democracy, the PAN victory ended the PRI's seventy-one-year monopoly on political power and signaled the shift from a hegemonic party system to a more pluralistic system with three major and several smaller parties vying for power. Several reforms were passed under the Fox administration in the areas of democracy and human rights, including a federal transparency law. However, the increased independence of the legislature and divisions within and among the three major parties blocked or weakened many of his proposed economic reforms. In addition, Mexico was negatively affected by the U.S. economic recession at the beginning of the decade, revealing Mexico's vulnerability to conditions in the United States, while the attack on the World Trade Center and Pentagon on September 11, 2001, ended the possibility of immigration reform sought by Fox.

The presidential elections of 2006 demonstrated some of the limitations of Mexico's electoral democracy. The PRD candidate, Andrés Manuel López Obrador, popular mayor of Mexico City and former president of the PRD, was initially expected to win, but an effective (although illegal) negative campaign by PAN and business groups as well as blunders on the part of López Obrador—including failure to appear at one of two schedules television debates—had reduced his lead by the day of the election. PAN candidate Felipe Calderón was elected president by a slim margin of less than 1 percent. López Obrador contested the results on the grounds of electoral fraud and illegal campaign practices by the opposition, but the Federal Electoral Tribunal rejected claims of fraud and, while it admitted that the opposition campaign practices had been illegal, ruled that the Calderón victory should stand. López Obrador and a significant sector of the PRD refused to recognize the Calderón victory, resulting in a split with a more moderate faction of the party that accepted the electoral outcome.

The Calderón presidency was overshadowed by the drug crisis and the impact of the global economic recession beginning in 2008. Shortly after taking office in December 2006, Calderón launched an antidrug campaign, sending some 100,000 military troops to areas of drug activity throughout Mexico. In 2007 the Bush administration expanded the drug war into Mexico and Central America with the Mérida Initiative, providing substantial military aid. But militarization of the drug war failed to curb the flow of drugs, and violence increased, resulting in an estimated 60,000 killed during Calderón's administration.

The 2012 election represented another watershed in Mexico's political trajectory, bringing the PRI back to the presidency with the election of Enrique Peña Nieto, former governor of the state of Mexico, by a comfortable margin. In the meantime, the PRD split, with López Obrador and his followers forming a new group, Morena (Movimiento Regeneración Nacional), from his campaign organization, which also attracted a number of intellectuals and leftists.

During his first months in office, Peña Nieto introduced several initiatives. The legislature passed an education reform measure that curbed the role of the powerful teachers' union (National Union of Education Workers; SNTE), returning education to government control and introducing regular teacher evaluation in an effort to improve the quality of education. The reform generated considerable resistance by teachers and particularly the CNTE (Coordinating Committee of Education Workers), a radical group within the SNTE, which has carried out a series of protests against the education initiative. In June 2016, government forces fired on CNTE protestors resulting in the death of several teachers and supporters.

Another initiative included efforts to reduce monopoly control in communications, for example, by opening up investment in Telmex and Telcel, owned by billionaire Carlos Slim, which control 70 to 75 percent of the telecommunications industry. The reform also created a new Federal Institute of Communications to regulate the system.

Legislation was passed to open PEMEX, the government-owned petroleum industry, which has been suffering from low productivity, deterioration, and declining investment, to foreign investment. However, the decline in oil prices has discouraged foreign investment, in addition to reducing Mexico's export earnings and government revenue, leading in turn to substantial budget cuts.

Although Peña Nieto promised a new strategy in the war on drugs focused on reducing violence rather than fighting cartels, his policies have been a continuation of previous policies. Among his major achievements to date were the capture of leaders of several cartels, especially Joaquín ("Chapo") Guzmán, head of the powerful Sinaloa cartel, who had twice escaped prison in the past but was extradited to the United States. But the U.S.-financed drug war has had little effect in reducing the violence associated with the drug trade, and the government has also failed to adequately respond to the large number of "disappearances." As of mid-2016, it is estimated that 100,000 people have been killed or "disappeared" since Calderón militarized the drug war in 2006.

Corruption continues to be a major problem extending to all levels of government, including a scandal as to how Peña Nieto and his wife obtained a new house and allegations that Peña Nieto plagiarized up to one-third of his thesis for a law degree. A grassroots movement, including community activists, intellectuals, and business leaders, took advantage of a new initiative that enables citizens to propose legislation if they can obtain 120,000 signatures in support. Believing that corruption was responsible for the inability of the government to respond effectively to the problems of crime and violence, poverty and lack of economic growth, and other issues, they proposed a *"3 de 3"* law that would require all government officials to reveal their assets, disclose all potential conflicts of interest, and prove they are paying taxes. The initiative obtained 660,000 signatures and was passed; although weakened, for example by allowing for private rather than public disclosure, it was recognized as an important step.

## GOVERNMENT STRUCTURES AND POLITICAL ORGANIZATIONS

Today, Mexico is an electoral democracy with a multiparty system, consisting of three major parties, the PRI, the PAN, and the PRD as well as a number of smaller parties, including the Green Party (Mexican Green Ecological Party; PVEM) and the Labor Party, and movements such as Morena. The executive is headed by the president who is elected by popular vote every six years. The president, governors, and the mayor of Mexico City cannot run for re-election, ensuring a periodic turnover, as was the case of legislative offices prior to 2013; currently deputies are allowed to serve four three-year terms, and senators can serve two six-year terms, as can mayors of other cities. Although electoral fraud and campaign violations have continued, particularly at the local level, the creation of an autonomous election board and tribunal and increased monitoring of the electoral process by the major parties, citizen groups, and international observers have helped reduce these problems in national elections.

The legislature consists of a Chamber of Deputies with 500 members and the Senate with 128 members. In the most recent legislative elections (2015), PRI and the affiliated Green Party won 67 percent of the vote, giving it half of the seats in

Congress, while the PAN won 20.9 percent and the PRD won 10.1 percent, having lost considerable support to Morena.

The judiciary has also been reformed and at least at the higher levels is independent of the executive and other political influences. The Supreme Court consists of twelve judges or ministers appointed by the president and approved by the Senate who serve for life. At the lower levels of law enforcement, however, there is substantial corruption as well as ineffectiveness in enforcing the law, including failure to prosecute criminals on the one hand and false arrests and forced confessions (including the use of torture) on the other. There have been efforts to reform these conditions, but the process is slow.

The military has been subject to civilian control since the early 1930s; its function has been chiefly to maintain domestic stability, including the repression of guerrilla movements and other dissidents. In recent years its role and visibility have expanded, largely a result of the use of military forces in the drug war beginning in the 1990s and particularly with the militarization of the drug war beginning in 2006. In contrast to the past history of mutual suspicion, there has been substantial cooperation between the military and U.S. agencies in combatting the drug cartels since 2000, including U.S. training of special forces, collaboration in gathering intelligence and planning and monitoring operations targeting the cartels, and financial aid. Although the increased reliance on the military was based on the assumption that it would be less subject to corruption than the police forces, soldiers and members of the U.S.-trained special forces have collaborated with the cartels and in some cases joined them. According to human rights groups, the militarization of the drug war has also resulted in increased human rights violations, including torture and murder, by military forces.

Political decentralization—the increased delegation of authority and transfer of financial resources from the federal government to state and local governments—began in the 1980s; by the end of the 1990s, subnational units were responsible for half of government expenditures. Combined with the increased recognition of opposition victories in state and municipal elections, decentralization resulted in greater autonomy and the emergence of new opposition strongholds, particularly at the state level, where the PAN gained control of several northern states, as well as Mexico City, where the mayor has been a member of the PRD since 1997. PRD control of this office has been particularly significant: Mexico City mayors have launched reforms at the local level that were at the time rejected at the national level (although some were subsequently adopted more widely), including legislation permitting gay marriage and adoption of children by gay couples. The office has also been a steppingstone to the PRD presidential candidacy, as in the case of Cuauhtémoc Cárdenas in 2000 and López Obrador in 2006.

# Interest Groups, NGOs, and Dissidents

## BUSINESS GROUPS

Between the 1940s and 1980s, the economy was dominated by a combination of state-owned firms, large private domestic conglomerates, and multinational corporations (MNCs). Much of the domestic private sector consisted of powerful economic groups, combining banks, manufacturing industries, commercial establishments, real estate agencies, and other assets under the control of a small number of investors, often a few families, through interlocking ownership and directorates. The economic groups and the large state-owned firms had growing access to foreign capital and technology through joint ventures, loans, and technology transfers.

Many of the larger economic groups were temporarily weakened by the economic crisis in the 1980s, but some succeeded in reconstituting themselves with significant help from the government, and several new groups formed through buying firms cheaply during this period. Both old and new groups subsequently benefited from the privatization of major state-owned firms. The reconcentration of wealth and economic power in a small number of economic groups became evident in the growth in the number of Mexican billionaires led by Carlos Slim, whose Grupo Carso had purchased controlling interest in telecommunications giant TELMEX, making him the wealthiest person in Mexico and one of the three wealthiest men in the world. Many of these groups have exercised direct influence on the government.

At the same time, a number of organizations represent Mexican business interests. Two business groups, CONCAMIN (Confederation of Industrial Chambers) and CONCANACO (Confederation of National Chambers of Commerce), were formed in the immediate aftermath of the revolution to represent industrial and commercial interests respectively. In 1928, business groups in the northern city of Monterrey formed COPARMEX (Employers' Confederation of the Mexican Republic) to oppose government intervention in the economy. Other organizations represent specific interests, such as AMB (Mexican Bankers Association), AMIS (Mexican Insurance Association), CANACINTRA (National Chamber of Manufacturing Industries), AMIB (Mexican Association of Stock Investment Firms), COECE (Coordinating Network of Foreign Trade Business Organizations), and CANACOPE (National Small Business Chamber). The CMHN (Mexican Council of Businessmen) represents Mexico's most powerful business interests, while the CCE (Businessmen's Coordinating Council) is an umbrella organization for business interests in general.

## Labor and Peasant Groups

The largest labor confederation in Mexico is the Mexican Labor Confederation (CTM), formed in 1935 and incorporated in the labor sector of the PRI corporate structure. In addition, unions of government workers, including the powerful teachers union (SNTE), were included in the so-called popular sector within the PRI. Several of these unions have been characterized by corruption, including selling jobs, and a general lack of democracy.

Over the years, individual unions and rank-and-file movements within the official union sector have challenged the leadership and promoted union democracy, and a number of independent unions have formed outside of the official sector. One example of the former is the CNTE, formed by dissident teachers within the SNTE opposed to corrupt leadership. The latter is epitomized by the Union of Telephone Workers, which broke off from the CTM and CT (Congreso del Trabajo) and in 1997 was instrumental in the formation of an independent labor confederation, the UNT (National Union of Workers), which also included autoworkers and electric power workers among others and became the second-largest labor confederation in Mexico.

Another independent confederation, FAT (Authentic Labor Front) continues to be active and has frequently collaborated with U.S. unions in cross-border activities.

The informalization of labor as a result of economic restructuring has reduced the size of the labor movement in recent years, which now often finds itself on the defensive. The informal sector today comprises approximately 60 percent of the labor force, while only 10 percent of the formal labor force is organized.

The CNC (National Peasant Confederation), formed to group regional peasant organizations, became the major organization of rural workers within the corporate PRI structure. As in the labor sector, independent organizations have emerged from time to time, many at the local level, to oppose corruption within the official organizations as well as government neglect, staging land invasions and sometimes taking up arms against corrupt and repressive local officials. There is considerable overlap between peasant and indigenous groups, particularly in southern Mexico, as demonstrated in the case of the Zapatistas, whose uprising was partly motivated by the agrarian legislation of 1991 and 1992, which in effect ended land distribution programs. Both labor and peasant organizations have joined together and formed coalitions with other groups in support of human rights, environmental protection, and democratization and, in some cases, have formed alliances with counterpoint organizations in other countries.

## Indigenous Groups

There are an estimated fifty-six different indigenous groups in Mexico, among which the best known are the Yaqui in the northwest; Otomi in central Mexico; Mixtec and Zapotec in the south (particularly the state of Oaxaca); Purépecha (Tarascans) in western Mexico; and various Mayan groups, among them the Mam, Tzotzil, and Tzeltal in the southeast.

Following the Spanish conquest, some indigenous communities were incorporated as debt peons into the colonial land tenure structures; others resisted the Spaniards, and later Mexican government forces, well into the nineteenth century. The Mexican Revolution led to a new emphasis on Mexico's indigenous past, evident in the works of Mexico's muralists in the 1920s and 1930s. But the policy of the postrevolutionary governments was based on the assumption that assimilation and cultural homogeneity were necessary for economic success and discouraged indigenous language and culture. Defined as peasants, indigenous communities benefited from agrarian reform as well as the elimination of debt peonage, although, similar to other rural groups, they subsequently suffered from government neglect, corruption, and repression.

In the early 1970s, indigenous groups in Mexico began to organize around their indigenous identity, often with the help of former student activists, religious groups influenced by liberation theology, and some government officials. National conferences united indigenous communities throughout the country around demands such as the restitution of communal lands, indigenous teachers, and improved health care incorporating traditional practices. During the 1980s, they succeeded in winning recognition, including a reform of Article 4 of the constitution to recognize the "pluricultural composition" of Mexico and to protect the languages and cultures of the indigenous people.

The Zapatista rebellion in 1994 brought increased visibility to the indigenous movement and its goals of territorial, political, and cultural autonomy for Mexico's Indian nations. The Zapatistas as well as other indigenous communities have organized autonomous municipalities and have continued to be active in resistance to government and corporate initiatives that threaten their communal lands.

## Women and Gender Issues

Like many Latin American countries, Mexico has traditionally been characterized by patriarchy, which often translates into fierce protectionism by men of their wives, sisters, and daughters. In extreme cases (notably in the countryside), the social life of women may be restricted to the private sphere of home and church. This syndrome has gradually broken down under the pressures of industrialization, urbanization, and, increasingly, women's political organizing. The percentage of Mexico's labor force who are women grew from 18 percent in 1978 to approximately 38 percent in 2012.

Women have long been at the forefront of reform movements and constitute a large portion of the leaders in nongovernmental organizations active in community organizing, civic action, and mobilization around human rights issues. In 1982, Rosario Ibarra de Piedra, a former housewife who became an activist on behalf of political prisoners and the "disappeared" when her own son was arrested and disappeared in the 1970s, became the first woman to run for president of Mexico. Since the 1970s, women's organizations have increasingly organized against traditional gender relations.

Also beginning in the 1970s, an increasing number of women have been recruited to top administrative positions in the government and have held several cabinet-level positions. Women also hold electoral positions, including state governor. Following the 1997 congressional elections, the Chamber of Deputies had eighty-five women (of a total of 500), or 17 percent of the total. This number declined in the 2000 elections but increased to 37 percent in 2013. A constitutional amendment in 2014 required that 50 percent of candidates for elected office be women, and in 2016 there are 211 women deputies, 42.4 percent of the total. Women also control an increasing portion of positions in the national executive committees of the three major parties, and the PRD and PRI have been headed by women in recent years.

Lesbian, gay, bisexual, and transgender (LGBT) groups have also become increasingly organized. In 2003, legislation was passed under the Fox government protecting sexual minority groups against discrimination, although these groups have continued to be attacked, with an estimated 1,200 killed between 1994 and 2006. Despite the conservative tenor of the national government and strong opposition by the Catholic Church, the PRD government in Mexico City has passed several laws affecting women and sexual minorities. In 2007 it passed a law decriminalizing abortion, the first such law in Mexico, and in 2010 it approved the rights of gays to marry and adopt children—the first such law in Latin America. When the law was contested by President Calderón and members of the PAN, the Supreme Court upheld it and required that such unions be recognized throughout the country. Currently, five states in addition to the Federal District recognize civil unions or marriages of persons of the same sex, and in May 2016 President Peña Nieto proposed a constitutional reform that would legitimize same-sex marriages throughout the country.

## RELIGION

The Catholic Church has been a major, if ambiguous, force in Mexican history since the colonial period. On the one hand, the official Church has been for the most part conservative, upholding authoritarian and hierarchical traditions and reinforcing the status quo. On the other, individual members of the clergy and Catholic laity have actively defended the rights of downtrodden sectors, evident in the role of priests such as Miguel Hidalgo in the early independence movements and more recently in the work of priests and catechists influenced by liberation theology in areas such as Chiapas, where they have had a role in the organization of indigenous peasants since the 1970s. Prior to his retirement in 1999, Bishop Samuel Ruiz of San Cristóbal de las Casas worked tirelessly on behalf of the indigenous groups of Chiapas and played a leading role in efforts to mediate the conflict between the Zapatistas and the government.

Its economic and spiritual power and social and political conservatism made the Church a major target of reformist groups and governments. In the mid-nineteenth century, the Liberal government succeeded in undermining the economic power of the Church through the expropriation of its landholdings and encouraged Protestant missionaries to come to Mexico in an effort to counter its spiritual influence. In the early twentieth century, the revolutionary governments restricted its ideological role through the establishment of state control of education. Draconian measures against the Church in the 1920s resulted in the Cristero rebellion, which ended with an agreement curtailing state persecution of the Church in return for noninterference of the Church in politics, with the result that the political role of the Church was quite limited throughout most of the twentieth century.

In 1991–1992, new legislation reversed many constitutional restrictions on the Church, which has become more outspoken on social and political issues. While socially conservative, particularly on issues such as abortion and homosexuality, Church officials have also denounced human rights violations, electoral fraud, and the gap between the wealthy and the poor. During his visit to Mexico in February 2016, Pope Francis strongly condemned Mexico's political and economic elite for inequality, corruption, injustice, and drug abuse and specifically targeted the dominant morality, which puts people at the service of capital. At the same time he demonstrated his sympathy for the downtrodden through addresses to indigenous groups and *maquiladora* workers.

According to the 2010 census, 84 percent of the population consider themselves Catholic; roughly 5 percent are Protestants. Evangelical movements have had a more limited role in Mexico than in some other Latin American countries but have been growing in recent years.

## Drug Cartels

Mexico has produced small amounts of heroin and marijuana since the nineteenth century, but drug trafficking became a major issue when Mexico replaced the Caribbean as a major route for drug transit to the United States, and Mexican cartels replaced those of Colombia, which were dismantled in the 1990s. Mexico has become the primary supplier of cocaine to the United States; production and trafficking of heroin and marijuana have expanded. Mexico has also become a major producer and exporter of methamphetamine.

Drug cartels now operate in every state in Mexico and control several cities; their expansion has been facilitated by the corruption of police officers, prison guards, politicians, and even the military. Drug trafficking has been accompanied by increased violence, fueled by struggles between cartels for control of territory and drug trade routes; the emergence of "enforcers" (armed militia formed by cartels to enforce their control and eliminate enemies); the expansion of government antidrug activities, including the extradition of cartel leaders to the United States after 2000; the expiration of the U.S. ban on assault weapons in 2004; and the militarization of the drug war under Calderón beginning in 2006. The government has estimated that 100,000 people had been killed due to crime and particularly as a result of drug trafficking and the drug war since 2006; over 27,000 people have disappeared, in some cases last seen in the control of Mexican police or military officials, and thousands more have been internally displaced. The violence has also been accompanied by increased brutality and viciousness, with bodies of victims showing signs of torture and mutilation.

The major cartel is the Sinaloa cartel, headed by Joaquin Guzmán prior to his arrest. A number of additional cartels maintain control in certain areas, in some cases subject to frequent turnover, as in Michocán, where the Sagrada Familiar was replaced by the Knights Templar, which was in turn replaced by the Nueva Generación cartel operating from the neighboring state of Jalisco. The cartels have also expanded their activities to include kidnapping, human smuggling, and extortion; in some cases they have gained control of legitimate businesses, such as lime and avocado production, mining, and logging in Michoacán.

Government efforts to eliminate the cartels have been stymied by corruption at various levels and widespread poverty, which has facilitated recruitment into the cartels. In 2007, the Bush administration launched a program of U.S. aid to fight drug trafficking in Mexico and Central America, the Mérida Initiative, which was continued and expanded under the Obama administration. While the program includes initiatives in areas such as cooperation in information gathering and support for judicial reform, the bulk of the funds have gone to military aid, including U.S. drone missions to hunt for suspects. (Mexico is now buying and using its own drones.) It has also resulted in a substantial increase in the United States' presence in Mexico, including the CIA, the DEA, and the FBI as well as other U.S. agencies.

Although the U.S. and Mexican governments have had some success in capturing cartel leaders and extraditing them to the United States, efforts to date have had a limited effect in reducing the influence of the cartels or curtailing the drug flow to the United States. The elimination of leaders is generally followed by struggles within the cartel among different groups for leadership that may in fact increase the level of violence. Corruption within government agencies has been a major factor inhibiting the effectiveness of antidrug policies, and several attempts to form special forces that would be immune from the influence of drug lords have failed as these, too, succumb to corruption.

## HUMAN RIGHTS, CIVIC, AND ENVIRONMENTAL ORGANIZATIONS

During the 1970s and 1980s, a large number of human rights, environmental, civic, and other NGOS emerged in Mexico, influenced by domestic conditions and changes, such as the increasing independence of the media beginning in the 1970s and the economic crisis and restructuring in the 1980s and 1990s; Mexico's increasing incorporation into the global economy; and international influences, including the growth of the environmental movement in the 1970s and the process of democratization in South America in the 1970s and 1980s. The growth of these groups was in turn instrumental in Mexico's own process of democratization, exposing civil and human rights violations of the government and promoting political and social reforms.

Some of these groups originated in local grassroots organization. The Civic Alliance can be traced to the formation of civic action groups in San Luis Potosí and other states in the 1950s and 1960s. The strength of the opposition candidate, Cuauhtémoc Cárdenas, in the 1988 elections provided an important impetus to these and other groups, which began to recognize the possibility of an eventual defeat of the PRI. The Civic Alliance organized civic action groups to monitor subsequent local and national elections and has promoted other electoral reforms as well as government transparency.

International NGOs also expanded their influence in Mexico, supporting national organizations and, in some cases, forming cross-national coalitions with their domestic counterparts. During the negotiations around NAFTA, coalitions formed by Mexican, Canadian, and U.S. environmental, civic, human rights, and labor organizations promoted the inclusion of measures protecting labor and the environment as well as the promotion of democracy. While they failed to include these provisions in NAFTA, two side agreements incorporated respect for the labor and environmental laws of the three member countries, although they have not been rigorously enforced.

## FOREIGN AND INTERNATIONAL GROUPS

Mexico's nationalism and resistance to foreign intervention following the revolution have not prevented foreign governments, MNCs, and international agencies from having an important presence in Mexico. While Mexico nationalized many of its key industries between the 1930s and 1970s, including oil, electric power, and telecommunications, foreign investment, primarily by U.S. companies, was important in manufacturing industries, such as the auto and chemical industries as well as the *maquiladoras*. With the economic crises of the 1980s and 1990s, the IMF as well as foreign governments provided loans tied to certain conditions to shore up Mexico's finances. Economic restructuring, including opening the economy by removing restrictions on trade and investment, as well as the privatization of state-owned firms further facilitated foreign investment and opened up previously restricted sectors, such as banks, to foreign ownership. Foreign firms, such as General Motors in Mexico, played an important role in NAFTA negotiations; foreign investment has also increased in areas such as food processing and commerce.

Mexico has expanded its free trade agreements, which include agreements with the European Union, Japan, and several other Latin American countries. Although approximately half of foreign investment is from the United States, investment from other countries is increasingly important.

As noted earlier, because of the expansion in drug trafficking and particularly because of the Mérida Initiative, U.S. government agencies such as the CIA, the DEA, and the FBI as well as the U.S. military have expanded their operations in Mexico, collaborating with Mexican counterparts in intelligence gathering, military training, and planning operations against cartels.

Finally, Mexican migrants in the United States have an important, although less visible, role in Mexico itself. Migrant remittances have sustained not only their families but also the Mexican economy. Hometown associations have provided funds for various civic projects and in some cases productive investments in their respective towns and villages. Through return migration, bi-national organizations, and, in some cases, voting, migrants have direct and indirect political and social influence.

## OTHER GROUPS AND ORGANIZATIONS

Throughout Mexico's history, new movements and grassroots organizations have formed around particular events or specific issues. Student groups have emerged periodically after the repression of the student movement in the 1960s and 1970s in response to conditions in their respective institutions and/or social and political conditions.

The disappearance of forty-three students from a rural college in Ayotzinapa, Guerrero (Oaxaca) in 2014 resulted in the emergence of groups throughout Mexico as well as internationally demanding their return. The students had commandeered a bus to go to a protest in Mexico City; forty-three were detained and not seen since. The government response that they had been seized by local police and turned over to drug cartels who subsequently killed them and burned the bodies is widely disputed, and investigations by international agencies have found no evidence to support the government story. It is widely believe that agencies of the federal government and police were involved, and protests in Mexico continue.

Two types of groups emerged in response to the drug violence and the inadequacy of government efforts to reduce it. One type consists of victims' rights groups that focus on organizing and negotiation, such as the movement Peace with Dignity and Justice formed by Javier Sicilia, a Mexican poet whose son was killed by a drug gang. In 2011–2012 it organized a caravan that traveled through Mexico and subsequently through several cities in the United States, holding meetings and demonstrations in which victims of drug violence and the drug war could speak about their experiences.

A second type consists of armed militia formed in several rural villages, notably in the western state of Michoacán, which establish checkpoints on roads leading to their respective villages and, in some cases, have set up their own courts to prosecute and convict those accused of drug-related violence and other crimes. They have had some success in combatting drug gangs, but government efforts to co-opt or neutralize them (e.g., through incorporating them in government rural forces) have weakened several groups; some have been accused of working for other cartels and engaging in vigilante violence.

Other social groups originate at the local level in response to specific issues. For example, indigenous groups have organized against specific government programs and corporations, such as mining companies that have targeted their land and livelihood. At the national level, the *3 de 3* initiative, previously described, involved various civil society groups coming together to support anti-corruption legislation.

## Conclusion

The twentieth century was one of profound change for Mexico, from a poor, largely rural society with a few industrial enclaves governed by a personalist dictatorship to a dynamic, relatively industrialized urban society with a large middle class and a modern state controlled for over seventy years by a hegemonic government party. Beginning in the late twentieth century, Mexico has also made significant progress toward a more democratic system, reflecting a combination of pressures by mobilized social and civic groups, the emergence and strengthening of opposition parties, and increased international visibility. Today, the hegemonic party system has been replaced by a pluralist system of competing parties, presidential power has been reduced by the increased autonomy of the legislative and judiciary branches of government, and centralization of control in the federal government has been replaced by a decentralized system providing greater authority to lower levels of government.

However, serious obstacles to socioeconomic development and an effective democratic system remain. Economic growth and development increased Mexico's wealth and the complexity of its social structure, but the gap between the wealthy and poor continues to be extreme. Foreign economic domination has been replaced by growing economic integration into the global economy and particularly with the United States, which continues to exert a strong influence on Mexico's economy.

The rule of law remains weak. Judicial reforms have increased the autonomy of the judiciary, and the Supreme Court has ruled against successive presidents on various issues. But other measures to reduce corruption and other violations have often been weakly enforced. Crime and insecurity, much of it drug related, have increased. Local police, prosecutors, politicians, and the military have been involved in complicity with the drug trade. The escalation of violence and brutality affects not only drug operatives but also officials and journalists that oppose the cartels and bystanders who have nothing to do with drugs.

The goals enshrined in Mexico's revolution and constitution for national sovereignty and social justice are still elusive. Economic inequality and the poverty of substantial sectors of the population, high levels of crime and official corruption, and the weakness of democratic institutions continue to present obstacles and challenges to authentic progress in Mexico. At the same time, the mobilization of numerous groups and organizations has been influential in introducing gradual change, including increased rights for women and LGBT groups, greater recognition of the claims of indigenous populations, and growing participation in civil society. These groups continue to challenge efforts to advance modernization without taking into account historical demands for social justice.

# Chronology

**150–900**  Classic period of Meso-American culture; rise of major cities including Teotihuacán, Palenque, Monte Albán

**900**  Decline of classic culture, rise of warrior tribes

**1325**  Building of Tenochtitlán, Aztec capital, now the center of Mexico City

**1521**  Conquest of Aztec Empire by Spaniards under Hernán Cortés

**1521–1821**  Spanish colonial period

**1810**  Beginning of independence movement with revolt against Spain led by Miguel Hidalgo; the revolt is defeated by the Spaniards but the date (September 16, 1810) continues to be commemorated as Mexican Independence Day

**1821**  Mexican independence achieved

**1846–1848**  Mexican-American War, culminating in Mexico's defeat; in the Treaty of Guadalupe Hidalgo, Mexico loses nearly half its territory to the United States

**1857**  Beginning of the Reforma; Liberals come to power, and a new constitution is adopted

**1862**  French intervention on behalf of Conservatives

**1867**  French and Conservatives are defeated by the Liberals under the leadership of Benito Juárez, who reestablishes the Liberal Republic

**1876–1910**  Porfiriato; coup carried out by General Porfirio Díaz, who controls power for the next thirty-four years

**1910**  Revolt against Díaz, led by Francisco Madero; beginning of the Mexican Revolution

**1911**  Success of revolt with abdication of Díaz; Madero elected president

**1913**  Madero assassinated by Victoriano Huerta, who becomes president and dissolves Congress; Constitutionalist Army formed under the leadership of Venustiano Carranza; Army of the South under Emiliano Zapata and Constitutionalist Army battle Huerta

**1914–1916**  Huerta defeated, but a split between Constitutionalists and forces of Zapata and Pancho Villa leads to conflict between the two sides; in 1915, Carranza gains control of Mexico City and in 1916 calls a constitutional convention

**1917** New constitution approved

**1927–1929** Cristero rebellion: uprising of pro-Catholic groups, especially rural populations in central Mexico, against anticlerical provisions of the government

**1929** Establishment of government party, National Revolutionary Party (PNR)

**1934–1940** Lázaro Cárdenas president

**1938** Expropriation of U.S.- and British-owned oil companies, which come under state control; government party restructured on corporate basis; name changed to Party of the Mexican Revolution (PRM); name changed to Institutional Revolutionary Party (PRI) in1947

**1939** Formation of National Action Party (PAN)

**1940–1970** "Mexican Miracle"

**1968** Student mobilization repressed when government agents and military surround student demonstration at Tlatelolco Plaza, firing into the crowd and killing an estimated 200–400 people

**1982** Debt crisis, beginning of economic restructuring

**1988** Opposition candidacy of Cuauhtémoc Cárdenas in presidential election, formation of Party of the Democratic Revolution (PRD)

**1988–1994** Salinas president; acceleration of process of economic restructuring, including privatization of government assets and negotiation of NAFTA with Canada and the United States

**1989** PAN wins gubernatorial election in Baja California, the first time an opposition candidate becomes a state governor

**1994** (January 1) Uprising of Zapatista National Liberation Army (EZLN) in Chiapas; (March) assassination of PRI presidential candidate Luis Donaldo Colosio; (September) election of Ernesto Zedillo in relatively open elections; (December) foreign exchange crisis and peso devaluation, again plunging country into major recession

**1997** Midterm elections, with Cárdenas becoming mayor of Mexico City, and loss of PRI control of Chamber of Deputies for the first time since the party was formed

**2000** (July 2) Vicente Fox, candidate of PAN, elected president

**2006** (July 2) Felipe Calderón of PAN wins narrow electoral victory over PRD candidate López Obrador in controversial presidential election. Militarization of drug war

**2012** Election of Enrique Peña Nieto returns PRI to the presidency

**2014** (September) Disappearance of forty-three students from rural teachers college in Ayotzinapa, Guerrero

**2015** Parliamentary elections give PRI 50 percent of Congress. Morena overtakes PRD in number of votes, 3.3 million to 1.9 million.

# Bibliography

Bethell, Leslie, ed. *Mexico since Independence*. Cambridge: Cambridge University Press, 1991.

Camp, Roderic A. *Politics in Mexico: The Democratic Transformation*. 6th ed. New York: Oxford University Press, 2013.

Eckstein, Susan. *The Poverty of Revolution: The State and the Urban Poor in Mexico.* Princeton, NJ: Princeton University Press, 1988.

Fox, Jonathan, and Gaspar Rivera-Salgado, eds. *Indigenous Mexican Migrants in the United States.* La Jolla: Center for U.S.–Mexican Studies and Center for Comparative Immigration Studies, University of California, San Diego, 2004.

Hamilton, Nora. *The Limits of State Autonomy: Post-Revolutionary Mexico.* Princeton, NJ: Princeton University Press, 1982.

Hamilton, Nora. *Mexico: Political, Social and Economic Evolution.* New York: Oxford University Press, 2011.

Harvey, Neil. *The Chiapas Rebellion: The Struggle for Land and Democracy.* Durham, NC: Duke University Press, 1998.

Hellman, Judith Adler. *Mexican Lives.* New York: New Press, 1994.

Hellman, Judith Adler. *Mexican Migrants: Between the Rock and the Hard Place.* New York: New Press, 2008.

Huber, Paul Lawrence. *Power from Experience: Urban Popular Movements in Late Twentieth Century Mexico.* University Park: Pennsylvania State University Press, 2004.

Knight, Alan. *The Mexican Revolution.* 2 vols. Lincoln: University of Nebraska Press, 1986.

Lustig, Nora. Mexico: *The Remaking of an Economy.* 2d ed. Washington, DC: Brookings Institution, 1998.

MacLeod, Dag. *Downsizing the State: Privatization and the Limits of Neoliberal Reforms in Mexico.* University Park: Pennsylvania State University Press, 2004.

Massey, Douglas, Rafael Alarcon, Jorge Durand, and Humberto Gonzalez. *Return to Aztlan: The Social Process of International Migration from Western Mexico.* Berkeley: University of California Press, 1987.

Meyer, Lorenzo. *Mexico and the United States in the Oil Controversy: 1917–1942.* Austin: University of Texas Press, 1977.

Middlebrook, Kevin J., ed. *Dilemmas of Political Change in Mexico.* La Jolla: Center for U.S.–Mexican Studies and Center for Comparative Immigration Studies, University of California, San Diego, 2004.

Middlebrook, Kevin J. *The Paradox of Revolution: Labor, the State and Authoritarianism in Mexico.* Baltimore: Johns Hopkins University Press, 1995.

Middlebrook, Kevin J., and Eduardo Zepeda, ed. *Confronting Development: Assessing Mexico's Economic and Social Policies.* Palo Alto, CA: Stanford University Press, 2003.

Moreno-Brid, Juan Carlos, and Jaime Ros. *Development and Growth in the Mexican Economy: A Historical Perspective.* Oxford: Oxford University Press, 2009.

Williams, Heather L. *Social Movements and Economic Transition: Markets and Distributive Conflict in Mexico.* Cambridge: Cambridge University Press, 2001.

Wise, Carol, ed. *The Post-NAFTA Political Economy: Mexico and the Western Hemisphere.* University Park: Pennsylvania State University Press, 1998.

Wise, Timothy A., Hilda Salazar, and Laura Carlsen, eds. *Confronting Globalization: Economic Integration and Popular Resistance in Mexico.* Bloomfield, CT: Kumarian, 2003.

## FILMS AND VIDEOS

*The Five Suns: A Sacred History of Mexico.* United States, 1996. A film by Patricia Amlen, University of California, Berkeley, Center for Media and Independent Learning.

*Memorias de un Mexicano.* Mexico, 1950. Documentary directed by Carmen Toscano, Salvador Toscano, with original film footage from the Porfiriato, the Mexican revolution, and the immediate postrevolutionary period. Available on video or DVD.

*Letters from the Other Side.* United States, 2006. Film by Heather Courtney, which documents the causes of migration and its impact, focusing on the lives of four women whose sons and/or husbands have migrated to the United States.

## WEBSITES

http://www.inegi.gob.mx/   Instituto Nacional de Estadística Geográfica e Informática (INEGI), official statistical agency

http://www.ueinternational.org/Mexicoinfo/mlna.php/   Mexican Labor News and Analysis, monthly analysis of labor issues and events

http://www.wilsoncenter.org/program/mexico-institute/   Mexican Institute of the Woodrow Wilson Center

http://www.gob.mx/   Official site of government of Mexico

http://www.lawg.org/Mexico/   Central America Migrant News Brief. Latin American Working Group

BOLIVIA

PARAGUAY

BRAZIL

Pacific
Ocean

Rio de la Plata

Córdoba

Rosario

URUGUAY

Buenos Aires

CHILE

Map of
**ARGENTINA**

N

W    E

S

100   0   100   200   300   Miles

Scale 1:45,000,000

**Falkland Islands
(Islas Malvinas)**

# THIRTEEN

# ARGENTINA

## *Aldo C. Vacs*

Argentina is located in the Southern Cone of South America. The country is shaped like an inverted triangle, with the northern base bordering on Bolivia, Paraguay, and Brazil; the eastern side on Brazil and Uruguay; the western side on Chile; and the apex pointing toward Antarctica. Its territory comprises about 2.8 million square kilometers, making it the eighth-largest country in the world and the second largest in Latin America (after Brazil). The Andes Mountains run from the Bolivian border to Tierra del Fuego and separate Argentina from Chile. Argentina exhibits a great diversity of physical features, productive capacity, and demographic patterns. The northern region has subtropical weather, the central has a temperate climate, and the southern displays cold temperatures. The northwest is quite arid and poor but has small subtropical areas and a string of fertile valleys where most of the population, including a substantial mestizo (people from mixed European and aboriginal descent) component, resides. Cuyo, in the western central region, is also arid but contains a number of oasis settlements that facilitate fruit and wine production and in which most of the population, largely of Spanish and Italian descent, is concentrated. The Gran Chaco, which includes savannas and subtropical forests, is located in the north central and eastern region, where most of the small remnants of the indigenous population live together with groups of European descent devoted to the production of cotton, tobacco, tea, and yerba mate. Patagonia, in the south, contains arid plateaus where sheep are raised and fertile valleys where fruit is produced, but it remains scarcely populated. The Pampas, in the central eastern portion of Argentina, are among the most fertile grasslands in the world; their temperate climate and adequate rainfall facilitate the large-scale production of grains and the raising of livestock. Most of the country's population live in large urban concentrations located in the Pampas region, including the capital city, Buenos Aires, as well as Rosario, La Plata, Mar del Plata, and Bahía Blanca and their respective suburban areas and satellite cities.

As of 2016, Argentina has a population of about 43.5 million people, most of European ancestry. In the late nineteenth and early twentieth centuries, massive waves of immigrants from Italy, Spain, central Europe, Russia, and the Middle East substantially altered the size and composition of the Argentine population. Between 1870 and 1914, the population grew from about 2 million to 8 million people, of whom close to one-third were foreign-born. After 1930, European immigration declined, but the country attracted large numbers of immigrants from neighboring countries. Most of these immigrants together with large contingents of the existing rural population settled largely in the cities, making Argentina one of the most urbanized countries in Latin America. By 1914 more than 50 percent of the population was living in urban concentrations; by 2000 it was estimated that close to 90 percent of the total population lived in urban areas.

From an economic perspective, Argentina has been a relatively rich country, particularly in the Latin American context. Between the 1870s and 1930, the country experienced rapid economic growth, which led to the emergence of large middle and urban working classes and expansion of political participation. The Great Depression brought about the end of economic prosperity, political stability, and social progress and inaugurated a period of growing confrontation during which Argentina's situation steadily declined. Between the 1940s and the early 1980s, the fluctuations between populist but fragile liberal democratic regimes and increasingly repressive military dictatorships contributed to economic stagnation, a growing concentration of income and wealth in the hands of the elites, and worsening poverty and marginality among the working and middle classes. Since the early 1980s, the establishment and consolidation of liberal democracy ended the darkest period of Argentina's political history, restoring the respect for human rights and providing for popular participation and political stability. However, the implementation of stringent free market policies reinforced inequitable patterns of income distribution, generated unemployment, increased poverty, fostered the multiplication of social problems, and led to political instability resulting in an electoral turn toward more populist and state-led policies in the early twenty-first century that were followed more recently, after domestic confrontations, by a return to neoliberal policies.

# Political Evolution

## FROM COLONY TO OLIGARCHIC REPUBLIC

Most of the territory currently occupied by Argentina was settled throughout the sixteenth and seventeenth centuries by two groups of Spanish colonizers: one arrived by land from Peru, occupying the northwestern area of current Argentina and spreading toward the south and southeast, and the other came by sea from Spain and colonized the areas comprising the Río de la Plata basin. The inhabitants of the northwestern region remained linked to the viceroyalty of Peru, supplying food, beasts of burden, and textiles demanded by the Peruvian and Upper Peruvian (Bolivian) silver-mining economy. The colonists who settled in the margins of the Río de la Plata and in the areas along the Paraná and Uruguay Rivers produced hides for export to Spain and engaged in legal as well as illegal commercial activities, including the smuggling of goods to and from Great Britain.

From the Spanish crown's perspective, the economic importance of both regions was limited. There were neither precious metals nor other valuable raw materials; there was only a scarce number of sedentary Indians whose labor could be exploited in agricultural activities, and the lack of conditions for a plantation economy prevented the introduction of large numbers of slaves. However, the strategic and commercial importance of the Río de la Plata area and specifically of Buenos Aires, its main city, increased in the late colonial period as it became a barrier against Portuguese territorial expansion and an entry point for commercial transactions with the hinterland. The continuous territorial disputes with Portugal transformed Buenos Aires into a crucial defensive outpost and led to the creation of local militias. The commercial role of the city and the Pampas region was bolstered during the eighteenth century by the increasing demand for hides in Europe and, in the late eighteenth and early nineteenth centuries, by the export of salted meat, particularly to the slave plantations of Brazil and the Caribbean.

The creation in 1776 of the viceroyalty of the Río de la Plata (comprising current Argentina, Uruguay, and portions of Bolivia, Paraguay, and Chile) with Buenos Aires as the government seat reinforced this trend and permanently shifted the balance of power in favor of the *porteño* (port city) elites. At the same time, this shift in the balance of power sharpened the conflict between the oligarchies of the interior, who zealously defended their political autonomy and tried to protect the regional economies from foreign competition, and the Buenos Aires elites, who tried to attain political supremacy and championed free trade.

Argentina's independence from Spain, secured between 1810 and 1816, was the culmination of a process involving growing tensions between the creole (people from Spanish descent born in the Americas) landed and commercial oligarchies, who had gradually concentrated most economic resources in their hands, and the Spanish rulers and administrators of a declining empire, who excluded these elites from political participation and wanted to preserve an outmoded mercantilist system. The first two decades after independence were marked by a succession of civil wars between the Unitarians—supporters of the prerogative of Buenos Aires to establish a centralized national government and promote free trade—and the Federalists—regional groups who steadfastly defended provincial autonomy and espoused economic protectionism. The confrontation between these two groups resulted in a period of civil wars accompanied by rapid economic decline.

This violent stalemate was temporarily broken after the inauguration in 1829 of Juan Manuel de Rosas as governor of Buenos Aires, a position he occupied with only a brief interruption until 1852. Rosas, a rich landowner from Buenos Aires province who defined himself as a Federalist, was able to establish his ascendancy on the federal *caudillos* (political-military strongmen) of the interior and to quell successive Unitarian challenges. Rosas's peculiar brand of federalism embodied the interests of the traditional cattle ranchers and exporters of hides and salted meat from Buenos Aires, who wanted a peaceful climate in which they could export their products, import manufactures, profit from the customs revenues generated by the port of Buenos Aires, and control the conduct of foreign relations. In exchange for this, they were inclined to leave provincial authority in the hands of local *caudillos*, maintaining harmonious relations with the provincial elites who shared their aversion to any change in the economic status quo, traditional class structure, and forms of political domination.

However, after two decades of dictatorial rule, the inability of the Rosas regime to promote the kind of political and economic changes that many among the elites believed were necessary to overcome the country's isolation and relative stagnation led to an alliance between interior and coastal groups interested in fostering a process of capitalist agrarian development. The fall of Rosas in 1852 was followed by a short period of internal conflict as the Buenos Aires and provincial elites clashed over the definition of the political and economic design of the emerging state. Finally, through a suitable combination of military force, political concessions, and economic might, the agrarian and commercial exporting elites of Buenos Aires were able to assert their hegemony and establish new conditions for political stability and economic growth, completing the occupation of the national territory, implementing free market and free trade policies, and creating a stable oligarchic political regime. This group consolidated its supremacy and prevented internal discord by forging an alliance between the Pampean and regional elites and appealing to the use of force and fraud when necessary to win elections.

Political stability facilitated Argentina's economic modernization and reinsertion into the world political economy as a producer and exporter of grains and beef. Between 1862 and 1916, successive administrations confronted the problems of the scarcity of labor, capital, skills, infrastructure, and technology by promoting massive immigration, attracting foreign investment, fostering education, implementing an ambitious program of public works, and encouraging the introduction of new techniques for cattle raising, grain cultivation, and food processing, storage, and transportation. Thus, by World War I, Argentina had become a major world exporter of beef, grains, and wool. The population had increased fivefold and was becoming mainly urban. There were a growing number of middle- and working-class people concentrated in the largest cities, especially in Buenos Aires, and the per capita income was higher than in several European countries.

However, the emergence of politically disenfranchised middle-class and urban working-class sectors and the existence of some provincial elites who felt excluded from the economic bonanza resulted in growing opposition to the oligarchic regime. Middle-class and marginal elite groups converged in the creation in 1892 of the Unión Cívica Radical (Radical Civic Union; UCR), the first and oldest mass party in Argentina, which fought for the expansion of political participation. In turn, the increase in the number of immigrants and urban workers led both to the rise of the anarchist movement and to the creation in 1894 of the Socialist Party, which sought significant political and socioeconomic changes.

## THE ASCENT AND FALL OF MASS DEMOCRACY

Between 1892 and 1912, the Radicals, under the leadership of Hipólito Yrigoyen, engaged in armed revolts and practiced electoral abstention to force the conservative elite to make political concessions. The emergence of militant labor and leftist political organizations, the growing pressure coming from the middle-class opposition, and the realization on the part of the oligarchy that the Radicals, despite their name, did not intend to alter the existing economic and social structures prompted the decision to liberalize the political system. In 1912, the reformist wing of the ruling Conservative Party passed a law instituting obligatory universal male suffrage and enacted guarantees to make voting secret and unconstrained. Afterward, the UCR began to participate successfully in a series of contests that culminated in 1916 with the election of Yrigoyen as president.

The period of 1916–1930 was one of democratic political stability characterized by the predominance of the UCR at the national and provincial levels. The Radical administrations focused their initiatives on the political arena, promoting the enlargement of the electorate and the displacement of conservative groups from power positions, but they introduced only minor changes in the socioeconomic domain. Federal interventions reduced the influence of conservative political groups that, unlike other Latin American traditional elites, could not rely on the electoral manipulation of a pliable peasantry, whose presence was practically negligible in the Argentine agrarian capitalist system. However, the oligarchic groups did not attempt to eliminate the democratic regime as long as the Radicals protected the existing socioeconomic structures. Thus, the Radical administrations' progressive policies were limited to favoring the urban and rural middle sectors through state patronage and social and educational policies and to satisfying some of the demands of the urban workers through the creation of an embryonic social security system, price controls of wage goods, and mediation in labor conflicts.

This period of political stability and social peace ended when the crash of 1929 and the ensuing Great Depression led to an abrupt decline in export revenues. The collapse of the economy led to an acute fight for economic shares between different socioeconomic groups. At the same time, the crisis reduced the margin of maneuver of the radical administration, which was unable to sustain its state patronage or to overcome the structural causes of the economic crisis. Moreover, in his old age, President Yrigoyen seemed to have lost the ability to deal effectively with the growing political and economic problems challenging his administration. In these circumstances, the landed and commercial elites were able to mobilize part of the discontented middle class and to incite some army officers to overthrow the elected government. The coup d'état of September 1930—orchestrated by the traditional oligarchy, supported by middle-class groups, and implemented by the armed forces—signaled the end of the era of Argentina's political stability and the beginning of more than five decades of continuous disarray.

The leader of the 1930 coup, General José F. Uriburu, attempted between 1930 and 1932 to establish an authoritarian regime whose corporatist features resembled Italian fascism. However, the oligarchy and a substantial portion of the military and middle sectors opposed Uriburu's project and forced him to allow the emergence of a facade democracy. The banning of the UCR and the use of electoral fraud and coercion facilitated the coming into power of Conservative administrations that attempted to restore the old oligarchic regime by limiting political participation and favoring export-oriented economic growth based on a close commercial association with Great Britain.

Throughout the so-called infamous decade (1930–1943), the ruling Conservative groups attempted to recreate the "paradise lost" of the oligarchic regime, when their political domination was uncontested and the export–import model of growth reigned supreme. However, it soon became clear that in the international and domestic circumstances engendered by the Great Depression, this goal was unattainable. The Conservative governments of the 1930s and early 1940s realized that even the substantial economic concessions made to Great Britain were not able to revive the prosperity based on the traditional export–import model. The rise of a new model of economic growth, import substitution industrialization, became inevitable as the decline in export revenues and the consequent scarcity of hard currency reduced the capacity to import and created opportunities and incentives for the rise of local manufacturing. This economic transformation would have significant social and political consequences that ultimately would lead to the end of Conservative rule.

The emergence of an industrial elite producing consumer goods for the domestic market, the decline in agricultural exports and the consequent rural stagnation, the escalating pace of rural–urban migration associated with the new employment opportunities in the emerging industrial sector, the influential political role played by the military after 1930, the growing discontent of the middle sectors with Conservative electoral fraud and economic policies, the demands of labor organizations, and the rise of nationalism created a volatile situation that could not be adequately controlled by the Conservative regime. The beginning of World War II reinforced some of these trends—such as the need to produce domestic manufactures, the growing importance of the military, and the rise of democratic and nationalistic demands by different groups—and created the opportunity for the military to oust the Conservative administration without significant opposition.

## The Rise and Decline of Peronism

The 1943 coup was plotted by a secret military lodge made up of nationalistic and authoritarian officers who sympathized with fascist ideology and wanted to maintain Argentina's neutrality during World War II. Among those who participated in the coup, Colonel Juan D. Perón rapidly emerged as the most skillful political figure. Palace coups engineered by Perón removed the two initial military presidents from office. Finally, a close Perón associate, General Edelmiro Farrell, became president (1944–1946), and, with his backing, Perón concentrated in his hands the vice presidency, the ministry of war, and the newly created secretariat of labor and social welfare. Afterward, using the power and resources of these offices, Perón organized a coalition that included his military supporters and an emerging state-controlled labor movement. Faced with Perón's growing power, his military and civilian adversaries tried to oust him, but this attempt failed when, after a few days of incarceration, Perón was rescued by a massive mobilization of workers who demanded his release on October 17, 1945. Eva Duarte, a young actress who had become Perón's companion in 1944, offered him continuous support during the crisis, and they married shortly afterward. Eva Perón—Evita, as she became popularly known—rapidly emerged as a prominent political figure in her own right, helping gather support for Perón among the poorer sectors of the population.

After Perón's release, a divided military heeded the growing demands for democratization and called for elections to be held in early 1946. Both Perón and his adversaries tried to mobilize and organize their supporters into broad political coalitions. On the Peronist side, the state-supported labor organizations created the Partido Laborista (Labor Party), while some former Radical and Conservative politicians established the so-called Renovating Junta of Radicalism, which counted on the support of several nationalistic middle-class groups and provincial political organizations. Both parties endorsed Perón as their presidential candidate but maintained separate lists for other offices. The opposition front included Radicals, socialists, communists, and Conservatives that formed an electoral alliance called Unión Democrática (Democratic Union). In the February 1946 elections, Perón won the presidency with 54 percent of the vote, and his supporters carried most provinces, securing substantial majorities in Congress.

A new political era, the era of populism, had started. The 1946 elections signaled the end of the radical electoral predominance, the Conservatives' ability to manipulate the political process, and the capacity of minor parties, such as the socialists, to gain congressional seats. Perón's victory rested on the support of the new urban working-class electorate fostered by the internal migrations and industrialization, the rural population and the inhabitants of the poorer provinces, and sectors of the lower middle class grateful for his economic and social initiatives. After his inauguration, Perón cemented a state-dominated populist alliance whose fundamental pillars were organized labor, the industrialists producing for the domestic market, and the nationalistic military groups favorable to rapid industrialization. This populist regime favored strong state intervention in the economy to promote industrialization, income redistribution policies favorable to organized labor and civilian and military bureaucracies, and nationalization of crucial sectors of the economy (public utilities, transportation, and foreign trade).

The Peronist government maintained the democratic forms (periodic elections, division of powers, and political party competition) but engaged in a number of semiauthoritarian practices, such as restricting the freedoms of expression, assembly, and strike; controlling the judiciary; manipulating the mass media and the educational system; imposing political constraints on public employees, union leaders, and education workers; and harassing and persecuting adversaries. As a result, the chances of the opposition parties to compete successfully for power were considerably reduced, and they began to favor a military coup as the only alternative to what they defined as an increasingly "totalitarian" regime.

The Peronist economic policies and political practices were relatively successful in the early postwar years as Argentina benefited from the use of war-accumulated reserves and the recovery of the international economy while workers, industrialists, and the military remained united behind a government that satisfied their demands. Meanwhile, Peronism expanded its basis of electoral support by extending the franchise to women in 1947 and establishing the women's branch of the party.

Evita played a central role in encouraging these decisions and became the leader of the women's branch of the Peronist Party. She also performed a crucial role in strengthening the regime by offering social welfare services through the Eva Perón Foundation, overseeing organized labor, and promoting the public veneration of Perón's leadership in her speeches and publications.

In 1949, Perón called for a constitutional convention that, amid strong objections from the opposition, instituted the possibility of presidential re-election, an option that had been forbidden by the 1853 constitution. Peronist union leaders, female activists, and some elected officials tried to nominate Evita as the vice-presidential candidate, but, faced with strong military opposition and affected by failing health, she was forced to decline the nomination. In 1951, Perón was re-elected president, gathering 65 percent of all votes cast.

First Lady Eva Duarte (Evita) and President Juan D. Perón in 1950, at a time when the couple had reached the peak of their popularity and political power in Argentina. Soon, in 1952, Evita would die and Perón would confront without her the economic and political crisis that led to his overthrow in 1955. *(Source: Caras y Caretas 2236)*

At the time of his second inauguration in 1952, Perón confronted growing difficulties as changes in the international economic situation, declines in domestic agricultural production, balance-of-payments deficits, inflation, and economic stagnation led to a renewed fight for economic shares among the members of the Peronist coalition. Perón's inability to restore economic prosperity and satisfy the conflicting demands of his followers reinforced the trend toward authoritarianism. The increasingly repressive characteristics of his political initiatives—declaration of a state of siege and internal war, takeover of newspapers and growing censorship, forced membership in the Peronist Party and other organizations, and open confrontation with the Catholic Church—weakened his regime and strengthened the resolve of the opposition to remove him by any means. Evita's death in 1952, the multiplication of the allegations of corruption, and a number of scandals involving Perón and his associates combined to undermine the regime's popularity and made it increasingly difficult to mobilize supporters in its defense. Perón's misguided policies, which fluctuated between using more repression and making concessions, fostered the unity of the anti-Peronist forces. Finally, in September 1955, after a series of failed revolts, a faction of the military supported by the opposition parties and the Catholic Church succeeded in overthrowing the regime. Perón fled the country and was replaced by a military administration, which very rapidly became involved in internal feuds concerning how to deal with the defeated Peronists and what kind of program to implement to replace Perón's populist policies.

## AUTHORITARIANISM AND LIMITED DEMOCRACY

After the fall of the Peronist regime, a succession of antipopulist civilian and military governments attempted with scarce success to overcome Argentina's political, economic, and social crises by introducing a new political economic model to foster growth and political stability. The forces that overthrew Perón agreed that the decline of the classic import substitution industrialization (ISI) model required the rejection of Perón's income redistribution and nationalistic policies and a new economic strategy that would include adjustment programs to reduce the growing balance-of-payments deficits, incentives for foreign investment to attract new capital and technology, and stabilization plans to eliminate inflation. Notwithstanding their different origins, composition, and ruling styles, the governments established during this period practiced exclusionary or repressive policies toward important sectors of the population, particularly against Peronists, who until 1973 were totally or partially banned from participating in elections. Meanwhile, to different degrees, these governments maintained state intervention in the economy while trying to shift the country's industrialization strategy in a new direction, one that combined relative protection and support for local producers with incentives for foreign investment and the welcoming of financial capital in an attempt to promote exports (especially of manufactures), foster international competitiveness, and modernize the most dynamic sectors of the economy.

These attempts failed due to a number of economic situations, including the relative scarcity of foreign investment, inflationary pressures, hard currency shortages, and state mismanagement. More important yet, the groups favored by the populist regime, such as organized labor and state-dependent industrialists, were able to outlast its fall and struggled to preserve or augment their respective shares of a dwindling economic pie while looking at the state as the means to attain their sectoral goals. Ultimately, this confrontation led to growing inflation, social conflict, and progressive government paralysis that intensified the economic crisis and heightened political instability.

Between 1955 and 1976, Argentina had a succession of authoritarian military and partially democratic civilian governments that were unable to overcome this stalemate. This failure affected the military administrations established in 1955–1958, 1962–1964, and 1966–1973, all of which were forced to step down and allow for a transition to civilian rule to escape political and economic disaster. The civilian governments of Arturo Frondizi (1958–1962) and Arturo Illia (1964–1966), elected thanks to the military ban on Peronism, were overthrown by the same military after they proved unable to solve the country's problems.

Finally, in the 1970s, faced with urban insurrections and the rise of guerrilla movements, the military and its allies allowed the electoral participation of Peronism—but not of Perón himself—in an attempt to restore some degree of stability. This led to the election in March 1973 of Perón's personal delegate, Héctor J. Cámpora, who resigned three months after his inauguration so that a new election, in which Perón could participate, could be held. Faced with the internal divisions affecting the Peronist movement, Perón attempted to maintain a neutral position by nominating his wife, María Estela Martínez de Perón (known as Isabel Perón), as the vice-presidential candidate. The formula of Perón–Perón won the October 1973 presidential elections with 62 percent of the votes, but Juan Perón died in July 1974. He was succeeded by his widow, who exacerbated, through a combination of governmental mismanagement, corruption, and authoritarian practices, the domestic strife. In early 1976, Argentina was in complete turmoil with Peronist and Marxist guerrilla groups, including the Montoneros and the Ejército Revolucionario del Pueblo (the Revolutionary Army of the Peopl; ERP), fighting against the military and paramilitary organizations while strikes, lockouts, and demonstrations proliferated in a context of economic stagnation, spiraling inflation, and political crisis.

## MILITARY REGIME AND STATE TERROR

In March 1976, the armed forces overthrew Isabel Perón and started the so-called process of national reorganization. This Argentine version of bureaucratic authoritarianism lasted until 1983. The military junta closed Congress and provincial legislatures, removed all elected officials and Supreme Court justices, banned the activities of political parties, placed labor and some business organizations under military control, and enacted other measures aimed at controlling political life. The new regime also unleashed a wave of repression that surpassed all previous authoritarian experiences. A brutal system of state terror was institutionalized, with multiple military, paramilitary, and police groups trying to annihilate the opposition. This campaign of extermination, which the military itself called a "dirty war," was aimed at eliminating not only the armed guerrilla groups and their sympathizers but also any kind of dissent. To achieve this end, the regime used multiple terrorist methods, including murder, "disappearance," incarceration in clandestine concentration camps, jailing, torture, exile, and looting opponents' property. More than 10,000—according to some estimates, as many as 30,000—people disappeared after being abducted, tortured, and assassinated by the security forces. Hundreds were killed in armed confrontations, and thousands more were forced into exile. The military rulers were also determined to eliminate the socioeconomic and political factors that led to Argentina's economic decline, social strife, and political instability. They agreed with a number of influential members of the elite and technocratic experts that the roots of the crisis were found in the existence of an interventionist state and a semiclosed economy typical of the ISI strategy. These advisers believed that the loosening of free market forces would not only create the conditions for renewed economic growth but also discipline the social actors' behavior, destroying the socioeconomic and political bases for the emergence of populist regimes. After a free market and trade liberalization program had been fully implemented, the different socioeconomic and political groups would perceive the futility of trying to influence public policies in their favor because the market, not the state, would assume the role of allocating resources and distributing income. As a result, the main cause of Argentina's high level of social conflict and political mobilization would be eliminated and governability would be restored. Once this happened, the military and its civilian allies envisioned the establishment of a more stable and less participatory political regime in which some form of restricted electoral competition would finally be authorized. However, the military regime was unable to attain its goals. The restrictions imposed by the armed forces on the monetarist economic team, which included a ban on reducing military budgets and privatizing military-controlled state enterprises, the formulation of misguided economic policies (especially those that led to overvaluation of the local currency), the persistent refusal of the economic agents to modify their state-oriented expectations and behaviors, and the worsening external financial conditions led to economic disaster. At the same time, growing domestic and foreign condemnation of the dictatorship's atrocious human rights violations helped to isolate and weaken the military regime. Domestically, this opposition was spearheaded by several human rights organizations, led by the Mothers of the Plaza de Mayo, a group of mothers of the disappeared that since 1977 congregated every Thursday at Buenos Aires's main public square in front of the presidential palace demanding information about their relatives and an end to illegal repression. Internationally, the courageous activities of the human rights groups and the shock generated by the state terrorist activities resulted in condemnation of the Argentine regime by nongovernmental human rights organizations (such as Amnesty International and Americas Watch), the United Nations and Organization of American States human rights commissions, and several developed nations' governments, including the United States under the Carter administration and Western European governments.

Members of the military junta that ruled after the 1976 military coup and waged a "dirty war" against their opponents, which resulted in thousands of assassinations and "disappearances." From left to right: Admiral Emilio Massera, General Jorge Videla, and Brigadier Orlando Agosti. *(Photo provided by the Department of Documentary Photographs, Argentine National Archive)*

In 1982, faced with a foreign debt crisis, economic stagnation, and growing domestic discontent, the government attempted to solve its problems by embarking upon an anticolonial military venture. The recovery of the Falkland Islands (Islas Malvinas), controlled by the British and claimed by Argentina, appeared to offer the perfect chance to unify the nation behind the government, regain some prestige for the military, and legitimize the regime. However, the confrontation with Great Britain ended in a complete Argentine defeat, and the domestic backlash forced the military to call for elections and transfer power to the civilians.

The authoritarian regime had failed to attain its ultimate goals but succeeded, through brutal repression and application of regressive economic policies, in changing Argentina's socioeconomic structure; reducing the power of organized labor; weakening the middle class; creating conditions for the growth of large, diversified domestic economic groups and foreign corporations devoted to export activities; and reducing the state economic role and its commitment to policies aimed at protecting low- and middle-income groups. The Argentine society that emerged from the military process was much more heterogeneous and fragmented than the one that had facilitated the rise of populism. These new economic and social conditions facilitated the acceptance of liberal political and economic prescriptions to promote stability and growth.

## THE RETURN TO DEMOCRACY

The collapse of the military government convinced a majority of the Argentine population not only that authoritarian regimes were unable to solve the country's problems but also that they inflicted a staggering cost in human lives, civil rights, and social welfare. This majority was inclined to support parties and candidates that offered the highest likelihood of consolidating a stable democracy and rejecting authoritarian deviations. Even those groups that had supported the military regime and benefited from its policies recognized that without a solid political foundation the free market model they favored was not going to last. At the same time, the acknowledgment that earlier state-led experiences had been unable to overcome the country's structural deficiencies and the simultaneous perception that socialist and populist regimes were crumbling the world over convinced many Argentines that liberal economic policies were the only option to solve the crisis.

The democratically elected administrations of Raúl Alfonsín (1983–1989) and Carlos S. Menem (1989–1995, re-elected 1995–1999) enjoyed the advantage of political legitimacy but confronted numerous economic obstacles inherited from the military. The basic elements of a liberal democracy, such as periodic elections, party competition, and majority rule with constitutional limitations, were preserved. However, there was also a growing concentration of power in the executive branch, which limited legislative participation and judicial control over important decisions as the country turned toward a free market economy.

The UCR, led by Alfonsín, won the 1983 elections by a wide margin of votes. It was favored in that occasion by the popular feeling that the Radicals would maintain their traditional respect for democratic liberties, the presidential candidacy of a relatively charismatic leader, and the fear that the Peronists would persist in embracing some of the authoritarian practices used in the past. Moreover, the military government's policies had promoted a process of deindustrialization that eroded Peronism's traditional basis of electoral support by substantially reducing the number of industrial workers and weakening the strength of organized labor. In these conditions, it was possible for the Radicals to consolidate their basis of electoral support among the middle class and to make inroads among the growing number of self-employed and nonunionized workers.

The Alfonsín administration implemented economic plans that combined orthodox liberal stabilization measures with some unorthodox ones aimed at protecting middle- and low-income sectors. At the same time, it attempted to fulfill its promises to bring the military personnel responsible for human rights violations to trial and to depoliticize the armed forces. However, these economic policies failed to overcome the domestic resistance of the Peronist Party and organized labor to neoliberal policies and the business groups' refusal to accept government controls on prices and exchange policies. As the civilian opposition grew, the military also defied the human rights policies of the administration and engaged in a series of revolts that compelled Alfonsín to make concessions, greatly reducing the number of officers that could be punished for their deeds during the dirty war. Moreover, foreign banks, the International Monetary Fund (IMF), and the governments of developed countries gradually withdrew their economic support for the administration, worsening the situation.

The growing disenchantment of large sectors of the population with the economic, social, and human rights policies of the Radical administration led to a decline in its popularity. Meanwhile, the Peronists were able to complete their process of internal reorganization on a more democratic basis, eliminating some unpopular figures from the party's leadership and projecting an image of moderation that attracted the support of not only the working class but also some middle-class sectors. On the right, other groups were also able to increase their appeal among middle- and upper-class groups by denouncing the Radicals' economic policies and by calling for a more coherent strategy of economic liberalization. In 1987, the Radicals were soundly defeated by the Peronists in the midterm congressional elections and lost a number of important governorships.

In 1988, Menem won the Peronist primaries and became the party's presidential candidate, emphasizing populist themes that appealed to the majority of the party members. Meanwhile, as the 1989 presidential elections approached, government attempts to regain control over the socioeconomic situation failed. In this context, Menem secured his victory with 51.7 percent of the votes, and the Peronists won a majority of the gubernatorial and congressional positions in dispute.

After the elections, the paralysis of the Alfonsín administration, combined with the misgivings concerning Menem's populist economic and social promises, worsened the crisis. The already high rate of inflation was replaced by hyperinflation, with prices rising more than 120 percent per month. Real wages collapsed, igniting a social explosion and forcing the presidential declaration of a state of siege. Finally, Alfonsín resigned in late June to facilitate Menem's early presidential inauguration a few days later.

## LIBERAL DEMOCRACY AND FREE MARKETS

To the surprise of his followers and adversaries alike, the new president embraced economic and political ideas opposed to the traditional Peronist policies. The populist promises of a "productive revolution" and huge wage raises were replaced by a free market economic program executed by some of the most representative figures of Argentina's economic and technocratic elites. Menem's project, the construction of a "popular market capitalism," required dismantling of the interventionist state conceived in the 1940s by Perón, which had survived the assault of successive military and civilian administrations. However, the Peronist tradition of personalistic leadership and the subordination of the Peronist Party and unions to the government continued, facilitating the concentration of power in the hands of the president.

The Menem administration formulated a series of ever more radical neoliberal economic and social policies that resulted in sweeping market reforms. All state enterprises and services were privatized and transferred to domestic or foreign owners, including the phone, airline, railroad, shipping, coal mining, highway, steel, armaments, and petrochemical companies; postal and insurance services; public television and radio stations; and an array of other public utilities and firms controlled by the state. Most economic activities were deregulated, a number of regulatory agencies were eliminated, and there were massive dismissals of public employees. Government monetary control was minimized, and a new currency was created (the peso replacing the austral) that was freely convertible in dollars at a parity rate of one for one. In the external sector, the opening of the economy included implementation of neoliberal policies, such as the removal of tariff and nontariff barriers and the elimination of most subsidies, liberalization of rules concerning financial and investment flows, and acceptance of a foreign debt-for-equity approach.

These economic policies accomplished some impressive results: inflation was contained, the economy grew at a significant rate (6.1 percent in 1990–1994), the rate of exchange remained unchanged, and capital inflows increased. At the same time, the program reinforced the trends toward regressive income distribution, higher unemployment, concentration of wealth, oligopolization of the economy, growing trade deficits, decline of the provincial economies most affected by federal budget cuts, and increasing unemployment. Nevertheless, electoral support for the administration among the population increased significantly as these measures generated economic stability and made the return of inflation unlikely.

In other areas, Menem followed a course that bolstered his political preeminence. The administration reacted forcefully against its labor opponents, dismissing state workers, imposing obligatory arbitration in private sector conflicts, and giving legal recognition only to pro-government unions. The right to strike was limited by presidential decree, wage and salary raises were linked to increases in productivity, and union control of workers' health and other social services was reduced.

Inside the Peronist Party, Menem supporters were appointed to the leading positions, reinforcing the subordination of the party and the congressional delegation to the president. The nomination and appointment of judges sympathetic to the administration eliminated many of the potential obstacles to the use of executive decrees to implement controversial policy initiatives while a law increasing from five to nine the number of justices packed the Supreme Court with Menem loyalists. At the same time, Menem cemented good relations with the military by pardoning the former members of the ruling juntas and other military personnel still incarcerated for their responsibility in human rights violations. Although internal military divisions and frictions were not completely eliminated, these concessions and the promotion of more professionally oriented officers made it possible to defeat new revolts of small discontented groups and considerably reduced military pressures on the administration.

In 1994, Menem successfully promoted a constitutional reform that permitted his re-election in the 1995 contest. These general elections resulted in a major victory for Menem, a tremendous defeat for the Radicals, and the rise of a center-left coalition, the Frente País Solidario (Front for a Country in Solidarity; FrePaSo), made up of leftist groups, Peronist dissidents, and some provincial organizations that opposed Menem's economic and human rights policies. Menem was re-elected for the 1995–1999 term with close to 50 percent of the votes, while the Peronists won most congressional and gubernatorial races. While the Radicals gathered less than 17 percent of the votes, FrePaSo obtained close to 30 percent of the votes, doubling its congressional representation.

# Economic Crisis, Political Upheaval, and the Return of Populism

Throughout his second administration, Menem was faced with a decline in economic growth, a dramatic rise in unemployment, and severe socioeconomic crises in some of the provinces. As the congressional elections of 1997 approached, the main opposition forces, the UCR and FrePaSo, realized that an electoral alliance would have excellent prospects of defeating the Peronists. The rise in unemployment, numerous allegations of corruption and police brutality, and the growing insecurity and distrust of the judiciary affected the government's popularity, particularly in the larger cities and most populated provinces. Thus, the leaders of the two main opposition groups agreed on establishing an electoral front—the Alliance for Work, Justice, and Education—and advocated a program calling for the creation of jobs, elimination of corruption, and increased educational, health, and other social expenditures. This political approach succeeded, and the alliance obtained more than 45 percent of the votes versus 36 percent for the Peronists, who lost their absolute majority in the Chamber of Deputies.

These results opened a period of intense political competition in anticipation of the presidential elections of 1999. The Peronists became involved in an internal struggle for the presidential nomination that pitted the governor of Buenos Aires province, Eduardo Duhalde, against Menem, who indicated his interest in running for a third term but ultimately failed to remove the constitutional ban on a third consecutive term. The alliance nominated the Radical mayor of the city of Buenos Aires, Fernando de la Rúa, for the presidency and Carlos Alvarez, a leader of FrePaSo, as the vice-presidential candidate.

Throughout the presidential campaign, the alliance benefited from the dissensions inside the Peronist Party; the Menem administration's inability to overcome the economic recession, reduce unemployment, and eliminate corruption; and Duhalde's incapacity to prevent a number of police scandals in Buenos Aires province. On October 24, 1999, the alliance won the presidential elections with 48.5 percent of the votes versus 38.1 percent for the Peronist candidate while increasing its congressional representation and gaining some governorships.

On December 10, 1999, de la Rúa and Alvarez were inaugurated president and vice president for the period 1999–2003. However, soon the alliance began to be affected by internal dissension as it became clear that the president and the Radical leaders were going to neither alter substantially the economic, social, and foreign policies followed by Menem nor engage in a strong anticorruption campaign. In October 2000, Vice President Alvarez resigned after his calls for a stronger stance against corruption were ignored by the president. The alliance remained in place but was considerably weakened by this resignation as well as by a ministerial reshuffle that indicated de la Rua's intention to follow a neoliberal course.

In the second half of 2001, amid growing recession and unemployment, the de la Rúa administration faced a rising tide of withdrawal of dollar-denominated deposits from the banks and was forced to suspend these withdrawals to prevent a generalized collapse of the financial system. This measure infuriated middle-class depositors, whose life savings were frozen, and led to multiple manifestations of discontent that very rapidly converged with the protests of the unemployed and impoverished groups, resulting in massive street demonstrations, lootings, and violent confrontations with the security forces. Groups of unemployed demonstrators known as *piqueteros* (picketers) blocked main highways and bridges demanding jobs, food, and subsidies while, at the same time, organizing soup kitchens and community health and educational services. Demonstrators took to the streets of the main cities, calling for the resignation of the authorities and the renewal of the political establishment, demanding *"Que se vayan todos!"* (They all must go!). Simultaneously, neighbors in different cities began to organize *asambleas de barrio* (neighborhood assemblies) in which, independent from the political parties, people organized demonstrations against the government and discussed proposals to solve local problems. As the intensity of the opposition and the level of the violence increased, the president attempted to solve the crisis by declaring a state of siege and trying to negotiate the creation of a national unity government with the Peronists. On December 20, after these attempts to control the situation failed, de la Rúa resigned his office.

The resignation marked the beginning of a chaotic political period in which the absence of a vice president led to successive congressional attempts to nominate a new president. In a matter of days, three different Peronist politicians were inaugurated and resigned as they could not control the situation. The convertibility of the peso into dollars ended, a default on the external debt was announced, and the peso declined to a third of its value. Finally, the fear that the crisis could end in a catastrophic collapse of the system led politicians and representatives to come to an agreement on supporting the appointment to the presidency of Eduardo Duhalde, the former governor of Buenos Aires, vice president, and defeated Peronist presidential candidate in 1999.

Duhalde was inaugurated on January 1, 2002, and remained in power until May 25, 2003. During this short period, the Duhalde administration was able to restore some degree of stability in the economic, social, and political realms. In the economic sphere, the "convertibility" experience came to a formal end, and the value of the peso stabilized at three pesos for a dollar. Depositors were forced to exchange their dollar-denominated funds at a third of their value in pesos or to accept promises of long-term repayment in dollars at low interest rates. Negotiations were initiated with the IMF, World Bank, and foreign lenders to restructure the debt and reschedule payments. Some progress was made in improving the socioeconomic situation by introducing payments to the unemployed, engaging in some public investment, and increasing some of the expenditures on health, education, and housing.

At the same time, Duhalde skillfully managed the political situation by announcing that he would not run for election in 2003, allowing different Peronist candidates to emerge, and selecting the relatively unknown Néstor Kirchner, the governor of the southern province of Santa Cruz, as his favorite. In the 1970s, Kirchner, together with his wife, Cristina Fernández, had been members of the leftist Peronist Youth while they were studying at La Plata, the capital of Buenos Aires province. After the 1976 coup, the Kirchners moved to Santa Cruz, keeping a low profile until redemocratization. In the 1980s and 1990s, they became again politically active in the Peronist movement. He had been elected governor of Santa Cruz while his wife became a federal senator. Duhalde supported Kirchner as a presidential candidate in the expectation that as governor of a small province with a good image but lacking a national political machine of his own, Kirchner would be able to defeat Menem but would remain unable to challenge Duhalde's control of the Peronist party.

The main contestants in the April 2003 presidential elections included three Peronist candidates (Kirchner, Menem, and Adolfo Rodríguez Saá, the brief December 2001 provisional president who had declared the debt in default), one Radical (Leopoldo Moreau), a former Radical who had been economic minister briefly under de la Rúa (Ricardo López Murphy), and another former Radical representative with left populist leanings (Elisa Carrió). The results showed an ample dispersion in the electoral preferences of the population: Menem received 24.5 percent of the votes, Kirchner 22.2 percent, López Murphy 16.4 percent, Rodríguez Saá 14.1 percent, and Carrió 14 percent. These results required a second voting round to be held in May 2003 between the two candidates with the most votes. However, it soon became clear through polls that Kirchner could count on sufficient support to easily beat Menem. After considerable hesitation and under strong political pressure, Menem finally decided to withdraw his candidacy, making it possible for Kirchner to be declared the winner and assume the presidency on May 25.

Once inaugurated, Kirchner increased his popularity by implementing a number of redistributive economic policies, progressive social measures, human rights initiatives, and nationalistic foreign policies in the context of a rapidly recovering economic situation. While the economy recovered and unemployment declined, favored particularly by the increase in the prices of export commodities, the Kirchner administration formulated policies aimed at promoting job creation, increasing unemployment benefits, improving health and educational services, and maintaining an adequate level of governmental expenditures, even when faced with pressure from the IMF and bankers to increase the fiscal surplus to repay the foreign debt. A tough stance was taken in the negotiations with private foreign creditors that resulted in the exchange of most of the debt at more favorable conditions and a considerable decrease in debt payments. With support from Venezuela, the debt with the IMF was cancelled, eliminating the IMF oversight of the country's economic policies and facilitating the abandonment of orthodox free market programs. The economy recovered steadily, and by the end of Kirchner's tenure it was growing at an annual rate of more than 8 percent. Hard currency reserves had risen to $35 billion, and the balance of trade remained highly positive. In this context of economic growth and increasing domestic consumption, the main problems faced by the administration were energy shortages, relative price misalignments, and increasing inflation.

The Kirchner administration supported and implemented a number of legal, judicial, and symbolic initiatives destined to punish human rights violations that had been forgiven by previous administrations. Thus, the nullification of the amnesty laws led to the detention, trial, and incarceration of a number of human rights violators who had escaped prosecution or been freed in previous years. Museums and memorial sites were created to remember the victims of the state terrorist activities, and the role of human rights organizations was officially recognized and supported. In the foreign policy sphere, the government distanced itself from the United States, particularly by refusing to support the Bush administration policies toward Iraq, the creation of an hemispheric free trade area, and militarization of the antidrug traffic efforts; established closer relations with Cuba and Venezuela; adopted a tougher position in negotiations with foreign lenders and multilateral credit institutions; and promoted closer integration with Brazil and the other members of Mercosur as well as the incorporation of Venezuela.

Politically, Kirchner took advantage of his growing popularity and the weakness of the opposition to build his own political base. His approach led to a series of internal Peronist confrontations that divided the party into different factions but succeeded in the creation of a substantial base of support that comprised Peronist groups as well as sectors of other organizations, including portions of Radical, provincial, and center-left parties. In the 1995 congressional and gubernatorial elections, "Kirchnerist" candidates running under different labels succeeded in winning a plurality of the disputed seats and governorships. Most important, President Kirchner's wife, Cristina Fernández, who had been until then a senator representing the province of Santa Cruz, ran for the Senate in the largest province—Buenos Aires—and defeated the wife of Eduardo Duhalde and his powerful political machine. With these electoral results, Kirchner secured control over the Peronist party, Congress, and most provincial administrations and was able to consolidate his administration's turn away from conservative market policies and toward center-left populist ones.

Kirchner's popularity remained high, and the expectations were that he would be re-elected in 2007. However, in a surprising decision, he chose not to run and to support the presidential candidacy of his wife, Cristina Fernández. In the general elections of October 2007, Cristina Fernández de Kirchner won in the first round with 45.3 percent of the votes over Elisa Carrió, who obtained 23 percent. For the first time in Argentine history, not only had a woman been elected president but also the two most voted-for candidates were women. The vice-presidential candidate who accompanied Cristina Fernández was Julio Cobos, the Radical governor of the Province of Mendoza, who had joined together with other Radical politicians the "Kirchnerist" electoral coalition Frente para la Victoria (Victory Front).

Cristina Fernández continued to implement domestic and international policies similar to those formulated by her husband, focusing on the elimination of poverty, promotion of social welfare, the pursuit of an independent foreign policy and regional integration, women's issues, and the defense of human rights. However, initially she confronted a number of challenges that affected her popularity. Particularly, when she tried to raise the export taxes on agricultural products, such as soybeans, the producers formed a united opposition front that included all major associations and counted on the support of many politicians (among them Vice President Cobos). After a number of lockouts and demonstrations, the measure was defeated in the Senate by the vote cast by the vice president (breaking the existing tie). Afterward, in 2008–2009, the international recession affected the prices and demand for agricultural exports, slowed economic growth, and reduced the government's capacity to maintain its expansionary economic and social policies. These problems led to the decline of the administration's popularity and the growth of the opposition (both inside and outside the Peronist movement). In the 2009 congressional elections, Kirchner's supporters lost their majority in Congress, although they maintained a plurality that made it possible to negotiate agreements with minor political groups to pass legislation. At the same time, internal disagreements concerning fiscal expenditures and the use of accumulated reserves to reduce the debt led to the removal of the Central Bank president and growing criticism in the press. Nevertheless, after the elections, the economic crisis receded, terms of trade improved, and in 2010 and 2011 the GDP grew around 9 percent each year. Thus, the Kirchner administration was able to resume some of its expansionary economic policies and to introduce new social initiatives (concerning job generation, family subsidies, and housing and pensions) while engaging in direct confrontation with the opposition media—especially the powerful Clarín and La Nación groups—over control of the main newsprint factory (Papel Prensa). Meanwhile, the unexpected death of Néstor Kirchner in October 2010 led to massive demonstrations of grief and resulted in renewed support for his widow to run for re-election in 2011.

In the general elections of October 2011, Cristina Fernández was re-elected for a second presidential term with 54 percent of the votes. In contrast, her main adversaries, Ricardo Alfonsín (son of former president Raúl Alfonsín and candidate of a front led by the Radical party), Eduardo Duhalde (Peronist dissident), Hermes Binner (candidate of a Socialist-led front), and Alberto Rodríguez Saá (other dissident Peronist) obtained between 12 and 8 percent of the votes each. Kirchner's Victory Front also obtained a majority of seats in the Chamber of Deputies, retained its plurality in the Senate, and won most provincial governorship contests.

These results strengthened the president and her supporters' position, but a number of economic, social, and political problems emerged after the elections that contributed to erode the administration's popularity. Economically, a slowdown (the GDP grew around 2 percent in 2012), increasing fiscal burdens, rising inflation, exchange rate devaluations, and growing pressure on foreign reserves made it difficult to maintain expansionary and redistributionist policies and generated discontent among the business and middle-class sectors because they felt threatened by the government's fiscal, monetary, and exchange policies. These groups (supported by the media) also blamed the government for the perceived deterioration in domestic security and growth in public corruption. Politically, the economic difficulties and these negative reactions were accompanied by the denunciation of governmental authoritarian practices that contributed to generate increased opposition to the administration. As a consequence, in the midterm elections of October 2013, the administration confronted a strengthened array of political challengers, both within and without the Peronist movement. Although Kirchner and her allies were able to retain a plurality of the votes (around 33 percent), the dissident center-right Peronists and a Radical–Socialist coalition obtained around 24 percent each, while Conservatives and leftist groups gathered around 8 and 6 percent, respectively. With these results, the government maintained its pluralities in Congress but lost a few seats and was unable to gain an absolute majority in either chamber. More damaging was the victory in Buenos Aires province of a dissident Peronist list and the inability to win in other large provinces and in the Federal District, which contain a majority of voters.

## Back to Neoliberalism

After the 2013 congressional elections, the political and economic situations continued to turn against the Kirchner administration amid accusations of corruption, economic slowdown, internal dissent among Peronists, and stronger opposition on the part of the Radicals, Socialists, and the center-right PRO (Republican Proposal) party led by the former mayor of Buenos Aires city, Mauricio Macri. Soon, the PRO, the Radical Party, and other minor groups established an electoral coalition called Cambiemos (Let's Change) to compete in the October 2015 general elections. In turn, the Peronists remained internally divided among groups that embraced more conservative or leftist populist positions, fluctuated between supporting or opposing Cristina Kirchner, and coalesced around personalistic leaders in different parts of the country. Between 2013 and 2015, The administration continued to lose popularity, as inflation, fiscal deficits, exchange controls, taxation inequalities, and corruption denouncements and investigations particularly affected the middle class and turned its members toward the opposition. Internal confrontations among Peronists weakened the capacity of the party to mobilize support among the working class and middle sectors. Finally, with the support of Cristina Kirchner, the former Peronist governor of Buenos Aires province, Daniel Scioli, became the candidate of the Frente para la Victoria (Front for the Victory—the Kirchner-supported coalition of Peronist and allied groups) but he remained debilitated by strong internal opposition and his own lack of national popularity. In the general elections of October 2015, Scioli obtained 37 percent of the presidential ballots while Macri trailed close behind with 34 percent of the votes. As no candidate obtained an adequate plurality, these results required a run-off election that took place on November 22. In this election Mauricio Macri obtained 51.3 percent of the votes and was elected president for the period 2015–2019 while Scioli came in close behind with 48.7 percent of the votes. This marked the first time that the candidate of a center-right nontraditional party had been elected president. In Congress, the Cambiemos coalition was unable to obtain a majority in either chamber and its different components (Radicals, PRO and others) announced that they will conform separate blocs, although cooperating with each other. The Frente para la Victoria retained a plurality in the lower chamber but lost its majority but gained a majority in the Senate. Other Peronist dissident groups and minor parties gained sufficient representatives as to be able to tip the balance in the House of Deputies. All of this indicated that the Macri administration would need to engage in negotiations with the different groups in Congress to advance its parliamentary initiatives. In the rest of the elections, the PRO won the two largest electoral districts, the province of Buenos Aires and the city of Buenos Aires, but diverse Peronist candidates, Radicals, and minor provincial parties won the governorships of the remainder of the provinces.

The first year of the Macri administration was characterized by a return to the implementation of neoliberal policies and the attempt to reverse the populist strategy pursued by its predecessors. In the first few months of 2016, the administration removed or reduced most agricultural exports taxes and eliminated the currency exchange controls, satisfying the demands of the middle class and exporters but generating an important devaluation and contributing to increase inflation. It also negotiated an agreement to pay the debt demanded by the so-called vulture funds, contributing to the removal of the country's default status in the international financial system but at the cost of reducing reserves. The attempts to reduce the fiscal deficit were concentrated in the elimination of subsidies and social expenditures as well as reducing public employment and the transfers of federal funds to the provinces. These measures slowed down the growth of the deficit but had a negative impact on employment and the fight against poverty while affecting domestic consumption and economic growth. Macri also moved in the direction of eliminating the legislation and agencies aimed to regulate the media. At the same time, Macri negotiated sometimes successfully with different blocs in Congress to approve some of these measures while appealing to presidential decrees to impose other decisions that could not gain parliamentary support.

In the foreign relations domain, Macri moved toward generating a rapprochement with the U.S. and the international financial community while distancing himself from populist and leftist governments (such as those of Venezuela, Cuba, Bolivia, and Ecuador) that had been closely associate with Kirchner. Meanwhile, the administration continued to support anticorruption campaigns and judicial investigations aimed at weakening, isolating, and criminally prosecuting Cristina Kirchner and her closest associates.

By mid-2016, although some of these measures guaranteed some popularity for the administration, particularly among the middle and upper sectors, growing domestic tensions and opposition had begun to emerge especially focused on the fiscal adjustment policies and the inability to contain inflation and generate economic growth. The attempt to impose huge increases in the prices of public services (between 300 and 400 percent for natural gas, electricity, and water, and around 100 percent in public transportation) led to an explosion of public discontent resulting in protests, marches, and demonstrations that unified working- and middle-class sectors in opposition to the administration even after some of these price raises were declared illegal and rescinded by the judicial authorities. After this backlash, Macri attempted to regain some popularity by introducing a few tax relief measures aimed at lower income groups and retirees and engaging in a more gradualist approach to economic adjustment, but by the end of 2016 his approval ratings were under 50 percent as the political attention began to be focused in the congressional midterm elections of October 2017 in which the opposition expected to make gains.

## Politics and Power

### Constitutional Framework and Political Institutions

The Argentine constitution, promulgated in 1853 and amended on different occasions, is currently in effect after having been rescinded or suspended during different periods of authoritarian rule. The 1853 constitution instituted a republican and representative political system with moderate federal features. It provided for a division of powers between the executive, legislative—divided into a Chamber of Deputies and a Senate—and judicial branches while upholding a presidentialist regime. The constitution guarantees a number of individual rights, among them freedom of association, speech, and press; protection of domicile, correspondence, and private activities against unwarranted government searches and interference; equality before the law; right to a public trial; and prohibition of retroactive application of any laws. Freedom of religion and freedom of public worship are also sanctioned, but the Catholic Church maintains a privileged position, enjoying economic support from the federal government. In economic terms, the 1853 constitution was extremely liberal, establishing the inviolability of private property, espousing free trade and market principles, promoting foreign immigration and investment, and opening internal rivers to free navigation.

The 1853 constitution was amended but remained largely unchanged until 1949, when a convention convened by President Perón—in circumstances defined as illegal by the opposition—introduced substantial reforms, including the possibility of presidential re-election and endorsing state economic intervention, limitations on private property rights, and nationalization of natural resources, public utilities, credit, and foreign trade. After Perón's overthrow, the military government declared the 1949 constitutional reform null and void and summoned a new constitutional convention, which adjourned after having approved a single new article guaranteeing workers' rights, minimum wages, and social security benefits.

In 1994, under Menem, a constitutional convention shortened the duration of the presidential and vice-presidential mandate to four years and established direct popular presidential elections with a system of run-off voting (that replaced the electoral college). It also introduced new constitutional rights and guarantees, including consumer, children's, and indigenous population's rights, and endorsed legislation establishing women's right to occupy at least one-third of all elective positions.

The executive branch consists of the president, the vice president, and the cabinet. Executive power is vested in the president, who can appoint and remove the ministers at will, except the chief of cabinet, who is answerable to the president but politically responsible to Congress and can be removed through a non-confidence vote. The president and vice president are elected directly by popular vote through a run-off system for a four-year term with the possibility of immediate re-election for one additional period. The president is the "supreme chief of the nation," whose powers include the general administration of the country, the appointment of administration officials, the implementation of laws, the right to introduce laws before Congress and to veto or approve legislation in part or as a whole, and the conduct of foreign relations. The president is the commander-in-chief of the armed forces and nominates Supreme Court justices and members of the diplomatic corps for confirmation by the Senate. The president can also declare, with the approval of the Senate, a state of siege, temporarily suspending some civil liberties in case of external attack or internal rebellion. Argentina follows a presidentialist tradition, concentrating in the presidents a large amount of power that makes it possible for them to often dominate the legislative and judicial branches.

The legislative branch consists of two houses: the Chamber of Deputies and the Senate. According to the constitution, the deputies represent the nation as a whole, while the senators represent the provinces and the Federal District. Congress has the power to make all laws and regulations, levy taxes and establish the budget of the central government, ratify or reject treaties and integration accords, authorize the executive to declare war, declare a state of siege and intervene in a province, and accept or reject the resignation of the president and vice president. Both chambers possess similar powers, and their approval is required to pass most legislation. To override a presidential veto, two-thirds of the votes in both chambers are required.

Judicial power at the national level is exercised by the Supreme Court of Justice and the lower courts created by Congress. The judicial branch is formally independent but, in practice, has been affected by external interferences and internal problems. The judiciary has often been subordinated to political authorities; judges and judicial personnel have been removed and replaced for political reasons, and the executive has disregarded judicial decisions. Compounding these problems, the judiciary has been plagued by slow procedures, frequent reversals of precedents, lack of citizen access, occasional corruption, and political disagreements between its members.

Traditionally, Argentina had a significantly large and diversified public sector composed of the central administration, decentralized agencies, and state enterprises. Since the rise of Peronism in the 1940s, the public sector grew very rapidly as the regulatory, distributive, and productive functions of the state expanded. The central administration has been highly bureaucratic in its procedures and clientelistic in its recruitment and composition. Attempts made by successive civilian and military governments to increase efficiency, reduce size, and attract better-qualified candidates were frustrated by the inability of these same administrations to forego clientelistic practices and risk political and social confrontations. Menem was more successful at reducing the size of the state, but clientelistic practices, bureaucratic procedures, and corruption continued to plague some areas of the public administration. The Kirchners' administrations reversed some of these moves and regained state control over a number of privatized enterprises (particularly in the areas of energy, transportation, and public services) while expanding the role of the state in economic and social areas.

According to the constitution, the twenty-three provinces and the Federal District retain all power not delegated to the federal government. Each province elects its own legislature and governor, but the constitution makes governors the "natural agents" of the federal government, in charge of enforcing the national constitution and laws. Contributing to reinforce the subordination of the provinces to the central authority is the federal government's power to take over and replace local officials with federal appointees when the "republican form of government" is endangered by internal conflicts. Because the courts have declined to define the notion of "republicanism," arguing that it is a political matter, federal authorities can define these circumstances very broadly and assume control of a province without judicial interference.

## MAIN POLITICAL PARTIES

**Unión Cívica Radical.** The Radical party emerged as the first Argentine modern mass party demanding the end of the oligarchic regime and renewal and moralization in the political, electoral, and administrative spheres. It was supported by diverse groups, including university students, marginal members of the elite, and middle- and low-income creole sectors. In 1896, Hipólito Yrigoyen became the leader of the party and began to expand its basis of support by recruiting new members among the immigrant-descent urban middle class and workers. The promulgation, in 1912, of an electoral law that guaranteed free, universal male, obligatory suffrage facilitated Yrigoyen's presidential victory in 1916. Under Yrigoyen, the Radicals favored some nationalistic and statist policies and implemented moderate redistributive and social policies, although without affecting the essential characteristics of the agriculturally based export–import model.

In the 1930s, after the overthrow of Yrigoyen, the Radicals were prevented from coming back to power by the use of repression, proscription, and fraud. After being defeated by the Peronists in 1946, Radicalism remained the main opposition and adopted a program calling for nationalization of natural resources, strategic industries and services, state intervention in the economy, income redistribution, and an independent foreign policy while denouncing the Peronist violations of civil liberties and political freedoms.

After supporting the military coup that ousted Perón, the Radicals split into two different parties: the Intransigent faction, led by Arturo Frondizi, and the People's faction, led by Ricardo Balbín. In the elections of 1958, after having reached an agreement with Perón, Frondizi was elected president with Peronist support but rapidly lost it and was overthrown in 1962. In 1964, taking advantage of the proscription of Peronism, the People's Radicals won the presidential elections. The new president, Arturo Illia, implemented some modest nationalistic and redistributive policies while respecting most constitutional freedoms and guarantees until he was overthrown by the military in 1966.

In the 1970s, the People's faction was able to obtain the exclusive use of the UCR name. Two major internal groups emerged during this period; one, led by Balbín, embraced moderate positions, favored alliances with other political parties, and maintained a friendly approach toward Perón; another, led by Raúl Alfonsín, favored more nationalistic and redistributive economic policies and opposed collaboration with Perón. Although losing two successive presidential elections to the Peronists in 1973 and being unable to prevent the military coup of 1976, Balbín remained leader of the party until his death in 1981. In 1982, when the military announced the call for elections, Alfonsín gained control over the party and became its successful presidential candidate. The Radical defeat in the 1989 presidential elections, hyperinflation, the electoral decline in successive congressional elections, and secret negotiations with Menem on constitutional reform eroded Alfonsín's popularity but were not enough to completely upset his control over the party machine. In the late 1990s, the Radicals were able to regain some popularity among the middle-class sectors by denouncing the socioeconomic difficulties and corruption associated with the Menem administration. The conformation of the alliance with the center-left FrePaSo helped facilitate this recovery, and by 1998 the Radicals were once again in a competitive political position. In November 1998, Fernando de la Rúa, president of the Radical Party and mayor of the city of Buenos Aires, won the open primaries organized by the alliance and became its presidential candidate for the 1999 elections. De la Rúa's victory in the presidential elections temporarily strengthened the Radical Party, but very soon the decline of his administration led to factional splits and reduced the party's popularity to its lowest historical level. During the 1990s and early 2000s, different groups, such as the one led by Elisa Carrió, split from the party and established their own political organizations while a number of Radical provincial factions became integrated into the Kirchnerist coalition (known as Radicals K), including the one led by Julio Cobos from the province of Mendoza, who became the vice-presidential candidate in the formula led by Cristina Fernández. In the 2007 general elections, the Radicals formed a coalition that came in third with only 17 percent of the votes, but the party was able to regain some popularity and improve its electoral performance, establishing coalitions, and gaining with its allies around one-quarter of the votes in the 2013 elections. In the 2015 general elections, the party established an electoral alliance called Cambiemos (Let's Change) with the PRO (Propuesta Republicana Party) of Mauricio Macri and was able to secure a minority but adequate representation in Congress and to win several governorships.

**Peronist Party.** The Peronist Party was created in 1946 after Perón's victory in the presidential elections. Throughout Perón's first presidency (1946–1952), the party, which after the introduction of women's suffrage in 1947 was divided into male and female sections, played a secondary role in the Peronist movement. The party was reduced to mobilize Peronist voters at election times and to disseminate the *doctrina justicialista*, an ideology advocated by Perón that represented a third option between capitalism and communism and called for social class cooperation, state intervention, nationalistic policies, and nonalignment to build an Argentina that would be economically independent, socially just, and politically sovereign. During Perón's unfinished second presidency (1952–1955), the party's importance increased as Perón's authoritarian turn led to attempts to establish partisan control over civil service and socioeconomic organizations.

After Perón's fall, the party became an underground political organization subordinated to the exiled leader, conveying Perón's orders to his followers. However, Perón was unable to prevent the emergence of the so-called neo-Peronist parties that, with the support of some union leaders, were determined to develop a "Peronism without Perón." Most of these parties had a brief existence, but a few of them established provincial roots and have remained active until today.

In the 1970s, Peronism was formally reorganized as the Justice Party (Partido Justicialista; PJ). Perón remained the party chief, with the right to appoint or remove the party authorities and select its electoral candidates. However, internal factions—including union leadership, guerrilla groups, professional politicians, and youth organizations—were vying for power. Perón tried to reestablish his authority and prevent further divisions by becoming president and nominating his wife for vice president, but his death in 1974 cleared the way for violent internal confrontations.

After the 1976 military coup, Peronism was banned, and many of its leaders were jailed, persecuted, or killed by the military. The party resurfaced in 1982 but split into a so-called *verticalista* faction—interested in maintaining the power of the traditional political and union bosses and continuing the tradition of hierarchical control from the top as practiced by Perón—and a number of anti-*verticalista* groups—which tried to introduce more democratic procedures and elect a new leadership. The *verticalistas* succeeded, appointing Isabel Perón president of the party and nominating traditional politicians and union bosses as candidates for most elective offices. The nondemocratic features of this process, the unsavory personalities and activities of some of the Peronist candidates, and the growing popularity of Alfonsín combined to produce the defeat of the PJ in the 1983 elections. The confrontation between *verticalistas* and anti-*verticalistas* resumed, with the former considerably weakened and the latter strengthened by these results.

By the late 1980s, Carlos Menem, a provincial governor and vice president of the party, appealed to populist and nationalistic rhetoric to prevail in the first open party primaries and went on to win the presidential election of 1989. After his inauguration, Menem reasserted his control over the party by becoming its president. Attempts made by groups opposed to Menem to maintain some influence failed, and the party remained under the control of the president's supporters, although new internal divisions emerged as Menem's second presidential term came to an end. In 1998 and 1999, Menem tried unsuccessfully to nullify the constitutional article that made it impossible for him to run for a third presidential term, but he confronted growing opposition from important party figures such as Eduardo Duhalde, the governor of Buenos Aires province, who finally became the Peronist presidential candidate in the 1999 elections. Duhalde's defeat left the party in disarray, and a number of Peronist leaders began to compete to gain control over the party machine in anticipation of the 2003 presidential elections. The collapse of the de la Rúa administration led to a period of dramatic internal confrontation within the party from which Duhalde emerged as the winner, consolidating his control over the party machine and becoming provisional president. After Duhalde supported the presidential candidacy of Kirchner, a new internal party struggle developed that ended with the victory of Kirchner, although the party remained divided into competing factions.

In the elections of 2007, 2011, and 2013, various Peronist groups competed for control of the party and supported different presidential, congressional, and gubernatorial candidates. The faction led by Cristina Kirchner maintained its hegemony until 2015 but after loss of that year's presidential elections several different groups have been formally established and compete with each other in the attempt to gain control over the party or by establishing dissident Peronist organizations.

**Other Parties and Coalitions.** Besides the Radical and Peronist parties, there has been a continuous presence in the Argentine political scene of a number of minor parties and coalitions. On the left, there have been multiple organizations—including socialists, communists, Trotzkyists, and other groups—that, at different times, played a role in the electoral contests, especially in the urban areas but that have been affected by their inability to overcome ideological divergences, avoid factionalism, and compete successfully for the working- and middle-class voters who support the Peronist and Radical parties. On the right, there have been a series of provincial parties that have remained influential at the local level but have been unable to organize a successful conservative alliance at the national level. In the last few years, there were also several leftist, center-left, and center-right parties and coalitions that attained relative success for brief periods but that disintegrated rapidly. At the time of the 2013 elections, the most relevant of these parties and coalitions were, on the left, the Leftist and Workers Front (FRIP) led by the Trotzkyist Worker Party; on the center-left, the Socialist Progressive Front led by Hermes Binner and the UNEN coalition led by Elisa Carrió; and on the center-right the Republican Proposal (PRO) led by Mauricio Macri, the mayor of the city of Buenos Aires. The PRO became formally established as a party in 2010 under the leadership of Macri and adopted a conservative, center-right ideology favorable to neoliberalism and strongly opposed to the populist policies. After creating an electoral coalition (Cambiemos) with the Radical and other minor parties, Macri won the run-off election of November 2015 and was elected president for the period 2015–2019.

## INTEREST GROUPS

**The Military.** The modern Argentine armed forces were organized as a professional institution during the late nineteenth century and remained subordinated to the civilian authorities until 1930. Since then, the military has not only organized coups and established authoritarian regimes but also played a crucial political role under most civilian administrations, exercising indirect control and vetoing government initiatives. Most officers have embraced conservative positions and supported the creation of a political system characterized by limited participation, hierarchical order, and an emphasis on domestic national security. However, agreement of these basic points has not prevented the emergence of factions that disagreed on the best methods to attain these goals or that were motivated by personalistic and group ambitions.

After overthrowing Perón in 1955, the coup leaders purged Perón's supporters from the officer corps but split into moderate and radical anti-Peronist factions, a division that would linger until the 1970s. The continuous capacity of Peronism to obtain electoral majorities and the civilian administrations' inability to suppress it resulted in the military coups of 1962 and 1966. In 1966, General Juan Carlos Onganía banned all political parties and established a bureaucratic authoritarian regime. However, growing economic and social problems accompanied by urban revolts and the rise of guerrilla movements led to Onganía's removal by his fellow officers and to a call for elections in which Peronism was finally allowed to participate.

In 1976, the armed forces overthrew Isabel Perón and inaugurated an authoritarian regime that, unlike previous ones, divided power equally among the three branches and attempted to create a system in which the military as an institution exercised power. However, as the difficulties accumulated, the military split once again into opposing factions: one group tried to implement less orthodox economic policies while establishing closer ties with conservative and provincial parties to co-opt their support; another group favored market policies and opposed any kind of political opening. The latter tried to overcome the crisis by increasing repression and arousing nationalistic feelings through the recovery of the Falkland/Malvinas Islands. The defeat on the islands forced the military to call for elections that resulted in a radical victory.

Under Alfonsín, the military budget was greatly reduced and the power of the civilian authorities was strengthened. The members of the three military juntas were tried and sentenced to prison for human rights violations. However, as the number of officers brought to trial increased, the military multiplied its demonstrations of discontent and refused to testify before civilian judges. Faced with growing disobedience, Alfonsín tried to limit the number of military officers under judicial investigation by supporting a law that extinguished any penal action against officers if they were not indicted within sixty days after the promulgation of the law. When this was not enough to satisfy the military and a revolt erupted, Alfonsín supported a "due obedience law" that exempted most officers from trial, with the exception of those who had been top commanders during the dirty war.

The concessions made by Menem, especially the pardons for the members of the juntas, satisfied most of the military and diminished support for the rebellious groups, making it possible to defeat and expel them from the ranks. After this, the military remained subordinated to the civilian government, performing its professional activities and exhibiting no signs of being interested in meddling in the political arena. This stance was not modified even when, in 2001, a judge declared the unconstitutionality of the laws passed under Alfonsín, renewing the possibility of bringing to trial those officers accused of human rights violations. Although vehemently opposed to this decision, the military did not revolt as it had done in the past, preferring, in this case, to appeal the decision to higher courts. In the last few years, the military and human rights policies implemented by the Kirchners, which included the replacement of the high military command, the reduction of military budgets, and the resumption of trials for human rights violations committed during the period of military rule, have displeased the armed forces, but, once again, the military has preferred to use constitutional channels and means to convey its dissatisfaction. The Macri administration has shown less inclination to confront the military on human rights issues but to a large extent dealing with the military human rights violations remains a judicial problem.

**The Catholic Church.** The Catholic Church has played an influential role in Argentine politics, as either a supporter or an opponent of specific policies implemented by different governments, particularly in the educational and social areas. The 1853 constitution instituted freedom of belief but granted Catholicism a privileged position by requiring the federal government to finance the Church and requiring the president and vice president to be Catholic, although this last provision was eliminated in 1994.

The Catholic Church has supported those governments that promised to implement policies that corresponded to a conservative interpretation of Catholic teachings, disregarding the authoritarian or democratic origins of these administrations. When some governments formulated policies that clashed with these notions, the Church conducted political campaigns aimed at reversing these measures and sometimes supported initiatives to remove from power those governments responsible for them. The majority of bishops and cardinals have been consistently conservative, even during the 1960s and 1970s when less traditional attitudes proliferated in the rest of Latin America. The emergence in Argentina of a group of progressive priests who embraced liberation theology was a phenomenon restricted mainly to the rank and file, though a few bishops sympathized with them. Most Church authorities welcomed the military coups of 1966 and 1976, especially because right-wing nationalistic figures associated with the Church were appointed to important positions.

Throughout the 1976–1983 period, most Church dignitaries supported the military regime or adopted neutral positions, and only a few bishops openly opposed the authoritarian government, even when some members of the Church (including bishops, priests, and lay associates) were killed, jailed, and persecuted. After the restoration of democracy in 1983, the most conflictive aspects of church–state relations were focused on family, cultural, and educational issues. Under Alfonsín, the Church hierarchy unsuccessfully opposed the passing of a divorce law and a more liberal family code. This defeat strengthened the influence of a more moderate group of bishops who emphasized the moral role of the Church but distanced themselves from open political actions. Under Menem, the Church hierarchy initially adopted a more supportive attitude than during the Alfonsín administration in the expectation that the new president, who had opposed the divorce law and advocated the Church's social teachings, would follow a less secular course. However, some members of the hierarchy criticized the application of economic policies that affected the poor and generated unemployment, while others denounced the pardons given by Menem to the military. During the Kirchner administrations, the Church confronted the government on issues such as reproductive rights, AIDS policies, gay marriage, sexual education, and private education, while being threatened by the resumption of human rights trials that resulted in the condemnation of some priests involved in repressive activities and the dismissal of military chaplains. In 2013, the election as pope of the cardinal archbishop of Buenos Aires, Jorge Mario Bergoglio, who adopted the papal name of Francis, helped the Argentine Church to regain some popularity among the population and strengthened its position but did not result in reversals of decisions that the hierarchy had opposed, such as the legalization of divorce and gay marriage and the reopening of the human rights trials that began to affect some members of the Church who cooperated with the military dictatorship.

**Organized Labor.** Argentina's long tradition of well-organized and relatively powerful labor organizations started in the late nineteenth century. The first unions were formed by European immigrants, particularly skilled workers, who embraced anarchist and socialist ideologies. In the 1940s, Perón was able to skillfully manipulate the labor movement through a combination of rewards for his supporters (collective bargaining, official recognition, social benefits) and elimination of his opponents (denial of legal recognition and benefits and removal from office). By 1945, the General Confederation of Labor (CGT) was under the control of Peronist union leaders, many of them newly elected, and the numbers of union-ized workers increased rapidly. In October 1945, a workers' mobilization forced the release of Perón from confinement and cleared the way for his presidential campaign. After Perón's inauguration, union membership became obligatory for most workers, the number of unionized workers greatly increased, and their wages and benefits improved. The CGT remained firmly under the control of Perón, who eliminated political dissidents and appointed loyal members of small unions to lead the organization.

After Perón's fall, the CGT and most unions were taken over by the military; however, in elections held in 1956, a majority of the unions elected Peronist leaders, and in the early 1960s the Peronists regained control of the CGT. Although perse-cuted and banned by different military and civilian governments, organized labor became an important political actor able to use its mobilization capacity to support Peronism and strengthen or weaken the administrations established between 1958 and 1976.

Under the 1976–1983 authoritarian regime, the CGT was taken over by the military, and some influential labor leaders who tried to oppose the military rulers were kidnapped and killed or forced into exile. As the economic crisis erupted, union leaders led some demonstrations and strikes but remained weak and disor-ganized. Only after the Falklands/Malvinas crisis were the multiple labor factions able to overcome part of their differences and to reestablish a unified CGT under Peronist control.

After the defeat of the PJ in the 1983 elections, confrontations within the CGT became more acute and created the opportunity for the rise of new labor leaders. In 1986, the CGT regained legal status and pursued a number of goals, among which the most important were the recomposition of real wages, the control of social ser-vices, and the promulgation of a new law on trade unions; but its ability to exact concessions from the government was limited by its lack of internal unity.

Some labor leaders negotiated with the Radical government and secured the appointment of one of their own as minister of labor. The Alfonsín administration sent to Congress a package of labor legislation reestablishing collective bargaining, maintaining union-provided social services, and strengthening the rights of orga-nized labor. However, after the Radical electoral defeats, this alliance collapsed and most union leaders went back to the Peronist fold and organized several gen-eral strikes.

After his inauguration, Menem saw an independent CGT as an obstacle to the smooth implementation of a neoliberal program. Collaborationist union leaders were appointed to government positions and tried to gain control over the CGT, which split into two rival organizations: one stated its complete loyalty to the ad-ministration and supported the neoliberal economic plan, and the other declared its support for Peronism but opposed the economic policies and warned that it would continue to fight for higher wages and against dismissals. In late 1992, public em-ployees' and teachers' unions joined by other smaller organizations formed a new labor organization, the Argentine Workers Central (CTA) that strongly opposed the neoliberal economic policies, denounced the official CGT as collaborationist, and established political links with the opposition. In 1994, a group of Peronist unions, led by the transportation workers' union, broke away from the CGT and formed another organization, the Movement of Argentine Workers (MTA), demanding tougher opposition to the government's labor and welfare policies. Meanwhile, as a result of Menem's neoliberal policies, the number of workers affiliated with unions had decreased from 50 to 35 percent while the number of self-employed, unemployed, and nonunionized workers had increased substantially.

In 2000, sectors of organized labor confronted the de la Rúa administration and called for strikes to oppose a new labor law that would weaken job stability and curtail the application of collective bargaining agreements. However, the divisions inside the labor movement prevented the creation of a unified front, and the labor reform promoted by the government was passed with the support of the CGT's moderate union leaders against MTA resistance. After de la Rúa's fall, the labor movement was reunified into a single CGT that by 2005 was led by Hugo Moyano, from the truck drivers' union. Under Moyano, the CGT initially maintained a relatively friendly approach toward the Kirchner administration, but there were internal labor disputes for the leadership positions, with the opponents to Moyano unsuccessfully asking for his replacement. Later on, Moyano demanded wage raises to compensate for inflation and clashed with Cristina Kirchner, who announced her intention to promote a "social pact" that would try to prevent wage and price increases while confronting Moyano. Ultimately, the clashes led to a formal break as Moyano called for strikes against Kirchner and sided with the Peronist dissidents while the president offered support to Moyano's adversaries in the labor movement By 2016, the Argentine labor movement was divided into five different organizations that competed with each other for hegemony and that fluctuated between supporting or opposing the administrations: the CGT led by the metalworker Antonio Caló (officially recognized); the CGT led by Moyano; the CTA led by Hugo Yasky; the Autonomous Workers Central led by Pablo Micheli; and the CGT–Blue and White led by Luis Barrionuevo.

In the late 1990s, in the context of the socioeconomic crisis, two important social movements emerged in Argentina: the *piqueteros* (pickets) and the recovered factories movement. The *piquetero* organizations are made up of unemployed workers that demand jobs and economic support by demonstrating in the streets and blocking important roads and bridges. They have evolved into a number of unemployed workers' groups that have been able to obtain subsidies from the government and exercise some degree of political influence, especially during the Kirchner administration, although they remain divided between softliners (open to cooperation with the government) and hardliners (embracing more radical positions). The recovered factory movement is made up of workers who have taken over closed factories and other enterprises (such as hotels and service companies), transforming them into self-managed units. There are around 150 of these recovered companies with more than 15,000 workers. They have counted on some moderate support on the part of the Kirchner administrations, but many of them face important economic and legal challenges while the movement itself remains divided into different currents, weakening the ability to advance its demands.

**Business Associations.** Argentine business associations are organized along sectors of economic activity, including agricultural, industrial, commercial, and financial interests. Among the agricultural associations, the most powerful are the Argentine Rural Society, which represents the interests of the largest and wealthiest landowners—cattle raisers and grain producers—and the Argentine Rural Confederation, which represents the interests of the medium to large agricultural producers, including cattle breeders and grain producers. Both organizations strongly defend private property rights—opposing any land reform—and advocate free market and trade policies. In the 1990s, they became the strongest supporters of Menem's economic policies, particularly welcoming the elimination of exchange controls and regulations and agricultural state boards and the measures directed to reduce labor costs. After the collapse of neoliberal policies, they maintained a strong opposition to any tax increases and introduction of new regulations becoming the leaders of the opposition to Cristina Kirchner's attempt to increase export taxes on agricultural commodities.

The Argentine Agrarian Federation initially represented tenant farmers and afterward small- and medium-sized farmers engaged in mixed agricultural and cattle-raising activities that produce mostly for the domestic market. Politically, it has usually opposed authoritarian regimes and supported democracy, favoring some degree of state intervention to enlarge the domestic market and protect small producers. It has been less supportive of neoliberal policies, expressing concern about the decline of the domestic market and the increase in agricultural imports, and maintained a close cooperation with the Néstor Kirchner administration, although it joined the other rural associations in opposition to Cristina Kirchner's attempt to raise export taxes.

The most important industrial association is the Argentine Industrial Union, whose membership and influence expanded as the ISI process developed. The organization was controlled by the large industrialists from Buenos Aires who opposed Perón's labor policies. After becoming president, Perón dissolved the organization and replaced it with another that represented the interests of the smaller industrialists of the interior and those that emerged as a result of the Peronist industrializing policies. After Perón's fall, the Industrial Union was restored and continued to represent the larger domestic and foreign industrial companies that supported a moderately liberal economic approach, although it also favored some state intervention and protection to promote its interests. The 1976–1983 military regime recognized the Argentine Industrial Union as representative of all industrial groups, but two factions emerged: one that represented the large industrial groups with liberal economic positions and another that represented the smaller industrial groups of the interior and favored some degree of state intervention. Under Menem, the former backed most of the neoliberal policies, while the latter expressed reservations concerning the rapid opening of the economy and the decline of the domestic market. Under the Kirchners, economic growth and redistribution policies led to an industrial recovery that benefited particularly those sectors producing for the domestic market.

The Argentine Chamber of Commerce represents the interests of the commercial sector but also includes among its members representatives of the insurance, transportation, and financial companies. It has always defended the free market system, advocated free trade, and called for the lifting of price controls and state regulations. In political terms, it has traditionally supported conservative civilian and military governments while opposing those that followed populist and state-led strategies. In the 1990s, it became one of the strongest supporters of Menem's neoliberal policies and stated its strong opposition to some of the redistributionist and state interventionist policies implemented by Duhalde and Kirchner.

Bank organizations include the Association of Banks of the Argentine Republic, the Association of Argentine Banks, and the Association of Banks of the Interior of the Argentine Republic. The first represents the interests of the largest banks, more than half of which are foreign owned. The other two associations represent the interests of smaller banks mostly of local capital. All of them support liberal economic principles, including free financial and exchange markets, but they differ on the roles to be played by foreign capital and the state. While the first supports unrestricted free movement of capital and complete lifting of most financial regulations, the other two favor some regulations to prevent the concentration of capital in the largest foreign and national banks.

## Women's Roles

Women's participation in Argentina's labor force has been increasing steadily since the 1940s, with 61 percent of women participating in the labor force as of 2007. However, around two-thirds of female workers were concentrated in the service sector, and wages for women were estimated to be, on average, one-third lower than those for men. In terms of education, women have fared better, having attained a higher level of literacy and high school attendance than men and representing a substantial proportion of university students, including those in traditionally male-dominated careers such as law, medicine, and engineering.

In the political realm, women have played an increasingly important role, particularly since their enfranchisement in the late 1940s. Since the turn of the century, Argentine women have fought for the right to vote and participated in political party activities, particularly in left and center-left parties. The emergence of Peronism in the 1940s was associated with the rise to prominence of Evita Perón, who became one of the twentieth century's leading political figures and has remained a revered icon for a substantial sector of the population. She was instrumental in securing the extension of the right to vote to women in 1947 and became the leader of the women's sector of the Peronist Party until her death in 1952. After 1947, women became active participants in many of the political parties, were elected to the national and provincial legislatures, and were appointed members of different cabinets, although in a lesser proportion than men. In 1973, Isabel Perón—Juan Perón's third wife—was elected vice president of the country in a formula headed by her husband. After Perón's death in 1974, she became the president of the country until she was overthrown by the military coup of March 1976.

Women played a crucial role during the last military dictatorship (1976–1983) in the struggle for human rights and democracy. The Mothers (and Grandmothers) of the Plaza de Mayo became the main opponents of the military junta, openly denouncing the terrorist tactics of the regime and demanding the return of the disappeared. Through their brave actions, which cost them heavily in terms of repression and persecution, the Mothers were able to call world attention to the brutality of the military government and to mobilize sectors of the Argentine population in the demand for respect for human rights and the establishment of democracy. After the transition to democracy, the Mothers and other human rights organizations in which women play a fundamental role have continuously demanded the investigation and condemnation of those responsible for terrorist practices and the return of the children of the disappeared.

In the 1990s, to increase women's formal political representation, a constitutionally endorsed law required that political parties reserve every third place on their lists of candidates for women. The implementation of this quota law, the first in the world of its kind, led to a rapid increase in the number of women elected to office; currently around 40 percent of the seats in Congress are occupied by women representing different parties. Also, there has been an increase in the number of women in ministerial and secretarial positions and running for executive office at the provincial level since the reestablishment of democracy, but the proportion of women appointed and elected to these offices remains relatively low. The 2007 general elections resulted in the presidential victory of Cristina Fernández de Kirchner while the runner-up was another woman, Elisa Carrió. The president emphasized that she will be guided by the example of Eva Perón and the Mothers and Grandmothers of the Plaza de Mayo in her attempts to eliminate poverty, defend human rights, and punish their violations. In 2011, Cristina Kirchner was re-elected president, while women's representation in Congress had risen to around 40 percent in both the upper and lower chambers, indicating that the trend toward gender equality continues uninterrupted.

## Looking Forward: Argentina's Political Prospects

In the 1980s and 1990s, the Argentine political-economic situation was characterized by the gradual consolidation of a liberal democratic regime and the implementation of neoliberal economic policies. This development surprised many analysts familiar with the country's evolution in the twentieth century. In the past, these elements were clearly antagonistic: liberal democratic governments felt threatened by the local versions of populism and were unable to stand the negative reactions generated by the attempts to implement free market policies; populist regimes were perceived as incompatible with liberal democracy and neoliberal economic programs because they often engaged in authoritarian practices and favored state intervention in the economy; and economic liberal programs were implemented through authoritarian means by the elites and the military due to their inability to gain electoral support and popular backing for free market policies. The inability to reconcile these elements became an important factor in fostering the periodic outbursts of political, economic, and social instability that resulted in Argentina's traditional merry-go-round of military and civilian governments since 1930.

The current situation, characterized by the existence of a constitutional, liberal democratic regime with successive elected administrations able to implement neoliberal and populist policies without generating the collapse of democracy, represents a scenario that would have been considered implausible in the past. Nevertheless, the stability of the emergent Argentine liberal democracy is still an issue when considering the strength and durability of the commitment to this regime by different domestic groups. In Argentina, support for liberal democracy has depended on a number of political variables, such as the degree of devastation brought about by authoritarian regimes and the intensity of the population's revulsion against these regimes, the depth of the popular belief in the legitimacy of democracy, the ability of democratic governments to establish effective institutional arrangements, and the existence of representative political parties. However, when confronted with the rise of tensions between market and democracy, the elected administrations turned in different degrees to solutions that, without eliminating the liberal democratic features of the regime, represented a consistent effort to concentrate political power in the executive branch, limit the participation or influence of organized political and socioeconomic groups in the decisions, and establish direct relations between personalistic leaders and an atomized civil society.

The fact that the concentration of power in the executive branch and the implementation of neoliberal policies facilitated a rise in corruption and generated unprecedented levels of unemployment and poverty among the population led in the early 2000s to changes in the political situation facilitating the growth of populist center-left coalitions interested in implementing policies aimed at reducing arbitrariness and corruption while lessening unemployment and poverty through the implementation of redistributive and welfare policies. However, by 2015, the neopopulist approach had also begun to show important drawbacks, including persistent inflation, economic slowdown, growing public deficits, and corruption that generated mounting opposition to the populist administration and led to the electoral return of neoliberalism to the presidency. In these conditions, the prospects for the continuous consolidation of democracy in Argentina remain brighter than they have been since the 1920s, but the stability of the democratic regime is still threatened by the existence of socioeconomic inequities and political weaknesses that could foster popular discontent and elite opposition, resulting in domestic upheaval.

# Chronology

**1516**  First Spanish expedition arrives at Río de la Plata
**1536**  First foundation of Buenos Aires; the city is abandoned in 1540
**1580**  Second foundation of Buenos Aires
**1776**  Creation of the viceroyalty of Río de la Plata
**1806–1807**  British invasions repelled by *criollo* militias

**1810** *Criollo* government junta replaces Spanish authorities

**1816** Declaration of independence

**1816–1829** Civil wars between federal and centralist factions

**1829–1852** Dictatorship of Juan Manuel de Rosas

**1853** National constitution modeled on U.S. presidentialist system adopted

**1853–1861** Sporadic civil war between Buenos Aires elites and provincial leaders

**1862–1880** Consolidation of oligarchic regime led by agro-exporting Buenos Aires elites

**1880–1916** Economic prosperity generated by export–import growth model and political stability under oligarchic regime

**1916–1930** Mass democracy under elected middle-class radical administrations: Hipólito Yrigoyen (1916–1922, 1928–1930) and Marcelo T. de Alvear (1922–1928)

**1930–1943** Great Depression and economic crisis in Argentina; military coup overthrows Yrigoyen; return of oligarchy to power and beginning of import substitution industrialization

**1943–1955** Rise and fall of Juan D. Perón's populist regime

**1955–1966** Political instability characterized by succession of military governments and limited democratic regimes

**1966–1973** Military regime in power; socioeconomic crisis, urban explosions, and guerrilla warfare

**1973–1976** Return to democracy under Peronist elected government; President Perón dies in office (1974) and is replaced by his widow and vice president, Isabel Perón; growing socioeconomic and political tensions; violent confrontations between guerrilla groups and military

**1976–1983** Military regime, dirty war, and economic crisis; invasion of Falkland Islands and defeat (1982); military call for elections (1983)

**1983–1989** Radical Party wins elections; Raúl Alfonsín elected president; growing economic and social problems; hyperinflation and political crisis

**1989–1995** Peronist candidate Carlos S. Menem elected president 1989–1995; Menem implements free market economic policies and attains political preeminence; constitution amended, allowing for presidential re-election (1994)

**1995–1999** Menem re-elected president; consolidation of market economy; growing socioeconomic problems and accusations of corruption

**1999** Electoral alliance between Radical Party and FrePaSo wins presidential election; Fernando de la Rúa and Carlos Alvarez elected president and vice president, respectively, 1999–2003

**2000** Vice President Alvarez resigns in October, denouncing lack of effective governmental action against corruption; alliance between Radicals and FrePaSo remains but is considerably weakened

**2001** President de la Rúa is forced to resign in December amid socioeconomic crisis and popular demonstrations; brief period of political turbulence with three different presidents

**2002** On January 1, Eduardo Duhalde is inaugurated president

**2003** Néstor Kirchner is elected president, 2003–2007

**2007** Cristina Fernández de Kirchner is elected president, 2007–2011

**2010**　Death of Néstor Kirchner on October 27 alters political landscape
**2011**　Cristina Fernández de Kirchner is re-elected president, 2011–2015
**2015**　Mauricio Macri is elected president for the period 2015–2019

# Bibliography

Brysk, Alison. *The Politics of Human Rights in Argentina: Protest, Change, and Democratization*. Stanford, CA: Stanford University Press, 1994.

Corradi, Juan. *The Fitful Republic: Economy, Society and Politics in Argentina*. Boulder, CO: Westview, 1985.

Epstein, Edward, ed. *The New Argentine Democracy: The Search for a Successful Formula*. Westport, CT: Praeger, 1992.

Hodges, Donald C. *Argentina's "Dirty War": An Intellectual Biography*. Austin: University of Texas Press, 1991.

Nouzeilles, Gabriela, and Graciela Montaldo, eds. *The Argentina Reader: History, Culture, Politics*. Durham, NC: Duke University Press, 2002.

O'Donnell, Guillermo. *Bureaucratic Authoritarianism: Argentina, 1966–1973, in Comparative Perspective*. Berkeley: University of California Press, 1988.

Page, Joseph. *Perón: A Biography*. New York: Random House, 1983.

Peralta Ramos, Mónica, and Carlos Waissman. *From Military Rule to Democracy in Argentina*. Boulder, CO: Westview, 1987.

Potash, Robert. *The Army and Politics in Argentina, 1928–1945: Yrigoyen to Perón*. Stanford, CA: Stanford University Press, 1969.

Potash, Robert. *The Army and Politics in Argentina, 1945–1962: Perón to Frondizi*. Stanford, CA: Stanford University Press, 1980.

Rock, David. *Argentina, 1516–1987: From Spanish Colonization to Alfonsín*. 2d ed. Berkeley: University of California Press, 1987.

Romero, Luis Alberto. *A History of Argentina in the Twentieth Century*. University Park: Pennsylvania State University Press, 2013.

Smith, William C. *Authoritarianism and the Crisis of the Argentine Political Economy*. Stanford, CA: Stanford University Press, 1989.

Snow, Peter, and Luigi Manzetti. *Political Forces in Argentina*. 3d ed. Westport, CT: Praeger, 1993.

Tedesco, Laura. *Democracy in Argentina. Hope and Disillusion*. London: Routledge, 2013.

Timmerman, Jacob. *Prisoner without a Name, Cell without a Number*. New York: Vintage, 1982.

### FILMS AND VIDEOS

*The Empty ATM* (Wide Angle 4). United States, 2003. Documentary examines the 2000–2001 economic, social, and political crisis and explores how Argentines dealt with the collapse of their economy.

*The Garden of Forking Paths* (Americas Program 1). United States, 1993. Documentary examining Argentina's political, economic, and social development in the twentieth century.

*Las Madres: The Mothers of Plaza de Mayo*. United States, 1985. Documentary about the courageous role played by the mothers of the disappeared.

*The Official Story*. Argentina, 1985. On the dirty war, the disappeared, and their repercussions on Argentine society.

*La República Perdida I/La República Perdida II* [The Lost Republic I and II]. Argentina, 1983/1985. Documentaries focused on the twentieth-century political history of Argentina that explore the causes of instability.

*The Secret in Their Eyes*. Argentina, 2009. Murder mystery reflects Argentine attempts to deal with the legacies of the dirty war.

*Tango Bar*. Argentina, 1988. The story of the tango is narrated against the background of Argentina's 1976–1983 dictatorship.

*The Take*. Canada/Argentina, 2004. The story of a closed factory recovered by its workers after the crisis of 2001.

## WEBSITES

Information on current Argentine events is available in English through the Foreign Broadcast Information Service–Latin America as well as the foreign news sections of the *Miami Herald, New York Times, Wall Street Journal,* and *Washington Post.* Access to the main Argentine newspapers and magazines is easily secured through the Internet on a daily and weekly basis. Among the main newspapers are the following: *Clarín* (http://www.clarin.com.ar), *La Nación* (http://www.lanacion.com.ar), and *Página/12* (http://www.pagina12.com.ar).

Political information can be obtained at different sites, including the Latin American Network Information Center (LANIC), maintained by the University of Texas, which offers a wealth of data and numerous links to different sites in Argentina and abroad dealing with governmental institutions, political parties, human rights, media, and academic research centers (http://info.lanic.utexas.edu/la/argentina/).

VENEZUELA

GUYANA

SURINAME

FRENCH
GUIANA

COLOMBIA

*Amazon River*

*AMAZON RAINFOREST*

PERU

*BRAZILIAN
HIGHLANDS*

*San Francisco River*

Recife

Salvador

Brasília
★

Belo Horizonte

BOLIVIA

CHILE

Rio de Janeiro

PARAGUAY

São Paulo

Map of
**BRAZIL**

N

W ✦ E

S

150   0   150  300   Miles

Scale 1:24,000,000

URUGUAY

ARGENTINA

# FOURTEEN

# BRAZIL

*Wilber Albert Chaffee*

## Introduction

Brazil occupies a unique position in Latin America due not only to its size but also as a result of major changes over the last twenty years that has taken it to a position of international leadership and given it a vastly improved domestic society. Even though Brazil experienced an economic down turn in 2016 and 2017, gross inequalities have been reduced, inflation that plagued the economy has been controlled, and democracy institutionalized. Today Brazil is more than Carnival and coffee; it is the seventh largest national economy, a power in global politics, and one of the BRIC (Brazil, Russia, India, and China) countries expected to be one of the major economies by 2050.

A continental nation, Brazil dominates South America, occupying half of the territory and bordering on all the other South American nations except Ecuador and Chile. One of the giants among nations, Brazil is fourth largest in area, fourth largest democracy, and the largest Catholic country. If Brazil were turned 180 degrees on the globe, its southernmost point would reach as far north as the border between North and South Carolina. The Amazon River, draining much of the land east of the Andes, carries twelve times the volume of water of the Mississippi and is navigable by ocean freighter across the width of Brazil, making the Peruvian city of Iquitos a seaport. The Amazon, itself, is the world's largest rainforest.

Now more than 200 million people, half of South America's population, Brazil's is the fifth largest in the world. Starting originally as a group of Portuguese colonies, today's population is a mix of the indigenous Amerindians; descendants of slaves brought from Africa; members of originally European immigrant families, especially Portuguese, Germans, Lebanese, and Italians; and over a million of Japanese ancestry. As a result, Brazil is second only to Nigeria in terms of persons of African ancestry and has the largest Japanese population outside of Japan. Twenty-five of Brazil's cities have metropolitan populations of 1 million or greater, with the metropolitan areas of Rio de Janeiro and São Paulo having 11 and 18 million people, respectively.

Brazil publishes 60 percent of the literature of South America and has an important national literature generally unknown in much of the rest of the world. *Autores* include Euclides da Cunha, Machado de Assis, Rachel de Queiroz, Carlos Drummond de Andrade, Guimarães Rosa, Jorge Amado, Cecília Meireles, and Clarice Lispector. The O Globo television system is one of the largest commercial networks in the world with its programming going into Portugal and Africa.

Proud of their country, Brazilians will tell you, "God is a Brazilian."

# A Brief Political History

Although Brazil is a part of Latin America, its first contacts with Europe and a history of being held together by a monarchy give it a significantly different history than its Spanish-speaking counterparts. European contact Brazil came with the landing in 1500 of Pedro Álvares Cabral at Coroa Vermelha in today's state of Bahia while sailing from Portugal to Asia via the Cape of Good Hope, the first permanent Portuguese settlement founded in 1532 at São Vicente in São Paulo. Subsequently, Portugal established colonies, called *capitanias* (captaincies) to harvest Brazilwood for textile dyes, beginning in the Northeast, the territory that bulges east toward Africa. Brazilian land proved to have good soil to expand the cultivation of sugar cane, brought from the Azores, which was followed by a massive slave trade from Portuguese colonies in Africa to tend the sugar cane and its processing in giant *engenhos* (sugar mills).

Political power was centered in *municipios* (municipalities) dominated by agricultural elites who also controlled the politics of the captaincies. Although the Portuguese crown eventually established a viceroyalty, the captaincies essentially reported directly to Lisbon.

In 1808, as a result of Napoleon's invasion and conquest of Iberia, the Portuguese royal family fled from Lisbon and established the new capital for their empire in Rio de Janeiro. For the first time, national politics in Brazil was centralized, technical schools were established, and printing presses brought in. A sense of nationhood began to develop as the captaincies became provinces. With the defeat of Napoleon, the royal family returned to Lisbon in 1821, leaving the crown prince, Dom Pedro de Bragança, as regent. At the urging of the Brazilians, Dom Pedro proclaimed the independence of Brazil in 1822, becoming its first emperor, Dom Pedro I. The independence under the emperor maintained Brazil as a single country, avoiding the disintegration that happened with Spanish colonies and the provinces now became states.

In 1831 Dom Pedro I abdicated in favor of his five-year-old son, Dom Pedro II, and the country was ruled by a regency until 1840 when the young emperor at the age of fifteen assumed full royal powers. Dom Pedro II reigned rather than ruled. During the latter part of the Portuguese colonial rule and much of the Brazilian monarchy, the British dominated Brazilian trade and its economy under special treaty rights. They supplied English manufactured goods and bought most of Brazil's exports, which were primary products, especially cotton, sugar, and minerals.

One of the few national actions was the war with Paraguay (1865–1870), which gave what may be the first real focus of nationalism and the first counterweight to the extreme federalism of Brazil in the form of an active national military. The Paraguayan War also highlighted the essential military weakness of Brazil, its lack of infrastructure, especially in its interior, and the difficulties in executing a war even against a nation as small and weak as Paraguay. The need for national economic development as a result came from the military, which saw itself as the only force really interested in the good of the nation as a whole.

Slavery became a continuingly contentious political issue, with the British pressuring Brazil to end the slave trade, and in 1871 the Law of the Free Womb made anyone born after that date a free person. In 1888, while the emperor was visiting Europe, his daughter, Princess Isabel as regent and under pressure from the army that had declared that hunting escaped slaves was beneath its honor, abolished slavery. The following year the military, headed by Marshall Deodoro da Fonseca, overthrew the monarchy and declared Brazil a republic.

The republic adopted a constitution, modeled on the American constitution, with a nationally elected president permitted one four-year term. Federal funds began to be used to create a national infrastructure of roads and railways, initiating a long period of economic growth. By 1894, politics became the politics of the governors, with no national political parties, each state having a Republican Party. By tacit agreement between the two major states, São Paulo and Minas Gerais, the presidency was traded between them every four years in *"café com leite"* (coffee with milk) politics; São Paulo's economy was dominated by the growing of coffee, and Minas Gerais was a producer of dairy goods. In this strongly federal system, Congress served as a meeting place where legislation covered only those points agreed to by the states, in negotiation with the federal president. Although there was a federal military, the states all had their own militias under the command of the governors, in some cases rivaling the national army in power. Opposition came from a group of military officers, dominated by young lieutenants (*tenentes*) who revolted against the government in the 1920s but failed to overturn the system. The 1929 depression brought about the loss of income from coffee exports and increasing discontent with the traditional politics of the Old Republic. Defeated in1930 as presidential candidate, Getúlio Vargas of the state of Rio Grande do Sul, along with dissident military including many of the *tenentes* successfully ousted the old government and inaugurated the Second Republic. Vargas was made provisional president by the Congress.

Vargas dominated Brazilian politics from 1930 until 1954, navigating among conflicting interests of the states, of differing military factions, and of ideological political parties such as the Integralistas, modeled on Europe's fascism, and the Communists, led by Plinio Salgado and former *tenente* leader Luis Carlos Prestes, respectively. Centralization of Brazilian politics became a reality for the first time since the early 1800s as Vargas replaced elected governors who did not support him with appointed *interventors*.

Vargas, who believed in the virtues of a rural culture and economy, faced a strong internal migration of agricultural workers who were streaming to the cities.

As increasing urban population without jobs threatened political order, he sought ways of increasing industrial employment to absorb the growing urban workforce, a process that developed into a strategy of import substitution. This fit the nationalist and developmentalist sentiments of the military that increasingly became the major support of Vargas. In 1934 a new constitution was written and the Congress elected Vargas to the presidency. The constitution, which did not allow for re-election, called for elections in 1938. As the election approached, political parties began to support candidates, but in 1937, backed by the army, Vargas declared the *Estado Novo* (New State), making his dictatorship official. He presented a new constitution, eliminated political parties, and further increased his authority by centralizing fiscal power. A corporative system of state-sponsored unions kept labor both under control and supportive of the government while a system of labor courts, modeled on the Italian system, was created to eliminate industrial conflict. Both strikes and lockouts were declared against the public interest, while other legislation established a minimum wage and protection for labor. Vargas cultivated his image as the *pai dos pobres* (father of the poor).

As World War II approached, Vargas sensed the eventual victory of the Allies and negotiated Brazilian involvement in the war with the United States. With American financial and technical support, he gained the construction of the first integrated steel plant of Latin America and the training of a Brazilian Expeditionary Force, which then sailed to Europe and fought alongside American troops in the Italian campaign. The involvement of the Brazilian military with U.S. troops created a long-term relationship between officers of the two militaries.

## Democratic Interlude

At a time when Brazilian troops were fighting in Europe against dictatorship, the Estado Novo of Vargas seemed out of place to many Brazilians and pressure for elections built. Vargas began the process of developing two political parties, encouraging the organization of the Social Democratic Party (PSD) by a group of *interventors* representing the interests of their states but also including industrialists and large landowners and the Brazilian Labor Party (PTB) built around urban labor and a system of control over workers. Opposition to Vargas, including many of the *tenentes*, created the National Democratic Union (UDN). General Eurico Dutra was launched as a candidate of a PSD–PTB coalition while the UDN-nominated Brigadeiro Eduardo Gomes, a *tenente* hero and head of the air force during World War II. Vargas was forced to resign in October 1945, and Dutra was elected president by popular vote. A new constitution, written in 1946, completed the move to democratic rule.

Vargas returned to the presidency in 1950, winning election as the PSD–PTB candidate. His term in office was marked by a tilt toward economic nationalism, especially the creation of Petrobras, the national oil company. The Vargas presidency was full of allegations of corruption, much of it coming from the pen and voice of Carlos Lacerda, newspaper publisher and governor of Rio de Janeiro. Told by the military leadership that he was no longer acceptable as president, Vargas committed suicide in the presidential palace in 1954, leaving behind a statement blaming his death on a "sea of mud" and a "campaign of international groups joined with national groups" seeking control of Brazilian resources. Vargas became a political martyr, which turned the tables on his tormentors.

Scheduled presidential elections went forward, the PSD–PTB candidate, Minas Gerais governor Juscelino Kubitschek. Kubitschek, a physician of Czech ancestry, campaigned with the slogan of "fifty years progress in five." With his inauguration in 1956, he quickly set out a "Program of Targets" including the construction of a new capital, christened Brasília, to be located in the country's interior. An automobile industry came into being, encouraged by special treatment of foreign manufacturers who were given a protected market, bringing a major surge of import substitution, while a program of roads and other infrastructure changed the map of Brazil. The fast-paced growth brought employment, increasing inflation, and charges of corruption. Kubitschek finished his term with a display of confidence and accomplishment, moving the capital from Rio de Janeiro to the newly constructed Brasília. However, rural unrest was beginning, and labor felt left out.

In early 1961, UDN candidate and São Paulo governor Janio Quadros became Brazil's new president. A major attempt to stabilize the economy failed, mostly due to the refusal of the Congress to approve harsh austerity measures. In August, after only seven months in office, Quadros tendered his resignation. João "Jango" Goulart, who had been Minister of Labor under Vargas and Kubitschek's vice president, had been elected vice president again under Quadros. The military refused to permit Goulart to assume office, but after negotiation Goulart was sworn in as president. Dissatisfaction with Goulart, the result of recession, increasing inflation, fears of his leftist rhetoric, and his failure to punish a military mutiny, resulted in a joint military–civilian coup at the end of March 1964, a coup hailed by the United States as saving Brazil from communism.

## Military Rule

Congress, pressured by the military, voted to make Army Chief of Staff General Humberto Castelo Branco president. He began the process of taming inflation, then running at more than 50 percent a year, by fiscal reform and monetary restriction. A series of Institutional Acts bypassed legislative approval. Old political parties were abolished and replaced with an official party, the National Renovating Alliance (ARENA), and a single opposition party, the Brazilian Democratic Movement (MDB). Political power was centralized in the executive, and Congress was temporarily closed. Election of presidents, governors, and mayors of major cities was transferred from popular vote to indirect election. During the military regime (1964–1985), elections continued, and generals who became president took off their uniforms and served only five-year terms. The military manipulated election laws, created and joined states, and used the economy to maintain control, especially where their dominance of voting in the smaller northeastern states meant a majority in the Senate.

A hardline military faction controlled the next election and made General Arthur Costa e Silva the president in 1967. He brought a new economic team into the government that increased available credit, especially in agriculture, and began a process of fast economic growth averaging almost 11 percent a year that lasted from 1968 to 1974 and dubbed the "Brazilian Miracle." Production costs were reduced by control of wages, and exports promoted. A massive cerebral hemorrhage incapacitated the president in mid-1969, and the military selected General Emílio Médici as the new president.

Médici met opposition to the government, including urban guerrilla warfare and the kidnapping of foreign diplomats, with increased repression. At the same time, the rapid growth of the economy brought increased social mobility and national pride. The continued growth in the economy served to legitimize military rule despite a rising vote for the opposition MDB.

General Ernesto Geisel became president in 1974 with an announced policy of moving the country back toward democracy. He brought in a new economic team that faced problems of increasing inflation and price increases in the purchase of petroleum. Geisel restored the political rights of many who had been exiled, only to find them winning contested elections for governorships and other offices. International borrowing and increased investment by the state sought to rekindle the growth pattern to offset the opposition's increased strength. General João Figueiredo, selected by Geisel to succeed him in 1979, faced continuing deterioration of the economy, with slowed growth and increasing inflation. A serious recession began in 1982 as foreign investment stopped, and the servicing of Brazil's debt, now the largest among developing countries, overwhelmed the budget. A new independent labor union formed under the leadership of autoworker Luiz Inácio da Silva, popularly known as "Lula," breaking the control that the government had maintained over workers since the administration of Vargas. Professional groups and the Catholic Church openly expressed the realities of military repression of civilians.

A new election law attempted to split the opposition by allowing new political parties to form. Lula organized the Workers' Party (PT), and Leonel Brizola, governor of Rio de Janeiro, founded the Party of Democratic Workers (PDT). In the next presidential election, both the candidates were civilians, and the opposition won the indirect election with a coalition of the PMDB and the PFL (which had split off from ARENA) called the Democratic Alliance.

## The "New Republic"

The day before the inauguration in March 1985, president-elect Tancredo Neves of the PMDB, underwent emergency surgery, and Vice President-Elect José Sarney assumed the presidency when Neves died.

Sarney faced a serious economic crisis of high inflation and slow growth. A group of young economists came forward with new theories on how to halt the inflation without the orthodox recessionary measures normally prescribed. At the end of February 1986, the theories were put into effect with the Cruzado Plan, which froze wages and prices while increasing the income of the lowest paid workers. The resulting new demands brought employment as industry used existing capacity for production. The plan's immediate success catapulted Sarney's popularity while preparations went ahead for an election of congressional deputies, many senators, and governors. The great importance of the election was that the combined deputies and senators would also become a constituent assembly, writing a new constitution to replace that of the military's. Sarney's allies overwhelmingly won the election, but the Cruzado Plan collapsed immediately after as inflation returned and growth came to a halt by the end of the year.

The new 1988 constitution provided liberal benefits for many formerly left out of social services and distributed a larger portion of the federal tax receipts to the states and municipalities. A split in the PMDB resulted in the creation of the Brazilian Social Democratic Party (PSDB), led by senators displeased with the rightward swing of the PMDB resulting from former ARENA members who had switched parties. Sarney completed his term in March 1990, while inflation soared to over 80 percent a month.

The new president, Fernando Collor de Mello, had beaten labor leader and organizer of the PT, Luiz Inácio Lula da Silva, in the first direct election for a president since 1960, winning 52.6 percent of the runoff election. Governor of the small northeastern state of Alagoas, Collor was the youngest president in Brazil's history, campaigning against corruption in politics and established politicians and running as a candidate of a new party he created solely for the election. He promised that no one who had served previous governments would be in his cabinet.

He believed that Brazil's import substitution strategy needed to be replaced with an economy open to the global market and began a process of privatization of the state-owned industries, including the National Steel Company at Volta Redonda. A scheduled lowering of tariffs on imports reduced the barriers that protected Brazilian industry from international competition. Thus Brazil embarked on a new economic course, sloughing off decades of state-led growth and protectionism.

Collor, secure in his popular election and coming into office at the Cold War's abrupt ending, began to reduce the influence of the military. He also continued reducing the long-standing antagonisms with Argentina. In the spring of 1991, Collor signed the Treaty of Asunción, creating a common market among the countries of Argentina, Uruguay, Paraguay, and Brazil. Known by its abbreviated name, Mercosul (Market of the Southern Cone) effectively increased the internal market for the products of the two largest economies in South America. Yet the economic stabilization policies of the new government proved ineffective and inflation returned.

In the spring of 1992, Collor's younger brother, Pedro, publicly stated that the president was receiving funds in exchange for political favors. A congressional investigation produced evidence that resulted in Collor's impeachment, followed by his resignation and a vote by Congress to remove his political rights for ten years. The impeachment proceedings of Collor were the first in Latin American history in which a president had been legally removed from office through constitutional processes.

Vice President Itamar Franco, succeeding to the presidency, continued Collor's privatization initiative and other stabilization programs. The most important action he took was the appointment of Senator Fernando Henrique Cardoso as finance minister. The president gave Fernando Henrique full support in a program to end the long-standing inflation that had plagued Brazil for decades and was then running at more than 20 percent a month. The new finance minister brought together a team of economists, many of whom had developed the Cruzado Plan, and with them instituted a new stabilization program, the Real Plan, named after the new currency put into circulation. By July 1994 the Real Plan had brought inflation down dramatically, and Fernando Henrique became a candidate for the presidency in the fall elections.

In the election, the only two significant candidates were Fernando Henrique, leader of the left-of-center PSDB in coalition with the right-of-center PFL, and PT candidate Luiz Inácio Lula da Silva who had narrowly lost in the previous election. Fernando Henrique won the election and enjoyed marked popularity as the continued success of the Real Plan meant a better standard of living for much of the population, especially the poor.

He came to office as the man who defeated inflation, and his continuing legitimacy largely depended on continuing success at holding inflation down. The policy of privatization continued during his administration. The constitution was amended to permit the president, governors, and mayors to run for a second consecutive term, allowing Fernando Henrique to run for re-election in 1998 claiming the need to finish the job of restructuring the economy. A constitutional amendment required all levels of government to be fiscally responsible and an expensive reform of banking cleaned up a failing banking system. The national telephone company was privatized creating a communications revolution making cell phones available inexpensively and extensively. He instituted the Bolsa Escola (School Supplement), which provided payments to poor families who kept their children in school. Fernando Henrique's presidency ended with major problems of unemployment and lack of growth unresolved and with a high level of federal debt.

Lula handily won the 2002 presidential election. He continued inflation control while launching the program Fome Zero (No Hunger) to guarantee sufficient food to the nation's poorest sectors. Later, the highly successful antipoverty program, the Bolsa Familia (Family Stipend), combined the Fome Zero program, the Bolsa Escola, and the Basic Benefit provided to persons in extreme poverty, covered 12 million families. The dramatic drop in inequality can be seen in the Gini index, a measure of income distribution, which dropped from 0.596 in 2001 to 0.548 in 2008. Many of the basic structural factors that caused inequality were not, however, fully addressed, and many still remained in poverty. Lula constructed a congressional coalition sufficient to amend the constitution, allowing for social security and tax reforms that had not been previously possible. At the same time, he began a drive to expand Brazil's exports, especially to South Africa, India, and China.

In 2006, despite a series of corruption scandals, Lula won a second term of office. The demand for Brazilian commodities, especially soya and iron ore, by China and the expanded exports to other developing countries along with increased domestic demand brought economic growth and a dramatic lowering of poverty. By 2009 China surpassed the United States as the destiny of Brazilian exports.

Dilma Rousseff, Lula's chief of staff and the daughter of Bulgarian immigrants, was chosen by Lula to be his successor and easily won the 2010 election. Major protests in June of 2013 registered increasing frustration with transit fares and government spending and related corruption on stadiums and other projects for the World Cup games and the Summer Olympics in 2016. Rousseff narrowly won re-election in 2014, but a serious recession including increasing inflation and unemployment and a serious corruption scandal led to a severe drop in her support. In 2016, Congress impeached her for misuse of funds, and the presidency fell to the vice president, Michel Temer.

## Political Economy

In many ways, Brazil's politics have been defined by its economy. Initial European interest in Brazil, especially by the Portuguese, focused on the export of primary products including Brazilwood as a dye, sugar, gold, diamonds, coffee, and rubber. By the first part of the twentieth century, coffee had become synonymous with images of Brazil. Today, primary products remain a major part of the export economy with iron ore, soybeans, orange juice, and frozen chickens surpassing coffee. However, industrial manufactures now exceed the value of primary products, with exports of steel, airplanes, automobiles and automotive parts, consumer durables, electronic equipment, weaponry, pharmaceuticals, petrochemicals, textiles, and footwear.

By the 1930s Brazilian economists and planners began to realize that the future development of the country required diversification and industrialization. The ability to compete in the international market of industrial goods was questioned, and Brazil under Vargas began implementing a strategy of import substitution with its allied policy of trade barriers, including high tariffs, to protect the new domestic industries. Brazilian governments, starting with construction of the National Steel Company at Volta Redonda in the 1940s, began the development of state-owned industry, soon followed by the creation of a state-owned oil company, Petrobras. Electric power and telephones also were taken over by the government along with major investment in transportation and many other areas.

The import substitution strategy of Vargas continued with the Kubitschek government, now increased by theoretical studies resulting from the Economic Commission for Latin America (ECLA) in Santiago, Chile. Promoted by Brazilian economist Celso Furtado, the ECLA analysis claimed lack of development resulted from a structural dependence on Europe and the United States. Inflation was seen as a stimulus to development. In the private sector, Kubitschek opened the country to the automobile industry, which brought with it many associated companies as parts suppliers and service industries grew.

The military governments, despite their opposition to Vargas and dislike of Celso Furtado, continued and expanded the strategy of import substitution, giving the federal government control over a major portion of the economy. Diversification of agricultural exports accompanied diversification in import substitution industry. The military gave negative interest loans to agribusiness for expansion and new products, knowing that it was the fastest way of increasing exports. Part of the increase came with the development of the alcohol-from-sugar program for automobile fuel in response to the dramatic rise in imported petroleum prices in the 1970s.

During the late 1960s and early 1970s, the rapidity of economic growth earned Brazil considerable international attention. The growth was financed by reducing the labor value of production through limitations on wage increases, funds from the national pension program, and foreign loans. Beset with persistent balance-of-payment problems, Brazil turned to foreign borrowing in the 1970s as banks pushed loans from the glut of petrodollar deposits accumulating from oil producers who had raised prices dramatically. The ability to borrow ended with the oil price collapse of the late 1970s drying up the ready availability of foreign loan capital.

Inflation became a characteristic of the Brazilian economy, as federal and state expenditures exceeded tax revenues. Much of industry was oligopolistic, faced little competition domestically and protected by high tariffs from less expensive foreign products. As a result, prices could be set to guarantee profits without regard to quality or costs. Wages were indexed to inflation, their value set by government standards rather than by collective bargaining.

During the 1980s the economy stagnated as inflation increased, the worst conditions since the 1929 depression, creating the "lost decade." The combination of depression and inflation was a major factor in the loss of power of the military their decision to allow a return to democratic rule. The civilian governments of José Sarney and Fernando Collor tried unsuccessfully to stabilize the economy with various anti-inflation plans.

The Collor government began a major change in Brazil's economic policies, privatizing state-owned companies, inviting greater foreign investment, and lowering tariff barriers to imports. The opening to the international market reversed a sixty-year policy of autarky, publicly owned industry, and import substitution. These actions continued under the brief administration of Itamar Franco and were followed by the first successful stabilization effort headed by Finance Minister Fernando Henrique, an action that propelled him into the presidency.

To the surprise of many, Lula continued many of the economic policies of the Fernando Henrique administration while promoting foreign trade. Brazil became the co-chair with the United States on negotiation for the Free Trade Area of the Americas but led opposition to it on the basis of American protectionism. Along with India, Brazil organized opposition to a new round of World Trade Organization talks due to the failure of Europe, the United States, and Japan to reduce agricultural subsidies and open their markets to goods from developing countries. The alcohol-from-sugar program expanded, giving Brazil an important initiative in reducing greenhouse gases and cars were designed to use it for fuel. Greatly increased exports moved Brazil's into a positive current account, especially supplying China with soy beans and iron ore.

The most significant policies of Lula's administration include the continuation of inflation targeting and the raising of the minimum wage, which along with the transfers of wealth have meant a significant drop in the level of poverty and the creation of a new consumer class, partly the result of a major increase in payroll-backed consumer credit. The middle class increased from 42 percent of the population in

2004 to 52 percent in 2008. Brazil became one of the two major recipients of foreign direct investment, which along with its export earnings made the country a creditor nation for the first time. In 2007 Petrobras, the national oil company, announced the discovery of extensive new deep water oil deposits that may be among the world's largest. The crowning achievements were the winning of the right to host the World Cup of Soccer in 2014 and the Olympics in 2016. Lula's popularity reached 80 percent of the voting population.

President Dilma Rousseff (PT) was inaugurated president in January 2011, having won the presidential election in October 2010. Her vice-presidential running mate came from the PMDB. Dilma, who had never before been elected to a political office, had distinguished herself when she was moved from the Ministry of Mines and Energy to take over as chief of staff for Lula. She gained visibility as the "Mother of the Programa de Aceleração Crescimento" (Program of Accelerated Growth) and was chosen by Lula as his choice as presidential candidate. During the military regime, she had been arrested and tortured for her antigovernment activities.

She spent much of her first year gaining independence from Lula's influence. In the first months in office she fired eight cabinet level ministers for alleged corruption. She has much less interest in foreign policy than her last two predecessors. She faced major problems of infrastructure and in her second term saw a drop in economic growth and increasing inflation as well as the massive 2013 street protests that saw a million people take to the streets in June of that year.

## Foreign Policy

Brazil is the only Latin American country today that plays a role of power and influence on the global stage. Foreign policy is managed by a highly professional foreign service, the Itamaraty. For decades Brazil maintained itself generally outside world politics with the exception of its decision to send troops to serve in the Italian campaign alongside American forces during World War II. At the end of the war, unlike other participants on the Allied side, Brazil did not get a permanent seat on the Security Council and soon returned to relative isolation. But in the 1980s, along with the insertion of Brazil into the global economy, it assumed a greater role in international politics, a change reflecting the experiences of presidents Fernando Henrique and Lula.

Fernando Henrique, an academic, spoke several languages and had taught or lectured at major universities in the United States and Europe. As president, he traveled broadly, recognized as one of the "third way" leaders along with British prime minister Tony Blair and U.S. president Bill Clinton. In addition, he pushed the expansion of Mercosul, bringing in Bolivia and Chile as associate members and including South Africa as visitor to their meetings. He also took an active role in South American politics, facilitating a border agreement between Ecuador and Peru and urging better relations between Colombia and Venezuela. One of the criticisms of Fernando Henrique's administration was the number of trips he made overseas.

Lula came to office with a history as labor leader who had traveled in Europe and the United Sates, became acquainted with much of the leadership of these countries and was heralded as one of the sources of democratic rule in Brazilian industry. Purchasing a new presidential airplane, he traveled almost 10 percent of his time in office, especially working to increase trade and gain political visibility for the country across the world. Brazil became a regularly invited guest to the G8 meetings and assumed a place of leadership on the new G20 gatherings. At the 2009 Copenhagen meeting on global warming, Lula was one of a half dozen world leaders that negotiated the final agreement with U.S. president Barack Obama. Lula also worked to broaden Mercosul, with Peru and Ecuador joining Chile and Bolivia as associate members and Venezuela becoming a full member. During Lula's administration thirty-five new embassies were established, with a concentration on Africa. Brazilian foreign policy has stressed the creation of a South–South economic and political reality, working with South Africa, India, and China in the negotiations at the Doha Round and promoting trade. The IBSA (Brazil, India, South Africa) Dialogue Forum was founded in Brasília, and a 2006 trade agreement linked Mercosul and the Southern Africa Customs Union. Brazil, along with France, took the initiative to create UNITAID to purchase and distribute drugs to fight important diseases.

A major foreign policy objective is a permanent seat on the Security Council of the United Nations, and since 2004 Brazil maintains peacekeeping troops as head of the United Nations Stabilization Mission in Haiti (MINUSTAH). The seat on the Security Council is part of a project that includes seats for Japan, India, and South Africa as major countries that should have that level of representation and reflecting the changes that have taken place in the world since the United Nation's foundation after World War II.

Dilma, similarly to both Fernando Henrique and Lula, included South Africa in BRIC meetings, and in 2013 it was the host to the planning for an international development bank by those countries, making them independent of the World Bank.

## Geography of Inequality

Brazil is divided into states, varying geographically in size from the huge state of Amazonas to small states like Alagoas. Populations of the states also represent great differences, with a population of more than 30 million in the state of São Paulo and only 300,000 in Amapá. Elected governors and state legislatures govern states, which, in turn, are divided into some 5,000 municipalities, in some way equivalent to U.S. counties, each with its mayor and municipal council.

The city of Brasília is the site of the federal government, located in the center-west of the country. Constructed in the late 1950s, today the region of the Federal District has over 2 million people and has become a hub that connects the interior of the country with the industrialized southeast.

The Brazilian Institute of Geography and Statistics (IBGE) divides the country into five regions: North, Northeast, Southeast, Center-West, and South. The North, comprised of the states of Pará, Amazonas, Acre, Rondonia, Roraima, Amapa, and Tocantins, is the area of the Amazon basin with Manaus and Belém as the only two major cities. This is the area of Brazil's vast rain forest, the home of most of Brazil's remaining Indians. This region borders the Guianas, Venezuela, Colombia, Peru, and Bolivia, yet has few roads or other land transport. The Northeast, a region of drought, desert, and poverty, has long existed with a sugar economy and subsistence farming. An Office for the Development of the Northeast (SUDENE), charged with improving the living condition among the northeastern states, has not made a significant difference in its forty years of existence. All the states have an Atlantic coast, and the cities of Fortaleza, Recife, and Salvador are major ports and state capitals. Northeastern states are Maranhão, Piauí, Ceará, Rio Grande do Norte, Paraíba, Pernambuco, Alagoas, Sergipe, and Bahia. The Northeast's population includes many descendants from the African slave trade and Salvador, Bahia, is known as the capital of African Brazil. The Southeast consists of the states of Rio de Janeiro, Espírito Santo, Minas Gerais, and São Paulo and is the economic powerhouse of Brazil and the region with the greatest population. The Center-West, a new frontier for Brazil, contains the states of Mato Grosso, Mato Grosso do Sul, and Goias, along with the Federal District of Brasília. The South is comprised of the states of Rio Grande do Sul, Santa Catarina, and Paraná, the most European part of Brazil with much of the population tracing ancestry back to Germany and Italy.

Brazil's geography of inequality underpins its system of economic and political power. The Northeast is poor, literacy is low, and infant mortality high. Political power still resides in the hands of traditional families while much of the population lives by subsistence farming and the area is devastated every few years by drought. The Southeast and South are industrialized, with the state of São Paulo's economy exceeding that of Argentina and that of the state of Minas Gerais being greater than Chile or Peru. In addition, São Paulo centers the country's banking, agribusiness, and service industries.

A shift in the population has taken place, changing the major locus of poverty. In the last sixty years Brazil has gone from an agrarian to an overwhelmingly urban society—now 80 percent of the population—with peasants, pushed off the land, especially in the Northeast, by drought and capital-intensive agriculture, moving to the major cities seeking work in the increasingly industrialized economy. The result is seen in the thousands of *favelas*, the squatter housing built on swamps, vacant lots, and hillsides, which are a prominent and permanent part of the urban landscape. Often lacking adequate running water or sewage, their populations run into the millions.

The geography of inequality is not only regional; it appears in the deep class divisions, in great differentials of educational opportunity, and in income maldistribution. The income of the upper 10 percent of society is twenty-six times the income of the lowest 40 percent. Brazil has the greatest wealth inequalities of any major nation in the world.

# A Culture of Discrimination

## Afro-Brazilians

To the first-time visitor to Brazil, the apparent lack of racial discrimination in a population that exhibits every human color seemingly demonstrates a colorblind society. In the 1940s Brazilian anthropologist Gilberto Freyre gave legitimacy to the concept of racial democracy with his studies of social history encapsulated in his book *The Masters and the Slaves* (*Casa-Grande & Senzala*). Census takers have found over a hundred words used to express the multitude of ethnotypes present in the society. Possibly the most popular and best-known Brazilian is soccer star Edson Arantes do Nascimento, better known as Pelé, an Afro-Brazilian; Machado de Assis, a mulatto and founder of the prestigious Brazilian Academy of Letters, has been called Latin America's greatest literary figure.

But behind this surface lies a pervasive racism. Despite the fact that a majority of Brazilians have some African ancestry, persons of color are poorly represented in politics and less so in the professions. A cursory examination of poverty shows income levels decreasing as completion darkens. A visit to the universities finds few of color among either the faculty or the students. The officer corps of the military, and especially the navy, remains almost exclusively white. Yet, discrimination is changing, and advances have been made in recent years. An Afro-Brazilian sat on the Supreme Court and became Chief Justice. An Afro-Brazilian was elected governor of one of the smaller states, and another elected mayor of Brazil's largest city, São Paulo, in 1996. In 1999, the second Afro-Brazilian was promoted to the rank of general.

Organized reaction against discrimination exists in muted form, not emerging as a significant interest group. Racial discrimination is constitutionally illegal. Furthermore, since the end of slavery in 1888, there have been no Jim Crow laws in Brazil. A result is that Afro-Brazilians have not had a focus in their battle for equality. In 2003 some universities instituted affirmative action programs to increase the number of Afro-Brazilians. This practice has grown.

## WOMEN

With the election of Dilma to the presidency, women have taken dramatically stronger role in political life. Traditionally, Brazilian culture calls for the man as breadwinner and the woman as housewife and mother, but with women entering the workforce in rapidly increasing numbers, this culture has been changing. Two forces have brought this change. First, the value of labor in production has decreased, partly the result of the "wage squeeze" during the military regime and partly due to restructuring of the economy. Both exacerbated income inequality and required more than one income to feed and sustain a family, forcing women into the workforce. Second, an increasing number of educated women are claiming the right to personal careers and professions. An additional element of change comes from the dramatic drop in the average number of children as the result of extensive family planning. In 1970, 5.3 children were born for each woman; the rate had dropped to 2.8 children by 1990 and to 1.8 by 2010.

The changing role of women also appears in Brazil's political life. The PT has been a vehicle for a number of them, with Dilma who had been Lula's chief of staff, winning the presidency in 2010. Women first emerged onto the political scene as elected officials and decision makers in the 1990s. Since then, they have been elected governors of several states, mayor of São Paulo, and held a number of cabinet positions. Two women have sat on the Supreme Court.

# The Political System

Unlike most Latin American countries, which became republics on gaining their independence from monarchical European countries, Brazil adopted a constitutional monarchy system including a bicameral legislature with a population-based lower house of deputies and a senate representing states. As mentioned earlier, Brazil became a republic but only at the end of the nineteenth century, in 1889.

A major problem in Brazilian elections is the manner in which federal deputies and state legislatures are elected; Brazil has an open-list, proportional election. Deputies and members of the state legislatures are not elected from individual districts but at large from the state with each state making up a single election district. The candidates of parties with the most votes win the seats of the state. As a result, candidates compete against other members of their own party. While it is necessary to be affiliated with a party to be a candidate, winners have little loyalty to their parties. In addition, this method of proportional representation strengthens various interest groups that would not be able to elect a representative in a local district but can win sufficient votes in the states to elect a favored candidate. This puts a premium on coalition building while weakening party structure and party discipline.

Election to executive positions, the president, governors, and mayors of larger municipalities requires a majority of valid votes cast. If no candidate obtains a majority on the first ballot, the two candidates with the most votes compete in a run-off election.

Voting is required in Brazil, and the 1988 Constitution extended the franchise both to illiterates and to sixteen-year-olds, greatly increasing democratization and essentially giving the franchise to all adults. This total opening was gradually obtained in different intervening constitutions until the one of 1988, which marked a final and major shift away from the restricted franchise adopted in 1891, when only literate males could vote.

Brazil's constitution, written in 1988 in an atmosphere of reaction against the centralization and excesses of the military regime, has a strong liberal content, including bringing rural workers into the social security system for the first time and expanding labor rights. The most important decentralizing provision of the constitution required that substantial federal revenues be passed on to the states and municipalities. The constitution has been amended, especially during Fernando Henrique administration, to change the distribution of funds to refederalize fiscal control to balance the federal budget, which is essential to the control of inflation. Yet governors have often successfully prevented amendments that would reallocate monies.

# The President

The president and vice president are elected directly every four years with the right of a single re-election. The presidential residence is the Palácio da Alvorada (Palace of the Dawn) and presidential offices are in the Palácio do Planalto (Palace of High Plain) in the capital Brasília.

Historically, the president of Brazil has been able to function largely independent of the Congress. The 1988 Constitution reduced the power of the presidency in relation to the Congress, giving the Congress virtual veto of any presidential action. In reality, however, the faction-ridden Congress has not used its power effectively, and the president has been able to use provisionary measures to legislate, which the Congress has accepted despite their power to overturn the measures. This power was reduced in a constitutional amendment that limited the use of the measures and required the Congress to act on them. A leader of the government in the Congress introduces legislation for the executive and tries to shepherd it into law. The president can veto legislation, but the veto can be overridden by a second congressional vote.

The president constructs his or her cabinet to give representation to various interest groups. The ministry of finance (Ministério da Fazenda) along with the president of the Central Bank administers the economic policies. Often there are serious rivalries between ministries, the president, and the personalities of the ministers determining which of them dominates policy. Usually the business community of São Paulo is consulted before the president makes his or her choice of economic ministers while the ministry of labor will go to someone who has links to unions. Cabinet positions are used to bring different parties into the government, with deputies and senators given positions. In this manner, presidents can form a legislative coalition to support his or her policies, with the expectation that the cabinet members will be able to obtain their parties' votes for executive-sponsored legislation. Accepting a cabinet or other executive position does not mean losing a legislative seat but only temporarily surrendering it to an elected alternate legislator and reclaiming the seat when he or she returns to the legislature. The foreign ministry, known as Itamaraty, is very professional and operates largely independent of the foreign minister, who acts more as a spokesman for foreign policy.

A major change has been the creation of a single ministry of defense in 1999 by President Cardoso, replacing the traditional ministries of the army, navy, and air force and the Chief of Staff of the Armed Forces. The Defense Ministry is headed by a civilian, and the military reports to the minister. This change has reduced the role of the military in Brazilian politics, possibly to its lowest point since the mid-nineteenth century.

The president also nominates federal judges. If the president leaves the country, the vice president, followed by the presidents of the Senate and the House, become acting president until his or her return.

The 1988 Constitution expanded the role of the office of the General Prosecutor of the Republic, giving him the ability to investigate and prosecute crime independent of political pressures. The office is in many ways equivalent to the attorney general in the United States, yet in other ways the General Prosecutor's office is a fourth branch of government as it has constitutionally guaranteed functional and administrative autonomy.

## The Legislature

Brazil has a bicameral legislature. In the lower Chamber of Deputies (Câmara dos Deputados) representation is based on the population of each state, with deputies elected every four years for a total number of 531 members. The Federal District and territories also have congressional representation. The constitution stipulates that each state has a minimum of eight and a maximum of seventy deputies. This distribution strongly favors the smaller and poorer states of the north and center-west over the more populous and richer state of São Paulo.

The upper house, or Senate (Senado) has three members from each state. Senators are elected for eight years, half of them every four years with a total number of 81 members. Each senator is elected with first and second alternates, who replace the senator if he or she leaves office, either through death, removal, or to accept another position. Senators frequently leave their seats, often to run for mayor or governor or to become a member of the cabinet. If a senator wishes to return to his or her seat, the alternate reverts to his or her previous position.

In addition to legislation, the houses of Congress can initiate Parliamentary Commissions of Inquiry to investigate possibly legal irregularities. Like the United States, the House of Deputies has the right of impeachment and the Senate, the trial of the impeachment.

# The Courts

A Supreme Court has eleven judges, nominated by the president and confirmed by the Senate. Justices serve until a mandatory retirement age of seventy, and the President of the Court serves a two-year term based on seniority. The Court deals with federal issues and constitutionality of legislation and is the final court of appeal. In addition, there is a Supreme Court of Justice, which rules as a final court of appeal on criminal cases. The judiciary also includes a number of separate courts systems to deal with specific areas of jurisdiction. The Supreme Court also has the responsibility to judge criminal acts of members of Congress who are protected from other courts due to their position.

A national Labor Court system arbitrates between labor and management. All the courts have regional and local lower courts. Labor courts were set up in the 1930s under the administration of Vargas to reduce the cost of strikes and to use labor unions as an arm of presidential power. Today the courts still serve to mediate industrial conflict, being a holdover of the corporatist institutions set up at that time. An electoral court system controls elections, making sure that candidates have the necessary credentials, that voting is honest, and that the elections take place in accordance with the law. A military courts system, as its name implies, handles cases involving members of the armed forces under military law.

The judicial system of Brazil is the weakest of the branches of government. This is partly a result of a lack of a tradition of judicial independence and partly the result of the fact that the legal system, carried over from the Portuguese colonial period, is based on the Napoleonic code rather than on English common law as in the United States. A constitutional amendment now requires lower courts to honor Supreme Court decisions, but decisions often are not final as there are a number of ways to appeal rulings. Yet the courts have been strong enough to declare some legislation unconstitutional and to play a significant political role. A fresh initiative against corruption has made the courts significantly stronger.

## Political Parties

Several parties have a significant representation in Brazil. The **Workers' Party (PT)** is the furthest left of the major parties but during Lula's administration moved to the center-left and maintained many of the policies of the previous administration. Originally the greatest support for the PT lay in the industrial cities of São Paulo in the South and major urban areas, but the antipoverty measures of Lula's administration have given it strong support in the Northeast. It is the only political party with party discipline and has grown in importance consistently since its organization.

The **Party of the Brazilian Democratic Movement (PMDB)** is a centrist party that originated as the opposition party that the military allowed during its regime. It is the largest of the parties and has been a part of the government's congressional coalition during both the Fernando Henrique and Lula administrations. The vice president, Michael Temer, was elected in a coalition ticket with President Rousseff and became interim president when Dilma was impeached.

The **Brazilian Social Democratic Party (PSDB),** which includes former president Fernando Henrique, split off from the PMDB in 1988. During the last five presidential elections, the PSDB and the PT have fielded the two most important candidates. The PSDB holds a number of important governorships.

The **Partido Socialista Brasileiro (PSB)** has become a significant party, winning more municipal elections that any other party and challenging the power of the PT in the Northeast.

In addition to these larger parties, there are many smaller parties with a few deputies in Congress. Among them is the former Brazilian Communist Party, which changed its name to the **Popular Socialist Party**. The **Communist Party of Brazil**, which earlier had split from the Brazilian Communist Party, remains. The **Liberal Party** has a strong base in the evangelical churches of Brazil. ARENA underwent a number of changes, first becoming the Party of Social Democracy (PDS) and finally becoming the **Progressive Party (PP)**, the most conservative of Brazil's major parties. The **Democratic Worker's Party (PDT)** takes a nationalist and left-of-center political position and is strongest in the states of Rio de Janeiro and the southern states.

Throughout these permutations, it bears repeating that the Brazilian genius for short-term coalition building at the expense of party building is the dominant style of political action, while federalism continues as the institutional matrix of its politics. Dilma increased her cabinet to thirty-nine positions.

## Interest Groups

Major interest groups have organized delegations within the legislature, largely made possible by the system of proportional representation that allows candidates identified with the group to receive sufficient votes in a state to win a seat. Many of these groups cross party lines and are formally organized in the legislature, among them are the agricultural interests, banking, soccer clubs, construction industry, private schools, evangelical churches, and retired persons.

## BUSINESS

Business in Brazil is organized within each state by federations of industry, a holdover from the corporatist 1930s. The São Paulo State Federation of Industries (FIESP) is the most powerful of these federations, as the state has close to half the country's industry. FIESP maintains a major research office and financially supports particular political candidates. More than any other group, FIESP represents the interests of Brazilian business, and presidents usually ask the advice of the federation in selecting finance ministers and consult with it in matters of the economy.

## UNIONS

Parallel to business are the labor unions, which function under the Consolidation of Labor Laws originally created by Vargas in 1943. The General Federation of Workers (CGT) is the official confederation of unions, based on the corporate structure put in place by Vargas and funded by union dues, equivalent to a single day's pay each year, collected and dispersed by the Ministry of Labor. The system of official unions gave the government virtual control of labor for almost fifty years. A second major confederation is the Central Union of Workers (CUT), an independent union originally organized under the leadership of Lula by the metalworkers of São Paulo's automobile industry in the early 1980s. The CUT has grown at the expense of the CGT as unions feel that their interests are better represented by the independent nature of the new federation. The CUT has been affiliated with the PT but over time developed an independent policy position. A union economic research institute, the Interunion Department of Statistics and Social Economics (DIEESE), sponsored by CUT in São Paulo, has been able to challenge government statistics on wages, employment, and buying power of wage earners. A third confederation is the Union Power (Força Sindical), which takes a less militant position than the CUT and has developed, in part, from efforts of the AFL-CIO to create a labor leadership modeled on the North American experience and today dominates the PDT. Rural workers, generally left out of traditional industrial unions, are represented by a National Confederation of Workers in Agriculture (CONTAG), growing first under military sponsorship and later independently using the right to administer government social programs for its membership as a means of enlisting members. CONTAG affiliated with the CUT in 1996.

## BANKING

Banking is big business in Brazil. Until the Real Plan stabilization, banking profits were extremely high, and with their financial power came political power. With inflation under control, many private banks went bankrupt, and the political power of the banking industry has diminished but they still maintain a substantial voice. A serious problem was the state banks, controlled by governors, who often used their financial power for political purposes. The restructuring of private banking and privatization of state banks required a major federal program in the mid-1990s to save the financial system and cost over $50 billion dollars. Foreign banks, especially from Spain, bought a number of the banks. The federally controlled National Bank for Economic and Social Development (BNDES) is four times the size of the World Bank.

## Public Employees

Public employment is well organized in Brazil at all levels. Federal employees are particularly well positioned and effective in protecting their jobs and salaries through the trade unions the Interunion Department of Legislative Staff (DIAP) and the National Confederation of Federal Public Servants (CNESF). On a number of occasions, presidents of Brazil have tried to reduce federal expenditures by cutting the oversized bureaucracy and its pension benefits, but they have often had their attempts defeated as members of Congress responded to the lobbying of the legislative staff. In 2003, CNESF, which represents some 900,000 civil servants, split off from the CUT, mostly over pension benefits.

## Agrarian Reform

A much-needed land reform has been long lacking in Brazil. A number of governments have placed laws on the books or made statements about its need, including the newly instituted military regime in 1964, but nothing adequate has yet been done to make land and agricultural credits available to the many who seek it. In the 1950s the Peasant Leagues gained headlines in their occupation of land in the Northeast. A Landless Movement (MST) has become a potent political force in Brazil. They have taken over land, called for a land reform program, and created dramatic demonstrations of their demands, including a massive march on Brasília and the occupation of government buildings. Battles with landowners have resulted in a number of deaths on both sides. The PT and the CUT have recognized the legitimacy of the claims of MST and allied with them, and the Catholic Church has called for recognition of their needs. Yet the power of the agro-commercial sector and its ties to the PT has meant that land reform has not yet come and that significant tension between the PT leadership and the MST has developed.

## Landowners

Strong opposition to land reform comes from *fazendeiros* (landowners) and the *coroneis* (colonels), traditional political bosses in the northeastern states. Well organized in the Rural Democratic Union (UDR), owners' interests are well represented in Congress as the Parliamentary Front of Agriculture. It can count on more than a third of the votes in the two houses and has successfully prevented any effective land reform. During the writing of the 1988 Constitution, they were a part of a coalition called the Big Center (Centrão), which wrote effective protection of their interests. Their continuing power comes from their ability to control voting in rural areas, particularly in the smaller states of the Northeast, which dominate the Senate because of their number. As a result, the UDR can block any legislation contrary to its members' interests and is necessary for any action that the executive wishes to get through Congress.

## STUDENTS

Politics in Brazil, as in most of Latin America, begins in the universities. Students seeking political careers first enter university politics, usually associating themselves with a national political party. Students were in the forefront of the protests calling for the impeachment of President Collor. Yet they have not regained their influence under the postmilitary governments.

## ORGANIZED RELIGION

Brazil is the most populous Catholic country, and the Church remains an important force. The Church historically has been identified with the social and political elite, and demonstrations by the faithful against the Goulart government were an important factor in legitimizing the 1964 coup. During the 1960s, much of the Church became strongly committed to liberation theology with its championing of the poor. Under the leadership of the Brazilian National Confederation of Bishops (CNBB), "base communities" were developed for worship and to provide needed services. The base communities fostered the organization of new groups that made demands on the government. Among the new groups that found their inspiration in the base communities was the new trade union movement. During the military regime, priests often were spokesmen of opposition to authoritarian rule. The Archdiocese of São Paulo gathered reports on human rights violations that were published in 1985 under the title *Brasil: Nunca Mais* (Brazil: Never Again), which went to fourteen editions. The military governments came to view many priests and bishops as supporters of left-wing policies and antithetical to their intentions of cleansing the country of communism. Like the military governments, the Vatican has seen danger in liberation theology. Liberal priests have been silenced, and, as the older generation of Brazilian bishops retired, new conservative bishops have replaced them. Yet the Church is by no means monolithic, as the CNBB, like Brazilian federalism itself, has proved a flexible institution capable of accommodating its different factions. The conservative policies of the Vatican have shifted due to the new emphases of Pope Francis.

The Church speaks out on questions of morality and doctrine. It has opposed artificial birth control but has not prevented its advocacy by the government, especially in the government's highly successful program to reduce infection of HIV.

The lack of an adequate number of priests along with a well-financed effort by evangelical groups has resulted in the fast growth of non-Catholic churches, especially evangelicals. The most prominent of them is the domestically created Universal Church of the Reign of God, with over 2,500 congregations, which has successfully used television to promote membership and has expanded abroad, including to the United States. With the open-list proportional elections, the evangelical churches have elected a significant number of representatives who form an important interest bloc in the Câmara dos Deputados.

Another religious interest in Brazil comes through Umbanda and Candomblé, based on West African Yoruba religion brought by slaves. Not well organized politically, its influence cannot be measured due to the blending of many of Umbanda's rituals and gods with Catholic worship. Yet politicians carefully honor its expression and accept its voice when raised.

## The Amazon

The Amazon region makes up almost 60 percent of Brazil's territory, thinly populated except for a few cities like Manaus, yet important in terms of its biodiversity and effects on the global climate. Brazil's borders with seven other countries run through the Amazon, and vast areas are set aside as homelands for Amerindians. The indigenous peoples have suffered dramatically as disease and occupation by persons seeking gold have decimated their populations. Others have seen the area in terms of potential economic development with the building of vast mining and hydroelectric projects.

Part of the concern has been the destruction of vast areas of the rain forest for lumber, minerals, or farm land. In response, environmental groups have tried to save the Amazon, most significantly by promoting sustainable development. Conflict between ranchers and the environmentalists climaxed in the 1988 assassination of Chico Mendes, a leader of the rubber tappers (*seringueiros*) by a local landowner and his son. Mendes had lobbied hard nationally and internationally, winning the "Global 500" award given by the United Nations for his work in organizing extraction reserves that restricted the destruction of the rain forest. In 2005, Sister Dorothy Stang, a seventy-four-year old American nun who had worked for sustainable development and had come into conflict with ranchers and loggers, also was assassinated.

## Brazil Today

Brazil must be counted as one of the world's great emerging economies. The country has embraced the global economy and the political consequences of that choice. Brazil has, however, experienced a severe economic slowdown beginning in 2016. The transition to democratic rule was managed successfully, with increased power to the legislature and to the judiciary and measures that reduced the role of the military in politics. Unlike many other major developing countries, Brazil has no serious domestic ethnic or religious conflicts that could threaten its future.

Politically, pervasive corruption remains a serious characteristic of Brazilian politics, undermining trust in the government and in democracy itself. Election to Congress is used as a protection against prosecution for public thievery. The presidents of both houses of Congress, members of Congress, governors, and cabinet members have been forced out of office for corruption, yet few have been incarcerated. In recent years corruption has become much less acceptable; in elections since 2002, a significant number of important politicians who had been accused of corruption were eliminated in the first round of voting, including former governors of Minas Gerais and São Paulo and the former mayor of São Paulo; others have been indicted and/or removed from office.

In 2010 a popular petition called on the Congress to pass the Clean Slate Law that prohibits anyone from running for elective office if under indictment, a law that was passed and in 2012 eliminated some candidates for the first time. The most important action has been the conviction by the Federal Supreme Court of twenty-five members of Congress and others associated with them in what is known as the Mensalão (big monthly payment). In 2005 it was discovered that Lula's chief of staff and other members of the leadership of the PT were paying members of Congress the equivalent of $12,000 per month to vote in favor of government legislation. In 2012 the case finally reached the Court with resulting convictions. It is the first time that corruption has been a Court issue and resulted in a set of convictions. The case greatly strengthened the Court. This was followed by a multibillion-dollar corruption scandal of the national oil company Petrobras that involved over $3 billion in bribes. In the consequent Operacão Lava Jato (Operation Car Wash), the courts indicted and convicted over 100 individuals and a number of major companies who had contracts with Petrobras. A major battle against corruption, it has resulted in investigations of Lula and the arrest of a number of persons close to Dilma Rousseff's administration.

Economically, the tradition of inflation, debt financing, and oligopolistic industry has been broken. New social programs in education, social security, and public health have been put into place. With almost no historic differences with neighbors and leadership in a regional economic bloc, Brazil has emerged as the leading power in both the politics and economy of South America. The military is out of politics. The discovery of a vast deep water oil field off its coast may make Brazil one of the world's greatest petroleum nations. Much of the growing economy depends on continuing demand for its commodities, but the domestic market has grown significantly. In the 2008 financial crisis, Brazil was one of the last countries to suffer from its effects and one of the first to recover. Commodities and mining products helped to weather this crisis, but the subsequent fall in commodity prices and lessening demand for these products in China have greatly contributed to the 2015–2017 economic downturn.

A number of Brazilian firms have become international, expanding by buying steel and food companies overseas. At the same time, protectionist barriers in industrialized countries limit purchase of Brazil's exports, especially of agricultural products. Yet greater availability of credit and higher incomes have increased the domestic market. Government statistics cite emergence of the middle class as the largest.

In many ways, over the last twenty years modern Brazil has been shaped by major institutional changes, first under presidents Fernando Henrique and Lula—political opponents yet together representing an end of the old political economy of Vargas. The country emerged as a democracy and an important actor in international politics, not only due to the two presidents who had international perspectives and experience but also due to the maturation of its economy and its expanded markets both globally and domestically. The economy is now diversified both in terms of trading partners and in terms of products. The domestic market is now big enough to permit productivity gains through efficiencies of scale. But Brazil fell into a serious recession with the drop in Chinese commodity purchases. This, along with other economic policy problems during the Rousseff administration led to

Expresident Dilma Rousseff.

drop in production, a major rise of unemployment, and increased inflation. Rising urban fare increases and corruption and spending for the World Cup and Olympics sparked massive street protests that shook the government in 2013 and initiated a decline in support for Dilma and the PT government.

In August 2016 President Rousseff was removed from office by impeachment, citing the breaking of budgetary laws in the run-up to her re-election. Behind the impeachment was a severe drop in her support due to a serious recession, a rise in unemployment, and a popular reaction against corruption as well as the maneuvering by her right-wing critics and then–Vice President Temer. Many of her supporters accused her detractors of carrying out a kind of congressional coup against her and the PT government.

Vice President Michel Temer, the son of a Lebanese immigrant, assumed the presidency and is scheduled to complete the two remaining years of the presidential term. He has moved the country back to the center-right and appointed banker Henrique Meirelles, who was Lula's president of the Central Bank, as finance minister. However, he is very unpopular, and there are strong demands for either his resignation or possible impeachment for receiving illegal money, actions that would bring a special election to replace him. Looking forward to the scheduled

2018 election, former Green Party and Socialist Party candidate Marina Silva polls better that Lula, who is strongly considering another run for the presidency. Lula, however, polls better than any of the other probably candidates.

Across Latin America there is a shift away from the left toward the right in politics and economics, a move that includes Argentina, Venezuela, Chile, and Brazil. In Brazil, there is a serious need for political reform including the problem that membership in the Congress is used to protect against criminal behavior.

A major foreign policy objective is a permanent seat on the Security Council of the United Nations. Brazil enjoys greater international prominence as Rio de Janeiro hosted the 2016 Olympics, an honor that required major expansion of transportation and sports facilities. It also meant answering the problems of criminal violence often centered in the *favelas*, major metropolitan areas where drug lords or armed militias dominate. Policing is hampered by low salaries, the firepower of the criminals, and organizational limitations on cooperation among police agencies. But the government of Rio has begun a process of occupying the *favelas*, urbanizing them, and driving out the drug lords who used to dominate them.

Brazil remains with a legacy of social problems: poverty, inequality, education, and now greater political instability. Infrastructure continues to fall behind need. Brazil must address growing environmental issues, among them serious urban pollution and the destruction of the Amazon rain forest.

Brazil is a nation of superlatives, but the question is whether Brazil's democracy and economic reforms can be maintained and advanced.

# Key Historical Events

**1500**  Sighting of Brazilian territory and landing by Pedro Álvares Cabral
**1808**  Portuguese royal family arrives in Brazil and makes Rio de Janeiro capital of the Portuguese Empire
**1822**  The Portuguese crown prince, Dom Pedro I, declares Brazil an independent nation and himself emperor
**1888**  Elimination of slavery
**1889**  Overthrow of emperor and establishment of the first republic by the military
**1922**  Week of Modern Art; Revolt of Copacabana Fort
**1924**  Revolt of the *tenentes* in São Paulo and the beginning of the Prestes Column's march through the interior
**1930**  Overthrow of the first republic and assumption of the presidency by Getúlio Vargas
**1937**  Vargas established the Estado Novo (New State)
**1945**  Vargas forced out of office, Marshal Dutra elected president
**1954**  Vargas, elected president in 1950, commits suicide
**1956**  Election of Juscelino Kubitschek and the beginning of the construction of Brasília
**1961**  President Jânio Quadros resigns, succeeded by Vice President João Goulart
**1964**  Military coup ousts Goulart and generals assume presidency beginning twenty-one years of military rule

**1985**  Tancredo Neves, a civilian, elected president, ending military rule

**1988**  New constitution written

**1990**  Direct election of Fernando Collor de Mello, defeating Luiz Inácio Lula da Silva

**1992**  President Collor de Mello impeached, resigns, and is succeeded by Vice President Itamar Franco

**1994**  Real Plan stabilizes economy; Fernando Henrique Cardoso elected president, defeating Luiz Inácio Lula da Silva

**1998**  Cardoso elected for a second term, again defeating Lula

**1999**  Military ministries replaced by a single civilian minister of defense

**2002**  Luiz Inácio Lula da Silva was elected president

**2006**  Lula re-elected for second term Brazil announced the liquidation of its debts with the International Monetary Fund and the Paris Club

**2007**  Announcement of discovery of major underwater oil field

**2008**  Government announces major drop in poverty

**2010**  Dilma Rousseff elected president.

**2012**  Supreme Court conviction of twenty-five involved in the Mensalão.

**2013**  Massive street demonstrations of more than 1 million people protesting increased transit fares and allocation of government resources to stadiums and not health and education. World Cup in Brazil; Dilma Rousseff re-elected president

**2016**  Rio de Janeiro hosted Olympics; Dilma removed from presidency by impeachment; Vice President Michel Temer assumes the presidency

# Bibliography

The following books in English will give a broad picture of various aspects of Brazil. In addition, there is a vast Portuguese-language literature for those able to read it. Fortunately, Spanish speakers can read Portuguese materials relatively easily.

Fishlow, Albert. *Starting Over: Brazil since 1985.* Washington, DC: Brookings Institution, 2011.

Hunter, Wendy. *The Transformation of the Workers' Party in Brazil, 1989–2009.* Cambridge: Cambridge University Press, 2010.

Monteiro, Alfred P. *Brazil's Reversal of Fortune.* London: Polity Press, 2014

Power, Timothy J., and Matthew M. Taylor, eds. *Corruption and Democracy in Brazil: The Struggle for Accountability.* Pittsburgh, PA: University of Pittsburgh Press, 2011

Roett, Riordan. *The New Brazil.* Washington, DC: Brookings Institution, 2010.

Skidmore, Thomas E. *Brazil: Five Centuries of Change.* Oxford: Oxford University Press, 1999.

Sweig, Julia E. *Global Brazil and U.S.–Brazil Relations.* New York: Council on Foreign Relations Press, 2011.

### Films and Videos

Brazil has an active film industry, and a number of films are available on DVD, some in English, but most with subtitles. The following Brazilian films are suggested.

*Black Orpheus.* Brazil, 1959.

*Carandiru.* Brazil, 2003.

*Central Station.* Brazil/France, 1998.

*City of God.* Brazil, 2002.

*City of Men (Cidade dos Homens).* Brazil, 2007.

*Elite Squad.* Brazil, 2007.

*The Year My Parents Went on Vacation.* Brazil, 2006.

WEBSITES

In addition to bibliographical resources, the Internet offers a vast library of material in both English and
    Portuguese. The following are addresses of a few of the most useful sites for further reading.
http://www.brasilemb.org   Brazilian embassy
http://www.lanic.utexas.edu   Latin American Network Information Center (LANIC)
http://www.brasa.org   Brazilian Studies Association
http://www.pt.org.br   Home page of the Worker's Party

PERU

BOLIVIA

BRAZIL

PARAGUAY

Antofagasta

Pacific
Ocean

ARGENTINA

URUGUAY

Viña del
Mar
Santiago

A N D E S   M O U N T A I N S

Concepción

Puerto
Montt

Map of
**CHILE**

N

W          E

S

100   0   100   200   Miles

Scale 1:40,000,000

Punta
Arenas

# FIFTEEN

# CHILE

*Eduardo Silva*

## Introduction

Long and narrow, Chile clings to the western edge of South America's Southern Cone. It is a heavily urbanized country; 85 percent of its 17 million people live in cities and towns, mostly in the central part of the nation. At just under 2 percent, the annual population growth rate is on the lower end for Latin America. Historically, Chile has a strong tradition of democratic rule punctuated by violent regime breakdown. The contemporary period is no exception. After forty years of democratic rule, Chile experienced near civil war in the early 1970s, economic chaos, and a harsh military dictatorship that had implanted a neoliberal development model only to emerge as an example of economic and political stability after redemocratization. Since 1990, democratically elected governments have managed the market economic model inherited from the military government in a manner that, with the exception of international crisis–induced economic slowdowns in 1998–2002 and 2008–2009, ensured sustained growth. Economic growth raised wages, which together with the expansion of social safety nets, public housing, and state support for local development projects, sharply reduced poverty to 12 percent of the population in 2015. Moreover, while political turmoil engulfed Venezuela, the central Andes, and Argentina in the late 1990s and early 2000s, Chile consolidated democracy. Between 1990 and 2010, four democratically elected governments of the coalition of center-left parties that emerged from the redemocratization process abrogated most of the antidemocratic provisions of the constitution imposed by the military government (1973–1989), which had established a "protected" or limited democracy. Those center-left governments also addressed the politically charged issue of human rights violations committed by the military during the dictatorship.

The victory of the candidate of a center-right coalition in the presidential election of 2010 was a major milestone. It established peaceful alternation in government, a key indicator of democratic consolidation. It was also the first time in fifty years that conservatives had won the presidency by democratic means. The center-left coalition survived out of power, learned how to behave as a democratic opposition, and crafted a strategy to regain the presidency in 2013. A combination of policy missteps, scandals, and internal tensions may tip the balance back to the center-right in December 2017. Should that occur the center-right could prove itself a viable electoral alternative.

The socioeconomic and environmental imbalances that are among the darker legacies of the free market model imposed by the military government temper Chile's significant achievements since redemocratization. In 2013, after twenty years of democratic rule, Chile's income distribution, while improved from the period of the military dictatorship, is not significantly better than the democratic period before it, say circa 1970. For all its growth, Chile's economy had not developed much beyond the agro-mineral export profile of traditional underdeveloped nations and paid a heavy cost in terms of environmental degradation and natural resource depletion. Its political stability rested, in part, on antidemocratic institutions. Those institutions protected the privileges of upper-class social groups. Although successive center-left governments abrogated most of those "authoritarian enclaves" by 2005, the political practices they created still affect electoral politics and the policy process. Those practices have deeply affected efforts to reform of the dictatorship-era labor code, regressive tax code, education system, and the electoral system during Michelle Bachelet's second government (2014–2017).

## Political Economy

The military government (1973–1989) imposed a radical program of free market economic restructuring in Chile that successive democratic governments of the center-left and center-right maintained. The center-left coalition did so partially because it was a condition of the military for the democratic transition. But the neoliberal socioeconomic model's success was also a powerful reason for its preservation. It delivered sustained, high economic growth rates between the mid-1980s and 2004. Although growth has slowed for a variety of reasons, the model itself is not under question in top circles of either coalition.

Following the prescriptions of the Washington Consensus, Chile's political economy stresses openness to international trade and finance. Openness to trade significantly diversified the economy. Although copper still contributes heavily to export earnings, the emphasis on comparative advantage has intensified agro-exports in fruits, timber, fish, wine, and other minerals, such as molybdenum. The financial services, construction, and commercial sectors also have expanded dramatically. Manufacturing, after a period of decline due to the dismantling of protection and subsidies of the earlier import substitution industrialization period, has restructured and stabilized. Rapid economic growth stimulated a tight labor market up to 1998, which, together with low inflation, contributed to rising wages. Privatized pension funds and health insurance, in addition to capital inflows from abroad, provided ample investment funds for the Chilean economy. Recessions induced by international crises in 1998–2002 and 2008–2009 had a negative impact on these trends, but in each case employment and investment picked up again albeit not to the levels of the 1990s. During the 2008–2009 crisis the economy contracted about 1.7 percent (less than expected) and recovered to robust growth averaging just under 6 percent per year since then. Unemployment, which peaked at around 10 percent in 2009, declined to about 6.4 percent in 2012. Chile has diversified its trading partners as well, with the United States declining in importance as trade with East Asia expands.

The socioeconomic model stresses macroeconomic stability, with a special emphasis on inflation control. Due to extensive privatization, with the exception of copper mining, the state renounced public enterprise as a development tool. It mainly relies on fiscal and monetary policy to direct the economy. Economic growth and increased welfare spending dramatically decreased from 40 percent of Chileans in 1990 to 12 percent by 2015.

On the down side, Chile's center-left governments neglected serious problems with the neoliberal model. Zealous inflation control overvalued the currency, hurting exporters and suppressing policies that reactivate economies during downturns. The stress on comparative advantage inhibited a transition from an agro-mineral extractive economy to one capable of adding value to those products and developing technology. Although absolute poverty has declined, it nonetheless has one of the most unequal distributions of income in South America. By the same token, Chile's education system and other barriers—such as the pro-business labor code—limit opportunity for social mobility for the majority, who are not members of the relatively small middle class or the tightly knit circles of the rich, the well-born, and the powerful.

As expected, Sebatián Piñera's center-right government did not waver from these macroeconomic policies. However, it kept its promise to maintain the social safety net established during twenty years of center-left rule, but it did not expand spending for those programs in any meaningful way. Moreover, its much-touted aggressive pro-growth economic policies failed to make a dent in inequality. Its faith in private education to increase job skills as its signature pro-social equity policy resulted in cycles of massive student protest beginning in June 2011. In May 2010, Chile became the first South American country to be accepted into the OECD, the club of developed countries. The 2012 OECD Chile Country Report slammed Chile for its unacceptable levels of income inequality. It recommended higher transfer payments, raising income taxes to do it, and thoroughgoing reform of its education system, including university.

Spurred by these events, Michelle Bachelet's second administration (2014–2017) promised to address Chile's lingering social debt, a dark legacy of the military government. Education reform, tax reform, labor reform, and constitutional reform became the centerpieces of her government's legislative initiatives. Although she delivered on the first three and began a process to accomplish the latter, many believe the reforms were too little too late. Coupled with other factors, public opinion turned against her and her government, putting in question the future of the center-left coalition.

## Political History

The structure of present-day Chilean society and political institutions has deep roots in the country's political history. This section notes some of the major milestones in their development and highlights their relevance for today. The next section analyzes politics and power in contemporary Chile; readers may go directly to that section if they prefer.

In colonial times the captaincy general of Chile was a far-flung outpost of the Spanish Empire. Lacking silver and gold, most creole wealth, power, and privilege

flowed from control over large estates. This system engendered a rigid class structure with harsh labor exploitation. This social system left an enduring legacy. From
colonial days until the present, relatively small, closely knit networks of elites have
vigorously defended the exploitative underpinnings of their wealth and privilege.

The autocratic republic (1833–1891) that followed independence from Spain in
1818 set the foundations for an enduring tradition of centralized, authoritarian government featuring strong presidentialism in Chile. After defeating Peru and Bolivia
during the War of the Pacific (1879–1883), Chile annexed the Bolivian province of Atacama and the Peruvian provinces of Tarapacá and Arica. This deprived Bolivia of its
access to the Pacific Ocean and gave Chile vast mineral wealth—first nitrate and then
copper. Foreign control of mining established enclave export firms at the heart of the
Chilean economy, a characteristic that, with some modifications, endures until today.

The parliamentary republic (1891–1924) was established after the civil war of
1891. During this period, Congress dominated the presidency. Political and fiscal
disorder sparked constitutional reform that culminated in the constitution of 1925.
This period witnessed the birth of the labor movement, socialist parties, and the
middle-class, anticlerical Radical Party. In addition to these political forces and institutions, the legacy of the parliamentary republic has been an enduring mistrust
of parliamentary political systems in Chile. They are associated with irresponsible
partisanship and ungovernability.

Classic Chilean democracy emerged from the constitution of 1925, which reestablished presidential rule and introduced direct popular elections for both chambers of Congress. In 1932, following a period of political, social, and economic
instability, Arturo Alessandri Palma's second administration ushered in forty years
of uninterrupted democratic rule. The period ended with the violent overthrow of
Salvador Allende in 1973. Classic Chilean democracy left a number of important
legacies. First, it reinforced a highly presidentialist and centralized political system
in which the presidency initiated most legislation and all-important decisions were
made in the capital, Santiago. Second, although their electoral fortunes varied over
time, many of today's major political parties consolidated during this period. On
the right were the Conservative and Liberal parties (later fused into the National
Party), the Radical Party and later the Christian Democrats dominated the center,
and the Socialist and Communist parties anchored the left. The dynamics of this
political system are critical to understanding the political regime that emerged after
redemocratization in 1990 and current debates over how to reform it. The military
government consciously designed a new constitution to "fix" many of its "perverse"
features, principally multipartyism and polarizing tendencies.

A key characteristic of classic Chilean democracy was that each pole of its
party system (right, left, and center) advocated distinctive ideologically charged
policies to promote economic development and social peace. The right supported
a good business climate and opposed labor rights. The reformist center proposed
greater state involvement in the economy to promote industrialization; sought
land reform to modernize agriculture; championed social reforms in education,
health, and housing; and pledged support for organized labor. The left embraced
the same causes but proposed more radical solutions. Influenced by Marxism, leftists unabashedly advocated greater state involvement in the economy, including

nationalization of private firms beyond that advocated by centrist parties and more radical land reform. Leftists believed in strong support for organized labor (higher wages, benefits, and rights) and generous fiscal expenditures for social reforms.

The flexibility of centrist parties was key to the political stability of Chile's tripolar multiparty system in which each pole mustered roughly a third of the votes. Thus, they had to be willing to enter into governing coalitions with either the moderate right or left, depending on circumstances. This ensured policy moderation and majorities in the Congress to pass legislation.

That flexibility was lost beginning with the conservative administration of Jorge Alessandri (1958–1964), son of the former president. Alessandri's government ushered in a period in which minority governments of the right, center, and left attempted to impose their own solutions to Chile's socioeconomic problems. These conditions fueled a leftward drift, radicalization, and polarization of Chilean politics. Alessandri's promarket, antilabor policies did little to solve Chile's socioeconomic problems; but they did alienate the center-left and the left, which perceived those policies to be an onslaught against hard-earned gains. The Christian Democrats under Eduardo Frei Montalva (1964–1970) followed with a reformist socioeconomic program. Political opposition and economic problems hampered implementation of the "Revolution in Liberty." This paved the way for the election of Socialist Salvador Allende at the head of a multiparty leftist coalition in 1970. His government's program addressing nationalization, planning, agrarian reform, and economic problems sparked mounting class conflict that polarized the nation, setting the stage for a violent coup d'état in 1973. It must be added that, from the beginning, the United States did everything in its power to help set that stage, promoting economic destabilization, supporting opposition mass mobilization, and aiding putschist military officers.

In the final analysis, despite high levels of confrontation, the ferocity of the military's coup against Allende on September 11, 1973, took everyone by surprise. It was a well-orchestrated combat operation against a revolution that was mostly rhetoric with respect to its capacity for armed resistance. In the terror that followed, thousands lost their lives, thousands more were arrested and tortured, and tens of thousands went into forced or voluntary exile.

## Military Government

The Chilean armed forces intervened in politics to resolve a deep societal crisis, which they attributed to the failings of a developmental model that fed class conflict. Therefore, during its first year of rule, the military junta searched for an altogether different development model. The junta found it in neoliberalism. Neoliberal ideology offered a vision of the economy, society, and the state capable of eradicating state-led development and Marxism. The military had largely achieved its goal when it handed the reins of power over to civilians in 1990.

The military inherited a chaotic economy. Extravagant fiscal deficits fed hyperinflation, expropriation paralyzed industry and commerce, and investment was nonexistent. The U.S.-trained neoliberal economists that advised the junta argued that sound, sustained economic growth depended on monetary stability, reestablishing a free market economy in which the private sector was the engine of growth, and building an economy open to international competition and foreign invest-ment. These advisors were known as the "Chicago boys," because most of them had received graduate degrees from the economics department of the University of Chicago, where many studied with Milton Friedman, a Nobel Prize–winning monetarist. To wring inflation and other price distortions out of the economy, they implemented an orthodox economic stabilization program between 1975 and 1979, along with radical privatization of state enterprises and trade and financial sector liberalization. Beginning in 1979, the Chicago boys privatized the pension system now largely administered by Pension Fund Administrators (AFPs), health-care in-surance by creating Private Health Insurance Plans (ISAPRES), and the educational system via vouchers. The Chicago boys crafted a labor code that institutionalized the emasculation of organized labor and decentralized political administration by giving regions and municipalities more authority over local issues.

The military government also restructured Chilean politics. It began the process by establishing a highly centralized, closed, authoritarian political system. It shut Congress indefinitely, banned all political parties, and purged state institutions and universities. The junta persecuted socialists, communists, and other far-left groups mercilessly, and many died or suffered torture, imprisonment, and exile at the hands of the consolidated intelligence services of the armed forces and the national police force. Pinochet, the commander-in-chief of the army, centralized power in his person and pronounced himself president of the nation.

Although Pinochet maintained order with iron-fisted rule, he and his support-ers wanted to legitimate authoritarianism. They wrote a new constitution, submitted it to a plebiscite in 1980, and had it approved by a wide margin under questionable electoral conditions. The constitution of 1980 was designed to guide Chile through a transition from military rule to a protected democracy. It awarded the military guardianship over the political system and safeguarded the privileges of property by making it virtually impossible to reform the free market economic system. The transi-tion itself was to begin in 1988 with a plebiscite to decide whether Pinochet would continue as president. If the plebiscite ratified him for another eight-year period (to 1997), elections for Congress would be held in 1989. If the plebiscite rejected Pinochet, then open elections for the presidency and for a Congress would be held in 1989.

Pinochet and his supporters fully expected to win the plebiscite by riding the crest of economic good times and the disarray of disheartened opposition politi-cal forces. But the economic cataclysm that beset Chile with the onset of the Latin American debt crisis changed that script. Between 1982 and 1983 GDP plunged 15 percent, unemployment soared to 33 percent, and the middle classes lost their savings as the financial system collapsed.

This economic crisis shook Pinochet's regime to the core. His unconditional sup-port for the Chicago boys and orthodox deflationary policies in a depressed economy aroused a powerful opposition movement. Mass mobilization demanding economic relief and rapid democratization swept the country between 1983 and 1986. Oppo-sition political parties quickly took over the protest movement. Two blocs vied for control of this movement: the Christian Democratic—led Democratic Alliance and the Communist-led Popular Democratic Movement. The resumption of economic growth and a failed attempt on Pinochet's life in 1986 ended the period of mass mobilization.

After 1986, the political transition followed the timetable and institutional structure set by the junta. The Democratic Alliance emerged as the more important of the two opposition movements, and its member parties learned how to work together more efficiently. This political force, now calling itself the Coalition of Parties for the No (the "no" vote was a ballot against Pinochet), soundly defeated him in the plebiscite (54.7 to 43 percent). The military, agreeing to abide by the terms of the 1980 constitution, and mollified by the opposition's promise not to alter the free market economic model, accepted defeat and set presidential and congressional elections for December 1989. The resurrection of political parties in the mid-1980s also extended to the center-right, which, being in full agreement with the military government, had disbanded their political organizations after 1973. The more traditional conservatives of the old National Party formed National Renovation, while libertarians (free marketers connected to the military government) established the Independent Democratic Union.

These were the political forces that contested the founding election of Chile's new democracy and that have dominated Chilean politics since then. In 1989, the center-left opposition bloc, now calling itself the Coalition of Parties for Democracy (CPD), backed the candidacy of Patricio Aylwin, a conservative Christian Democrat. On the center-right, National Renovation and the Independent Democratic Union supported the candidacy of Hernán Büchi, a successful minister of finance. A populist banker-businessman, Francisco Javier Errázuriz, also ran on the right. The presidential election results mirrored the plebiscite. Aylwin won with 55.2 percent of the vote. Conservatives garnered 44.8 percent, but those votes were split between Büchi (29.4 percent) and Errázuriz (15.4 percent). The far left, by contrast, fared poorly. Aylwin and the CPD took office in March 1990.

## Power and Politics

In March 2010 the inauguration of Sebastián Piñera, the presidential candidate of the center-right Coalition for Change, marked the end of an era in contemporary Chilean politics. His victory over Eduardo Frei Ruiz-Tagle brought to a close twenty years of uninterrupted rule by the CPD, the center-left coalition that had governed Chile since the end of the dictatorship and the electorally most successful political party coalition in Chilean history. This turn of events invites an assessment of the successes and shortcomings of the CPD and the reasons for its defeat in the presidential elections of 2009–2010. It also calls for a reflection on Piñera's government One of the biggest surprises was his pledge to support the social programs established by the CPD and to increase their funding and efficacy. Did Piñera succeed in laying the foundations for a new conservatism? Could the CPD reinvent itself sufficiently to recapture the presidency in 2014?

From 1990 to 2010, four administrations of the CPD governed Chile: Patricio Aylwin (1990–1994); Eduardo Frei Ruiz-Tagle (1994–2000); Ricardo Lagos (2000–2006); and Michelle Bachelet (2006–2010), Chile's first female president. The first two were Christian Democrats, and the last two were moderate Socialists. The CPD achieved notable successes during their presidencies. It guided the transition from military dictatorship to democratic consolidation. Chile enjoyed steady economic growth,

permitting incomes to rise and poverty to fall. The social safety net expanded significantly during those twenty years, as did the inclusiveness of society in general.

Three pillars sustained the consolidation of democracy, a task in which the CPD
had to gain the trust of the armed forces and the social forces that had supported the
dictatorship. First, the CPD retained the free market economic model. Second, it governed within the institutional framework established by the 1980 constitution. Third,
the CPD focused its social programs on the eradication of poverty. A decision to value
governability above all else anchored the CPD's political philosophy. The emphasis
on governability responded to the public perception that the parties of the CPD had
been responsible for the breakdown of "classic" Chilean democracy, a perception the
CPD to a large extent shared. We turn now to a discussion of those three pillars.

True to their promise, CPD governments maintained the free market political
economy inherited from the dictatorship. Ideological conversion among their ranks
and rapid, sustained economic growth and its benefits consolidated support for
neoliberal economics in the CPD. Between 1984 and 1997, the neoliberal economic
model produced rapid, sustained economic growth of approximately 7 percent per
year with low inflation, virtually balanced budgets, and a high investment rate.
Growth slowed in the 2000s largely due to the Asian financial crisis and to the global
financial crisis of 2008–2009. Because all four administrations of the CPD supported
the free market economy and exercised policy moderation, serious challenges to
conservatives on the issues that had torn Chile apart in the past—property, profits,
and the social order—were no longer on the political agenda.

The military dictatorship's constitution of 1980, designed to constrain the sovereign will of the people, structured much of power and politics after 1990. These
institutions established a "protected democracy" that conferred extraordinary
powers on conservative political forces to defend the neoliberal socioeconomic
model imposed by the military government from anything but modest reform. They
shaped a policymaking process that generally produced a compromise bill in which
the core interests of the center-right were strongly protected, or else the bill died.

All four CPD presidencies patiently chipped away at these authoritarian enclaves. Significant constitutional reform to restore Chile to full political democracy
proved beyond the powers of the first two CPD administrations. Constitutional
amendments require two-thirds support of all deputies and senators. Given the conservatives' interest in the maintenance of military guardianship and veto power over
socioeconomic policy, up to 2005 they had approved only relatively minor changes.

In 2005, in a breakthrough for Chilean democracy, the CPD and the opposition
negotiated significant constitutional reforms. These included, first, the abolition of
appointed senators, of whom the first nine had been Pinochet appointees (four legally
had to be the commanders-in-chief of the armed forces and the militarized police).
Second, presidential authority to dismiss military commanders and the reduction of
the National Security Council to an advisory role curtailed the autonomy of the armed
forces. Third, presidential terms were cut from six years to four in an effort to rein in
excessive presidentialism. Analysts believe the opposition negotiated these reforms
for several reasons. The CPD by then had appointed five nonmilitary senators loyal to
the government; Pinochet and close identification with the dictatorship had become
an electoral liability; and those at odds with the CPD had, by then, mostly resigned.

Conservatives steadfastly blocked CPD proposals to change the party and electoral system. They kept proportional representation off of the agenda. Conservatives also blocked reform of the binomial electoral system, which overrepresented conservative parties in the Congress. In the binomial electoral system, each district elects two candidates. A party coalition must obtain double or more votes than the competing coalition to win both seats. If it does not, the minority coalition automatically wins a seat. This system ensures that the second largest bloc, frequently conservative parties, can win one out of every two contested seats with only one-third of the vote, which is the historic percentage of the vote for the right. The binomial electoral system—with its explicit rejection of proportional representation—was designed to encourage coalition building in a multiparty system and competition for centrist votes. These effects blunt ideological polarization and party system fragmentation that contributed to the collapse of democracy in 1973. In the final analysis, the binomial electoral system, coupled with high quorum rules to change most existing legislation—much of it fundamental laws that support the free market socioeconomic model—granted conservatives important veto power during the period of CPD rule. But, as will be shown, these institutions also give power to the CPD now that they are not government. In short, given the difficulties of winning supermajorities, congressional opposition to executive-generated bills has real teeth in Chile.

Social equity and human rights policy comprised the third pillar of CPD rule. Overall, poverty rates declined, in part because of increased spending for an expanded social safety net. Aid to families and individuals in the form of cash transfers rose, especially during Bachelet's administration. The percentage of Chileans officially classified as poor fell from 38 toward the end of the military government to 15 percent in 2009 (up from 13 percent in 2007). Government expenditures for public health, on which 75 percent of Chileans rely, doubled between 1990 and 2004 and expanded even more during Bachelet's government. The Lagos administration passed a law (Plan AUGE) that reformed the financing of the public and private health-care system to make quality service more accessible to all for a predetermined list of illnesses regardless of whether individuals are enrolled in the public or private system. Because the private pension system (AFP) contained serious flaws and excluded large numbers of people, the Bachelet administration passed mild pension system reform. The principal feature was the establishment of a small guaranteed pension to various vulnerable groups. In addition to these traditional issues, the CPD embraced new social movements whose issues had received scant, if any, recognition by the military government. These included the feminist, environmental, and indigenous people's movements (see the section on interest groups).

CPD governments consistently failed to make much headway in two areas. Labor code reform was disappointingly weak. The military government had imposed a harsh antiunion labor law. Successive CPD governments were unable to overcome both internal differences and conservative opposition to pass a major overhaul. Education reform was another weak point. The military government had privatized and decentralized education. The system included public municipal schools; private schools with state subsidies (the student voucher system); and elite, exclusive, totally private schools. After surprising, massive protests by high school students in 2006, the Bachelet administration sponsored a reform of the education system to address the worst inequities. Unfortunately, conservative forces hijacked the reform process, passing only mild reforms to ensure quality across the system. Significantly, municipalities still controlled schools and subsidized private schools remained for-profit businesses.

Surprisingly, one of the most positive developments occurred in the area of human rights. The military government had unleashed a ferocious campaign of terror, especially between 1973 and 1977, in which over 3,000 persons died and 30,000 were subjected to torture. Since 1990, the issue has divided the Chilean polity, arousing strong passions on both sides: on one side are conservatives, who feel the violence was justified; on the other side are leftists and reformists who either suffered it or believed human rights violations to be crimes against humanity. The CPD built its approach on three principles: truth, justice, and reparation. At first, justice was beyond reach. There was no question of overturning the amnesty law the military government had decreed for itself in 1978. Amnesty had strong backing from conservative political forces who considered the military—and Pinochet personally—to be the saviors of Chile and the guardians of neoliberal order. The Aylwin administration concentrated on truth by establishing the Truth and Reconciliation Commission, also known as the Rettig Commission. The commission gave a full account of victims, the methods used by the security branches of the armed forces and the police, and the judiciary's condoning of state terror. The Aylwin government also instituted compensation for the families of victims who had died or disappeared. Justice had to wait until the Lagos and Bachelet administrations. As late as 1998, the military's position seemed unassailable. But by 2005 Pinochet's political fortunes had suffered a dramatic reverse due to unrelenting efforts to prosecute him after the British government placed him under house arrest for human rights violations during a visit to that country for medical reasons in 1998. That paved the way to prosecute other military officers for their crimes after a horrifying and sobering public accounting of state terror. Equally important, several branches of the armed forces publicly admitted to institutional excess and committed to never again engage in such excesses.

Why did the CPD lose its grip on power after twenty years in the presidency? A number of factors sapped its electoral appeal and weakened its internal structures. First, presidentialism weakened the linkages between political parties and the presidency. Presidents assembled teams of technocrats to govern and neglected the party leadership. Over time the political parties of the CPD devoted themselves more and more to the task of negotiating quotas for employment in the executive branch. Second, the top political class of the CPD formed cross-party agreements on policy agendas, consequently ignoring important issues because they were too conflictive. Third, the CPD's presidential candidate, Eduardo Frei, symbolized the exhaustion of a ruling coalition that had run out of ideas for governing. Frei, a Christian Democrat, had already been president and was considered a tired, lackluster candidate who was a party man (and political parties were in decline with voters). Once voters put all these dynamics together, they lost a great deal of respect for the coalition, its parties, and its candidate. Born in the 1980s out of the crucible of democratization, the CPD had lost touch with the Chile of 2010. The CPD had little to offer. The CPD's problems were magnified by internal splits, where a maverick presidential candidate—former socialist Marco Enríquez-Ominami—ran an independent campaign for the presidency after he lost a rigged primary process. The primary process itself was a hoary public testament to backroom deals among party elites that defied mounting calls for genuine internal democratization. In first-round balloting in December 2009, he drew 20 percent of votes from Frei and only half-heartedly endorsed him days before the second round in January 2010. Frei lost with 48.4 percent to Piñera's 51.6 percent.

Sebastián Piñera, who had run against Bachelet in the presidential election of 2005–2006, capitalized on negative voter perceptions of the CPD. He formed a coalition that expanded on the traditional electoral union of Renovación Nacional (RN) and the Unión Democrática Independiente (UDI)—the Alianza por Chile. He called his organization the Coalition for Change. He presented a moderate stance, softening the hard edges of RN's and, especially, UDI's conservatism. Gone were exhortations to privatize the rest of the economy, to slash taxes and government spending, and to cut back on the creeping welfare state. The goal was to wrestle moderate voters away from the CPD—especially Christian Democrats—and to invite political and technocratic figures among them to participate in his government. Piñera aspired to recast Chilean conservatism in moderate center-right terms to empower it to win many terms in the presidential office—to become a winning electoral force.

Piñera's campaign (and subsequently his government) stressed efficiency in government to do more with the same amount of resources. In terms of political economy, his focus is on setting the conditions necessary to restore sustained high growth and to generate employment. On social issues Piñera emphasized greater efficiency in the delivery of services. In the areas of education and health care he pledged to expand public–private partnerships (the system of operating licenses for private companies). With respect to welfare, much to the consternation of CPD politicians, he vowed to maintain the popular social safety net established by President Bachelet and even to increase resources for it, largely through administrative efficiency measures. After a brief honeymoon, Piñera's government proved unable to recast Chilean conservatism for long-term rule. The devastating earthquake that struck south-central Chile in February 2010, just a month before he was to take office complicated his task. Piñera had to plan for reconstruction to repair billions of dollars in damage. His administration shepherded through legislation on temporary corporate tax increases to finance reconstruction. In a first blow, however, planning and implementation did not live up to the efficiency he had promised. Corruption, delays, and shoddy construction plagued the effort.

Piñera's government failed to pass major legislation, although there were some successes. These included extending prenatal leave for working expectant mothers and a bonus for elderly couples completing fifty years of marriage. It also instituted voting law reform. Chileans are now automatically registered to vote, and voting is voluntary instead of compulsory. Overhaul of the binomial electoral system, meaningful education reform, expansion of health care, and tax reform, however, were not on the table.

Administrative efficiency did not improve either. The new government came in with a zeal to replace as many administrators as possible. Political appointees and temporary contract personnel went first. A campaign to prosecute permanent public service personnel for malfeasance or worse and deteriorating relations between arrogant new superiors and personnel convinced many to leave or take early retirement before they became embroiled in legal proceedings or otherwise harassed. This resulted in a dearth of experienced administrators across the entire public administration system with the corresponding negative impacts on program administration.

Historical tensions between the two major coalition partners further debilitated Piñera's administration. The president was from the more traditional conservative RN Party, which received many important ministries. UDI, a militant libertarian party born of the military dictatorship, felt slighted, especially because it was electorally far more successful. Indeed, it held more seats in the legislature than any party. Conflicts over policy and appointments raged, became public, and sullied the Coalition for Change's image. Policy differences were especially strong over lifestyle issues, taxation, privatization, and welfare rollback, where UDI consistently took harder lines.

Last but not least, after initial disarray from being out of power for the first time in twenty years, the CPD learned how to function as an opposition bloc. First, the coalition did not dissolve, as some pundits speculated. Second, it learned how to challenge the government's legislative initiatives in the Congress and in the court of public opinion. On seemingly progressive social, tax, and administrative reforms, the CPD pointed to the "fine print" (*letra chica*) and explained how it actually reduced or restricted benefits. This tactic, plus its slender majority in the Senate, permitted the CPD to delay passage and negotiate changes. Its parties also established a primary system to democratize them, bring in new leadership, and increase voter appeal.

One of the biggest problems for the Coalition for Change's government was the resurgence of mass protests on a scale not seen since the democratization movement of the 1980s. It began with large, up to nearly 40,000 strong, demonstrations by environmentalists in April–June 2011 against a plan to develop hydroelectric power that involved the construction of megadams in pristine Patagonia. These demonstrations built on Mapuche hunger strikes, gay rights activism, and rumbling public sector unions.

Then, in June 2011, a cycle of massive university-led student demonstrations and occupations of educational establishments began that rocked the political system. University and high school students protested high costs, uneven quality, and the corruption in the education system. They demanded free education as a right, the end to education as a commodity, quality across the system, and the strengthening of state universities and K–12 public schools. In short, they demanded the abolishment of the education system inherited from the dictatorship and turned their critique of its inequalities into an indictment of the inequalities of Chile's neoliberal political economy as a whole. This framing resonated with Chilean public opinion and became a focal point for rallying the movements that had already been protesting, generating demonstrations of over 100,000 strong. Protests continued into 2012 and beyond.

The student movement was also militantly autonomous. It rejected all political parties and declared the Chilean political system hopelessly sclerotic. The CPD, taken completely by surprise, did not know how to react to the movement, and the movement disdainfully rejected its clumsy efforts to capitalize politically on the protests. Meanwhile, the students resolutely rejected all overtures from the government, especially early ones designed to demobilize them without concrete offers on the table. In the end, the students did negotiate after a fashion when the authorities advanced concrete proposals. All of them broke down, but significant increases in low-cost, government-backed loans and grants were legislated, and a new superintendence to oversee educational quality was established.

Infighting within Piñera's government over how to handle the student protests further debilitated the Coalition for Change's public image. UDI pressured to gain the upper hand, but its hardline stance over policy resulted in plummeting public approval ratings. The negative effects of these tensions carried over to the presidential elections of November 2013, as the center-right coalition torpedoed its front running candidates. Eventually, Evelyn Matthei, a former RN senator and Piñera government cabinet minister, stood for the Coalition for Change.

Meanwhile, the CPD and the Communist Party allied to form the New Majority, with hugely popular former president Michele Bachelet as its candidate. Marco Enríquez Ominami stood for the newly formed Progressive Party in a crowded field of center-left candidates. Bachelet gained first plurality by a large margin in the November 2013 general election but did not reach an absolute majority, thus forcing a second-round election in December. Marco Enríquez Ominami was third with a scant 10 percent of the vote. Moreover, not only did Evelyn Matthei come in a distant second, but also the center-right coalition lost seats in both the lower and upper chambers of the legislature. In the run-off election, Bachelet triumphed by 62 percent to 38 percent. Moreover, for the first time in ten years the center-left coalition enjoyed a majority in both chambers of the Congress, albeit a slender one in the senate. This gave her a chance of pushing through elements of her ambitious legislative program, which included tax reform, education reform, labor code reform, changing the binomial electoral system, and constitutional reform.

Bachelet immediately began to deliver on her program, although given significant opposition from conservatives in the legislature and tensions within her own coalition, reforms involved significant compromises. Tax reform, introduced in March 2014, was signed into law in February 2016. It modified corporate and personal income tax, introduced new exceptions to value-added taxes, and simplified the tax code. In January

Michelle Bachelet, President of Chile GP.

2015, the lower chamber of the Congress approved a bill that had already passed in the Senate to change the binomial electoral system for a proportional representation system. District lines were redrawn and the number of deputies increased from 120 to 155 and senators from 38 to 50. It stipulated that 40 percent of candidates must be females. It is to go into effect for the 2017 presidential and legislative elections.

Upon taking office in March 2014, Bachelet also introduced what was to be her signature legislation, a bill to reform the education system that addressed the central demands of the student movements. This bill proposed guaranteed free education; it prohibited selectivity in private schools that participated in the state-funded voucher program and ordered them to incorporate as not-for-profit foundations over three years.

The bill clearly threatened the education system's vested interests. Unfortunately, education minister Nocolás Eyzaguirre, a pillar of the consensus politics establishment, former Western Hemisphere Director of the World Bank, and former finance minister in Bachelet's first government, was unable to orchestrate workable compromises among intense conflicting interests. Still, there were reforms. State voucher-funded schools had profit-making loopholes closed and were brought under closer scrutiny, and public municipal schools were strengthened. Students with family income under a certain level had the option to attend university tuition-free.

Despite these advances, in trying to please everyone Eyzaguirre's compromises pleased no one. Students continued protesting and support from Nueva Mayoría eroded as more progressive and conservative members alike rejected them—all to the drumbeat of relentless opposition from the conservative coalition, now called Chile Vamos.

The troubles of Batchelt's second administration did not end there. In addition to student protests, she faced unrest from other social movements as well. The labor movement, long dormant, awakened. Labor disputes over subcontracted worker conditions in the copper mines flared up as did strikes and demonstrations from public sector unions worried about job security and eroding wages and salaries, including incidents at the time of this writing. Meanwhile, protests against mega projects in the mining sector spiked, and regional territorial movements continued to demand greater decentralization and special economic subsidies given their remoteness from Chile's main markets that drove up the prices of goods and services. In 2016 a protest movement demanding an end to Chile's private pension system erupted due to the certainty of paltry payouts.

In midst of these difficulties, scandals further rocked Bachelet's government. Problems began when her government accused prominent party leaders of UDI and RN of involvement in financial wrongdoing, bringing an end to the political career of some. However, conservatives counterattacked implicating Batchelet's son by association in his wife's alleged illicit influence pedaling in lucrative real estate development deals. They accused Batchelt of deliberately turning a blind eye and then publicly rising to his defense rather than distancing herself from him.

The combination of multiple arenas of protest, scandals, ministerial instability, tensions between the progressive and conservative (read Christian Democrat) factions of Nueva Mayoreia, and the public perception that the same old consensus politics that only benefited the establishment prevailed had significant consequences.

For one, it produced a precipitous drop in Batchelet's popularity; as of October 2016 it was the lowest of any government since democracy was restored in 1991—a precipitous drop after triumphing with 67 percent of the vote to the Alianza por Chile's 37 percent in the December 2013 presidential elections. A second important consequence was Nueva Mayoría's defeat in the municipal elections of October 23, 2016. It lost a number of important municipalities to Chile Vamos. The biggest number, however, was the 65 percent abstention rate.

These developments have had an impact on the 2017 presidential race that's beginning to shape up. In the absence of the binomial electoral system, Nueva Mayoría is unable to to settle on a consensus candidate for the 2017 presidential election. The Christian Democratic party has decided to run a candidate of its own. Chile Vamos is likely to offer up Sebastián Piñera again. If the election were held today, bets are that Piñera would win.

## Chilean Government Structures

### POLITICAL INSTITUTIONS

The military government's administrative decentralization program divided Chile's territory into fifteen regions, including the Santiago metropolitan area. Each region is headed by an intendant (*intendente*) appointed by the president. Regions are divided into the traditional fifty-one provinces, each headed by a governor also appointed by the president. In 1991, the Congress approved direct election of formerly appointed mayors.

Executive power is vested in the president, who serves a four-year term, and successive re-election is not allowed. Presidents are directly elected by absolute majority; in the absence of a clear-cut majority, the two top vote-getters compete in a run-off election (or second-round vote). The presidency is the strongest branch of the political system. It initiates most bills, and the presidency's full weight behind a bill can overcome opposition through compromise. Moreover, the presidency has a strong role in the maintenance of internal order. The presidency initiates all legislation that has a fiscal impact.

The legislative branch consists of a bicameral Congress located in the port city of Valparaíso (about an hour and a half by road from Santiago, the capital city). It is not as powerful an institution as it had been before 1973, since it meets fewer days than it did before 1973, and its oversight capacity and the competence of its committees are diminished. As of this writing the Senate consists of thirty-eight members, and the Chamber of Deputies has 120 seats, but they will expand to 50 and 155, respectively, after the December 2017 national elections.

The judicial branch of government consists of a twenty-one-member Supreme Court, sixteen appellate courts, major claims courts, and local courts. Supreme Court justices are appointed by the president of the republic from a slate of five names proposed by the Court itself. Each appellate court has jurisdiction over one or more province(s). The Supreme Court exercises its duties in separate chambers consisting of at least five judges each. These chambers are presided over by the most senior member or the president of the court. The judicial system also includes special courts, such as juvenile courts, labor courts, and military courts in time of peace.

The 1980 constitution granted the armed forces significant tutelary power over civilian political forces, especially center-left ones. However, by 2010 most either had been rescinded or the military routinely did not invoke them. Still, military doctrine and promotion of general officers are free of civilian oversight. The president of the republic may nominate the commander-in-chief of the armed forces only from a list of five names submitted by the military and can only remove him before the four-year term is up under the most extraordinary of circumstances. Moreover, internal security laws give military courts expanded jurisdiction over judicial issues that are usually the purview of civilian courts. This hampers expeditious investigation of human rights abuses committed during the military government.

## MAIN POLITICAL PARTIES

Chile has a well-institutionalized political party system. It remains a multiparty system with many of the traditional parties still active. The old National Party formed National Renovation (RN), a center-right party based on traditional conservative values that included some moderates and was willing to negotiate key policy issues with the CPD. A "new right" also developed. Close collaborators of the military government, especially among the economic technocrats, formed the Independent Democratic Union (UDI). The UDI, a libertarian party, is less inclined to compromise with centrist or center-left political parties. UDI's populist approach has transformed it into Chile's most successful party. The RN and UDI form electoral coalitions for presidential races, now called the Alliance for Chile, but relations between the two parties are frequently strained.

The Christian Democratic Party (PDC) dominates the center. Ideologically, the PDC continues to rely on social-Christian doctrine and has a significant conservative faction. The Radical Party is another traditional centrist party. It has moved to the center-left ideologically and has joined the Socialist International.

The left changed substantially, especially the Socialist Party (PS). After significant internal turmoil, dissension, and splits, the PS experienced an ideological transformation by renouncing Marxism and the class struggle and becoming a European-style social democratic party. It is, essentially, a moderate "third way" socialist party, a center-left organization seeking a middle ground between free market capitalism and orthodox socialism. The Party for Democracy (Partido por la Democracia; PPD) is another moderate center-left party that formed following one of the initial splits of the PS. Both the PS and the PPD renounced social revolution and socialist state building. They no longer supported nationalization, extensive industrial policy, the strong mixed economy, full employment, or the comprehensive welfare state. They softened their commitment to labor rights and more equal distribution of the national wealth. Party leadership accepted free market economics and settled for putting a human face on capitalism, meaning a commitment to maintaining social safety nets, education, health care, and civil society participation in political decision-making. Meanwhile, the Communist Party of Chile (PCCh) retains its Marxist roots, although it no longer actively advocates violent revolution. In that sense, it seems to have embraced an ideological posture similar to that of European communists in the 1980s. Further to the left but also, for the moment, eschewing violence is the Revolutionary Movement of the Left (MIR). Marco Enríquez

Ominami's rupture with the PS during the 2009–2010 presidential elections led to the creation of a new party—the Progressive Party. The party's platform emphasizes internal party democracy, greater social equality, and effective political participation. Among other things, it seeks to pull the CPD away from the right and embrace a broader coalition of social forces. It failed to win any seats in Congress.

In a significant departure from Chile's "classical" democracy, the electoral system encouraged coalition building among political parties. The center-left formed the CPD, which now consists of the PDC, the PS, the PPD, and the Radical Party. The CPD's structure strongly encouraged consensual politics among top leadership, which heavily conditioned the policy agenda by leaving out conflictual issues. In the wake of the massive student protests and citizen groundswell for government to address Chile's deeply entrenched social, political, and economic inequality exacerbated by the legacies of the dictatorship, the CPD expanded to include the Communist Party, calling itself Nueva Mayoría (New Majority). For municipal election of 2016 it also included new parties, such as Movimiento Amplio Social Región and Izquierda Ciudadana.

RN and UDI also formed electoral pacts on the center-right. Alliance for Chile candidates did well running against Lagos and Bachelet. A slightly expanded coalition, the Coalition for Change, won the 2010 presidential election but lost to the New Majority coalition (the CPD with the Communist Party) in 2013. In 2015, following resounding electoral defeat in the 2013 presidential election, conservatives altered their coalition yet again, now under the name Chile Vamos. In addition to the classic conservative parties, Chile Vamos includes independents and new conservative regional movements, as well as a women's branch, Vamos Mujer. Independent and regional parties include Evolución Política and Partido Regionalista Independiente.

We are, then, seeing some changes in the party system, namely the formation of new regional and independent parties and movements as a result of citizen discontent with the perceived complacency of the "establishment" and social mobilization against it. Many of these parties align with the dominant center-left and center-right coalitions, although they are formally independent. In addition, an autonomous far left coalition, Pueblo Unido, has also formed. It includes the Partido Igualdad and Partido Frente Popular. The relaxation of barriers to entry for new parties—from 0.5 to 0.25 percent of voters in three contiguous or eight discontiguous regions—contributed to the proliferation of these and other new political parties in the north, central, south, and extreme southern regions of Chile.

# Interest Groups

## WOMEN

Chilean women have a history of second-class citizenship and discrimination in relation to men. However, as the twentieth century progressed, they made advances. They won the right to vote in 1949 and obtained wide access to education, including university education. Women have also become more visible in the business world at the mid-management level, although the board room remains a predominantly male preserve. Female participation in the nonprofessional labor force has also increased since the 1970s, especially in nondomestic services (food services, sales, secretarial) and nontraditional industry (fruit packing, canneries, poultry dressing and packaging). Thus, traditional gender roles are increasingly under challenge among both the middle and working classes.

Women have become an important political force in Chile. The women's movement played a vital role in the opposition to the military regime, especially in organizing the vote that defeated Pinochet in the decisive plebiscite of October 5, 1988. In newly redemocratized Chile, female politicians in municipalities and in the national legislature are more numerous than ever before, representing the full political spectrum. They also occupy numerous government posts, including cabinet posts. In December 2005 former defense minister Michelle Bachelet became the first female president of Chile. She appointed many more women to cabinet posts, reaching parity with men. Former foreign minister Soledad Alvear headed the Christian Democratic Party in 2007; Carolina Tohá led the PPD from July 2010 until recently. Also in 2004, the passage of a divorce law—over strenuous objection of the Catholic Church—heralded a victory for gender relations in Chile. Despite these advances, women still suffer from gender discrimination not only in the workplace but also in society in general.

In the governments of the CPD, gender issues received far more attention than in the past. In January 1991, the Aylwin administration created the National Women's Service (SERNAM) to incorporate a gender perspective into public policy. SERNAM's immediate focus was to reduce discrimination against women in access to employment, housing, education, and credit. Longer term objectives were aimed at improving the position of women with respect to men. They included dismantling institutionally rooted gender inequalities that hindered equal rights for women, easing the responsibility of females for home and child care, and stopping the sexual division of labor by integrating women into the labor market.

Overall, SERNAM did not succeed in promoting its longer term goals or, sadly, many of its shorter term ones either. This was largely due to the agency's firmly subordinated place on the CPD's policy agenda. The agency did not enjoy cabinet rank and had only a small administrative budget. As a result, SERNAM concentrated on forming working teams with the relevant departments of other ministries. Within these limitations, Bachelet's administration introduced many initiatives to improve women's lives. These included expansion of day care spaces, small pensions for low-income women, more resources to address violence against women, and an increase in the availability of emergency contraception.

In her second presidency, Michelle Bachelet continued to champion gender equality. In March 2014 she submitted a bill to Congress to form a Ministry for Women and Gender Equality, which became law in January 2015. Gender equality is an integral part of education, electoral system, labor, and constitutional reforms. She also sponsored a bill, still being debated, to decriminalize therapeutic abortions (risk to mother) and has passed laws strengthening civil unions and same-sex unions.

## INDIGENOUS PEOPLES

Although the vast majority of Chileans are mestizos, or of European heritage, some 3 percent of the population are native peoples, mostly Araucanian or Mapuche, who still inhabit the forested region of south central Chile (Bío-Bío and Araucanía).

In the twentieth century, the vanquished Mapuches (whose armed resistance continued into the 1880s) suffered from widespread discrimination and second-class citizenship. Until 1973, close-knit Mapuche communities based on family groupings retained common lands called *reducciones*, which they worked communally or as individual family parcels. Communal property and a separate identity for indigenous peoples clashed with the dictatorship's neoliberal ideals. In 1978, the military government broke up the *reducciones* and replaced them with family farms, which could be bought, mortgaged, and sold to cultivate individualistic, competitive, and economic-maximizing behavior among the Mapuche. Thus, the dictatorship hoped to obliterate Mapuche identity and culture, a strategy begun after the coup when the military broke Mapuche organizations by subjecting their leaders to death, torture, imprisonment, and exile.

The governments of the CPD attempted to redress some of the worst discriminatory policies of the military government and earlier periods. A vibrant indigenous peoples' movement has also emerged after redemocratization. All told, approximately 900,000 people claiming Mapuche heritage currently live in Chile, most of them exploited and poor. In 1989, while Patricio Aylwin was still a candidate for the presidency, the CPD signed an agreement with the indigenous peoples of Chile. In it, the CPD committed itself to the promulgation of a new law that would recognize ancestral culture and rights. Aylwin's government partially delivered on this promise by passing a new Indian law in 1993. The law recognized ancestral lands. It protected those lands by making them inalienable and established a fund to buy back lands that had been usurped by Chileans since the beginning of the century, when the reservations originally had been established. The law also promoted multiethnicity, legally recognized Indian communities, encouraged participation in policy-making, and acknowledged the need for socioeconomic development. The National Corporation of Indigenous Development (CONADI) now administers indigenous affairs, although it would benefit from more independence from the presidency.

Some advances were also achieved during the Lagos and Bachelet administrations. Under Lagos, the peoples of Rapa-Nui (Easter Island) achieved a measure of territorial autonomy. During Bachelet's government, the Chilean Congress finally ratified ILO Convention 169, which commits countries to recognize the pluriethnicity of their populations and the rights of indigenous peoples. In April 2008, president Bachelet launched "Recognition: Social Pact for Multiculturalism." Its policy agenda emphasized (i) greater indigenous participation in the political process; (ii) the resolution of property rights issues and the expansion of infrastructure for human development (health, education, and culture); and (iii) the promotion of multicultural relations and diversity.

Piñera's administration did not dismantle these initiatives; it essentially just ignored them. Instead, it emphasized controlling and repressing transgressive indigenous collective action (read: land invasions, road blocks, destruction of property, and occasional violence—sometimes armed—against persons). It also applied Pinochet-era antiterrorism laws, a practice begun during the Lagos administration, more vigorously.

The conflict has not abated in Bachelet's second administration, neither has its criminalization under the Pinochet-era antiterrorist law, which was questioned by special United Nations rapporteur missions as late as 2013. Her government responded rather belatedly in 2016 by setting up a dialogue roundtable. It includes repesentatives of the Mapuche people, landowners, the Catholic Church, academics, and the government.

## Environmental Movement

Chile has a relatively small but active environmental movement centered on a number of nongovernmental organizations (NGOs). Most of them have devoted themselves to consultancy or watchdog functions in relation to government environmental agencies. Part of this emphasis is due to the importance of environmental impact reporting requirements for development projects—this is the space for civil society challenges to such projects in the policy process. Some NGOs also organize public campaigns that may include protests and demonstrations. Issues include biodiversity protection, natural resource degradation (mining, forestry, and agriculture), urban pollution, and, more recently, climate change.

Environmental policy is governed by the Comprehensive Environmental Act of 1994. Mandatory environmental impact reporting is the main environmental policy instrument. The "polluter pays" principle is the second major instrument to force compliance with environmental regulations. However, the requirement is weak because the burden of proof rests with the prosecution. The act emphasizes gradualism. This means prioritizing problems and applying only small, incremental changes to deal with the most urgent ones. Still, the environmental movement has used environmental impact reporting provisions to mount legal challenges to new ventures in resource extraction, which are sometimes successful.

Until 2008 the National Commission for the Environment (CONAMA)—created during the Aylwin administration—was the government institution responsible for the sector. CONAMA was a small agency without cabinet rank. It was structured as an interministerial commission chaired by the minister of the general secretariat of the republic. Pollution abatement, rather than natural resource extraction, was CONAMA's principal focus.

Bachelet's government turned one of the environmental movement's enduring political demands into reality. It replaced CONAMA with a Ministry of the Environment in charge of policy and regulation. This elevates the saliency of environmental policy. Cabinet rank places environment on a more equal footing with other sectoral ministries. The law that created the Ministry of the Environment also established an Environmental Evaluation Service to administer environmental impact reporting. An Environmental Superintendency supervises the implementation of the four major environmental policy instruments, which are environmental resolutions, pollution prevention and clean-up plans, environmental regulations, and zoning rules. The same law obligated Piñera (who supported conservation) to send bills to Congress for the establishment of Environmental Tribunals (an appeals court to challenge government fines and rulings) and the creation of a Biodiversity and Protected Areas Service to rationalize existing institutional capacity in that area.

In June 2014, shortly after President Bachelet took office, her government ruled against a hydroelectric megaproject to dam a series of pristine Patagoian rivers to generate electricity for Chile's central and northern mining regions. This was a major victory for the environmental movement that had campaigned against it since 2008. Her government also signed into law a measure supported by environmentalists to ensure that 20 percent of Chile's energy would be supplied by renewable sources by 2025. Meanwhile, stepped-up local community protest to mining has delayed a number of projects.

## ORGANIZED BUSINESS

The most influential economic interest groups are business, finance, and agriculture. Each of the major economic sectors has a sectoral peak association. The most powerful ones are the Industrial Development Society (SFF), the National Agriculture Society, and the National Chamber of Commerce, which organize industrialists, landowners, and merchants, respectively. The SFF takes a very hard line with respect to the maintenance of Chile's protected democracy. The National Mine Owners' Society, the Chilean Builders' Chamber, and the Banking and Financial Institutions Association round out the most important business interest groups. In practice, these associations mostly represent the interests of large-scale businesspeople. The six major sectoral associations have formed an encompassing peak association, the Confederation for Production and Commerce (CPC). The CPC defends the general interests of business in the policy process. Its views represent a consensus of those of its six member organizations. In 2016 organized business once again closed ranks to gut labor code reform.

## ORGANIZED LABOR

Labor organizations emerged significantly weakened after eighteen years of military rule and repression. The old, Marxist-dominated Sole Workers' Center (Central Unica de Trabajadores; CUT) was broken up by the military government, which allowed labor organizations only at the plant level. With democratization, CUT became Chile's principal labor confederation. It is a group of industrial, professional, and mining unions led by leftist Christian Democrats and elements of the left, including the Communist Party. Overall, the union movement is not as strong as it was before the military government. Restricted collective bargaining, weak strike laws, open shops, low membership (around 11 percent of all employed workers in 2009), and other measures have limited organized labor's ability to represent its interests. As of 2006, however, the labor movement has become more militant in its frustration over its electoral support being taken for granted by the CPD. Piñera's government failed to avoid raising tensions with public sector unions over administrative efficiency policies that contributed to public sector employee dismissals, rollbacks of severance payments for years of service, and other human resource cost-saving measures. Fears over employment security and working conditions led to sharply increased strike activity. Labor unrest did not abate in Bachelet's second government. Copper mine workers in private and state-owned enterprises struck over pay increases. Public sector unions, coordinated by the Public Sector Roundtable (Mesa del Sector Público), which includes the CUT, demonstrated repeatedly alongside students, protesting over job security and salaries.

## CATHOLIC CHURCH AND UNIVERSITY STUDENTS

The Catholic Church, students, and intellectuals also play a role in Chilean politics. During the Pinochet period, the Church promoted human rights and gave aid to the poor and dispossessed. Its political role has declined with redemocratization, dedicating itself mainly to defending traditional family mores. In practice, that has translated into opposition to abortion, divorce, and contraceptives such as the morning-after pill. Despite their efforts, Chile passed a divorce law in 2004, after which the Church retrenched in defense of right to life, although the morning-after pill is also legally dispensed now. Chile's Church has also been rocked by sexual molestation scandals.

After redemocratization in 1999, the student movement was not as active as it had been historically, but its organizations continued to produce future leaders of the major political parties. Student movement quiescence, however, ended beginning in 2006 when high school students, with support from university students and some professors, mobilized massively for a month, frequently clashing with police who were strenuously repressing them. This action precipitated a revision of the Pinochet-era education law. However, the revised law did not reform the fundamental features of the Chilean educational system, especially in the relationship between public and private institutions. This contributed to rising student militancy and cycles of protest previously described. In addition, intellectuals have become very influential in Chilean politics, especially if they possess advanced degrees from foreign universities (with a heavy concentration in economics). They swell the ranks of the technocracy that advises all elected political leaders in and out of government.

# Conclusion

In twenty years of rule, the center-left CPD consolidated democracy and a free market economy in Chile. Since 1990 Chile has enjoyed regular, fair, and free elections among institutionalized political parties with freedom of expression and association. Most of the authoritarian institutions that initially "protected democracy" have either been eliminated or so weakened that they no longer pose a threat, as in the case of military autonomy. Moreover, Chile's basic state institutions—the executive, the legislative, the judiciary—function reasonably well and, in comparison to other Latin American countries, have been relatively free of corruption, occasional scandals notwithstanding. By the same token, all four CPD governments maintained the free market economy inherited from the military dictatorship. In contrast to the dictatorship, they steadfastly implemented mild social reforms to put a more "human face" on neoliberalism, especially in poverty reduction, health, and pensions. Equally important, huge strides were made on human rights issues, to the point where some of the perpetrators have gone to trial and prison and reparations have been paid to survivors of the disappeared and to persons who were tortured. Unresolved problems remain. Poverty may have been reduced, but inequality (both of income and opportunities) remains an issue. The middle class, which has expanded, feels its life chances threatened because most social policy is directed toward the poor. Maintaining their standard of living while at the mercy of market forces is a daunting task. Political parties are in disrepute. The environment and indigenous peoples, for all of the advances discussed herein, remain under threat.

Piñera's administration squandered an opportunity to address these issues from a moderate position and thus recast Chilean conservatism for lasting rule. Its emphasis on administrative efficiency, public–private sector partnership, and the creation of an "opportunity society" did not improve on those unresolved and pending issues. Instead its blunders, missteps, and internal conflicts paved the way for the return of Michelle Bachelet as the head of the New Majority coalition. However, her government, for all of its legislative initiatives and reforms, has fared no better. Demonstrations continue, the public massively withdrew support from her due to scandals and political and administrative blunders arising from the coalition's internal divisions. This leaves Chile Vamos, as of this writing, in a good position to win the December 2017 presidential elections. If that comes to pass, Chile's democracy will have entered into a new phase of democratic alternation but under conditions of growing voter disaffection. This could have consequences for the party system that one should keep an eye out for.

# Chronology

**1536**   Diego de Almagro extends Spanish conquest to Chile

**1810**   Chile begins independence movement from Spain

**1818**   Chile becomes a republic

**1833**   Autocratic republic begins with Diego Portales's new authoritarian constitution

**1836–39**   Chilean military defeats in war against Peru–Bolivia confederation

**1879–83**   War of the Pacific against Peru and Bolivia; Chile gains provinces of Arica, Tarapacá, and Antofagasta

**1891**   Civil war against President José Manuel Balmaceda ends autocratic republic, beginning of parliamentary republic

**1925**   Chile's Portilian constitution replaced by the constitution of 1925

**1949**   Women receive the right to vote

**1970**   Salvador Allende elected president at the head of Popular Unity; Chile begins the democratic road to socialism

**1973**   (September 11) The armed forces, headed by General Augusto Pinochet, overthrow the Popular Unity government and a U.S.-backed military junta takes political power

**1980**   A new constitution with many authoritarian enclaves is approved in a questionable plebiscite

**1988**   End of military rule; General Pinochet is defeated in a plebiscite on his continued rule in October

**1990**   Christian Democrat Patricio Aylwin becomes president of redemocratized Chile at the head of a broad center-left coalition of political parties known as the CPD

**1998**   Pinochet taken into custody in Britain pending extradition charges to Spain for human rights violations

**2000**   Pinochet returns to Chile to face legal proceedings for human rights violations; economic growth resumes

**2004**   Army and air force admit institutional responsibility for systematic human rights violations in Chile

**2005** CPD candidate Michelle Bachelet becomes the first female president of Chile in second-round voting

**2006** General Pinochet dies without standing trial

**2010** President Sebastián Piñera heads first elected conservative government in fifty years

**2014** Michelle Bachelet returns to the presidency after landslide electoral victory over the conservative opposition

# Bibliography

Angell, Alan, and Benny Pollock, eds. *The Legacy of Dictatorship: Political, Economic, and Social Change in Pinochet's Chile.* Liverpool, UK: University of Liverpool Press, 1993.

Baldez, Lisa. *Why Women Protest: Women's Movements in Chile.* Cambridge: Cambridge University Press, 2002.

Bauer, Arnold J. *Chilean Rural Society from the Spanish Conquest to 1930.* New York: Cambridge University Press, 1975.

Borzutzky, Sylvia. *Vital Connections: Politics, Social Security, and Inequality in Chile.* Notre Dame, IN: University of Notre Dame Press, 2002.

Borzutzky, Silvia, and Lois Hecht Oppenheim, eds. *After Pinochet: The Chilean Road to Democracy and the Market.* Gainesville: University Press of Florida, 2006.

Borzutzky, Silvia, and Gregory Weeks. *The Bachelet Government: Conflict and Consensus in Post-Pinochet's Chile.* Gainesville: University of Florida Press, 2010.

Collier, Simon. *Chile: The Making of a Republic, 1830–1865.* Cambridge: Cambridge University Press, 2003.

Collins, Joseph. *Chile's Free Market Miracle: A Second Look.* Monroe, OR: Food First, 1995.

Donoso, Sofía, and Marisa von Bülow, eds. *Social Movements in Chile: Organization, Trajectories, and Political Consequences.* New York: Springer, 2017.

Drake, Paul. *Socialism and Populism in Chile, 1932–1952.* Urbana: University of Illinois Press, 1978.

Drake, Paul W., and Iván Jaksic, eds. *The Struggle for Democracy in Chile, 1982–1990.* Rev. ed. Lincoln: University of Nebraska Press, 1995.

Edwards, Sebastián, and Alejandra Cox-Edwards. *Monetarism and Liberalization: The Chilean Experiment.* Cambridge: Ballinger, 1987.

Ffrench-Davis, Ricardo. *Economic Reforms in Chile: From Dictatorship to Democracy.* Ann Arbor: University of Michigan Press, 2002.

Foxley, Alejandro. *Latin American Experiments in Neoconservative Economics.* Berkeley: University of California Press, 1983.

Garretón, Manuel Antonio. *Incomplete Democracy: Political Democratization in Chile and Latin America.* Chapel Hill: University of North Carolina Press, 2003.

Gil, Frederico, Ricardo Lagos, and Henry Landsberger, eds. *Chile at the Turning Point: Lessons of the Socialist Years, 1970–1973.* Philadelphia: Institute for the Study of Human Issues, 1979.

Kaufman, Robert. *The Politics of Land Reform in Chile, 1950–1970.* Cambridge, MA: Harvard University Press, 1972.

Kay, Cristóbal, and Patricio Silva, eds. *Development and Social Change in the Chilean Countryside: From the Pre-Land Reform Period to the Democratic Transition.* Amsterdam: Centrum voor Studie en Documentatie van Latijns Amerika, 1992.

Loveman, Brian. *Chile: The Legacy of Hispanic Capitalism.* 2d ed. Oxford: Oxford University Press, 1988.

Mamalakis, Markos. *Growth and Structure of the Chilean Economy: From Independence to Allende.* New Haven, CT: Yale University Press, 1976.

Martínez, Javier, and Alvaro Díaz. *Chile: The Great Transformation.* Washington, DC: Brookings Institution, 1996.

Montecinos, Verónica. *Economists, Politics, and the State: Chile 1958–1994.* Amsterdam: Centrum voor Studie en Documentatie van Latijns Amerika, 1998.

O'Brian, Philip. *Allende's Chile.* New York: Praeger, 1976.

O'Brian, Philip. *The Pinochet Decade.* London: Latin American Bureau, 1983.

Oppenheim, Lois Hecht. *Politics in Chile: Democracy, Authoritarianism, and the Search for Development.* Boulder, CO: Westview, 1993.

Oxhorn, Philip D. *Organizing Civil Society: The Popular Sectors and the Struggle for Democracy in Chile.* Philadelphia: Pennsylvania State University Press, 1995.

Petras, James, and Fernando Leiva, with Henry Veltmeyer. *Democracy and Poverty in Chile: The Limits of Electoral Politics.* Boulder, CO: Westview, 1994.

Pollack, Marcelo. *The New Right in Chile, 1973–97.* New York: St. Martin's, 1999.

Posner, Paul W. *State, Market, and Democracy in Chile: The Constraint of Popular Participation.* New York: Palgrave Macmillan, 2008.

Roxborough, Ian, Philip O'Brien, and Jackie Roddick, eds. *Chile: The State and Revolution.* London: Macmillan, 1977.

Sehnbruch, Kirsten, and Peter M. Siavelis, eds. *Democratic Chile: The Politics and Policies of a Historic Coalition, 1990–2010.* Boulder: Lynne Rienner, 2013.

Siavelis, Peter. *The President and Congress in Postauthoritarian Chile: Institutional Constraints to Democratic Consolidation.* University Park: Pennsylvania State University Press, 2000.

Sigmund, Paul. *The Overthrow of Allende and the Politics of Chile, 1964–1976.* Pittsburgh, PA: Pittsburgh University Press, 1977.

Silva, Patricio. *In the Name of Reason: Technocrats and Politics in Chile.* University Park: Pennsylvania State University Press, 2009.

Stallings, Barbara. *The Breakdown of Democratic Regimes: Chile.* Baltimore: Johns Hopkins University Press, 1978.

Stallings, Barbara. *Class Conflict and Development in Chile.* Stanford, CA: Stanford University Press, 1978.

Valenzuela, Arturo, and Samuel Valenzuela, eds. *Military Rule in Chile: Dictatorship and Opposition.* Baltimore: Johns Hopkins University Press, 1986.

Verdugo, Patricia. *Chile, Pinochet, and the Caravan of Death.* Coral Gables, FL: North-South Center, 2001.

Vylder de, Stephen. *Allende's Chile.* Cambridge: Cambridge University Press, 1976.

Weeks, Gregory. *The Military and Politics in Postauthoritarian Chile.* Tuscaloosa: University of Alabama Press, 2003.

Winn, Peter. *Victims of the Chilean Miracle: Workers and Neoliberalism in the Pinochet Era, 1973–2002.* Durham, NC: Duke University Press, 2004.

Winn, Peter. *Weavers of Revolution.* New York: Oxford University Press, 1986.

## FILMS AND VIDEOS

*The Battle of Chile.* United States, 1976.
*Chile, Obstinate Memory.* United States, 1997.
*Estadio Nacional.* Chile, 2001.
*I Love Pinochet.* Chile, 2001.
*In Women's Hands.* United States, 1993.
*Neruda.* Chile/France, 2016.
*NO.* Chile/France/United States, 2012.
*The Pinochet Case.* Chile, 2001.
*Under Construction.* Chile, 2000.
*Wichan: The Trial.* Chile, 1995.

## WEBSITES

http://www.lanic.utexas.edu/ Latin American Information Network, LANIC, best source for data, mostly in Spanish
http://www.iadb.org/ Inter-American Development Bank
http://www.larcdma.sdsu.edu/humanrights/ San Diego State University, Human Rights
http://www.ILO/ International Labor Organization
http://www.labl.com/countries/chile/ Chilean–American Chamber of Commerce

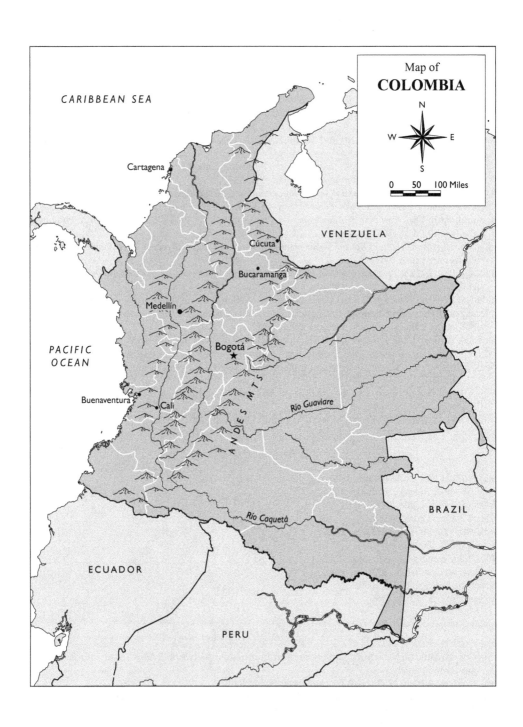

Map of
**COLOMBIA**

N
W    E
S

0   50   100 Miles

CARIBBEAN SEA

Cartagena

VENEZUELA

Cúcuta

Bucaramanga

Medellín

PACIFIC
OCEAN

Bogotá

Buenaventura

Cali

A N D E S   M T S.

Río Guaviare

Río Caquetá

BRAZIL

ECUADOR

PERU

# COLOMBIA

*John C. Dugas*

On December 10, 2016, in an elaborate ceremony at the Oslo City Hall in Norway, Colombian President Juan Manuel Santos received the Nobel Peace Prize "for his resolute efforts to bring the country's more than 50-year-long civil war to an end." The prize underscored the successful negotiation of an agreement to end the armed conflict with Latin America's largest and oldest guerrilla movement, the Fuerzas Armadas Revolucionarias de Colombia (FARC). Despite the celebratory atmosphere in Oslo, the peace agreement confronted numerous obstacles back home to ensuring its full implementation. Moreover, Colombians continued to face another leftist guerrilla movement, the Ejercito de Liberación Nacional (ELN), along with vicious right-wing paramilitary groups, state security forces that frequently violated fundamental human rights, and some 6 million internally displaced persons who had fled violence in the countryside. These problems were compounded by a deeply entrenched drug trade based on the cultivation and processing of coca and opium poppies and pressure from the United States to stop the drug trade at the source. Despite these seemingly intractable problems, Colombians could rightfully take pride in the dynamism of their cities and the entrepreneurial spirit of their people. In the cultural realm, Colombian artists, writers, and performers displayed impressive creativity. Not least, the political arena itself was striking for the sheer valor of many nonviolent activists, the historical capacity for compromise of political elites, and the notable ability of ordinary citizens to "muddle through" repeated crises.

Colombia is located in the northwest corner of South America, adjoining the Panamanian isthmus and sharing borders with Venezuela, Brazil, Peru, and Ecuador. At 440,000 square miles in area, it is the fourth-largest Latin American country in size, slightly larger than the states of California and Texas combined. Colombia is dominated by the Andes Mountains, which enter the country at its southern border with Ecuador and split into three principal ranges running northward. The country's two most important rivers, the Magdalena and the Cauca (which eventually joins the Magdalena), flow in a northward direction between these ranges, ultimately emptying into the Caribbean. The majority of Colombians live in cities and towns located in the intermountain basins and plateaus of the Andes. The country's extensive low-lying areas are known as "hot country" (*tierra caliente*) since the temperature is significantly warmer than the more temperate clime of the mountains. In the north, a vast expanse of largely flat hot country begins toward the lower course of the Magdalena River and lies adjacent to the Caribbean Sea. The other major area of hot country lies to the east of the Andes; here are located Colombia's great plains, known as the *llanos*, as well as the Amazon rain forest farther south and east. Most of *tierra caliente* is relatively sparsely populated, particularly the *llanos* and the Amazon region. Colombia's population of 49 million is the third largest in Latin America, exceeded only by Brazil and Mexico. Most Colombians are mestizos, that is, of mixed indigenous and European origin, with smaller numbers of Caucasians, Afro-Colombians, indigenous peoples, mulattos (of mixed African and European origin), and *zambos* (of mixed African and indigenous origin). Spanish is the principal language, although indigenous languages are still spoken in some regions and are recognized as official by the 1991 Constitution. The vast majority of Colombians identify themselves as Roman Catholic; nevertheless, evangelical Protestantism is growing rapidly, and there are small Jewish and Muslim communities. Some indigenous communities also practice their traditional religions.

## Economic and Social Context

### ECONOMIC DEVELOPMENT

In the aftermath of independence, Colombia's economic development was constrained by the destruction wrought by the war as well as by the high costs of transportation due to its mountainous terrain. Nonetheless, economic elites made concerted efforts to introduce tropical commodities that could be profitably exported. One significant commodity was tobacco, which by the mid-1860s began to exceed gold in export earnings. Ultimately, the most important export commodity introduced to Colombia during the nineteenth century was coffee, first cultivated in the easternmost range of the Andes but soon grown throughout the Colombian Andes, particularly in the central Andean range in the region of Antioquia and to its south. Coffee accounted for less than 2 percent of export earnings during the early 1840s but grew to nearly 50 percent of export earnings by 1898. By 1950, coffee accounted for over 70 percent of Colombia's export earnings and provided much of the foreign exchange required for the country's incipient industrialization. While some coffee was produced on large estates, the predominant mode of cultivation was by small- to medium-sized family farms. Some scholars have suggested that this pattern had a conservatizing effect on Colombian society, since the country's leading industry was overwhelmingly Colombian owned and operated.

In the second half of the twentieth century, the Colombian economy underwent significant changes, becoming both more industrialized and more diversified in its economic output. The economic dominance of coffee gradually declined, and by 2010 coffee accounted for less than 5 percent of the country's legal export earnings. Simultaneously, the country experienced a significant growth in nontraditional exports, such as cut flowers, bananas, palm oil, textiles, shoes, clothing, and processed food. Even more significant was the expansion of mining and the production for export of coal, nickel, and especially oil. Although Colombia remained a major producer and exporter of unprocessed commodities into the twenty-first century, it also experienced a notable process of industrialization, particularly after 1950. Like most Latin American countries, Colombia adopted a policy of import substitution industrialization after mid-century, designed to promote domestic industry by encouraging the production of goods that had previously been imported from abroad. Such a policy was an amalgam of protectionist tariffs, preferential credit, tax incentives, and subsidized electricity rates for industry as well as the creation of state-owned industries where private capital was unwilling to invest. In the 1950s and 1960s, most industrial production occurred in relatively light industries; however, by the 1970s industrialization had expanded into more technologically sophisticated areas, such as plastics, petrochemicals, and automobile assembly.

Despite their embrace of import substitution industrialization, Colombian policymakers avoided the high degree of state intervention pursued by other Latin American countries. Indeed, from the mid-twentieth century to the present, economic policy has been broadly conservative in nature: import substitution was complemented by a growing emphasis on export promotion, monetary and fiscal policy remained fairly cautious, agrarian reform was minimal, and labor policy was markedly conservative. Such policies clearly responded to the interests and pressures exerted by economic elites, as opposed to the demands of labor unions or peasant movements. Nonetheless, Colombia's macroeconomic policies also helped it avoid many of the harsh extremes experienced by its neighbors. For example, during the "lost decade" of the 1980s, Colombia was the only South American country that did not experience a single year of negative economic growth; it avoided the extreme hyperinflation that plagued many of its neighbors and was the only major debtor country in Latin America that did not have to restructure its debt. Colombia was also among the last of the countries in the region to embrace economic liberalization (doing so in the early 1990s), and its immediate effects were less harsh than those experienced by many other Latin American countries.

## Peasants and Urban Workers

Caution and moderation have thus been the prevalent watchwords of economic policymakers in Colombia for decades; however, this has certainly not implied a broad societal satisfaction with the socioeconomic status quo. In the countryside, capitalist agricultural development has caused tremendous social upheaval for Colombian peasants by promoting a development model entailing the concentration of land ownership, the availability of cheap wage labor, the introduction of advanced agricultural techniques, and large-scale farm production. This has conflicted with an alternative "peasant model" of agrarian development based upon widespread distribution of land among numerous small holders engaging in more traditional agricultural production based upon family labor. As a result of this basic clash, contemporary Colombia has experienced numerous agrarian conflicts, which continue to occur and are largely rooted in disputes over land ownership.

Land distribution has long been skewed in favor of large landholders. A 2016 Oxfam study found Colombia to have the most unequal distribution of land in all of

Latin America, with 84 percent of farms occupying less than 4 percent of productive land, whereas 0.4 percent of landowners held more than 67 percent of productive land. Such a condition reflects, in part, the historical limits of agrarian reform in Colombia as well as the absence of an effective national peasant movement. The most important peasant movement in Colombian history, the National Association of Peasant Users (Asociación Nacional de Usuarios Campesinos; ANUC), was founded in 1967 but largely disintegrated by the early 1980s as a result of internal divisions and state repression. Unfortunately, the inequality of land distribution worsened since the 1980s as the drug trade produced a "counteragrarian reform" in the countryside: large traffickers invested their profits in the countryside, frequently using coercion to force peasants off their land. Indeed, a 2005 report by the Colombian Comptroller's Office estimated that as a result of forced displacement drug traffickers controlled 48 percent of the most productive land in the country. In turn, both leftist guerrillas and right-wing paramilitaries recruited the bulk of their forces from among peasants, who encountered few viable alternatives in the countryside other than direct participation in the drug trade as cultivators of coca or opium poppy. All this constitutes part of the internal armed conflict in Colombia (discussed in the Political History section), which has produced some 6 million internal refugees, most of them peasants fleeing the crossfire among guerrillas, paramilitaries, and state security forces. A study commissioned by Colombia's Constitutional Court estimates that the armed conflict has resulted in nearly 5.5 million hectares being forcibly taken over or abandoned. Notably, in 2011 President Juan Manuel Santos signed the Victims and Land Restitution Law, designed to return millions of acres of stolen and abandoned land to internally displaced persons. Nonetheless, implementation of the law has been exceedingly slow—by April 2016, courts had ordered restitution for only 3,426 of the more than 67,000 legitimate land claims filed with the government.

In contrast to the peasantry, urban workers in Colombia have had a fairly long tradition of national organization and a somewhat greater influence on state policy. In 1936, the first important national labor confederation, the Confederation of Colombian Workers (Confederación de Trabajadores de Colombia; CTC), was established and became an ardent supporter of the liberal administrations of the 1930s and early 1940s. A new labor confederation, the Union of Colombian Workers (Unión de Trabajadores de Colombia; UTC), was founded in 1946 under the auspices of the Catholic Church. The UTC shared certain ideological affinities with the Conservative Party, and Conservative politicians in turn saw value in promoting an alternative to the Liberal-dominated CTC. The 1960s and 1970s witnessed the growing autonomy of the CTC and the UTC from the traditional political parties, but the labor movement was plagued by a divisiveness that sharply restricted its power. For example, in 1964 a communist-dominated labor confederation, the Trade Union Confederation of Colombian Workers (Confederación Sindical de Trabajadores de Colombia; CSTC), was formed, followed in 1971 by a fourth national labor confederation, the General Confederation of Labor (Confederación General de Trabajo; CGT), rooted in Christian Democratic principles. The lack of a single national labor confederation, the weakening of the two traditional labor confederations, and the growing importance of unaffiliated independent trade unions clearly diluted the potential power of the labor movement.

Beginning in the 1980s, however, attempts were made to consolidate the Colombian labor movement. In 1986, the United Central Organization of Workers (Central Unitaria de Trabajadores; CUT), was founded, bringing together the former CSTC, the majority of independent trade unions, and a significant number of trade unions and federations previously affiliated with the CTC and the UTC. By 2009, the labor movement was divided into the majority CUT, representing 64.2 percent of unionized workers; the CGT (14.6 percent of unionized workers); the CTC (5.5 percent of unionized workers), with the remaining 15.7 percent of unionized workers unaffiliated with any of the labor confederations. The strength of the Colombian labor movement is also undermined by its limited extension among the working class. In 2015, only 1,002,555 Colombian workers were unionized, representing just 4.6 percent of the working population. The organized labor movement has also been among the foremost victims of Colombia's ongoing political violence. For example, during the first five years of the presidency of Juan Manuel Santos (2010–2015), there were 186 murders of trade unionists in Colombia. Although this marked a decline from the 564 killings of trade unionists during the eight-year administration of Alvaro Uribe (2002–2010), Colombia continues to be one of the deadliest places in the world to be a trade union member. While pressure from organized labor has been instrumental in achieving legislation that provides limited material benefits for the Colombian working class, such legislation has also placed constraints on labor protests and organizing. This double-edged nature of labor legislation underscores that the organized labor movement shares with the peasantry a relatively weak position in the balance of power among social classes in Colombia.

## DOMINANT ECONOMIC CLASSES

The dominant classes in Colombia, comprised largely of national economic elites who own or control the principal private productive assets of land and capital, exercise significant power in the economic realms of agriculture, industry, finance, and commerce. The interests of these sectors are articulated and defended by a variety of producer associations (*gremios*), ranging from relatively small regional groups to large national organizations. Although particular sectoral interests of the dominant classes occasionally come into conflict, there exists substantial consensus on such fundamental issues as the defense of private property, limited state intervention, conservative social policies, and opposition to leftist guerrilla movements. The first Colombian producer association, the Agricultural Society of Colombia (Sociedad de Agricultores de Colombia; SAC), was founded in 1871 to promote the interests of large farmers. The SAC was followed by the creation in 1927 of the National Federation of Coffee Growers (Federación Nacional de Cafeteros; FEDECAFE). Perhaps the most prominent of all the producer associations is the National Association of Industrialists (Asociación Nacional de Industriales; ANDI), which was established in 1944. This organization primarily represents Colombian industrial enterprises but has extended membership to businesses in the areas of agriculture, commerce, finance, and insurance. A number of other producer associations wield significant influence, although their efforts have been dedicated largely to the promotion and defense of their particular sectoral interests. Thus, producer associations have been formed to represent the specific interests of cattle ranchers and of commercial farmers of rice, cotton, sugarcane, milk, poultry, and flowers. This pattern is repeated in the industrial realm, where producer associations emerged to foster the development of specific industries such as plastics, textiles, paper, cement, and pharmaceuticals. Retail establishments and the banking and financial sectors also have their own national associations.

Colombian producer associations, in contrast to the peasantry and the labor confederations, have traditionally exerted considerable influence on the formation of state policy. Although it would be misleading to portray them as controlling the reins of the state, the producer associations have enjoyed relatively easy access to state policymakers, and their concerns have received significantly more attention than those raised by the peasantry or by organized labor. This is not to say that their proposals or critiques have always been accepted. Indeed, the relative autonomy of the state has allowed it to occasionally enact policies seemingly in opposition to the interests of producer associations. One example of this was the neoliberal "economic opening" carried out during the administrations of Virgilio Barco and César Gaviria in the early 1990s, which subjected many Colombian industries to greater international competition. Nonetheless, there is little to suggest that national economic elites have lost significant power relative to the peasantry or organized labor in the first decades of the twenty-first century.

## DEMOGRAPHIC AND SOCIO-ECONOMIC CHANGES

Despite these significant societal divisions, all Colombians have experienced major demographic transformations since the mid-twentieth century. Between 1950 and 2016, the population quadrupled in size, growing from 12.6 million to 48.9 million. Moreover, this growth in population was accompanied by significant urbanization. Colombia moved from being a predominantly rural society in 1950 to a largely urban society by 2010, when 75.1 percent of the population resided in urban areas. However, the latter half of the twentieth century also witnessed a rapid decline in population growth, from 3 percent per year in the early 1960s to 1.2 percent per year by 2010. Population growth slowed primarily as the result of a sharp decrease in the country's total fertility rate, which dropped from an average of nearly seven children per woman in the 1950s to an average of 2.2 children per woman by 2010. The marked decline in population growth also accompanied a significant improvement in the living conditions of the average Colombian. Between 1950 and 2010, life expectancy at birth increased by more than twenty years, giving the average Colombian born in 2010 a life expectancy of seventy-four years. At the same time, the infant mortality rate dropped from 123 deaths per 1,000 live births in the early 1950s to 17 deaths per 1,000 live births in 2010.

Despite these improvements in socioeconomic conditions, Colombia was characterized by the World Bank in 2012 as having the seventh highest level of income inequality in the world, on par with Haiti and Angola. It is also marked by high levels of poverty, with 28.5 percent of the population living below the poverty line in 2015. Nonetheless, the country has experienced a steady decline in poverty since 2002, when 49.7 percent of the population lived below the poverty line. This reduction in poverty is partially the result of relatively strong economic growth in the first decade and a half of the twenty-first century, accentuated by significant increases in both exports and foreign investment. Despite this record, Colombia has also suffered from a stubbornly high rate of unemployment in recent years, registering at 8.3 percent in October 2016.

# Political History

## NINETEENTH-CENTURY POLITICAL DEVELOPMENT

Colombia achieved its political independence in the violent revolutionary struggles that shook the continent after Napoleon deposed King Ferdinand VII of Spain in 1808. Although the struggle for independence began in 1810, royalist forces were not defeated in Colombia until August 7, 1819, when Simón Bolívar routed the Spanish at the Battle of Boyacá. Even then, fighting continued in various parts of Colombian territory until 1823. The nineteenth century was tumultuous for the new country. Just a decade after its independence, the Republic of Colombia experienced a severe dismemberment as both Venezuela and Ecuador broke away to form independent countries in 1830. The remainder of the century was marked by a series of civil wars between the Liberal and Conservative parties, which today are among the oldest continuously functioning political parties in all of Latin America.

The parties originated in disputes between the followers of Bolívar (who died in December 1830) and those of Francisco de Paula Santander, Bolívar's vice president during the war for independence and later president of Colombia (1832–1837). Bolívar's followers emphasized the need for social order and favored a leading role for the Catholic Church in society; in the 1840s, they formally organized themselves into the Conservative Party. Santander and his followers, meanwhile, stressed the importance of liberty and sought a greater separation between church and state. By the 1840s they, too, had congealed into a political organization, the Liberal Party. Conservatives also tended to favor centralized political administration and economic protectionism, while Liberals supported federalism and free trade; nonetheless, these distinctions were not always clear and, in any case, were subordinate to the church–state controversy. Ideological differences between the two parties helped to foment seven major civil wars in Colombia during the second half of the nineteenth century: 1851, 1854, 1860–1862, 1876, 1885, 1895, and 1899–1902. In only one of these conflicts, the civil war of 1860–1862, was the challenging party (in this case, the Liberal Party) able to conclusively defeat the political party in power. Nevertheless, the wars helped reinforce party identity among both elites and lower-class Colombians, who did much of the fighting and dying. The bloodiest of these conflicts, the War of a Thousand Days (1899–1902), produced an estimated 100,000 deaths. This war also weakened Colombia significantly, facilitating the separation of Panama in November 1903.

## EARLY TWENTIETH CENTURY POLITICAL DEVELOPMENT

U.S. complicity in the separation of Panama is one of the more dismal episodes in U.S.–Latin American relations. The U.S. and Colombian governments had negotiated the Hay-Herrán Treaty of 1903, which authorized the United States to construct and operate a canal across the isthmus of Panama, which was then the northernmost department of Colombia. Nevertheless, the Colombian Senate, concerned about the amount of payment as well as the abrogation of Colombian sovereignty in the proposed Canal Zone, rejected the treaty unanimously in August 1903. President Theodore Roosevelt was outraged by the decision, charging, "You could no more make an agreement with the Colombian rulers than you could nail currant jelly to a wall." The United States thereupon encouraged secessionist leaders in Panama, intervened to ensure that Colombian military forces could not put down the insurrection, and then quickly recognized the independence of the rebel government. Within two weeks, the Roosevelt administration negotiated a new canal treaty with representatives of the fledgling Panamanian government. Colombians bitterly held the United States responsible for the Panamanian secession. In 1921, the U.S. government belatedly agreed to pay Colombia an indemnity of $25 million for the loss of Panama.

Despite the recurring political violence between Liberals and Conservatives, Colombia lacked sustained periods of military rule, a factor that helped the two political parties establish themselves as the primary actors in Colombian politics. Indeed, much of Colombia's political history can be understood as a struggle between the Liberal and Conservative Parties for control of the state. Between 1863 and 1885, the Liberal Party dominated, governing under a constitution that was federalist, secular, and politically liberal. From 1886 to 1930, the Conservative Party ruled under a constitution that centralized political authority and reestablished Church privileges. Unfortunately, the exclusion of the opposing party from positions of power during these periods of party dominance fomented both ill will and the frequent civil wars. In 1930, the Conservative Party split in the presidential election, allowing the Liberal candidate to win and ushering in a new era of Liberal Party dominance. The Liberals expanded the electorate, limited the influence of the Church, and responded to the demands of peasant and urban labor movements. Growing urbanization consolidated the Liberal Party as the majority party during this time period. Nonetheless, in the 1946 presidential elections, the Liberal Party split, fielding two presidential candidates, which permitted Conservative candidate Mariano Ospina Pérez to win.

## La Violencia

The period from 1946 to the early 1960s has come to be known as *La Violencia*, a bloody sectarian conflict between the Liberal and Conservative parties in which approximately 200,000 people died. *La Violencia* began in the aftermath of the 1946 elections as Conservatives and Liberals fought over the spoils of political office at the local level. This violence greatly intensified after the assassination of the popular Liberal Party leader Jorge Eliécer Gaitán on April 9, 1948. Gaitán was a populist politician of lower middle-class background who had become a self-made man, a brilliant criminal lawyer, and in 1947 the leader of the Liberal Party. Gaitán was a charismatic speaker who appealed directly to the lower and lower middle classes, often through mass rallies and parades. He employed an anti-elite discourse, arguing that oligarchs from both political parties exploited the state for their own benefit while ignoring the needs of the masses. In contrast, Gaitán explicitly identified himself with the lower classes, proclaiming famously, "I am not a man, I am a people!" Gaitán was the most likely presidential candidate of the Liberal Party for

the 1950 elections. His unfortunate assassination marked both the end of his populist movement and the escalation of *La Violencia*.

Gaitán's murder produced a massive urban insurrection in Bogotá (the Bogotazo), which destroyed large parts of the city. Shocked by the violence of the Bogotazo
and afraid of losing its political control over the masses, a faction of the Liberal
Party joined the Conservative administration of Ospina in an effort at bipartisan
government. Nonetheless, partisan friction and violence continued, and in May
1949 the Liberal Party withdrew from the Ospina administration. When Liberals
in Congress subsequently threatened to impeach President Ospina, the Conservative government declared a state of siege, closed Congress, and suspended civil
liberties. The Liberals, alleging a lack of electoral guarantees, withdrew from the
presidential election of November 1949, resulting in the unopposed election of Conservative Laureano Gómez.

The election of Gómez represented a victory for the most extreme wing of the
Conservative Party. Militantly partisan, the Gómez administration precipitated a
heightening of *La Violencia*. Indeed, of the approximately 200,000 deaths during the
period of *La Violencia*, over 50,000 of them occurred in the first year of the Gómez
administration. By this time, Liberal guerrilla movements had organized in several
areas, while Conservatives utilized the military apparatus of the state to defend
their partisan cause. Violence was prevalent throughout most of the Andean region.
In much of the countryside, traditional rivalries between villages that were chiefly
Liberal or Conservative erupted into conflict. In the cities, the violence was less
intense, but prominent acts of political violence did occur. Moreover, while largely
partisan in nature, *La Violencia* often spiraled out of control in the form of rural
banditry, local political vendettas, and violent efforts to confront large landowners or, alternatively, to plunder small landholders. The continuation of *La Violencia*
prompted more moderate Conservatives, led by former President Ospina, to con-
spire with the military against Gómez. This eventually led to Gómez's ouster in a
military coup by General Gustavo Rojas Pinilla in June 1953.

Rojas Pinilla came to power with the support of both Liberals and the Ospinista
wing of the Conservative Party. This support was grounded in the belief that the
general could stem the tide of violence and pave the way for a return to civilian
rule. Although the military government of Rojas Pinilla did have notable initial success in quelling *La Violencia*, it was unable stop the conflict completely. Moreover,
although Rojas Pinilla had assumed power with no evident desire to consolidate
his position, it soon became clear that he sought to remain in power by creating
a political base of support through populist social reforms and appeals to labor.
Disillusioned with this course of events, leaders from both political parties began to
oppose Rojas Pinilla. In July 1956, Liberal politician (and former president) Alberto
Lleras Camargo met with former Conservative president Laureano Gómez in Spain,
where he was living in exile. The two leaders signed the Pact of Benidorm, which articulated the decision by their respective political parties to oppose Rojas Pinilla and
which led to a series of subsequent agreements aimed at establishing a bipartisan civilian government. Resistance to the military regime culminated in May 1957 when
Rojas Pinilla was removed from power by a five-man military junta that served as
an interim government until civilian rule was restored in 1958.

## THE NATIONAL FRONT REGIME (1958–1974)

The new bipartisan civilian regime was known as the National Front. It epitomized the notion of a "pacted democracy," wherein political elites negotiate compromises that protect their fundamental interests, thereby facilitating the process of democratization. In the case of the National Front, the pacted democracy was secured by a rigid agreement that provided for power-sharing by the two traditional parties and extensive mutual guarantees to protect the parties' interests. Specifically, the National Front was founded upon the twin pillars of alternation in power and parity of power. With regard to alternation, the agreement provided that the presidency was to alternate every four years between the Liberal Party and the Conservative Party for a period of sixteen years. Parity, in turn, referred to the strictly equal division of political power between the two parties. First, all elected bodies were to be equally divided between the Liberal and Conservative Parties regardless of the electoral results in a given district. This provision applied to the Senate and the Chamber of Representatives, departmental assemblies, and municipal councils. Within each party's (equal) allotment, seats were to be awarded by proportional representation according to the number of votes won by different party factions. Second, all cabinet appointments as well as all positions in the judicial branch were to be divided equally between the two parties. Third, appointed officials at all levels of government were to be named on the basis of parity between Liberals and Conservatives. Finally, the National Front agreement required a two-thirds majority vote for the approval of nonprocedural measures in all elected bodies, thus giving added assurance to the parties that their fundamental interests would be protected.

In effect, the National Front agreement institutionalized bipartisan rule in Colombia. It created a political regime that was civilian, but not particularly democratic. This restricted democracy generally respected civil liberties but limited political participation to the Liberal and Conservative parties. Third parties were formally excluded from direct participation in politics. The political regime allowed for elections, but these had no bearing on the partisan composition of elected bodies since parity was predetermined. Such restrictions on democratic rule were justified as necessary for bringing stability to a deeply divided society. Notably, the National Front system survived the sixteen-year period intact, with two Liberal presidents (Alberto Lleras Camargo, 1958–1962, and Carlos Lleras Restrepo, 1966–1970) alternating with two Conservative presidents (Guillermo León Valencia, 1962–1966, and Misael Pastrana Borrero, 1970–1974). The National Front was successful in restoring and consolidating civilian rule in Colombia, as well as in bringing an end to the fierce party-based violence that had been ubiquitous since the mid-1940s.

Unfortunately, the National Front regime also had the consequences of fragmenting and depoliticizing the traditional Liberal and Conservative Parties, of entrenching clientelism as their primary means of mediating between the state and society, and of reducing their responsiveness to the demands of a modernizing and restive country. These changes, in combination with the exclusion of other political parties and movements from power, provided fertile ground for incipient left-wing guerrilla movements. The Colombian guerrillas were themselves rooted in *La Violencia* since many of their leaders were former combatants from that period. Nonetheless, unlike the Liberal guerrillas of the previous era, the leftist guerrillas of the 1960s and 1970s sought to overthrow the established political and socioeconomic order. By the 1970s, four principal guerrilla movements were active in Colombia: the Colombian Armed Revolutionary Forces (Fuerzas Armadas Revolucionarias de Colombia; FARC); the Army of National Liberation (Ejército de Liberación Nacional; ELN); the Popular Liberation Army (Ejército Popular de Liberación; EPL); and the April 19th Movement (Movimiento del 19 de Abril; M-19).

The FARC originated in response to a 1964 military campaign against a number of communist-oriented, peasant self-defense groups in regions of southern Tolima and southwestern Cundinamarca. From its beginnings, the FARC attempted to establish ties to the peasantry, particularly in areas of recent colonization. It also maintained close links to the Colombian Communist Party. The ELN was a Cuban-inspired guerrilla movement begun by Colombian students who sought to establish a socialist regime. It initiated military operations in January 1965 and became the most orthodox of the Colombian guerrilla movements, unwilling to waver from its original goal of socialist revolution or its view of the government as "bourgeois" and thus an absolute enemy with which negotiations were impossible. The EPL originated in the Sino-Soviet split of the mid-1960s, which caused a division in the Colombian Communist Party and the creation of the Maoist-oriented Marxist–Leninist Communist Party of Colombia (Partido Comunista de Colombia–Marxista-Leninista; PCC-ML). The EPL was established in 1967 as the armed wing of the PCC-ML and was originally heavily influenced by Maoist thought, with its focus on the peasantry and its strategy of a prolonged popular war. However, the EPL broke with Maoism in 1980 and expanded its radius of action to include urban areas. The M-19 was born in 1973 by the merging of two sectors that were dissatisfied with the existing revolutionary movements: one sector consisted of individuals who had been expelled from the Communist Party and the FARC, and the other was comprised of members of the socialist wing of the National Popular Alliance (Alianza Nacional Popular; ANAPO), a political movement led by the former dictator Rojas Pinilla. Indeed, the name of the guerrilla movement came from the date of April 19, 1970, when the presidential election was allegedly stolen from Rojas Pinilla. The M-19 was the least orthodox of the Colombian guerrilla movements, highly nationalistic and originally urban in nature.

## The Post–National Front Period (1974–1990)

The National Front regime formally ended in 1974 with the termination of bipartisan presidential alternation and congressional parity. Nonetheless, other aspects of parity remained in place until 1991. Specifically, a 1968 constitutional reform extended for ten years bipartisan parity in the appointment of cabinet officers, governors, mayors, and non–civil service administrative positions. Even after 1978, the constitution required the president to "give adequate and equitable participation" to the principal opposing party in appointments to these positions. Despite these restrictions, 1974 marked the return of unrestrained party competition for the presidency, Congress, departmental assemblies, and municipal councils. Elections between 1974 and 1990 showed that the Liberal Party clearly had become predominant in Colombia, winning the majority of seats in the Chamber of Representatives and the Senate in every election. Its congressional domination peaked in 1990 when it won 61.8 percent of the seats in the Chamber and 63.1 percent of the seats in the Senate. The Conservative Party retained its position as a solid minority, generally capturing between 30 and 40 percent of the seats in Congress. Third parties, meanwhile, typically garnered less than 5 percent of congressional seats.

The Liberal Party also dominated the presidency between 1974 and 1990: of the five presidents elected in this period, four were Liberals. The sole Conservative elected to the presidency in this period (Belisario Betancur, 1982–1986) was able to achieve office only after a split in the Liberal Party caused it to field two presidential candidates. Nonetheless, in one sense, competition between the two dominant political parties no longer mattered. In the aftermath of the National Front, ideology had largely ceased to differentiate the Liberal Party and the Conservative Party. Although factions of the Conservative Party spoke with greater insistence about the need to return to traditional morality and to maintain close relations with the Catholic Church, few programmatic differences remained between Colombia's two historic parties. Both could be described as mainstream catch-all parties dependent upon clientelism to ensure multiclass support.

Despite their electoral dominance, by the 1980s both the Liberal Party and the Conservative Party appeared to be in crisis. Although both parties defended the interests of the upper strata of Colombian society, neither had shown itself willing to address effectively the concerns of the lower and middle sectors of society. In addition, the rigidity of the political regime, deep-seated clientelism, and widespread political violence hindered the emergence of new political parties that might serve as real alternatives to the bipartisan monopoly of power. The result was a deepening crisis of political legitimacy, reflected in declining party identification, widespread political apathy, high rates of electoral abstention, a growing number of civic strikes and protests, and the intensification of organized violence against the political regime.

In particular, the repressive policies of the Liberal administration of Julio César Turbay (1978–1982) generated growing sympathy for the guerrilla movements, especially for the M-19, which came to symbolize opposition to the unpopular Turbay government. Ironically, although Turbay sought to crush the guerrillas militarily, the FARC, the EPL, and the ELN all grew in numbers and expanded their activities during his administration. This period also witnessed the emergence of some new, although relatively small, guerrilla movements: the indigenous Quintín Lame Armed Movement (Movimiento Armado Quintín Lame), the Workers' Revolutionary Party, (Partido Revolucionario de los Trabajadores; PRT), and the Movement of the Revolutionary Left (Movimiento de Izquierda Revolucionaria; MIR).

The Conservative administration of Belisario Betancur (1982–1986) sought to radically change the repressive approach of its predecessor by carrying out a policy of democratic reform and peace negotiations with the guerrilla movements. The policy achieved limited success, most notably in the passage of an amnesty law in 1982 and the signing of ceasefire accords with the FARC, EPL, and M-19 in 1984. Nonetheless, the Betancur peace process soon confronted a number of obstacles, including military opposition and the failure of all sides to comply with the accords.

By the end of the Betancur administration, the ELN, the EPL, and the M-19 were once again engaged in armed conflict with the state. For its part, the FARC maintained a tenuous ceasefire with the state and launched a legal political movement, the Patriotic Union (Unión Patriótica; UP). Lamentably, soon after its founding, the assassinations of literally thousands of UP members began, largely by right-wing paramilitary forces but with the participation or acquiescence of state security forces. This systematic campaign against UP militants, which would continue for years, is one of the great human rights tragedies of recent Latin American history.

The Liberal administration of Virgilio Barco (1986–1990) was marked by increased violence on the part of all the armed actors, with the attendant worsening of the human rights situation. The first two years of Barco's government saw heightened guerrilla violence, including the return of the FARC to direct combat with the state and the failure to initiate any substantive peace talks. Nonetheless, by 1988 the M-19 had become convinced of the need to demobilize and reenter civilian life. After a period of lengthy negotiations, the M-19 signed a peace accord and turned in its arms in March 1990. Meanwhile, right-wing paramilitary groups, which had taken root in the early 1980s, began to flourish as they benefited from an influx of drug money and the collaboration of sectors of the state security forces. The principal strategy of the paramilitaries was to kill individuals who constituted the support network of the guerrillas as well as anyone who was believed to sympathize with the guerrillas.

The Barco administration also had to confront the growing power and violence of drug cartels. In 1989, the violent activities of drug traffickers, particularly the Medellín cartel, reached a critical threshold, highlighted by the assassination of several prominent political figures. The most notable of these was Luis Carlos Galán, a popular Liberal senator and the clear favorite to become president in the 1990 elections. After Galán's murder in August 1989, Barco announced a series of far-reaching state-of-siege decrees intended to break the back of the drug cartels, which were labeled by the president as "the common enemy." In the face of an intense state crackdown, the Medellín cartel issued its own declaration of war against the Colombian state and began a campaign of terror marked by intimidation, dynamite attacks, car bombs, kidnappings, and assassinations, primarily of civilians. It was during this period that the United States began a policy of massive security assistance for the war on drugs. The George H. W. Bush administration supported President Barco's declaration of war against the Medellín cartel by announcing the five-year, $2.2 billion Andean Initiative. Beginning with the Andean Initiative and continuing through the present, the bulk of the counternarcotics aid that the United States has sent to Colombia has been military in nature.

---

## THE DRUG TRADE IN COLOMBIA

To the outside world—and to the chagrin of most of its citizens—Colombia is synonymous with drug trafficking. The powerful drug cartels of the 1980s and 1990s developed from modest and disperse drug-trafficking activities in Colombia in the 1960s and 1970s.

Originally focused on the production and transportation of marijuana, by the late 1980s the drug trade had shifted largely to cocaine and had come under the control of the Medellín and Cali cartels. The cartels were estimated to control between 75 and 80 percent of the Andean cocaine traffic, employ nearly 100,000 Colombians, and derive annual incomes of between $2 billion and $4 billion. In the 1990s, both the Medellín and Cali cartels were dismantled but without any significant drop in the amount of cocaine exported. Instead, the drug industry became fragmented, with dozens of small- to medium-sized trafficking organizations taking over the terrain of the big cartels. Colombia also became a major producer of opium poppy, from which heroin was refined and exported to the United States.

The effects of the drug trade on the Colombian economy have been decidedly mixed. On the positive side, drug trafficking has contributed to the nation's foreign exchange earnings, provided employment for significant numbers of Colombians, and opened channels of upward mobility for some members of the lower social classes. On balance, however, the economic effects of drug trafficking have been negative. The influx of narcodollars has tended to revalue the Colombian peso, which has placed pressure on the country's traditional industries. Moreover, the climate of violence associated with drug trafficking has encouraged domestic capital flight and generally discouraged investment. Of particular concern, the violence accompanying the drug trade has increased the costs of doing business by forcing companies to spend significant amounts on security measures. The enormous profits of the drug trade have grossly inflated the price of land, goods, and services in the trafficking areas and in major cities. The drug trade has also contributed to making Colombia a net importer of food as a result of the conversion of cropland into coca fields and the employment of peasants to grow and process the drug crops. Massive aerial spraying to eradicate coca crops has produced serious environmental and health consequences, without significantly decreasing coca cultivation. Finally, the drug trade has enormously increased the level of corruption throughout the economic system.

Nevertheless, the more lasting consequences for Colombia have occurred in the political realm. In the 1980s and 1990s, drug cartels relied extensively on both bribery and violence against state officials to protect their trafficking activities. All too often, Colombian police officers, soldiers, judges, and elected officials were faced with the excruciating choice of *plata* or *plomo*; that is, they could accept "silver" (*plata*) in the form of a bribe to look the other way or "lead" (*plomo*) in the form of a bullet if they chose to confront the traffickers. More recently, drug-trafficking organizations have sought to enter the political realm directly, primarily through the paramilitary organizations that they have long financed or controlled. In the "para-political" scandal that began unfolding in 2006, sixty-eight members of Congress were investigated for their close ties to the paramilitaries. Most analysts agree that the principal factor that prompted the paramilitaries to enter the political realm was to ensure protection from extradition and long prison sentences in the United States for drug-trafficking offenses. Despite the tremendous amount of resources dedicated by U.S. and Colombian officials to fight the drug trade over the past three decades, the U.S. Drug Enforcement Administration stated in 2016 that 90.2 percent of cocaine reaching the United States originated in Colombia. Moreover, the United Nations Office on Drugs and Crime estimated that in 2015 alone there was a 46 percent increase in the amount of processed cocaine produced in Colombia.

## THE 1991 CONSTITUTION AND BEYOND

Paradoxically, the Medellín cartel's vicious war against the state during 1989–1990 was key to the subsequent effort to democratize the Colombian political regime. The drug traffickers' violence, in combination with the apparent incapacity of the state to respond adequately to it, highlighted public discontent with the existing political regime. An enterprising movement of student activists took advantage of this crisis of legitimacy and successfully pushed for the election of a National Constituent Assembly to draft a new constitution. In 1991, the assembly met for five months to draw up the constitution, with the explicit purpose of broadening and deepening Colombian democracy. The possibility of participating in the assembly served as a concrete incentive for the reincorporation into civilian life of the EPL and two smaller guerrilla movements, the PRT and the Quintín Lame. All of them signed peace accords with the government, demobilized, and engaged actively alongside former guerrillas of the M-19 in helping write the new constitution.

The 1991 constitution represented a significant step toward the democratization of the Colombian political regime. Among other measures, it eliminated all vestiges of the exclusionary National Front regime, introduced an extensive bill of citizen rights, provided for a variety of new participatory mechanisms (including the popular election of governors), and curtailed the president's state-of-siege emergency powers. The new constitution, however, did not undertake significant reforms to the political party system or the state security forces. As well, the 1991 Constitution did not function as a viable political pact to end the ongoing armed conflict, primarily because neither the FARC nor the ELN guerrillas participated in its drafting and, thus, did not feel compelled to respect the new constitutional order.

Much of the violence perpetrated by drug traffickers eased during the Liberal administration of César Gaviria (1990–1994). The Gaviria government prioritized ending the violence of the drug cartels and, to that end, guaranteed traffickers a reduced sentence and nonextradition if they surrendered to authorities and confessed to at least one crime. However, most of the key traffickers, including the notorious leader of the Medellín cartel, Pablo Escobar, waited until the National Constituent Assembly passed a constitutional article explicitly banning extradition before taking advantage of Gaviria's generosity. In June 1991, Escobar and his top lieutenants surrendered to Colombian authorities. However, when the Gaviria administration decided to transfer them to a more secure prison in July 1992, Escobar and nine of the top leaders of the Medellín cartel escaped. Drug-related violence again surged until state security forces killed Escobar in December 1993 and the Medellín cartel was dismantled. The victory, however, was ephemeral since the rival Cali cartel quickly took over the Medellín cartel's business and no significant reduction in drug trafficking took place. Meanwhile, Gaviria engaged in peace negotiations with both the FARC and the ELN in Caracas, Venezuela (1991), and in Tlaxcala, Mexico (1992); however, neither of these efforts came to fruition.

Colombia's armed conflict deepened during the Liberal administration of Ernesto Samper (1994–1998). Unfortunately, Samper's term quickly became mired in a serious drug scandal, in which the president was accused of receiving several million dollars from the Cali drug cartel for his election campaign. Although Samper steadfastly denied the charges, the accumulation of evidence led to two unsuccessful attempts in Congress to impeach the president. The Clinton administration never believed Samper's claims of innocence and exerted tremendous pressure to force his resignation. U.S. pressure had contradictory effects. On one hand, it provoked angry charges of U.S. intervention in Colombian internal affairs and rallied many Colombians to the defense of Samper. On the other hand, it pushed the Samper administration to dismantle the top leadership of the Cali cartel in 1995, to strengthen penalties for drug trafficking, and to reform the 1991 Constitution to once again allow for the extradition of Colombian citizens to stand trial abroad. Unfortunately, Samper's preoccupation with the drug scandal and his accompanying loss of credibility undermined his administration's efforts to deal with the armed conflict. Both left-wing guerrilla movements and right-wing paramilitary groups expanded significantly during the Samper administration, and both became increasingly reliant upon the drug trade, directly or indirectly, to finance their armed activities.

The Conservative administration of Andrés Pastrana (1998–2002) engaged in a fitful dialogue with the FARC leadership for more than three years, during which the guerrillas were ceded a 16,000-square-mile demilitarized zone intended to facilitate peace talks. Nonetheless, the talks ultimately failed to produce much more than a detailed agenda for negotiations. Over time, the Pastrana administration grew increasingly concerned about abuses committed by the FARC in the demilitarized zone, whereas the FARC repeatedly charged the government with failing to act decisively to curtail the cruel actions of the paramilitary forces. The peace talks broke down definitively in February 2002 when the government ordered the military to retake the demilitarized zone. Even as Pastrana talked peace with the FARC, he was determined to repair strained relations with the United States. As a result, the war on drugs in Colombia became notably more militarized under Pastrana, particularly under the auspices of "Plan Colombia." In principle, Plan Colombia was a multifaceted program designed to eradicate illicit crops; support a negotiated settlement with the guerrilla movements; revive the moribund Colombian economy; and provide aid for judicial institutions, human rights, and alternative development. In practice, however, Plan Colombia largely became a conduit for U.S. military and police assistance. Most of the U.S. funds went to train and equip new counternarcotics battalions within the Colombian army, which then moved into areas of coca production, such as Putumayo and Caquetá that were dominated by the FARC guerrillas. Critics rightly feared that the United States was being drawn ever more deeply into Colombia's long-standing internal armed conflict.

The election of Álvaro Uribe (2002–2010), a hardliner and former Liberal, as president reflected the growing frustration of many Colombians regarding the armed conflict. Uribe, the former governor of Antioquia, had been critical of Pastrana's peace process and promised to establish firm state authority throughout the country. Once in office, Uribe strengthened the state security forces and deployed them aggressively against the FARC and ELN guerrillas, whom he labelled as "terrorists." Indeed, much of Uribe's popularity was due to the successive military blows that his administration rained down upon the FARC, whose strength is estimated to have declined precipitously from 18,000–20,000 armed combatants to 8,000–10,000 over the course of his eight years in office. By the end of his second term in 2010, Uribe's security policies had resulted in a considerable decline in kidnappings, extrajudicial killings, and massacres. Much of this decline is explained not by the weakening of the guerrilla movements but by the demobilization of some 31,000 right-wing paramilitary fighters across the country. The paramilitaries had been far more violent than the guerrillas, committing nearly 60 percent of the massacres in Colombia's armed conflict. The reincorporation process, begun by Uribe in 2003 and concluded in 2006, was subjected to heavy criticism for its lax penalties for egregious crimes committed by paramilitary forces, as well as for the emergence of new armed groups. Called BACRIM (short for *Bandas Criminales*) by the Colombian government, these neo-paramilitary forces came to number between 3,000 and 5,000 members and focused on drug trafficking and extortion, while engaging in the same types of massacres, killings, and rapes perpetrated by previous paramilitary groups. Nevertheless, Uribe's relative success in improving the security situation in Colombia, along with a steady improvement in the economy, made him the most popular Colombian president in decades. Uribe rode this popularity to re-election as president in May 2006 with 62.4 percent of the vote. Despite his high approval ratings, Uribe was the object of sustained criticism from labor organizations, which disapproved of his neoliberal economic policies, and human rights groups, which expressed concern over the growing number of extrajudicial killings perpetrated by state security forces and the impunity in which these cases remained.

## THE HUMAN RIGHTS MOVEMENT IN COLOMBIA

The human rights movement is among the most overlooked, yet crucial, social movements working to change Colombia today. The Colombian human rights movement began during the repressive years of the presidency of Julio César Turbay (1978–1982) with the creation of the Permanent Committee for Human Rights (Comité Permanente para los Derechos Humanos). It was soon joined by a variety of national and regional human rights organizations, many of which focus on specific groups whose rights have been violated, such as political prisoners, disappeared persons, displaced individuals, victims of state violence, kidnapping victims, and human rights activists themselves. Other human rights organizations have a broader focus, such as the Colombian Commission of Jurists (Comisión Colombiana de Juristas; CCJ), which produces sophisticated studies of human rights and international humanitarian law in the context of Colombia's civil conflict, and the Center for Research and Popular Education (Centro de Investigación y Educación Popular; CINEP), which maintains the country's most widely consulted database on human rights violations. Given the country's internal armed conflict, the promotion and defense of human rights places human rights defenders at considerable risk. Indeed, Colombian rights activists have been subjected to assassinations, disappearances, torture, death threats, and smear campaigns seeking to undermine their work. These attacks have been carried out primarily by paramilitary units and sectors of the state security forces and have been aimed at creating a climate of fear to deter human rights workers from their activities. For example, between 2010 and 2015, some 345 human rights defenders were killed. The Colombian human rights movement today plays an essential role in keeping the issue of human rights at the forefront of national and international consciousness, particularly at a juncture in which the FARC has agreed to disarm and engage in the nonviolent pursuit of political power.

Riding on the coattails of the popular Uribe, his former defense minister, Juan Manuel Santos, was elected president in June 2010. Santos initially confirmed his intention to follow Uribe's unyielding stance against the FARC. Despite this early hard-line position, in September 2012 Santos announced that his administration and the FARC would enter into formal peace negotiations. For its part, the FARC announced that it would stop kidnapping for ransom and subsequently released its last ten military and police captives. Formal negotiations, which were based in Havana, Cuba, began in October 2012, but the process was excruciatingly slow. Moreover, former president Alvaro Uribe and many of his followers felt betrayed by Santos's decision to negotiate with the FARC, leading them to withdraw from the governing coalition and form a new political party, the Democratic Center Party. The 2014 presidential election was largely a referendum on the Santos peace process. Ultimately, Santos won in a run-off with the Democratic Center candidate, Óscar Iván Zuluaga, but with a mere 50.95 percent of the vote.

Despite the slow, halting progress of the negotiations, the Santos administration and the FARC finally announced a comprehensive peace accord in August 2016. Under the terms of the accord, the 7,000 members of the FARC were to hand over all of their weapons within six months to the United Nations. In return, the government was to provide amnesty for all rank-and-file guerilla fighters, lenient penalties (which excluded jail time) for guerrilla leaders responsible for war crimes or crimes against humanity, and a guarantee of ten seats for the FARC in the Colombian Congress for the next two legislative terms (2018–2026). Moreover, the accord contained specific commitments with regard to agrarian reform, programs to provide alternatives to illicit drug crop production, and the demining of the Colombian countryside. Nonetheless, the peace agreement was quickly met with the implacable and vociferous opposition of former president Alvaro Uribe and his followers. Uribe's campaign against the accord was successful in defeating it in a national plebiscite held on October 2, 2016, but only with a paper-thin majority of 50.2 percent of the votes.

President Santos immediately began a process of consultation with all parties, including Uribe. This process produced some 500 recommendations of amendments to the peace accord, which the government sorted into fifty-seven themes before returning to the bargaining table in Havana. After two weeks of intense negotiations, the Santos administration and the FARC announced a revised agreement on November 24, 2016, which incorporated changes in fifty-six of the fifty-seven thematic areas but continued to reject prison sentences for the guerillas and to provide for FARC representation in Congress. Instead of holding a new plebiscite, Santos sent the revised accord to Congress, where by December 1, 2016 it had been approved overwhelmingly in both houses, albeit without a single vote of support from the Democratic Center Party of Álvaro Uribe.

Beyond his determination to negotiate a peace accord with the FARC, President Santos has demonstrated a notable degree of pragmatism, working to repair previously frayed relations with neighboring Venezuela and Ecuador and promoting the Victims and Land Restitution Law. Of some concern to the United States, Santos has also played a leading role in questioning the effectiveness of the ongoing war on drugs, pushing the Organization of American States to draft a report in 2013 that examined alternative scenarios for dealing with illicit drugs—a theme that he reiterated in his Nobel Peace Prize address in December 2016. As Santos entered his final years in office, he faced the challenge of guaranteeing the smooth demobilization of the FARC, ensuring the passage of legislation to enact the many programs envisioned in the peace accord, and locating the necessary financing for these programs. He also confronted the challenge of negotiating a successful peace accord with the ELN, the last remaining Colombian guerrilla movement. Formal negotiations with the ELN were to begin in January 2017; a successful peace accord would finally bring an end to five decades of internal armed conflict during which over 220,000 Colombians have lost their lives.

Finally, the role played by the United States in Colombia needs to be explicitly considered. Between 2000 and 2016, the United States provided $9.94 billion in aid under the auspices of Plan Colombia, making it the largest recipient of U.S. aid outside the Middle East and Afghanistan. This money went primarily toward purchasing dozens of helicopters, the creation of new army and navy brigades, and the training of thousands of Colombian military and police. Hundreds of U.S. troops and private contract personnel worked on the ground in Colombia as military trainers, intelligence gatherers, spray pilots, mechanics, and in other roles. Meanwhile, congressional opponents of U.S. security assistance to Colombia successfully introduced human rights conditions that needed to be met for the full amount of military aid to be released. However, despite unequivocal evidence of continuing human rights violations by Colombian state security forces, the U.S. State Department repeatedly certified Colombia's human rights record, allowing the aid to be disbursed.

While the Obama administration reduced U.S. aid to Colombia and shifted it more toward civilian programs and economic assistance, it continued to certify Colombia's human rights record and to supply high levels of military assistance to the Colombian state security forces. Moreover, in 2009 the Obama administration signed an agreement with the Uribe administration giving U.S. military personnel extensive access to seven Colombian military bases to conduct joint counternarcotics and antiterrorism activities over a ten-year period. This agreement was vigorously opposed by neighboring Venezuela and Ecuador, which felt directly threatened by the expanded U.S. involvement in the region, and it was subsequently declared unconstitutional in August 2010 by Colombia's Constitutional Court. In the face of the military bases agreement setback, the Obama administration sought to strengthen ties to Colombia by ensuring passage of the U.S.–Colombia Free Trade Agreement in October 2011. This accord had faced stiff opposition from U.S. and Colombian labor unions, the left-wing Alternative Democratic Pole party, and Democrats in the U.S. Congress, all concerned about the negative effects on poor peasant farmers and vulnerable Afro-Colombian and indigenous communities as well as the ongoing violence against trade unionists. The Obama administration facilitated congressional approval by negotiating a "Labor Action Plan" meant to improve the rights and conditions of Colombian workers and labor activists. Despite this plan, there were twenty killings of trade unionists in 2015 alone, along with fifteen assassination attempts and 106 death threats. Moreover, impunity for labor violence remained extremely high, with 95 percent off labor rights violations committed between 2011 and 2015 failing to result in the conviction of a perpetrator. In the economic realm, the trade pact had lopsided results in its first four years. According to official U.S.

and Colombian sources, Colombia's trade balance with the United States went from a $8.4 billion surplus in 2011 to a $5.6 billion deficit in 2015. This result was not entirely surprising, given that many Colombian products had already entered the U.S. market duty-free prior to the trade agreement, that falling commodity prices (especially oil) undermined the value of Colombian exports, and that the accord immediately eliminated duties on 80 percent of U.S. exports of consumer and industrial products to Colombia.

# The Colombian Political Regime

## Constitutional Structure

State authority is formally exercised in Colombia today in accordance with the 1991 Constitution. Administratively, the country is divided into thirty-two departments, each of which has an elected governor and a departmental assembly that can pass administrative decrees governing areas such as public works, tourism, and socioeconomic development. Departments, in turn, are subdivided into municipalities (roughly the equivalent of U.S. counties), each of which has an elected mayor and municipal council. Despite appearances to the contrary, Colombia is a unitary state—not a federal state—since departments and municipalities are strictly limited in their competencies by the constitution and national legislation.

At the national level, the executive branch is led by the president, who is both head of state and head of government. The president and vice president are elected by national popular vote for four-year terms. If no candidate receives a majority of votes in the presidential election, a run-off election is held between the top two candidates. Although the 1991 constitution originally limited the president to one term in office, a 2005 constitutional amendment allows the president to be re-elected for a second consecutive term. The president governs with the aid of a cabinet of appointed ministers and traditionally has exercised tremendous political power. The 1991 Constitution placed limits on that power by removing the ability to appoint departmental governors, weakening the president's veto power, limiting the president's ability to issue legal norms, and restricting the president's ability to govern under state-of-siege decrees. Nevertheless, the presidency remains the key political office in Colombia. This is especially true since the executive branch enjoys extraordinary fiscal powers: all budgetary bills must originate in the executive branch, and Congress can only increase spending in a given area with the written authority of the respective cabinet minister.

The legislative branch consists of a bicameral congress elected through a system of proportional representation for four-year terms. There are no term limits that restrict re-election. The 102-member Senate has 100 members elected in a single national electoral district and two indigenous members elected by indigenous communities. The Chamber of Representatives is elected in departmentally based districts, with each department granted a minimum of two representatives and an additional representative for every 365,000 inhabitants. In addition, the Chamber has set aside seats for Afro-Colombians (two), indigenous citizens (one), and Colombians living abroad (two). In the 2014–2018 legislature, this translated into 166 representatives.

The 1991 Constitution strengthened the legislative branch by giving Congress the power to override presidential vetoes more easily, to censure executive cabinet members, to modify legislative decrees issued by the president, and to limit the president's authority under the declaration of a state of siege.

In the aftermath of the 1991 constitution, the Liberal and Conservative parties initially continued to dominate Colombian politics. However, the traditional two-party system was undermined both by the popularity of President Álvaro Uribe (who deliberately sought a break with the traditional parties) and by a package of constitutional amendments approved in 2003 aimed at establishing more cohesive and responsible parties. Thus, by the 2014 congressional elections, the Liberal and Conservative parties together garnered only 34.3 percent of the seats in the Senate (down from 83.3 percent as recently as 1998) and 40.4 percent of the seats in the Chamber of Representatives (down from 81.4 percent in 1998). Several new parties have emerged since 2002, including the Social Party of National Unity (Partido Social de Unidad Nacional, better known as the Partido de la U), which was originally created to support Álvaro Uribe and is now the mainstay of support for Juan Manuel Santos; the Democratic Center party (Centro Democrático), created as the pro-Uribe party after his political break with Santos in 2012; the center-right Radical Change (Cambio Radical), largely a political vehicle for the rising politician Germán Vargas Lleras, and the Alternative Democratic Pole (Polo Democrático Alternativo), the major democratic leftist party in contemporary Colombia. Although the Colombian party system has been in considerable flux over the past two decades, the days of the exclusive two-party system appear to be definitively over.

The judicial branch is organized into three functional jurisdictions. The "ordinary" jurisdiction covers civil, criminal, commercial, labor, and family law matters and works through a hierarchical system of municipal courts, circuit courts, superior courts, and the twenty-three-member Supreme Court, which hears appeals from lower-level courts and has the authority to investigate the president, members of Congress, and other top government officials. This function became particularly important during Uribe's second term, when the Supreme Court spearheaded the investigation of dozens of members of Congress accused of close ties to illegal right-wing paramilitary organizations. The "administrative" jurisdiction deals with disputes arising from official public acts as well as the acts of private entities performing public duties. It adjudicates these matters through departmental courts and the Council of State, a twenty-seven-member body that serves as the highest administrative court in the country. Finally, the "constitutional" jurisdiction is the realm of the Constitutional Court, a nine-member body created by the 1991 Constitution and dedicated to determining the constitutionality of a wide range of laws, bills, referenda, and treaties. During the Uribe administration, the Constitutional Court served as an important check on presidential power; for example, it declared unconstitutional both a national referendum that would have allowed Uribe to run for a third term in office and the 2009 military bases agreement with the United States. The justices of the Supreme Court, the Council of State, and the Constitutional Court all serve for eight-year, nonrenewable periods. However, the magistrates of the Constitutional Court are elected by the Senate, from slates of three candidates nominated by the president, the Supreme Court, and the Council of State, respectively, whereas new justices of the Supreme Court and the Council of State are chosen by the courts themselves from lists of eligible candidates proposed by the Superior Council of Judicial Affairs, a body created by the 1991 Constitution to ensure judicial independence.

The 1991 Constitution transformed the previous judicial system from an inquisitorial model, in which judges were responsible for the entire sequence of investigating a crime, issuing a verdict, and sentencing the criminal, to an accusatorial system, in which a separate, independent body investigates the crime and prosecutes the accused before the judge, whose responsibility is now limited to that of judging and sentencing. The leading role is played by the newly created Office of the General Prosecutor (the Fiscalía General), which is charged with "investigating crimes and accusing the suspected infractor before the corresponding courts of law" (Article 250). The general prosecutor, who serves for a period of four years, is selected by the Supreme Court from among three nominees chosen by the president. Another 1991 reform related to the judicial branch was the establishment of the Human Rights Ombudsman (Defensor del Pueblo), whose task is to promote and protect human rights in Colombia. As such, the ombudsman has a number of responsibilities, including education, preparation of legislation, petitioning of habeas corpus, and preparation of special legal actions to defend the basic rights of citizens. The Human Rights Ombudsman is chosen by the Chamber of Representatives from a slate of three candidates nominated by the president. Finally, the 1991 Constitution establishes special indigenous legal jurisdictions. Within these jurisdictions, indigenous authorities are allowed to exercise judicial functions in accordance with their own norms and procedures, as long as these are not contrary to the law and constitution.

## LIMITATIONS ON DEMOCRATIC GOVERNANCE

The formal, constitutional exercise of power as delineated in the 1991 Constitution is constrained in actual practice by several significant factors. First, the historic weakness of the Colombian state means that its territorial reach is often limited, particularly in more rural, inaccessible parts of the country. Although the Uribe administration successfully established a police presence in all 1,105 Colombian municipalities, this presence is frequently limited to a single small station incapable of fully controlling the municipality, particularly in its rural zones. The lack of an effective state presence and the absence of education, health, and other public services has historically allowed for the de facto control of certain areas by guerrilla movements, drug-trafficking organizations, or paramilitary units. Second, despite the good intentions of the 1991 Constitution, the Colombian political system continues to function largely through a system of broker clientelism, especially outside of the major urban areas. That is, politicians use their access to office to distribute specific state benefits such as government jobs, scholarships, and access to social services in return for votes on election day. Such a system subverts the notion that all citizens should have equal access to state benefits regardless of their political ties. Third, beyond the distorting influence of broker clientelism, Colombian elections continue to be marred by outright vote-buying and by the occasional armed intimidation of voters and candidates in some areas. Such practices clearly undermine the ability of Colombian authorities to conduct free and fair elections.

Fourth, even though the Colombian judiciary has served as a real check on the power of the executive branch, the administration of justice for ordinary citizens has been highly problematic, with the rate of impunity for criminal cases reaching an appalling 80 percent. The World Bank in 2012 ranked Colombia 178 out of 183 countries in judicial efficiency, with the sixth-slowest judicial system in the world and the third slowest in Latin America. Finally, Colombian democracy continues to be weakened by the direct and indirect participation of the state security forces in human rights abuses. An enduring resolution of Colombia's long-standing civil conflict will only happen if state security forces start to fully respect the civil and political rights of all Colombian citizens, particularly human rights activists, trade unionists, and the newly reincorporated former guerrilla fighters.

# Chronology

**1526**  Santa Marta, the oldest permanent Spanish city in Colombia, is established

**1819**  Patriot troops led by Simón Bolívar defeat the Spanish at the Battle of Boyacá

**1830**  Venezuela and Ecuador separate from Colombia

**1899–1902**  The War of a Thousand Days between Liberals and Conservatives produces 100,000 deaths and contributes indirectly to the loss of Panama

**1903**  A Panamanian uprising occurs with the complicity and armed intervention of the United States, which ensures the independence of Panama from Colombia

**1948**  Liberal leader Jorge Eliecer Gaitán is assassinated, producing mass rioting in Bogotá and deepening an undeclared civil war between Liberals and Conservatives—*La Violencia*

**1949**  Laureano Gómez, an extreme Conservative, wins election to the presidency after the Liberal Party withdraws from the race; political violence intensifies

**1953**  General Gustavo Rojas Pinilla overthrows Gómez in a military coup

**1957**  Rojas Pinilla resigns and goes into exile; the National Front establishes shared government between Liberals and Conservatives for a period of sixteen years

**1964–1967**  Three guerrilla organizations take up arms against the state—the Ejército de Liberación Nacional (ELN), the Fuerzas Armadas Revolucionarias de Colombia (FARC), and the Ejército Popular de Liberación (EPL)

**1973**  The Movimiento 19 de Abril (M-19) guerrilla movement takes up arms

**1974**  The National Front regime formally comes to an end

**1982**  Belisario Betancur, a Conservative, assumes the presidency and achieves cease-fire agreements with the M-19, the FARC, and the EPL

**1985**  The Unión Patriótica (UP) is created as part of the peace negotiations with the FARC; thousands of its militants are subsequently killed

**1989**  President Virgilio Barco declares war against the Medellín drug cartel, which responds with car bombings, terrorist attacks, and kidnappings

**1990**  The M-19 turns in its arms and becomes a legal political movement

**1991**  A new constitution is drafted to deepen Colombian democracy; Pablo Escobar, leader of the Medellín cartel, turns himself in to Colombian authorities

**1993**   State security agents kill Escobar, who had escaped from prison the previous year, and the Medellín cartel is dismantled

**1994**   Ernesto Samper, a Liberal, assumes the presidency amid charges that he accepted money from the Cali drug cartel to finance his presidential campaign

**1995**   Colombian state security forces dismantle the Cali cartel

**1998**   Andrés Pastrana, a Conservative, assumes the presidency and begins peace talks with the FARC, ceding them a 16,000-square-mile demilitarized zone

**1999–2000**   Pastrana and the Clinton administration promote Plan Colombia, greatly increasing U.S. military and police assistance

**2002**   Peace negotiations with the FARC break down; Alvaro Uribe is elected president, promising to take a hard line against the leftist guerrilla movements

**2003**   President Uribe enters negotiations with right-wing paramilitary movements, producing the demobilization of 31,000 armed fighters by 2006

**2006**   Alvaro Uribe is re-elected president with 62.4 percent of the vote

**2010**   Juan Manuel Santos, Uribe's former minister of defense, is elected president

**2012**   President Santos begins peace negotiations with the FARC

**2014**   Juan Manuel Santos is re-elected with 50.95 percent of the vote

**2016**   The Santos administration and the FARC reach a final peace agreement; after its defeat in a national plebiscite, the agreement is renegotiated and passed overwhelmingly by Congress; Santos is awarded the Nobel Peace Prize

# Bibliography

Brittain, James. *Revolutionary Social Change in Colombia: The Origin and Direction of the FARC-EP*. New York: Pluto, 2010.

Bouvier, Virginia, ed. *Colombia: Building Peace in a Time of War*. Washington, DC: United States Institute of Peace, 2009.

Bowden, Mark. *Killing Pablo: The Hunt for the World's Greatest Outlaw*. New York: Penguin, 2001.

Bruce, Victoria, and Karin Hayes. *Hostage Nation: Colombia's Guerrilla Army and the Failed War on Drugs*. New York: Alfred A. Knopf, 2010.

Carroll, Leah Anne. *Violent Democratization: Social Movements, Elites, and Politics in Colombia's Rural War Zones, 1984–2008*. South Bend, IN: University of Notre Dame Press, 2011.

Chepesiuk, Ron. *Drug Lords: The Rise and Fall of the Cali Cartel*. Wrea Green, UK: Milo, 2003.

Civico, Aldo. *The Para-State: An Ethnography of Colombia's Death Squads*. Oakland: University of California Press, 2016.

Crandall, Russell. *Driven by Drugs: U.S. Policy toward Colombia*. 2d ed. Boulder, CO: Lynne Rienner, 2008.

Dudley, Steven. *Walking Ghosts: Murder and Guerrilla Politics in Colombia*. New York: Routledge, 2004.

Henderson, James D. *Colombia's Narcotics Nightmare: How the Drug Trade Destroyed Peace*. Jefferson, NC: McFarland, 2015.

Kirk, Robin. *More Terrible than Death: Massacres, Drugs, and America's War in Colombia*. New York: Public Affairs, 2003.

LaRosa, Michael J., and Germán R. Mejía. *Colombia: A Concise Contemporary History*. Lanham, MD: Rowman & Littlefield, 2012.

Safford, Frank, and Marco Palacios. *Colombia: Fragmented Land, Divided Society*. Oxford: Oxford University Press, 2002.

Welna, Christopher, and Gustavo Gallón, eds. *Peace, Democracy, and Human Rights in Colombia*. South Bend, IN: University of Notre Dame Press, 2007.

WEBSITES

http://www.cinep.org.co/  CINEP is a Jesuit human rights organization that maintains the country's most widely consulted database on human rights violations

http://www.coljuristas.org/  The Comisión Colombiana de Juristas produces serious studies on the violation of human rights in Colombia's civil conflict

http://www.semana.com/  *Semana* is the principal Colombian newsweekly

http://es.presidencia.gov.co/Paginas/  The homepage of the Colombian presidency also contains links to all of the ministries of government

http://www.hchr.org.co/  The U.N. High Commissioner for Human Rights Office in Colombia is dedicated to promoting and defending human rights in Colombia

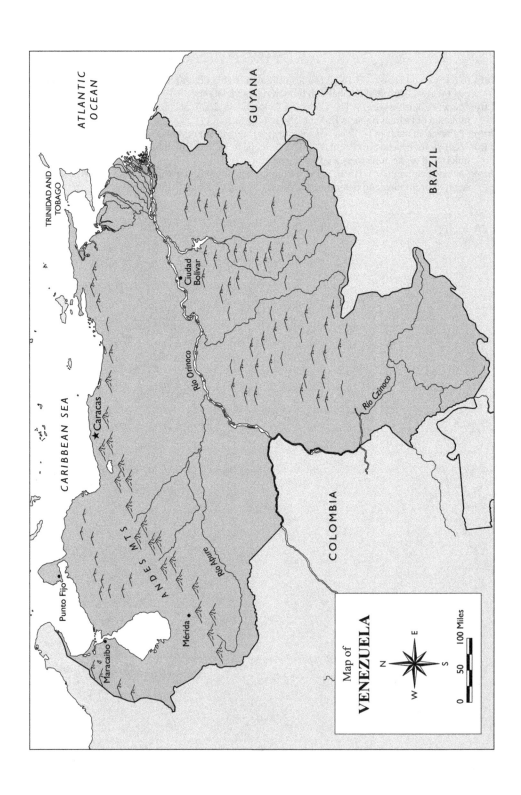

Map of
**VENEZUELA**

# SEVENTEEN

# VENEZUELA

*Daniel Hellinger*

In December 1998, former Lieutenant Colonel Hugo Chávez Frías was elected president of Venezuela, inaugurating an era of change not only for Venezuela but for much of the hemisphere. Leftist presidents espousing various types of socialism would come to power in Bolivia, Brazil, Argentina, Ecuador, Chile, Nicaragua and other countries, all part of a "pink tide." By September 2016, the tide seemed to be receding. Corruption, falling prices for raw material exports (which threatened programs to reduce poverty and inequality) and rising crime rates contributed to these setbacks to the left.

Chávez would not live to see this swing. On March 5, 2013, three months after having been reelected to a third six-year term, he died, but only after designating his vice president to succeed him. Nicolás Maduro had to face voters in a new election on April 14. His opponent, Henrique Capriles Radonski, had lost to Chávez 55 to 44 percent the previous December. Despite a wave of sympathy for the fallen president, Maduro barely won, by 50.6 to 49.1 percent.

In January 2016, the United Socialist Party of Venezuela (PSUV) and its left allies were soundly defeated in elections for the National Assembly, leaving with opposition tantalizingly close to a super-majority in the legislature that would have allowed them to dismantle many of Chávez's programs and policies. By May, Maduro's approval ratings had fallen to 26 percent, and the opposition began a campaign to gather signatures for a recall election, as permitted under the 1999 Constitution. By October, it was evident that a recall, if it took place, would occur late enough in Maduro's term not to force a new election; instead, his vice president would take power and finish out his term until new elections in 2018. Meanwhile, street violence, a long-standing plague that Chávez tried but failed to relieve, and scarcity, brought on by falling oil prices and poor governance, afflicted Venezuelans. People wondered openly wondered not only whether the military might stage a coup, but whether it would be on behalf of Maduro or the opposition.

**TABLE 21.** Conventional Oil Reserves by Country, 2012

| Rank | Country | Proved Reserves (Billion Barrels) |
|------|---------|-----------------------------------|
| 1. | Venezuela | 297.7 |
| 2. | Saudi Arabia | 265.9 |
| 3. | Iran | 157.3 |
| 4. | Iraq | 140.3 |
| 5. | Kuwait | 105.1 |
| 6. | United Arab Emirates | 97.8 |
| 7. | Russia | 80.0 |
| 8. | Libya | 48.5 |
| 9. | Nigeria | 37.1 |
| 10. | Kazakhstan | 30.0 |
| 11. | Qatar | 25.2 |

*Source*: OPEC Annual Statistical Bulletin, 2013.

The world was watching, partly because it is Venezuela's fortune—or misfortune, say some—to possess the world's largest reserves of oil (see Table 21). One Venezuela oil minister called oil, which was used by indigenous people in pre-Columbian times to caulk their canoes, "the devil's excrement." Among anxious observes was the government of Cuba, which relied upon Venezuela for oil supplied on generous financial and trade terms. Venezuela's polarized politics remain today too important to ignore.

# Geography and People

Venezuela is approximately the size of Texas and Oklahoma combined. Oil and gas mostly are exploited around Lake Maracaibo and in the eastern region, which is also rich in bauxite and iron and in hydroelectric power provided by the mighty Orinoco River. The high Andes run along the border with Columbia; a lesser spur (although some peaks reach nearly 9,000 feet) runs along the northern, Caribbean coast. Most of Venezuela's 30.4 million people, 87 percent of them urban, live in these northern highlands; one of every five Venezuelans lives in metropolitan Caracas.

The eastern and southern slopes of the Andes give way to plains (*los llanos*) where cattle ranches predominate. The *llanos* are like one big airport landing strip, which has not escaped the attention of Colombian drug lords, guerrillas, and right-wing paramilitary groups. Further south is the Sabana Grande, famous for diverse and exotic flora and fauna, home to most of Venezuela's small indigenous population; some are also found in the peninsula west of Lake Maracaibo. The border with Colombia runs over 1,600 miles through mountains and plains.

The majority of Venezuelans are *pardos*, racially mixed people of European, African, and (to a lesser extent) indigenous ancestry. In the Andean west, the population is more generally mestizo. Northeast of Caracas, in coastal region Barlovento, some of the world's most prized cacao (for chocolate) has been cultivated since colonial times, and descendants of enslaved Africans are the majority. Many lighter-skinned

Venezuelans today are descendants of immigrants who came in the late 1800s or post–World War II. After 1970, hundreds of thousands of Colombians fleeing civil war and, also attracted by an oil boom, took up residence in the barrios and the informal sector of the economy.

Chávez, a *pardo*, grew up the son of a poor school teacher in the small city of Barinas, where the *llanos* meet the Andes. While there is no one-to-one correlation, much of his opposition came from upper and middle class Venezuelans who tend to be lighter-skinned and live in more affluent parts of the Caracas valley. Chávez's charismatic appeal was to people inhabiting the world of barrios, poor neighborhoods perched on hillsides, far above the glittering skyscrapers and cafes below. Alejandro Moreno, a priest and sociologist who lives in a barrio, once said of Chávez, "What is important is not what he speaks but what speaks inside him. In him speaks the convivial relations of popular Venezuela, of convivial man. . . . An elderly woman expressed it very well: 'For me, it's like my own son is president'" (Moreno, 1998: 5).

Paradoxically, no country in the world makes a fetish of Western standards of female beauty than does Venezuela. Venezuelans have won more beauty contests than any other nationality, and beauty queens often move on to professional careers in journalism and politics. Yet Venezuela has a strong women's movement. The 1999 Constitution stands as the first in the world to use gender neutral language, speaking not of *ciudadanos* (citizens) but of *ciudadanos y ciudadanas*.

## Venezuela's History and Its Uses Today

In 1982 then-Lieutenant Hugo Chávez met with other young officers to form the Bolivarian Revolutionary Movement (MBR). They swore an oath under the same tree that according to legend shaded Simón Bolívar, "the Liberator" and his collaborators when they swore to liberate the country from Spain. Disillusioned by the squandering of the oil boom of the 1970s, the young officers pledged to fight corruption, reform the armed forces, and "rescue the values of the nation."

Bolívar is more than a national hero in Venezuela; he is a secular saint. After defeating Spanish forces near Maracaibo in 1821, he and his allies achieved freedom from Spain for present-day Ecuador, Peru, Colombia, Panama, and Venezuela. Bolívar wanted educational, social, and economic reform to lay the basis for republican government. He championed the Pan-American ideal of a united continent, capable of dealing equitably with the United States, which, he feared, would one day impose on Latin America "misery in the name of democracy." But his *criollo* allies joined the independence cause to escape economic controls imposed by Spain, not to make social revolution. As his dream of a united and progressive republic slipped away, Bolívar bitterly ruminating he had attempted to "plow the sea." Chávez the solider fashioned himself a leader to finish Bolívar's dreams, and like his hero, he increasingly tried to accomplish this in a top–down way, contradictory to the participatory ideals of the 1999 Constitution that he helped fashion.

The civil war for independence saw over 400 battles on Venezuelan soil, reducing the population by one-third. Of 900,000 people populating Venezuela in the late colonial period, 10 percent were enslaved. Slavery was abolished in 1854, but rural Venezuela continued to be a land of heavily indebted peons. *Pardos* from the *llanos* filled the ranks of *caudillo* armies, hoping for land and freedom, but usually gaining neither. The most devastating conflict was the Federal War of 1858–1863, fought between Liberals and Conservatives, which took between 60,000 and 100,000 lives, approximately 5 percent of the population.

A Liberal general, José Antonio Gúzman Blanco, held power for the next forty years and undertook modernization, accumulating debt to build ports, railroads, and public buildings. To create a national identity, he encouraged a cult around the figure of Bolívar, and today every town, no matter how humble, has a Plaza Bolívar with a statue of the Liberator. Gúzman promoted European immigration was encouraged to "whiten" the population—a racist "solution" to the problem of social indolence in a country where only 19 percent of the population was literate. The economy remained dependent, agrarian, and export oriented; regional *caudillos* ran local fiefdoms.

In 1899 rebellion originated from the Andean states, where coffee growers and dairy farmers harbored resentment against bankers, merchants, and government officials in Caracas. Its leader, General Cipriano Castro, was nationalist, authoritarian, and populist. He ran afoul of European powers when he refused to honor foreign debts contracted by the old regime and rival *caudillos*. In 1902, Britain, France, Germany, and Italy blockaded Venezuelan ports. The United States invoked the Monroe Doctrine and brokered a compromise. But Washington had little use for Castro and leapt at the opportunity to oust him by supporting a coup in 1908.

Juan Vicente Gómez replaced Castro and earned a reputation as the "tyrant of the Andes," running the country from 1908 until 1935 like it was his personal hacienda. But he was also a state-builder. He put Venezuela's fiscal house in order by improving the customs bureaucracy, and he continued Castro's work of training Venezuela's first professional army, which suppressed uprisings by regional caudillos. Gómez, the last *caudillo*, ruled until he died in bed in 1935.

## Oil Changes Everything

In 1922, with Gómez entrenched in power, oil drillers struck an enormous gusher, and Venezuela was forever changed. By 1935, oil export earnings were sixteen times what traditional exports (coffee and cacao) earned. The flow of petrodollars enriched Gómez, his family, and his cronies, but it also unleashed a socioeconomic tidal wave. Peasants fled rural indolence for opportunities in oil camps and cities. The new working class in the oil camps was joined in the cities by bus and truck drivers, port and railroad workers, construction workers, and so forth. Imports soared, creating opportunities for merchants. A small but growing middle class began to think about wresting power away from the *gómecista* oligarchy.

In 1928, a group of university students was arrested after a protest, and most were sent into exile. One member of this "Generation of 1928," Rómulo Betancourt, would powerfully shape Venezuelan politics for the next forty years. He founded a party called Acción Demócratica (AD) that pledged itself to (i) challenge the oil companies (*imperialismo petrolero*) and capturing a "just share" of profits for the nation; (ii) use the profits to modernize and diversify the economy and to improve living conditions ("sowing the oil"); and (iii) establish democracy based on universal suffrage. After 1935, moderate but unelected governments sought to follow a middle course between democratic reformers and the *gómecistas*. Betancourt's AD and the Venezuelan Communist Party (PCV) formed the opposition. The PCV had a strong base in labor, especially in the oil fields; Betancourt worked tirelessly to organize not only workers but also peasants and the middle class.

In 1943, President (and General) Medina Isaías Angarita forced the foreign oil companies to renegotiate their oil leases and to accept both higher royalties and Venezuela's sovereign right to raise their taxes. Venezuela's share of oil profits increased the next year from about one-eighth to over one-half. Medina also prepared a democratic transition, but the deal collapsed once a consensus candidate suffered an incapacitating illness. Next, middle-class military officers, eager to cleanse their ranks of unprofessional *gómecista* officers, cut a deal with Betancourt and in 1945 overthrew Medina. For three years (the *trienio*), Betancourt and AD, backed by strong majorities in three national elections, implemented a program of housing construction, education reform, limited land reform, peasant and labor organizing, and public investment. Betancourt abandoned harsh criticism of *imperialism petrolero* and brokered a deal with the companies to stabilize oil profit-sharing at "fifty–fifty."

The government had powerful enemies. Communists were furious as AD used the Labor Ministry to push them out of the unions, especially in the oil fields. Businessmen railed against government support for unions. A Catholic student leader, Rafael Caldera, organized a Christian Democratic party, the People's Independent Electoral Organizing Committee (COPEI), and mounted street protests against AD's attempt to break the Church's monopoly on education. In November 1948 some of the officers involved in the 1945 coup overthrew Venezuela's first directly elected president (novelist Rómulo Gallegos). In 1952 General Marcos Pérez Jiménez seized full power. Betancourt fled to exile in New York, even as the Cold Warriors of the Eisenhower administration backed the dictatorship.

## The Rise and Fall of the Punto Fijo Regime

Pérez Jiménez combined populism, including lavish spending on massive housing projects, with heavy-handed authoritarianism. By 1958, his corruption, inefficiency, and the cold-blooded murder of political opponents alarmed even many in the military. Young Communist and AD cadres led resistance in the swelling slums of Caracas and other large cities. In January 1958, Pérez Jiménez fled the country. A provisional government took power and held elections in December 1958. The winner was Rómulo Betancourt.

Before the election, Caldera, Betancourt, and other party leaders signed a power-sharing pact in October 1958 at Caldera's Caracas villa, Punto Fijo. They deliberately excluded the Communists from the deal. For the next forty years, AD and COPEI, bitterly contested each other in elections but also banded together to protect their joint control of the state—and its petrodollars—a system that came to be called "*puntofijismo.*" Other pacts assured Church leaders, the military, business groups, and labor unions (those affiliated with AD, not the PCV) that the new regime would not threaten their vital interests. The goals were to exclude the PCV and prevent a repetition of the *trienio* collapse.

Soon, Washington and the Venezuelan business community had a new reason to prefer Betancourt, as Fidel Castro marched into Havana, Cuba, in January 1959. But not all was well in relations with Washington; new Middle Eastern production was threatening Venezuela's share of the U.S. oil market. After Washington rebuffed Venezuela's entreaties for a special trade agreement, Betancourt dispatched his oil minister, Pérez Alfonzo, to the Middle East to propose cooperation. This eventually led to the founding of OPEC, sowing the seeds of a new oil boom in the 1970s.

Betancourt's limited reform agenda and anticommunism alienated young leftists in both his own party and the PCV. They had borne the human cost of resistance to the dictatorship. Inspired by the Cuban Revolution of 1959, the radicals launched armed struggle, forming, with Cuban support, the Armed Forces of National Liberation (FALN) in 1962. Many Venezuelans were disappointed with Betancourt but not ready to overthrow an elected government. Backed by U.S. arms and training in counterinsurgency, the military defeated the insurrection.

COPEI's Rafael Caldera won the 1968 election, and most rebels accepted his amnesty offer. Some formed a new party, Movement Toward Socialism (MAS). Their hopes were high as the 1973 election approached, but AD and COPEI together obtained 85 percent of the vote. MAS became a junior partner in the system dominated by the two large parties. Some leftists turned to a longer-term strategy of organizing workers dissatisfied with the Venezuelan Workers Confederation (CTV), dominated by AD, and residents of the barrios. Some became allies of Chávez's MBR, which was still in the shadows.

In the Punto Fijo era, Venezuela's political parties insinuated themselves into almost every area of organized social life: unions, neighborhood associations, women's groups, student organizations, peasant associations, and so forth. The parties ran slates of candidates against one another for control of these organizations. Victory meant a larger share of the state's oil income (called "rent"), which subsidized all these organizations. For example, unions were mostly funded by state revenues, not dues. Union leaders controlled major banks and services (e.g., tourist facilities), distancing them from the lives of workers; many were corrupt. Iron discipline prevailed in internal party and legislative matters. A vote against the directive of the party leadership was political suicide. People could only vote for slates, not individuals, and many "elected" leaders were "parachutists" dropped into leadership of groups or state and local governments by party leaders. One analyst called this state of affairs "partyarchy."

Nonetheless, Venezuela seemed a political success story compared to other Latin American countries. It escaped a wave of military rule in the 1970s. A new oil boom, partly a result of OPEC's power, brought unprecedented fiscal resources. In 1974 (Table 21), oil earnings shot up from $2.6 billion in 1973 to $8.9 billion in 1974. The AD president, Carlos Andrés Pérez, winner of the 1973 election, used the windfall to raise the minimum wage, eliminate unemployment, create vast new steel and aluminum industries, subsidize industries and agriculture, and expand social benefits. Inflation was controlled by keeping prices capped, but subsidies to businesses kept them profitable. The bolívar was fixed at 4.3 to the dollar, which made it cheap to travel abroad and to buy imported goods. Venezuelans on shopping sprees in Miami exclaimed, "¡*Tan barato, dame dos*" (So cheap, I'll take two!).

In 1976 Venezuela nationalized the oil companies and placed them under a state holding company, Petróleos de Venezuela (PDVSA). It was the companies that suggested accelerating nationalization. They were well compensated and relieved of responsibility for making new investments in depleted fields, and their old ones were going to expire in 1983 anyway. And the foreign companies had already placed Venezuelan engineers and managers in charge of local operations. And the law contained a provision that would eventually be used to allow the companies to return to the fields, beginning the late 1980s under operating contracts of various types.

Seeking to transform Venezuela overnight into an industrial powerhouse, Pérez borrowed heavily against the company's future earnings; very little investment was made in the oil industry itself. PDVSA's "success" depended on high prices, and by the early 1980 the consuming, importing countries had begun to turn the tables on OPEC. By 1978, COPEI's Luis Herrera Campíns, elected president in 1978, promised frugality; instead, he rode a new wave of petrodollars generated by the 1978 Iranian Revolution. This proved a short respite.

In 1981, the government derived 90 percent of its revenues from oil exports. In 1982 oil earnings fell about 25 percent, and the price per barrel was in free fall. The massive new industries started by Pérez were uncompetitive, riddled with corruption, and in need of continual subsidies to set off losses. International banks, struggling under a global recession, were eager to lend. Servicing foreign debt was draining dollar reserves. To cope, Herrera Campíns bled PDVSA of profits and capital in a desperate effort to keep the bolivar at 4.3 to 1.

The reckoning came on "Black Friday," February 28, 1983, when Herrera Campins devalued the bolívar. The days of 4.3 to 1 and zero unemployment were over. Between 1983 and 1987, Venezuela suffered a net loss of $17.3 billion in capital due to debt payments and capital flight. The poverty rate soared, rising from 20 to 80 percent of the population. Venezuelans asked who was to blame. No longer could anyone blame *imperialismo petrolero*. Elites blamed the people, claiming that oil rents had made Venezuelans lazy. The people in the barrios had a different view. Visible to the majority living on the mountainsides, a small class in the Caracas valley continued to live the high life—"*a la adeco*," many said, referring to members of AD. The country was wealthy; the people were poor; the parties were to blame.

Between 1983 and 1988, the administration of President Jaime Lusenchi (AD) corruption touched new depths. Generals, senators, ministers, and businessmen siphoned millions of dollars into their pockets and then went safely abroad. Contracts included lucrative commissions for middlemen. At the grassroots, petty corruption became a way of life. Toll booth operators would turn in only a fraction of their collection, cutting in their bosses and keeping their jobs as long as they belonged to the right party. Bureaucrats demanded bribes to attend to public business. The military seemed integrated into the system of graft and patronage. Few knew that in its ranks were officers disillusioned with *puntofijismo* and inspired by the ideals of Bolívar.

When Pérez won a second term in 1988, he campaigned as a populist who would restore the good times. He staged a lavish inauguration, reinforcing popular beliefs that the country remained wealthy. Venezuelans were shocked, then, when Pérez announced an austerity program—a structural adjustment agreement with the International Monetary Fund (IMF). Public employment was to be frozen, price controls eased, state enterprises sold off, wages held in check, and so forth.

## Rise of Chavismo

On the morning of Monday, February 27, 1989, gasoline prices were due to rise in accord with the IMF pact. Microbus owners attempted to pass the hike to their riders. An angry mob burned a microbus on the outskirts of Caracas, lighting a fuse. By the end of the day, widespread looting and rioting, the *caracazo*, had spread to twenty-two cities. Pérez sent the army to occupy neighborhoods and recover looted goods. In the violence, human rights groups estimate that over 1,000 people died.

This use of the army emboldened the young Bolivarian officers, increasing their numbers and determination to act. On February 14, 1992, they launched a coup against Pérez. When it failed, Pérez asked the captured leader to appear on television to appeal to his supporters to lay down their arms. Lieutenant Colonel Hugo Chávez, uniformed and wearing his red paratrooper's beret, told his comrades that their objectives had failed "for now." He spoke for less than a minute, but the effect was electrifying. The politicians expected people to rally to democracy; instead, thousands of youths started sporting red berets. Only Caldera, the elder statesman and a founder of the regime, recognized the depth of the crisis. He condemned the coup but called for reflection on why Venezuelans had lost faith in the system.

A second failed coup in November 1992 showed that normalcy had not returned. Street demonstrations became daily occurrences. In 1993, Congress ousted Pérez on a trumped-up charge of illegally diverting funds. Later that year, Caldera's dissent proved to be his ticket to back to the presidency, but only after he split from COPEI and promised to abandon neoliberal economic policies. He sought national reconciliation by freeing Chávez and other officers. Then the banking system, rife with corruption, collapsed. Backed against the wall financially, Caldera implemented neoliberal policies resembling those of Pérez.

Caldera's presidency was the last gasp of the old regime. As the December 1998 elections approached, it seemed likely that Venezuela's next president would come from outside the traditional party system. Mild political reforms, especially direct election of governors, had opened the political system a crack, but AD and COPEI resisted the deeper reforms, angering a variety of social movements, including women, indigenous groups, neighborhood organization, and worker-democracy movements. Prohibited by law from using Bolívar's name for partisan purposes, Chávez entered the contest as the candidate of a left coalition headed by the Movimiento Quinta República (MVR; V here is a Roman numeral, referring to founding a fifth Venezuelan republic). He won 56 percent of the vote heading a coalition of the MVR and some smaller parties. The centerpiece of his campaign was an outright call for a constituent assembly to rewrite the constitution—something his opponents would not do out of fear of the influence of popular movements.

Chávez benefited from a new collapse in oil prices, which undermined the Caldera's neoliberal oil policy. In the 1990s, PDVSA executives had pushed through an *apertura petrolera* (oil opening), permitting foreign capital into the oil fields through service contracts, joint ventures, and shared risks. Offering terms as lucrative to investors as those in the Gómez era, the executives sought to boost production with little investment by PDVSA. Company executives wanted Venezuela to quit OPEC and its quota system; some floated the idea of selling private shares in the company. Chávez did not campaign against their scheme, but as a nationalist and populist he distrusted PDVSA's managers. They in turn would form the nucleus of forces that tried to oust Chávez in 2002 via a coup and then an oil industry shutdown.

## Survival Politics

In his first two years, Chávez focused on sweeping away the old political class. He won a referendum to call the constituent assembly. In the subsequent election, the new constitution was approved and COPEI and AD were roundly defeated then—and again in new elections in July 2000. The constitution declared that the new "Bolivarian Republic of Venezuela" would be a "participatory and protagonistic" democracy. Among new participatory mechanisms were involving civil society in choosing judges and officials to defend human rights, an ombudsman, and national auditor. Venezuela became the first country to create the possibility for citizens to recall the president, not just other elected officials. The era of Punto Fijo was over, and most Venezuelans, including many who had not voted for Chávez, were pleased.

In the early period, Chávez's economic policies were not radical, but in 2000 he began to implement programs aimed at improving social conditions. He assigned the army responsibility for projects aimed at repairing and building housing, schools, clinics, and subsidized markets in the barrios. He called these programs "missions" that attacked the poverty that had come to afflict nearly 80 percent of the population of the oil-rich nation. The presence of many former officers in key government posts and the use of the military in these missions touched off a debate between those who distrust an intrusion of the military into civic life and those who praise the military for alleviating social and economic exclusion. That debate continues today.

Opposition to Chávez began to intensify in November 2001 when he used emergency powers granted by the National Assembly to issue decree laws to carry out education reforms, land reform, urban housing, oil policy, and a host of other issues. The laws alarmed the middle class and wealthy, especially a new oil law that restored some measure of state control over PDVSA. PDVSA was not just a source of wealth but also, in the view of the middle class, their main link to the modern developed world that seemed within reach during the 1970s. Oil executives, business elites, politicians, and labor leaders longing for a return to the old regime found a willing ally in the private media, which ratcheted up a mass propaganda campaign against Chávez and provoked protests, some violent. The campaign culminated in the astounding events of April 11–14, 2002, when Chávez was overthrown by a coup—only to be restored to power forty-eight hours later.

The events began on April 10 when all four major private TV networks, most radio stations, and the most influential newspapers called for a mass demonstration in front of PDVSA headquarters to demand the ouster of Chávez. Once assembled, opposition leaders directed the hundreds of thousands of protesters to march on the presidential palace, where thousands of Chavistas (followers of Chávez) had gathered. Suddenly sniper fire broke out in the area around the palace. Twenty people were killed, and 200 were injured. There were casualties on both sides, but the media blamed everything on Chávez, a sensitive matter to soldiers who remembered Pérez's repression of the *caracazo*. The military hierarchy detained Chávez and installed a junta headed by the president of FEDECARMAS, the country's most important business organization. Prominent TV journalists and coup makers celebrated openly how they had collaborated in calling the demonstration and instigating the coup.

The coup began to unravel almost as fast as it had happened. Some of its supporters became alarmed when the junta started hunting down government ministers, dissolved the National Assembly, and abrogated the 1999 Constitution. Some garrisons around the country remained loyal to Chávez, and thousands of barrio residents descended from the hills and surrounded the presidential palace. Popular pressure and military units loyal to Chávez brought down the junta and allowed the president to return.

A second showdown came in December 2002 when PDVSA executives, business elites, and the old CTV union leadership shut down the oil industry in an attempt to bring the government to its knees. With some help from other OPEC countries, loyal employees and the military restored the flow of oil. In the end 18,000 of PDVSA's most skilled workers and professionals were fired. The government won and production recovered, but PDVSA suffered a blow to its longer-run capacity.

Finally, the opposition turned to a constitutional strategy. Throughout 2003 and 2004, Venezuelan politics were almost entirely focused on efforts to use the innovative recall provision of the constitution to "revoke" Chávez's mandate. As required, the opposition gathered the signatures of more than 20 percent (2.4 million) of registered voters. Neither side trusted the other, but with the help of international mediation, especially by former U.S. President Jimmy Carter and the Carter Center of Atlanta, the recall took place in August 2014. Chávez had looked vulnerable to defeat in 2003. Unemployment was high and social conditions remained precarious, but his popularity rose as the "social missions" began to take effect. The signature programs were Barrio Adentro (Inside the Neighborhood, which put 12,000 Cuban doctors in clinics in poor areas) and Misión Robinson, which eradicated illiteracy. Rising oil prices and new taxes and royalties imposed by his government helped. Chávez appealed as a fellow *pardo* (mixed race) to the lower classes, which felt excluded and alienated from the traditional politicians backing recall.

The president's smashing 59 percent victory reaffirmed his legitimacy internationally and gave him new political capital at home. Chávez announced his intention to accelerate land reform, raise royalties, and expand the social missions. The opposition was demoralized, and the president seemed secure in power. Another loser was the Bush administration, which encouraged ousting Chávez by extraconstitutional means, providing financial aid to the main opposition organization, the so-called Democratic Coordinator, through the U.S. taxpayer funded National Endowment for Democracy. U.S. State Department documents indicate that United States funneled more than $40 million annually to opposition groups through various nongovernmental organizations. Given its past history of intervention in the region, it is likely that more support was channeled covertly.

However, the recall also revealed a weakness in the Bolivarian revolution. The politicians of the MVR proved so incapable of organizing rejection of Chávez's recall that the Venezuelan leader had to step in to reorganize his supporters and vest more power in grassroots leaders drawn the missions. In 2006 Chávez found the PSUV, which was supposed to be more rooted in grassroots organizers than was the MVR. However, almost immediately the same tensions between grassroots leaders at the social base and politicians reasserted itself. Although the PSUV used a primary to choose most of the pro-government candidates for the 2010 National Assembly elections, an unprecedented event in Venezuelan politics, many grassroots Chavistas felt the old party system was reemerging in a new guise.

Chávez benefited from an opposition that failed to cast off the taint of the past, but that began to change after Chávez won a smashing victory in the December 2006 presidential election. His main opponent recognized defeat, unlike many in the opposition who had cried "fraud" after the recall with little credibility. Chávez seen to be in command, and he decided now to try to march forward with plans to rapidly transform Venezuela into a socialist state, shifting power from elected officials, including governors and mayors, to territorial communes where locally elected representatives would distribute financing of economic and social projects. This proved to be a bridge too far. In 2007, Chávez lost (though narrowly) a bid to amend the constitution to facilitate his call to build "twenty-first century socialism" based on local communal councils and a new system of property rights that included private ownership but also created several new forms of public ownership.

High oil prices and the new oil laws certainly were keys to Chávez's success in reducing poverty and inequality. Poverty was literally cut in half between 2002 and 2012, from 62 to 32 percent. But the oil boom but also facilitated a repetition of some of the mistakes of the 1970s, as the government borrowed large sums against expectations of continued high oil prices. When prices began to fall after 2014, Maduro's government followed the earlier script, borrowing heavily, especially from China, to sustain oil production and social programs.

Instead of Pérez's grandiose plans to industrialize the country overnight, Chávez embraced ideas for "socialism of the twenty-first century," which centered around encouraging worker-run farms and factories that would be environmentally friendly (Few advocated this for the vital oil industry!), exchange based on solidarity and fairness rather than the market, and a diversified economy. Funds to these programs, as well as the social missions, would come directly from the executive branch and PDVSA (now controlled by the executive).

The political counterpart to economic experiments was the Communal Council movement. The movement had both a bottom–up and top–down character. On the one hand, such local neighborhood assemblies had sprung up in some places during the years of mass protest against *puntofijismo* and neoliberal economic policies; others manifested themselves early in the Chávez presidency in the form of Bolivarian Circles. They were also spurred by education and health missions and were most often led by women.

The top–down impetus came in 2006 when Chávez decided, as part of his plan to create "socialism of the twenty first century," to pass a law by which the government would actively promote communal councils throughout the country. They would form of representatives called "*voceros/as*" elected by neighborhood assemblies. The plan was that they would decide community priorities for financing from funds controlled by the executive branch and by PDVSA, respectively, thereby bypassing local and state politicians as well as the National Assembly—something that was unwelcome not only to the opposition but also to politicians in the PSUV.

In this way, Chávez hoped to undermine clientelism and bureaucratic obstruction, but it also placed distribution of oil rents under his own control. Many councils were simply co-opted by politicians. Many others were not, but even the grassroots leaders inevitably prioritized preserving Chavista victories in elections, given that an opposition victory would likely reverse many of the missions. Altogether as many as half of the 19,500 Communal Councils originally registered with the government may no longer be functioning. However, others have continued and provided significant experience in democratic participation. The council movement, though battered by economic crisis and political frustrations, remains a force to be reckoned with but also far from achieving the idealist, if not utopian, vision that Chávez had in promoting them.

Counterpart to his domestic programs, Chávez undertook several foreign policy initiatives, including founding a hemispheric television network (Telesur), providing discounted oil to Caribbean and Latin American nations that would otherwise been punished by high prices, and joining with Brazil and other countries to create new diplomatic organizations (the Community of Latin Amirian and Caribbean Nations [CELAC] and the Union of South American Nations [UNASUR]), directly challenging the Organization of American States, headquartered in Washington, D.C.

Chávez took the lead in 2005 in rallying Latin American countries to reject the U.S. proposed Free Trade Area of the Americas, modeled on the neoliberal NAFTA accord. He founded the Bolivarian Alliance for the Peoples of Our America (ALBA) as an alternative economic bloc to serve as an international counterpart to his economic experiment at home, attracting like-minded governments, including Ecuador, Bolivia, Cuba, and Nicaragua. These moves, as well as Chávez's criticism of wars waged by the United States in Central Asia and Iraq and his warm relationship with Iran, earned him membership in the eyes of the Bush administration

(2000–2008) in an "Axis of Evil." Recent shifts rightward in Latin America and the economic troubles in Venezuela jeopardize all these initiates.

# Venezuela's Bolivarian Constitution and Institutional Framework

The Constituent Assembly of 1999 renamed the country the "Bolivarian Republic of Venezuela," an affirmation that Chávez's revolution intended to invoke the Liberator's philosophy for its underlying principles. The constitution established a unicameral National Assembly elected by a combination of proportional and uninominal systems. It is weighted to favor larger parties, which worked to the advantage of the PSUV in the Chávez years but had the opposite effect in the assembly elections of December 2015 when the opposition won nearly two-thirds of the seats with only 56 percent of the vote.

The 1999 charter guarantees people an extensive list of social and economic rights aimed at broadening social inclusion. Indigenous rights (including seats in the National Assembly reserved for indigenous representatives) are given unprecedented recognition. All rights typically associated with liberal democracy were recognized, although there were potential areas of conflict. For example, although freedom of speech and press are guaranteed, the right of the people to "truthful information" was also guaranteed. The constitution provides that all international human rights treaties to which Venezuela is a signatory take precedence over national law.

In addition to the usual three branches (executive, legislative, judicial), the constitution creates a "citizen's power" branch, an attempt to incorporate Chávez's idea of "protagonistic" democracy. Venezuela's new system would be representative and pluralist on the one hand but on the other hand also promote direct participation by the people. The attorney general, a national ombudsman, and a comptroller were to be chosen by the National Assembly after consultation with a council composed of groups in civil society, such as human rights organizations. Provisions permitting recall of elected officials and referendums were also designed to give citizens a protagonistic role in Venezuela's new democracy.

Too often the constitutional ideal and reality diverge. For example, instead of subjecting new, major legislation in 2001 to widespread popular debate, Chávez used decree powers granted by the Assembly to make new laws. In November 2013 Maduro was given emergency powers to deal with corruption and economic issues, with little input from below. Reform of the judiciary has been very controversial. In the Punto Fijo era, the courts were heavily politicized. Rich and powerful figures unhappy with the decision of one court could usually find a judge tied to their party to reverse a ruling or verdict. The National Assembly, controlled by the Chavistas, expanded the size of the Supreme Court and facilitated the removal of judges deemed corrupt or derelict in their duties. Chávez probably sincerely sought judicial reform, but the courts now show little capacity to act independently of the executive, especially on constitutional issues and criminal cases involving opposition politicians.

## Political Actors in Bolivarian Venezuela

The PSUV's main electoral advantage today is that many Venezuelans perceive the opposition as no better and likely to dismantle the social and economic programs that lifted millions out of poverty at the height of the Chávez years. Although it has held primaries to choose candidates, it has not definitively broken from the practices associated with "partyarchy" in the Punto Fijo era.

Having won the 2009 referendum allowing him to run indefinitely for president every six years, Chávez, though gravely ill with cancer, launched his campaign for reelection in December 2012. But that election also saw the emergence of Henrique Capriles as a more formidable challenger, successful to some degree in separating himself from the past.

### THE OPPOSITION

The main opposition coalition between 2010 and 2016 has been the Democratic Unity Roundtable (MUD). It included traditional parties (AD, COPEI, and some of the smaller, leftist parties of the Punto Fijo era), new parties, and parties put together by regional political personalities. The MUD replaced an earlier alliance that was identified too much with the *puntofijista* past and with the failed coup of 2002. AD, though much weaker than in its halcyon Punto Fijo days, is the largest party in the MUD and the only one that retains a network of offices around the country. In the Caracas area, the middle class tends to support a different party, Primer Justicia (Justice First), which tends toward more neoliberal policies than any other significant party. The MUD also counts some smaller leftist parties among its members, but they have much less weight in the coalition.

But MUD has been divided. AD's leaders seem mostly to want to reclaim political power, that is to restore the place it had under *puntofijismo*, which would probably mean an attempt to rewrite the constitution. It is the largest party in the coalition, the only one with a truly national presence. However, the MUD's two most prominent personalities are Capriles and Leopoldo López, another former mayor of a Caracas municipality. Both came from the Justice First party in the Caracas, but both have also founded their own personalist parties. Capriles sought to position himself as a center-leftist for the 2013 and 2014 presidential elections. He promised to maintain the government's social policies but to run them more efficiently. Capriles prefers to compare himself to Brazil's Lula. The Chavistas see him as a wolf in sheep's clothing, pointing out that he is the scion of the country's wealthiest families and charging that, as mayor of the wealthy suburb of Baruta at the time of the short-lived coup of 2002, he encouraged a mob attack on the Cuban embassy (located in Baruta).

More than Capriles, López has aligned himself with sectors that have little interest in working through the constitution for a legal recall. While carefully avoiding an open call for violence, he pointedly called for street protests at the same time as some protests were turning violent. He was arrested and jailed on charges of promoting violence, and he was convicted after a trial criticized as unfair by many human rights organizations. He rivals Capriles today for leadership of the MUD.

FEDECAMARAS, the largest business organization, always opposed Chávez, but some sectors of business have developed a working relationship, if not cooperative one, with the government. Business organizations are extremely weak in comparison to the behemoth that is PDVSA. Many of the PDVSA high executives ousted after the end of the company shutdown 2003 live abroad but remain active opponents of the Bolivarian government.

While it might seem that Chavismo would have a strong ally in organized labor, the situation with this actor is complicated. In 2000 the Chavistas launched a rival confederation (National Workers Union; UNT) that is now larger than the CTV, but the UNT is divided on how closely to work with the government. Workers in general seem to reject the corrupt and unresponsive leadership of the past, but they also resist being subordinated to the interests of any political party, including the PSUV. The UNT is also deeply divided among factions that support radicalization and socialism and those that take a more traditional approach to labor relations.

Perhaps the most potent actor that opposed Chávez was the private media. From 2002 until 2004, the private media were not just biased; they assumed an overtly political role in organizing the opposition. Coup plotters in 2002 met in the home of one of Venezuela's most powerful media magnates just beforehand. Not surprising, the government responded afterwards. In 2007 the government refused to renew the broadcasting license of one major station, RCTV, which was especially active in promoting the 2002 coup, limiting the station to cable and satellite operations. In 2012, the government moved against a less influential but just as vitriolic opposition station, Globovisión, though this time through a financial maneuver.

Despite these actions, independent and opposition broadcasting stations continue to operate. However, all have adopted more moderate and balanced political coverage. For their part, Chávez and Maduro used the state radio and television outlets as partisan tools for their own ends. The audience share for state TV is small, but it has helped the government respond to the private media, whose audience dwarfs that of the state channel.

After the *caracazo*, Venezuelan society experienced an explosion of popular organizations among women, barrio residents, indigenous peoples, environmentalists, human rights activists, and others. Subsequently, many of these movements aligned with or were coopted by Chavismo, and others have jealously guarded their autonomy. Still others are somewhere in between these endpoints, trying to balance support for social program with political defense of Chavismo. A few social movements, notably among some students, are more closely aligned with the opposition than the government. Intellectuals have divided as well and not only along an axis of pro- or antigovernment. A significant sector, called Marea Socialista (Socialist Tide), has split from the PSUV and sought to carve out an opposition space to that party's left.

In regard to human rights, two of the more influential organizations are PROVEA, the Venezuelan Program of Education and Protection of Human Rights, and the Center for Peace and Human Rights at the Central University of Venezuela. These organizations have criticized the government in many respects but also recognized irresponsible behavior on the part of the opposition. Their criticisms include recognition of serious failings of the government to apply laws equally and to reform the notoriously corrupt criminal justice system. Some members of the human rights community in Venezuela criticized the main organizations for allegedly focusing too much on government abuses and not enough on opposition violence.

The Church is relatively weak. Most of the hierarchy opposed Chávez and Maduro, but many clergy working in the poor barrios were inclined toward Chávez, who often wore a crucifix. In general, the growing evangelical Christian population was friendlier to the president than church-going Catholics.

The situation is more opaque for another pillar of Bolivarianism, the military. The failure of the April 2002 coup gave Chávez an opportunity to purge disloyal elements. Many soldiers have embraced their participation in missions (many funded directly by PDVSA) in the barrios and poor rural areas, but there are reports that some officers feel these activities do not befit their vocation and training. A major question is whether the military feels the same loyalty to Maduro, who came out of the unions, as it did toward Chávez, one of their own.

## Economic and Development Strategies in Bolivarian Venezuela

Between 2001 and 2003, the government had to contend with the impact of the short-lived coup and three-month oil stoppage. The stoppage cost the country $9 billion, 9 percent of its annual gross domestic product. The economy contracted by 8.9 percent in 2002 and 9.4 percent in 2003. After 2004, the economy began to grow at a very high annual rate (between 7 and 12 percent). Certainly soaring oil prices helped, as they soared above $50 per barrel in 2004. They would reach $140 before falling back in the face of a global supply glut in 2014. Although world market conditions (especially rising consumption in China) partly explained the boom period, Chávez's leadership in restoring the strength of OPEC must also be given some of the credit. In October 2004 the government hiked royalties from 1 to 16 percent, and in 2007 the government forced companies operating as partners with PDVSA to sell enough shares to the state company to give it ownership. High prices and these reforms provided the export revenues that the government channeled not only to benefit the lower classes but also sectors of the bourgeoisie, some uncomfortably close to the government from the perspective of the grassroots.

Chavismo is strong in rural areas. Under land reform policies, over 130,000 families received state-owned land, alleviating inequality in a country where 70 percent of agricultural land was owned by 3 percent of the population. The reform is supposed to extend to unused private lands, but the state bureaucracy has often been slow to act. Peasants have used land occupations to try to force the government bureaucracy to act, increasing tensions. Agriculture remains a severe weakness, with much food imported, and much of it now distributed at discounted prices in state-run markets.

Overall, in terms of improvements in health care, literacy, nutrition, and education, some significant gains were recorded, making Venezuela the only country in the hemisphere to have met some of the poverty-reduction targets set at the United Nation's Millennium Summit of 2000, with particular progress in reducing infant mortality and increasing women's access to education and the labor market.

However, even before Chávez died, there were signs of serious failures of governance that put the entire Bolivarian project in doubt. Since 2009, severe electricity shortages have disrupted lives and the economy. Record-high homicide rates were the top issue on voters' minds, polls showed. Corruption scandals disheartened many Bolivarian activists. The opposition media loses few opportunities to bash the government, but government supporters are also frustrated by the failure of state media to respond to complaints, forcing them to go to the private media.

Grave shortages of foodstuffs and medical supplies are undermining support for Maduro and the PSUV. The government blames unscrupulous speculators that buy up subsidized medicines and food and then sell their wares in middle-class areas. It also claims that the opposition and the United States are engaged in an "economic war" to subvert the regime. One cannot simply dismiss these charges, as U.S. and Latin American conservatives have historically resorted to such intervention against left-wing governments (e.g., Chile in the 1970s; Nicaragua in the 1980s). However, there is little doubt that government ineptitude and falling oil prices are the underlying forces behind the economic crisis.

## Challenges after Chávez

Chávez's charismatic appeal was based on his ability to connect closely to most Venezuelans both in his persona and through redirection of oil wealth toward the poor. But he was much less successful institutionalizing participatory democracy, much less "twenty-first century socialism." Two major events exposed the weakness of the Bolivarian Revolution: the death of Hugo Chávez in March 2013 and the collapse of global oil prices.

Chávez clearly failed to prepare for his disappearance from the stage. Maduro has tried to rally Chavistas around the same kind of populist, nationalist rhetoric, but he has so far been overwhelmed by a triple challenge of (i) stepping into the rather large shoes of Chávez, (ii) the collapse of oil prices from a high of $130 to between $40 and $50 in 2016, and (iii) Chávez's failure to leave behind and efficient and institutionalized system of governance.

Besides the immediate problem of failing oil revenues, there are longer-term problems with PDVSA that must be addressed. The company has borrowed heavily to finance new exploration and drilling meanwhile spending much of its capital to carry out many of the programs assigned to it by Chávez. Many of these loans, especially from China, are repaid in future oil production. The company is turning to foreign investment partners to develop new fields and to loans to carry out production in existing ones. In other words, whether the PSUV or the MUD wins the next presidential election, sovereign control over the natural resource is in jeopardy. And to fill the void, the government in 2016 opened remote areas of the country to major new investments in mining.

In summer of 2016, the MUD decided to accelerate street protests (a concession to its right wing, led by López) and simultaneously to collect signatures to force a recall of President Maduro. The National Election Council, with a four-to-one government majority, agreed to oversee the process but interpreted the rules in such a way to make it harder for the opposition to achieve recall. Eventually, it became clear that no recall would take place. Also, the Council suspended scheduled regional elections. In 2017 Maduro called for a constituent assembly to rewrite the constitution, putting the 2018 presidential election in doubt.

Various protests were staged throughout 2016 not only by the opposition but also by barrio residents. However, the latter actions seemed to target shortages and other immediate issues, not the demands of the opposition for a recall or Maduro's resignation. The opposition staged a massive rally (and the Chavistas a similar one in response) in early September 2015, then wanned. After Maduro moved to emasculate the National Assembly's they surged in 2017.

Neither the Bolivarians nor the MUD were actually addressing the longer-term issues facing the country. Should the country seek a way out of the economic crisis through opening its subsoil treasures to foreign investment? If cuts in programs are needed to put the country's financial house in order, who should pay? Can the country continue to play the major role it undertook in leading Latin America away from hemispheric and global trade deals and in experimenting with new regional diplomatic and economic organizations?

# Chronology

**Pre-1499**   Sparsely inhabited—estimated 350,000 inhabitants

**1499–1810**   Colony of Spain; hides and cacao are chief exports

**1810**   Independence wars begin

**1813**   Simón Bolívar assumes command

**1823**   Last Spanish garrison falls in 1823

**1830**   Conservative General José Antonio Páez establishes Venezuela as independent republic; by 1888, 730 battles and twenty-six major insurrections take place

**1858–1863**   Federal War: population falls from 1.9 million to 1.6 million, heads of cattle fall from 12 million to 1.8 million

**1870–1888**   Antonio Guzmán Blanco rules as head of alliance of *caudillos*

**1899**   Andean General Cipriano Castro takes power

**1901**   Europeans blockade Venezuelan coast; United States intercedes to settle European demands

**1908–1935**   Juan Vicente Gómez, ousts Castro with U.S. support. Builds army, defeats last *caudillo* uprisings, reforms finances and pays off debt; rules with iron fist

**1922**   Oil boom commences; Gómez enriches family and cronies

**1935–1945**   Gómez dies; period of liberalization; parties emerge

**1943**   President (General) Isaías Medina reforms oil laws and forces companies to accept state's sovereign right to tax profits

**1945–1948** Rómulo Betancourt and his Democratic Action (AD) party govern; first direct elections with universal suffrage; 50–50 profit-sharing agreement between government and oil companies

**1948** Coup leads to repressive dictatorship of General Marcos Pérez Jiménez

**1958** Dictatorship overthrown; pact of Punto Fijo among parties; Betancourt, leader of AD, wins presidency in December elections

**1960–1968** Guerrilla warfare; defeat of leftist insurgency

**1973** Election of Carlos Andrés Pérez; (OPEC) oil boom begins

**1976** Oil companies nationalized; Petróleos de Venezuela S.A. (PDVSA) formed

**1983** Devaluation of bolívar marks end of oil boom; economy in free fall

**1989** Pérez wins new term, announces IMF structural adjustment; Caracazo riots in twenty-three cities; repression leaves 1,000 dead

**1992** (February 12) Colonel Hugo Chávez leads unsuccessful coup against Pérez; (November) Second failed coup

**1993** Pérez forced from office early by Congress

**1994** Rafael Caldera becomes president following break from his party, COPEI; oil company managers begin "oil opening" policy and urge break from OPEC

**1998** President Hugo Chávez elected in December as AD and COPEI support collapses

**1999** Constituent Assembly writes constitution of Bolivarian Republic of Venezuela

**2000** Chávez elected to six-year term under new constitution

**2001** Oil reform raises royalties and requires majority Venezuelan ownership of joint ventures; land reform and other measures generate middle-class protests

**2002** In April, attempted coup by opposition reversed by mass pressure unleashed from barrios and loyal military officers; in December, PDVSA executives lead three-month shutdown of oil industry; production restored by April 2003

**2003** Government launches "missions" to improve literacy and health care in barrios

**2004** Chávez wins nearly 59 percent of vote, to win recall election marked by high turnout; opposition divided and demoralized

**2005** (January) Chávez declares "twenty-first century socialism" in speech at the World Social Forum in Porto Alegre, Brazil; (December) pro-government coalition sweeps National Assembly election as divided opposition abstains

**2006** Chávez reelected with 63 percent of vote in election marked by high turnout

**2007** Chávez forms United Socialist Party of Venezuela (PSUV) but suffers first electoral defeat when package of constitutional reforms is defeated in a popular referendum

**2008** PSUV wins, but opposition gains in regional elections

**2009** Chávez wins referendum to permit indefinite reelection of the president

**2010** National Assembly elections result in an almost even split between PSUV and opposition, but PSUV retains majority in the Assembly

**2011** Chávez diagnosed with cancer, undergoes treatment in Cuba

**2012** Chávez, with 54 percent of vote, defeats Henrique Capriles Radonski in presidential election; designates Nicolás Maduro as successor as he leaves for Cuba for cancer treatment

**2013**   (March 5) Chávez dies; (April) Maduro barely defeats Capriles presidential election; opposition protests, but recount reaffirms Maduro victory

**2014**   Student protests against insecurity and economic conditions; protest intensify with dozens of deaths among protesters, security forces, and bystanders; (August) oil prices reach over $130 but enter into freefall

**2015**   Sweeping opposition victory in National Assembly elections

**2016**   Maduro approval hovers around 20 percent in polls; opposition seeks recall

# Bibliography

Betancourt, Rómulo. *Venezuela: Oil and Politics*. Boston: Houghton Mifflin, 1998.

Buxton, Julia. *The Failure of Political Reform in Venezuela*. Aldershot, UK: Ashgate, 2001.

Ciccariello-Maher, George. *Building the Commune: Radical Democracy in Venezuela*. London: Verso. 2016.

Coppedge, Michael. *Strong Parties and Lame Ducks: Presidential Partyarchy and Factionalism in Venezuela*. Stanford, CA: Stanford University Press, 1998.

Coronil, Fernando. *The Magical State: Nature, Money and Modernity in Venezuela*. Chicago: University of Chicago Press, 1997.

Ellner, Steve, and Daniel Hellinger, eds. *Venezuelan Politics in the Chávez Era: Class, Polarization, and Conflict*. Boulder, CO: Lynne Rienner, 2003.

Ewell, Judith. *Venezuela and the United States: From Monroe's Hemisphere to Petroleum's Empire*. Athens: University of Georgia Press, 1996.

Hawkins, Kirk. *Venezuela's Chavismo and Populism in Comparative Perspective*. Cambridge: Cambridge University Press, 0214.

Hellinger, Daniel. *Venezuela: Tarnished Democracy*. Boulder, CO: Westview, 1991.

Jones, Bart. *Hugo! The Hugo Chávez Story from Mud Hut to Perpetual Revolution*. Hanover, NH: Steerforth, 2007.

Kozlof, Nicolas. *Hugo Chávez. Oil, Politics and the Challenge to the U.S.* London: Palgrave MacMillan, 2007.

Lynch, John. *Simón Bolívar, A Life*. New Haven, CT: Yale University Press, 2006.

Mallén, Ana, and María Pilar García-Guadilla. *Venezuela's Polarized Politics: The Paradox of Direct Democracy under Chávez*. Boulder, CO: Lynne Rienner, 2017.

McCoy, Jennifer, and David Myers, eds. *The Unraveling of Representative Democracy in Venezuela*. Baltimore: Johns Hopkins University Press, 2004.

Mommer, Bernard. *The Political Role of National Oil Companies in Exporting Countries: The Venezuelan Case*. Oxford: Oxford Institute for Energy Studies, 1994.

Smilde, David, and Daniel Hellinger, eds. *Venezuela's Bolivarian Democracy: Participation, Politics and Culture under Chávez*. Durham, NC: Duke University Press, 2011.

Tinker-Salas, Miguel. *The Enduring Legacy: Oil, Culture, and Society in Venezuela*. Durham, NC: Duke University Press, 2009.

Velasco, Alejandro. Barrio *Rising: Urban Popular Rising and the Making of Modern Venezuela*. Berkeley: University of California Press, 2015.

Wilpert, Gregory. *Changing Venezuela by Taking Power: The History and Politics of the Chávez Government*. London: Verso, 2007.

## FILMS AND VIDEOS

*¿Puedo Hablar?* United States, 2007. Documentary about 2006 presidential election attributes Chávez's popularity to genuine concern for poor but raises issues about his personal accumulation of power.

*The Revolution Will Not Be Televised*. Ireland, 2003. Irish film crew in Caracas to make pro-Chávez documentary finds itself in the presidential palace during the April 2002 coup.

*Shoot to Kill*. Venezuela, 1990. Carlos Azpurua's feature film on violence and law in a Caracas barrio.

## WEBSITES

http://www.derechos.org.ve/   The best independent reports on Venezuela are from the respected human rights agency PROVEA (website is in Spanish)

http://www.venezuelananalysis.com/   A well-organized and readable English-language website with a decidedly pro-Chávez slant

http://www.analitica.com/   More staid but clearly anti-Chavista

http://www.petroleumworld.com/   Oil-related developments affecting Venezuela

http://www.aporrea.org/   Venezuela's burgeoning grassroots media sector

Map of
**BOLIVIA**

| 0 | 100 | 200 km |
| 0 | 100 | 200 miles |

66

60

BRAZIL

Rio Mamore

Riberalta

Cobija

PERU

Amazon Basin

Rio Beni

Trinidad

Rio Mamore

Lake
Titicaca

A

N

*LA PAZ

D

E

Cochabamba

Nevado
Sajama

Oruro

Santa
Cruz

S

Sucre

Puerto
Aguirre

Rio Lauca

Potosi

ATACAMA DESERT

A
l
t
i
p
l
a
n
o

SOUTH
PACIFIC
OCEAN

Tarija

PARAGUAY

Rio Paraguay

CHILE

ARGENTINA

66

60

12

12

16

16

# EIGHTEEN

# BOLIVIA

## *Waltraud Q. Morales*

## Introduction

Bolivia, one of Latin America's most ethnically diverse and up-and-coming countries, remains an outlier among its neighbors as conservative political and socioeconomic governance reclaims the region. Landlocked within the heart of the continent and a land of ancient indigenous civilizations and great geographical and social contrasts, Bolivia represents a model of radical change and an ongoing experiment in populist governance. A long history of rebellious instability, social inequality, and oppression of the Indian majority culminated in 1952 in a national social revolution. Despite major reforms, the revolution stalled. In the 1990s, however, the rise of militant social movements and the election in 2005 of Evo Morales Ayma as Bolivia's first indigenous president initiated an historic "refounding" revolution. Implementation of a radical new constitution and populist policies of economic redistribution and indigenous empowerment ended the hegemony of traditional elites and restructured the state and the economy.

Re-elected in 2009 and 2014, Evo Morales is Bolivia's longest-serving president with over a decade in office to consolidate reforms and ensure his legacy beyond 2020 when his third term ends. Morales further sought to amend the constitution and retain the presidency until 2025. Despite his continued popularity, voters narrowly rejected a nationwide referendum in February 2016 to revise term limits and allow Morales another consecutive term. This unexpected defeat delivered a serious blow to Morales and his Movement Toward Socialism (MAS) government and loyal social movement supporters; it precipitated urgent questions of succession and heightened uncertainty over the leadership and the future of the Refounding Revolution.

## Geopolitical Overview

Bolivia is the sixth-largest country in Latin America—larger than Texas and California combined—and in 2017 had a population of 11 million people. The country is diverse in topography and climate, ranging from the frigid high Andes and Andean plateau (Altiplano) and the temperate intermountain valleys to the lush, tropical savannahs and forests of the Amazon basin. Bolivia shares with Peru Lake Titicaca, South America's highest and largest lake. Ancient Indian peoples of the Altiplano developed hundreds of potato varieties and tended various camelid animals like llama, alpaca, and vicuña—as their descendants do today. At lower elevations, the rich earth provided fruits, vegetables, and grains that sustained the inhabitants.

Bolivians argue that the country is a prisoner of its landlocked geography and the post-independence territorial losses that have hindered economic development. For most of its postconquest history, the economy was dependent on rich silver and tin mines in the western spine of the Andean range. Mining was both a blessing and curse, skewing economic development and the country's social and political life. The apt description of Bolivia as "a beggar on a throne of gold" characterizes the country's extreme dependence on the extractive, boom-to-bust, mining mono-culture. Mining's demand for cheap labor ensured the enslavement of Bolivia's majority highland indigenous Aymara and Quechua peoples. The infamous Cerro Rico of the colonial city of Potosí once provided Spain and industrializing Europe mountains of silver for their monetary and mercantilist expansion.

During the heyday of the tin era in the first half of the twentieth century, Bolivian tin mines provided 30 percent of the world's annual production. Although current production ranges around 10 percent of exports, mining remains an important, if greatly diminished, economic activity. Despite the depletion of the major mines after the great tin collapse in 1985, small-scale miners continue to eke out a meager livelihood scavenging what remains of the great silver and tin empires. The decline of the tin economy and massive layoffs and mine closures promoted another resource boom—illegal coca leaf cultivation. Bolivia's traditional and legal coca leaf economy soon became enmeshed in illegal production serving the Andean and global drug trade. Thousands of unemployed indigenous and mestizo (people of mixed European and indigenous heritage) miners migrated to the central and eastern lowlands to cultivate coca leaf. Without transportation and basic infrastructure, coca was the only marketable crop in high demand. Soon coca was shipped raw or semiprocessed as cocaine paste to the refiners, middlemen, and exporters who were part of the Colombian drug cartels. For a time, millions of dollars in illicit drug profits fed state coffers and staved off poverty but also distorted long-term economic development.

Traditionally, wealth and power meant land, which belonged to a handful of land-owners, probably less than 2 percent of the post-independence and prerevolutionary population. The predominantly Indian peoples of the Altiplano, inter-Andean valleys, and semitropical and tropical lowlands were largely landless, having been stripped of their communal holdings (or *ayllus*) by the twentieth century. On the eve of the 1952 revolution, Indian peasants (called *Indios* before the revolution and *campesinos* after) were engaged primarily in agriculture but were basically landless while some 6 percent of landowners held 92 percent of cultivable land. Despite significant land reform in the decade after 1952, reconcentration of ownership since then has generated a powerful Landless Movement (Movimiento Sin Tierra; MST), especially in the Oriente, or eastern lowlands.

Historically, regionalism was a dominant force because political power inevitably followed economic power. Before the silver boom of the sixteenth century, Sucre—still Bolivia's constitutional capital—was also the political capital. Later Potosí—the city of silver—became a thriving metropolis and the colony's political-economic center. With the demise of the silver economy and rise of the great tin empires in the nineteenth century, both economic and political power shifted to La Paz—today's de facto capital—but only after a brief civil war in 1898. By the end of the twentieth century, the relocation of Bolivia's population and economic center to Santa Cruz and its wealth to the Camba (lowlander) elites has shifted political power away from La Paz. However, the shift is incomplete and is contested by the Kollas, or highlanders of the Altiplano, especially by President Morales and the Aymara and Quechua indigenous social movements that he represents.

Because Bolivia's population originally centered on the Altiplano, often it is described as an Andean and Indian country. However, two-thirds of Bolivia's land mass lies in the semitropical and tropical eastern lowlands, or Oriente. Migration and economic expansion, especially in the department and city of Santa Cruz (today Bolivia's largest city), shifted the economic and much of the political power away from the indigenous and mestizo populations of the highlands and into the hands of the European-looking lowlanders. President Morales's reforms directly challenged those interests, and inflamed regional and racist tensions.

Economics, as well as geography and demographics, fuel the ongoing conflict. In the Oriente, land is concentrated in the hands of cattle barons and soybean producers, and the expanding hydrocarbon sector, especially natural gas, is located there. This region, historically rife with secessionist movements, in many ways represents the "other," "white" Bolivia. Nevertheless, the Oriente is also home to marginalized indigenous groups that have become politically mobilized in the last two decades through the land reform movement. In 2011, lowland Indian communities fiercely opposed a proposed road through the Isiboro Sécure National Park and Indigenous Territory (Territorio Indígena y Parque Nacional Isiboro Sécure; TIPNIS) and challenged the official Morales–MAS development model.

## Early History

From 7500 B.C.E. until 1532 C.E. the pre-Columbian empires of the Tiwanaku, Aymara, and Incan peoples dominated the territory from the Pacific coast to the Andean highlands. Despite the absence of written records, these early indigenous cultures were rich in oral traditions and artifacts. They domesticated the Andean llamas and alpacas and developed a complex agricultural system of farming and grain supply. Of these cultures, the Tiwanakan peoples were ancestors of the Aymara, the pre-Incan Indians of Bolivia, who had established a vast empire and capital at Tiwanaku. Their cosmology and religion influenced the Incan and other pre-Incan peoples, who copied their complex social and economic organization. The civilization's demise is a mystery—perhaps ecological disaster or conquest. In its place on the Altiplano around Lake Titicaca emerged the regional kingdoms of the Aymara.

Around 1,460 soldiers of the Quechua Empire of the Incas defeated the decentralized Aymaras and, despite numerous rebellions, incorporated them into their Pan-Andean empire of 8 to 10 million inhabitants. The Incan social structure evolved into a rigid pyramid of agriculturally based classes wherein land was held in common through *ayllus* (agricultural cooperatives), and royal monopolies controlled the mines and animal and forests resources. An ancient involuntary labor system, the *mita*, provided the armies of workers and soldiers for the empire. By the sixteenth century, despite its high development and relative prosperity, the empire began to decline. Assisted by treachery and firepower, the Spanish invaders conquered it in 1532.

## Colonial Rule (1532–1809)

During the sixteenth century, the Spanish established colonial Bolivia's governing center on the mineral-rich Altiplano, under the Audiencia of Charcas (Upper Peru) with its administrative seat in Sucre. Mining dominated the colonial economy and established a two-class society of wealthy Spaniards and impoverished Indians. By 1650, Potosí, the Villa Real of Carlos V, was the richest and most populated city of the New World reportedly with 160,000 inhabitants. Mineral exploitation, however, dislocated the indigenous population, distorted the rural economy, and increased class and race inequities. Although there was a caste system under Incan rule, the *encomienda* system of the Spanish overlords destroyed the indigenous way of life, and abuses of the *encomienda* and *mita* worsened the exploitation of the indigenous underclass. In the mines, hundreds of thousands Indian slaves perished because of subhuman conditions and disease—perhaps 15 percent of the population in the first fifty years of the colony. And on the land, Indians served as the feudal aristocracy's serf labor, their lives determined by their overlord. In 1776, administrative centralization relegated the relative autonomy of the Audiencia of Charcas to the newly established Viceroyalty of Buenos Aires. This reorganization and the exclusive rights of the Spanish-born to official positions and property ownership reduced the influence of local elites. Ultimately, the French Enlightenment and Spanish colonial misgovernment, which had provoked the bloody indigenous uprising by Túpac Katari in 1781 and 1783, inspired the *mestizo* and *creole* independence movement.

## Independence and *Caudillo* Rule (1809–1879)

In July 1809, an independence uprising in La Paz, led by Pedro Domingo Murillo, established a popular citizens' council and a governing junta but was quickly quashed by troops from Lima and a countercoup in La Paz. However, the next year when the Viceroyalty of La Plata in Buenos Aires rebelled, uprisings erupted throughout Bolivia. Although Bolivian forces fought the Fifteen Years' War, liberation awaited major victories elsewhere by Generals José de San Martín, Antonio José de Sucre, and Simón Bolívar. Finally, the Battle of Tumusla in April 1825 assured Alto Peruvian independence from Spain. Bolívar never intended an autonomous Alto Perú; however, as competition among postindependence power centers began to interfere with his plans of a united South America, the idea of an independent Bolivia as a buffer state gained favor.

In July 1825 highland patriots assembled to decide their future: independence, incorporation with Lower Peru, or annexation by Argentina. Since both Peru and Argentina now supported an independent Alto Perú, the highland delegates had only Bolívar's opposition to overcome. To that end, they named the new country after Bolívar and declared him its first president. Official independence of the Republic of Bolívar became August 6, 1825, celebrating Bolívar's victory at the Battle of Junín. Despite being elected for life, Bolívar served as president for mere months and soon returned to Gran Colombia to pursue his dream of a greater South America, which never materialized.

Bolivia's first constitutionally elected president was José Antonio de Sucre (1826–1828), who struggled to rebuild the war-torn and bankrupt country but was soon removed when Peru invaded in 1828. Finally, the 1829 election of Andrés de Santa Cruz realized a decade of relative stability and a series of legal, educational, and fiscal reforms. Santa Cruz had a Quechua mother who claimed to be the direct descendant of the last Incan ruler; thus he is considered Bolivia's first mestizo *caudillo*. Santa Cruz dreamed of a greater Peruvian–Bolivian confederation that would mirror the ancient Incan political system, and he briefly unified the two countries in 1836. In so doing he upset the fragile South American status quo; both Argentina and Chile declared war and exiled Santa Cruz and abolished the confederation in 1839.

Great political turmoil followed as military strongmen or *caudillos* fought for control. In 1848, General Manuel Isidoro Belzú seized the presidency. A mestizo with pronounced Indian features, he was affectionately called "Tata Belzu" by the indigenous masses. He was the typical larger-than-life *caudillo*, terrified of assassination and revolt, but whose populist policies courted the Indians and the oppressed classes. Finally, José María Linares became Bolivia's first civilian president in 1854 and pursued sweeping fiscal, administrative, and judicial reforms. He turned to authoritarian rule to thwart the incessant coup plotting; nevertheless, in 1861, General José María de Achá, his minister of war, overthrew him and became president.

In 1864, Mariano Melgarejo, the most reviled of Bolivia's mestizo tyrants whose brutality and corruption earned him the epithet *el caudillo bárbaro*, became president and initiated events that culminated in the loss of Bolivia's rich Matto Grosso region to Brazil and Atacama province to Chile. His secret deals with Chilean nitrate companies and the 1866 Mejillones Treaty hastened the War of the Pacific. That same year, his unpopular land decree seized and sold off communal Indian lands and instigated peasant riots. In 1871, General Agustín Morales overthrew Melgarejo and annulled the agrarian law and renegotiated the disastrous agreements.

Finally, in 1873, the civilian governments of Adolfo Ballivián and Tomás Frías briefly curtailed the military rivalries to resolve the looming territorial crisis with Chile. Nevertheless, the hawks in the army and General Hilarión Daza seized power. Foolishly underestimating the Chilean threat, in 1878 Bolivia's Congress levied a 10 cent tax on nitrate exports by the British-Chilean Nitrates and Railroad Company of Antofagasta. This tax provided Chile and allied foreign capitalists the perfect pretext for war.

# The War of the Pacific (1879–1884)

More than a territorial dispute, the War of the Pacific was the first of several resource wars that dismembered and impoverished Bolivia. Geopolitical rivalry and economic imperialism were two important external causes, but Bolivia's internal instability and regionalism were also to blame. The Altiplano remained the country's center of gravity, and the fledgling republic, weakened by revolts and corrupt and inept leaders, failed to exert control over its distant provinces and resources. Until the discovery of fertilizer riches, the Pacific coast was sparsely settled and ignored by highland governments. And the poverty and backward economy meant there was scant Bolivian capital available to develop the guano and nitrate resources. Meanwhile, Chilean entrepreneurs and British commercial interests quickly formed a profitable partnership mining and exporting the natural agricultural fertilizers from Bolivia's Atacama region to European markets. Chile was also a fierce rival of Peru and Argentina and was intent on dominating the Pacific Coast.

Guano and nitrate deposits were discovered in 1840. Competing Chilean–Bolivian territorial claims provoked conflicts in 1857 and 1863, but Bolivia was simply too weak to defend its sovereignty militarily and turned to diplomacy. So, in 1866 the First Treaty of Limitation between Bolivia and Chile (the Mejillones Treaty) established the boundary at the 24th parallel and a shared exploitation zone between the 23rd and 25th parallels. A Second Treaty of Limitation in 1874 ended the zones of shared economic exploitation and, most important, exempted Chilean companies operating in Bolivian territory from any new taxes for the next twenty-five years.

Unfortunately, in 1878, President Daza implemented a 10 cent tax on each hundred pounds of nitrates exported from Bolivian territory, violating the 1874 treaty. In response, the British-Chilean Nitrates and Railroad Company of Antofagasta refused to pay the tax, and the Chileans sent a battleship, which seized the Bolivian port of Antofagasta in February 1879. Chile gave Bolivia a twenty-four-hour ultimatum to accept arbitration. When Bolivia refused, Chile occupied the entire Pacific coast south of the 23rd parallel and, in April 1879, declared war against Bolivia and Peru.

Bolivia's forces were demolished early on; they were unprepared, and their leaders were inept and irresponsible. By 1880 Bolivia was spent, and Peru was forced to bear the brunt of the war. Finally, in October 1883, Peru signed a separate peace treaty with Chile, ceding a large swath of its coastal territory. Bolivia signed a truce in 1884, which left Chile in de facto possession of all Bolivia's coastal territory. A final peace treaty was not signed until 1904, and even this treaty, as far as Bolivia is concerned, remains in dispute.

In large part, the War of the Pacific was a natural consequence of growing Chilean hegemony and the aggressive expansion of global capitalism. Nevertheless, Bolivia's misgovernment contributed to the country's defeat. In reaction, civilians took over.

# Republican Government (1880–1932)

Civilian rule centered on competing elites and their political parties representing special ethnic and class interests. These civilian politicians were members of a new white and mestizo ruling class of silver- and tin-mining barons, their business associates, and remnants of the old landed aristocracy. For fifty years, until the Great Depression and Bolivia's tragic involvement in the Chaco War, they relied on a system of limited franchise and control of government by personalist leaders beholden to the mining plutocracy. In effect, this made Bolivia "a state that tin owned." And despite its serious drawbacks, this ruling system provided the necessary political stability for state formation and economic growth.

Two major political parties developed during the War of the Pacific. The Liberal Party wanted to continue the war and the Conservative Party pressed for a negotiated peace. The Conservatives represented the interests of the silver magnates who dominated Bolivian politics until the Civil War of 1899, which ended the era of the Conservative Party oligarchy and the regional influence of Potosí and Sucre— Bolivia's official capital. The Liberals, victors in the regional clash, were allied with the up-and-coming tin-mining elite and the increasing economic power of the highland industrial and commercial interests in Oruro and La Paz, which became Bolivia's effective capital after the revolt. In addition, Liberals favored secular and federalist rule, and Conservatives supported Roman Catholicism and unitary government. However, these were superficial differences; leaders of both parties represented civilian rule and the predominantly white, privileged class. In principle, both parties believed that constitutional government would bring the stability and national unity needed for economic prosperity.

With the franchise limited to less than 5 percent of the population, instability and violence were contained as partisan, and electoral disputes replaced military coups. But representative government remained precarious as Bolivian politicians generally lacked a civic culture of compromise and honest stewardship. Nevertheless, despite the elite infighting and outright electoral manipulation by the ruling party, the opposition could obtain a sizeable legislative representation in the early decades of republican rule. After a relatively free election in 1884, the election of 1888 turned violent, and the Conservative Party winner controlled the presidency until the Liberal revolt of 1899. In turn, from 1900 to 1920 the Liberal Party oligarchy monopolized power until a coup by disaffected Liberals, who had founded the new Republican Party and ended the Liberal monopoly.

By 1920 the regional and economic power base that dominated the country until 1952 was firmly in place. Between 1900 and 1927 the world demand for industrial metals—especially tin—reached its zenith. The incredible profits bankrolled Bolivia's "Big Three" tin magnates—Carlos Aramayo, Mauricio Hochschild, and Simon Patiño—and their control of the country's economy and government. The Patiño holdings alone provided 50 percent of Bolivia's total tin production. A mestizo, "white collar" mine worker, Patiño struck it rich with a small mine in Potosí and consolidated his mining empire by buying out British and Chilean mining interests in 1910 and in 1924.

The state treasury was so dependent on the low taxes on tin exports that the Big Three tin barons in effect exerted a virtual veto power over the government. Tin production, which was controlled by the companies and the volatile global market, increased Bolivia's economic dependency. The state promoted free market and free trade policies that benefited and enriched the mining capitalists but assuaged the governments' chronic budget deficits. However, the government was in a bind: tin provided essential employment, foreign exchange, and government revenue. Reforms were not only impossible but also unthinkable as long as the private tin companies "owned" most politicians and public officials and were protected by the conservative military. This entrenched political-economic control of the tin oligarchy and associated establishment interests was known as *la Rosca*.

The Republican Party's seizure of power in 1920 marked the shift from two-party oligarchic rule to a volatile populist multiparty system. The Republicans soon split into the rival factions of the aristocrat Daniel Salamanca and populist Bautista Saavedra. As president, Saavedra (1921–1925) put down labor and Indian unrest, and he indebted Bolivia to Wall Street bankers and encouraged Standard Oil of New Jersey to prospect for oil in the Chaco region. The opposition, including the new Nationalist Party of Hernán Siles, which won the 1925 elections, denounced his policies.

By 1930, the country was in deep economic and political crisis. The U.S. stock market crash a year earlier precipitated the collapse of global tin prices. With the treasury virtually bankrupt and the economy in shambles, the country's dependence on tin became a double-edged sword. In July 1930 President Siles attempted to change the constitution and remain in office, but a bloody citizens' revolt, the "constitutionalist" revolution, removed him. Daniel Salamanca was elected president. In all respects his presidency was a failure. Not only were his domestic policies ineffective and repressive but his foreign policy was also catastrophic. He aggressively expanded Bolivian control over the Chaco region and escalated a minor border clash with Paraguay into war.

Already by the eve of war, major changes were underway. The 1930 revolt marked a shift in Bolivian politics from palace coups to populist mass action and direct street democracy. The economic depression and the war undermined the political power of the tin oligarchy and made it vulnerable to a populist and nationalist backlash. Most important, the war turned the military against the Rosca and its political hegemony.

## The Chaco War and the Coming of Revolution (1932–1952)

Bolivia's defeat in the Chaco War created the social and political preconditions for revolution in 1952. The defeat was an unexpected and devastating blow to Bolivian national pride. Bolivians had expected a quick, easy victory over Paraguay, which they considered a weaker, third-rate power. As with the War of the Pacific a century earlier, the war was not simply for territory but for resources. The Gran Chaco was largely a sparsely populated wasteland of a quarter-million square miles in the heart of the continent, and the boundary dispute between Bolivia and Paraguay preceded independence. In 1920 rumors of rich oil deposits revived the competition between the two countries, and to this day many Bolivians believe that foreign oil companies, Standard Oil and Royal Dutch Shell, had a surreptitious role in the war.

A hawk, President Salamanca surrounded himself with like-minded ultranationalists. He had pilloried his predecessor for cowardice and was obsessed with restoring Bolivia's honor. Despite the economic recession, he sank millions of pesos that Bolivia did not have into armaments, preparing for the right moment to strike against Paraguay. As diplomatic efforts stalled and tensions escalated, on July 18, 1932, Salamanca ordered the army to preemptively seize a strategic water source in the desert-like region. The war had begun. Despite speeches and parades, the war was not popular; the general staff had warned that the country was not ready and that many Bolivians and Paraguayans favored a diplomatic solution. The military's warnings proved prescient as the war bogged down into a litany of defeats. In early 1935 Paraguayan forces had advanced within miles of Bolivia's oil centers and the war's command center. The Bolivians drove them back and recaptured the oil region. With both sides spent, a protocol of peace and ceasefire was signed in June 1935.

Why had Bolivia lost the war when observers (including the Paraguayans) had anticipated victory? Who was to blame for defeat? Bolivia in 1932 had three times Paraguay's population and seven times its soldiers, and Bolivia outgunned Paraguay by as much as ten to one. From the outset, military and civilian dissension, corruption, and incompetence were to blame. On the eve of war, the general staff resigned in protest because Bolivia was not prepared for war. There had been four commanders in three years; three armies were destroyed in the field; and, in the middle of the war, the army mutinied and arrested the president. Defeat was costly. Over 100,000 men died on both sides, and both countries were crippled with massive national debts. However, for Bolivia the social and political consequences of the Chaco defeat were revolutionary. The war and defeat were catalysts for fundamental social change that swept away the tin oligarchy and the traditional political class and began the gradual integration of Bolivia's indigenous peoples into national life. War and defeat created both the psychological and structural conditions for radical change.

In the postwar period, an antiestablishment political coalition emerged composed of veterans, unionized labor, peasant syndicates, and student activists, led by two populist military reformers, Colonels David Toro and Germán Busch. Foremost, the military reformers were nationalists who also stood for social justice, economic development, and popular participation. Anti-imperialism united them; they rejected the stranglehold of foreign capital and the tin Rosca on Bolivia; and they were harbingers of the 1952 revolution. In 1936 Colonels David Toro and Germán Busch, who believed that Bolivia's problems could not be solved within the traditional political system but were the direct consequences of that system, preempted the May elections with a military coup. As president of a civilian–military junta, Toro promised to defend the interests of workers and veterans, reduce poverty, and restore Bolivia's economic sovereignty. His government had allied with old-style Republican Socialists and a new Socialist Party of syndicalist and Marxist persuasions. The mix was highly volatile.

Fearing a coup against him, Toro made a bold move: he nationalized the U.S.-owned Standard Oil of Bolivia. The 1937 expropriation was the first seizure of a U.S. company in Latin America, and it was immensely popular: Standard Oil had come to represent all the evils of imperialism. Toro and Busch favored nationalist and corporatist economic policies and rejected the special privileges of the tin interests and foreign investors. They were soon under attack by conservatives and radicals alike. As partisan dissension increased, Busch overthrew Toro in July 1937 but upheld the nationalization. He institutionalized the reforms of the 1936 revolution through a constitutional convention, which elected him president in May 1938, and began to draft a new constitution. For the first time, the political left took part.

The 1938 Constitution was radical and progressive. It established the social function of private property and state control over the economy. An educational reform promised free, universal education and indigenous schools. The 1939 Busch Labor Code granted the right to unionize and strike and improved working conditions. However, unable to control the political turmoil that the reforms unleashed, in April 1939 Busch assumed dictatorial powers. Before his suicide in 1939, he nationalized the Mining Bank and secured the state's right over the nation's mineral wealth.

In the end, the Toro and Busch constitutional reforms were beaten back by the forces of financial privilege and radical extremism alike—a valuable lesson for later reformers and revolutionaries. The military was unable to impose social change without the support of a united civil society, and postwar political life was hopelessly polarized and contentious. The war had discredited the traditional oligarchic parties, allowing antiestablishment nationalist and Marxist parties to emerge and challenge them.

Formed in 1941, the Nationalist Revolutionary Movement (Movimiento Nacionalista Revolucionario; MNR) spearheaded the 1952 revolution and was the most important nationalist party. Its middle-class founders were student activists, war veterans, and journalists who denounced imperialism and the Rosca as the enemies of the people. Led by Víctor Paz Estenssoro—Bolivia's first revolutionary president—the MNR program emphasized its patriotic, socialist, revolutionary, and nationalist character. A central goal was the country's economic independence. Another nationalist party, the Bolivian Socialist Falange (Falange Socialista Boliviana; FSB) was founded in 1937 and survived several decades after 1952 as the only organized opposition to the MNR. Influenced by Spanish fascism, the party was fundamentally anticommunist and elitist.

Several Marxist parties were also founded in the 1930s and 1940s but lost importance after the revolution. The Party of the Revolutionary Left (Partido de la Izquierda Revolucionaria; PIR) had antecedents in the leftist student and workers movements and mirrored the MNR, proposing a multiclass, nationalist bourgeois revolution. Its program called for a statist economy, agrarian reform, and nationalization of mining and petroleum resources.

The Revolutionary Workers' Party (Partido Obrero Revolucionario) was more radical than the PIR. Its leader, Tristán Marof, provided the historic phrase—"mines to the state, land to the Indian"—that became the fighting words of the 1952 revolution. The party favored a proletarian socialist revolution. Although the Revolutionary Workers' Party appealed primarily to university students and middle-class Marxist intellectuals, it became the party of the Bolivian Mine Workers' Federation (Federación Sindical de Trabajadores Mineros de Bolivia; FSTMB) that was founded in 1944.

Threatened by postwar radicalism, the oligarchy formed a coalition of traditional parties, propertied classes, and conservative military personnel and began to dismantle the Busch reforms. In 1940 the oligarchy's candidate and popular war hero, General Enrique Peñaranda, won the presidency handily. He established warm relations with the United States and received substantial economic and military assistance; as a result, U.S. influence over Bolivia's internal affairs increased. Bolivia became the major supplier of tin for the U.S. war effort and signed a tin agreement favoring the United States. The Peñaranda government also renewed debt payments (suspended since 1931) to U.S. banks and indemnified Standard Oil for the expropriation of its properties.

These conservative policies mobilized opposition. As dissension in Congress and labor unrest increased, the government declared martial law and cracked down on the MNR and strikers. In December 1942, a massacre at the Catavi Mine left hundreds of striking miners dead. Such repression forged an alliance among the miners, labor, the MNR, and the reformist military. In December 1943 Lieutenant Colonel Gualberto Villarroel overthrew Peñaranda and was elected president in August 1944. The new government included the MNR and younger officers of the nationalistic military lodge. The United States and the oligarchy denounced Villarroel's government as "Nazi." But the reformers were ideologically divided and confused: the common denominator was nationalism and anti-imperialism. The government stood with the dispossessed—miners, labor, and the indigenous peoples. Villarroel held the first Indian congress in 1945 that abolished involuntary servitude. Although the reform was not enforced, it provided hope and momentum to the indigenous movement.

The oligarchy instigated an uprising in July 1946. A mob attacked the presidential palace, murdered Villarroel, and hung his body from a lamp post in the main plaza. For the next six years the oligarchy and conservative military repressed all political and social opposition. In 1949 a Catavi mine massacre left several hundred striking miners dead, and a brief MNR-led civil war ended violently. However, in May 1951 the MNR presidential candidate, Víctor Paz Estenssoro, ran from exile and won a plurality. Before the National Congress could decide the outcome, the oligarchy handed the government to the military, which annulled the elections and appointed a general as interim president. These unconstitutional actions, culminating two decades of frustrated reforms, prompted a revolutionary uprising.

## From Revolution to Military Dictatorship (1952–1982)

The Bolivian Revolution began with the Battle of La Paz on April 9, 1952. The revolt by the MNR, workers, and miners was aided by the city's police force, which provided the rebels with arms. After three days of heavy fighting, the urban rebellion triumphed and Víctor Paz Estenssoro returned from exile and was sworn in as president on April 16. As Latin America's second social revolution since the Mexican Revolution, the Bolivian Revolution initiated radical political and socioeconomic change. Among the revolution's major reforms were universal suffrage and education, land reform, nationalization of the mines, and incorporation of Indians into national life. By abolishing literacy tests, the 1952 voting law established real democracy for the first time as eligible voters quintupled to a million voters. Most of these were illiterate indigenous peoples, who comprised 60 percent of the population and had never been accorded full citizenship rights. In 1951 a mere 5 percent of

Bolivians voted; in 1960 it had risen to 26 percent. To win elections, political parties would now have to appeal to an increased and more diverse electorate.

The 1953 Agrarian Reform Decree abolished feudal debt servitude and restored the collective properties of indigenous communities. However, because the MNR had delayed enactment, the reform legalized premature seizures by indigenous peasants and confiscated only large estates. Nevertheless, land reform broke the hold of the landed aristocracy and helped empower the Indian. In 1952 land ownership was highly inequitable: some 5 percent of landowners held over 90 percent of the land. Of the over 70 percent of Bolivians in agriculture, most were indigenous peasants who were largely landless.

The 1952 Act of Bolivia's Economic Independence nationalized major mining enterprises and created the state Bolivian Mining Corporation (Corporación Minera de Bolivia; COMIBOL). The state now controlled most of the country's tin production and foreign exchange earnings, and although the economic impact was huge, the benefits to the government and people of Bolivia were less than anticipated. First, to gain diplomatic recognition and economic assistance from the United States, the MNR government (against the opposition of the radical labor sector of the party) compensated the tin barons at a significant loss to the treasury. Second, by 1952 the private mines were aging and had limited production and capitalization so that, in effect, the state assumed additional expenses and liabilities. Lastly, Bolivia was in an economic crisis because of the drastic cuts in the U.S. tin quota. On the other hand, U.S. aid to Bolivia, among the most generous in the region, was conditional and served to control and moderate the revolution. For example, the government's new Petroleum Code privileged U.S. corporate investment over the Bolivian State Petroleum Enterprise. U.S. aid was also linked to the draconian stabilization program imposed by the International Monetary Fund (IMF) in 1956 to control crippling inflation. Thus, despite revolutionary rhetoric, MNR policies could not achieve the country's economic independence.

Opponents' charges of communism notwithstanding, the revolution was primarily nationalist and was led by a middle-class party. MNR leaders had forged a multiclass coalition of intellectuals, students, miners, workers, and peasants; indeed, Víctor Paz Estenssoro had argued that a Bolivian revolution would succeed only by a broad alliance of classes. However, the party's ideological and class diversity—an asset in making the revolution—became a liability once in power. The MNR's original program of national autonomy and economic development was moderate and purposely vague, but the alliance with workers and miners and the struggle for power radicalized the party. Nevertheless, as the government's revolutionary legislation transformed the landscape of traditional Bolivia, the MNR became more divided between moderate and radical wings.

Influenced by the Mexican model, the MNR attempted to institutionalize the revolution by a corporatist system of party control over civil society and the military. The MNR government created a new military loyal to the party and co-opted national peasant and labor unions. To harness the powerful labor movement, the MNR formed the Bolivian Workers' Central (Central Obrero Boliviano; COB) and affiliated labor with the MNR, including the largest union of mine workers, the FSTMB. Although the leftist MNR labor leader Juan Lechín Oquendo headed both unions, the party's hold over labor remained partial. Not only was the proletarian left at odds with the MNR's mainstream, middle-class orientation, but also labor zealously guarded its autonomy.

In the rural sector, the MNR government founded the National Peasant Confederation (Confederación Nacional de Trabajadores Campesinos de Bolivia; CNTCB). Nevertheless, indigenous peasant leaders were suspicious of political parties, and, despite MNR affiliation, peasant organizations could not always be controlled. Instead, as with labor, the MNR exerted its influence indirectly and contained the potentially powerful indigenous movement by manipulating internal leadership and factional struggles. This divisive governing strategy, rather than providing a loyal base for the MNR government, split the party. During the presidency of Hernán Siles Zuazo (1956–1960), the party's ruling coalition was fragmented further as the government turned against labor interests and ordered the military to quell peasant unrest.

The MNR was composed of three factions: the pragmatic reformers of Víctor Paz, the conservative nationalists of Hernán Siles, and the proletarian left of Juan Lechín. By 1960 the MNR was unraveling as sectors split off and formed independent parties. A governing pact had promised each leader a presidential term, but the pact was broken when Lechín was denied his turn and Paz was re-elected in 1960 and 1964, ironically to reduce party dissension and maintain U.S. support. By 1964, with only the Paz wing of the original MNR remaining, the party's failure to unite Bolivian society and to institutionalize the revolution invited a military counterrevolution.

A junta of officers of the reorganized army and Air Force General René Barrientos Ortuño removed Paz Estenssoro. A key motivation behind the coup was the need for social order; days earlier the army had clashed with striking miners, students, and teachers. Barrientos, in a populist, charismatic style not unlike that of Evo Morales, cultivated the Quechua indigenous leaders of his native Cochabamba and justified the military takeover as a restoration of the revolution. In 1966 Barrientos was elected president with the help of his new Military–Campesino Pact. This alliance gave him (and subsequent military presidents) the ability to control civil society, especially the miners and proletarian left, and impede the return of civilian democratic rule. Although Barrientos preserved major reforms, he pursued conservative and repressive policies. Military takeover of and bloody confrontations in the mines and military administration of the unions "disciplined" labor. A new investment code and probusiness climate favored U.S. corporations and the new homegrown moneyed elite. The military, imbued with U.S. counterinsurgency training, viewed any political opposition as communist subversion. This was the political and social climate when Ernesto "Ché" Guevara launched his guerrilla foco experiment in Bolivia in 1967.

Ché Guevara misunderstood the Bolivian reality and miscalculated the opposition to Barrientos. As a result, his attempt to spark a popular insurgency in Bolivia, which would provoke an aggressive, Vietnam-style U.S. military intervention and incite a continental-wide revolution, failed. The clandestine guerrilla front established in Bolivia's inaccessible and isolated southeastern jungles never generated more than a handful of recruits or the curiosity of local inhabitants. An effective counterinsurgency effort among the Bolivian military, the U.S. military, and the CIA ended in Guevara's capture and death in October 1967. This was Barrientos's finest hour; subsequently, his hold on the government slipped, and he died unexpectedly in a helicopter crash in 1969.

After his death, a brief civilian interregnum was cut short by General Alfredo Ovando Candia, a nationalist reformer intrigued by the Peruvian military model of "revolution from above." Ovando organized a civilian–military cabinet of the "national left" and reversed Barrientos's policies. Labor unions were permitted to reorganize, miners' wages were increased, and civil liberties were restored. However, the leftist ruling coalition of progressive military and young civilian reformers was unstable and lacked broad support. In a popular move in October 1969, Ovando nationalized the installations of U.S. Gulf Oil, which had paid close to $2 million to the Barrientos government for special concession in oil and gas production. Gulf (and the major oil producers) retaliated with a boycott of Bolivian crude, causing the Ovando government to lose $14 million in revenues. In turn, the United States severely reduced economic aid. In September 1970, a besieged Ovando promised Gulf Oil $78 million in compensation.

A month later, General Juan José Torres seized power and forged ahead with his military-led revolutionary populism. Torres summoned a Popular Assembly of progressive and Marxist parties and social movements, which debated and enacted revolutionary policies. As the country became more ideologically polarized, direct action by students, and property seizures by workers and peasants contributed to instability and violence. Finally, in August 1971, the conservative military sector of Hugo Banzer Suárez, supported by the regional business interests in Santa Cruz, terminated Torres's radical experiment.

President Banzer patterned his elitist and authoritarian rule—a Bolivian-style bureaucratic authoritarianism—on that of the Brazilian military and its brand of repressive order and progress. While Banzer's policies protected the newly prosperous middle class and economic elite of the Media Luna (southeastern lowlands, especially Santa Cruz) whose interests in mining, import–export, petroleum, and agribusiness fueled economic growth, he repressed labor, peasants, students, and most political parties. By 1974 he dispensed with democratic pretense altogether and in an *auto-golpe* established a personalist dictatorship. Banzer's neoliberal economic policies provided foreign investors with generous investment laws; a new Petroleum Code invited new exploration by a number of U.S. oil companies. Foreign banks provided hefty loans, and the U.S. government tripled the level of military and economic assistance.

However, by 1977 the political pressure for a return to civilian government erupted in demonstrations and a hunger strike in La Paz. Relations with Washington soured as the Carter administration championed democracy and human rights. Facing an economic crisis as well, Banzer was forced to expedite elections. The three elections held between 1978 and 1980 were sullied by fraud and military intervention. In November 1979 in an interim appointment, Lydia Gueiler Tejada, president of the Chamber of Deputies, briefly served as Bolivia's first woman president. She narrowly escaped an assassination attempt staged to derail the 1980 elections. Hernán Siles received 39 percent of the vote, short of the required absolute majority.

The military preempted the run-off vote in Congress, and General Luis García Meza seized power. Known as the infamous cocaine general, García Meza was cozy with the major Andean drug cartels. Bolivia became an international pariah—the country that cocaine bought—and the United States and Latin American governments refused to recognize the rogue regime. García Meza aped Chilean dictator Augusto Pinochet and justified the military's yearlong bloody rampage as a battle against Bolivia's "Marxist cancer." In August 1981, the military high command ousted García Meza and normalized relations with the United States. Nevertheless, as protests against military rule escalated over the next fourteen months, the generals turned to Congress, which revalidated the 1980 elections.

## Transition to Democratic Rule

Hernán Siles assumed the presidency in October 1982, but after eighteen years of militarism the return to democracy proved chaotic and precarious. Conspiracies, bankruptcy, and strikes engulfed Siles's three years in office (1982–1985) and ultimately derailed his populist agenda. His government inherited a staggering $5 billion foreign debt and faced default. In 1984 a harsh IMF neoliberal stabilization program reduced 2 million Bolivians to starvation levels. Unable to contain extreme labor militancy and political contention, Siles was forced to rule by executive decree. As coup plotting proliferated, even within the governing coalition, two army colonels attempted a "cocaine coup" to stop an investigation into the military's narcotics connections. In June 1984 Bolivia's elite antinarcotics unit kidnapped President Siles, but the U.S. ambassador soon secured his release. By the end of the year, a desperate Siles announced early elections.

In August 1985, incoming President Víctor Paz, who had presided over the 1952 revolution, reverted to counterrevolution and "democracy with authority." Paz engineered the Pact for Democracy between the MNR and the National Democratic Action (ADN), which provided the legislative majority he needed to govern. To address an economy in free fall with sky-high inflation and reduced export earnings, Paz imposed a draconian neoliberal austerity program. The New Economic Policy (Nueva Política Económica; NPE) devalued the peso and cut wages and jobs. The government closed eleven state mines after the global tin market collapsed in 1985 and fired more than 13,000 miners. Bolivia's workers protested with a massive nationwide strike. Paz in turn arrested and exiled hundreds of union leaders. As elections neared, he terminated the pact altogether and governed by executive decree and martial law. His signature NPE, despite improvements in inflation and international credit, had worsened social inequities and threatened democracy.

The major contenders in the May 1989 elections were described as the "three look-alikes": Hugo Banzer of the ADN; Gonzalo Sánchez de Lozada of the MNR, nicknamed "Goni" and mocked for his gringo Spanish; and Jaime Paz Zamora, former vice president and leader of the Leftist Revolutionary Movement (MIR) party. Dominated by the economy, the campaign ended with no clear winner. Sánchez de Lozada and Banzer each garnered 23 percent of the vote and Paz Zamora only 20 percent. But a surprise deal in Congress between old political enemies handed Paz Zamora the presidency and created the MIR–ADN "National Unity" governing pact.

Paz Zamora's policies continued neoliberal austerity and martial law against strikers and demonstrators. Conservative policies consolidated civilian rule and provided the stability needed for economic growth. At the same time, economic "rationalization," which had decimated traditional labor, provoked the rise of new challengers to the status quo: indigenous groups and coca leaf farmers.

Pressured by the United States, Bolivian governments implemented a militarized antinarcotics program during the 1980s. Domestic legislation and the 1990 U.S.-Andean Initiative controlled cultivation and distribution of coca leaf through aggressive policing and eradication. Traditional and new migrant coca growers were dependent on the crop, which was the raw material for the illegal paste and refined cocaine of the Andean drug cartels. Most Bolivians viewed the drug war as a demand rather than a supply problem and rejected U.S. policies targeting coca leaf farmers. Paz Zamora made this position public, promoting the "coca is not cocaine" and "Coca for Development" campaign.

In the 1990s the pro-coca campaign took off with the election of Evo Morales as leader of the Cochabamba Coca Growers' Confederation and his rise as a major political contender. The hard-line antidrug and neoliberal economic policies of presidents Sánchez de Lozada and Hugo Banzer also played a role in Morales's increasing political influence. President Sánchez de Lozada (1993–1997) enacted constitutional and economic reforms that privatized major state enterprises, including mining and petroleum, thereby reversing two key milestones of the revolution. Indigenous citizens, despite the token vice presidency of Víctor Hugo Cárdenas, an Aymara Indian, remained marginalized.

President Hugo Banzer (1997–2001) expanded forcible coca eradication and economic austerity, further radicalizing the coca growers and worker-peasant unions. Like his predecessor, Banzer aggressively suppressed the escalating strikes and demonstrations, so that by 1999, with economic growth the lowest in a decade, the country seemed at war. Nevertheless, the United States and international aid agencies praised Bolivia as a "miracle" of economic stabilization and coca eradication. The IMF and World Bank granted Bolivia over $1 billion in debt forgiveness and Banzer's "Zero Coca" campaign reduced the traditional crop to the lowest level in decades. Then, in 2000 a corruption and drug-trafficking scandal and violent protests in Cochabamba against water privatization (the Water War) shook the Banzer government. The old dictator, dying of cancer, left office early and his vice president, Jorge Quiroga Ramírez (2001–2002), took over.

The young U.S.-educated technocrat failed to stem the political and social unrest. Cochabamba erupted again in violent demonstrations and clashes with the military in the Water War against the government's water privatization contract with the multinational corporation Bechtel. Most Bolivians viewed water as a natural birthright and resisted the staggering increase in rates. At the same time, the peasant coca growers in the Chapare and Yungas regions increased their protests and roadblocks against forcible coca eradication. Violent clashes between the military and coca growers finally forced Quiroga to suspend eradication.

The new social movements of "water warriors," coca growers, and indigenous peoples opposed the reactionary policies of the post-1982 pseudo-democratic regimes. They rejected the privatization (Law of Capitalization) and globalization agenda of the ruling class, which benefited the elite and foreign corporations at the expense of the poor and indigenous. The 1994 and 1995 constitutional reforms (Law of Popular Participation and Law of Administrative Decentralization, respectively), however, recognized the nation's multiethnic and pluricultural character. The reforms, which extended resources to hundreds of newly created municipalities, local communities, and regional governments, benefited marginalized groups. The laws expanded the political participation of civil society and mobilized the indigenous movement to challenge the political establishment in the 2002 and 2005 presidential elections.

## Indigenous Resurgence and Populist Democracy

Early postrevolution peasant unions generally promoted indigenous interests. Founded in the late 1970s, the Confederation of Peasant Unions (Confederación Sindical Única de Trabajadores Campesinos de Bolivia; CSUTCB) was headed until 1988 by an Aymara Indian, Genaro Flores, who also led the indigenist party, the Túpac Katari Revolutionary Liberation Movement. By the 1980s, new peasant and indigenous groups were formed to protest coca eradication and neoliberalism. They used direct action tactics—strategic roadblocks, property seizures, hunger strikes, mass marches, and customary "chew ins" of the sacred coca leaf—to pressure and even topple governments.

---

### SOCIAL MOVEMENTS AND INDIGENOUS PEOPLES

Bolivia's new social movements have achieved unprecedented influence. The 1994 Law of Popular Participation and the 1994 Law of Civic Associations and Indigenous Peoples permitted indigenous and traditional communities (*ayllus* and *markas*), civic associations, and neighborhood committees to participate in the electoral process directly independent of political parties. Candidates could run for the presidency, Congress, mayoral offices, and constituent assemblies, and women were allotted 50 percent of association seats.

The reform laws empowered marginalized groups and new social movements and political parties at the expense of the older traditional parties. In 2004, hundreds of citizens' associations organized for municipal elections with many candidates representing indigenous and native peoples' organizations. In 2005, hundreds of civic and indigenous organizations participated in the presidential election and the first direct elections for departmental prefects (state governors). A large contingent of indigenous and social movement candidates were elected to the Constituent Assembly in 2006 and drafted the new 2009 Constitution that expanded and formalized their participation. In the 2009 presidential elections these movements and civic and indigenous associations helped ensure victory for the Morales–MAS government and provided the two-thirds majority in the new Plurinational Legislature needed to pass pro-indigenous reforms.

## INTEREST GROUPS AND SOCIAL MOVEMENTS

Since the return to democracy, interest group representation and social movements have organized to promote indigenous and cultural rights, gender equality, and citizenship and human rights generally. Newer associations joined traditional groups and represent all sectors of Bolivian life. Since 2000, antiglobalization movements, coca growers' federations, indigenous peoples' organizations, and autonomy movements have been prominent.

- Assembly of Guaraní People (Asamblea del Pueblo Guaraní; APG): promotes land and citizenship rights for lowland Indians
- Bolivian Permanent Assembly of Human Rights (Asamblea Permanente de Derechos Humanos de Bolivia; APDHB)
- Confederation of Indigenous Peoples of Bolivia (Confederación de Pueblos Indígenas de Bolivia; CIDOB): represents the indigenous movement
- Confederation of Intercultural Communities of Bolivia (Confederación Sindical de Comunidades Interculturales de Bolivia; CSCIB): union of lowland peasant communities
- Confederation of Peasant Unions of Bolivia (Confederación Sindical Única de Trajajadores Campesinos de Bolivia; CSUTCB)
- Coordinating Committee in Defense of Water (Coordinadora en Defensa del Agua): led by Oscar Olivera of the Cochabamba Water War
- Federation of Neighborhood Councils of El Alto (Federación de Juntas Vecinales El Alto; FEJUVE): supported the El Alto Water War and Gas War
- Federation of Peasant Women of the Tropics of Cochabamba (Federación de Mujeres Campesinas de Trópico de Cochabamba): women's coca growers' union once led by Leonilda Zurita
- Indigenous Council of the South (Consejo Indígena del Sur; CONISUR): council of eastern region's coca colonists and indigenous communities that supported the government's trans-Amazonian road
- Landless Movement (Movimiento Sin Tierra; MST): indigenous land reform movement
- National Democratic Council (Consejo Nacional Democrático; CONALDE): anti-Morales association of pro-autonomy governors of eastern departments
- National Coordination for Change (Coordinadora Nacional por el Cambio; CONALCAM): pro-Morales association of grassroots organizations and leftist political parties
- National Confederation of Peasant, Indigenous and Native Women of Bolivia "Bartolina Sisa" (Confederación Nacional de Mujeres Campesinas Indígenas Originarias de Bolivia "Bartolina Sisa"; CNMCIO-BS)
- National Council of Markas and Ayllus of Qullasuyo (el Consejo Nacional de Markas y Allus del Qullasuyo; CONAMAQ): a confederation of self-governing highland indigenous communities
- Pro-Santa Cruz Civic Committee (Comité Cívico Pro-Santa Cruz): Santa Cruz organization for autonomy that opposed the new constitution and Morales's policies
- Six Federations of Coca Growers of the Tropics of Cochabamba (Seis Federaciones del Trópico de Cochabamba): represents six regional federations of local coca growers unions and some 40,000 peasant coca growers; the federation supported the founding of MAS
- Union of Cruceño Youth (Unión Juvenil Cruceñista): Santa Cruz pro-autonomy student group active in anti-Morales demonstrations

---

## RADICAL WOMEN ACTIVISTS

The role of Bolivian women in grassroots movements increased exponentially in the last decades. Marches and hunger strikes by wives and mothers against authoritarian rule mobilized civil society to demand democracy and human rights. Two women representing different generations and experiences were part of this struggle.

Domitila Barrios de Chungara was the head of the Housewives Committee of Siglo XX (Comité de Amas de Casa de Siglo XX) during the military governments of the 1960s and 1970s. She was arrested and beaten defending her livelihood and home. As a pioneer of the women's movement, Domitila challenged the macho society of the mines and state oppression of the miners. Although of indigenous (Aymara and Quechua) descent, she did not identify with her Indian roots but with her class as a miner's wife.

Leonilda Zurita Vargas, a younger empowered activist of Quechua ancestry, was leader of the National Confederation of Peasant, Indigenous and Native Women of Bolivia and served as a senator in Bolivia's legislature representing the Movement Toward Socialism (MAS). President of the women's peasant coca growers' federation of Cochabamba, she led marches and hunger strikes against forcible eradication and drug war violence.

Activism was a necessity, not a choice. Both women grew up poor with heavy family responsibilities. Leonilda, whose family survived growing coca on a meager bit of land, explained: "We are organized, because we are traumatized." Women's ranks have multiplied in Congress, municipal and regional offices, civic and neighborhood associations, political parties, and Morales's government.

---

By 1988, the national Peasant Coca Growers' Union and Juan Evo Morales Ayma became the voice of the *cocalero* (peasant coca leaf grower) movement. Soon the Indians' right to grow the sacred leaf led to demands for greater indigenous rights and autonomy. The drug war produced hundreds of confrontations between the military and the peasantry, rupturing the decades-old Military-Peasant Pact, which had served to control the indigenous and *campesino* majority. As a consequence of the rupture and the participation and decentralization reforms, the peasant, workers, and indigenous unions and social movements allied with the parties of the left and elected an unprecedented number of *campesino* and Indian delegates to the legislature.

The Aymara leader, Felipe Quispe Huanca, known as "el Mallku" (the Eagle), headed both the CSUTCB and an Indian political party, the Pachakuti Indigenous Movement (MIP) that often competed with Morales's MAS party for the indigenous vote. In 2002 Morales nearly won the presidency because the U.S. Ambassador Manuel Rocha criticized his candidacy, and in 2005 the Indian majority, the country's largest voting bloc, made Morales Bolivia's first democratically elected indigenous president. The election marked a historic power transfer from traditional establishment parties to new, socialist, and pro-indigenous parties. Why and how did this major shift occur?

The re-election of the MNR's Sánchez de Lozada in 2002 set the stage for the transition to social movement governance. The outcome revealed a country divided and major contenders tied with less than a quarter of the electorate. The socialist and pro-Indian vote was on the rise (MIP and MAS with 27 percent), and the latter promised to end coca eradication and nationalize sectors of the economy that had been privatized. The electoral campaign was rife with scandal and was expensive—over $5 million—while the majority of the population lived below the poverty line and the national debt was in the billions. Morales remained popular despite being labeled a drug trafficker and Marxist. Nevertheless, Sánchez de Lozada, the least popular candidate in the polls, became president because an unstable governing pact and run-off in Congress decided the outcome.

Sánchez de Lozada's presidency lasted a mere fifteen months as protests erupted against higher taxes in February 2003 and against proposed exports of Bolivia's natural gas via Chile in the bloody September–October Gas War. National outrage over the deaths of over 100 protestors in confrontations between the military and the popular social movements forced his premature resignation. Vice President Carlos Mesa Gisbert, a historian without political experience or party backing, became interim president. When a referendum on gas in 2004 and higher hydrocarbon taxes on new fields in 2005 failed to defuse the crisis, Mesa called early elections.

The presidential election of December 2005 marked a historic power transition between Bolivia's nonindigenous ruling elite and its indigenous majority. A diverse, multiclass, multiethnic cross-section of voters backed Morales and his agenda to "Refound the Nation." The landslide victory of 54 percent of votes represented a popular mandate for a second revolution: a new constitution, renationalization of hydrocarbons and mines, voluntary coca eradication, socialist economics, and indigenous and regional autonomy.

# Refounding Bolivia

The Refounding Revolution that President Morales instituted and consolidated during two terms in office (2005–2014) unleashed a protracted struggle among disparate interests and intensified persistent divisions: economic, ethnic, class, partisan, ideological, and regional. During Morales's first term, an alliance of indigenous and popular social movements forced the temporary retreat of the conservative and primarily white and mestizo ruling class, the so-called new Rosca. Regional conflict between the highlander, pro-Indian and social movement central government and the lowlander, non-Indian eastern elites escalated. With political and economic power concentrated in the Oriente, its rich, privileged classes—especially Santa Cruz entrepreneurs—were threatened by reforms. The Camba elites of four southeastern departments or states (Santa Cruz, Tarija, Beni, and Pando) revived demands for regional autonomy and secession. These Media Luna departments ("Half-Moon" because of the crescent shape of the region), often joined by the Cochabamba department, were the center of anti-Morales opposition.

---

## BOLIVIAN GOVERNMENT

Under the new Political Constitution of the State (Constitución Política del Estado; CPE), which was passed by national referendum on January 25, 2009, and became law on February 7, 2009, Bolivia's governing structure was reorganized. The country was renamed the Plurinational State of Bolivia (Estado Plurinacional de Bolivia) to reflect its multicultural population and orientation. There are four organs or branches of government: the executive, the legislative, the judicial, and the electoral. The executive branch includes the president, the vice president, and cabinet ministers. The president serves as both head of state and head of government for a five-year term and, along with the vice president, may be re-elected for only one consecutive term of office. To win, a presidential candidate must receive an absolute majority of the popular vote (51 percent) or at least 40 percent of the vote and a 10 percent margin over the next highest candidate. Otherwise, a second election is held within sixty days, and the candidate with the most votes (plurality) wins. In the general elections of 2005, 2009 (held a year early according to the new constitution), and 2014, Morales won historic majorities in the first round.

The bicameral legislative branch was renamed the Plurinational Legislative Assembly (Asamblea Legislativa Plurinacional) and increased to 166 seats with special seats reserved for rural peasant, indigenous, and native peoples. The Cámara de Diputados (Chamber of Deputies or House of Representatives) of 130 deputies, and the Cámara de Senadores (Chamber of Senators) of thirty-six senators (four for each of the nine departments) serve five-year terms.

Judicial and electoral branches of government included the Tribunal Supremo de Justicia (Supreme Tribunal of Justice) and the Órgano Electoral Plurinacional (Plurinational Electoral Organ). Justices in the Supreme Tribunal are nominated by two-thirds of the legislature and directly elected by simple majority for a six-year term with no re-election. Also the new Tribunal Agroambiental (Agro-Environmental Tribunal) adjudicated land, water, natural resource, and environmental issues. An independent jurisdiction of native and indigenous peoples applied community justice. The Plurinational Electoral Organ of seven members had at least two representing the original native, indigenous, and peasant peoples.

---

Morales's first term furthered open representation and economic nationalism. In 2006 the May Day "nationalization" of petroleum and gas resources resulted in more lucrative state contracts with transnational firms. A Constituent Assembly of 255 delegates, heavily comprised of indigenous, civil, and social movement members, was elected to draw up a new constitution. After a year and a half of fierce dissension, the assembly passed a final draft in December 2007. The Media Luna backlash over the draft charter, especially by the Pro-Santa Cruz Civic Committee, and frustrated referendums for self-rule polarized the country and engulfed it in violence for most of 2008. The killing of pro-government supporters (the Massacre of Porvenir) in a small town in Pando department in September forced President Morales to briefly impose martial law. Finally, the legislature ratified the revised constitution on October 21.

In a national referendum on January 23, 2009, voters approved the new Political Constitution of the State (Constitucíon Política del Estado; CPE) with a majority of 61 percent. Nevertheless, in three Media Luna departments (Beni, Santa Cruz, and Tarija) voters rejected it. Facing a determined opposition bloc and without a two-thirds legislative majority, the first Morales administration had great difficulty implementing the new constitutional provisions and resorted to direct street action by social movements and indigenous supporters to pressure Congress. Opposition groups launched counterprotests, resulting in another chaotic and violent year. Much of the dispute was over two key provisions: the legislation detailing autonomy and self-rule and the interim electoral law that regulated the upcoming December elections.

Autonomy had divergent meanings for reformers and opponents. The new CPE defined autonomy as decentralization and greater self-rule and citizenship rights for indigenous communities. Opponents, primarily in the Media Luna, rejected self-rule and land rights for native communities as fragmenting the country into tribal fiefdoms. Media Luna leaders insisted upon autonomous and exclusive regional control over natural resources and policing and two-thirds of their departments' tax revenues. Their reading of regional autonomy sought to insulate Bolivia's richest departments—where most oil and gas, timber, and land resources were located—from the indigenous and socialist encroachments of Morales's Refounding Revolution.

As his first term neared its end, the conservative opposition fielded a number of contenders hoping to block Morales's re-election. Three indigenous-peasant candidates and a female candidate challenged him as well. However, a feverish voter registration campaign inscribed impressive numbers of rural and indigenous voters as well as hundreds of thousands of overseas Bolivians, who were permitted to vote abroad for the first time. The top conservative and pro-autonomy opposition tickets split and collectively received only 33 percent of the vote. Evo Morales was easily re-elected in December 2009 with a 64 percent absolute majority of the vote and a greater popular mandate than in 2005. His governing coalition of MAS and the Movement Without Fear (Movimiento Sin Miedo; MSM) party made up of social movement and indigenous supporters, seized majority control of the new legislature.

## Consolidating Reform

Most of President Morales's second term focused on the implementation of the progressive constitution. The 411-article CPE guaranteed extensive political, social, and economic rights of citizenship: social benefits, land reform, environmental protection, sovereignty over natural resources, economic development, and greater legal protections and self-governance for Bolivia's peasant, indigenous, and original native peoples. However, the process quickly became mired in discord. Conservative and pro-autonomy opposition was expected but not the degree of dissension and division within the MAS coalition of social movements. In late summer of 2010, the city of Potosí saw massive antigovernment protests by civic and indigenous peasant associations and small mining cooperatives headed by the mayor, who had run against Morales and been supported by the department's MAS governor. In 2012, as unrest spread, the MAS coalition lost its two-thirds majority in Congress.

Pro-indigenous marches by the major peasant and Indian movements of the eastern lowlands demanded land reform, native autonomy, and control of natural resources. In August 2011, the Eighth March of the Indigenous Peoples of the East, Chaco, and Bolivian Amazon joined the 360-mile march of indigenous communities within the Isiboro Sécure National Park and Indigenous Territory (TIPNIS) against the construction of a highway through the park. In October, when the thousands of marchers flooded La Paz, Morales hastened to sign Law 180 banning the road and designating the park a protected, "untouchable" reserve. But in December, a pro-government countermarch for the road by the region's coca colonists and indigenous communities of Indigenous Council of the South (CONISUR) arrived in La Paz. Therefore, in February 2012 the government passed the Law of Consultation whereby a referendum of TIPNIS residents would decide the road's future. Although the referendum's results were contested, the government insisted that the majority of indigenous communities desired the road. To date, despite Morales's determination and political and legal maneuvers, the highway project remains on hold.

The confrontations exposed glaring contradictions between rhetoric and policy at home and abroad given Morales's high profile pro-environmental, anticapitalist, and anti-imperialist campaigns internationally. For example, in 2010 he hosted the First World Conference of the Peoples on Climate Change in Cochabamba; and in New York at the 65th UN General Assembly, he promoted the slogan, "Planet or death, we shall overcome," and secured the adoption of Bolivia's resolution declaring water a human right. Championing the protection of *Pacha Mama* (Mother Earth) at subsequent multilateral forums, Morales gave global environmental activism high priority in his second term.

President Morales also remained a vocal critic of U.S. imperialism and intervention and routinely faulted the U.S. embassy for meddling in Bolivia and encouraging opposition and antigovernment protests, such as the TIPNIS crisis. He expelled the U.S. DEA in 2008 and has roundly criticized the hypocrisy of the U.S. State Department's annual drug reports that routinely decertified Bolivia for failing demonstrably in antinarcotics control. However, his voluntary coca eradication and cooperative self-policing by coca growers' unions has reduced violence and human rights abuses and limited coca cultivation. His "coca yes, cocaine no" policy sought legal commercialization and export of coca leaf products. In 2011 Bolivia withdrew from the United Nation's Single Convention on Narcotic Drugs but rejoined in 2013 with a formal reservation rejecting the ban on coca leaf chewing. Morales is engaged in an aggressive international campaign to amend the convention and remove coca from the list of hard drugs, a necessary precursor to legalization of coca cultivation in Bolivia.

## Third-Term Victory

In 2013 protests and leadership disputes intensified over Morales's bid for a third consecutive term, a controversial and conceivably unconstitutional move (since only two consecutive terms were permitted). However, the Constitutional Tribunal ruled in April that Morales could run again in 2014 because his first presidency had predated the new constitution and did not count. Despite a fierce opposition campaign that denounced him as a Chávez-style "totalitarian," Morales bested all competitors. Among these, former president and Christian Democratic Party candidate Jorge Quiroga; the Green Party and TIPNIS indigenous leader Fernando Vargas; and Juan Fernando del Granado, an ex-ally and former La Paz mayor of the Movement Without Fear, mounted no serious challenge. Samuel Doria Medina of Democratic Unity secured second place with 25 percent of votes cast. Consequently, on October 12, 2014, Evo Morales again emerged victorious with 61 percent of the popular vote and a solid legislative majority.

The MAS landslide was made possible by a reconfigured electoral alliance of entrepreneurial sectors of peasants, indigenous, and conservative elites who prospered in the hydrocarbon-fueled economy. Nevertheless, opposition voices were becoming increasingly strident. The unresolved TIPNIS resistance movement exposed a house deeply divided, especially over the government's extractivist development of natural resources and endangerment of fragile ecosystems and native communities. The crisis pitted segments of Morales's original social movement base against one another and against the government, and fractured inter- and intra-indigenous and peasant communities and organizations. More clashes followed after passage of the May 20, 2015 decree that opened up hydrocarbon exploration in protected areas and facilitated new contracts and joint ventures with foreign investors. In October 2016, the alarm was raised when a still-uncontacted indigenous tribe, living in isolation in Bolivia's remote rainforest bordering Peru and east of the Madidi National Park, was exposed by the extensive exploration of a subsidiary of the state-owned China National Petroleum Corporation (CNPC).

An aggressive strategy of resource nationalism has been essential to the Morales–MAS administration's goal to turn Bolivia into a regional energy power. The government has further committed to building the country's first nuclear reactor. At the same time, environmentalist and climate change advocacy has been central to Morales's global activism despite blatant inconsistencies and contradictions between domestic and foreign policies. His high-profile climate diplomacy has focused the international spotlight on Bolivia and enhanced the country's stature in the global hierarchy. In December 2015, Bolivia signed the landmark Paris Agreement on climate change and ratified the accord in October 2016. As Bolivia assumes its seat as a nonpermanent member of the UN Security Council in 2017 and more developing countries like China focus on global warming, Morales will have a greater opportunity to pursue a leadership role in climate-change reform.

Bolivia's relations with the United States remained hostile during Morales's third term as attempts to renew the exchange of ambassadors failed. Indeed, 2013 marked a particularly low point: Morales blamed U.S. imperialists for the death of Hugo Chávez, expelled the U.S. Agency for International Development (USAID), and offered asylum to Edward Snowden, the former National Security Agency whistleblower. The latter precipitated an international incident when, at the behest of the United States, four European countries detoured Morales's plane returning from a Moscow summit because of fears that Snowden was hidden aboard. The United States repeatedly rejected requests for the extradition of ex-president Gonzalo Sánchez de Lozada, indicted for the 2003 Black October deaths of protestors.

In turn, Morales reciprocated with hostile, anti-imperialist denunciations and expanded friendly relations with adversaries of the United States like Venezuela, Cuba, Iran, China, and Russia. He remained a steadfast defender of the region's populist pink tide presidents, blaming their troubles on Washington's machinations and conspiracies (such as the released WikiLeaks cables of the U.S. Embassy's close engagement with disaffected Bolivian opposition and indigenous leaders). Morales roundly denounced Brazilian president Dilma Rousseff's impeachment in August 2016 and continued to champion Nicolás Maduro, Chávez's beleaguered successor, even as Maduro's political fortunes and U.S.–Venezuelan relations deteriorated further in 2016. At the UN General Assembly in September, he condemned the "warmongering policies" of Israel and the United States and blamed humanity's problems on imperialism and capitalism.

On the other hand, by taking advantage of neoliberal capitalism, the Bolivian economy grew around 5 percent during Morales's third term even as a slowdown because of the global glut in oil and gas took hold. Despite expanded state control of the economy and modified nationalizations, foreign investment and assistance increased with traditional and nontraditional partners like Russia and China and supplanted reliance on U.S. aid. Economic nationalism, central to Morales's economic revolution, clearly paid off in fiscal stability, increased revenue for social spending, and voter popularity. However, the critical question ahead was whether Bolivia could continue to develop and alleviate poverty without further neoextractivist dependence on mining and raw materials, especially hydrocarbons and lithium reserves.

With over a decade in office, Morales's approval rating hovered around 60 percent. His Patriotic Agenda (Agenda Patriótica) toward Bolivia's socialist and communitarian alternative to capitalism that had served as the roadmap for electoral success in 2014 reaffirmed core revolutionary goals: sovereign access to the sea, economic sovereignty over natural resources, freedom from finance capital, respect for the environment and Mother Earth, an end to poverty and food insecurity, and the administration of public goods according to the indigenous ethic of do not lie, steal, or be lazy. Despite mixed progress on these fronts and relative accommodation with upper class elites and business leaders, by 2016 persisting discontent and personal scandal obstructed Morales's path to re-election.

## Bid for a Fourth Term

In a critical referendum on February 21, 2016, voters rejected by a slim 51 percent the constitutional amendment to allow Morales a fourth term. Had the referendum passed as expected, Morales could have been re-elected and retained the presidency until 2025, the bicentennial year of Bolivian independence. The narrow defeat indicated that a voter majority of disaffected indigenous and social movement sectors and average Bolivians feared a monopoly on power and that a corruption scandal days before the voting proved detrimental. A former girlfriend employed in a Chinese company with hundreds of millions in state contracts had allegedly benefited from her association with Morales and was later arrested for influence peddling. Reports that their son—who Morales believed had died in infancy—was alive mired the campaign in soap opera sensationalism until the prodigal proved to be an imposter. In the end, Morales was not implicated and denounced the attacks as a dirty media war orchestrated by Washington and the right-wing opposition. He blamed the "No" vote on fraud and floated the option of a referendum redo. Supporters increasingly felt that "we may have lost a battle, but not the war."

In August a bitter confrontation between the government and the informal cooperative mining sector of the National Federation of Mining Cooperatives (Federación Nacional de Cooperativas Mineras de Bolivia; FENCOMIN) contributed to political uncertainty and unrest. The striking minerworkers blockaded major roads and demanded repeal of the August 19 amendment to the mining law that tightened state control over cooperatives, imposing higher taxes, stricter environmental standards, and prohibiting direct contracts with transnational mining companies. Larger private and corporate mining interests also resisted the seminationalization and made common cause with the small cooperative miners. Conflict escalated on August 25 with the killing of several miners and of Deputy Minister Rodolfo Illanes who had been taken hostage and beaten to death. The strike proved serious economically and politically, causing millions in damages and lost export earnings and weakening further Morales's base and core constituency. Although the FENCOMIN mineworkers were closely allied with Morales and had helped him achieve and maintain power, the federation president and a hundred miners were arrested. Morales blamed the social agitation (as he had in previous conflicts) on the ongoing conspiracy against him. However, with popular sectors increasingly disaffected by neoliberal and extractivist economics and the trust between the governed and the government declining, more unrest was inevitable.

In September, after months of clamor for a repeat referendum, Morales publicly ruled out a fourth term run. Nevertheless, several allied social sectors began amassing signatures for a Citizen Legislative Initiative to modify the constitutional term limits. The MAS decision to postpone debate on the presidential succession until 2018 and repeated reminders by Morales and top officials that it was up to the people to decide fueled supporters' hopes. The opposition remained fearful that adroit maneuvering by Morales while still in office would pave the way for his reelection in 2019.

## The Challenge of *Vivir Bien*

As Morales nears the end of his presidency, a great number of critical questions remain that only time may resolve. Foremost is whether Bolivia's experiment in democratic social movement governance and indigenous-based revolution will persist if Morales is not re-elected. or even if he is, will serious corruption and creeping authoritarianism (as opponents have charged) eventually destroy the re-founding revolution from within as has happened with reforms in the past? Will the mounting contradictions between rhetoric and policy on climate change and indigenous rights incite more conflict and violence? Is a future water war imminent as global warming prolongs extreme drought and water rationing into 2017? Can the country escape the dependency of extractivist development as export profits shrink and advances in economic and social welfare suffer? And will Morales soften his anti-imperialist, anticapitalist campaigns to normalize U.S.–Bolivian relations? Or will he continue to promote socialist and indigenous alternatives to global capitalism in his efforts to transform the world system?

As the political tide in the hemisphere shifts away from left-wing populist leaders, perhaps Evo Morales will remain an exception. In an important sense, Bolivia's politics of resistance have been a harbinger as well as an outlier in the process of radical social change within the region and beyond. Internationally, a growing number of nationalist populist leaders and social movements have arisen and are struggling with the challenges of globalization, multiculturalism, identity politics, and indigenous resurgence. For Bolivia, these struggles cover well-trod territory and have delivered meaningful achievements and relevant lessons.

On many fronts, Morales's refounding revolution represents a success story. There has been over a decade of relative political stability and continuity in the land of coups and revolutions. Extreme poverty in one of the hemisphere's poorest countries has radically declined by nearly a half, and social spending has increased by a similar amount. Bolivia has been singled out by the Economic Commission on Latin America and the Caribbean and the World Bank as one of the few countries that greatly reduced economic inequality. Rejecting Washington Consensus orthodoxy, modified nationalizations and state socialism have achieved steady economic growth that has rivaled many other countries. Moreover, Bolivia has been widely recognized as an innovative and successful model of humane antinarcotics control.

In particular, Bolivia's indigenous ethic of *vivir bien* (living well) provides an essential moral check against exploitation of the planet and its peoples. It severely challenges the government's economic pragmatism and conflicted compromises between development and environmental protection. In final analysis, even as the Morales administration falls short of the environmental stewardship that *vivir bien* entails, its message and goals of shared community and well-being resonate far beyond Bolivia and encourage progressive social and sustainable economic development.

---

## BOLIVIAN PRESIDENTS SINCE 1930

Carlos Blanco Galindo, 1930–1931
Daniel Salamanca Urey, 1931–1934

José Luis Tejada Sorzano, 1934–1936
David Toro Ruilova, 1936–1937

Germán Busch Becerra, 1937–1939
Carlos Quintanilla Quiroga, 1939–1940
Enrique Peñaranda del Castillo, 1940–1943
Gualberto Villarroel López, 1943–1946
Víctor Paz Estenssoro, 1964–1964
René Barrientos Ortuño, 1964–1969
Alfredo Ovando Candia, 1969–1970
Luis Adolfo Siles Salinas, 1969–1969
Juan José Torres Gonzáles, 1970–1971
Hugo Banzer Suárez, 1971–1978
Juan Pereda Asbún, 1978–1978
David Padilla Arancibia, 1978–1979
Wálter Guevara Arze, 1979–1979
Alberto Natusch Busch, 1979–1979
Lidia Gueiler Tejada, 1979–1980
Luis García Meza Tejada, 1980–1981
Néstor Guillén Olmos, 1946–1946
Tomás Monje Gutiérrez, 1946–1947
Enrique Hertzog Garaizabal, 1947–1949

Mamerto Urriolagoitia Harriague, 1949–1951
Hugo Ballivián Rojas, 1951–1952
Víctor Paz Estenssoro, 1952–1956
Hernán Siles Zuazo, 1956–1960
Víctor Paz Estenssoro, 1960–1964
Celso Torrelio Villa, 1981–1982
Guido Vildoso Calderón, 1982–1982
Hernán Siles Zuazo, 1982–1985
Víctor Paz Estenssoro, 1985–1989
Jaime Paz Zamora, 1989–1993
Gonzalo Sánchez de Lozada, 1993–1997
Hugo Banzer Suárez, 1997–2001
Jorge Quiroga Ramírez, 2001–2002
Gonzalo Sánchez de Lozada, 2002–2003
Carlos Mesa Gisbert, 2003–2005
Eduardo Rodríguez Veltze, 2005–2005
Evo Morales Ayma, 2005–

## BOLIVIA: MAJOR POLITICAL PARTIES SINCE 1952

- Civic Solidarity Union (Unión Cívica de la Solidaridad; UCS)
- Conscience of the Fatherland (Conciencia de Patria; CONDEPA)
- Democratic Popular Unity (Unidad Democrática y Popular; UDP)
- Democratic Unity (Unidad Demócrata;UD)
- Democratic Social Power (Poder Democrático Social; PODEMOS)
- Green Party (Partido Verde; PV)
- Leftist Revolutionary Movement or Movement of the Revolutionary Left (Movimiento de Izquierda Revolucionaria; MIR)
- Movement Toward Socialism (Movimiento al Socialismo;MAS)
- Movement Without Fear (Movimiento Sin Miedo; MSM)
- National Convergence (Convergencia Nacional; CN)
- Nationalist Democratic Action (Acción Democrática Nacionalista; ADN)
- National Unity Front (Frente de Unidad Nacional; UN)
- Nationalist Revolutionary Movement (Movimiento Nacionalista Revolucionario; MNR)
- New Republican Force (Nueva Fuerza Republicana; NFR)
- Pachakuti Indigenist Movement (Movimiento Indígena Pachakuti; MIP)
- Túpac Katari Revolutionary Liberation Movement (Movimiento Revolucionario Túpac Katari de Liberación; MRTKL)

# Chronology

**900–1000**   Classical period of Tiwanaku

**1100–1400**   Rise and development of Aymara Kingdoms

**1400–1500**   Incan conquest of Aymara and establishment of the Kollasuyo

**1532**   Spanish conquest of Inca Empire by Francisco Pizarro

**1538**   Spanish colonize Upper Peru and establish the Viceroyalty of Lima

**1545**   Discovery of Cerro Rico (Silver Mountain) of Potosí

**1548**   Establishment of the Audiencia of Charcas with its seat in Sucre

**1730**   Indigenous rebellion in Cochabamba against Spanish authorities

**1780–1782**   Indian rebellion of Túpac Amaru (José Gabriel Condorcanqui)

**1825**   Liberation of Upper Peru and declaration of Bolivian independence

**1825–1828**   Marshall Antonio José de Sucre is elected president and establishes Bolivia's first republican government

**1829–1839**   Rule by General Andrés de Santa Cruz

**1835–1839**   Creation of the Peru-Bolivian Confederation by General Santa Cruz; Chile invades and defeats Santa Cruz

**1841**   Peru invades but is defeated ending attempts to annex Bolivia

**1860s–1870s**   Guano, nitrates, and silver discovered in Atacama region

**1879–1884**   War of the Pacific; Bolivia is defeated and becomes landlocked

**1880–1899**   Civilian and Conservative Party rule of the Silver Oligarchy

**1899**   Federal Revolution of the Liberal Party; power shifts to La Paz and the tin oligarchy

**1904**   Peace treaty of War of the Pacific signed

**1920**   Rebellion by Bolivia's indigenous peoples is repressed

**1923**   Miners' revolt is suppressed with violence and bloodshed

**1932–1935**   Bolivian defeat in Chaco War with Paraguay

**1936–1939**   Military reform governments of Colonel David Toro and Colonel Germán Busch

**1937**   President Toro nationalizes Standard Oil Company

**1939–1943**   Conservative government of General Enrique Peñaranda

**1943–1946**   Military reform government of Major Gualberto Villarroel and MNR

**1944**   Founding of the Bolivian Mine Workers' Federation (FSTMB)

**1945**   First National Indigenous Congress

**1946**   Overthrow and hanging of President Villarroel

**1946–1952**   Return of rule by mining oligarchy

**1951**   Nationwide elections are overturned and military takes over

**1952**   Bolivian National Revolution (April)

**1952–1964**   MNR governments of Víctor Paz Estenssoro and Hernán Siles Zuazo

**1952**   Universal Suffrage Decree

**1953**   Land reform; and nationalization of the mines

**1955**   Educational Reform Decree

**1964–1969**   "Restorative Revolution" of General René Barrientos

**1965–1967**   Ernesto "Ché" Guevara in Bolivia; death of Ché (October 1967)

**1969–1970**   Military populist government of General Ovando and nationalization of the Bolivian Gulf Oil Company (October 1969)

**1970–1971**   Military leftist government of General Juan José Torres

**1971–1978**   Military coup and dictatorship of General Hugo Banzer Suárez

**1978**   Miners' wives launch hunger strike in La Paz cathedral to protest government repression and demand national amnesty

**1979**   "Massacre of All Saints" by military results in over 200 dead; Lydia Gueiler Tejada heads an interim government as Bolivia's first woman president

**1980**   Cocaine coup by General Luis García Meza preempts electoral process; U.S. and European governments suspend aid

**1982**   Return to democracy; Congress revalidates 1980 election of Hernán Siles Zuazo

**1982–1985**   Left of center civilian government of Hernán Siles Zuazo; hyperinflation and instability forces early elections

**1985–1989**   MNR government of Víctor Paz Estenssoro; his "democracy with authority" imposes neoliberal New Economic Policy (NPE)

**1985**   Crash of world tin market sends Bolivian economy into recession

**1986**   Mine closings and 23,000 miners lose jobs; escalation of U.S.–Bolivian antinarcotics operations

**1988**   Law on the Regulation of Coca and Controlled Substances (Law 1008) criminalizes coca leaf cultivation in most of the country

**1989–1993**   Presidency of Jaime Paz Zamora

**1989**   Chapare coca-growing federations sponsor first national "Día de Acullico" or "Day of Coca-Leaf Chewing"

**1990**   Andean Drug Summit in Colombia officially militarizes the Bolivian drug war; lowland indigenous peoples' "March for Territory and Dignity" secures land rights

**1993–1997**   Presidency of Gonzalo Sánchez de Lozada and Víctor Hugo Cárdenas as Bolivia's first indigenous vice president

**1997–2001**   Presidency of Hugo Banzer; forcible coca eradication and militarization of the 1998 "Zero Coca" or "Plan Dignity" policy and economic austerity provokes strikes and roadblocks by coca growers and worker-peasant unions

**2000**   Water War protests in Cochabamba over water privatization by the Bechtel Corporation forces government to impose martial law (February–April); month-long peasant roadblocks seal off La Paz (September–October); rise of Bolivian Landless Movement (MST)

**2001**   An ill Banzer resigns a year early, and Vice President Jorge Quiroga Ramírez takes over

**2001–2002**   President Jorge Quiroga continues political and neoliberal policies; cancellation of the Bechtel water privatization project; unrest as coca growers protest coca eradication; Evo Morales, leader of the coca growers' federation, is ousted from Congress but runs for president in 2002 elections in which Morales's MAS party has strong showing

**2002**   Gonzalo Sánchez de Lozada wins elections on June 30

**2003**   Bloody January–February protests over proposed tax hike; more bloodshed during September–October Gas War protests derails Sánchez de Lozada presidency on October 17; Vice President Carlos Mesa Gisbert becomes interim president

**2004** President Mesa holds July referendum and 80 percent of voters approve proposed new Hydrocarbon Law

**2005** Congress approves new Hydrocarbon Law increasing taxes on gas and oil for new fields, but Mesa does not sign it and is forced by rising protests to call elections; Evo Morales wins the presidency in a landslide victory as Bolivia's first elected president of indigenous heritage and promises to "Refound the Nation"

**2006** May Day renationalization of Bolivia's Hydrocarbons and Energy sector; Constituent Assembly elections (July) to rewrite the constitution; Santa Cruz approves autonomy agenda

**2007** Bolivia charges ex-president Gonzalo Sánchez de Lozada with genocide; bloody clashes in Sucre between pro- and anti-Morales supporters and Constituent Assembly delegates pass draft of new constitution in military garrison; Constituent Assembly moves to Oruro and approves proposed constitutional charter despite boycott by opposition delegates from eastern lowlands

**2008** Morales announces construction of a transamazonian road; national and departmental referendums on the new constitution and autonomy provisions; on August 10, voters support (67 percent) President Morales in the National Recall Referendum; U.S. Ambassador Philip Goldberg declared "persona non grata," and Morales denounces the attempted "civil coup" against his government at the 63rd UN General Assembly; in November, the ouster of U.S. DEA

**2009** National Plebiscite on January 25 approves (by 61 percent) New Political Constitution of State; Morales calls for decriminalization of coca-leaf chewing at UN Commission on Narcotic Drugs in Vienna in March; December 6, Morales is re-elected by majority vote of 64 percent; re-elected Morales attends the Copenhagen climate summit where he defends "Mother Earth," denouncing climate and environmental violations by capitalist countries

**2010** Morales is inaugurated on January 22; in April Morales hosts the First World Conference of the Peoples on Climate Change in Cochabamba; in July the UN General Assembly adopts a Bolivian-sponsored resolution recognizing access to clean water and sanitation as a human right; in September Morales criticizes capitalism and interventionist policies of the United States and proposes the new slogan "Planet or death, we shall overcome!" at the 65th UN General Assembly

**2011** Construction of transamazonian road beings in June; Bolivia withdraws in July from the UN Single Convention on Narcotic Drugs; in August First (VIII) Indigenous March in Defense of TIPNIS; violent repression of marchers in Yacumo, Beni on September 25; October 24 Law 180 declaring TIPNIS "untouchable"; in December CONISUR pro-highway march begins

**2012** United States denies Bolivia's request for the extradition of Sánchez de Lozada charged with genocide; in January CONISUR pro-road march arrives in La Paz, and Bolivia reapplies to join the UN Convention with reservations; in April at Summit of Americas Morales calls on US to integrate Cuba, and Second (IX) Indigenous March in Defense of TIPNIS begins; in May Bolivia nationalizes electricity grid; in June TIPNIS marchers arrive in La Paz; in December Bolivia joins Mercosur

**2013**   In January Bolivia rejoins the UN Convention with a reservation protecting the coca-chewing tradition and Morales announces the Patriotic Agenda for the Bicentennial; in April Bolivia seeks arbitration of the seacoast dispute with Chile by International Court of Justice; in May expels USAID; in June Bolivia files second extradition request for Sánchez de Lozada; in July Morales's plane is banned from several European countries' airspace and Morales offers Edward Snowden asylum in Bolivia; in September United States decertifies Bolivia for the sixth time for its antidrug control record

**2014**   Morales re-elected on October 12 and calls it "a victory for anti-imperialism; announces plans to build a nuclear reactor

**2015**   UN approves Bolivian initiative making April 22 International Mother Earth Day; on May 20 Supreme Decree 2366 opens up national parks to oil and gas extraction; Pope Francis visits in July; in August Morales visits Castro on his eighty-ninth birthday; in September Congress passes law revising term limits, and the International Court of Justice agrees to hear Bolivia's seacoast dispute claim; in October Peoples Climate Change Conference in Cochabamba; in November Morales visits Tehran, the First World Summit of Decolonization in Bolivia, Morales attends UN Climate Change Conference in Paris; in December Bolivia signs the Paris Agreement on Climate Change

**2016**   On February 21 voters reject referendum on revised term limits law to allow Morales's re-election; in April Morales denounces drug war at UN drug summit; in May Morales visits Cuba and receives the Order of José Martí and rejects the Transnational Drug Trafficking Act; in June Bolivia elected to UN Security Council; in August first lithium exports to China, Morales visits Castro on his ninetieth birthday, Iranian Foreign Minister Mohammed Javad Zarif visits Bolivia and is awarded the Condor of the Andes, the anti-imperialist military academy is inaugurated in Santa Cruz, cooperative mineworkers' strike, and death of Deputy Minister Rodolfo Illanes; in September Morales denounces "imperialism and warmongering" of Israel and the United States at UN General Assembly; in October ratifies Paris Agreement; in November Morales declares national emergency over water crisis

**2017**   Bolivia begins two-year term as nonpermanent member of UN Security Council

# Bibliography

Arnade, Charles W. *The Emergence of the Republic of Bolivia.* New York: Russell & Russell, 1970.
Barrios de Chungara, Domitila. *Let Me Speak! Testimony of Domitila, a Woman of the Bolivian Mines.* New York: Monthly Review, 1978.
Crabtree, John, and Ann Chaplin. *Bolivia: Processes of Change.* New York: Zed, 2013.
Crabtree, John, and Laurence Whitehead, eds. *Unresolved Tensions: Bolivia, Past and Present.* Pittsburgh, PA: University of Pittsburgh Press, 2008.
Dangl, Benjamin. *The Price of Fire: Resource Wars and Social Movements in Bolivia.* Oakland, CA: AK, 2007.
Dunkerley, James. *Bolivia: Revolution and the Power of History in the Present.* London: Institute for the Study of the Americas, University of London, 2007.

Dunkerley, James. *Rebellion in the Veins: Political Struggle in Bolivia, 1952–1982.* London: Verso, 1984.

Fabricant, Nicole. *Mobilizing Bolivia's Displaced: Indigenous Politics and the Struggle Over Land.* Chapel Hill: University of North Carolina Press, 2012.

Gill, Lesley. *Teetering on the Rim: Global Restructuring, Daily Life, and the Armed Retreat of the Bolivian State.* New York: Columbia University Press, 2000.

Grindle, Merilee, and Pilar Domingo, eds. *Proclaiming Revolution: Bolivia in Comparative Perspective.* London: Institute of Latin American Studies, University of London, 2003.

Guevara, Ernesto Ché. *The Bolivian Diary of Ernesto Ché Guevara.* Edited by Mary-Alice Walters. New York: Pathfinder, (1994) 2000.

Harten, Sven. *The Rise of Evo Morales and the MAS.* New York: Zed, 2011.

Healey, Susan. "Ethno-Ecological Identity and the Restructuring of Political Power in Bolivia." *Latin American Perspectives* 36, no. 4 (July 2009): 83–100.

Hylton, Forrest, Sinclair Thomson, and Adolfo Gilly. *Revolutionary Horizons: Past and Present in Bolivian Politics.* London: Verso, 2007.

Klein, Herbert S. *Bolivia: The Evolution of a Multi-Ethnic Society.* 2d ed. New York: Oxford University Press, 1992.

Klein, Herbert S. *A Concise History of Bolivia.* Cambridge: Cambridge University Press, 2003.

Kohl, Benjamin H., and Rosalind Bresnahan, eds. *Special Issue: Bolivia under Morales: National Agenda, Regional Challenges, and the Struggle for Hegemony. Latin American Perspectives* 37, no. 4 (July 2010).

Kohl, Benjamin H., and Linda C. Farthing. *Impasse in Bolivia: Neoliberal Hegemony and Popular Resistance.* New York: Zed, 2006.

Kohl, Benjamin H., and Linda C. Farthing, with Félix Muruchi. *From the Mines to the Streets: A Bolivian Activist's Life.* Austin: University of Texas Press, 2011.

Lazar, Sian. *El Alto, Rebel City: Self and Citizenship in Andean Bolivia.* Durham, NC: Duke University Press, 2008.

Lehman, Kenneth. D. *Bolivia and the United States: A Limited Partnership.* Athens: University of Georgia Press, 1999.

McNeish, John-Andrew. "Extraction, Protest and Indigeneity in Bolivia: The TIPNIS Effect." Nancy Postero, ed., *Special Issue: The Politics of Indigeneity in Bolivia. Latin American and Caribbean Ethnic Studies* 8, no. 2 (2013): 221–242.

Malloy, James M. *Bolivia: The Uncompleted Revolution.* Pittsburgh, PA: University of Pittsburgh Press, 1970.

Malloy, James M., and Eduardo A. Gamarra. *Revolution and Reaction: Bolivia, 1964–1985.* New Brunswick, NJ: Transaction, 1988.

Mitchell, Christopher. *The Legacy of Populism in Bolivia: From the MNR to Military Rule.* New York: Praeger, 1977.

Morales, Waltraud Q. *Bolivia: Land of Struggle.* Boulder, CO: Westview, 1992.

Morales, Waltraud Q. "Bolivia's Foreign Policy Toward the Middle East (2000–2015): Promoting a Populist and Radical Agenda Abroad." In *Latin American Foreign Policies Towards the Middle East: Actors, Contexts, and Trends,* edited by Marta Tawil Kuri. New York: Palgrave Macmillan, 2016, pp. 179–200.

Morales, Waltraud Q. *A Brief History of Bolivia.* 2d ed. New York: Facts on File, 2010.

Morales, Waltraud Q. "The TIPNIS Crisis and the Meaning of Bolivian Democracy Under Evo Morales." *The Latin Americanist.* 57, no. 1 (March 2013): 79–90.

Morales, Waltraud Q., and Annabelle Conroy. "New Social Movement Governance in Bolivia: Contention in a Multiethnic Democracy." In *The New Global Politics: Global Social Movements in the Twenty-First Century,* edited by Harry E. Vanden, Peter N. Funke, and Gary Prevost. New York: Routledge, 2017, pp. 29–45.

Nash, June. *We Eat the Mines and the Mines Eat Us: Dependency and Exploitation in Bolivian Tin Mines.* New York: Columbia University Press, 1979.

Olivera, Oscar. *Cochabamba: Water War in Bolivia.* Translated by Tom Lewis. Cambridge, MA: South End, 2004.

Postero, Nancy Grey. *Now We Are Citizens: Indigenous Politics in Postmulticultural Bolivia.* Stanford, CA: Stanford University Press, 2007.

Powers, William. *Whispering in the Giant's Ear: A Frontline Chronicle from Bolivia's War on Globalization.* New York: Bloomsbury, 2006.

Sanchez-Lopez, Daniela. "Reshaping Notions of Citizenship: the TIPNIS Indigenous Movement in Bolivia." *Development Studies Research* 2, no. 1 (2015): 20–32.
Siekmeier, James F. *The Bolivian Revolution and the United States: 1952 to the Present.* College Station: Penn State Press, 2011.
Sivak, Martin. *Evo Morales: The Extraordinary Rise of the First Indigenous President of Bolivia.* New York: Palgrave Macmillan, 2010.
Smale, Robert L. *I Sweat the Flavor of Tin: Labor Activism in Early Twentieth-Century Bolivia.* Pittsburgh, PA: University of Pittsburgh Press, 2010.
Shulz, Jim, and Melissa Draper. *Dignity and Defiance: Stories from Bolivia's Challenge to Globalization.* Berkeley: University of California Press, 2008.
Webber, Jeffrey R. *From Rebellion to Reform in Bolivia: Class Struggle, Indigenous Liberation, and the Politics of Evo Morales.* Chicago: Haymarket, 2011.
WikiLeaks. *The WikiLeaks Files: The World According to US Empire.* New York: Verso, 2015.

## FILMS AND VIDEOS

### Films by Director Jorge Sanjines

*Banderas del Amanecer.* Bolivia, 1982. Political events of 1979–1982, including the failed elections, military repression, coup of García Meza, and the return to democracy.

*El Coraje del Pueblo* (The Courage of the People; The Night of San Juan). Italy/Bolivia, 1971. Repression during the government of General Barrientos, especially of labor and peasant groups under pretext of fighting Ché's guerrilla threat.

*La Nación Clandestina.* Bolivia, 1989. Indian Sebastían Mamani denies his class and indigenous roots and culture and plays a repressive role during dictatorships.

*Ukamau.* Bolivia, 1966. Indian peasant and abuse by *hacendado* as peasant tries to get revenge for the rape of his wife.

*Yawar Malku* or *Blood of the Condor.* Bolivia, 1969. Classic film on Bolivia.

### Other Bolivian Films and Documentaries about Bolivia

*The Bolivian Diary.* France/Switzerland, 1996. Ché Guevara is executed by the Bolivian army (aided by the CIA). Guevara's diary, a personal account of his attempt to foment revolution in Bolivia.

*The Devil's Miner.* United States/Germany, 2006. Independent Lens Documentary of two Bolivian brothers who live in poverty with their mother in mountains of Bolivia and work in Cerro Rico mine.

*Evo Pueblo.* Bolivia, 2007. Dir. Tonchy Antezana; the history of a young farmer of the Bolivian plateau that becomes the first indigenous president of Bolivia.

*Fire on the Amazon.* United States/Peru, 1993. Dir. Luis Llosa; in Bolivia's Amazon basin, corporate cattle ranches are replacing the rain forest, rubber-tapper union leader Santos, forges an alliance with Indians to protest deforestation and is assassinated.

*Hijos de la Montaña de Plata.* Spain, 2006. Dir. Juan Betancor; hard life of Bolivia's miners.

*On the Road with Evo.* United States/Bolivia, 2006. Dir. Túpac Mauricio Saavedra and Gabriel Dvoskin; a "Rough Cut," Frontline/World, PBS documentary by Bolivian filmmaker covering the newly elected indigenous president Evo Morales and his impact on Bolivian politics. Available online: http://www.pbs.org/frontlineworld/rough/2006/05/bolivia_on_the.html.

*Our Brand Is Crisis.* United States, 2005. Dir. Rachel Boyton. About the selling of Bolivian presidential election of Gonzalo Sánchez de Lozada in 2005.

*The Real Thing: Coca, Democracy and Rebellion in Bolivia.* Canada, 2004. Dir. Jim Sanders; a "guerrilla-styled documentary" that focuses on the U.S. drug war and its impact on the peasant farmers of Bolivia.

*Wara Wara.* Bolivia, 1930. This classic silent film by José María Velasco Maidana of the doomed love between a Spanish conqueror and a captive Aymara princess was rediscovered in 1989, restored in Germany, and rescreened after eighty years in La Paz in September 2010.

WEBSITES

### Bolivian Information and News

Twitter: @evoespueblo  Evo Morales Ayma
http://www.boliviaweb.com/  Boliviaweb
http://www.bolpress.com/  Bolivia Press
http://ain-bolivia.org/  Andean Information Network
http://lanic.utexas.edu/la/sa/bolivia/  LANIC links to Bolivia media resources
http://www.cedib.org/  Bolivia press by CEDIB (Centro de Documentación e Información Bolivia)
http://www.democracyctr.org/  Democracy Center
http://www.erbol.com.bo/  News and information portal
http://www.noticiasbolivianas.com/  Noticias Bolivianas: news aggregator for all Bolivian newspapers

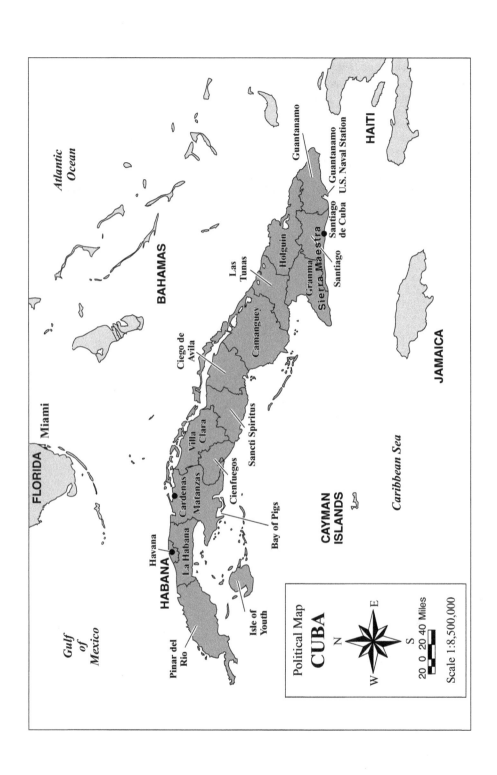

# CUBA

*Gary Prevost*

## Introduction

Cuba is an archipelago of two main islands, Cuba and the Isle of Youth, and about 1,600 keys and inlets. The total area of 42,803 square miles is nearly as large as Pennsylvania. Cuba lies just ninety miles south of Key West, Florida. Low hills and fertile valleys cover more than half the country. Tropical forests and high mountains in the east, which sheltered the revolutionary movement in the 1950s, are contrasted with the prairies and western hills and valleys. Cuba's subtropical climate is warm and humid, with an average annual temperature of 75 degrees. The climate contributes to Cuba's attraction as a year-round tourist destination.

In 1959, Cuba began a social revolution under the leadership of the 26th of July Movement, named for the date in 1953 when movement leaders tried to overthrow the dictatorial regime of Fulgencio Batista with an ill-fated attack on the Moneada army barracks in Santiago, the country's second-largest city. The movement, under the leadership of Fidel Castro and Ché Guevara, carried out profound changes in Cuban society, including the establishment of a socialist economic system. Today, the revolutionary movement that took control in 1959 is still in power despite a more than fifty-year economic blockade by the government of the United States and the collapse of Cuba's main trading partner, the Soviet Union. It is the character of Cuba's revolution and its success in resisting years of efforts by the United States to regain control of the island that have made Cuba far more prominent in world affairs than its small size would indicate.

Cuba's current population is 11.2 million, with no significant growth in the last decade. More than 70 percent of the population lives in urban areas, with the capital, Havana, having 2.5 million residents. Cubans of Spanish descent make up approximately 40 percent of the population, while 12 percent have African ancestry and approximately 50 percent are mulatto (mixed heritage of Spanish and African). There is a small community of persons of Asian heritage (less than 1 percent).

More than half of all Cubans are under the age of thirty—born and raised since 1959. Over 1 million Cubans live in the United States, primarily in south Florida, where they have a major impact on political, social, and economic life. The core of this Cuban American community was roughly 150,000 middle- and upper-class Cubans who left between 1959 and 1961 during the dramatic changes brought on by the revolution. The community has been augmented through the years by tens of thousands of others who have migrated for both political and economic reasons. The government of the United States treats all refugees from Cuba who arrive on U.S. soil as political refugees, a privilege extended to no other Latin American nation. Such a designation grants them the right to live and work in the United States.

Education is a priority in Cuban society, and the state provides free primary, secondary, technical, and higher education to all citizens. Cuba has an average of one teacher for every forty-five inhabitants, and the literacy rate of 99 percent is one of the highest in Latin America. Cuba's health-care system has been a priority for the revolution and is a well-regarded model for the developing world, with more than 260 hospitals and 420 clinics. Family doctors are assigned to each community, and there is a doctor for every 260 Cubans. The average life expectancy is seventy-eight years, and the infant mortality rate is 5.1 per 1,000—both numbers are slightly better than the United States. Cuba also sends thousands of doctors annually to work in the lesser developed world in a program that has become an increasingly important component of the Cuban economy.

Women and Cuban citizens of African descent suffered from widespread discrimination prior to 1959, and the increased prominence of both groups in Cuban society is one of the major achievements of the revolution, although racism and sexism are still prevalent factors in society. Racism is rooted in the importation of millions of slaves to Cuba to cultivate sugar cane from the eighteenth century onward. Prior to 1959, women worked outside the home only as domestic servants and prostitutes, but today, women have been integrated fully into the workplace and have equal access to education and equality before the law. Women also have much greater control over their lives through the widespread availability of contraceptives and abortion. As a result of the equal access to education at all levels since 1959, women now occupy prominent positions in almost all institutions of the society, especially in financial institutions, academia, and management of enterprises. The prominence of female leaders in society has continued to grow as the postrevolutionary generation assumes power. However, women remain underrepresented at the highest levels of the Communist Party, the country's only party, and in the government.

Racial discrimination was formally outlawed at the outset of the revolution, and long-standing customs that barred black Cubans from many public facilities were overcome. As the result of equal access to education, Afro-Cubans have risen to high places in the government, armed forces, education, and commerce. Recent years have seen a significant increase in the study and appreciation of the contributions made by persons of African heritage to the development of Cuba's distinctive culture. The links of this community to Africa were strengthened during the 1970s and 1980s when Cuba developed close political and military ties with the African nations of Angola and Ethiopia. However, racist attitudes still persist in the society;

and although no formal statistics are available, black Cubans seem to make up a greater percentage of those at the bottom end of the economic ladder. As a result, there has been renewed public focus on the issue in the last decade.

Cuba is a predominantly secular society, the result of both a relatively weak Catholic Church prior to 1959 and policies of the revolution. Among the believers, Catholicism is the dominant faith, although many people combine it with ideas of African origin in the religion Santería. Santería is probably the most widely practiced religion in the country, and in recent years it has benefited the most from a more tolerant attitude toward religion by the government. A number of Protestant churches also function, and there is a small and growing presence of evangelicals, who have become important players in other parts of Latin America. At the time of the revolution in 1959, the Catholic Church sided with the Batista regime and many foreign priests, especially Spanish priests, were expelled from the country. While guaranteeing freedom of religious practice, the government actively discouraged religious participation for many years, barring believers from membership in the Communist Party and promotions in most areas of Cuban life until 1991. The changing role of religion in Cuban society was embodied in the visits of Pope John Paul II in 1998, Pope Benedict in 2012, and Pope Francis in 2015. Church attendance and baptisms have risen significantly in recent years, but the number of practicing Catholics is still probably under 200,000.

# History

Prior to the arrival of Columbus in 1492, Cuba was inhabited mainly by the indigenous Taino, Siboney, and Guanahatabey people. In 1511, a Spanish colony was established and the indigenous were forced into slavery and wiped out, mostly by disease. As a result, contemporary Cuba, unlike much of Latin America, retains no indigenous subculture. In 1519, the Spanish governor of Cuba sent Hernán Cortés to conquer Mexico. Cuba became the last stop before Spain for ships delivering the riches of Spanish America and the Philippines. In 1762, Havana fell into British hands for a short period until it was returned to Spain in exchange for Florida the following year. Generally, the Spaniards had little interest in the island until the increased demand for sugar in Europe resulted in its selection for significant cultivation in the eighteenth century, when African slaves were brought to work on the plantations.

When Napoleon invaded the Iberian Peninsula in 1807, Latin American nations began to use the occasion to gain independence, but Cuba remained Spanish, in significant measure because of the successful sugar industry and the close identification of the local elites with Madrid. However, Spanish control was resisted as three wars for independence were fought in the last decades of the century. The first, known as the Ten Years War, had an abolitionist component. It began in 1868 with the leadership of landowner Carlos Manuel de Céspedes, who freed his own slaves, and ended with minor Spanish concessions in 1878. Slavery was abolished two years later. A second inconclusive war lasted a year and ended in 1880. The final struggle began in 1895, led by Cuba's national hero, writer-poet José Marti, who was killed early in the war, and by General Antonio Maceo, an Afro-Cuban who had become a hero when he refused to accept the earlier peace agreement with the Spanish.

A park (Parque de la Iglesia) in San Antonio de los Baños, Cuba. Bust of 1959 Cuban revolutionary hero Camilo Cienfuegos is seen against the background of a colonial-style church (La Iglesia Villa Ariguanado) built in 1826. *(Photo by Miguel Collazo)*

When the fight for independence seemed almost won, the U.S. battleship Maine blew up in Havana Harbor. Spain's resulting war with the United States ended Spanish rule in 1898. Cuba expected immediate independence but instead gained only American occupation. The occupation government of General Leonard Wood began reordering Cuban life along the lines of North American society. The U.S. Congress made the provision that an amendment to an appropriations bill introduced by Senator Orville H. Platt be incorporated in the Cuban constitution of 1901. The amendment limited Cuban sovereignty in fiscal and treaty-making matters and allowed the United States to intervene at any time to maintain a "government adequate for the protection of life, property, and individual liberty." The Platt Amendment also provided for a North American naval base at Guantanamo, a site still occupied by the United States against the objections of the Cuban government. Cuban products now went to North American markets, and the island became in essence a political protectorate of the United States. Twice, in 1905 and in 1917, the United States intervened militarily under the Platt provision. The U.S. Federal Reserve Bank established its only foreign branch in Havana. By 1926 U.S. direct investment on the island totaled nearly $1.4 billion.

Two political parties developed, the Liberals and the Conservatives. In 1925 Liberal candidate Gerardo Machado was elected president for a four-year term. In 1927, Machado changed the constitution, extending the presidential term to six years and had himself re-elected, which in essence destroyed the party system in Cuba. During the Machado presidency, student and university activism grew. Julio A. Mella, a law student and secretary-general of the Student Federation, organized a national student congress. Strongly anti-imperialist and highly critical of the role of the United States, Mella worked with the Mexican Enrique Flores Magón to organize the Cuban Communist Party in 1925. Mella's efforts, though he was exiled and eventually assassinated in Mexico, led to the formation of a strong student movement at the University of Havana known as the Student Directorate. Though strongly repressed by Machado, the student leaders, known as the Generation of 1930, combined with the labor movement and dissident segments of the army to force Machado from power in August 1933. Over the following year, various political factions battled for control of post-Machado Cuba with the United States maneuvering behind the scenes to temper the revolutionary character of the change and defend U.S. economic interests on the island. The primary vehicle for that tempering was Sargent Fulgencio Batista, a former army stenographer who emerged as head of the anti-Machado military forces. Batista would go on to be a dominant political figure in the country over the next twenty-five years, sometimes in formal leadership of the country and other times from behind the scenes.

A new constitution was adopted in 1940 that included radical progressive ideas, including labor rights and health care. Batista was elected president later that year but stepped aside in 1944 under constitutional provisions prohibiting re-election. Ramon Grau San Martin was elected president in 1944. He ran on the ticket of the Cuban Revolutionary Party (Auténtico), which was an outgrowth of the student movements of the 1930s. A second Auténtico president, Carlos Prío Socarras, a student leader of the 1930s, was elected in 1948. The Auténtico program stressed progressive policies but quickly became identified with extremes of corruption. A new political party, the Cuban People's Party (Orthodox), formed around the leadership of Eduardo Chibas, also a member of the Generation of 1930. The party's youth wing was led by Fidel Castro, a law student at the University of Havana. The popularity of the new party indicated that it would win the presidency in the 1952 election, even though Chibas had committed suicide a year earlier. Castro was an Orthodox candidate for Congress.

In a surprise move, Batista launched a military coup in March 1952, removing Prío Socarras. He canceled the upcoming election and appointed himself president. The new Batista government catered to U.S. policy interests by adopting an anti-communist position and by breaking formal diplomatic relations with the Soviet Union. Washington responded with military assistance grants of $1.5 million annually from 1954 to 1956 and doubled this figure during the 1957–1958 period. A military mission assisted in training Batista's army. Cuba was opened up to increased U.S. investment, and Havana became an ever more popular gambling and nightclub center just a few miles off the Florida coast. In the 1950s, organized crime and the Batista government cooperated in personal enrichment.

# Revolution

The opposition to the new Batista government was centered in the urban areas. Following the example of the Generation of 1930, students organized urban guerrilla warfare, using the universities as sanctuaries from the national authorities. In

Havana, students formed the Revolutionary Directorate under the leadership of José Antonio Echeverría. On the other end of the island, in the city of Santiago de Cuba, Frank Pais, son of a Protestant minister, organized students at the University of Santiago.

Castro gathered a number of students and workers around him and sought to begin a national uprising by capturing the army barracks at Moneada, Santiago, and the Céspedes barracks in Bayamo. They attacked on July 26, 1953. In the ensuing battles, most of the attackers were killed, and Castro was captured. He was sentenced to prison on the Isle of Pines (now renamed the Isle of Youth) but released after twenty-two months as part of a general amnesty by Batista under popular pressure. An agreement between Castro and Pais created the 26th of July Movement (M-26-7), named for the date of the Moneada barracks attack. After Castro had made a number of appearances in continued opposition to Batista, he was advised to leave the country and began to enlist and train a guerrilla army in Mexico. There, he met and began work with an Argentine doctor, Ernesto "Ché" Guevara, who had been in Guatemala with the government of Jacobo Arbenz until the CIA-backed overthrow of that government in 1954. After successful fundraising among anti-Batista Cubans, Castro bought a yacht, the Granma, from a retired American couple. In November 1956, he loaded the Granma with eighty-two men and sailed for Cuba, landing in Oriente Province. In a coordinated effort, Pais tried to divert the attention of Batista's forces to the city of Santiago, but the invaders were met by army units and almost completely defeated. The survivors, including Castro, his brother Raúl, and Ché Guevara, took refuge in the Sierra Maestra Mountains.

The Museum of the Revolution, located on the edges of Old Havana, is the former presidential palace. It was constructed between 1913 and 1920. Tiffany's of New York decorated the interior. The palace was the site of an unsuccessful assassination attempt on Fulgencio Batista in March 1957. *(Photo by Catherine A. Kocy)*

For the next two years, the war against Batista proceeded on two fronts, the 26th of July Movement guerrilla campaign in the Sierra Maestra of eastern Cuba and an urban resistance campaign consisting of several different political groupings. During 1957 the guerrillas worked to consolidate their position in the mountains by recruiting local peasants to join them and to provide logistical support. Meanwhile, many Cubans were already bombing government installations, executing police, and undermining confidence in the Batista government. In March 1957, the Revolutionary Directorate under the leadership of Echeverría tried to kill Batista in an armed attack on the presidential palace. The attempt failed and resulted in the death of Echeverría and most of the directorate leadership. Batista responded to the rebellion with widespread repression. Close to 20,000 Cubans would die in the struggle between 1953 and 1959, mostly civilians.

The ultimate military success of the revolutionary uprising was surprising in both its quickness and its small numbers at the beginning. Of the eighty-two men who boarded the Granma in Mexico, only twelve made it to the mountains. After a year of accumulating a few hundred cadre, the guerrillas launched their first attacks in early 1958, just a year before their ultimate triumph. Batista's defeat began in May 1957 when his army carried out an ill-fated offensive against the rebels in the Sierra Maestra. The turning point was a ten-day battle in Jigue when the rebels surrounded a government unit of greater firepower and defeated them. Following that defeat, the morale of Batista's primarily conscript army was very low. Seizing the moment, the 26th of July Movement went on the offensive. In the decisive battle at Santa Clara in December 1958, the rebel forces under the leadership of Ché Guevara and Camilo Cienfuegos totally routed Batista's forces, and the army collapsed. Batista had no reliable defenses around him in Havana, and on December 31, 1958, he fled the country.

Beyond the broad outlines of the military campaign just detailed, the triumph of the movement was a complex phenomenon. It was not a mass-based revolutionary war by a peasant army like those that occurred in China or Vietnam. Peasants were recruited to the movement and gave it important support, but the guerrilla army, 800 as late as September 1958, was primarily a force of students, professionals, and workers from Cuba's middle sectors. The Cuban insurrection was not an urban proletarian revolution. Organized labor, whose ranks were heavily influenced by the communist People's Socialist Party (PSP), opposed the 26th of July Movement until almost the very end, when the communists gave their belated support.

The 26th of July Movement also carried out a broad alliance strategy that culminated at a July 1958 meeting in Caracas, Venezuela, where the Revolutionary Democratic Civic Front was organized, encompassing almost all the anti-Batista forces. The front, combined with the military weakening of Batista, eroded U.S. government support for the regime. In March 1958, under pressure from the Senate, the U.S. State Department placed an arms embargo on Cuba. In December, the Eisenhower administration repeatedly placed pressure on Batista to step down. However, the U.S. opposition to Batista was predicated on the assumption that the moderate anti-Batista forces would dominate the new government. That assumption proved erroneous.

## Revolution in Power

On January 8, 1959, Castro and his followers entered Havana. He noted that the U.S. military had prohibited the Liberator Army under General Calixto García from entering Santiago de Cuba in 1898 and that history would not be repeated. Castro took no position in the new government but set about consolidating Cuba's military forces under his command. Castro and his allies from the Sierra Maestra were committed to a program of radical social and economic reform, and they soon set out on a course to consolidate control over state power.

The victory over Batista came so quickly that most of the old political structures were intact. Only a few thousand of Batista's closest allies left the country. Most of the landowning elite, businesspeople, professionals, and clergy stayed, hoping that they could influence the course of the new government and protect their considerable privileges. Well aware that their radical plans would encounter stiff resistance among those committed to only minor change, Castro and his allies moved to isolate his opponents one by one. In mid-February 1959, Castro accepted the position of prime minister and began to push through measures that would distribute wealth and increase support in the rural areas. In May, an agricultural reform act limited the size of most farm holdings to fewer than 1,000 acres. This measure destroyed the largest holdings, including U.S.-owned sugar properties, several of which exceeded 400,000 acres. Land was distributed to thousands of rural workers, and the government moved to improve conditions on the large farms it now controlled. As a result, support for the revolution increased throughout the countryside. The passage of the Rent Reduction Act resulted in the transfer of about 15 percent of the national income from property owners to wage workers and peasants.

A literacy campaign sent thousands of young volunteers to rural areas. Literacy was increased, and the young supporters of the revolution learned firsthand about the conditions of the rural areas. The government also began building hundreds of new schools and training thousands of additional teachers. Health care was extended to the entire population for the first time with the construction of rural clinics and hospitals. Many private and racially segregated facilities such as clubs and beaches were opened to the public. These radical social and economic measures carried out in the first years of the revolution often involved mass mobilizations, which served to unite the poor majority of Cuban citizens behind the government. These measures also served to identify the movement's political enemies, who exposed themselves through their vociferous opposition to the changes. Moderates in the government, such as acting President Manuel Urrutia Lleo, resigned in protest in June 1959, taking much of the leadership of the old democratic parties and landed elite into exile with him. Simultaneously, the use of revolutionary tribunals to judge and then execute approximately 500 members of Batista's police and security agencies was popular with the Cuban masses but forced many of those who had been associated with the old regime to seek refuge abroad. One by one those political forces that opposed the radical direction of the revolution dropped away until only the revolutionary core remained, primarily the cadre of the 26th of July Movement from the Sierra Maestra and a few allies from the Revolutionary Directorate, who increasingly assumed key cabinet posts and took control of the government bureaucracy.

Mobilized literacy workers in Cuban Literacy Campaign

The increasingly radical direction of the revolution in 1959–1960 led to direct confrontation with Washington. The U.S. government had begun to realize that it had a potential major problem with Cuba when Castro left Washington following a visit in 1959 without requesting significant U.S. aid. Up until that point, U.S. officials had expected to control Cuba through the normal give-and-take of foreign aid. By April 1959, the Cuban leadership had already decided on a series of radical changes, and they were not seeking approval in Washington. At the time Castro left Washington, Cuba still maintained the Batista policy of nonrecognition of the Soviet Union. However, this policy began to change. In February 1960, Soviet First Deputy Premier Anastas Mikoyan paid a visit and a Soviet–Cuban trade agreement was signed. Ché Guevara went to Eastern Europe soon after and lined up $100 million in credits for industrialization in Cuba. Relations with the Soviet Union offered a balance and an alternative to the dominance of American power in Cuban affairs.

The Cuban economy depended on the sale of sugar. A U.S. quota system had allocated Cuba a 2.8-million-ton market at a predetermined and subsidized price considerably above that of the world market. One of the first actions of friendship by the Soviet Union was the February 1960 purchase of Cuban sugar. As U.S.–Cuban relations worsened, the Soviet Union agreed to purchase 2.7 million tons of Cuban sugar if the American government reduced its quota. The Soviet Union also began to supply Cuba with oil. In April 1960, the first shipment of Soviet oil arrived in exchange for Cuban products. American oil companies, which owned Cuba's refineries, advised by the U.S. secretary of the treasury, refused to refine the oil. The refineries were taken over by the Cuban government, and Washington responded by eliminating Cuba's sugar quota, the backbone of the Cuban economy.

The confrontation between Havana and Washington had been building through-out 1959 and 1960. The confrontation over the oil refineries resulted in the first nation-alizations in July 1960, and they were followed quickly by the seizing of U.S.-owned sugar plantations in August and foreign banks in September. Late in 1960 the United States broke diplomatic relations with Cuba, and in January 1961 the Eisenhower administration instituted an embargo on most exports to Cuba. By December 1959 the CIA began to recruit Cuban exiles, and in March 1960 Eisenhower decided to arm and train an exile force for the purpose of invading the island and precipitating the overthrow of the Castro government.

John Kennedy assumed the presidency of the United States in January 1961 and with it the responsibility for the group of Cuban exiles, now training in Central America under CIA direction. In April, the exiles invaded Cuba at the Bay of Pigs but were stalled by local militias, while in the cities the government-organized Committees for the Defense of the Revolution quickly pointed out persons in op-position, who were immediately arrested before any of them could support the invasion. The major result of the American intervention was the consolidation of Castro's position by creating a solid identification between the anti-imperialism of Cuban tradition and the victory of the forces under Castro. Soon after the defeat of the exile force at the Bay of Pigs, Castro declared the "socialist" character of the Cuban Revolution.

From the declared commitment to socialism in April 1961 to the campaign to produce 10 million tons of sugar cane in 1970, the Cuban Revolution moved through its most idealistic period. Domestically, the revolution sought to create a thoroughly homegrown socialist economy marked primarily by a lack of market incentives. Shared sacrifice and a drive for self-sufficiency were the primary driv-ing forces in economic development. The leadership sought to diversify the Cuban economy while instituting a policy of industrialization. New products such as cotton were introduced to the island with the hope of reducing the island's depen-dence on foreign inputs. As part of its sugar agreements with the United States, Cuba had limited its industrial development. There were numerous distortions—Cuba exported raw sugar but imported candy; it produced vast quantities of to-bacco but imported cigarettes. Cuban economic policy of the 1960s was designed to reverse this reality. The determination to end dependence on sugar production took the extreme form of plowing over vast acreage of sugar lands and planting new crops, but these efforts largely failed due to the lack of expertise and appropri-ate climatic conditions.

During the 1960s, the Cuban government also borrowed a strategy of heavy in-dustrialization from the Soviet Union, but these efforts yielded only limited success because of Cuba's particular conditions and the lack of trained personnel. Follow-ing the failure of the "balanced growth" model, Cuba turned to an approach labeled the "turnpike model." Instead of seeking to diversify the economy immediately, Cuba would give priority to sugar production by increasing the cultivated acreage and increasing mechanization. Earnings from sugar export would be used to import machinery to diversify agricultural and industrial production on a sounder basis. Other sectors were also developed, especially the production of cattle, fishing, and citrus fruit. Cement, nickel, and electricity were also expanded with assistance of machinery from the Soviet Union. During this period (1964–1970), the nationalization of the Cuban economy was completed. All industry, commerce, and finance; and 70 percent of agricultural land were controlled by the state.

The turnpike model culminated in the 1970 sugar harvest that was intended to further industrialization without incurring further debt. The harvest was a massive undertaking that involved workers from all sectors and volunteers from around the world; although close to 10 million tons were cut, major processing problems cut the final harvest to 8.5 million tons, far short of the goal. It was a significant blow to the prestige of the revolution, and production dropped in several key sectors outside of sugar. The failure of the revolutionary offensive led to a reassessment of the goals and strategies of the revolution in economic development as well as in other areas. It was recognized that more attention had to be paid to productivity, perhaps at the sacrifice of some egalitarian goals. It was also realized that economic independence from the Soviet Union could not be achieved in the short run.

Concurrent with the changing economic realities, the end of the 1960s brought some changes on the international front. During the 1960s, the Cuban leadership advocated an uncompromising stance toward Latin American elites and the United States. Castro's Second Declaration of Havana saw revolution as inevitable in Latin America due to class oppression, economic exploitation, and oligarchic domination by pro-U.S. repressive regimes. As a strategy, Castro called for armed revolution on a continental scale. The Cubans gave direct material support to revolutionary movements in Nicaragua, Guatemala, Venezuela, and Colombia. Guevara, a leader of Cuba's own revolution, went to fight in Bolivia, where he was killed in 1967. In 1966, Castro convened the Conference of Solidarity of the Peoples of Asia, Africa, and Latin America, where, in his keynote speech, the Cuban leader attacked U.S. imperialism, Latin American elite governments, and all political movements that opposed the necessity of armed struggle, including communist parties. While this strategy struck a responsive chord among revolutionaries throughout the Americas, the policy did isolate Cuba within the hemisphere. Its support for armed guerrilla movements made normal relations with most governments in Latin America impossible and even served to bring Castro in conflict with significant leftist forces in the region.

## Decade of the 1970s—Economic Changes

The decade of the 1970s in Cuba saw a more sober approach in economic policy-making, internal governance, and foreign affairs. In hindsight, this was the decade where the Cuban Revolution was successfully institutionalized. The longevity of the Cuban revolutionary project was secured in a series of crucial policy shifts following the failure of the sugar harvest. As a starting point, the party and Castro himself took full responsibility for the shortfall. There was no significant scapegoating, nor did the events result in a purge of party leadership. The response to the failure was policy initiatives in economics and politics that were probably long overdue. The changes were not instituted hastily but rather introduced gradually over the course of the next decade.

The changes in the economic arena were considerable. The failure of the economic projects of the 1960s led the Cuban leadership to reluctantly conclude that the only viable economic strategy was to move toward economic integration with the East European Council for Mutual Economic Assistance (CMEA). Integration into the CMEA meant that Cuba would primarily concentrate on the production of sugar, nickel, and citrus products in return for oil, manufactured goods, and canned foods. This arrangement worked in large measure because Cuba received a guaranteed return for its exported primary products, something it could not likely have obtained in the open, world capitalist market. Cuba received an especially favorable exchange rate on Soviet oil for its sugar. This arrangement essentially shielded Cuba from the dramatic rise in world energy prices that occurred between 1973 and 1982, devastating many third-world economies. By the mid-1980s, 85 percent of Cuba export–import was with the CMEA countries. The only major trade that remained with the capitalist world was the prized Cuban tobacco. During this period, Cuba did not abandon its goal of increasing food self-sufficiency and developed more domestic industries, but inevitably these efforts did take a back seat to meeting the production goals for the CMEA.

During this time, the Cuban consumer did not always directly benefit from the overall growth of the economy because of its primary export orientation, but the wealth redistribution policies of the revolution did result in a significant sharing of the benefits of CMEA membership. In 1970, virtually all consumer goods were rationed; but by the mid-1980s, only 30 percent of income was being spent on rationed goods, and by 1989 the ration had all but been eliminated. By the end of the 1980s, Cuba had constructed one of the most egalitarian societies in the world, free of the malnutrition and hunger that marked most of its Central American and Caribbean neighbors. However, even at Cuba's height, the Cuban consumer still suffered from a lack of variety and quality of goods available to buy. When the economic shocks of 1989 intervened, Cuba had not yet achieved a fully developed socialist economy.

## Cuban Response to the Collapse of the Soviet Union

Dramatic changes began in Cuba with the fall of the Berlin Wall in November 1989 and were accelerated by the collapse of the Soviet Union at the end of 1991. These events impacted Cuba strongly because, at the beginning of 1989, virtually all of Cuba's foreign trade (85 percent) was with the Soviet Union and other socialist countries of CMEA. Cuba was dependent on CMEA for most of its energy supplies, fertilizer, machine tools, and canned foods. The CMEA arrangement to purchase Cuban sugar, nickel, and other primary products had led to significant economic and social progress after 1970, but the sudden and unexpected loss of these markets wrecked the Cuban economy. In 1989, Cuba imported 13 million tons of oil from the Soviet Union, but by 1992 it was able to import only 6 million tons, all of it at world market prices. The importing of canned food from Eastern Europe was ended altogether. By 1993 Cuba had lost 75 percent of its import capacity, and the country's economic activity contracted by 40 percent. Outside the context of war, no modern economy had been so devastated in the twentieth century. The destruction of the economy resulted in the return of rationing for basic necessities.

The return to rationing was clearly a setback for Cuba, but it also meant that the country was not abandoning its socialist principles. In announcing what he called the "special period in a time of peace," President Fidel Castro declared that the hardships were to be shared, and no one was to be left on his or her own. The equitable rationing of goods was in stark contrast to most of the rest of Latin America, where "structural adjustment programs" often resulted in food prices beyond the means of the majority, who are poor and experience consequent malnutrition. No medical facilities or schools were to be closed. The Cuban government honored this pledge over the ensuing years. To earn immediate hard currency, a program to dramatically increase the tourism industry was implemented despite the social problems, such as drugs and prostitution that come along with it. From just a $165 million industry in 1989, tourism revenues grew to $850 million in five years as successful foreign investments in new facilities were attracted from Europe and Latin America. Today, tourism is a primary engine of the Cuban economy; with 3.5 million visitors annually and revenues of more than $4 billion. The tourism sector thrives even though U.S. visitors make up less than 10 percent of the total, the majority coming from Canada, Latin America, and Western Europe. In addition, after many years of sharp growth, tourism revenues leveled off in recent years. To meet tourist and national needs, Cuba's purchases abroad and subsequent debt has risen.

To spur foreign investment, changes were made in Cuban law to allow full recovery of investments in three years and relatively easy repatriation of profits. Latin American businesspeople, particularly Mexicans, were seriously courted by the Cuban government. By 1994 over 150 foreign-Cuban joint ventures were under way, comprising over $1.5 billion invested from many other countries, including Spain, Canada, Germany, and Israel. These efforts have been limited by the aggressive efforts of the U.S. government to prevent foreign business investment in Cuba. First, the Torricelli bill in 1992 and then the Helms–Burton legislation of 1996 tightened the long-term U.S. embargo on Cuba by punishing firms that make investments on the island. Although the legislation, especially Helms–Burton, has caused friction between the United States and its allies, its presence does represent an obstacle to Cuba's further reintegration into the current world economy. The Obama administration, as part of its 2014 opening to Cuba, called on the U.S. Congress to end the embargo but as of this writing no action had been taken.

Several other factors beyond the turn to tourism have also been crucial to Cuba's economic survival in the post-Soviet period. Recognizing the worldwide demand for mineral commodities, Cuba has invested heavily with foreign assistance in nickel mining and is in the process of becoming the second-leading supplier worldwide and is also a major producer of cobalt. Also crucial to Cuba's economic health has been its relationship with Venezuela, which provides Cuba with the bulk of its imported oil needs in return for the presence of more than 40,000 Cuban professionals, primarily medical. The Cuban medical presence in Venezuela is just one part of a major Cuban economic engine. The exportation of Cuban professionals to more than fifty countries worldwide provides both important medical services in the lesser developed world and billions of dollars annually to the Cuban economy. Cuba also manufactures drugs that are gaining a foothold worldwide.

Mechanized Cuban-made, sugar-cane harvesters, and their proud operators in a Cuban cane field. *(Photo by Patrice Olsen and Harry E. Vanden)*

Also important to the Cuban economy, like others in Latin America and the Caribbean, are remittances sent by Cubans living abroad, mainly in the United States. While exact figures are difficult to ascertain, the amount probably surpasses $2.5 billion. Also crucial to Cuba's economic transformation has been its move away from sugar. Cuba once supplied 35 percent of the world's sugar exports, but that figure is now less than 10 percent, with fewer and fewer Cuban workers in the sugar sector, and much less state investment in the sector.

Despite the transformation of the Cuban economy and robust annual economic growth after 1995, the economy has remained a major challenge for the country, especially in the last several years. First, hurricanes did major infrastructure damage; and then tourism, remittances, and nickel prices all took a hit during the 2008–2009 international economic crisis. Combined with ongoing problems of productivity, especially in the agricultural sector, by 2010 the Cuban economy was at a crossroads as the Communist Party prepared for its first congress in twenty years. The Cuban leadership responded to the economic challenges by proposing the most significant economic reforms since the 1960s. The government announced that it would ultimately reduce government employment by approximately 20 percent—1 million workers—and move those workers into a market-oriented service sector and increase agricultural production by enticing people back to the land. In the six years since the reforms were announced, there have been some significant developments. Thousands of Cubans have opened small businesses, selling items ranging from used clothes to food as the government has authorized hundreds of occupations for private work. In another important nod to the market, Cubans are now allowed to sell homes and cars, and a vibrant market has developed in both arenas. The government's effort to revitalize the agricultural sector has met with limited success, and the process of reducing jobs in the state sector has moved very slowly in part due to relatively high taxes placed on the new businesses.

While the reforms are significant, they leave the overall economy under state control. Further, there is no clear indication whether such wholesale changes will be successful in the short term or whether the government will follow through with all the planned job reductions in the state sector. The government has also announced that the basic food ration will be phased out and replaced by a system that targets only the neediest, but, as of this writing, that change has not occurred. The reforms will need to tap into the long-latent entrepreneurial instincts of segments of the Cuban population and if successful will create wealthier Cubans who will challenge the long-held egalitarian values of the Cuban system and potentially form an independent political force.

## Political Process

The 1970s saw an overhaul of the Cuban political process with the institutionalizing of the formal organs of government power, known as People's Power. These institutions, created island-wide in 1976, represented a shift in governance structures from the first phase of the revolution. The 1960s had seen the consolidation of the Cuban Communist Party (PCC) and the utilization of the neighborhood-based Committees for the Defense of the Revolution (CDR) as dual governing organs. The CDR was designed in 1960 for security purposes, reporting on the activities of counterrevolutionaries and supporting governmental policy. The leadership recognized that the CDR could not rule the country, and that task was given to the PCC created in 1965. The PCC's origins can be traced to 1961 when the alliance with the old Communist Party (PSP) was formalized with the creation of the Integrated Revolutionary Organization (ORI). It was viewed as temporary, and with 16,000 members it was reorganized in 1963 into the United Party of the Cuban Socialist Revolution (PURSC). The PURSC was then acknowledged by the Soviet Union as a legitimate communist party. The final stage of party development began in October 1965 with the launching of the PCC, an organization modeled after the Soviet one. It had a small politburo at the top composed primarily of Sierra Maestra veterans and a handful from the old PSP, a central committee of a few hundred members, and a National Party Congress that was to meet every five years to establish broad policy guidelines. Actually, there was little change in governance style for several years. The first Party Congress was not convened until 1975; in the interim, decision-making revolved almost exclusively around the small core of 26th of July Movement veterans who had led the revolution from its beginning. However, after 1975 the party and its formal structures grew in importance. By 1980 party members occupied nearly all the important positions with the state ministries, the armed forces, and the education system. Like other communist parties, it was a limited-membership organization, acknowledging 800,000 members at its 2011 Congress. Most members start early, beginning as Young Pioneers when teenagers, then becoming Young Communists when they enter adulthood, and finally party members a few years later. Their material rewards are generally limited, yet they have always been favored by somewhat easier access to housing and consumer goods.

The Cuban government never functioned as smoothly or as efficiently as the creators intended. During the early years, costly planning and administrative mistakes were made, some the result of inexperience and others the result of adopting inappropriate Soviet models. In response, popular participation in policy implementation was proposed through newly created government organs called People's Power. Following a trial run in Matanzas province in 1974, the institutions were established nationwide in 1976. Still in operation today, People's Power is composed of municipal, provincial, and national assemblies that are assigned the task of supervising government agencies within their jurisdictions and, at the national level, formulating laws and regulations for the society as a whole. Cuba has 168 municipalities under Cuban Law Number 1304 of July 3, 1976 and reformed in 2010 with the abrogation of the municipality of Varadero and the creation of two new provinces: Artemisa and Mayabeque in place of former La Habana Province. These municipalities are then divided into electoral districts where roughly every 1,000 to 1,500 voters (fewer in some rural areas, more in other areas) elect one representative to a Municipal Assembly of People's Power for a term of two and a half years. In each of these constituent districts, an electoral committee is appointed to oversee the nomination of candidates. The district is broken down into subdistricts, each of which can propose one candidate. This process produces from two to eight candidates maximum from each district; by law there must be at least two nominees—an uncontested election is not permitted. The electoral commission, in collaboration with each candidate, posts the candidate's biography and photo in all public places such as schools, markets, convenience stores, and local clinics for electors to conveniently consult. There is no cost incurred by the candidate. Candidates are not permitted to campaign and can be disqualified if they are judged to be doing so. Run-off elections are often necessary to obtain a majority vote. In the 2012 municipal elections as a first step in the National elections of 2012–2013 from a total of 32,183 candidates, 13,127 municipal delegates were elected in the first round. In 1,410 districts none of the candidate got the required minimum 50 percent of the valid vote; thus, there was a second round election between the two aspirants who got the highest vote.

Of the elected delegates, 33.5 percent are women, and 14.07 percent are young people between the ages of sixteen and thirty-five. Municipal delegates are not paid for this work. Thus, they carry it out on a voluntary basis. Municipal deputies must spend one evening per week available to their constituents to receive their complaints or opinions. However, in practice many delegates receive visits several times a week by their neighbors who are their constituents. Every six months there is a formal accountability session at which complaints, suggestions, and other community interests are raised with the delegate. Delegates are not professional politicians and are generally given time off from their full-time jobs to carry out these functions. There is traditionally considerable turnover among municipal delegates varying from more than one-half to one-third as a result of various factors—for example, delegates not willing to be elected for another term because of the difficulty working as a volunteer after work or study hours or citizens not renominating an incumbent because of perceived lack of competence. Some have compared their position to that of county supervisors in the U.S. system, providing a link to the local population with only limited powers of their own. The municipal assembly has committees responsible for such areas as education, health, and economic affairs. In 1989 people's councils—groups of delegates from within a municipality—were created in Havana to make government more accessible. By 1993 the people's councils were adopted throughout the country.

The Provincial People's Power Assemblies can propose projects and assign priorities to housing, hospitals, and other projects. The provincial legislatures and their executives act as intermediaries between national policy and its execution at the local level. The provincial government allocates its budget, received from the national level, among the various municipal units. This is done by collecting requests and advice from the lower levels. The assemblies are responsible for selecting the directors for industries, for moving personnel from one job to another, and for replacing persons who are removed or retire. However, not all enterprises report to the provincial level; some report directly to the national level.

The highest organ of government is the 612-member National Assembly of People's Power. It is elected by an innovative Cuban notion whereby up to 50 percent of the deputies are made up of the local municipal delegates (in 2013, 46.41 percent). The idea is to maintain as close as possible of a link between the Parliament and the electors, and thus the municipal elections are the first of two steps in the national elections held every five years. The other half is composed of political, social, scientific, cultural, and sports figures. As the legislative body of Cuba, the assembly passes the budget, confirms heads of ministries, makes laws, selects Supreme Court justices, and sets basic economic policies. It meets only infrequently to ratify decisions and draw public attention to national issues. The primary work of the assembly, as in many other legislative bodies worldwide, is done in standing committees. These committees investigate and prepare reports and propose laws to be debated during National Assembly sessions. Their role is mainly consultative and investigative, and they conduct public hearings. The assembly, whose deputies are elected for five-year terms, also elects from among the deputies a thirty-one-member Council of State, including the president and first vice president. The Council of State nominates with the approbation of the National Assembly, the Council of Ministers or cabinet. Both councils run the government on a day-to-day basis between assembly sessions to whom they are accountable.

The president of the Council of State is both head of state and head of government. This gives him the power to nominate members of the Council of Ministers, all of whom are subject to confirmation by the assembly. Raúl Castro was elected president in 2008 when his brother, Fidel, stepped aside for health reasons. Raúl was re-elected in 2013 for a second term but has declared he will not seek re-election in 2018 based on a new Party Congress decision limiting the presidency to two terms. This decision has yet to be amended in a reformed constitution. In addition to its executive functions, the Council of State can legislate by issuing decree laws when the assembly is not in session. The Council of State also is responsible for the court system. The 2013 mandate of the National Assembly is composed of 48.86 women, the third highest in the world. The assembly has 62.91 percent white and 37.09 percent black or mullato deputies. The average age is 48 years old. Typically, the largest group of delegates are leaders of local government, the second largest group are industrial workers, farmers, educators, and health service employees, and others directly tied to production and services. Not surprising, the Communist Party apparatus has at least fifty of its operatives in the assembly.

The PCC is not legally an institution of the government, but by constitutional mandate and in political practice it rules the country. As stated, party members dominate the legislative bodies at all levels. The direction of the Communist Party officially lies in its National Congress, but the body meets rarely. The 2016 Congress was only its seventh in more than fifty years. When the Congress meets, it adopts a set of broad policy goals and elects the Central Committee, the ongoing policymaking body of the party. The committee meets in plenary session at least once every year and officially is the highest body of the party between sessions of the party congresses. Selection to the committee is prized, a mark of honor and prestige in Cuban society. The 150-member Central Committee works as a planning body and shadows the implementation of party policies by the government. Virtually every person of importance in Cuba is a member or alternate member of the Central Committee, from generals and provincial heads to top medical people and administrators. Little is known about the internal workings of this body, but it is said to operate on the basis of consensus since the formal existence of factions is prohibited.

The Secretariat, selected from the membership of the Central Committee, is officially its executive body and is responsible for carrying out the committee's policies between yearly meetings. To oversee the work of the Secretariat, the Political Bureau (or Politburo) is elected from the Central Committee to run the party. In the Political Bureau lies the political power of decision. The Political Bureau's twenty-four members control both the party and important posts in the government. Until his illness Castro was not only the first secretary of the party but also commander-in-chief and president of the Council of State and the Council of Ministers. His brother Raúl was second secretary, first vice president, and minister of the armed forces.

The unions, with a special place in Cuban politics, differ from other organizations and interest groups. The unions' general secretary is a member of the Political Bureau, and the national committee of the Confederation of Cuban Workers (CTC) and its national directorate have the right to initiate laws, a power otherwise restricted to government organs. Normally, the minister of labor is a member of the CTC and the trade unions are guaranteed positions on the Central Committee and in the leadership of the provincial and municipal party organizations. Within the National Assembly and other government bodies, the CTC acts as an interest group, not independent of the PCC, but sometimes representing an alternative perspective.

The primary question facing the aging revolutionary generation is how to stage a political transition to a new generation of leaders who have both the capacity and commitment to retain the social and political achievements of the revolution while adapting to a wider world context dominated by the free enterprise system. While the day-to-day administration of the Cuban government has passed into the hands of the next generation, at the highest levels, control is still significantly in the hands of the Sierra Maestra generation, men in their eighties. Initially, Raúl Castro, the new president, relied on officials with whom he worked in the armed forces to lead key ministries, in the process postponing the transition to a younger generation. Younger leaders have appeared in the membership of the all-important Party Central Committee, elected at the long-delayed sixth Party Congress. As previously mentioned, in an important reform, the Congress supported a constitutional change limiting the service of the Cuban presidency to two terms, meaning that Raúl Castro will step down no later than 2018. In an important nod to the younger generation, the newly elected Cuban parliament in 2013 chose fifty-two-year-old Miguel Diaz-Canal as first vice president, making him the early favorite to succeed Raúl Castro in the presidency. However, only time will tell if a successful generational transition has occurred in the PCC and political system.

Formal, legal political opposition in Cuba does not exist. The PCC is the only legal political party, and throughout the years of the revolution those persons who have sought to pursue a political position against it have faced significant state repression, usually in the form of jail terms. The great majority of the political dissidents have gone into exile, and as a result political opposition inside Cuba today is weak. With active support of the U.S. government representatives on the island, political opposition has shown some signs of life in recent years. The Verela Project succeeded in collecting thousands of signatures calling for constitutional reform; however, the government rejected the petition, and in 2003 seventy-five political dissidents were arrested and many jailed and given long prison terms. The dissident movement received considerable attention in 2010 when hunger striker Orlando Zapata Tamayo died while in captivity, and a few months later the Cuban government agreed to release fifty-two prisoners following intervention by the head of the Cuban Catholic Church and the Spanish government. Most went into exile in Spain. Beyond formal political opposition, is it possible to speak of a civil society in Cuba independent of the PCC and the government? In the mid-1980s, the government permitted society to form new associations "from below." It was a recognition that neither the huge mass organizations (CDR, CTC, etc.) nor the specialized professional associations provided diversity in Cuban society. The civil associations grew slowly at first and then, during the economic crisis of the 1990s, rapidly. Today, there are some 2,150 associations registered in Cuba. The greatest number are fraternal-philosophical, including 420 Masonic lodges. The others range from sports clubs to scientific and technical groups. The approval process is tightly controlled by the government and demonstrates the wariness with which such independence is viewed in party circles.

## Cuba's International Relations

The 1970s and 1980s also saw a reorientation of Cuba's foreign relations. The 1960s had been marked by an uncompromising revolutionary internationalism that clearly aligned Cuba with revolutionary causes throughout the world, especially in Latin America. As a consequence, Cuba was largely in a position of diplomatic isolation except for its growing political and economic ties with the Soviet Union and its allies. All Latin America, with the exception of Mexico, had broken relations with Cuba in the 1960s. However, two events in the late 1960s helped foster a shift in Cuba's international relations. First, in 1967, Castro's confidant Ché Guevara was killed in Bolivia attempting to lead revolutionary forces. Guevara's death came at the end of a series of defeats suffered by revolutionary groups that the Cubans had backed in Latin America. Guevara's defeat led to a reevaluation of the perspective that had argued that the Cuban model of insurrection could be easily copied elsewhere in Latin America. Second, Soviet pressure on Cuba began to take effect. The Soviets had always been uneasy about support for guerrilla warfare and Cuba's outspoken criticism of reform-oriented Latin American communist parties, but the pressure did not become severe until Castro was brought into line following his initial criticism of the Soviet invasion of Czechoslovakia.

Soon after, the election of Richard Nixon brought the prospect of U.S–Soviet detente and with it a strong desire by the Soviet Union to downplay revolutionary rhetoric in the third world. Cuba largely complied with Soviet pressure and began to stress diplomatic initiatives in Latin America, resulting in the reestablishment of relations with Argentina, Peru, and Chile. These three countries had undergone shifts to the left and saw the reestablishment of relations with Cuba as part of a foreign policy shift away from total domination by the United States. Later political changes, particularly the military coups in Chile and Argentina, damaged these relations, although ties with Argentina were never suspended. By the mid-1970s Cuba had shifted its own policy toward more normalized relations with other countries of the Americas, but the general political circumstances, particularly the domination of Latin America by military regimes, made a significant breakdown of isolation difficult.

Cuba's role in Africa in the 1970s signaled the beginning of a new era of foreign policy that was to be marked by an expansion of Cuban power and influence and an end to Cuba's isolation. By the end of the decade, Cuba had 35,000 troops on the continent aiding the revolutionary governments of Ethiopia and Angola against foreign invasions while also providing wide-ranging civilian support from medicine to education. Crucial to the respect Cuba gained throughout the entire third world was the role that Cuban troops played in repelling a South African incursion into Angola in the 1980s.

Cuba's successes in Africa led directly to a prominent role for Castro in the Non-Aligned Movement (NAM), an organization of third-world countries that grew in prestige during the 1970s. In 1979, at the ministerial conference of NAM, Cuba received strong endorsement of its Africa policies, and in September 1979, at the sixth NAM summit in Havana, Castro was elected as president of the organization. The presidency of NAM represented a new high of prestige for Castro and revolutionary Cuba, yet Castro's term as president was not without its setbacks. Cuba lost prestige within the organization when it backed the unpopular Soviet invasion of Afghanistan. However, Cuba's setbacks over Afghanistan were reversed during the crisis over the Falklands/Malvinas in 1982. Overt U.S. support for the

British during that brief war gave Cuba the opportunity to rally Latin American nations on a nationalistic basis against the United States, thus helping to break down Cuba's isolation from Latin America. By the end of the decade, Cuba was extending its trade with most of Latin America, and Cuban leaders, including Castro, were welcome and prominent participants at Latin American and Caribbean political meetings.

Parallel to successes in Africa and with NAM, Cuba also played an important role in the Central American–Caribbean region in the early 1980s as a supporter of the revolutionary governments that emerged in Grenada and Nicaragua in 1979. Cuba's relationship with the Nicaraguan revolutionaries was long-standing, going back to the founding of the Sandinista National Liberation Front (FSLN) in 1961. During the dark days of the FSLN, its leaders often lived in exile in Cuba before returning in the late 1970s to lead a successful revolution against the Somoza dictatorship. The Sandinista uprising received more direct support from countries such as Costa Rica and Venezuela, but once the FSLN attained power, Cuba and Nicaragua established a close relationship. Cuba provided important material support and considerable revolutionary advice.

By 1983 Cuba's fortunes in the international arena were on a strong upward path, but there was a cost for these gains. As it had in earlier times, Cuba became a target of the United States because of its successes. There had been a brief thaw in U.S.–Cuba relations after 1977 when diplomatic missions were reopened in each country and the ban on U.S. citizens traveling to Cuba was lifted. However, the long-standing trade embargo was not lifted, and by 1979 Cuba was being harshly attacked for its policies in Africa. When Ronald Reagan assumed the presidency in 1981, Cuba's relations with Grenada and Nicaragua were attacked, and the ban on U.S. citizen travel to Cuba was reinstated. Cuba's deep involvement continued in Nicaragua through the decade, but the Sandinistas lost power in the 1990 elections after a long and debilitating war with the United States.

The new century has seen the end of Cuba's relative isolation. By 2010 Cuba had full diplomatic relations with more than 175 countries, including all Latin America. In 2009 it was granted full membership in the Rio Group of the Latin American countries. However, Cuba's most important relations are with its fellow members of the Bolivarian Alliance, especially Venezuela, which provides important aid to Cuba in return for thousands of doctors and educators who work in support of the Bolivarian Revolution. The full integration of Cuba into Latin America contributed to the decision in 2014 of the United States to seek full diplomatic relations with the island.

# U.S.–Cuban Relations

Cuba underwent significant changes in the last twenty-five years, but those changes generally did not extend to its relations with the United States until 2014. As Cuba plunged into an economic crisis at the beginning of the decade of the 1990s, U.S. policy focused on attempting to prevent Cuba from reintegrating into the world economy. In 1992, Congress passed and President George H. W. Bush signed the

Cuba Democracy Act, which sought to tighten the thirty-year-old embargo by cutting off third-country trading to Cuba by U.S. companies. The legislation also specified that the only acceptable political change in Cuba was the total removal of the PCC from power. U.S. policymakers fully expected the revolutionary government to fall quickly in the absence of its socialist allies in Europe. When the collapse did not occur, new legislation drafted in Congress by Jesse Helms and Dan Burton sought an even tighter embargo on Cuba by punishing virtually every enterprise from any country that sought to make new investments on the island. Initially opposed by the Clinton administration because of vigorous opposition from U.S. allies, the Helms–Burton legislation was passed into law in 1996 following an incident in the Straits of Florida when the Cuban Air Force shot down airplanes of a Miami-based exile group that had entered Cuban airspace. Tensions between the two governments also grew over continued U.S. government support for groups seeking the overthrow of the Cuban government.

However, opposition to the embargo within the United States continued to build. In early 1998, the U.S. Chamber of Commerce began a public campaign against the embargo, citing worldwide opposition to it and its inconsistency in light of U.S. trade with China and Vietnam, other countries where the Communist Party remains in power. As a result of the campaign, many Republican lawmakers, especially in Midwest farm states, began calling for a lessening of the embargo to allow for the sale of food and medicines. In 2000, legislation permitting the sale of food and medicine was passed by the U.S. Congress and signed by President Clinton. Today Cuba purchases close to $400 million per year in U.S. agricultural products, placing it in the top thirty receivers of such products among U.S. trading partners. However, Cuba received no reciprocity of access to U.S. markets other than a limited number of U.S. citizens traveling to Cuba and U.S. citizens sending remittances to relatives in Cuba. It remained the basic policy of the U.S. government to work for the overthrow of the Cuban socialist system, and the U.S. government stepped up those efforts on a number of fronts. In 2002, the U.S. interests section in Havana became bolder in its cooperation with Cuban opponents of the government, and then in 2004 stepped up its effort to tighten the embargo. Travel of U.S. citizens to the island, including that of Cuban Americans, was sharply curtailed, and efforts were made to significantly reduce the amount of U.S. remittances sent to the island. President Barack Obama assumed power in 2009, promising a new policy for Cuba and Latin America. On December 17, 2014 Obama delivered on his promise when he announced simultaneously with President Raul Castro that following year long secret negotiations brokered by Canada and the Vatican the two countries were ready to achieve full diplomatic relations and that President Obama would work with the U.S. Congress to end the embargo and travel ban to facilitate greater exchange between the two countries. In the two years since the dramatic announcement full diplomatic relations have been achieved and agreements have been signed by the two governments on health and environmental matters, but the U.S. Congress has not moved to end the embargo, severely limiting the creation of a normal trading relationship and significant U.S. corporate investment on the island. The election of Republican Donald Trump has raised questions as to whether the U.S. overtures will continue.

# Conclusion

Cuba in the second decade of the new millennium is as interesting as ever. Fidel Castro passed away in November 2016 after ten years of retirement from public life during which time even Fidel himself admitted the Cuban economic model no longer works, and as a result, the government launched the dramatic economic reforms described earlier in the chapter. They are clearly intended to preserve Cuba as a socialist system under the leadership of a new generation of Cuban Communists. The market mechanisms being adopted threaten the island's vaunted egalitarianism, but if they succeed, not for the first time Cuba will be an inspiration to those in the world looking for a successful model of social justice.

# Chronology

**1898**   Cuba achieves independence from Spain during Spanish–American War; Cuba occupied by U.S. troops until 1902

**1901**   Platt Amendment to new Cuban constitution gives the United States the right to intervene in Cuba to "maintain government adequate for the protection of life, property, and individual liberty"

**1906**   American governor appointed to replace Cuban president

**1925**   Gerardo Machado becomes president and rules in dictatorial manner

**1933**   Machado overthrown by popular revolt

**1934**   U.S. President Franklin Roosevelt abrogates Platt Amendment; provisional government overthrown by "sergeants' revolt" led by Fulgencio Batista

**1940**   Batista elected president under a new constitution

**1952**   Batista takes over government in a coup

**1953**   Young rebels, led by Fidel Castro, attack Moneada military barracks in Santiago and are captured and jailed

**1955**   Batista declares amnesty; Castro flees to Mexico

**1956**   In July, rebels led by Castro travel by boat to east end of Cuba; only a dozen escape battles with armed forces and take refuge in Sierra Maestra Mountains

**1958**   Guerrilla war starting in mountains spreads and defeats Batista's force at end of year

**1959**   Castro creates coalition government in January; in June, moderates in cabinet resign, leaving effective control to Castro and the 26th of July Movement

**1961**   In January, United States breaks relations with Cuba and imposes trade embargo; invasion at Bay of Pigs by CIA supported by Cuban exiles defeated by Cuban army

**1962**   United States confronts Soviet Union over its placement of missiles in Cuba; Cuban Missile Crisis ends with Soviets pulling missiles out in exchange for U.S. promise never to invade Cuba

**1970**   Failed 10-million-ton sugar harvest leads to economic and political reform 1976; new system of local, provincial, and national assemblies creates People's Power

**1989**   Collapse of communist regimes in Eastern Europe begins process of economic reform

**1994** Confrontation with the United States over refugee exodus; private agricultural markets reinstated
**1998** Visit of Pope John Paul II
**2006** Fidel Castro enters hospital with undisclosed illness; presidential duties temporarily transferred to Raúl Castro
**2008** Raúl Castro is elected president for a five-year term
**2010** Cuban government announces major economic reforms
**2013** Raúl Castro is re-elected for a second five-year term and declares it will be his last based on newly enacted term limits
**2014** Presidents Raul Castro and Barack Obama announce that they will reestablish full diplomatic relations and that the United States move to end its embargo on the island
**2016** Fidel Castro dies at the age of ninety.

# Bibliography

Anderson, Jon. *Che Guevara: A Revolutionary Life*. New York: Grove, 1997.

August, Arnold. *Cuba and Its Neighbours: Democracy in Motion*. London: Zed, 2012.

Blight, James, and Philip Brenner. *Sad and Luminous Days: Cuba's Struggle with the Super Powers after the Missile Crisis*. Lanham, MD: Rowman & Littlefield, 2007.

Deutschmann, David, and Deborah Shnookal. *Fidel Castro Reader*. Melbourne: Ocean, 2007.

Gleijeses, Piero. *Visions of Freedom: Havana, Washington, and Pretoria, and the Struggle for Freedom in Southern Africa, 1976–1991*. Chapel Hill: University of North Carolina Press, 2016.

Guevara, Ernesto "Ché." *Episodes of the Cuban Revolutionary War*. New York: Pathfinder, 1996.

Hart, Armando. *Aldabonazo: Inside the Cuban Revolutionary Underground*. New York: Pathfinder, 2004.

Kirk, John M., and H. Michael Erisman. *Cuban Medical Internationalism*. New York: Palgrave Macmillian, 2009.

Leogrande, William, and Peter Kornbluh. *Back Channel to Cuba: The Hidden History of Negotiations Between Washington and Havana*. Chapel Hill: University of North Carolina Press, 2015.

Matthews, Herbert. *Revolution in Cuba*. New York: Charles Scribner's, 1975.

Mesa-Lago, Carmelo, and Jorge, Perez-Lopez. *Cuba under Raul Castro: Assessing the Reforms*. Boulder, CO: Lynne Reinner, 2013.

Morales Dominguez, Esteban. *Race in Cuba: Essays on the Revolution and Racial Inequality*. New York: Monthly Review, 2013.

Morales Dominguez, Esteban, and Gary Prévost. *U.S.–Cuban Relations: A Critical History*. Lanham, MD: Lexington, 2008.

Pérez, Louis A. *The Structure of Cuban History: Meanings and Purpose of the Past*. Chapel Hill: University of North Carolina Press, 2015.

Saney, Isaac. *Cuba: A Revolution in Motion*. London: Zed, 2004.

Smith, Wayne S. *The Closest of Enemies: A Personal and Diplomatic Account of U.S.–Cuban Relations since 1957*. New York: Norton, 1987.

Strieker, Pamela. *Toward a Culture of Nature: Sustainable Development and Environmental Policy in Cuba*. Lanham, MD: Lexington, 2007.

Whiteford, Linda, and Laurence Branch. *Primary Health Care in Cuba: The Other Revolution*. Lanham, MD: Rowman & Littlefield, 2007.

## FILMS AND VIDEOS

*Fidel*. Cuba, 2000.

*If You Only Understood*. Cuba, 1998.

*The King Does Not Lie: The Initiation of a Shango Priest*. United States, 1992.

*Memories of Underdevelopment.* Cuba, 1968.
*The Uncompromising Revolution.* United States, 1992.
*Will the Real Terrorist Please Stand Up.* United States, 2011.

WEBSITES

http://www.granma.cu/   Granma International (newspaper of the Communist Party)
http://www.radiohc.org/index.html/   Radio Havana
http://www.cubagov.cu/   Cuban government (official)

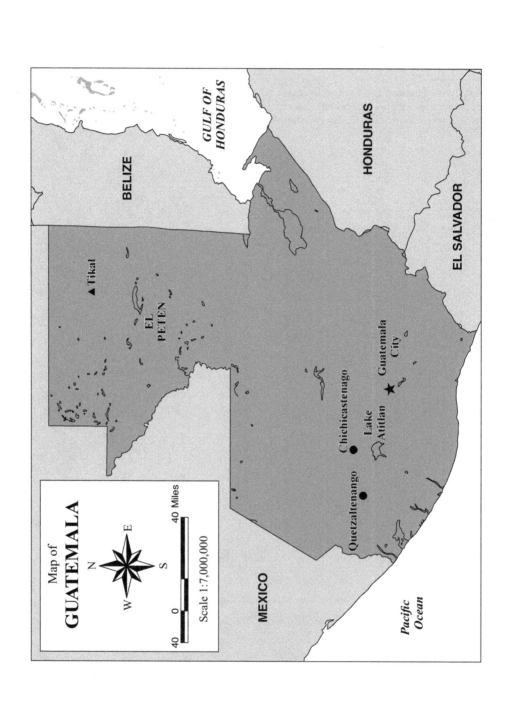

# TWENTY

# GUATEMALA

*Susanne Jonas*

How is it possible that a country as small as Guatemala has taken on such grandiose and dramatic proportions in Latin America? Already in the 1960s, the late Uruguayan writer Eduardo Galeano (1969) referred to Guatemala as "the key to Latin America" and "a source of great lessons painfully learned." During the second half of the twentieth century, Guatemala also loomed large in the saga of U.S.–Latin America relations. Guatemala suffered one of Latin America's longest and bloodiest Cold War civil wars, lasting thirty-six years and leaving some 200,000 civilians dead or "disappeared." In the early years of the twenty-first century, Guatemala's difficult postwar process holds important lessons for the entire hemisphere.

Located just to the south of Mexico and slightly smaller than Tennessee (42,042 square miles), Guatemala is the most populous Central American country. (Ironically, even as Guatemala's demographics are changing very rapidly, there has been no formal census since 2002; hence, demographic statistics are projections from that census and from a variety of other national and international sources.) Its population reached over 16.5 million by 2016 and continued to grow rapidly. The ethnic diversity of its population, which is around 40 percent Mayan (and as recently as the late twentieth century was over 50 percent), is both a rich human/cultural resource and a source of the country's particularly turbulent history. The extreme polarization of Guatemala's social structure stems largely from the compounding of class divisions and exploitation with ethnic divisions, discrimination, and racism, during some periods reaching genocidal proportions.

The Mayan population, subdivided into twenty-two language groups, is dispersed today throughout almost all regions of Guatemala, but historically it was concentrated in the western highlands, or *Altiplano*, bordering on Mexico to the north. The highlands area, world famous for its spectacular beauty, contains a chain of volcanoes, some of them sloping directly into the also world-famous Lake Atitlán. The country's other major regions are the southern Pacific coastal lowlands, site of major agro-export plantations, and the large lowlands Petén area in the north, home to one of the continent's major tropical rain forests as well as the major Mayan ruins at Tikal. In the eastern half of the country, the Sierra de las Minas and Lake Izabal on the Rio Dulce lead to an Atlantic coastal lowland; this area on the Atlantic coast has remained primarily *ladino* (mestizo), with Garifuna and Xinca indigenous populations—and more recently, some Mayan. Guatemala City, the capital, is located on a mesa surrounded by the central highlands.

About half of Guatemala's population has been rural, although urbanization is increasing rapidly. Guatemala City has come to concentrate a significant percentage of the population (projected at 30 percent in 2016), followed by the highlands city of Quetzaltenango, and Los Angeles, California. The urban primacy of Guatemala City is even more striking in regard to political power and availability of social services.

## Precolonial, Colonial, and Neocolonial History

Pre-Hispanic indigenous Guatemala was by no means "primitive"; what the Spanish conquerors found in 1524 was a complex, stratified, proto-class society torn by multiple social tensions. Despite these class divisions, the population was unified by a common belief system. The ruling elites were priests rather than warriors, which explains the predominance of temples in the Mayan ruins. Preconquest Mayan society had developed sophisticated technologies—more advanced and scientific in some areas (e.g., mathematics and astronomy) than those of Europe during the Middle Ages. By the sixteenth century, it was a society in transition; had it not been interrupted by the conquest, it might well have developed into a society as advanced as those in Western Europe.

Despite the class divisions in pre-Hispanic Guatemala, at no time before the conquest did the Maya suffer the systematic material deprivation that has characterized Guatemala since 1524. Malnutrition, for example, was not a chronic condition of the population, as it is today. Prior to 1524, Guatemala was a primarily agricultural society in which land was cultivated both individually and communally to produce food and other necessities for the population itself, rather than for export to the world market, that is, for consumption and profit by foreigners thousands of miles away. In this sense, underdevelopment as we know it today did not exist in Guatemala prior to 1524 but was the direct outcome of the conquest and Guatemala's integration into an expanding capitalist world economy.

The Spanish conquest itself, a violent clash of two socioeconomic systems and two cultures, forcibly integrated the Maya into Western civilization: several million were killed immediately, and by 1650 an estimated two-thirds to six-sevenths of the indigenous population in Central America and Mexico had died, largely through disease epidemics. Following the military conquest, the colonization of Guatemala was carried out by Spanish state functionaries, Spanish settler planters and merchants, and the Catholic Church, which maintained a very close relationship with the state.

The conquest and the subsequent three centuries of colonialism (1524–1821) integrated Guatemala into an expanding capitalist world market that determined the colony's production priorities and systematically channeled its surplus into the pockets of foreign ruling classes. This dependent relationship also left internal legacies that endured far longer than the colonial relation to Spain itself: agricultural mono-export (at the expense of food production, tying the ups and downs of the entire economy to the fortunes of export prices), concentration of landholding in the hands of a small minority, and various forms of unfree/forced indigenous labor as the underpinning of the entire socioeconomic structure. The overlap between the degrees of class and racial oppression was notable: unlike *indios*, as they were disparagingly called by the *criollo* (European) elites, and unlike African slave labor imported into areas where the indigenous populations had been exterminated, the *ladinos*, or mixed-origin populations, acquired greater freedom and social mobility and eventually formed the nuclei of the urban working and middle classes.

Independence from Spain in 1821 (led by the elites but supported by nearly all sectors of the population, each for its own reasons) brought little change in internal structures, although it initiated a diversification of Guatemala's external contacts. Spain's previous economic and commercial monopoly was replaced by British interests and (later in the nineteenth century) by German and U.S. interests. Within Guatemala, power alternated between Liberals and Conservatives from 1821 until the "Liberal Revolution" of 1871. Both the Liberal and Conservative parties were dominated by *criollo* elites, but they differed on issues such as the state's relation to the Catholic Church and the degree of centralization versus federalism.

The 1871 triumph of the Liberals led by General Justo Rufino Barrios came in the wake of the rise of coffee as the dominant export. The land for the coffee estates, which required large concentrations of land and labor, came from the newly consolidated Liberal (anticlerical) state's confiscation of Catholic Church properties, once that Church had been disestablished, and from a major new wave of expropriations of indigenous communal lands. The Liberal Revolution also saw the consolidation of the army as the principal labor mobilizer and enforcer; the army viewed its mission as maintaining order in the countryside. Ironically, the Liberal Revolution, touted as a necessity for development, modernization, and progress, proved far more costly than previous governments to the indigenous populations, who were now subjected to harsher forms of forced labor. Except for a brief democratic interlude in the early 1920s, Liberal military dictators ruled with an iron hand on behalf of the coffee oligarchy and foreign investors for over seventy years.

The other major change during the late nineteenth and early twentieth centuries was the expansion of U.S. private corporate interests into Guatemala and several other Central American countries. The most notable of the U.S. corporate investors in Guatemala, the United Fruit Company (UFCo), began monopolistic operations in banana production; UFCo became the largest landowner in Guatemala, writing its own contracts with the government and operating virtually unrestricted by any Guatemalan government regulations—functioning, in essence, as "a state within a state." UFCo also owned the only railroad and hence could dictate transportation prices. U.S. interests reinforced the interests of Guatemala's coffee growers: concentration of land ownership and coercion applied to the subjugated indigenous labor force.

This period also saw the rise of the United States as a world power and a great expansion of U.S. influence over internal Guatemalan political affairs, in alliance with the local landed oligarchy. This alliance was the key to the longevity of the Liberal dictatorships. Washington's support was crucial to the last of these dictators, Jorge Ubico, who ruled from 1931 to 1944. The Ubico regime contained social tensions, particularly after the world depression left hundreds of thousands of rural workers unemployed during the 1930s, through top–down repression rather than reform. The model of the "pressure cooker" in Guatemala and other Central American nations contrasted sharply with the "safety valve" reforms and industrialization programs of the 1930s in larger Latin American countries such as Mexico, Chile, and Brazil. Although the purely repressive Central American model gave the appearance of guaranteeing stability, subsequent events revealed the fragility of that model.

# The Revolution of 1944–1954 and the 1954 CIA Intervention

Under the weight of the economic and social crises caused by the world depression of the 1930s, Guatemala's neocolonial order cracked in 1944, when a broad middle-and working-class coalition (including young army officers) overthrew the Ubico dictatorship. Thus was initiated the Revolution of 1944–1954, the only genuinely democratic experience in Guatemala's entire history. The two governments of Juan José Arévalo (1945–1950) and Jacobo Arbenz (1951–1954) for the first time guaranteed basic democratic liberties (including free elections and the formation of political opposition parties), abolished forced labor (which had been nearly universal for the indigenous population), granted minimum wages and basic organizing and bargaining rights for workers and peasants, and established basic social welfare institutions. In addition, the Revolution modernized Guatemalan capitalism, undertaking agricultural diversification and industrialization programs, fomenting national enterprises, and regulating foreign investment to serve national priorities.

Most significant in this nationalist democratic revolution was Arbenz's far-reaching (but capitalist) agrarian reform of 1952, which distributed land to over 100,000 peasant families. The principle underlying the land reform was the government's expropriation of large tracts of land that were not being used by their owners, with compensation based on the value declared for tax purposes. The land would be used to produce, and the large numbers of landless would own enough land to have some disposable income; in short, the producers could become consumers, forming the basis for an internal market and reducing dependence on the world market. (This basic principle has always associated industrialization and modernization of the economy with labor guarantees and land reform.)

Coming on top of other nationalistic moves by Arbenz, the expropriation of unused land belonging to UFCo (the largest landowner in Guatemala, which had been using a mere 15 percent of its holdings) prompted an angry response from the U.S. government. (Not so coincidentally, John Foster Dulles, secretary of state beginning in 1953, and CIA director Allen Dulles had been major lawyers for UFCo.)

More broadly, Washington feared the spread of the example of reform and popular mobilization from Guatemala to other Central American countries. The fact that the Guatemalan Revolution was occurring at the height of the Cold War enabled the United States to charge that Guatemala was serving as a "beachhead for Soviet expansion" in the Western Hemisphere (although in reality the Soviets were virtually uninvolved in Guatemala) and gave the CIA the justification it needed to plan the ouster of Arbenz.

After mid-1952, the CIA worked with Guatemalan rightist opposition forces (e.g., many of the large landowners, rightist politicians, and the Catholic Church) to organize the overthrow of the Arbenz government in June 1954 and install in its place a pro-U.S. counterrevolutionary regime led by (U.S.-chosen) Colonel Carlos Castillo Armas. In general, the "Liberation," as its Guatemalan supporters called it, marked the first major U.S. Cold War covert intervention in the Western Hemisphere and a turning point in U.S.–Latin American relations. Many elements of that CIA covert operation were subsequently used against other leftist governments in Latin America, for example, the Castro government in Cuba (1961), the Allende government in Chile (1973), and the Sandinista government in Nicaragua (1980s).

## Aftermath: Chronic Crisis

The Castillo Armas regime immediately reversed the democratic and progressive legislation of the Revolution, including everything from the land reform and labor laws to literacy programs that were deemed "procommunist indoctrination." All pro-Revolution organizations and political parties were declared illegal; under direct U.S. supervision, the government also unleashed a wide-ranging witch hunt and McCarthy-style repression campaign that cost the lives of some 8,000 supporters of the Revolution and forced thousands of others into exile or hiding. The legacy of the Revolution and its violent termination was to compound the social polarization already characteristic of Guatemala, throwing the country into permanent crisis.

---

THE U.S. COVERT OPERATION IN GUATEMALA, 1954

- A team of ambassadors to Central America instructed to collaborate with the ouster of Jacobo Arbenz; head of the team was John Peurifoy as ambassador to Guatemala, an extreme anticommunist with prior experience in defeating the rebels in the Greek civil war.
- CIA chose Colonel Carlos Castillo Armas to be the Guatemalan pointman to lead the anti-Arbenz operation.
- CIA fully trained, equipped, and funded the anti-Arbenz mercenary army (in Honduras) of Guatemalan rightists, led by Castillo Armas.
- CIA carried out psychological warfare through clandestine "Radio Liberty" in Guatemala and through aerial propaganda leaflets dropped from planes.

- Funded and worked with anti-Arbenz elements in the Guatemalan military leadership while neutralizing those loyal to Arbenz.
- Maneuvered on the diplomatic front to get the OAS to approve a resolution (March 1954) condemning Guatemala as posing a threat of "communist aggression" to the entire hemisphere.
- Imposed embargo on arms to Guatemala by all U.S. allies and subsequently used the shipment of (obsolete) arms from Czechoslovakia as a pretext for a final move against Arbenz.
- Helped Castillo Armas's mercenary army "invade" Guatemala from Honduras on June 18, 1954; as soon as they were over the border, flew Castillo Armas (in Ambassador Peurifoy's private plane) to Guatemala City.
- Simultaneously, CIA planes, manned by U.S. pilots, strafed and bombarded Guatemala City and other cities, to demoralize Arbenz and get him to resign (which he did on June 27).
- Despite having promised to allow pro-revolution military officers to take charge following Arbenz's resignation, the United States double-crossed them and installed Castillo Armas in power.
- Organized powerful lobby (largely United Fruit Company–orchestrated) in the U.S. Congress, media, and elsewhere to secure "consensus" in U.S. public opinion supporting the coup and to suppress criticism of the operation (at the height of the McCarthy era in the United States.)

Nevertheless, even under the post-1954 counterrevolutionary order, history could not be reversed, since the same underlying structural dynamics and contradictions that had caused the Revolution continued to develop. The Guatemalan economy, like that of all Central America, enjoyed a thirty-year period (1950–1980) of growth based on the expansion and diversification of agricultural exports to the world market; a minimal industrialization program during the 1960s and 1970s was carried out mainly by U.S. companies within the context of the Central American Common Market. However, even export-led growth generated turmoil because of the extreme inequities in resource and income distribution. To take the most telling indicator for Guatemala as an example, after the reversal of the land reform, 2 percent of the population controlled 67 percent of the arable land. In the 1970s, the diversification of agricultural exports brought significant new land expropriations from peasants and new concentrations of land tenure; the main beneficiaries were army generals using their control over the state apparatus to accumulate personal wealth. Thus, impoverishment stemming from land concentration intensified exponentially as Guatemala became virtually the only country in Latin America not to have sustained even minimal land reform.

At the social level, the diversification of the productive structure significantly modified Guatemala's traditional class structure and reshaped the ruling coalition between the army and economic elites, the latter represented in a tightly knit umbrella organization, the Coordinating Committee of Agricultural, Commercial, Industrial, and Financial Associations (CACIF). Among other things, diversification of the ruling class meant incorporation of the upper ranks of military officers and a redefinition of the alliance between the army and the bourgeoisie (economic elites). Rather than opening up the class structure, these modifications only accentuated its overall polarization.

At the bottom of Guatemalan society, meanwhile, industrialization and agricultural diversification did not significantly expand the proletariat as a fully employed labor force. Rather, the countryside saw the growth of a semiproletariat: land-starved peasants from the highlands were forced to work on southern coastal plantations as seasonal migrant laborers during part of the year. In the cities, migrants from rural areas swelled the ranks of an underemployed informal proletariat. As a consequence, the "development" of the 1960s and 1970s actually left a decreasing proportion of the economically active population fully employed on a permanent basis. These tendencies were disastrously compounded during the 1980s, Latin America's "Lost Decade."

The profound changes in society after 1954 produced new generations of social movements (labor, peasant, indigenous, student, community, and human rights)— first in the 1960s, then in the late 1970s, and (after they were destroyed in the late 1970s and early 1980s) again in the second half of the 1980s. In the absence of any serious attempt to meet the needs of the poor or the indigenous or to use the benefits of growth during the 1960s and 1970s to redistribute wealth, these movements continually exerted new pressures upon the state and the established social order. These pressures were contained by a level of repression at times unmatched anywhere else in Latin America; one generation after another of social movement leaders and activists, as well as moderate leftist political opposition leaders, was eliminated by the army and illegal paramilitary forces. Even systematic repression failed to stop the reemergence of popular movements in one or another form, although it severely restricted their functioning.

These massive social conflicts defined Guatemalan politics during the last four decades of the twentieth century. Within an overall framework of direct military rule, there was a civilian interlude under President Julio César Méndez Montenegro (1966–1970) and a more definitive return to civilian rule beginning in 1986; in both cases, the army dominated politics from behind the scenes. However, largely as a legacy of the experience of the 1944–1954 revolution and its violent overthrow, hardline regimes, whether military or civilian, faced constant challenges. It was precisely the refusal to permit even moderate reformist political options that created the conditions for the growth of a revolutionary guerrilla movement attempting to repeat the experience of the 1959 Cuban Revolution. Quite literally, there was no alternative within the political system.

The first wave of guerrilla insurgency, during the 1960s, was centered in the eastern region, where the peasants were *ladino* rather than Mayan. Although small and without a base among the indigenous population, the insurgency of the Fuerzas Armadas Rebeldes (Rebel Armed Forces; FAR) was contained only after a major counterinsurgency effort (1966–1968), organized, financed, and run directly by the United States along the lines of its operations in Vietnam. This was a turning point in Guatemala, with U.S. military advisers playing a decisive role in transforming the Guatemalan army (previously "weakened" in Washington's view by nationalist tendencies and inefficiency) into a modern, disciplined counterinsurgency army. The military grew to some 46,000 troops during the 1980s; it became known as the most brutal in Latin America—a literal "killing machine"—and during the 1970s and 1980s came to dominate the state directly.

The counterinsurgency state was institutionalized after 1970, when the head of the 1966–1968 army campaign, Colonel Carlos Arana Osorio (the "butcher of Zacapa"), used that victory to win the 1970 presidential election. Since the goal of this first "dirty war" had been to eradicate the civilian support base of the guerrillas, it cost the lives of over 8,000 civilians. It was also within this context, in Guatemala, that Latin America first experienced the artifacts of counterinsurgency war: semiofficial death squads (based in the security forces and financed by economic elites, with such names as "White Hand" and "An Eye for an Eye") and disappearances of civilian opposition figures. Since that time, Guatemala has had more than 40,000 civilian disappearances, accounting for over 40 percent of the total for all Latin America. The army's temporary victory by 1968 over FAR insurgents thus ended the first phase of Guatemala's thirty-six-year civil war.

## Insurgency and Counterinsurgency in the 1970s–1980s

As suggested earlier, the structural transformations of the 1960s–1980s caused Guatemala's Mayan populations to redefine their class identity. These same factors profoundly affected their self-conception and identities as indigenous. Economic growth followed by economic crisis broke down the objective barriers that had kept the Maya relatively isolated in the highlands. This was greatly intensified by the economic and political crises of the 1970s and 1980s, when growing numbers of Maya were forced to migrate to the southern coast as seasonal laborers and to Guatemala City. These changes and displacements brought them into increased contact with the *ladino*, Spanish-speaking world. Rather than "*ladinizing*, or acculturating, them, however, these experiences reinforced their struggle to preserve their indigenous identity, although in new forms—as Guatemalan Jesuit priest-scholar-activist Ricardo Falla put it, to discover "new ways of being indigenous." These factors form the background for understanding why Guatemala's Mayan peoples became one of the powerful social forces driving the insurgency of the 1970s and 1980s.

In the countryside, structural contradictions—the crisis in subsistence agriculture compounded by a massive earthquake in 1976—uprooted and displaced thousands of indigenous peasants, causing them to redefine themselves in both class and cultural terms. As producers, they were being semiproletarianized as a seasonal, migrant labor force on the plantations of the southern coast, meanwhile often losing even the tiny subsistence plots of land they had traditionally held in the highlands. The combination of their experiences of being evicted from their own lands and their experiences as a migrant semiproletariat radicalized large numbers of highlands Mayas. Even the more developmentalist influences were contradictory in that they raised hopes and expectations in the 1960s, only to dash them in the 1970s. The clearest examples of this dynamic were those peasants who received land from the government's colonization programs in the 1960s, only to have it taken away again in the 1970s, as powerful army officers grabbed profitable lands in colonization areas.

Culturally, highlands indigenous communities were being transformed and redefined throughout the 1960s and 1970s as they came into contact with the *ladino* world. Increased contact had the paradoxical effect of reinforcing their defense of their ethnic and cultural identity, and this became a factor in mobilizing their resistance to the *ladino* state. Politically, "reformist" parties such as the Christian Democrats came into indigenous communities, raising expectations of change—only to leave those hopes unfulfilled for most people. Meanwhile, Mayan organizations were defined by the government as "subversive" and excluded from "normal" political expression. Even their self-help organizations, formed in response to the devastating 1976 earthquake, were viewed as a threat.

Finally, increased army repression against indigenous communities had contradictory effects: rather than terrorizing the Mayas into passivity, by the late 1970s it stimulated some of them to take up arms as the only available means of self-defense against state violence. All these contradictory experiences of the 1970s occurred in interaction with the transformation of grassroots organizations of the Catholic Church, the rise of Christian Base Communities(CBCs), and the gradual emergence of a "Church of the Poor." These new religious currents became central to the radicalization of the Mayan highlands.

All these strands were woven together by 1976–1978 in the emergence of the Comité de Unidad Campesina (CUC) as a national peasant organization, including both peasants and agricultural workers and both Mayas and poor *ladinos*, but led primarily by Mayas—by definition a subversive organization from the viewpoint of the ruling coalition. CUC came into the limelight after a major massacre at Panzós, Alta Verapaz, in 1978 and the 1980 massacre at the Spanish embassy, in which Guatemalan security forces burned alive more than three dozen indigenous protesters. Among the victims was Vicente Menchú, father of Rigoberta Menchú. In February 1980, CUC staged a massive strike of workers on the southern coast sugar and cotton plantations; from the viewpoint of landowners and the army, this strike was their worst nightmare come true.

Equally important in the growth of a politicized indigenous movement was a change in the stance of the revolutionary insurgents vis-à-vis the Mayan population, within the context of a broader reevaluation of strategy and organizational recomposition after the defeat of 1968. This involved recognition of the failures of the foco strategy (see Chapter 10) of the 1960s as fundamentally militaristic and not rooted in a solid mass base. Even more serious, the insurgents had virtually ignored the indigenous population during the 1960s. By the time of their resurgence in the early 1970s, the three major organizations had generally come to understand some of these errors in their organizing strategies; two of them, Ejército Guerrillero de los Pobres (EGP) and Organización del Pueblo en Armas (ORPA), spent several years being educated by the indigenous population and organizing a political support base in the western highlands (and other areas) before renewing armed actions later in the 1970s.

In sum, veterans of the 1960s insurgency were able to reorganize and reinitiate their struggle in the early 1970s, this time in the western indigenous highlands and with Mayan communities becoming central participants. The active involvement of up to 500,000 Mayas in the uprising of the late 1970s and early 1980s was without precedent in Guatemala, indeed, in the hemisphere. Coming in the wake of the 1979 Sandinista victory in Nicaragua and the outbreak of civil war in El Salvador, also in 1979, this remarkable awakening in the indigenous highlands provoked a revolutionary crisis, threatening the army's century-old domination over rural Guatemala.

The guerrilla military offensive reached its height in 1980–1981, gaining 6,000 to 8,000 armed fighters and 250,000 to 500,000 active collaborators and supporters and operating in most parts of the country. In the context of the Sandinista triumph in Nicaragua and the outbreak of civil war in El Salvador,, both in 1979, the new wave of armed struggle in Guatemala was taken very seriously by the ruling coalition as heralding a possible seizure of power by the insurgents. In early 1982, the various guerrilla organizations united in the Guatemalan National Revolutionary Unity (URNG), overcoming years of sectarian divisions.

Even as unity was proclaimed, however, and even as the revolutionary movement achieved its maximal expression during 1980 and 1981, a change in the balance of forces between the insurgents and the army began during the second half of 1981 as the army initiated an all-out "scorched-earth" counteroffensive. By the spring of 1982, the revolutionary movement had suffered serious losses to its infrastructure in the city, where security forces had previously, in 1978–1980, decimated the leadership and ranks of the unions and other popular movements and political opposition forces. In the highlands, the army unleashed a virtual holocaust upon the indigenous communities. Blinded by its own triumphalism, the URNG had in fact lost the initiative, and some of its fundamental weaknesses came to the surface. As a result of the URNG's weaknesses and of major changes within the ruling coalition, the army gained the upper hand and dealt decisive blows against the insurgents. For the next several years, the URNG was on the defensive; it did not recover a capacity to take new initiatives until the late 1980s.

A major reason for this second defeat of the guerrillas and the suffering inflicted on its supporters among the population was the failure to have anticipated the scorched-earth, genocidal war unleashed by the Guatemalan security forces in mid-1981; hence, tens of thousands of highlands Mayas were left unprepared to defend themselves. The statistics are staggering: from mid-1981 to 1983 alone, 440 villages were entirely wiped off the map and up to 150,000 civilians were killed or disappeared. There were over 1 million displaced persons (1 million internal refugees, up to 200,000 refugees in Mexico). Accompanying these massive population displacements was the deliberate destruction of huge areas of the highlands (burning of forests, etc.), causing irreversible environmental devastation. The

This billboard was at the entrance to Chichicastenango until after the signing of the Peace Accords at the end of 1996. It shows the degree of control by the army and the Civilian Self-Defense Patrols (PACs), misnamed "Comités Voluntarios," since there was nothing voluntary about them. *(Photo by S. Jonas)*

aim of these genocidal policies was not only to eliminate the guerrillas' popular support base but also to destroy the Mayan culture, identity, and communal structures.

The army carried out these goals in the first stage (1981–1983) through scorched-earth warfare and in the second stage (after 1983) through the imposition of coercive institutions throughout the countryside that were designed to consolidate military control over the population. Among these institutions were mandatory paramilitary Civilian Self-Defense Patrols (PACs; at one point involving 1 million peasants, one-quarter of the adult population); "development poles," rural forced resettlement camps where every aspect of people's lives was subject to direct army control; and militarization of the entire administrative apparatus of the country. These counterinsurgency institutions were legalized in the new constitution of 1985, which provided the juridical framework for civilian government in the late 1980s.

## Transition to Restricted Civilian Rule

As discussed earlier, the beginning of revolutionary insurgency in Guatemala during the 1960s generated a counterinsurgent response on the part of the United States and the Guatemalan ruling coalition, which was institutionalized in state power after 1970. During the late 1970s, the ability of the military regimes to govern Guatemala deteriorated seriously as a consequence of relatively weakened internal cohesion within the ruling coalition and the lack of any consensual basis or societal legitimacy. The clearest examples were the openly fraudulent elections of 1974, 1978, and 1982. By 1982, these divisions were serious enough to spark recognition of the need for a change in the nature of military rule; to recover some modicum of legitimacy, at least among the ruling sectors; and to end Guatemala's international isolation as a pariah state and hence its restricted access to international financial assistance.

The shift is often seen as beginning with the military coup of March 1982 (following the third successive electoral fraud), which brought to power the regime of General Efraín Ríos Montt. But this was a false start, as the Ríos Montt government (March 1982–August 1983) presided over the bloodiest era and the majority of the massacres. It was only after this most brutal phase of the counterinsurgency war had accomplished its goals under Ríos Montt that army leaders and their civilian allies, now under the military government of General Oscar Mejía Víctores (1983–1985), took concrete steps toward a return to civilian rule. They recognized that a facade of constitutional democracy was needed to overcome the contradictions of direct military dictatorship. This understanding was the background for the political process of 1983–1985, during which a constituent assembly was elected to write a new constitution containing basic guarantees of citizens' rights, at least on paper (alongside institutionalization of PACs, etc.). Finally, presidential elections were held in late 1985.

The 1985 presidential election, although free of fraud, was severely restricted and unrepresentative of large sectors of the population as only rightist and centrist parties that had reached agreement with the military were allowed to participate. Aside from the exclusion of the left, there were no real choices on substantive issues. Nevertheless, the election did permit nonmilitary candidates for the first time in fifteen years; it was overwhelmingly won by Christian Democrat Vinicio Cerezo, the most progressive of the candidates. Cerezo's victory was greeted with high hopes for a real change from the many years of military dictatorship.

Despite these hopes and despite having come into power with a significant popular mandate, however, Cerezo chose not to fully use the space that he had— that is, not to wage the struggle that would have been needed to achieve a real transfer of power from the military to civilians. His government did very little to control the army or address the country's underlying social and economic problems; he accepted the army's priority of defeating popular and revolutionary forces, and this significantly limited the possibility for genuinely pluralistic politics or for ending the civil war. In this regard, the Cerezo period (1986–1990) turned out to be not so much a genuine transition to democracy as a necessary adjustment for trying to deal with Guatemala's multiple crises and reestablish minimal international credibility. It evolved into a civilian version of the counterinsurgency state, in some respects a continuation of what had been imposed in the late 1960s.

A second nonfraudulent election was held in 1990; it was viewed as significant insofar as it established the continuity of civilian rule, between Cerezo and newly elected Jorge Serrano. Nevertheless, abstention was extremely high, with only 30 percent of eligible voters participating; and once again, no leftist opposition parties were permitted. By 1990, however, there were new currents in the "informal" arena of Guatemalan civil society (outside the electoral process), and these began to undermine the foundations of the counterinsurgency state. One major expression of these currents was an emerging national consensus, articulated primarily in dialogues led by the Catholic Church, for an end to the civil war. Virtually all political sectors began to recognize that Guatemala could not be truly democratized until the civil war was ended through political negotiations (rather than a military victory by either side), until the country was demilitarized, and until underlying structural inequalities and ethnic discrimination were acknowledged and addressed.

## Social Crisis and Reemergence of Social Movements

Structural social crisis—ironically, a product of macroeconomic growth during the 1970s—was compounded during the 1980s when the international capitalist crisis hit Central America (and all Latin America) as severely as the depression of the 1930s had. Among its principal manifestations were rising prices for all industrial imports (largely a consequence of the oil shocks) coupled with falling prices for Central American exports. These crises left the Guatemalan economy suffering negative growth rates during the 1980s; both unemployment and inflation soared to unprecedented levels. As a result, purchasing power in 1989 was 22 percent of what it had been in 1972, and the overall poverty levels jumped markedly during the late 1980s.

The central social characteristic of Guatemala during the 1980s (and into the 1990s) remained increasing concentration of wealth amid pervasive poverty. All the Central American countries shared this characteristic, but Guatemalan poverty has been particularly extreme on several counts. First, the inequality of resource and income distribution has been greater, and no measures have been taken since the overthrow of Arbenz to alleviate it (i.e., there has been no land or tax reform). The second particularity of Guatemalan poverty has been the number of social indicators on which it ranks worst (illiteracy, physical quality of life, and infant mortality). The third particularity is the ethnic component of poverty: all statistics for the Mayan population are far worse than the national average. As elsewhere, there has also been a marked feminization of poverty, with increasing numbers of women becoming heads of households and low-wage workers (see details later in this chapter).

These characteristics of extreme underdevelopment and inequality were not new to Guatemala, but a number of things did change dramatically during the 1980s. First, under the impact of the international crisis of the 1980s, all Guatemala's economic and social problems were seriously aggravated. Even at the macroeconomic level, Guatemala lost over fifteen years of growth during the 1980s, reversing the growth pattern of the previous thirty years. Second, after the mid-1980s, the government began to implement austerity policies more aggressively, culminating in the neoliberal structural adjustment measures of the late 1980s and early 1990s; these policies further aggravated the grave social crisis. Third, informalization of the urban economy left only slightly over one-third of the workforce fully and permanently employed.

This last indicator was among the important modifications in Guatemala's class structure during the 1980s, which left close to 90 percent of the population living below the official poverty line by the end of the decade (up from 79 percent in 1980); nearly three-quarters of the population lived in extreme poverty and were unable to afford a basic minimum diet. During the late 1980s, the impact of the economic and social crisis in regenerating social ferment among the poor proved greater than the ability of the counterinsurgency state to repress such ferment. Despite the reescalation of repression against labor and other popular movements, the constitution of this huge majority of the population that was united by being poor led to a slow rebuilding and reemergence of popular movements after the disasters of the early 1980s; a stream of austerity protests began even under the military government in 1985 and continued with surprising vigor.

Guatemala's new popular movements were the product not only of austerity measures but also of the country's multiple crises, including the many crises of uprooted populations. The war alone left over 10 percent of the population displaced. Natural disaster (the 1976 earthquake), war, and economic crisis during the late 1970s and 1980s brought significant migration to the capital, causing its population to double. Increasingly, the urban poor were indigenous, and more than half the households came to be headed by women. A significant number of the new urban poor (250,000–500,000 people) lived in the city's massive shanty towns in precarious squatter settlements. The absence of basic social services (running water, sewage, electricity, and transportation) sparked new community struggles that became as important as more traditional labor union struggles among organized sectors of the labor force. Residents of one such community protested by leaving the body of a child who had died from typhoid on the steps of the National Palace.

In the rural areas, meanwhile, hundreds of thousands of those displaced within the highlands or to the southern coast joined together with the landless already living there to form a national movement for land. The reconstituted popular movements of primarily rural Mayas also included human rights groups organized around demands that were openly political and directly related to the ongoing counterinsurgency war: for example, the Group of Mutual Support (GAM), an organization of wives and mothers of the disappeared and other human rights victims; the mainly indigenous widows' organization, the National Coordinating Committee of Guatemalan Widows (CONAVIGUA); the Council of Ethnic Communities "Everyone Is Equal" (CERJ), founded to empower the highlands Mayas to resist service in the PACs; and the Council of Displaced Guatemalans (CONDEG), representing internal refugees. Many thousands of Mayas also defied army relocation and control programs by fleeing to remote mountain areas and forming permanent Communities of People in Resistance (CPRs), which began to gain formal recognition nationally and internationally in the early 1990s.

Among the main new characteristics of Guatemala's social movements in the late 1980s and early 1990s were the following. The first and most important was the centrality of the indigenous population and its double condition of exploitation and ethnic discrimination in both rural and urban settings. This was reflected in the rise of diverse movements and organizations fighting for a broad range of indigenous rights. These movements were bolstered by working with indigenous organizations throughout the Americas (the 1991 continental meeting was held in Guatemala) and by the awarding of the 1992 Nobel Peace Prize to Guatemalan Mayan and political opposition leader Rigoberta Menchú. The second novelty was the growing role of the Catholic Church alongside Guatemala's social movements. Liberation theology was a major influence throughout the 1970s and 1980s, and even after the appearance and rapid growth of evangelical Protestant groups during the 1980s (reaching up to one-third of the population), the Catholic Church remained a leading force in articulating the demands of the popular movements.

The third new element of the late 1980s and 1990s movements was the slowly emerging and increasingly visible protagonism of women. (By this time, women were also becoming more central to the labor force and as single heads of household.) Women had been excluded from traditional politics in Guatemala (voting as well as office holding), and their political activities had generally been very limited. Traditional political parties had excluded women from virtually all positions of political leadership. Only in the late 1980s did women begin to increase their participation in electoral (and nonelectoral) politics, although such participation remained limited by the traditional problems of discrimination and illiteracy. On the economic front, women began to organize in workplaces where they were overrepresented (e.g., *maquiladora* industries, schools), although their presence in union leadership remained less visible. In their communities, by contrast, women became visible as the principal organizers of austerity protests in the 1980s and ongoing community mobilizations in the 1990s (e.g., for social services in shantytown neighborhoods). Women were also very prominent in human rights organizations such as GAM and indigenous human rights organizations such as CONAVIGUA, CERJ, and CONDEG. It was only in the 1990s, however, that Guatemalan women founded organizations designed explicitly to achieve their rights as women and began to demand equal participation for their organizations in broader coalitions. In short, Guatemala experienced the gradual emergence of a bloc of popular and indigenous organizations.

By the late 1980s, the context for political action was also shaped by the resurgence of the URNG. Even having destroyed much of the URNG's social base in the highlands in the early 1980s, the army had been unable to inflict a "final" defeat upon the insurgent forces or to win the war definitively. Hence, the organizations of the URNG survived the holocaust; they remained the nuclei of future resistance even at their low point and gradually began to recover their ability to take initiatives, both militarily and politically. Nevertheless, their inability to resist the army's counteroffensive of the early 1980s combined with the "civilianization" of the counterinsurgency state in the mid-1980s required once again a profound reorganization and redefinition of strategy.

This redefinition became necessary, first, in response to the clear lesson of the early 1980s that "taking state power" through military victory over the counterinsurgency forces was a totally unthinkable objective and that the cost of the second round of the war for the civilian population had been so high as to preclude a strategy based simply on continuing the war. Guatemala was one of the few countries in Latin America where the armed insurgent movement operated continuously since the 1960s. However, armed struggle is not what people choose unless they see no other options; after thirty years of counterinsurgency war, particularly after the holocaust of the early 1980s, the URNG could not simply propose another decade of war. (In fact, the mid-1980s saw several splits within the organizations of the URNG, with dissidents arguing that the insurgents should have laid down their arms after the defeat of 1981–1983.) Second, in view of the 1985 election and transition to civilian rule, that is, to a potentially legitimate government, the left had to find new ways of becoming a significant force in civil society. Hence, shortly after the 1985 election, the URNG began to propose dialogue and negotiations for a political settlement to the war.

To summarize, because of its profound contradictions, the Guatemalan counterinsurgency project could not be stabilized. First, it did not and could not win the battle for legitimacy, given its intrinsic brutality. Second, its basic premise that the army had definitively won the war against the guerrilla insurgency was disproven in practice, causing discontent and destabilization within the ruling coalition. Finally, this was combined with neoliberal economic policies designed to expand the economy solely through world market-oriented nontraditional exports. Aside from intensifying social conflicts, these policies limited economic growth precisely because they did nothing to develop the internal market. By the late 1980s, then, Guatemala was by no means in an insurrectionary situation or ungovernable, but it was in a chronic social crisis.

For four years the Guatemalan government stubbornly insisted that the insurgents must "lay down their arms" and disarm unilaterally without negotiating any substantive issues. They maintained this stance even after the 1987 Central American Peace Accords negotiated (in Guatemala City) primarily to end the Contra War against the Sandinista government in Nicaragua but also to address the need for negotiated peace in El Salvador and Guatemala. Only several years later did Guatemalan army and government spokespeople finally acknowledge the significant upsurge in guerrilla actions. The implicit admission that the war could not be won militarily by either side created the conditions, for the first time beginning in 1990–1991, for serious discussions about ending the war.

## Guatemala's Peace Process (1990–1996)

This section summarizes the saga of the Guatemalan peace process and the accords signed in December 1996. It is important to keep in mind that as recently as 1992–1993, hardliners among Guatemala's military and civilian elites were determined not to negotiate a settlement permitting a legal presence or political participation by the insurgent left or its allies, and they regarded virtually all the organizations of civil society as the guerrillas' allies or facades. Particularly after the signing of a negotiated peace in neighboring El Salvador in January 1992, the elites vowed never to tolerate such an outcome in Guatemala. The extraordinary story of how and why, from 1994 to 1996, the Guatemalan army and government found themselves involved in very much the same kind of process as the Salvadorans, with the United

Nations as moderator and verifier of the process, is chronicled in detail elsewhere (Jonas 2000).

By 1990, considerable political pressure for peace had built up within Guatemala as well as internationally. During 1989, the National Reconciliation Commission (established by the 1987 Central American Peace Accords) sponsored a National Dialogue. Although boycotted by the army, the government, and the business elites, this dialogue expressed a clear national consensus among all other sectors in favor of a substantive political settlement to the war. The dialogue process projected a series of URNG meetings with the political parties, social sectors (private enterprise, popular, and religious movements), and finally with the government and the army.

In early 1991, the newly elected government of Jorge Serrano opened direct negotiations with the URNG. For the first time, top army officials agreed to participate in meetings to set the agenda and procedures for peace talks without demanding that the URNG first disarm, although they still hoped to win URNG demobilization in exchange for minimal, pro forma concessions. During the next year, there were agreements in principle on democratization and partial agreements on human rights. The precariousness of the process became evident when it stagnated in mid-1992 and moved toward total breakdown during the last months of Serrano's crisis-ridden government.

The entire peace process was derailed by the May 1993 *Serranazo*, or attempted *auto-golpe*. Serrano's suspension of the constitution and dissolution of Congress to seize absolute control (initially but briefly supported by some factions of the army) unleashed a major political and constitutional crisis. After being repudiated by virtually all sectors of civil society and the international community, the *Serranazo* was resolved in June through the (most unexpected) ascendance of Human Rights Ombudsman Ramiro de León Carpio to the presidency. However, the peace process remained at a standstill during the rest of 1993. In January 1994, with the new government's obstructionist tactics having run their course, the negotiations were resumed, this time on a significantly different basis. During the 1991–1993 rounds, Guatemala's peace talks had been moderated by Monsignor Rodolfo Quezada Toruño of the Catholic Bishops' Conference, with the United Nations in an observer role. As of January 1994, both sides agreed that the United Nations should become the moderator; this paved the way for significantly increased involvement by the international community, raising the stakes in the negotiations and giving the entire process a less reversible dynamic.

Furthermore, the January 1994 Framework Accord established a clear agenda and timetable. This accord also formalized a role for the broad-based multisector Assembly of Civil Society (ASC), which included virtually all organized sectors of civil society (even, for the first time, women's organizations) and the major political parties. Only the big business sectors represented in CACIF decided not to participate. Having gained new experience during the *Serranazo*, grassroots organizations had become increasingly vocal in demanding participation in the peace process. The ASC was also striking in the diversity or plurality of political and ideological positions represented within its ranks; unlike El Salvador's popular organizations in relation to the Farabundo Martí National Liberation Front (FMLN), the ASC was by no means a simple instrument of the URNG. As the main agreements were being hammered out, the ASC—after itself engaging in a fascinating process of consensus building among widely divergent positions—offered proposals to the negotiating parties on each issue. While not binding, their proposals had to be taken into account by the two parties, and the URNG adopted many of the ASC proposals as its own negotiating positions. The formation of the ASC also gave Guatemala's organized popular sectors their first sustained experience of participating in the political process and was the precursor to the eventual participation by many of those sectors in the 1995 election.

The breakthrough Human Rights Accord was signed in late March 1994, calling for the immediate establishment of international verification mechanisms to monitor human rights. After the mandated UN Verification Mission in Guatemala (MINUGUA) finally arrived in November 1994, its functioning on the ground throughout Guatemala created a political climate that was much more positive for ending systematic human rights violations (as well as mechanisms for denouncing such violations, an important change in a country previously dominated by fear). At the negotiating table, meanwhile, two new accords were signed in June 1994, on the Resettling of Displaced Populations (mainly Guatemalan refugees returning from Mexico) and a Truth Commission empowered to *esclarecer*, or shed light on, past human rights crimes but without judicial powers and without naming the individuals responsible—which sparked fierce criticism from popular and human rights organizations.

The next item on the agenda, the Accord on the Identity and Rights of Indigenous Peoples, was the subject of negotiation for nine months, until March 1995. The signing of this accord was a landmark achievement for a country whose population is 60 percent indigenous. This accord went far beyond antidiscrimination protections for Guatemala's indigenous majority to mandate a constitutional reform redefining Guatemala as a multiethnic, multicultural, and multilingual nation. If fully implemented, this agreement would require profound reforms in the country's educational, judicial, and political institutions. It laid the formal basis for a new entitlement of Guatemala's indigenous majority and established their right to make claims upon the state—all of which is a precondition for democracy and genuine pluralism in Guatemala. This accord together with independent initiatives by a variety of indigenous organizations also created a new context for social and political interactions and for a more democratic political culture. As an example of this new culture, after its signing, the residents of Sololá, a town in the heart of the conflict zone, decided to base the 1996 competition for the "Queen of Sololá," traditionally a beauty contest, on who could best explain the Accord on Indigenous Rights.

Nationally, the peace process was directly impacted by the dynamics of the campaign for the November 1995 general election, and vice versa. The most important novelties of this electoral process were the URNG's early 1995 call, urging participation in the vote, and the formation of a left-of-center electoral front of popular and indigenous organizations (the "left flank" of the ASC), the New Guatemala Democratic Front (FDNG), to participate in the elections. In the November 1995 general elections, no presidential candidate received an absolute majority. The major surprise was the stronger-than-expected showing of the newly formed FDNG, which won six seats in Congress; in addition, alliances between the FDNG and locally based indigenous "civic committees" (unaffiliated with the traditional political parties) won several important mayoralties, including Xelajú (Quetzaltenango), Guatemala's second-largest city, half of whose residents are *ladino* and half indigenous. A January 1996 run-off for president pitted modernizing conservative Alvaro Arzú of the National Action Party (PAN) against a stand-in for the rightist former dictator Efraín Ríos Montt of the Guatemalan Republican Front (FRG), who opposed the peace process. Arzú won by a scant 2 percent margin.

Even before taking office, Arzú had already held several direct, secret meetings with the URNG. Shortly after taking office, Arzú immediately signaled his intention to bring the ongoing peace talks to a successful conclusion. Once the formal peace negotiations were reinitiated and following intensive consultations with the private sector, the Accord on Socio-Economic Issues was signed in May 1996—this time, finally, with CACIF support. The accord did not directly resolve Guatemala's most fundamental problems, such as grossly distorted land ownership and income distribution, widespread poverty, and unemployment combined with underemployment. However, it did commit the government to increase spending on health and education and to carry out a much-needed tax reform, the latter being the key to financing virtually all the reforms from the Peace Accords and the minimum basis for any future change. Meanwhile, the most difficult issues of social justice were deferred to the future.

The crowning achievement of the peace process came in September 1996, with the signing of the Accord on Strengthening of Civilian Power and Role of the Armed Forces in a Democratic Society. This accord mandated constitutional reforms subordinating the army to civilian control and restricting the army's role to the sole function of external defense, a stark contrast to the army's past practices of involving itself in all areas of government. Most important, the accord created a new civilian police force to handle all internal security matters. The army's size (46,000) and budget were also to be reduced by one-third; the PACs and other counterinsurgency units were to be eliminated. This accord also contained important provisions for reforms of the corrupt and dysfunctional judicial system.

After a serious crisis in October 1996 that nearly derailed the entire process, the talks were resumed and operational accords were signed in December. These dealt with a definitive ceasefire, constitutional and electoral reforms, the legal reintegration of the URNG (entailing a partial amnesty for both the URNG and the army), and a timetable for fulfillment of all the accords. Following the dramatic return of the URNG leadership to Guatemala on December 28, the historic Final Peace Accord was signed in Guatemala's National Palace on December 29, 1996, amid considerable national celebration and international attention. Thus ended the first phase of the peace process that the Guatemalan elites had vowed never to permit in Guatemala.

How did this "never" turn into acceptance? Aside from the role of the United Nations and four international "friend" governments, within Guatemala, slowly but surely and despite fierce resistance and significant delays, the peace process acquired credibility. Even the recalcitrant army and CACIF could no longer afford to resist the process openly and found themselves having to defend their interests by participating in the negotiations. In short, none of the major Guatemalan players could afford to boycott the process.

Seen in its totality, the peace process was a great step forward for Guatemala's democratic development, although not for social justice. Rather than being imposed by victors upon vanquished, the negotiations represented a splitting of differences between radically opposed forces, with major concessions from both sides. In addition, most of the accords contained provisions for citizen participation in decision-making (including by the Mayan population) and provided innovative mechanisms, such as the Women's Forum, for training and participation by those previously excluded. (Although there was no accord on women's rights, several of the main accords contained provisions specifically designed to expand women's rights.)

Taken as a whole, the accords and the provision for UN verification of government compliance represented a departure from forty-two years of painful Cold War history and provided the framework for institutionalizing political democracy. If fully implemented, the accords had the potential to open an opportunity for significant transformations of Guatemalan society. However, even after the signing and initial implementation of some accords, the road remained full of minefields: the efforts to fully implement the accords were bound to encounter very serious resistances from those who held power in the old system.

## Postwar Guatemala (1997–2013)

By the early 2000s, sixteen years after the signing of the final Peace Accords, it remained evident that the implementation phase of Guatemala's peace process was just as difficult and dangerous as the negotiations had been. Guatemala's "peace resisters" lost no time in sharpening their knives to defend the old order, taking every opportunity to challenge the substance and the continuity of the peace process. Just getting the entire complex of new laws and constitutional reforms through Congress sparked battles on many fronts. The Arzú government, which had taken such bold initiatives to finalize the peace negotiations, was much more timid—on many occasions, resistant—with regard to compliance with the accords. This became particularly evident in early 1998, when it pulled back from its commitment to carry out a reasonable tax reform that was to have been a long-range mechanism for internal financing of the Peace Accords. Meanwhile, the rise in common crime, a problem intrinsic to postwar situations around the world, provided a pretext for keeping the army involved in policing and other internal security matters, in violation of the demilitarization accord.

An extremely difficult moment for postwar Guatemala came in May 1999, with the referendum on constitutional reforms required to put into effect some of the most significant provisions of the accords on indigenous rights and on strengthening civilian power (limiting the functions of the army and making judicial reform). Although polls had shown ahead of time that the reforms were likely to be approved, a well-financed last-month blitzkrieg campaign by peace resisters (who urged a "no" vote, using blatantly racist arguments) succeeded in defeating the reforms—that is, in getting a 55 percent majority among the bare 18.5 percent of the electorate that voted. Clearly, the main winner of this vote was abstention, and the main loser was the peace process itself. This political disaster raised a basic question as to whether Guatemala's fragile democracy could be consolidated. (For detailed analysis, see Jonas 2000, Chapter 8.)

---

### PRESIDENTS/REGIMES SINCE THE 1930S

- Jorge Ubico (1931–1944; military dictatorship)
- Juan José Arévalo (1945–1950; freely elected)
- Jacobo Arbenz (1951–1954; freely elected, overthrown)
- Col. Carlos Castillo Armas (1954–1957; military coup)
- Gen. Miguel Ydígoras Fuentes (1958–1963; military dictatorship)
- Col. Enrique Peralta Azurdia (1963–1966; military coup and dictatorship)
- Julio César Méndez Montenegro (1966–1970; freely elected, Partido Revolucionario)
- Col. Carlos Arana Osorio (1970–1974; elected, military dictatorship)
- Gen. Kjell Laugerud (1974–1978; electoral fraud, military dictatorship)
- Gen. Romeo Lucas García (1978–1982; electoral fraud, military dictatorship)
- Gen. Efraín Ríos Montt (1982–1983; military coup and dictatorship)
- Gen. Oscar Mejía Víctores (1983–1985; military coup and dictatorship)
- Vinicio Cerezo (1986–1990; freely elected, Democracia Cristiana Guatemalteca)
- Jorge Serrano (1991–1993; freely elected, Movimiento de Acción Solidarista; 1993 attempted *auto-golpe*)
- Ramiro de León Carpio (1993–1995; appointed transition government)
- Alvaro Arzú (1996–1999; freely elected, Partido de Avanzada Nacional)
- Alfonso Portillo (2000–2003; freely elected, Frente Republicano Guatemalteco)
- Oscar Berger (2004–2007; freely elected, Gran Alianza Nacional)
- Alvaro Colom (2008–2011; freely elected, Unidad Nacional de la Esperanza)
- Otto Pérez Molina (2012–2015; freely elected, Partido Patriota)
- Jimmy Morales (2016–2019; freely elected, Frente Convergencia Nacional)

---

The late 1999 general elections gave a strong victory to Alfonso Portillo, the presidential candidate of FRG, the party founded by ex-dictator Ríos Montt, one of the principal architects of the 1980s genocide. Politically, the FRG's victory resulted from an astute populist campaign by Portillo combined with a "punishment vote" against the Arzú government—primarily for the PAN's failure to take even the most basic measures to improve people's daily lives (socioeconomic situation and personal security), while maintaining the privileges of the rich. In this sense, it was a vote about citizens' most immediate concerns. Within the FRG delegation that was to dominate the new Congress were former army officials who had been key architects and henchmen of the scorched-earth dirty war of the 1980s—not to mention Ríos Montt himself, who was to preside over Congress.

At the same time as this shift from a moderate-rightist to an extreme-rightist government occurred, the election also featured a stronger-than-expected showing of the Alianza Nueva Nación (ANN), the leftist coalition constructed by the newly legalized URNG together with other progressive forces. Despite its scarce resources, internal divisions, and many other disadvantages, the ANN won 13 percent of the national vote and nine seats in Congress. Structurally, the participation of the left as the third force, albeit a very weak and splintered one, was a step toward normalizing Guatemalan politics; for the first time since 1954, all political and ideological tendencies were represented. But 1999 was a high point for leftist electoral forces; in the 2003, 2007, and 2011 elections, they declined significantly from 1999 and were increasingly reduced to a bare minimum.

Meanwhile, pro-peace forces in Guatemalan civil society—particularly Mayan and women's organizations—continued to pressure the government to honor and implement the Peace Accords. Although their efforts gained limited immediate results, they established for the first time the presence of counterhegemonic forces in a society where traditionally the only social sector to exercise any real power was the business elite (CACIF). Despite these pressures for change, Guatemala's political (state) and social institutions remained weak and dysfunctional, beyond the capacity to conduct fraud-free elections after 1985. A major legacy of the counterinsurgency state was the decades-long subordination of all state institutions to the army.

As late as the early 2000s, Guatemala's institutions were still unable to guarantee basic rights in practice, despite the attempted reforms of the judicial system and the army through the Peace Accords and despite UN monitoring efforts. The new Civilian National Police force, independent of the army, and the weak and corrupted justice system were characterized by pervasive impunity (nonpunishment of blatant crimes, including human rights crimes). The most heinous peacetime crime was the April 1998 assassination of Auxiliary Bishop Juan Gerardi just two days after the Archbishop's Human Rights Office, which he had founded, released a report attributing 85 percent of the killings during the war to state security forces (the armed forces and PACs). This assassination, along with other major assassinations and crimes from the thirty-six-year war, remained unsolved and unpunished for many years.

The official Truth Commission (Historical Clarification Commission) established by the Peace Accords released a far-reaching report in February 1999, based on 9,000 interviews; the report attributed 93 percent of the human rights crimes committed during the war to the army and its paramilitary units (versus 3 percent to the URNG) and established that some actions and policies of the Guatemalan government during the 1980s constituted "acts of genocide." The report also sharply criticized the U.S. role in supporting the apparatus of terror for decades. However, implementation of the Truth Commission's follow-up recommendations would require new battles (discussed later).

## GOVERNMENT INSTITUTIONS

**Executive:** President (elected every four years), cabinet, and armed forces (technically subordinated to the president as commander-in-chief but actually has functioned autonomously, including a host of subunits, such as the presidential guard and military intelligence, which were slated by the Peace Accords to be radically changed).

**Legislative**: One-chamber Congress, with 158 members.

**Judicial System**: Regular court system consists of sixty-five courts with jurisdictions for different regions of the country, appeals courts, and the Supreme Court. Members of the Supreme Court are elected by Congress, and other court judges are nominated by the Supreme Court and approved by Congress. There is also an active Public Prosecutor's office. In addition, Guatemala has a Constitutional Court that has far-reaching powers in matters beyond traditional constitutional issues (e.g., striking down new taxes).

The Peace Accords mandated thorough overhaul and reform of the judicial system, to eliminate ingrained problems of corruption and impunity, vulnerability to threats, and incompetence. In addition, the accords mandated incorporation of Mayan customary law (*derecho consuetudinario*) into the legal system. While some of these reforms have been discussed, most reforms have not yet been made, and some are being reversed.

**Semigovernment Institutions**: Supreme Electoral Tribunal, Constitutional Court, Ombudsman's Office for Human Rights.

**Local Government**: Twenty-two departments, 330 municipalities; departmental governors are appointed by the executive, and municipal mayors are elected.

The Portillo government (2000–2003) remained under the shadow of the party dominated by retired General Ríos Montt, one of the principal architects of the 1980s genocide. The Portillo years sent the incipient healing process into reverse gear. Instead of reparations to war victims, for example, this government initiated the payment of compensation to former members of the PACs, which were reconstituting themselves, although they had been identified by the Historical Clarification Commission and by virtually all human rights agencies as principal perpetrators of human rights crimes; they had been slated by the Peace Accords to be totally dissolved. The Portillo government was also notable for its total incompetence and unprecedented corruption in every sphere of public and private life.

The November 2003 election marked a significant step forward as voters decisively rejected the presidential candidacy of Ríos Montt. After a December run-off election, the new government of the Grand National Alliance (GANA) that took office in January 2004 was led by conservative businessman Oscar Berger as president and public servant Eduardo Stein as vice president. In theory, this new government had one last opportunity to return to the agenda of the Peace Accords and had promised to do so. But it was heavily dominated by the business elites, deflating the widespread hopes among civil society organizations. The Berger government presented itself as less corrupt than its predecessor, but it was dominated by the interests of CACIF. Social conflicts (e.g., over land) proliferated.

The country was still marked by strong army influence in many spheres, combined with the reconstruction and coordinated actions of the ex-PAC networks and the prominence of retired military officers in virtually every political party in Congress except the small leftist parties. The executive branch remained beholden to clandestine "parallel powers" within public institutions. Institutionalized justice remained a distant goal in Guatemala as impunity reigned supreme and honest judges continued to be killed, threatened, or forced into exile. Meanwhile, social activists also continued to face human rights threats and crimes by "unidentified" forces.

Finally, another particular wave of human rights crimes emerged after 2000, specifically targeting women. "Feminicide" has meant not simply female victims of generalized social violence but specific violence and brutality directed against women—assassinations accompanied by rape, torture, and bodily mutilation. Despite the absence of any single logic or profile of the victims, there were more than 5,000 known cases between 2000 and 2010, not counting the many unreported cases. Equally notable and equally central to feminicide has been the systematic indifference of governmental officials and institutions to this phenomenon and a refusal to investigate specific cases. Despite strong pressure from antifeminicide human rights organizations, only 2 percent of cases have been solved. Once again, impunity has remained the order of the day.

---

### INTEREST GROUPS

By far the most powerful interest group is the umbrella organization for big business, the Coordinating Committee of Agricultural, Commercial, Industrial, and Financial Associations (CACIF); labor unions and peasant federations have existed since the Revolution of 1944, but since the 1954 coup, they have been relatively weak. During the 1980s and 1990s, interest groups became organized in the following additional areas: human rights, both in general and with respect to indigenous concerns (reflecting the fact that the Mayan population was the main target of state repression); indigenous cultural, political, and economic issues; community organization, particularly in the urban shantytowns; student organization, at both the high school and university levels; women's rights, both as part of the broader popular movement and (more recently) for specifically women's issues; and small and medium businesses as well as "guilds" of lawyers and other professionals. The most effective interest group activities during the 1990s were those undertaken in the broad cross-sector coalition, the Assembly of Civil Society, during the peace negotiations. After the signing of the Peace Accords, the most effective organizing was among Mayas and women. In the early 2000s, indigenous organizations participated in broad coalitions against the incursions of foreign mining corporations into their communities, with some of these protests developing a very high profile, even as they faced severe governmental repression.

---

Like the rest of Central America, Guatemala has been in the throes of neoliberal "reform," with all of its negative consequences for income distribution and social justice. The structural problems that gave rise to the thirty-six-year war are further than ever from being resolved, poverty statistics are geometrically higher than in the 1950s and 1960s, and official policies no longer even promise a "trickle-down" effect to eradicate poverty. Indeed, to mention just one example, while agrarian reform was considered a "procommunist" idea during the Arbenz era in the 1950s, it has simply disappeared from the vocabulary of the new world order. Neoliberal economic policies emanating from Washington, combined with the ongoing refusal of Guatemala's own economic elites to pay taxes or redistribute land, have been obstacles to resolving problems of extreme poverty, inequality, joblessness, and landlessness.

In addition to these massive socioeconomic problems, social violence of many different types has proliferated to alarming levels, especially in urban areas; this violence has been linked to rampant drug trafficking by organized crime including elements within the national police and armed forces as well as youth gangs and antigang vigilantes engaged in "social cleansing." Indeed, rapidly escalating postwar social violence has largely replaced the pervasive political violence of the civil war years (although there are still some notable instances of the latter), maintaining "security" as a top concern of many Guatemalans. Rather than controlling social violence, state institutions (the army and police) have been allegedly involved in perpetuating it through clandestine connections.

The other major consequence of the preceding conditions, particularly the lack of adequate jobs and social programs to guarantee decent living standards, has been a continuing stream of Guatemalan migration to the United States, which began in the late 1970s and the 1980s—an extremely perilous journey by foot through Mexico. But in this postwar era, the principal factors have shifted from political persecution as the primary cause to economic and social conditions and environmental disasters—most notably, Hurricane Stan in the fall of 2005 and droughts alternating with deluges and massive mudslides in 2010 and subsequently.

By the latter part of the decade, over 800,000 Guatemalans lived and worked in the United States, sending home remittances that became a main pillar of the economy. U.S.-based Guatemalans have engaged in broad campaigns for their rights to legalization in the United States, while Guatemala-based migrant rights organizations held their own government responsible for the socially inequitable development that forced so many people to migrate. But actual living conditions for Guatemalan migrants also deteriorated seriously in the United States. For several years after 2008, the great U.S. recession slashed job opportunities for low-wage Latino migrants. Meanwhile, deportations of Guatemalan migrants increased exponentially, including a high-profile May 2008 mass raid and deportation of nearly 300 Guatemalans working at Agriprocessors, Inc., a kosher meatpacking plant in Postville, Iowa, in 2008.

The United States, as always, has retained a powerful influence over decision making in Guatemala. Particularly after September 11, 2001, U.S. foreign policy priorities have been centrally concerned with antiterrorism and security, promoting a stronger role for the Guatemalan army in general. Washington's obsession with national security matters since 2001 and its free trade agreement with Central America and the Dominican Republic (CAFTA-DR) that took effect in 2006 strongly impacted the agendas of successive Guatemalan governments.

The 2007 general election raised once again the issues of national priorities. The initial round of elections, held in September, with presidential candidates from numerous parties, was marked by significant violence, as well as some financing of almost all parties from drug traffickers and organized crime. The November run-off election pitted retired General Otto Pérez Molina (Partido Patriota) against Alvaro Colom Caballeros (Unidad Nacional de la Esperanza; UNE). Colom projected himself as a social democrat, using the rhetoric of "hope." In contrast, Pérez appealed to the quest for "security" among many Guatemalans and campaigned on a platform of *mano dura* (iron fist) or crackdown, against many different "threats." Despite general expectations that Pérez would win, the victory went to Colom (53 percent vs. 47 percent). Analysts emphasized that this was the first time that the electoral primacy of Guatemala City, where Pérez won handily, was trumped by a strikingly unified vote for Colom in rural departments, particularly Mayan areas.

But the Colom government never carried out its reformist agenda. In addition to UNE itself being compromised by commitments to some business elites, corruption, and opaque forces within the party, the structural realities of Guatemala did not permit major change. Despite the government's social democratic ideology, it did not implement the moderate tax reform and fiscal agreements at the heart of the Peace Accords, which were supported even by the World Bank and International Monetary Fund but fiercely opposed by Guatemalan business elites. These policies would have strengthened the Guatemalan state, broadened social services, and reformed the tax base to pay for a stable peace, contribute to poverty reduction, and mitigate the long-range deficit of decent formal-sector jobs.

The lack of public sector financial resources combined with other factors to maintain the Guatemalan state as a structurally and institutionally "weak state," regardless of the political leanings of particular governments—in large measure a consequence of not implementing the reforms envisioned in the Peace Accords. The accords had addressed many of these weaknesses, such as the imperative of reforming and strengthening the judicial system to correct the embedded issues of impunity; corruption; inefficiency; inaccessibility to the courts, especially for non-Spanish-speaking Mayan communities; and the generalized lack of justice guarantees. A multisectoral commission on strengthening the judicial system had made comprehensive recommendations, but these were minimally implemented.

The accords had also envisioned new laws governing the functioning of the electoral system and of political parties to make them more substantively democratic and ultimately more stable. This topic was debated in Congress, which itself required reforms to become more transparent and legitimate, but little changed. Many political parties survived only one electoral cycle. All these factors undermined the legitimacy of the political system.

Most seriously, these accumulated and multiple deficiencies in formal state institutions left a large opening for uncontrolled criminal activities and social violence. The operations of previously existing Guatemalan groups (gangs, organized crime, drug traffickers, and clandestine powers) were compounded by the increasing penetration of major drug cartels from Mexico late in the first decade of the twenty-first century; they recruited from Guatemala's former military forces, among other sectors. In some areas of the country, entire communities were coerced into participating in the drug trade. Overall, Central America's Northern Triangle—Guatemala, Honduras, and El Salvador—is considered by UN agencies to be the world's most violent peacetime region (i.e., one that is not in a state of civil war).

Meanwhile, the ultraconservative opposition forces dedicated themselves to destabilizing the Colom government. This became clearest in the 2009 Rosenberg scandal, in which the opposition used the assassination of lawyer Rodrigo Rosenberg (who made a video beforehand, blaming Colom if he were killed) to demand Colom's resignation. In a new twist for Guatemala, the case was investigated by the International Commission against Impunity in Guatemala (CICIG), mandated by a 2006 Guatemalan government agreement with the United Nations to probe pervasive impunity and the clandestine criminal "parallel powers" that had infiltrated the country's judicial and security systems. Under the leadership of Spanish judge and law professor Carlos Castresana, CICIG's thorough investigation brought to light the truth in a January 2010 report that exonerated Colom and revealed the intricate details of the self-planned assassination. This victory and the continued operations of CICIG revealed that it was occasionally possible, if difficult and frustrating, to make advances against impunity.

But the limits of change were revealed once again in the general elections of September 2011. This time, retired general Pérez Molina (Partido Patriota) had the upper hand from the beginning against nine other candidates, several from new parties. The relatively established UNE party was left without a candidate, once Colom's ex-wife Sandra Torres was eliminated from running. Pérez continued with his "law and order" platform, which by 2011 had broader appeal amid pervasive citizen insecurity. But Pérez won only 36 percent of the votes, much less than predicted by virtually all polls, forcing him into a November run-off. He won the run-off easily, but among far fewer voters than in the initial election. Even before taking office, he appointed a number of wartime counterinsurgency officials to key positions—some, like Pérez himself, linked to the 1980s scorched-earth policies and acts of genocide.

In many respects, the Pérez government was characterized by a militaristic style of rule. In the case of a large peaceful demonstration protesting various government policies in Totonicapán in October 2012, soldiers opened fire on the Mayan peasants, killing six and wounding thirty-four, which was the first open massacre in peacetime Guatemala. This was just the worst instance of official violence and states of siege against popular protests. In the context of security arguments, the army also resumed police functions far more prominently than at any time since 1996. None of this improved citizen security, and during 2012 and 2013, this government did not fulfill its own law-and-order goals.

Nevertheless, Pérez made a crucial initial decision not to remove Attorney General Claudia Paz y Paz, who had established an outstanding record of integrity and of pursuing justice for victims' families and survivors of wartime army massacres. This opened the path, after decades of intense activity and an ongoing genocide trial in Spain, to a historic trial *in* Guatemala. In early 2013, having lost his parliamentary immunity, General Efraín Ríos Montt was put on trial for genocide and crimes against humanity in the Ixil region during 1982–1983. The eyes of the world were fixed on Guatemala, as the fearless, persistent war survivors and victims' families, most from poor Mayan Ixil communities, testified for weeks in an extraordinary collective project of testimony and revelation. On May 10, the "high risk" court headed by Judge Yassmín Barrios found Ríos Montt guilty as charged and sentenced him to eighty years in prison. Ten days later, in the face of pressures from CACIF and ultraright organizations, the sentence, verdict, and part of the process were annulled by a divided Constitutional Court, with the trial to be resumed in 2014. Nevertheless, the trial remained a worldwide example in the annals of transitional justice, insofar as it marked the first time a former head of state had been tried and found guilty of genocide in a court of the country where the genocide had occurred. There was little doubt that the protagonists on all sides would continue their decades-long struggle.

Aside from the outcome of the trial itself, the process sparked a major institutional crisis and a revival of Guatemala's ultrapolarized political dynamics and rhetoric at a level not seen since the civil war. "Antiterrorist" and ex-military organizations launched a barrage of accusations of "communism" against many sectors and individuals, but the targets of the attacks denounced and organized against these tactics. With the wounds of war being ripped open again, this scenario highlighted the ongoing challenges of transforming Guatemala.

Even as the efforts to reopen the Ríos Montt trial were stalled as of late 2016, several other trials for "grave war crimes" were taking place in Guatemala. Among the most significant was the Sepur Zarco case. In February 2016, two important military officials during the Ríos Montt regime were convicted of crimes against humanity that had occurred at the Sepur Zarco military base where fifteen Q'eqchí Maya women were subjected to sexual violence and domestic and sexual slavery (serial rape and forced labor). Based on both victim and expert testimony, this was the first time a Guatemalan court—or any domestic court—had tried a case involving sexual violence and slavery that were determined to be crimes against humanity. Bringing the gendered dimension of the scorched-earth war to the forefront and convicting the responsible military officials promised to mark a major advance in transitional justice, although this case has also been contested by defense appeals to have the results overturned.

As of late 2016, several other cases of grave war crimes were at various stages of being heard and decided in Guatemala's high-risk courts. Among the most prominent were the trials of Guatemalan soldiers and army officials in the 1982 massacre at Las Dos Erres, Petén. That case began to be prosecuted in Guatemala in 2011–2012, after a 2009 sentencing by the Inter-American Court of Human Rights (of the Organization of American States) that the massacre involved massive crimes against humanity and that those responsible were therefore excluded from amnesty by the 1996 Peace Accords. Justice has not been achieved, and victims have not received material reparations. Nevertheless, by persistently seeking justice in Guatemala and sometimes prevailing, the survivor victims and their allies are very slowly making dents in Guatemala's decades'-old tradition of unassailable impunity.

In another realm of the previously unimaginable, 2015 saw a massive nonviolent social upheaval against the Pérez Molina regime, leading ultimately to the forced resignation of Pérez. In April 2015, CICIG, now under the leadership of (Colombian) Iván Velásquez, published a report, carrying out independent investigations but coordinating with Guatemalan Public Prosecutor Thelma Aldana, and strongly supported by the United States. The report revealed details of widespread and massive corruption, specifically with customs offices and tax collection agencies taking bribes to benefit importers by reducing duties (network "La Linea"). Corruption rings also operated within the health-care and social security systems. All of these involved top officials and cabinet members in the Pérez regime, including the vice president and eventually naming the president.

Sparked by social media calls for peaceful protest, a broad-based, cross-class grassroots coalition of 30,000 people took to the streets of Guatemala City on April 25 and soon thereafter also in smaller cities and rural areas, demanding the resignation of Vice President Roxana Baldetti and subsequently President Pérez as the top players in the network of massive fraud and bribery, cover-up, and use of public institutions for private gain. These peaceful protests (#RenunciaYa) continued weekly for four months, from late April through the end of August. On August 27, after CICIG published tapes proving Pérez's involvement, an estimated 100,000 people participated in a general strike, with demonstrations in over 140 municipalities and rural areas. Public pressure finally pushed Congress (itself full of *"corruptos"*) to strip Pérez of his immunity from prosecution on September 1. The breadth of the coalition was notable, ranging from CACIF and Guatemala City's middle class to young social justice activists, students, and indigenous and peasant organizations from around the country. They articulated unparalleled public demands for accountability and transparency against corruption and generalized impunity and, from some, demands for justice (#JusticiaYa).

What ended in a potentially transformational moment—Pérez stripped of his immunity by Congress, forced to resign on September 2, and sent to jail to await trial to prevent his flight from Guatemala—was almost immediately undermined by electoral politics as usual. Only a few days after Pérez's resignation, the September 6 general and presidential elections were held, without any congressional reforms of the Electoral and Political Parties Law. In essence, this move—ignoring calls by some sectors to postpone the election and establish a transitional government until after reforms had been made—returned politics to the traditional system of parties, financing, and candidates. Comedian Jimmy Morales campaigned as the consummate "outsider" against traditional and corrupt party politicians but was supported by some of the most virulent rightist ex-military and intelligence forces and the army veterans' association, themselves implicated in corruption as well as human rights crimes. Morales himself had almost no policy positions beyond describing himself as "not corrupt, not a thief."

After a strong showing in the initial September election, Morales won the October 26 run-off election, with 70 percent of the vote against UNE's Sandra Torres. As he took office in January 2016, Morales's appointed traditional officials, many from the military or with ties to the military, incorporated virtually nothing from the demands of the 2015 uprising. Although many critics vowed to monitor every move of the new government, the euphoric sense that "Guatemala will never be the same" (after the events of 2015) dissipated and became an open question.

Meanwhile, Guatemala's underlying neoliberal socioeconomic structures were never seriously challenged; in fact, they were taken to extremes by the extractivist mining/hydroelectric model that dominated twenty-first-century foreign mega-investments by U.S. and Canadian companies. This model also had political implications, insofar as governmental agencies as well as private security forces were involved in repression against antimining protests, in some cases leading to deaths of protest leaders and other serious human rights violations. Operating especially on Mayan lands and areas of the country, some of these investments ended up being challenged internationally by Mayan victims and activists, and illuminated the intersection between the twenty-first-century political economy and human rights.

Despite macro-economic growth from 2001 to 2015, this did not stimulate human development, as documented in the United Nations Development Program's (UNDP) Human Development Report for 2015–2016. The UNDP's

Human Development Index, which measures access to health care, educational level, and living standards, increased an annual average of 2.3 percent between 2000 and 2006, but subsequently (2006–2014) grew by less than 0.3 percent per year. The most dramatic figure was the poverty rate—as measured, for example, by per capita income, which fell from 72 percent to 58 percent between 2000 and 2006 but rose back up to 67 percent by 2014. The decrease in purchasing power reduced the middle class from 12 percent to 9 percent, increasing the level of inequality. At least 3 million Guatemalans fell below the poverty line between 2000 and 2013. All of these tendencies were largely a consequence of reduced public spending on social programs covering health and education, which many experts attributed to the failure to meet the Peace Accords goals regarding tax policy.

Given the structural neoliberal economic policies previously mentioned and increasing social violence perpetrated by organized crime and drug rings as well as youth gangs (not only in Guatemala but also in El Salvador and Honduras), many Northern Triangle Central Americans saw no option for a safe and decent life in their home countries. These conditions, and particularly the violence of daily life, led to a major surge in migration to the United States through Mexico, particularly by unaccompanied children and families (mothers with young children), beginning in the first half of 2014 and continuing through 2016; this created a massive humanitarian crisis on the U.S.–Mexico border. The United States responded to the surge of asylum-seekers fleeing social violence with harsh measures of detention and deportation, designed to deter further migration, and pressured Mexico to carry out massive deportations to prevent Central Americans from ever arriving at the U.S.–Mexico border.

Guatemala has had its highs and lows in the last two decades, and the country is still a study in contradictions between the old and the new. The year 2016 marks the twentieth anniversary of the 1996 Peace Accords, which, while mostly unfulfilled, have opened up space for some important new justice processes. The genocide and war crimes convictions have set international precedents, even when they were annulled, as in the case of Ríos Montt. The spontaneous uprising of 2015 may give rise to new movements to strengthen and cleanse state institutions. Once again, the dramas of Guatemala remain in the international spotlight.

# Chronology

**1524**  Spanish conquest, beginning of colonial era

**1821**  Independence from Spain

**1871**  "Liberal reform" begins under presidency of General Justo Rufino Barrios; disestablishment of the Church

**1901**  United Fruit Company (UFCo) arrives in Guatemala

**1931**  Jorge Ubico takes over presidency

**1944**  Ubico overthrown in military coup; civilian–military uprising subsequently ousts military junta and begins Revolution of 1944–1954

**1945**  Juan José Arévalo elected president; new democratic constitution is promulgated

**1947**  New labor code establishes basic workers' rights

**1949**  Formation of Partido Guatemalteco de Trabajo (Communist Party; PGT), not legalized until 1951

**1950**  Jacobo Arbenz elected president

**1952**  Agrarian Reform Law passed

**1954**  (June) Arbenz overthrown in CIA-organized "Liberation"; U.S.-backed Carlos Castillo Armas takes power

**1957**  Castillo Armas assassinated

**1958**  General Miguel Ydígoras Fuentes elected president

**1959**  Cuban Revolution

**1960**  (November) Major military uprising against Ydígoras suppressed, some participants become rebels, beginning of guerrilla insurgency

**1962**  Mass student, labor demonstrations, formation of revolutionary guerrilla organizations

**1963**  Overthrow of Yidígoras in coup led by Colonel Enrique Peralta Azurdia to prevent 1963 elections

**1966**  Julio César Méndez Montenegro (Revolutionary Party) elected president

**1966–1968**  United States sends Green Berets, finances and directs counterinsurgency campaign led by Colonel Carlos Arana Osorio; founding of death squads; by 1970, around 8,000 unarmed civilians killed by security forces

**1970**  Arana elected president

**1972**  Entry of Ejército Guerrillero de los Pobres (EGP) guerrillas into Guatemala

**1974**  General Kjell Laugerud becomes president through electoral fraud

**1975**  Guerrilla activities resume, primarily in Mayan highlands

**1976**  (February) Massive earthquake; formation of National Committee of Trade Union Unity (CNUS), increased popular organizing

**1977**  Large protest march by mine workers from Ixtahuacán to Guatemala City

**1978**  (March) General Romeo Lucas García becomes president through electoral fraud; (April) formation of Comité de Unidad Campesina (CUC); (May) massacre of Kekchi Indians at Panzós, U.S. Congress bans arms sales to Guatemalan government

**1979**  (July) Sandinista victory in Nicaragua

**1980**  (January) Government massacre and burning of Nebaj protestors in Spanish embassy; Spain breaks diplomatic relations; increase in guerrilla activity in Mayan highlands

**1981**  Beginning of army counteroffensive, involving numerous massacres and destruction of over 400 Mayan villages by 1983

**1982**  (February) Formation of Guatemalan National Revolutionary Unity (URNG) by EGP, ORPA, FAR, and PGT Nucleus; discontented army officers led by Efraín Ríos Montt seize power in coup; Ríos Montt presidency begins worst phase of scorched-earth counterinsurgency war

**1983**  (January) United States resumes military sales to Guatemala; (August) General Oscar Mejía Víctores seizes power in military coup; counterinsurgency war continues

**1984**  Constituent Assembly draws up new constitution

**1985**   Official U.S. economic and military aid resumed; (December) Christian Democrat Vinicio Cerezo wins presidency, takes office in January 1986, return to civilian rule

**1987**   (August) Esquipulas II, Central American Peace Accords signed in Guatemala; (September) Guatemalan army begins "year's end" counterinsurgency offensive

**1988–89**   Aborted military coup attempts by rightist civilians and military officers

**1990**   Beginning of dialogue process of discussions between URNG and political and social sectors; (November) first round of presidential election

**1991**   (January) Jorge Serrano wins runoff election; (April) beginning of government-URNG peace negotiations; (October) major continental indigenous conference held in Guatemala, with march from Quetzaltenango to capital

**1992**   (October) Awarding of Nobel Peace Prize to Rigoberta Menchú

**1993**   (May–June) Serrano attempts *auto-golpe*, or *Serranazo*; reversed and resolved by ascendance to presidency of Ramiro de León Carpio, former human rights ombudsman

**1994**   (January) Framework Accord signed, establishing United Nations as moderator of peace negotiations and formation of Assembly of Civil Society; (March) Human Rights Accord signed; (June) signing of accords on Resettlement of the Uprooted and Truth Commission (Historical Clarification Commission); (November) Arrival of MINUGUA, UN verification mission

**1995**   (March) Signing of Indigenous Peoples' Rights Accord; (March) eruption of scandal involving CIA-paid Guatemalan army officers in previous assassinations of U.S. citizen Michael Devine and guerrilla husband of U.S. lawyer Jennifer Harbury, Efraín Bámaca; (November–January 1996) in second election round, Alvaro Arzú wins presidential election; first-time electoral participation of leftist New Guatemala Democratic Front (FDNG)

**1996**   (January) New president Arzú takes office; (March) informal cease-fire between army and URNG; (May) signing of Accord on Socio-Economic Issues; (September) signing of Accord on demilitarization; (December) operational accords signed; (December 29) final Peace Accord signed in Guatemala City, ending thirty-six-year civil war

**1997**   (January) International community (donor nations and agencies) pledges $1.9 billion to implement Peace Accords, conditioned on Guatemalan government compliance with accords

**1998**   (February) Government retreat on tax reform; (April) assassination of Auxiliary Bishop Juan Gerardi two days after release of major human rights report under his supervision; (October–November) Central America hit by devastating Hurricane Mitch

**1999**   (February) Historical Clarification Commission releases report on human rights crimes during the war; (March) U.S. President Clinton, in Guatemala, apologizes for U.S. role in Guatemalan counterinsurgency war; (May) Constitutional reforms defeated in referendum; (November–December) in second elections round, Alfonso Portillo and party of ex-dictator Ríos Montt win; first-time participation of (now legal) URNG in election as part of coalition "New Nation Alliance"

**2003** (November–December) General elections: in second round, Oscar Berger wins, Ríos Montt decisively defeated

**2006** (July) Despite widespread protests in 2005–2006, CAFTA takes effect in Guatemala

**2007** (September, November) General elections; in second round, self-denominated social democrat Alvaro Colom narrowly wins election over Otto Pérez Molina

**2009–2010** Destabilization activity against Colom government and major struggles over structural impunity; successful investigation by UN-cosponsored International Commission against Impunity in Guatemala (CICIG)

**2011** General elections; in second round, ex-general Pérez Molina wins presidency

**2012-present** War crimes trials against perpetrators held in Guatemala

**2013** Historic trial of Ríos Montt in Guatemala for genocide and crimes against humanity; guilty verdict annulled by Constitutional Court

**2014** Beginning of surge in migration to United States from Northern Triangle countries by unaccompanied children and families fleeing extreme social violence

**2015** (April–August) widespread peaceful uprising against government corruption and impunity; (September) forced resignation of President Pérez; General elections, in second round, "outsider" Jimmy Morales wins presidency

**2016** Sepur Zarco trial and other war crimes trials continue

# Bibliography

This bibliography includes only references in English, although many of the best analyses written by Guatemalans are available only in Spanish; wherever possible, I include translated works by Guatemalans and other Latin Americans. For students who read Spanish, see, for example, the works of Edelberto Torres Rivas, Gabriel Aguilera, Ricardo Falla, and a host of Mayan analysts. For reasons of space, this bibliography does not include journal and newspaper articles.

Adams, Richard. *Crucifixion by Power.* Austin: University of Texas Press, 1970.

Barry, Tom. *Inside Guatemala.* Albuquerque, NM: Inter-Hemispheric Education Resource Center, 1992.

Berger, Susan. *Guatemaltecas: The Women's Movement, 1986–2003.* Austin: University of Texas Press, 2006.

Carmack, Robert, ed. *Harvest of Violence.* Norman: University of Oklahoma Press, 1988.

Chase-Dunn, Christopher, Susanne Jonas, and Nelson Amaro, eds. *Globalization on the Ground: Post-Bellum Guatemalan Development and Democracy.* Boulder, CO: Rowman & Littlefield, 2001.

Falla, Ricardo. *Massacres of the Jungle.* Boulder, CO: Westview, 1994.

Falla, Ricardo. *Quiché Rebelde: Religious Conversion, Politics & Ethnic Identity.* Austin: University of Texas Press, 2001.

Galeano, Eduardo. *Guatemala: Occupied Country.* New York: Monthly Review Press, 1969.

Gleijeses, Piero. *Shattered Hope: The Guatemalan Revolution and the U.S.* Princeton, NJ: Princeton University Press, 1991.

Goldman, Francisco. *The Art of Political Murder: Who Killed the Bishop?* New York: Grove, 2007.

Grandin, Greg. *The Blood of Guatemala.* Durham, NC: Duke University Press, 2000.

Grandin, Greg. *The Last Colonial Massacre.* Chicago: University of Chicago Press, 2004.

Immerman, Richard. *The CIA in Guatemala.* Austin: University of Texas Press, 1982.

Jonas, Susanne. *The Battle for Guatemala: Rebels, Death Squads and U.S. Power.* Boulder, CO: Westview, 1991.

Jonas, Susanne. *Of Centaurs and Doves: Guatemala's Peace Process.* Boulder, CO: Westview, 2000.

Jonas, Susanne and Nestor Rodríguez. *Guatemala–U.S. Migration: Transforming Regions.* Austin: University of Texas Press, 2014.

Jonas, Susanne, and David Tobis, eds. *Guatemala.* Berkeley, CA: NACLA, 1974.

Levenson, Deborah. *Adios Niño: The Gangs of Guatemala City and the Politics of Death.* Durham, NC: Duke University Press, 2013.
Lovell, W. George. *A Beauty That Hurts: Life and Death in Guatemala.* 2d ed. Austin: University of Texas Press, 2010
Manz, Beatriz. *Paradise in Ashes.* Berkeley: University of California Press, 2004.
Melville, Thomas. *Through a Glass Darkly.* Bloomington, IN: XLibris, 2005.
Menchú, Rigoberta, with Elisabeth Burgos-Debray. *I . . . Rigoberta Menchú.* New York: Verso, 1980.
Nelson, Diane. *A Finger in the Wound.* Berkeley: University of California Press, 1999.
Payeras, Mario. *Days of the Jungle.* New York: Monthly Review Press, 1983.
Perera, Victor. *Unfinished Conquest: The Guatemalan Tragedy.* Berkeley: University of California Press, 1993.
Schirmer, Jennifer. *The Guatemalan Military Project.* Philadelphia: University of Pennsylvania Press, 1998.
Schlesinger, Stephen, and Stephen Kinzer. *Bitter Fruit.* expanded ed, Cambridge, MA: Harvard University Press (David Rockefeller Center for Latin American Studies), 1999.
Smith, Carol, ed. *Guatemalan Indians and the State: 1540–1988.* Austin: University of Texas Press, 1990.
Warren, Kay. *Indigenous Movements and Their Critics: Pan-Mayanism and Ethnic Resurgence in Guatemala.* Princeton, NJ: Princeton University Press, 1998.

## CENTRAL AMERICAN CONTEXT

Booth, John, Christine Wade, and Thomas Walker. *Understanding Central America.* 6th ed. Boulder, CO: Westview, 2014.
Dunkerley, James. *Power in the Isthmus.* New York: Verso, 1988.
LaFeber, Walter. *Inevitable Revolutions.* New York: Norton, 1984.
Pérez Brignoli, Hector. *A Brief History of Central America.* Berkeley: University of California Press, 1989.
Robinson, William. *Transnational Conflicts: Central America, Social Change and Globalization.* London: Verso, 2003.
Torres Rivas, Edelberto. *Repression and Resistance.* Boulder, CO: Westview, 1989.
Vilas, Carlos. *Between Earthquakes and Volcanoes: Market, State, and the Revolutions in Central America.* New York: Monthly Review Press, 1995.
Walker, Thomas, and Ariel Arimony, eds. *Repression, Resistance, and Democratic Transition in Central America.* Wilmington, DE: Scholarly Resources, 2000.

## LITERATURE, POETRY, AND PHOTOS

Arias, Arturo. *After the Bombs.* Translated by Asa Zatz. Willimantic, CT: Curbstone, 1990.
Asturias, Miguel Angel. *The President.* Translated by Frances Partridge. Prospect Heights, IL: Waveland, 1997.
Castillo, Otto René. *Let's Go.* Translated by Margaret Randall. Willimantic, CT: Curbstone, 1971.
Goldman, Francisco. *The Long Night of White Chickens.* New York: Atlantic Monthly, 1992.
Moller, Jonathan. *Our Culture Is Our Resistance.* New York: Powerhouse, 2004.
Montejo, Víctor. *Testimony: Death of a Guatemalan Village.* Translated by Victor Perera. Willimantic, CT: Curbstone, 1987.
Simon, Jean-Marie. *Guatemala: Eternal Spring, Eternal Tyranny.* New York: Norton, 1987.
Tobar, Héctor. *The Tattooed Soldier.* New York: Penguin. 1998.
Zimmerman, Marc. *Literature and Resistance in Guatemala.* Athens: Ohio University Center for International Studies, 1995.

## FILMS AND VIDEOS

*AbUSed: The Postville Raid.* United States, 2010.
*Devils Don't Dream.* Guatemala, 1995.
*Discovering Dominga.* United States, 2003.
*El Norte.* United States/Guatemala, 1985.
*Finding Oscar.* United States, 2016.

*Granito: How to Nail a Dictator.* Guatemala, 2011.
*Ixcanul.* Guatemala, 2016.
*La Jaula de Oro.* Mexico, 2013.
*Mayan Voices/American Lives.* Guatemala, 1994.
*Men with Guns.* Mexico, 1997.
*When the Mountains Tremble.* Guatemala, 1983.

WEBSITES

http://www.ijmonitor.org/category/guatemala-trials   International Justice Monitor, a project of Open
    Society Foundation. Guatemala trials since 2013–2014

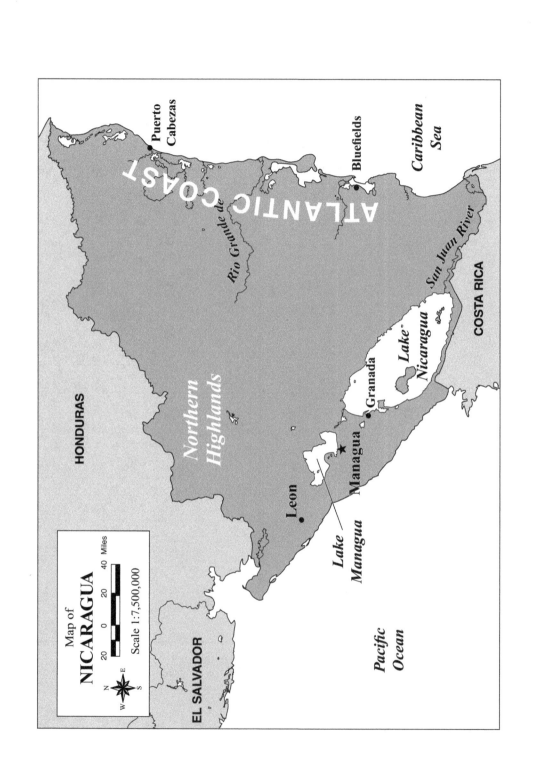

Map of
**NICARAGUA**

Scale 1:7,500,000

20   0   20   40 Miles

HONDURAS

EL SALVADOR

Pacific
Ocean

Leon

Lake
Managua

Managua

Granada

Lake
Nicaragua

Northern
Highlands

Rio Grande de

ATLANTIC COAST

Puerto
Cabezas

Bluefields

Caribbean
Sea

San Juan River

COSTA RICA

# TWENTY ONE

# NICARAGUA

*Gary Prevost and Harry E. Vanden*

## Introduction

Nicaragua has been a land of conflict and struggle for power. It is located at the geographic center of Central America and is the largest and most sparsely settled of the Central American republics. Its 57,143 square miles make it about the size of the state of Iowa. Its population of 6.2 million, which has grown rapidly in the last two decades, is concentrated on the Pacific coast side of the country. It has three distinct geographic regions: mountains in the north, a narrow Pacific coastal plain containing two large lakes, and a wider Atlantic coastal plain. The Pacific plain is part of a trough that connects the Atlantic and Pacific Oceans through the San Juan River Valley. For more than a century, this region has been viewed as having great potential for a new interoceanic canal, and recent interest by China has brought that possibility to the fore once again. There is considerable volcanic activity in the country, with three volcanoes reaching 5,000 feet emerging from Lake Nicaragua.

Most of Nicaragua has considerable potential for agricultural production. Occupying nearly half the country, the Caribbean lowlands are composed primarily of hot, humid tropical rain forest and swamps. They are not conducive to long-term productive agriculture, and less than 10 percent of the population lives there. The central highlands and western lowlands have been much more hospitable to human habitation and agricultural production. The central region is especially good for coffee production, while the western lowlands support a wide range of agricultural products, such as cotton, rice, and sugar.

Nicaragua is favored not only with above-average natural resources and climatic conditions but also with several other advantages. Unlike some Latin American countries, it is not overpopulated. Arable land is adequate for the size of the population. Much of the country has a relatively homogeneous population, with no significant racial, linguistic, or religious differences. Most Nicaraguans are Roman Catholic, speak Spanish, and are mestizo (mixed Spanish and Indian ancestry).

The exception to this homogeneity is the Atlantic coast region, which is quite different. This region has an English-speaking black population with a Caribbean heritage and a small native indigenous population of Sumo and Miskito Indians. In recent years the demographic composition of the region has changed with significant migration of mestizos. Despite its abundant natural resources, Nicaragua has remained one of the poorest countries in the hemisphere, with low per capita income and short life expectancy. It is also a country that has had more than its share of political violence and oppression. However, Nicaragua also falls within a select group of countries worldwide that has experienced a highly unusual phenomenon—social revolution. The events of the 1970s and 1980s in Nicaragua, the era of the Sandinista revolution, warrant Nicaragua's inclusion as a case study in this volume. It shares many characteristics with its Central and Latin American neighbors, but it was the brief period of revolutionary fervor that makes Nicaragua stand out. Yet, to understand the historical context of the events of 1978–1990, it is necessary to review Nicaraguan history.

The patterns of conflict that have marked modern Nicaragua did not begin with the Spanish conquerors of the sixteenth century. The region was inhabited by indigenous groups of South American origin that occupied the less hospitable eastern regions, while the western side was colonized by Meso-American groups from the north. There was little contact between the two groups, but within the western region there were clear patterns of warfare, slavery, and involuntary servitude. Spanish conquerors reached Nicaragua from Panama in 1522, making their first contact with indigenous people on the western plains. The expedition, under the leadership of Gil González, was seeking to obtain gold and converts to Christianity and was apparently successful on both counts. It also discovered the possible water link between the Atlantic and Pacific using the San Juan River and Lake Nicaragua. The initial contact was not without violence, however, as a legendary chief, Diriangen, offered armed resistance to the Spanish. In 1524, under the leadership of Francisco Hernández de Córdoba, the Spanish imposed their control over the region and founded the settlements of Grenada and León.

The Spanish conquest of Nicaragua had a profound and devastating impact. The existing indigenous population of around 1 million was reduced within a few decades to just tens of thousands. Some deaths occurred in battles with the Spanish, but most came from diseases that the Spanish introduced, such as measles and influenza, for which the local population had no immune defenses. By the 1540s the Indian population of western Nicaragua had dropped below 50,000 and continued to decline afterward. The legacy of this devastation is that the more populated western part of Nicaragua is predominantly a mestizo culture with little trace of its indigenous past except for a significant number of cities and towns with native names.

Another legacy of the colonial period is the rivalry between the cities of León and Grenada. Grenada was originally designated by the Spanish to be the administrative center. As a result, it was populated by the aristocratic class, while colonizers of lower social status settled León, which was projected to be primarily a fortress city on the northern reaches of the colony. However, León emerged as the administrative capital, and aristocratic Grenadans had to endure centuries of rule by a city they viewed to be inferior. This resentment boiled into open warfare on occasion as the two cities also developed an economic rivalry. Wealth in aristocratic Grenada was based primarily on cattle, while the León economy was more commercially oriented and included international trade. For much of the colonial period, Nicaragua was an underpopulated, impoverished corner of the Spanish Empire.

The end of the colonial era did not bring any great relief to Nicaragua's difficult position. It won its independence in stages, first as a part of the Mexican Empire in 1821. It then became a member of the Central American Federation in 1823 and finally emerged as a sovereign state in 1838, when it withdrew from the federation. Internally, most of the nineteenth century after independence was marked by constant battles between León and Grenada for control of the country. By then, the Leonese had come to call themselves "Liberals" and the Grenadinos had identified themselves as "Conservatives." In a pattern that was to repeat itself, the chaos created by the internal conflict combined with the departure of the Spanish allowed outside forces to exert significant influence over Nicaragua.

British interests established a protectorate over the Atlantic region, known as the Autonomous Kingdom of Mosquitia (the Mosquito Coast), which lasted for most of the nineteenth century. U.S.-based Commodore Cornelius Vanderbilt's transit company became involved in moving California-bound gold prospectors across Nicaragua in 1849. Simultaneously, the British claimed control over the mouth of the San Juan River on the Atlantic coast, threatening the Vanderbilt operations. In 1850, the United States and Great Britain attempted to diffuse the conflict by signing the Clayton–Bulwar Treaty, in which they agreed to cooperate on the development of any transoceanic transit route. The treaty was negotiated and signed without involving the government of Nicaragua, establishing a pattern of disregard for Nicaragua's sovereignty that has continued to the present.

The Clayton–Bulwar Treaty did not end conflict in Nicaragua. In 1855 the Liberals of León hired an American soldier of fortune, William Walker, to lead their army against Grenada. Under Walker's leadership, the Liberal army triumphed, and Walker became the de facto president of Nicaragua. He instituted Liberal reforms, including the encouragement of foreign investment and development of Nicaragua's natural resources. Initially, Walker's activities were supported by the U.S. government. However, the British and other Central American governments were taken aback by what seemed to be a bold imperialist act by the United States. Nicaraguans of both political parties also began to turn against Walker when he legalized slavery and established English as the country's official language. Now seen as a hated foreigner, Walker came under attack from forces armed by the British, other Central American governments, and even private U.S. interests who feared he had become a liability to stable commerce in the region. In 1857, the U.S. government brokered a deal that sent Walker into exile. He returned in 1860 but was unsuccessful in regaining control and was defeated and executed. The final defeat of Walker in 1860 by a combined Central American force ushered in a thirty-year period of rule by the Conservatives, who quelled numerous uprisings and established a semblance of a stable, yet traditional, government.

# The Modern Era

The beginning of a modern national consciousness in Nicaragua that included the Indian and mestizo masses emerged toward the end of the nineteenth century. Although the Liberal reform movement did not develop in Nicaragua until the late nineteenth century, it carried a vision of society similar to movements in Mexico (under Benito Juárez) and elsewhere in Latin America. José Santos Zelaya's Liberal revolution of 1893 marked the beginning of the modern Liberal movement in Nicaragua. Although constrained by traditional European-style liberalism, Zelaya endeavored to centralize state power. He introduced some progressive ideas and began to challenge the traditional oligarchy and the power of the Catholic Church. His successful drive to recover the Atlantic coast from British colonialism also stimulated the growth of a national consciousness. Supported by elements of the national bourgeoisie, Zelaya introduced reforms that soon alarmed the Conservative forces and threatened the interests of the United States, which was antagonistic to the growth of a vigorous, independent national capitalist class in Nicaragua.

As Zelaya faced increasing internal and external pressure, his regime degenerated into a dictatorship. In 1909, Washington forced him to resign before he could implement his plans to modernize Nicaragua. Using various pretexts, the United States sent in marines to reinstate Conservative rule and ensure the dominant position of U.S. capital. As U.S. intervention increased over the next years (the marines again landed in 1912, to prop up the regime of Adolfo Díaz, and did not leave until 1924), anti-interventionist sentiment grew among the Nicaraguan people. With the outbreak of a new Liberal uprising against a Conservative coup in 1925 and the U.S.-inspired reinstallation of Adolfo Díaz as president, the struggle began to take on clear nationalist and anti-imperialist overtones. The marines once again intervened. It was at this point that Augusto César Sandino returned from Mexico and joined the now strongly nationalist Liberal struggle. Although Sandino encountered open hostility from the upper-class head of the Liberal army, José M. Moneada, he was able to arm and organize his own Liberal band and participate in the increasingly successful offensive.

Sandino was born into poverty in southern Nicaragua in 1895. Between 1923 and 1926 Sandino worked in Mexico as a mechanic in the oil industry of Tampico; it was there that his eclectic political philosophy was formed through contacts with anarchists, Free Masons, and supporters of the Mexican Revolution. The Liberal struggle was met with enthusiastic support from the masses, who participated in growing numbers. However, as these forces were in sight of a clear military victory, the United States arranged a compromise solution that was accepted by Moneada and eventually supported by all the Liberal generals, save one—Sandino. Thereafter, large numbers of peasants, miners, artisans, workers, and Indians who had fought with Sandino followed him to the Segovias, a remote mountain region in the north. From there, he began a guerrilla war.

The first Sandinista struggle continued from 1927 to 1933, and Sandino's growing army made life very difficult for the marines. Their political work and the increasing sophistication and tenacity of their popular guerrilla war had gained the support of many Nicaraguans, growing numbers of Latin Americans, and a few informed North Americans.

This was one of the first modem examples of the power of a guerrilla army with popular support against a technologically superior invader, even when the latter was bolstered by a significant national mercenary military force. Mobile guerrilla bands as the components of an egalitarian people's army, political as well as military organization, integrated political and military actions, close ties to the peasants, and, most important, popular support and involvement—such were the legacies from Sandino's war. More than three decades later, these lessons were put to use by the leadership of the next generation, the Sandinista National Liberation Front (FSLN).

Yet, although Sandino's political support had enabled him to gain a military victory, he disbanded his army before he could achieve far-reaching political and economic change. After his death at the hands of Anastasio Somoza's National Guard (1934), most of Sandino's followers were soon killed by the U.S.-trained National Guard. Some Sandinista columns fought on for a few more years in remote areas, but they too were eventually forced to abandon systematic armed resistance. All that remained was the legacy of Sandino and the example of his army, which lived on in the popular mind for some time, nourished by eyewitness accounts and firsthand stories from Sandinista survivors.

Nicaragua returned to more traditional authoritarian rule as Somoza took direct control of the government in 1936. He instituted an increasingly repressive family dictatorship that—mostly because of its close ties to the United States—would endure until militarily defeated by the FSLN in 1979. However, despite bloody repression and the intense vilification of Sandino and his followers, sporadic popular struggle continued through the 1930s, 1940s, and 1950s, although at a relatively low level. Somoza proved to be one of the best friends of the United States and was warmly received by Franklin Roosevelt in Washington. By the 1950s Nicaragua was a fully dependent producer of primary goods (mostly coffee and cotton) and an integral part of the U.S. system of political and economic control in the Western Hemisphere. Opposition to the dictatorship came to be symbolized by the sincere but elitist Conservative Party. Even the Nicaraguan Socialist Party (founded as a pro-Moscow communist party in 1944) often collaborated with the traditional politicians and Somoza-controlled unions, at the workers' expense. Somoza had taken over the Liberal Party and even went so far as to make pacts (in 1948 and 1950) with the Conservative Party in an attempt to co-opt the only major focal point of opposition to his regime.

## Carlos Fonseca and the Roots of the FSLN

It has been said that Nicaragua is a land of poets and that poets often reflect the popular will. Rigoberto López Pérez was one of the Nicaraguan intellectuals who directly felt the far-reaching cultural implications of a dependent dictatorship that was subservient to the United States. He, like Cuban poet José Marti, felt compelled to exchange pen for pistol to liberate his country. In 1956, the young poet assassinated Somoza. In so doing he not only avenged Sandino but also spurred a

his brother Luis, Anastasio Jr. was a military man, and his arrival at power signaled the end of an era of cosmetic liberalization and a return to more blatant authoritarian dictatorship. By 1970, corruption and incompetence became more widespread as the family more openly used public office for private enrichment.

## Turning Point for Revolution

Most observers argue that a key turning point for the regime was the Christmas earthquake of 1972, which cost the lives of 10,000 people and destroyed central Managua. Passing on the opportunity to be magnanimous with the family fortune in the face of the disaster, Somoza chose to turn the catastrophe to short-term personal advantage. He and his associates used their control of the government to channel international relief funds into their own pockets, primarily through the self-awarding of government contracts and the purchase of earthquake-damaged land and industries. Popular resentment against the government began to build among all classes when it became clear that Somoza used the tragedy to his own advantage. Donated international relief supplies were often sold by the government or given to friends of the Somoza family. Somoza lost not only whatever support he may have had among the poorer classes but also the loyalty of the country's economic elite. Somoza's competitors in the business world were outraged by the manner in which he largely shut them out of the earthquake reconstruction. After 1973, large segments of the business community went elsewhere with their political support, eventually to the revolutionaries.

The political crisis of the Somoza regime and the earthquake came at a time when the FSLN was not well poised to take advantage. After Pancasán, the movement survived but did not prosper. By 1972, the revolutionaries had fewer than 500 cadres within Nicaragua, and much of the leadership, including Fonseca, was living in exile in Cuba. Realizing that popular sentiment against the dictatorship was building, the FSLN made a spectacular reentry into Nicaraguan politics on December 27, 1974, with the seizure of the home of a wealthy Somoza supporter who was hosting a party for the U.S. ambassador. An FSLN commando unit held more than a dozen foreign diplomats and Nicaraguan political leaders hostage for several days and forced Somoza to release Sandinista political prisoners, pay a large sum of money, and broadcast and publish FSLN communiqués.

Somoza's response to the FSLN action served to deepen the crisis of his regime. He imposed martial law and sent his National Guard into the countryside to destroy the FSLN. In pursuit of that objective, the Guard carried out arbitrary imprisonment, torture, and murder of hundreds of peasants. Catholic priests in rural areas documented these actions, and the Nicaraguan Church hierarchy, which had previously supported the Somoza dynasty, denounced its human rights violations.

However, even as the regime weakened, the path to political change was not entirely clear. For its part, the FSLN was severely divided over the proper strategy to employ against Somoza. Three tendencies emerged, formalized at a meeting of the National Directorate in Cuba in 1975, the first convening of that body since 1970. The three tendencies were called Prolonged People's War, Proletarian, and Insurrectionist, or Tercerista.

The three tendencies finally converged around the tactical and strategic questions brought to the fore by the upsurge of mass struggle that opened in late 1977 and as the urban masses moved into action after the murder of Conservative opposition leader and well-respected newspaper publisher Pedro Joaquin Chamorro in early 1978. After the first serious confrontation between the urban masses and the National Guard—the uprising in the Indian community of Monimbó in February 1978—the Insurrectionist tendency shifted its strategy almost exclusively to prepare for insurrection in the cities. The Insurrectionists also participated in the Broad Opposition Front (FAO) through their supporters in the "Group of Twelve." The twelve were prominent middle- and upper-class opponents of Somoza, including Sergio Ramírez, later elected vice president on the FSLN ticket in 1984. All opposition forces soon united under the banner of the National Patriotic Front (FPN).

As the summer of 1979 approached, the Somoza dictatorship became increasingly isolated. Despite his increasingly dismal prospects, Somoza was unwilling to compromise and launched what proved to be a fatal strategy He ordered the bombing of civilian areas to deny his adversaries food and shelter. It failed because the FSLN suffered few casualties, and the bombing served to further rally popular support behind the rebels. Faced with imminent defeat, Somoza fled the country on July 17, 1979. He went first to the United States and then into exile in Paraguay, where he was assassinated fourteen months later by Argentine revolutionaries. His demise ended one of the most durable dictatorships—forty-six years—in Latin American history.

On July 19,1979, the Sandinistas marched into Managua and established a revolutionary government that was dominated by the FSLN but also contained political actors from the non-Sandinista opposition to Somoza, including Chamorro's widow, Violeta. The new government reflected the relationship of forces that existed at the time that the guerrilla war triumphed. The FSLN, confident that it had a mandate for significant social, political, and economic change, set about the process of creating a revolution in Nicaraguan society. The Sandinistas remained in power for eleven years, until 1990, when, following an electoral defeat at the hands of a coalition headed by Violeta Chamorro, the FSLN handed over power and retreated to the position it held through the first years of the twenty-first century—that of leading opposition party.

## The FSLN in Power

As the Sandinistas consolidated their political control after July 1979, more moderate elements of the victorious coalition left the government. After the initial euphoria of the revolutionary victory died down, the revolutionary leadership engaged in actions that concentrated power in the upper echelons of government and in the FSLN's National Directorate. Later, as the United States and its allies pressured the Nicaraguan leadership to bring the regime more in line with Western-style political systems, steps were taken toward a system of representative democracy that the dominant group in the Sandinista leadership hoped would satisfy many of its detractors and thus increase the legitimacy of the Nicaraguan government in the eyes of the West—a legitimacy that was never received.

many observers, the Sandinistas handed over the reins of power to the incoming Chamorro administration in April 1990. In doing so the FSLN became the first revolutionary group in Latin American history to cede power to an opposition force through an election.

## The 1990 Election and After

After 1990, three conservative governments largely reversed the policies and programs of the Sandinistas. Violeta Chamorro's National Opposition Union (UNO) and Arnoldo Aleman's Constitutional Liberal Party (PLC), elected in 1996, succeeded in significantly undermining FSLN programs. However, they did not succeed in their goal of marginalizing the FSLN. The Sandinistas emerged from the 1990, 1996, and 2001 elections as the leading opposition force with political control in several municipalities and regained the presidency in 2006.

In retrospect, it would seem that the 1990 election marked the beginning of a return to political decision-making by political and economic elites that was conducted far from institutions in which the masses could exercise any real power. Indeed, the next six years saw the development of a political system that was increasingly characterized by intense competition among political elites. Nor were important concerns addressed; as unemployment and poverty became more generalized and income and wealth more concentrated, it became increasingly clear that those aspects of economic democracy that had grown during the earlier years of Sandinista rule were severely eroded by successive waves of neoliberal policies and elite politics. These policies were continued in successive administrations. In 1990, it seemed that the real benefactors were not the majority who voted for the UNO but the external and internal economic elites who had engineered the Sandinista electoral demise. It was their demands—and not those of the common people—that would get the greatest attention. What the majority of those that voted for the UNO did not realize was that Violeta Chamorro had been chosen as an electoral tool to unseat the Sandinistas. Thus, there would be strong pressure to dismantle the type of state apparatus and policies that had developed under Sandinista rule, implement a conservative neoliberal economic program, strengthen traditional parties, and further reduce the power and size of the mass organizations and the Sandinista party. Nor would these changes give the masses any appreciable power in the new system.

The National Assembly became a focal point for political competition and deal-making. A dispute between the president and many assembly members of her own UNO coalition in 1992 worsened the situation. This angered the other UNO delegates, who questioned the legitimacy of the institution and began to boycott assembly sessions. They believed that the understanding on which their coalition was based had been betrayed and further accused Chamorro and Antonio Lacayo of collaborating with the Sandinistas in a co-government. On the left, worker and peasant organizations and the increasingly militant ex-Sandinista fighters (*recompas*), who had still not received land, accused the Sandinista leadership of collaborating with the government at their expense. Former contras (*recontras*) who had not received their promised land also became increasingly militant.

President Daniel Ortega (left, wearing hat and bandana and shaking hands) campaigning in the 1990 Nicaraguan elections. Recast in jeans, cowboy boots, and bandana, Ortega was portrayed by FSLN as a rock star-like friend of the people. He lost to UNO candidate Violeta Chamorro. Defeated again in 1996 and 2001, Ortega returned in triumph to the presidency in the 2006 elections and was re-elected by a wide margin in 2011 and 2016. *(Photo by H. Vanden)*

As the 1996 elections approached, the FSLN began to ally itself with Minister of the Presidency Antonio Lacayo's newly formed National Project. The Sandinista Renovation Movement (MRS) was making common cause with the Christian Democratic Union, Virgilio Godoy's Independent Liberal Party, Miriam Arguello's Popular Conservative Alliance, the Nicaraguan Democratic Movement (MDN), and the National Conservative Party (PNC). The strongest contender for the 1996 presidential election was Managua's conservative mayor, Arnoldo Alemán. Alemán was using his PLC to gain control of the now-factionalized old Liberal Party (including Liberal groups who were allied with Somoza). In the end, this strategy and his successful public works campaign in Managua combined to give him victory in the first round of the election. His Liberal Alliance was also a big winner elsewhere, winning many municipalities, including Managua, and forty-two of ninety-three seats in the National Assembly. The FSLN won thirty-six seats in the assembly, and the smaller parties won fifteen.

In 1996, it was the vestiges of the old Liberal Party reorganized as the Liberal Alliance that had once again united to claim victory. The FSLN's eleven years of party dominance had been refuted in the 1990 and 1996 elections. Although still a power contender, it was far from being the dominant party in Nicaragua. There were twenty-four parties on the ballot, but Aleman's Liberal Alliance and the FSLN secured 89.8 percent of the votes. (Sandinista presidential candidate Daniel Ortega came in a distant second with 38 percent of the vote compared to Aleman's 51 percent.) In the first months of Aleman's rule, there was a strong upsurge in returning Somocistas, and shortly after the election Somoza's nephews returned to

Nicaragua to reclaim much of Somoza's property. Indeed, Aleman's administration soon became known for its favoritism, if not outright corruption. When it entered into a pact with Alemán, the FSLN further eroded its legitimacy in the eyes of many. This helps explain Ortega's significant loss to Enrique Bolaños and the PLC-led Liberal Alliance in 2001.

The election in November of that year saw a similar outcome to the 1996 election as old-line politician and former head of the major business grouping (COSEP) Bolaños led the Liberal Alliance to victory over Sandinista candidate Ortega with a resounding 56 percent of the vote compared to Ortega's 42 percent. After less than two years in office, the Liberal Alliance splintered. In the municipal elections in November 2004, the Sandinistas swept at least ninety of the country's 152 municipalities, including Managua and fifteen of the seventeen department capitals. Ortega and the FSLN forged an alliance with the Alemán wing of the Liberal Alliance, who had turned against Bolaños after he spearheaded an anticorruption drive that implicated Alemán. After Alemán was removed from the National Assembly and forced to submit to a criminal trial, he was convicted of taking more than $7 million and sentenced to a prison term of twenty years.

## The Sandinistas Return to Power

By making this controversial alliance with former enemy Alemán and his PLC, the Ortega-led FSLN became a potent force in the legislature with the ability to move the National Assembly to pass legislation increasing the legislative body's power at the expense of the president. But cooperation between the former enemies did not stop there. A further pact was made before the 2006 election that allowed the winner of a plurality in the first round of voting to assume the presidency. The FSLN also signaled its cooperation with the Catholic Church by supporting a stringent abortion law in 2006. These moves and a more cooperative stance toward private business allowed Daniel Ortega to narrowly win the presidency with 38% of the vote in 2006 and assume the office in 2007. Once in office the Sandinistas used their power and a close alliance with Venezuela under Hugo Chávez, which yielded substantial aid and abundant petroleum, to embark on new social programs and consolidate their power. This led to an even larger election victory for Daniel Ortega in 2011 when he garnered 62.46 percent of the vote. In the municipal elections in November of 2012, the FSLN took 134 of the country's 153 municipalities. The FSLN continued its stronghold on Nicaraguan politics in 2016 when Ortega and his running mate, wife, Rosario Murrillo, gained 72 percent of the vote and a continuing FSLN majority of seats in the National Assembly. Opponents accused the Ortegas of instituting family rule as the Somozas had before. As in other recent Nicaraguan elections the FSLN's political opponents claimed significant fraud, which, in the absence of significant international observation, is almost impossible to verify.

Those challenges notwithstanding, Daniel Ortega has emerged as one of the most popular politicians in the hemisphere through a variety of means. Part of Ortega's success has been in successfully pitting the traditional Liberal and Conservative opposition parties against one another so that he faced no credible opposition in either of the last two elections. Ortega used the division within the opposition to successfully push through constitutional changes in 2014 placing no limits on presidential re-election and thus paving the way for his successful 2016 presidential bid.

However, as Walker and Wade argue in *Nicaragua: Emerging from the Shadow of the Eagle*, equally important to Ortega's political maneuvers in securing control of Nicaragua's electoral has been the policies pursued over the past decade in the service of the country's poor majority. Upon returning to power in 2007, the FSLN worked quickly to recover the social gains of their revolution that had been lost in sixteen years of neoliberal governments. A new literacy campaign, with Cuba's renewed help, reduced illiteracy from 21 percent to 5 percent. Also, the government eliminated all school fees. With more students in school and greater school funding, primary school completion rates went from 64.2 percent to 77.8 percent between 2010 and 2014. Programs of the Bolivarian Alliance assisted with housing, medical care, and agricultural production. The Zero Hunger program targeted hunger in the rural areas with land and livestock distribution reaching more than 32,000 families. These programs had positive impacts on Nicaragua's social indicators. More significant, the poverty rate decreased from 48.3 percent to 29.6 percent in 2014. Another basis of governmental support is that compared to the drug trade driven violence of its Northern Triangle neighbors, Nicaragua is a relatively low-crime country. During 2014 when unaccompanied minors were fleeing Central American violence at a high level, not a single child was from Nicaragua.

## Nicaragua's Economy

As noted earlier in the chapter, Nicaragua's economy has historically been one built around the export of primary agricultural products including coffee, sugar, and beef. However, in the recent years the economic profile of Nicaragua has begun to shift. Agriculture products have remained important export crops, but they have been supplemented by new agricultural products like peanuts and sesame. Industrial production and extraction have become increasingly important to the country's GDP approaching 20 percent, compared to 30 percent for agriculture. The industrial sector is driven primarily by a renewal of gold mining and the manufacture of textile apparel, which was done with significant foreign investment over the last twenty years. Services now account for 50 percent of the economy led by a booming tourism industry (second highest foreign income earner) and remittances from Nicaraguans working abroad, amounting to $1.2 billion in 2015.

The diversification of Nicaragua's economy has contributed to annual growth rates in recent years in the vicinity of 5 percent, the best in Central America. Nicaragua has benefited from greater diversity of its foreign trade relations. Exports to the United States have increased significantly during the era of the Central America–Dominican Republic Free Trade Agreement (CAFTA-DR) but do represent only 56 percent of the destination of the country's exports. Its imports are much more diversified with Latin America leading the way with over 40 percent compared to 20 percent from the United States. Though now threatened by that country's political and economic instability, Venezuela's economic relations with Ortega's Nicaragua has been highly beneficial. Starting in 2007 Nicaragua received over $600 million in support from Venezuela and the Bolivarian Alliance of the Americas (ALBA). Half was in grants; the other half in subsidized oil, greatly reducing the country's energy bill. However, foreign support also came from other sources. Nicaragua received more than $1.5 billion in renewable energy investments between 2007 and 2012. In 2015 renewable energy generated half of the country's electricity with plans to reach 90 percent by 2025. Nicaragua was now seen as a sound investment location, validated by the World Bank, resulting in a new relationship with Panama, Taiwan, Russia, and Chile.

While its future is uncertain, following the expansion of the Panama Canal, Nicaragua has been in serious negotiations with a Chinese businessman for the building of a $40 to $50 billion interoceanic canal through southern Nicaragua. A significant social movement comprised environmentalists and indigenous activists have raised significant objections to the project. Ironically, many of Nicaragua's successes are the result of a good relationship between Ortega and the Nicaraguan business community.

## Nicaraguan Government Structures

Similar to other Latin American governments, Nicaragua has four independent branches of government: executive, legislative, judicial, and electoral. As is often the case in Latin America, the executive branch has been the most powerful. The president heads the state's executive branch, where he is both head of state and head of government. The administrative apparatus under presidential control is rather large, with sixteen ministries and thirty-five independent agencies having cabinet rank. The appointive powers of the president are extensive, including all ministers in the Council of Ministers and vice ministers and numerous other high-level functionaries. The president chooses the chief and associate justices of the Supreme Court but from a list provided by the National Assembly. In recent years the FSLN under Daniel Ortega has consolidated power in all three branches of government and in the Supreme Electoral Court as well.

The National Assembly is composed of ninety members elected by proportional representation from nine administrative regions, plus the past-president and runner-up in the last presidential election. The assembly's most important powers, in addition to the aforementioned ratification of appointments, are budgetary oversight; the ability to summon the president and ministers; and a role in naming Supreme Court justices, members of the electoral council, and the controller general. The National Assembly also has an extensive system of standing and special committees, although the work of the body is weakened by limited resources. When the National Assembly acted primarily to back up the president during the Sandinista years, it never developed an independent stance. Divisions within UNO between 1990 and 1996 allowed the assembly to become more of a player in its own right, but the assembly is once again being subordinated to presidential control as Ortega and the FSLN consolidate power.

Courts in Nicaraguan and Latin American history have not played a role similar to that of their North American neighbors. Nicaragua does not have a formal checks-and-balances system. The lack of judicial review of laws leaves the Nicaraguan courts with the role of applying and interpreting laws rather than making them. The Supreme Court has sixteen judges elected for five-year terms by the National Assembly upon the recommendation of the president. It is organized into four divisions, each responsible for a specific realm of law: civil, criminal, constitutional, and administrative.

The fourth branch of government, the Supreme Electoral Council, is intended to ensure that electoral administration is nonpartisan. Established in 1983, it performed well in the 1984 elections and was in significant measure responsible for the legitimacy of the hotly contested 1990 elections. Under the leadership of Sandinista Mariano Fiallos, it set a high standard for honesty and competence. Unfortunately, this organ's reputation was damaged by widespread irregularities in the 1996 election and a restructuring in 2000 that guaranteed partisan appointees from the Liberal Party and FSLN. Its reputation was further tainted by irregularities in recent elections that may have amplified FSLN vote totals.

## Interest Groups

The Sandinistas were out of political power at the national government level from 1991 to early 2007, but discussion of interest groups in contemporary Nicaragua deserves input from the Sandinista era. Many of the key sectors and organizations that influence politics in Nicaragua today emerged during the 1980s. Many were originally a part of FSLN structures, but after 1990 they moved to a more independent position. They include the National Workers Front (FNT), which includes the Farm Workers Association (ATC), Health Workers Federation (FETASALUD), Heroes and Martyrs Confederation of Professional Associations (CONAPRO), National Association of Educators of Nicaragua (ANDEN), National Union of Employees (UNE), National Union of Farmers and Ranchers (UNAG), Sandinista Workers Central (CST), and Union of Journalists of Nicaragua (UPN). There is also the Nicaraguan Workers' Central (CTN), which is an independent labor union. The Superior Council of Private Enterprise (COSEP) is a powerful business organization.

As is true elsewhere in Latin America, the most powerful traditional groups, such as large landowners and large-scale entrepreneurs, did not work through organizations but maintained direct links with the governments, even those headed by the Sandinistas.

### WOMEN

In the area of women's rights, the gains of the 1980s were numerous, including the institutionalization of AMNLAE, the national women's organization; paid maternity leave; equal access to education; legal equality in relation to divorce, adoption, and parental responsibility; a measure of economic independence; and the inclusion of sex education in the school curriculum. Of course, these gains occurred in the context of a very traditional male-oriented society and during a Sandinista

small private producers and the cooperatives were responsible for 47 percent of all agricultural production. The campesino sector benefited from the government's policy of easy credit terms and technical assistance along with state-run processing and storage facilities, but heavy-handed government control in the countryside eroded Sandinista support. In one of its final acts in 1990, the outgoing Sandinista-led National Assembly passed laws designed to protect the agrarian reform from its possible dismantling by future governments. While the laws could not make up for ten years of failure to grant the necessary titles, they provided a legal basis to struggle for the maintenance of the reform's gains.

The large-scale return of former owners, mainly self-exiles who had developed business interests in Miami, led to many confrontations and mobilizations in the 1990s. These mobilizations led to the July 1990 general strike, which demanded the repeal of new government decrees undermining land reform. The National Workers' Federation FNT received assurances that no further land would be returned to previous owners, but in reality the government continued its privatization and land-return policies behind the scenes. The ability of the rural union movement to carry out a resolute struggle against the return of lands was undermined by cross-cutting interests. In some instances, farm workers welcomed former landlords, hoping that their return would bring new capital into their farms. In other instances, the government's firmness in moving forward with privatization persuaded some farmers to accept what they thought was the best deal they could get. Initially, the Association of Rural Workers (ACT) sought to prevent the privatization process entirely, but it retreated from this position as a result of division within its ranks. Eventually, the union accepted the government's policy with several stipulations. The speed with which this privatization was carried out is demonstrated by the fact that by the end of 1993 the ACT reported that the agricultural Area of People's Property (APP) had been 100 percent privatized.

## ARMED FORCES

Sometimes overlooked in recitations of revolutionary achievements, especially by outside observers, was the elimination of the repressive apparatus of the Somoza regime and its replacement by an army and police force under civilian political control. When the Sandinistas handed over state power in 1990, they left behind army and police institutions imbued with a revolutionary consciousness and insulated from penetration by North American institutions. At the time of the 1990 elections, there were about 96,000 soldiers, and by mid-1994 the number stood at 17,000. By the end of 1995, the Sandinista label had been removed from the organization.

The nature of the strongly Sandinista military changed over time. The army was not absorbed into the framework of U.S. domination, as was true for virtually every other Latin American army except that of Cuba. Nor had it engaged in the systematic human rights abuses so common in Nicaragua's northern neighbors in Central America. Nicaraguan citizens did not have to fear arbitrary death or detention as they did during the Somoza era. The army also remained strictly neutral during the protracted political stalemate between the executive and legislative branches in 1994 and 1995. The professionalism of the army helped defuse the potentially volatile confrontation. In numerous incidents, the army was deployed in labor disputes, especially in the countryside, where it acted in support of former landowners attempting to recover their land from occupying workers. Such bias has not been repeated with the return of the FSLN to power.

The deterioration of the police as a progressive force occurred with even greater speed. The Ministry of the Interior was renamed the Ministry of Government, and the Sandinista police became the national police. New uniforms were issued, and police units in riot gear were commonly deployed in the capital, a departure from the Sandinista era. In 1992, Managua mayor Amoldo Alemán created a new municipal police force (highly visible in the capital with their red berets). During the 1980s the Sandinista police gained a reputation for honesty and discipline. Much of that reputation is now gone. Bribery and corruption have developed on a widespread basis in the context of the desperate economic situation and low police salaries. Both the military and the police have, however, remained under civilian control and are not prone to intervention in the political process, as is the case in Guatemala and Honduras.

## INDIGENOUS PEOPLE

After initial serious mistakes, the Sandinista government enacted an autonomy statute for Nicaragua's Atlantic coast that is a significant achievement for the rights of the indigenous peoples of the Americas. Nicaragua's Atlantic coast, rich in minerals and other natural resources, had long been exploited with no care for the environment or the non-Hispanic population that lived there. The region encompasses 56 percent of Nicaragua's territory, but with a population of some 350,000, it has less than 10 percent of the population. Roughly two-thirds of the region's people are mestizo immigrants who came to the region from the west in search of land. However, the rest of the population is indigenous, with the largest group (75,000) being Miskitos who live in small communities throughout the Atlantic coast region. There are also small communities of creoles, the name used by descendants of Africans. Initially, the Pacific coast-based Sandinistas continued the same pattern of dominant relations with the Atlantic coast. After serious confrontation with CIA-sponsored Indian rebel groups in the early 1980s, however, the government entered into dialogue with the Atlantic coast residents. This dialogue resulted in a 1987 autonomy statute that guaranteed the rights of the indigenous groups to their own language, culture, and communal forms of land ownership. In addition, the statute recognized the rights of the different groups in regard to the development of natural resources. Also established were regional government assemblies with direct representation from each ethnic group. The statute allowed for the transference of considerable authority to these governments, especially in the areas of taxation and resource development.

Post-Sandinista governments of 1990–2007 challenged the autonomy process. Basically, Managua used flanking tactics to undermine the rights of the residents of Nicaragua's Atlantic coast. Rather than seeking any formal reversal of the autonomy statute, the central government simply ignored the law and created its own approach to the region. In April 1990, Chamorro created the Institute for the Development of the Atlantic Coast (INDERÀ). For four years, the meager resources allotted for the coast were channeled through INDERÀ rather than the

Nicaragua. Once in power, the Ortega government largely continued the economic policies of his neoliberal predecessors but did institute a series of popular social welfare measures and align itself with the Latin American left, including membership in ALBA that resulted in tangible assistance from Venezuela and benefits for ordinary Nicaraguans. The FSLN deepened its hold on power by winning all elections from 2008 forward, including the 2016 presidential and legislative elections.

### Liberal Parties

With the disintegration of the anti-Sandinista UNO coalition in the mid-1990s, the Liberal PLC emerged as the key anti-Sandinista force. The PLC broke with the official Liberal Party of the Somozas, the PLN, in the late 1960s over Anastasio Somoza Jr.'s decision to assume the presidency in the 1967 elections. It participated as part of the FSLN's opposition in the Council of State but before the mid-1990s was not a significant force. However, solid party-building activities after 1990, previously unused by any party other than the Sandinistas, quickly catapulted the party into a strong position. Its first national presence came with its 1994 victories in the Atlantic coast regional elections.

Although Alemán became the party's central leader and won the presidency in 1996 under the PLC banner, he was not a long-time member. The PLC recruited Alemán, the mayor of Managua under the UNO government, calculating that his reputation as a strong leader who got things done would make him an excellent candidate.

The other strong partner in the Liberal Alliance that contested the 1996 election was the Independent Liberal Party. Founded in 1944 to oppose the continuation of the Somozas in power, this party had strong anti-Somoza credentials and participated in the revolutionary struggle and the first revolutionary government. Its senior leader, Virgilio Godoy, was elected vice president under Violeta Chamorro in 1990, although sharp divisions within the UNO coalition reduced the power of the vice president.

In the 2001 elections, Bolaños became the standard bearer of the PLC, easily defeating Ortega. The combined Liberal Alliance also won a clear majority of fifty-three seats in the National Assembly. As a movement developed for the prosecution of Alemán for his legendary corruption, fissures began to appear among the Liberals. By vigorously supporting the eventual trial and imprisonment of Alemán, Bolaños alienated the bulk of the PLC, which sought leniency for their leader. By 2004 the Alemán faction of the PLC had entered a temporary coalition with the Ortega-led Sandinistas to try to force President Bolaños from office. This effort failed but in the process weakened the Liberal Alliance and paved the way for the FSLN victory in 2006. In the 2016 National Assembly, the FSLN has a strong majority (seventy of ninety seats), followed by Aleman's PLC with thirteen seats and the PLI with two seats.

## Conclusion

Characterization of contemporary Nicaragua is not easy. What can be said of this country forty years after the 1979 Sandinista revolution, almost thirty years after the unprecedented removal of the FSLN from power by election, and ten years after the triumphant return to power of Daniel Ortega in 2007? Ortega and the FSLN's return to power did not mean that the revolution in full force had gained power. During the seventeen years of neoliberal government between 1990 and 2007, Nicaragua was fully reintegrated into an economic and political system dominated by the United States and the capitalist economic system of the Western Hemisphere. Because of the collapse of the socialist bloc and Cuba's own economic crisis, reintegration was inevitable, but, under the leadership of Chamorro and those that followed her, the move against the radical character of the Sandinista revolution was undertaken with particular vengeance. The result was that the majority poor who had begun to make some progress under FSLN rule were pushed back into grinding poverty.

Reminiscent of its traditional dependence, Nicaragua became ever more closely tied to the advanced industrial countries of the West as a producer of primary products and recipient of their aid. Starting with the presidential term of Arnoldo Alemán, the country returned to traditional personalistic policies marked by increasing authoritarian tendencies, frequent accusations of blatant favoritism and corruption, and ever more partisan party politics conducted by the political elite. Power and personalism came to overshadow government and party institutions. Pacts and political arrangements often defined the rules of political competition and lawmaking more than courts or the constitution. This orientation by Nicaragua's traditional parties was not surprising, because that was in part how the country was ruled by them prior to 1979. What was significant was that once in opposition, the FSLN adapted quickly to this style of insider politics while still clinging to a core base of support that had been energized during the years of Sandinista rule. Elements of this core stayed active during the years of neoliberal power mainly through strikes and demonstrations carried out by mass organizations created in the 1990s. In 2006, the FSLN, under Daniel Ortega's strong personalistic style, was able to regain the upper hand through playing by the rules of the traditional elites, which included a pact between the Alemán faction of the Liberal Party and Ortega's FSLN. As a result, they returned to power as a social democratic, not a revolutionary, party committed to pursuing a narrow and constrained agenda to reverse some of the most blatant aspects of neoliberal rule. Ortega and his tightly controlled FSLN further consolidated their power in the 2011 and 2016 elections when he was re-elected and the party maintained a strong majority in the National Assembly.

Many inside and outside the FSLN worry that Ortega, like a traditional *caudillo*, wields too much personal power. Yet, as described in the previous section, the FSLN in its ten years in power has been modestly successful in the efforts to reduce illiteracy, improve health care, and reduce extreme poverty. It has signed an agreement for a Grand Canal and closely allied Nicaragua with Latin America's move to the left, Venezuela, and ALBA. This is far less than the 1979 revolution promised, but it may be enough to propel the FSLN to continued victories in coming elections and confirm Daniel Ortega as the dominant political figure in the party and country.

# Chronology

**1522**  Spanish reach Nicaragua 1821 Nicaragua becomes independent

**1823-1838**  Nicaragua becomes part of Central American Federation 1855 William Walker takes over Nicaragua 1908 Marines occupy Bluefields 1912–1924 Marines occupy Nicaragua

**1926-1933**  Marines again occupy Nicaragua; Sandino leads guerrilla war

**1934**  Sandino assassinated

**1936-1957**  Anastasio Somoza dictatorship

**1957**  Anastasio Somoza assassinated; son Luis becomes president 1961 FSLN founded in meeting in Tegucigalpa, Honduras 1967 Anastasio Somoza Jr. becomes president

**1960s**  FSLN guerrilla fronts repeatedly destroyed, forcing shift to coordinated political and military action 1974 Reemergence of FSLN guerrilla activity with seizure of Somoza associates at a holiday party

**1975-1977**  Carlos Fonseca Amador killed; FSLN splits into three factions; Insurrectionists (Tercerista faction) shift strategy from rural guerrilla warfare to urban insurrection and broad alliances

**1978**  FSLN commandos seize National Palace; September insurrection in major cities defeated by National Guard

**1979**  Reunification of FSLN; final offensive defeats Somocista forces and Junta of National Reconstruction (JGRN) takes power on July 19

**1980**  National literacy crusade; Violeta Chamorro and Alfonso Robelo leave Governing Council of National Reconstruction (JGRN); Council of State, dominated by Sandinista mass organizations, assumes legislative power

**1981**  U.S. government begins covert financing of ex-National Guardsmen

**1982**  Nicaraguan government imposes state of emergency after contra attacks

**1983**  Visit of Pope John Paul II highlights conflict between official Church and revolution; Nicaragua joins Contadora peace process

**1984**  Elections held; Daniel Ortega elected president, and Sandinistas win 63 percent of the seats in the National Assembly

**1985**  United States declares economic embargo against Nicaragua

**1986**  World Court rules that United States is in violation of international law for its support of the contras; National Assembly elaborates new constitution

**1987**  Constitution approved; National Assembly passes autonomy statute for the regions of the Atlantic coast

**1988**  Nicaraguan government institutes harsh austerity measures in the face of declining productivity and 36,000 percent inflation; Sapoa agreement is signed between the contras and the Nicaraguan government; Hurricane Joan devastates the country, particularly the Atlantic coast region

**1990**  Elections held in Nicaragua, and the final results give 55 percent to the UNO and 41 percent to the FSLN; Violeta Chamorro assumes the presidency; the FNT is formed with 200,000 members

**1996**  Arnoldo Alemán elected president, defeating Daniel Ortega and the FSLN

**1998**  Hurricane Mitch hits Nicaragua, causing many deaths and widespread destruction

**2001** Enrique Bolaños elected president as head of the PLC for 2002–2007 term, defeating Sandinista candidate Daniel Ortega, 56 percent to 42 percent

**2004** Arnoldo Alemán found guilty of corruption and sentenced to twenty years; Sandinistas win vast majority of municipalities in countrywide municipal elections

**2006** Daniel Ortega and the FSLN return to power in narrow electoral victory

**2011** Daniel Ortega re-elected president with 62 percent of vote, but many voting irregularities

**2012** Agreement signed with Chinese company to build Grand Canal across Nicaragua, Sandinistas triumph in municipal elections

**2016** Ortega re-elected with 72 percent of the vote over a divided opposition, takes office January 2017

# Bibliography

Black, George. *The Triumph of the People*. London: Zed, 1981.

Close, David. *Nicaragua: Navigating the Politics of Democracy*. Boulder: CO: Lynne Rienner, 2016.

Close, David, Salvador Marti, and Shelley A. McConnell, eds. *The Sandinistas and Nicaragua since 1979*. Boulder, CO: Lynne Rienner, 2012.

Dye, David R. *Democracy Adrift, Caudillo Politics in Nicaragua*. Cambridge, MA: Hemispheric Initiatives, 2004.

Gilbert, Dennis. *Sandinistas*. Oxford: Blackwell, 1988.

Millett, Richard. *Guardians of the Dynasty*. Mary Knoll, NY: Orbis, 1977.

Leigh, Jennifer. *Women's Activism and Feminist Agency in Mozambique and Nicaragua*. Philadelphia: Temple University Press, 2008.

Norsworthy, Kent. *Nicaragua: A Country Guide*. Albuquerque, NM: Inter-Hemispheric Education Resource Center, 1990.

Plunkett, Hazel. *Nicaragua: A Guide to the People, Politics and Culture*. New York: Interlink Books, 2004.

Prévost, Gary, and Harry E. Vanden, eds. *The Undermining of the Sandinista Revolution*. London: Macmillan, 1997.

Robinson, William. *A Faustian Bargain*. Boulder, CO: Westview, 1993.

Schoultz, Lars. *Beneath the United States: A History of U.S. Policy Toward Latin America*. Cambridge, MA: Harvard University Press, 1998.

Spalding, Rose. *Capitalists and the Revolution in Nicaragua*. Chapel Hill: University of North Carolina Press, 1995.

Vanden, Harry E., and Gary Prévost. *Democracy and Socialism in Sandinista Nicaragua*. Boulder, CO: Lynne Rienner, 1993.

Vilas, Carlos. *State, Class, and Ethnicity in Nicaragua*. Boulder, CO: Lynne Rienner, 1989.

Walker, Thomas, ed. *Nicaragua Without Illusions*. Wilmington, DE: Scholarly Resources, 1997.

Walker, Thomas, and Christine J. Wade. *Nicaragua: Living in the Shadow of the Eagle*. 6th ed. Boulder, CO: Westview, 2017.

## FILMS AND VIDEOS

*Deadly Embrace: Nicaragua, the World Bank and the International Monetary Fund*. United States, 1999. Available through Ashley Eames, Wentworth, NH 03282.

*Fire from the Mountains*. United States, 1987.

*Nicaragua: From the Ashes*. United States, 1982.

*Thank God and the Revolution*. United States, 1981.

# APPENDIX 1
## *Presidential Elections*

### Argentina

2015 Presidential Elections Round 1

| Candidate | Party | Percentage |
| --- | --- | --- |
| Daniel Scioli | Front for the Victory | 36.9 |
| Mauricio Macri | Let's Change | 34.3 |
| Sergio Massa | United for a New Alternative | 21.3 |

2015 Presidential Elections Round 2

| Candidate | Party | Percentage |
| --- | --- | --- |
| Mauricio Macri | Let's Change | 51.3 |
| Daniel Scioli | Front for Victory | 48.7 |

2011 Presidential Elections

| Candidate | Party | Percentage |
| --- | --- | --- |
| Cristina Fernandez de Kirchner | Front for the Victory Alliance | 54.0 |
| Hermes Juan Binner | Broad Progressive Front | 17.0 |
| Ricardo Luis Alfonsin | Union Alliance for Social Development | 11.2 |

### Bolivia

2014 Presidential Elections

| Candidate | Party | Percentage |
| --- | --- | --- |
| Juan Evo Morales Ayma | Movement Toward Socialism (MAS) | 61.4 |
| Samuel Doria Medina | National Unity Front | 24.2 |
| Juan Del Granado | Movement Without Fear | 9.0 |

2009 Presidential Elections

| Candidate | Party | Percentage |
| --- | --- | --- |
| Juan Evo Morales Ayma | Movement Toward Socialism (MAS) | 64.2 |
| Manfred Reyes Villa | Progress Plan for Bolivia, National Convergence (PPB-NC) | 26.5 |
| Samuel Doria Medina | Alliance for National Unity | 5.7 |

# Brazil

2014 Presidential Elections: Round 1

| Candidate | Party | Percentage |
| --- | --- | --- |
| Dilma Rousseff | Workers' Party (PT)/Liberal Party (PL) | 41.6 |
| Aecio Neves | Brazilian Social Democratic Party (PSDB) | 33.6 |
| Marina Silva | Brazilian Socialist Party | 21.3 |

2014 Presidential Elections: Round 2

| Candidate | Party | Percentage |
| --- | --- | --- |
| Dilma Rousseff | Workers' Party (PT)/Liberal Party (PL) | 51.7 |
| Aecio Neves | Brazilian Social Democratic Party (PSDB) | 48.4 |

2010 Presidential Elections: Round 1

| Candidate | Party | Percentage |
| --- | --- | --- |
| Dilma Rousseff | Workers' Party (PT)/Liberal Party (PL) | 46.9 |
| Jose Serra | Brazilian Social Democratic Party (PSDB) | 32.6 |
| Marina Silva | Green Party (PV) | 19.3 |

2010 Presidential Elections: Round 2

| Candidate | Party | Percentage |
| --- | --- | --- |
| Dilma Rousseff | Workers' Party (PT)/Liberal Party (PL) | 56.0 |
| Jose Serra | Brazilian Social Democratic Party (PSDB) | 44.0 |

# Chile

2013 Presidential Elections: Round 1

| Candidate | Party | Percentage |
| --- | --- | --- |
| Michelle Bachelet | Socialist Party of Chile | 46.7 |
| Evelyn Matthei | Independent Democratic Union | 25.0 |

2013 Presidential Elections: Round 2

| Candidate | Party | Percentage |
| --- | --- | --- |
| Michelle Bachelet | Socialist Party of Chile | 62.2 |
| Evelyn Matthei | Independent Democratic Union | 37.8 |

2009 Presidential Elections: Round 1

| Candidate | Party | Percentage |
| --- | --- | --- |
| Sebastian Piñera Echeñique | Coalition for Change | 44.1 |
| Eduardo Frei-Ruiz Tagle | Concert of Parties for Democracy | 29.6 |
| Marco Enriquez-Ominami Gumucio | New Majority for Chile | 20.1 |

# El Salvador

2014 Presidential Election: Round 1

| Candidate | Party | Percentage |
|---|---|---|
| Salvador Sánchez Cerén | National Liberation Front Farabundo Martí (FMLN) | 48.9 |
| Norman Quijano | National Republican Alliance (ARENA) | 39.0 |
| Antonio Saca | Grand Alliance for National Unity (UNIDAD) | 11.4 |

2014 Presidential Election: Round 2

| Candidate | Party | Percentage |
|---|---|---|
| Salvador Sánchez Cerén | National Liberation Front Farabundo Martí (FMLN) | 50.1 |
| Norman Quijano | National Republican Alliance (ARENA) | 49.9 |

2009 Presidential Elections

| Candidate | Party | Percentage |
|---|---|---|
| Mauricio Funes | National Liberation Front Farabundo Martí (FMLN) | 51.3 |
| Rodrigo Ávila | National Republican Alliance (ARENA) | 48.7 |

# Guatemala

2015 Presidential Elections Round 1

| Candidate | Party | Percentage |
|---|---|---|
| James Ernesto Morales | National Convergence Front | 23.9 |
| Sandra Julieta Torres | National Unity of Hope | 19.8 |
| Manuel Antonio Baldizon Mendez | Renewed Democratic Liberty | 19.6 |

2015 Presidential Elections Round 2

| Candidate | Party | Percentage |
|---|---|---|
| James Ernesto Morales | National Convergence Front | 67.4 |
| Sandra Julieta Torres | National Unity of Hope | 32.6 |

2011 Presidential Elections: Round 1

| Candidate | Party | Percentage |
|---|---|---|
| Otto Perez Molina | Patriotic Party (PP) | 36.0 |
| Manuel Antonio Baldizon Mendez | Renewed Democratic Liberty | 23.2 |
| Jose Eduardo Suger Cofino | Commitment, Renewal and Order (CREO) | 16.3 |

2011 Presidential Elections: Round 2

| Candidate | Party | Percentage |
| --- | --- | --- |
| Otto Perez Molina | Patriotic Party (PP) | 53.7 |
| Manuel Antonio Baldizon Mendez | Renewed Democratic Liberty | 46.3 |

# Haiti

2016 Presidential Elections

| Candidate | Party | Percentage |
| --- | --- | --- |
| Jovenel Moïse | Haitian Tèt Kale Party | 55.6 |
| Jude Célestin | Alternative League for Haitian Progress and Empowerment | 19.6 |
| Jean-Charles Moïse | Platform Pitit Desalin | 11.0 |

2011 Presidential Elections: Round 1

| Candidate | Party | Percentage |
| --- | --- | --- |
| Mirlande Manigat | Rally of Progressive National Democrats | 31.4 |
| Jude Célestin | Unity | 22.5 |
| Michel Martelly | Farmers' Response | 21.8 |

2011 Presidential Elections: Round 2

| Candidate | Party | Percentage |
| --- | --- | --- |
| Michel Martelly | Farmers' Response | 67.6 |
| Mirlande Maniga | Rally of Progressive National Democrats | 31.7 |

# Honduras

2013 Presidential Elections

| Candidate | Party | Percentage |
| --- | --- | --- |
| Juan Orlando Hernandez | National Party (PNH) | 36.9 |
| Xiomara Castro | Liberty and Refoundation (LIBRE) | 28.8 |
| Mauricio Villeda | Liberal Party (PLH) | 20.3 |
| Salvador Nasralla | Anti-Corruption Party | 13.4 |

2009 Presidential Elections

| Candidate | Party | Percentage |
| --- | --- | --- |
| Porfirio Lobo Sosa | National Party (PNH) | 57.0 |
| Elvin Santos | Liberal Party (PLH) | 38.0 |

# Mexico

2012 Presidential Elections

| Candidate | Party | Percentage |
|---|---|---|
| Enrique Peña Nieto | Institutional Revolutionary Party (PRI) | 38.2 |
| Andres Manuel López Obrador | Party of the Democratic Revolution/ Civil Platform/Workers' Party (PRD-PT-MC) | 31.6 |
| Josefina Vázquez Mota | National Action Party (PAN) | 25.4 |

2006 Presidential Elections

| Candidate | Party | Percentage |
|---|---|---|
| Felipe Calderón | National Action Party (PAN) | 35.9 |
| Andres Manuel López Obrador | Party of the Democratic Revolution/ Civil Platform/ Workers' Party (PRD-PT-MC) | 35.3 |
| Roberto Madrazo | Institutional Revolutionary Party (PRI) | 22.2 |

# Nicaragua

2016 Presidential Elections

| Candidate | Party | Percentage |
|---|---|---|
| Daniel Ortega Saaverda | Sandinista National Liberation Front (FSLN) | 72.5 |
| Maximino Rodriguez | Liberal Constitutionalist Party (PLC) | 15.0 |
| Jose del Carmen Alvarado Ruiz | Independent Liberal Party (PLI) | 4.5 |

2011 Presidential Elections

| Candidate | Party | Percentage |
|---|---|---|
| Daniel Ortega Saavedra | Sandinista National Liberation Front (FSLN) | 62.5 |
| Fabio Gadea Mantilla | Independent Liberal Party (PLI) | 31.0 |

# Panama

2014 Presidential Elections

| Candidate | Party | Percentage |
|---|---|---|
| Juan Carlos Varela | Panameñista Party | 39.1 |
| Jose Domingo Arias | Democratic Change | 31.4 |
| Juan Carlos Navarro | Revolutionary Democratic Party (PRD) | 28.2 |

2009 Presidential Elections

| Candidate | Party | Percentage |
|---|---|---|
| Ricardo Martinelli | Democratic Change/National Republican Liberal Movement (MOLIRENA)/Panamanian Party/ Patriotic Union Party | 59.9 |
| Balbina Herrera | Revolutionary Democratic Party (PRD) | 37.6 |

# Paraguay

2013 Presidential Elections

| Candidate | Party | Percentage |
|---|---|---|
| Horacio Cartes | National Republican Association–Colorado Party | 48.5 |
| Efrain Alegre | Authentic Radical Liberal Party | 39.1 |

2008 Presidential Elections

| Candidate | Party | Percentage |
|---|---|---|
| Fernando Lugo | Patriotic Alliance for Change (APC) | 40.9 |
| Blanca Ovelar | National Republican Association–Colorado Party | 30.6 |
| Lino Oviedo | National Union of Ethical Citizens (UNACE) | 21.9 |

# Peru

2016 Presidential Elections: Round 1

| Candidate | Party | Percentage |
|---|---|---|
| Keiko Fujimori | Popular Force | 39.8 |
| Pedro Pablo Kuczynski | Peruvians for Change | 21.0 |
| Veronika Mendoza | Broad Front for Justice, Life, and Liberty | 18.8 |
| Alfredo Barnechea | Popular Action | 7.0 |

2016 Presidential Elections: Round 2

| Candidate | Party | Percentage |
|---|---|---|
| Pedro Pablo Kuczynski | Peruvians for Change | 50.1 |
| Keiko Fujimori | Popular Force | 49.9 |

2011 Presidential Elections: Round 1

| Candidate | Party | Percentage |
|---|---|---|
| Ollanta Humala | Peruvian Nationalist Party (GP) | 27.8 |
| Keiko Fujimori | Force 2011 | 20.7 |
| Pedro Pablo Kuczynski | Alliance for the Great Change | 16.2 |
| Alejandro Toledo | Possible Peru | 13.7 |

2011 Presidential Elections: Round 2

| Candidate | Party | Percentage |
|---|---|---|
| Ollanta Humala | Peruvian Nationalist Party (GP) | 48.2 |
| Keiko Fujimori | Force 2011 | 45.5 |

## Uruguay

2014 Presidential Elections Round 1

| Candidate | Party | Percentage |
|---|---|---|
| Tabare Vazquez | Broad Front (FA) | 49.5 |
| Luis Alberto Lacalle de Herrera | National Party–Whites (PN-B) | 31.9 |
| Dr. Pedro Bordaberry Herrán | Colorado Party (PC) | 13.3 |

2014 Presidential Election Round 2

| Candidate | Party | Percentage |
|---|---|---|
| Tabare Vazquez | Broad Front (FA) | 56.6 |
| Luis Alberto Lacalle de Herrera | National Party–Whites (PN-B) | 43.3 |

2009 Presidential Election Round 1

| Candidate | Party | Percentage |
|---|---|---|
| José Alberto Mujica Cordano | Broad Front (FA) | 48.1 |
| Luis Alberto Lacalle de Herrera | National Party–Whites (PN-B) | 28.9 |
| Dr. Pedro Bordaberry Herrán | Colorado Party (PC) | 16.9 |

2009 Presidential Election Round 2

| Candidate | Party | Percentage |
|---|---|---|
| José Alberto Mujica Cordano | Broad Front (FA) | 52.4 |
| Luis Alberto Lacalle de Herrera | National Party–Whites (PN-B) | 43.5 |

# Venezuela

2013 Presidential Elections

| Candidate | Party | Percentage |
|---|---|---|
| Nicolas Maduro Moras | United Socialist Party of Venezuela(PSUV) | 50.6 |
| Henrique Capriles Radonski | Justice First (PJ) | 49.1 |

** Note: Special election was held following the death of President Hugo Chávez.

2012 Presidential Elections

| Candidate | Party | Percentage |
|---|---|---|
| Hugo Chávez | United Socialist Party of Venezuela (PSUV) | 55.1 |
| Henrique Capriles Radonski | Justice First (PJ) | 44.3 |

*Sources:* Georgetown University and Organization of American States Political Database of the Americas, http://www.georgetown.edu/pdba. Derksen, Wilfried. Elections Around the World, http://www.agora .stm.it/Electionss/Elections.htm. Electionsguide.org, http://209.50.195.230/eguide/resultsum/uruguay_ pres04.htm.

2010 Chamber of Representatives Election/Senate of the Republic Election

| Party | Percentage (Deputies/Senators) | Number of Seats (Deputies/Senators) |
|---|---|---|
| Social National Unity Party (PSUN) | 25.9/25.2 | 47/28 |
| Colombian Conservative Party (PC) | 21.4/20.6 | 38/22 |
| Colombian Liberal Party (PL)/Radical Change (CR) | 19.3/15.8 | 37/17 |

## Costa Rica

2014 Legislative Assembly Election

| Party | Percentage | Number of Seats |
|---|---|---|
| National Liberation Party (PLN) | 25.5 | 18 |
| Citizen Action Party (PAC) | 23.8 | 14 |
| Broad Front (FA) | 13.1 | 9 |

2010 Legislative Assembly Election

| Party | Percentage | Number of Seats |
|---|---|---|
| National Liberation Party (PLN) | 37.1 | 23 |
| Citizen Action Party (PAC) | 17.6 | 11 |
| Libertarian Movement Party (PML) | 14.4 | 10 |

## Dominican Republic

2016 Chamber of Deputies and Senate Elections

| Party | Percentage | Number of Seats (Deputies/Senators) |
|---|---|---|
| Dominican Liberation Party (PLD) | 41.8 | 106/26 |
| Modern Revolutionary Party (PRM) | 20.4 | 42/2 |
| Social Christian Reformist Party | 9.2 | 18/1 |
| Dominican Revolutionary Party (PRD) | 7.8 | 16/1 |

2010 Chamber of Deputies and Senate Elections

| Party | Percentage | Number of Seats (Deputies/Senators) |
|---|---|---|
| Dominican Liberation Party (PLD) | 54.6 | 105/31 |
| Dominican Revolutionary Party (PRD) | 41.9 | 75/0 |

## Ecuador

2017 National Congress Election

| Party | Percentage | Number of Seats |
|---|---|---|
| Pais Alliance | 39.0 | 74 |
| Creating Opportunities (SUMA) Movement | 20.0 | 34 |
| Social Christian Party | 15.9 | 15 |

2013 National Congress Election

| Party | Percentage | Number of Seats |
|---|---|---|
| PAIS Movement (MPAIS) | 66.4 | 91 |
| Creating Opportunities Movement | 8.8 | 12 |

# El Salvador

2015 National Congress Election

| Party | Percentage | Number of Seats |
|---|---|---|
| National Republican Alliance (ARENA) | 38.8 | 32 |
| Farabundo Marti National Liberation Front | 37.2 | 31 |
| Grand Alliance for National Unity | 9.2 | 11 |

2012 National Congress Election

| Party | Percentage | Number of Seats |
|---|---|---|
| National Republican Alliance (ARENA) | 39.8 | 33 |
| Farabundo Marti National Liberation Front | 36.7 | 31 |
| Grand Alliance for National Unity | 9.7 | 11 |

# Guatemala

2015 Congress of the Republic Election

| Party | Percentage | Number of Seats |
|---|---|---|
| Renewed Democratic Liberty Party | 19.1 | 44 |
| National Unity for Hope | 16.3 | 36 |
| Everyone Together for Guatemala | 10.6 | 18 |
| National Convergence Front (FCN) | 9.4 | 11 |
| Patriotic Party (PP) | 8.5 | 17 |

2011 Congress of the Republic Election

| Party | Percentage | Number of Seats |
|---|---|---|
| Patriotic Party (PP) | 26.2 | 56 |
| Grand National Alliance (GANA) | 22.6 | 48 |
| National Change Union | 9.5 | 14 |
| Renewed Democratic Liberty | 8.9 | 14 |
| Commitment, Renewal and Order | 8.7 | 12 |

# Haiti

2015 Chamber of Deputies and Senate Elections

| Party | Percentage (Deputies/Senators) | Number of Seats (Deputies/Senators) |
|---|---|---|
| Unity | NA/NA | 7/3 |
| Truth | NA/NA | 12/3 |
| Haitian Bald Head Party | NA/NA | 22/2 |
| Organization of People in Struggle | NA/NA | 7/1 |

2011 Chamber of Deputies and Senate Elections

| Party | Percentage (Deputies/Senators) | Number of Seats (Deputies/Senators) |
|---|---|---|
| Unity | NA/NA | 33/15 |
| Alternative for Progress and Democracy | NA/NA | 14/9 |
| Ansanm Nou Fo | NA/NA | 10/2 |

# Honduras

2013 National Congress Election

| Party | Percentage | Number of Seats |
|---|---|---|
| National Party (PN) | 33.6 | 48 |
| Liberty and Refoundation (LIBRE) | 27.5 | 37 |
| Liberal Party of Honduras (PLH) | 17.0 | 27 |
| Anti-Corruption Party | 15.2 | 13 |

2009 National Congress Election

| Party | Percentage | Number of Seats |
|---|---|---|
| National Party (PN) | 56.5 | 71 |
| Liberal Party of Honduras (PLH) | 38.1 | 45 |

# Mexico

2015 Legislative Elections

| Party | Percentage (Deputies/Senators) | Number of Seats (Deputies/Senators) |
|---|---|---|
| Institutional Revolutionary Party (PRI) | 29.2/NA | 203/58 |
| National Action Party (PAN) | 21.0/NA | 108/44 |
| Party of the Democratic Revolution (PRD) | 10.9/NA | 56/19 |

2009 Legislative Elections

| Party | Percentage (Deputies/Senators) | Number of Seats (Deputies/Senators) |
|---|---|---|
| Institutional Revolutionary Party (PRI) | 31.9/33.1 | 163/58 |
| National Action Party (PAN) | 25.9/27.9 | 114/44 |
| Party of the Democratic Revolution (PRD) | 18.5/19.7 | 104/19 |

# Nicaragua

2016 National Assembly Elections

| Party | Percentage | Number of Seats |
|---|---|---|
| Sandinista National Liberation Front (FSLN) | 66.8 | 70 |
| Liberal Constitutionalist Party (PLC) | 14.7 | 13 |
| Independent Liberal Party (PLI) | 6.6 | 2 |

2011 National Assembly Election

| Party | Percentage | Number of Seats |
|---|---|---|
| Sandinista National Liberation Front (FSLN) | 63.0 | 63 |
| Independent Liberal Party (PLI) | 32.7 | 27 |

# Panama

2014 Legislative Assembly Election

| Party | Percentage | Number of Seats |
|---|---|---|
| Democratic Change | 33.7 | 30 |
| Democratic Revolutionary Party (PRD) | 31.5 | 25 |
| Panamenista Party | 20.2 | 12 |

2009 Legislative Assembly Election

| Party | Percentage | Number of Seats |
|---|---|---|
| Alliance for Change (APC) | 56.0 | 42 |
| One Country for All (UPPT) | 40.6 | 27 |
| Democratic Revolutionary Party (PRD) | 23.4 | 14 |

# Paraguay

2013 Chamber of Deputies/ Chamber of Senators Election

| Party | Percentage (Deputies/Senators) | Number of Seats (Deputies/Senators) |
|---|---|---|
| Republican National Association–Colorado Party (ANR) | 40.1/35.8 | 44/19 |
| Authentic Liberal Radical Party (PLRA) | 29.3/24.4 | 27/12 |
| Front Guasu | 5.7/9.6 | 1/5 |

2008 Chamber of Deputies/Chamber of Senators Election

| Party | Percentage (Deputies/Senators) | Number of Seats (Deputies/Senators) |
|---|---|---|
| Republican National Association–Colorado Party (ANR) | 29.1/33.0 | 29/15 |
| Authentic Radical Liberal Party (PLRA) | 28.9/28.3 | 26/14 |
| National Union of Ethical Citizens (UNACE) | 19.2/18.5 | 16/9 |

# Peru

2016 Congress of the Republic Election

| Party | Percentage | Number of Seats |
|---|---|---|
| Popular Force | 36.3 | 71 |
| Peruvians for Change | 16.4 | 20 |
| Broad Front for Justice, Life and Liberty | 13.9 | 20 |
| Alliance for the Progress of Peru | 9.2 | 9 |
| Popular Alliance | 8.3 | 5 |

2011 Congress of the Republic Election

| Party | Percentage | Number of Seats |
|---|---|---|
| Peru Wins | 25.3 | 47 |
| Force 2011 | 22.9 | 37 |
| Electoral Alliance Possible Peru | 14.8 | 21 |
| Alliance for the Great Change | 14.4 | 12 |
| National Solidarity Alliance | 10.2 | 9 |

# Uruguay

2014 Legislative Elections

| Party | Percentage (Deputies/Senators) | Number of Seats |
|---|---|---|
| Broad Front (EP) | 49.5 | 50/15 |
| National Party-Whites (PN-B) | 31.9 | 32/10 |
| Colorado Party (PN) | 13.3 | 13/4 |

2009 Chamber of Deputies and Chamber of Senators Elections

| Party | Percentage | Number of Seats |
|---|---|---|
| Broad Front (EP) | 49.5 | 50/16 |
| National Party–Whites (PN–B) | 31.9 | 30/9 |
| Colorado Party (PN) | 13.3 | 17/5 |

2009 Chamber of Deputies and Chamber of Senators Elections

| Party | Percentage | Number of Seats (Deputies/Senators) |
| --- | --- | --- |
| Broad Front (EP) | 47.4 | 50/15 |
| National Party–Whites (PN–B) | 28.5 | 32/10 |
| Colorado Party (PN) | 16.6 | 13/4 |

## Venezuela

2015 National Assembly Election

| Party | Percentage | Number of Seats |
| --- | --- | --- |
| Democratic Unity Roundtable | 56.2 | 109 |
| Great Patriotic Pole | 40.9 | 55 |
| Indigenous Seats | NA | 3 |

2010 National Assembly Election

| Party | Percentage | Number of Seats |
| --- | --- | --- |
| United Socialist Party of Venezuela (PSUV) | 48.2 | 98 |
| Coalition for Democratic Unity (MUD) | 47.1 | 67 |
| Homeland for All | 3.1 | 2 |

*Sources:* Georgetown University and Organization of American States Political Database of the Americas, http://www.georgetown.edu/pdba/. Derksen, Wilfried. Elections Around the World, http://www .welections.wordpress.com

# Authors and Contributors

## Authors

**Gary Prevost** is Professor of Political Science at St. John's University/College of Saint Benedict, Minnesota. He received his PhD in political science from the University of Minnesota and has published widely on Latin America and Spain. His books include *Democracy and Socialism in Sandinista Nicaragua*, coauthored with Harry E. Vanden; *The Undermining of the Sandinista Revolution*, co-edited with Harry E. Vanden; *Cuba: A Different America*, co-edited with Wilber Chaffee; *The Bush Doctrine and Latin America*, and *Cuban-Latin American Relations in the Context of a Changing Hemisphere*, both co-edited with Carlos Oliva Campos; *Revolutionaries to Politicians*, co-edited with David Close and Kalatowie Deonandan; *United States–Cuban Relations—A Critical History*, coauthored with Esteban Morales; *Latin America: An Introduction*, coauthored with Harry E. Vanden; and *Social Movements and Leftist Governments in Latin America: Confrontation or Co-optation* and *U.S. National Security Concerns in Latin America and the Caribbean: Failed States and Ungoverned Spaces*, both co-edited with Carlos Oliva Campos and Harry Vanden. In addition, he has authored and coauthored numerous articles and book chapters on Nicaragua and Spanish politics. His research on Latin America has been supported by a number of grants, including a Fulbright Central American Republics Award.

**Harry E. Vanden** is Professor in Government and International Affairs and the Institute for the Study of Latin America and the Caribbean at the University of South Florida, Tampa. He received his PhD in political science from the New School for Social Research and also holds a graduate certificate in Latin American Studies from the Maxwell School of Syracuse University. He has lived in several Latin American countries, including Peru, where he was a Fulbright Scholar and later worked in the Peruvian government's National Institute of Public Administration, and Brazil, where he held a second Fulbright grant and taught at the State University of São Paulo. His scholarly publications include numerous articles and book chapters and more than fifteen books, including *Democracy and Socialism in Sandinista Nicaragua* coauthored with Gary Prevost; *The Undermining of the Sandinista Revolution*, co-edited with Gary Prevost; *Inter-American Relations in an Era of Globalization: Beyond Unilateralism?* co-edited with Jorge Nef; *Latin American Social Movements in the Twenty-First Century*, co-edited with Richard Stahler-Sholk and Glen Kuecker; *Latin America: An Introduction*, coauthored with Gary Prevost; *José Carlos Mariátegui: An Anthology of His Writings*, translated and edited with Marc Becker (U.S. and Indian editions); *Social Movements and Leftists Governments in Latin America*, co-edited with Gary Prevost and Carlos Oliva; *Rethinking Latin American Social Movements: Radical Action From Below*, co-edited with Richard Stahler-Sholk and Marc Becker; *U.S. National Security Concerns in Latin America and the Caribbean: The Concept of Ungoverned Spaces and Sovereignty*, co-edited with Gary Prevost, Luis Fernando Ayerbe, and Carlos Oliva; and *The New Global Politics: Social Movements on a Global Scale*, co-edited with Peter N. Funke and Gary Prevost.

## Contributors

**Wilber Albert Chaffee** is Professor Emeritus at Saint Mary's College of California and presently lives in Brazil. He has been a Senior Research Associate at the Instituto Universitário de Pesquisas do Rio de Janeiro and a Fulbright scholar. He received his PhD in government from the University of Texas, Austin. In addition to his numerous articles and book chapters, he has published *The Economics of Violence in Latin America; Cuba: A Different America*, co-edited with Gary Prevost, and *Desenvolvimento: Politics and Economy in Brazil*. He is currently working on a study of institutional change in Brazil.

**Nora Hamilton** is Professor Emerita of Political Science at the University of Southern California. She received her PhD in sociology from the University of Wisconsin. She has published *The Limits of State Autonomy: Post-Revolutionary Mexico; Crisis in Central America* (editor); *Modern Mexico, State Economy and Social Conflict*, co-edited with Timothy Harding; and several articles and book chapters on political and economic change in Mexico and Central America. She has also published on Central American migration and recently published *Seeking Community in a Global City: Guatemalans and Salvadorans in Los Angeles*, coauthored with Norma Chinchilla.

Susanne Jonas is a professor (ret.) of Latin American & Latino Studies at the University of California, Santa Cruz, where she taught for 24 years and received a Distinguished Teaching Award. Her PhD is in political science from the University of California, Berkeley. A scholar of Latin America for five decades, she has particular expertise on Guatemala and Central America. Since the 1990s, she has become a specialist on Guatemalan/Central American migration and is co-author, with Nestor Rodríguez, of *Guatemala-U.S. Migration: Transforming Regions* (University of Texas Press, 2014). Her book, *Of Centaurs and Doves: Guatemala's Peace Process*, published in English and Spanish in 2000, was designated a Choice "Outstanding Academic Book." *The Battle for Guatemala: Rebels, Death Squads, and U.S. Power* (1991) was also published in Spanish. Overall, she has written 9 books, several translated into Spanish, and has co-edited 13 books/journal issues. She has published over 75 major analytical articles/book chapters, and many shorter and OpEd articles. Her current work focuses on Central American migration.

**Eduardo Silva** is Lydian Professor of Political Science at Tulane University. He received his PhD in political science from the University of California, San Diego. He is author of *Challenging Neoliberalism in Latin America* and *The State and Capital in Chile: Business Elites, Technocrats, and Market Economics*. He is coeditor of *Organized Business, Economic Change and Democracy in Latin America*; and *Elections and Democratization in Latin America, 1980–1985*. He has also published over thirty articles that have appeared in professional journals, edited volumes, and public affairs outlets.

**Aldo C. Vacs** is Professor and Chair of the Department of Government, Skidmore College, a Research Associate at the University of Pittsburgh, and a contributing editor for the *Handbook of Latin American Studies*. He holds a PhD in political science from the University of Pittsburgh. Dr. Vacs has published many articles and book chapters and has authored *Discreet Partners: Argentina and the USSR since 1917; The 1980 Grain Embargo Negotiations: The U.S., Argentina and the USSR*; and *Negotiating the Rivers*. He is currently researching political democratization, economic liberalization, and the process of political economic transformation in Latin America.

**John C. Dugas** is Associate Professor and Chair of the Department of Political Science at Kalamazoo College. He received his PhD in political science from Indiana University. He has worked for over a decade on issues of political reform in Colombia and is the coauthor of *Los Caminos de la Descentralización: Diversidad y retos de la transformación municipal* and editor of *La Constitución de 1991: ¿Un pacto político viable?*, both published by the Universidad de los Andes in Bogotá, Colombia. He has also published articles in the *Journal of Latin American Studies*, the *Latin American Research Review, Third World Quarterly*, and *America Latina Hoy*.

**Daniel Hellinger** is Professor of Political Science at Webster University in St. Louis, Missouri. He received his PhD in political science from Rutgers University and has authored *Venezuela:*

*Tarnished Democracy,* many scholarly articles on Venezuela and Latin America, and coedited (with Steve Ellner) *Venezuelan Politics in the Chávez Era: Class, Polarization and Conflict.* He is presently working on a comparative study of the nationalizations of copper in Chile and oil in Venezuela.

**Waltraud Q. Morales** is Professor Emeritus of Political Science at the University of Central Florida. She received her MA and PhD from the Graduate School of International Studies of the University of Denver. She has published articles on Bolivian domestic and foreign policies, women and gender in Latin America and the third world, the Andean drug war, Andean indigenous peoples, and sustainable development and human security. Publications include *A Brief History of Bolivia,* and "Responding to Bolivian Democracy: Avoiding the Mistakes of Early U.S. Cuban Policy," *Military Review* (July/August 2006). She has been the recipient of grants from the National Endowment for the Humanities and Fulbright teaching, research and study grants to Bolivia in 1990 and 2004.